BY JOHN MCPHEE

Giving Good Weight

Coming into the Country

The Survival of the Bark Canoe

Pieces of the Frame

The Curve of Binding Energy

The Deltoid Pumpkin Seed

Encounters with the Archdruid

The Crofter and the Laird

Levels of the Game

A Roomful of Hovings

The Pine Barrens

Oranges

The Headmaster

A Sense of Where You Are

Giving Good Weight

John McPhee

GIVING GOOD WEIGHT

Farrar · Straus · Giroux

NEW YORK

Library of Congress Cataloging in Publication Data
McPhee, John A. Giving good weight.
CONTENTS: Giving good weight. The keel of Lake Dickey.
The pinball philosophy. The Atlantic Generating Station.
Brigade de cuisine.
I. Title. AC8.M2658   081   79–17572

The text of this book originally appeared in The New Yorker,
*and was developed with the editorial counsel
of William Shawn, Robert Bingham,
and C. P. Crow.*

For Laura

Contents

GIVING
GOOD
WEIGHT

You people come into the market—the Greenmarket, in the open air under the downpouring sun—and you slit the tomatoes with your fingernails. With your thumbs, you excavate the cheese. You choose your stringbeans one at a time. You pulp the nectarines and rape the sweet corn. You are something wonderful, you are—people of the city—and we, who are almost without exception strangers here, are as absorbed with you as you seem to be with the numbers on our hanging scales.

"Does every sink grow on your farm?"

"Yes, ma'am."

"It's marvellous. Absolutely every sink?"

"Some things we get from neighbors up the road."

"You don't have no avocados, do you?"

"Avocados don't grow in New York State."

"Butter beans?"

"They're a Southern crop."

"Who baked this bread?"

"My mother. A dollar twenty-five for the cinnamon. Ninety-five cents for the rye."

(3)

"I can't eat rye bread anymore. I like it very much, but it gives me a headache."

Short, born abroad, and with dark hair and quick eyes, the woman who likes rye bread comes regularly to the Brooklyn Greenmarket, at Flatbush and Atlantic. I have seen her as well at the Fifty-ninth Street Greenmarket, in Manhattan. There is abundant evidence that she likes to eat. She must have endured some spectacular hangovers from all that rye.

Farm goods are sold off trucks, vans, and pickups that come into town in the dark of the morning. The site shifts with the day of the week: Tuesdays, black Harlem; Wednesdays, Brooklyn; Fridays, Amsterdam at 102nd. There are two on Saturdays—the one at Fifty-ninth Street and Second Avenue, the other in Union Square. Certain farms are represented everywhere, others at just one or two of the markets, which have been primed by foundation funds and developed under the eye of the city. If they are something good for the urban milieu—tumbling horns of fresh plenty at the people's feet— they are an even better deal for the farmers, whose disappearance from the metropolitan borders may be slowed a bit by the many thousands of city people who flow through streets and vacant lots and crowd up six deep at the trucks to admire the peppers, fight over the corn, and gratefully fill our money aprons with fresh green city lettuce.

"How much are the tomatoes?"

"Three pounds for a dollar."

"Peaches?"

"Three pounds for a dollar twenty-five."

"Are they freestones?"

"No charge for the pits."

"How much are the tomatoes?"

(4)

"Three pounds for a dollar. It says so there on the sign."

"Venver the eggs laid?"

"Yesterday."

"Kon you eat dum raw?"

We look up from the cartons, the cashbox, the scales, to see who will eat the eggs raw. She is a good-looking big-framed young blonde.

"You bet. You can eat them raw."

"How much are the apples?"

"Three pounds for a dollar."

Three pounds, as we weigh them out, are anywhere from forty-eight to fifty-two ounces. Rich Hodgson says not to charge for an extra quarter pound. He is from Hodgson Farms, of Newburgh, New York, and I (who come from western New Jersey) have been working for him off and on for three months, summer and fall. I thought at first that I would last only a week, but there is a mesmerism in the selling, in the coins and the bills, the all-day touching of hands. I am often in charge of the peppers, and, like everyone else behind the tables by our truck, I can look at a plastic sack of them now and tell its weight.

"How much these weigh? Have I got three pounds?"

"That's maybe two and a quarter pounds you've got there."

"Weigh them, please."

"There it is. Two and a quarter pounds."

"Very good."

"Fantastic! Fantastic! You see that? You see that? He knew exactly how much it weighed."

I scuff a boot, take a break for a shiver in the bones. There are unsuspected heights in this game, moments that go right off the scale.

(5)

This is the Brooklyn market, in appearance the most cornucopian of all. The trucks are drawn up in a close but ample square and spill into its center the colors of the country. Greengage plums. Ruby Red onions. Yellow crookneck squash. Sweet white Spanish onions. Starking Delicious plums.

Fall pippins ("Green as grass and curl your teeth"). McIntoshes, Cortlands, Paulareds. ("Paulareds are new and are lovely apples. I'll bet they'll be in the stores in the next few years.")

Pinkish-yellow Gravensteins. Gold Star cantaloupes. Patty Pan squash.

Burpless cucumbers.

Cranberry beans.

Silver Queen corn. Sweet Sue bicolor corn, with its concise tight kernels, its well-filled tips and butts. Boston salad lettuce. Parris Island romaine lettuce. Ithaca iceberg crunchy pale lettuce. Orange tomatoes.

Cherry Bell tomatoes.

Moreton Hybrid, Jet Star, Setmore, Supersonic, Roma, Saladette tomatoes.

Campbell 38s.

Campbell 1327s.

Big Boy, Big Girl, Redpak, Ramapo, Rutgers London-broil thick-slice tomatoes.

Clean-shouldered, supple-globed Fantastic tomatoes. Celery (Imperial 44).

Hot Portugal peppers. Four-lobed Lady Bell glossy green peppers. Aconcagua frying peppers.

Parsley, carrots, collard greens.

Stuttgarter onions, mustard greens.

Dandelions.

The people, in their throngs, are the most varied we see—or

that anyone is likely to see in one place west of Suez. This intersection is the hub if not the heart of Brooklyn, where numerous streets converge, and where Fourth Avenue comes plowing into the Flatbush-Atlantic plane. It is also a nexus of the race. "Weigh these, please." "Will you please weigh these?" Greeks. Italians. Russians. Finns. Haitians. Puerto Ricans. Nubians. Muslim women in veils of shocking pink. Sunnis in total black. Women in hiking shorts, with babies in their backpacks. Young Connecticut-looking pants-suit women. Their hair hangs long and as soft as cornsilk. There are country Jamaicans, in loose dresses, bandannas tight around their heads. "Fifty cents? Yes, dahling. Come on a sweetheart, mon." There are Jews by the minyan, Jews of all persuasions —white-bearded, black-bearded, split-bearded Jews. Down off Park Slope and Cobble Hill come the neo-bohemians, out of the money and into the arts. "Will you weigh this tomato, please?" And meantime let us discuss theatre, books, environmental impacts. Maybe half the crowd are men—men in cool Haspel cords and regimental ties, men in lipstick, men with blue eyelids. Corporate-echelon pinstripe men. Their silvered hair is perfect in coif; it appears to have been audited. Easygoing old neighborhood men with their shirts hanging open in the summer heat are walking galleries of abdominal and thoracic scars—Brooklyn Jewish Hospital's bastings and tackings. (They do good work there.) A huge clock is on a tower high above us, and as dusk comes down in the autumn months the hands glow Chinese red. The stations of the hours light up like stars. The clock is on the Williamsburgh Savings Bank building, a skyscraper full of dentists. They go down at five into the Long Island Rail Road, under us. Below us, too, are all the subways of the city, in ganglion assembled.

"How much are the cabbages?"

"Forty cents a head."

"O.K. Weigh one, please."

We look around at empty storefronts, at J. Rabinowitz & Sons' SECURITY FIREPROOF STORAGE, at three gold balls (Gem Jewelers Sales), at Martin Orlofsky's Midtown Florist Nursery. Orlofsky has successfully objected to our presence as competitors here, and we can sell neither plants nor flowers. "HAVE YOU HAD ANY LATELY? CLAMS, STEAMERS." Across Fourth Avenue from the Greenmarket is the Episcopal Church of the Redeemer, a century and a quarter old, with what seem to be, even in the brightest morning light, black saints in its stained-glass windows. Far down Fourth, as if at rest on the paved horizon, stands a tower of the Verrazano-Narrows Bridge. To the northwest rises the Empire State. Not long after dawn, as trucks arrive and farmers begin to open boxes and set up wooden tables, a miscellany of whores is calling it a day—a gradual dispersal, quitting time. Their corner is Pacific and Fourth. Now and again, a big red Cadillac pauses at the curb beside them. The car's rear window is shaped like a heart. With some frequency, a squad car will slide up to the same curb—a week-in, week-out, endless duet with the Cadillac. The women hurry away. "Here come the law." The Greenmarket space, which lies between Atlantic and Pacific, was once occupied by condemned buildings— spent bars and liquor stores. The block is fenced and gravelled now, and is leased by the Brooklyn Academy of Music, which charges the Greenmarket seventy-five dollars a Wednesday. The market does not fill the lot—the rest is concession parking. Here in the din of the city, in the rivers of moving metal, some customers drive to the Greenmarket as if it were a roadside stand in Rockland County, a mall in Valley Stream.

On a sidewalk around the corner, people with a Coleman stove under a fifty-five-gallon drum are making sauce with our tomatoes. Tall black man in a business suit now picks up a slim hot pepper. Apparently he thinks it sweet, because he takes most of it with a single bite and chews it with anticipant relish. Three . . . two . . . one. The small red grenade explodes on his tongue. His eyeballs seem to smoke. By the fistful, he grabs cool stringbeans and stuffs them into his mouth.

I forget to give change to a middle-aged woman with bitter eyes. I charged her forty-five cents for a pound and a third of apples and she gave me half a dollar. Now she is demanding her nickel, and her eyes are narrower than the sides of dimes. She is a round-shouldered person, beaky and short—short-changed. In her stare at me, there is an entire judiciary system —accusation, trial, and conviction. "You give me my nickel, mister."

"I'm sorry. I forgot. Here is your nickel."

She does not believe my mistake a mistake. She walks away in a white huff. Now she stops, turns, glowers. She moves on. Twice more, as she departs from the market, she stops, turns, and stares angrily back. I watch her all the way to the curb. She waves at the traffic and gets into a cab.

A coin will sink faster through bell peppers than it will through water. When people lose their money they go after it like splashing bears. Peppers everywhere. Peppers two deep over the apples, three deep over the plums. Peppers all over the ground. Sooner or later, the people who finger the eggs will spill and break the eggs, and the surface they walk on becomes a gray-and-yellow slurry of parking-lot gravel and egg—a Brooklyn omelette. Woman spills a dozen now. Her purse is hanging open and a falling egg plops in. Eleven smash on the ground. She makes no offer to pay. Hodgson, who is young and whimsical, grins and shrugs. He is not upset. He is authentically amused. Always, without a sign of stress, he accepts such losses. The customer fingers another dozen eggs, and asks if we are sure they are good.

I err again, making change—count out four ones, and then a five, "and ten makes twenty."

The customer says, "I gave you a ten-dollar bill, not a twenty."

I look at her softly, and say to her, "Thanks very much. You're very nice."

"What do you mean I'm very nice? I gave you a ten-dollar bill. Why does that make me very nice?"

"I meant to say I'm glad you noticed. I'm really glad you noticed."

"How much are the tomatoes?"

"Weigh these, please."

"Three pounds for a dollar."

"How much the corn?"

"Ten cents an ear. Twelve for a dollar."

"Everything is so superior. I'd forgotten what tomatoes taste like."

"Will you weigh these, please?"

"The prices are so ridiculously cheap."

"How can you charge so little?"

"In nine years in the city, I've never seen food like this."

"How much are these?"

"Fifty-five cents."

"Wow! What a rip-off!"

"Three pounds for a dollar is too much for tomatoes. You know that, don't you? I don't care how good they are."

"How much are these?"

"A dollar-ten."

"A dollar-*ten*?"

"Three eggplants. Three and a half pounds. Three pounds for a dollar. You can have them for a dollar-ten."

"Keep them."

"In the supermarket, the vegetables are unspeakable."

"They are brought in from California."

"You can't see what you are getting."

"When the frost has come and you are gone, what will we do without you?"

Around the market square, some of the trucks have stickers on them: "NO FARMERS, NO FOOD." Alvina Frey is here, and Ronald Binaghi, from farms in Bergen County, New Jersey. John Labanowski and his uncle Andy Labanowski are from the black-dirt country, the mucklands, of Orange County, New York. Bob Engle and Jim Kent tend orchards in the Hudson Valley. Bill Merriman, the honey man, is from Canaan, Connecticut; Joan Benack and Ursula Plock, the bakers, from Milan, New York. Ed and Judy Dart grow "organic" on Long Island, Richard Finch in Frenchtown, New Jersey. John Henry. Vincent Neglia. Ilija Sekulovski. Don Keller. Cleather Slade completes the ring. Slade is young, tall, paunchy, silent, and black. His wife, Dorothy, sells with him. She has a nicely lighted smile that suggests repose. Their family farmland is in Red Springs, North Carolina, but the Slades are mainly from Brooklyn. They make occasional trips South for field peas, collards, okra, yams, and for the reddest watermelons north of Chichicastenango.

Jeffrey Mack works for Hodgson part time. He has never seen a farm. He says he has never been out of the city. He lives five blocks away. He is eight years old, black. He has a taut, hard body, and glittering eyes, a round face. He piles up empty cartons for us and sometimes weighs tomatoes. On his better days he is some help.

"Jeffrey, that's enough raisin bread."

"Jeffrey, how many times do I have to tell you: get yourself out of the way."

"What are you doing here, Jeffrey? You ought to be in school."

He is not often pensive, but he is pensive for a moment now. "If you had a kid would you put him up for adoption?" he asks.

"What is that supposed to mean, Jeffrey? Why are you asking me that?"

"My mother says she's going to put me up for adoption."

With two, three, and four people working every truck, the farmers can occasionally take breaks, walk around—eat each other's apples, nectarines, and pears. Toward the end of the day, when their displays have been bought low and the crowd is becoming thin, they move around even more, and talk in small groups.

"What always surprises me is how many people are really nice here in the city."

"I was born in New York. My roots are here, you know. I'd throw away a bad cantaloupe, anything, so the people would come back."

"We have to leave them touch tomatoes, but when they do my guts go up and down. They paw them until if you stuck a pin in them they'd explode."

"They handle the fruit as if they were getting out all their aggressions. They press on the melons until their thumbs push through. I don't know why they have to handle the fruit like that. They're brutal on the fruit."

"They inspect each egg, wiggle it, make sure it's not stuck in the carton. You'd think they were buying diamonds."

"They're bag crazy. They need a bag for everything, sometimes two."

"They're nervous. So nervous."

"Today I had my third request from someone who wanted to come stay on the farm, who was looking for peace and quiet for a couple of days. He said he had found Jesus. It was unreal."

"I had two Jews in yarmulkes fighting over a head of lettuce. One called the other a kike."

"I've had people buy peppers from me and take them to another truck to check on the weight."

"Yeah, and meanwhile they put thirteen ears of corn in a bag, hand it to you, and say it's a dozen. I let them go. I only get after them when they have sixteen."

"They think we're hicks. 'Yeah,' I say. 'We're hicks and you're hookers. You're muggers and you breathe dirty air.' "

"I hardly smoke in the city. Down home I can smoke a whole pack of cigarettes and still have energy all night. You couldn't pay me to live here. I can't breathe."

If the farmers have a lot to say about their clients, they have even more to say about each other. Friendly from the skin out, they are deep competitors, and one thing that they are (in a sense) competing for is their right to be a part of the market. A high percentage of them seems to feel that a high percentage of the others should be shut down and sent away.

The Greenmarket was started in 1976. Farmers were recruited. Word got around. A wash of applicants developed. There was no practical or absolute way to check out certain facts about them—nor is there yet. For example, if some of the goods on a truck were not grown by the farmer selling them, who did grow them, and when, and where? The Green-market quickly showed itself to be a prime outlet for the retailing of farm produce. On a good day, one truck with an eighteen-foot box could gross several thousand dollars. So every imaginable kind of seller became attracted. The ever-present problem was that anyone in jeans with a rustic address painted on his truck could load up at Hunts Point, the city's wholesale fruit-and-vegetable center, and head out at 5 A.M. for the Greenmarket—a charter purpose of which was to help the regional farmer, not the fast-moving speculator, survive. Authentic farmers, moreover, could bring a little from home and a lot from Hunts Point. Wholesale goods, having been grown on big mass-production acreages (and often shipped in underripe from distant states), could be bought at Hunts Point and retailed—in some instances—at lower prices than the custom-grown produce of a small Eastern farm. Prices, however, were an incidental issue. The customers, the people of the city, believed—and were encouraged to believe—that when they walked into a Greenmarket they were surrounded by true farmers who had grown the produce they displayed and were offering it fresh from the farm. That was the purpose and promise of the Greenmarket—if not the whole idea, an unarguably large part of it—and in the instances where wholesale, long-distance, gassed-out goods were being presented (as some inevitably were) the principle was being subverted. In fact, the term Greenmarket had been coined—and registered in Albany—to set apart these markets in the public mind from certain "farmers' markets" around the city that are annually operated by Hunts Point hicks.

"Are you a farmer, or are you buying from an auction?" was a challenge the farmers began to fling around. Few were neighbors at home—in positions to know about each other.

They lived fifty, a hundred, a hundred and fifty miles apart, and came to the city to compete as strangers. They competed in sales, and they competed in slander. They still do. To a remarkable—and generally inaccurate—extent, they regard one another as phonies.

"He doesn't even know what shoe-peg corn is."

"Never trust a farmer who doesn't know shoe-peg corn."

"What exactly is shoe-peg corn?"

"Look at *him*. He has clean fingernails."

"I happen to know he has them manicured."

"I bust my hump seven days a week all summer long and I don't like to see people bring to market things they don't grow."

"Only farmers who are not farmers can ruin this market."

"These hustlers are going to work us off the block."

"There's farmers selling stuff they don't know what it is."

"What exactly is shoe-peg corn?"

"I like coming here. It gets me out of Vineland. Of course, you pick your ass off the night before."

"Look at Don Keller's hands. You can see the farm dirt in them."

"His nails. They'll never be clean."

"Rich Hodgson. See him over there? He has the cleanest fingernails in New York State."

"That Hodgson, he's nice enough, but he doesn't know what a weed looks like. I'll tell you this: he's never even *seen* a weed."

AROUND THE BUILDINGS of Hodgson Farms are some of the tallest volunteers in New York, topheavy plants that sway

(1 5)

overhead—the Eastern rampant weed. With everybody working ninety hours a week, there is not much time for cosmetics. For the most part, the buildings are chicken houses. Rich's father, Dick Hodgson, went into the egg business in 1946 and now has forty thousand hens. When someone in the city cooks a Hodgson egg, it has quite recently emerged from a chicken in a tilted cage, rolled onto a conveyor, and gone out past a candler and through a grader and into a waiting truck. A possible way to taste a fresher egg would be to boil the chicken with the egg still in it.

Dick Hodgson—prematurely white-haired, drivingly busy —is an agrarian paterfamilias whose eighty-two-year-old mother-in-law grades tomatoes for him. His wife, Frances, is his secretary and bookkeeper. He branched into truck farming some years ago specifically to keep his daughter, Judy, close to home. Judy runs the Hodgsons' roadside stand, in Plattekill, and her husband, Jan Krol, is the family's vegetable grower, the field boss—more than a hundred acres now under cultivation. Rich, meanwhile, went off to college and studied horticulture, with special emphasis on the fate of tropical houseplants. To attract him home, his father constructed a greenhouse, where Rich now grows wandering Jews, spider plants, impatiens, coleus, asparagus ferns—and he takes them with him to Harlem and wherever else he is allowed to sell them. Rich, who likes the crowds and the stir of the city, is the farm's marketer.

The Greenmarket, even more than the arriving Hodgson generation, has expanded Hodgson Farms. Before 1976, the family had scarcely twenty acres under cultivation and, even so, had difficulty finding adequate outlets for the vegetables Jan grew. The roadside stand moved only a minor volume.

Much of the rest was sold in New Jersey, at the Paterson Market, with discouraging results. "Paterson is semi-wholesale," Rich says. "You have to sell in units of a peck or more. You're lucky if you get three dollars for a half bushel of tomatoes. You ask for more and all you hear all day is 'That's a too much a money. That's a too much a money.' " (A half bushel of tomatoes weighs twenty-six pounds, and brings at least eight dollars at the Greenmarket, giving good weight.) The Hodgsons tried the fruit-and-vegetable auction in Milton, New York, but the auctioneer's cut was thirteen per cent and the farmers were working for him. They also tried a farmers' market in Albany, but sold three bushels of peppers and a couple of bags of corn in one depressing day. They were more or less failing as small-scale truck farmers. Dick Hodgson's theory of family cohesion through agricultural diversification was in need of an unknown spray. NBC News presented a short item one evening covering the début of the Greenmarket. The Hodgsons happened to be watching.

"The first place we went to was Fifty-ninth Street, and the people were fifteen deep waiting to get to the eggs. I couldn't believe it. There were just masses of faces. I looked at them and felt panic and broke into a cold sweat. They went after the corn so fast I just dumped it on the ground. The people fell on it, stripped it, threw the husks around. They were fighting, grabbing, snatching at anything they could get their hands on. I had never seen people that way, never seen anything like it. We sold a full truck in five hours. It was as if there was a famine going on. The people are quieter now."

Quietly, in a single day in the Greenmarket, Rich has sold as many as fifteen hundred dozen eggs. In one day, nearly five thousand ears of corn. In one day, three-quarters of a ton of tomatoes.

"How much are the tomatoes?"

"Fifteen hundred pounds for five hundred dollars."

Rich is in his mid-twenties, has a tumbling shag of bright-red hair, a beard that comes and goes. When it is gone, as now, in the high season of 1977, he retains not only a mustache but also a pair of frontburns: a couple of pelts that descend from either end of the mustache and pass quite close to his mouth on their way to his chin. He is about six feet tall and wears glasses. Their frames are pale blue. His energy is of the steady kind, and he works hard all day with an easygoing imperturbability—always bemused; always a controlled, sly smile. Rarely, he looks tired. On market days, he gets up at four, is on the Thruway by five, is setting up tables and opening cartons at seven, has a working breakfast around nine (Egg McMuffin), and, with only a short break, sells on his feet until six or seven, when he packs up to drive home, take a shower, drop into bed, and rise again at four. His companion, Melissa Mousseau, shares his schedule and sells beside him. There is no market on Mondays, so Rich works a fourteen-hour day at home. He packs cartons at the farm—cartons of cauliflowers, cartons of tomatoes—and meanders around the county collecting a load for Harlem. The truck is, say, the six-ton International with the Fruehauf fourteen-foot box—"HODGSON FARMS, NEWBURGH, N.Y., SINCE 1946." Corn goes in the nose—corn in dilapidating lath-and-wire crates that are strewn beside the fields where Jan has been bossing the pickers. The pickers are Newburgh high-school students. The fields, for the most part, are rented from the State of New York. A few years ago, the state bought Stewart Air Force

Base, outside Newburgh, with intent to lengthen the main runway and create an immense international freightport, an all-cargo jetport. The state also bought extensive farms lying off the west end of the base. Scarcely were the farmers packed up and on the road to Tampa Bay when bulldozers flattened their ancestral homes and dump trucks took off with the debris. The big freightport is still in the future, and meanwhile the milieu of the vanished farms is ghostly with upgrowing fields and clusters of shade trees around patches of smoothed ground where families centered their lives. The Hodgsons came upon this scene as farmers moving in an unusual direction. With the number of farms and farmers in steady decline in most places on the urban fringe, the Hodgsons were looking for land on which to expand. For the time being, rented land will do, but they hope that profits will be sufficient to enable them before long to buy a farm or two—to acquire land that would otherwise, in all likelihood, be industrially or residentially developed. The Greenmarket is the outlet—the sole outlet—that has encouraged their ambition. In the penumbral world of the airport land, there are occasional breaks in the sumac where long clean lines of Hodgson peppers reach to distant hedgerows, Hodgson cantaloupes, Hodgson cucumbers, Hodgson broccoli, collards, eggplants, Hodgson tomatoes, cabbages, corn—part vegetable patch, part disenfranchised farm, with a tractor, a sprayer, and a spreader housed not in sheds and barns but under big dusty maples. The family business is integrated by the spreader, which fertilizes the Greenmarket vegetables with the manure of the forty thousand chickens.

Corn in the nose, Rich drives to the icehouse, where he operates a machine that grinds up a three-hundred-pound block and sprays granulated snow all over the corn. Corn snow. He stops, too, at local orchards for apples, Seckel pears, nectarines, peaches, and plums. The Greenmarket allows farmers to amplify their offerings by bringing the produce of neighbors. A neighbor is not a wholesale market but another farmer, whose farm is reasonably near—a rule easier made than enforced. The Hodgsons pick things up—bread included —from several other farms in the county, but two-thirds to three-quarters of any day's load for the city consists of goods they grow themselves.

In the cooler of E. Borchert & Sons, the opiate aroma of peaches is overwhelming, unquenched by the refrigerant air. When the door opens, it frames, in summer heat, hazy orchards on ground that falls away to rise again in far perspective, orchards everywhere we can see. While loading half-bushel boxes onto the truck, we stop to eat a couple of peaches and half a dozen blue free plums. Not the least of the pleasures of working with Hodgson is the bounty of provender at hand, enough to have made the most sybaritic Roman prop himself up on one elbow. I eat, most days, something like a dozen plums, four apples, seven pears, six peaches, ten nectarines, six tomatoes, and a green pepper.

Eating his peach, Rich says, "The people down there in the city can't imagine this. They don't believe that peaches come from Newburgh, New York. They say that peaches come only from Georgia. People in the city have no concept of what our farming is like. They have no idea what a tomato plant looks like, or how a tomato is picked. They can't envision a place with forty thousand chickens. They have no concept how sweet corn grows. And the people around here have a false concept of the city. Before we went down there the first time, people up here said, 'You're out of your mind. You're going to get robbed. You're going to get stabbed.' But I just don't have any fears there. People in black Harlem are just as nice as people anywhere. City people generally are a lot calmer than I expected. I thought they would be loud, pushy, aggressive, and mean. But eighty per cent of them are nice and calm. Blacks and whites get along much better there than they do in Newburgh. Newburgh Free Academy, where I went to high school, was twenty-five per cent black. We had riots every year and lots of tension. Cars were set on fire. Actually, I prefer Harlem to most of the other markets. Harlem people are not so fussy. They don't manhandle the fruit. And they buy in quantity. They'll buy two dozen ears of corn, six pounds of tomatoes, and three dozen eggs. At Fifty-ninth Street, someone will buy one ear of corn for ten cents and want it in a bag. The reason we're down there is the money, of course. But the one-to-one contact with the people is really good—especially when they come back the next week and say, 'Those peaches were really delicious.' "

IN THE MOONLESS NIGHT, with the air too heavy for much sleep anyway, we are up and on the road, four abreast: Anders Thueson, Rich Hodgson, David Hemingway . . . A door handle is cracking my fifth right rib. Melissa Mousseau is not with us today, and for Hemingway it is the first time selling. He is a Newburgh teen-ager in sneakers and a red football shirt lettered "OKLAHOMA." Hemingway is marking time. He has mentioned January half a dozen ways since we started out, in a tone that reveres the word—January, an arriving milestone in his life, with a college out there waiting for him, and, by implication, the approach of stardom. Hemingway can high-jump seven feet. He remarks that the Greenmarket will require endurance and will therefore help build his stamina for January. He is black, and says he is eager to see Harlem, to be "constantly working with different people—that's a trip in the head by itself."

When the truck lurches onto the Thruway and begins the long rollout to the city, Hodgson falls asleep. Anders Thueson is driving. He is an athlete, too, with the sort of legs that make football coaches whistle softly. Thueson has small, fine features, light-blue eyes, and short-cropped hair, Scandinavian yellow. He is our corn specialist, by predilection—would apparently prefer to count ears than to compute prices from weights. When he arrives in Harlem he will touch his toes and do deep knee bends to warm himself up for the corn.

Dawn is ruddy over Tappan Zee, the far end of the great bridge indistinct in mist. Don Keller, coming from Middletown, broke down on the bridge not long ago, rebuilt his starter at the toll-booth apron, and rolled into market at noon. Days later, Jim Kent's truck was totalled on the way to Greenmarket—Hudson Valley grapes, apples, peaches, and corn all over the road. Gradually now, Irvington and Dobbs Ferry come into view across the water—big square houses of the riverbank, molars, packed in cloud. In towns like that, where somnolence is the main resource, this is the summit of the business day. Hodgson wakes up for the toll. For five minutes he talks sports and vegetable prices, and again he dozes away. On his lap is a carton of double-yolk eggs. His hands protect them. The fingernails are clean. Hodgson obviously sees no need to dress like Piers Plowman. He wears a yellow chemise Lacoste. The eggs are for Derryck Brooks-Smith, a

Brooklyn schoolteacher, who is a regular Hodgson city employee. Brooks-Smith is by appearances our best athlete. He runs long distances and lifts significant weights. He and Thueson have repeatedly tried to see who can be the first to throw an egg over an eight-story building on Amsterdam Avenue. To date their record of failure is one hundred per cent—although each has succeeded with a peach.

We arrive at six-fifteen, to find Van Houten, Slade, and Keller already setting up—in fact, already selling. People are awake, and much around, and Dorothy Slade is weighing yams, three pounds for a dollar. Meanwhile, it is extremely difficult to erect display tables, open boxes, and pile up peppers and tomatoes when the crowd helps take off the lids. They grab the contents.

"Weigh these, please."

"May I have a plastic bag?"

"Wait—while I get the scales off the truck." The sun has yet to show above the brownstones.

This is the corner of 137th Street and Adam Clayton Powell Jr. Boulevard, known elsewhere in the city as Seventh Avenue. The entire name—Adam Clayton Powell Jr. Boulevard—is spelled out on the street sign, which, as a result, has a tip-to-tip span so wide it seems prepared to fly. The big thoroughfare itself is of extraordinary width, and islanded, like parts of Broadway and Park Avenue. A few steps north of us are the Harlem Performance Center and the Egbe Omo Nago African Music Center, and just east along 137th Street from our trucks is the Mother A.M.E. Zion Church. For the Tuesday Greenmarket, the street has been barricaded and cars sent out, an exception being an old Plymouth without tires that rests on flaking steel. On the front wall of the church is a decorous advertisement: "Marion A. Daniels & Sons, Funeral Directors." The block has four young sycamores, and contiguous buildings in every sort of shape from the neat and trim to broken-windowed houses with basements that are open like caves. On 137th Street beyond Adam Clayton Powell are two particularly handsome facing rows of brownstones, their cornices convex and dentilled, their entrances engrandeured with high, ceremonious flights of stairs. Beyond them, our view west is abruptly shut off by the City College cliffs in St. Nicholas Park—the natural wall of Harlem.

The farm trucks are parked on the sidewalks. Displays are in the street. Broad-canopied green, orange, purple, and red umbrellas shield produce from the sun. We have an awning, bolted to the truck. Anders Thueson, with a Magic Marker, is writing our prices on brown paper bags, taping them up as signs. "Is plums spelled with a 'b'?" he asks.

Hemingway tells him no.

A tall, slim woman in a straw hat says to me, "I come down here get broke every Tuesday. Weigh these eggplants, please."

"There you are. Do you want those in a bag?"

"You gave me good weight. You don't have to give me bags."

Minerva Coleman walks by, complaining. She is short and acidulous, with graying hair and quick, sardonic eyes. She wears bluejeans and a white short-sleeved sweatshirt. She has lived in this block twenty-three years. "You farmers come in too early," she says. "Why do you have to come in so early? I have to get up at four o'clock every Tuesday, and that don't make sense. I don't get paid."

Not by the Greenmarket, at any rate. Minerva works for Harlem Teams for Self-Help, an organization that is something like a Y.M.-Y.W.C.A. It is housed, in fact, in a former Y, the entrance to which is behind our truck. Minerva is Director of Economic Development. As such, she brought the Greenmarket to 137th Street—petitioned the city for it, arranged with the precinct to close off the street. While her assistants sell Harlem Teams for Self-Help shopping bags (fifteen cents), Minerva talks tomatoes with the farmers, and monitors the passing crowd. As the neighborhood kleptos come around the corner, she is quick to point them out. When a middle-aged man in a business suit appears on the scene wearing a sandwich board, she reads the message—"HARLEM TEAM FOR DESTROYING BLACK BUSINESS"—and at once goes out of her tree. "What do you mean, 'destroying black business'? Who is destroying black business? *What* is destroying black business? Get your ass off this block. Can't you see this market is good for everybody? The quality and the price against the quality and the price at the supermarket—there's no comparison."

Exit sandwich board.

"How much are the apples?"

"Three pounds for a dollar, madam."

"Are they sweet?"

"You can eat them straight or bake them in a pie."

"Give me six pounds of apples, six pounds of tomatoes, and three dozen extra-large eggs. Here the boxes from the eggs I bought last week."

Mary Hill, Lenox Avenue. Florrie Thomas, Grand Concourse. Leroy Price, Bradhurst Avenue. Les Boyd, the Polo Grounds. Ylonia Phillips, 159th Street. Selma Williamson, 141st Street. Hattie Mack, Lenox Avenue. Ten in the morning and the crowd is thick. The sun is high and hot. People are drinking from fireplugs. A white cop goes by, the radio on his buttock small and volcanic, erupting: ". . . beating her for two hours." In the upstairs windows of the houses across the street, women sit quietly smoking.

"Are these peppers hot?"

"Those little ones? Yeah. They're hot as hell."

"How do you know how hot hell is? How do you know?"

The speaker is male and middle-aged, wears a jacket and tie, and is small, compact, peppery. He continues, "How do you know how hot hell is? You been over there? I don't think you know how hot hell is."

"Fifty cents, please."

The hundreds of people add up into thousands, and more are turning the corner—every face among them black. Rarely, a white one will come along, an oddity, a floating moon. Just as a bearded person becomes unaware of his beard and feels that he looks like everyone else, you can forget for a time that your own face is white. There are no reminders from the crowd.

Middle-aged man with a woman in blue. She reaches for the roll of thin plastic bags, tugs one off, and tries to open it. The sides are stuck together and resist coming apart. She looks up helplessly, looks at me. Like everyone else on this side of the tables, I am an expert at opening plastic bags.

"These bags are terrible," I tell her, rubbing one between my thumb and fingers. When it comes open, I hand it to her.

"Why, thank you," she says. "You're nice to do that for me. I guess that is the privilege of a lady."

Her husband looks me over, and explains to her, "He's from the old school." There is a pause, some handling of fruit. Then he adds, "But the old schools are closing these days."

"They're demolished," she says. "The building's gone."

They fill their sack with peppers (Lady Bell).

The older the men are here, the more likely it is that they are wearing suits and ties. Gray fedoras. Long cigars. The younger they are, the more likely it is that they are carrying shoulder-strapped Panasonics, turned on, turned up—blaring. Fortunately, the market seems to attract a high proportion of venerable people, dressed as if for church, exchanging news and some opinion.

Among our customers are young women in laboratory smocks with small gold rings in the sides of their noses— swinging from a pierced nostril. They work in Harlem Hospital, at the end of the block, on Lenox Avenue.

Fat man stops to assess the peppers. His T-shirt says, "I SURVIVED THE BERMUDA TRIANGLE." Little boy about a foot high. His T-shirt says, "MAN'S BEST FRIEND."

Our cabbages are in full original leaf, untrimmed, each one so broad and beautiful it appears to be a carnation from the lapel of the Jolly Green Giant. They do not fit well in collapsible shopping carts, so people often ask me to strip away the wrapper leaves. I do so, and sell the cabbage, and go back to weighing peppers, making change, more peppers, more change. Now comes a twenty-dollar bill. When I go into my money apron for some ones, a five, a ten, all I come up with is cabbage.

I prefer selling peppers. When you stay in one position long enough, a proprietary sense develops—as with Thueson and the corn. Hodgson, the true proprietor, seems to enjoy selling anything—houseplants and stringbeans, squash and pears. Derryck Brooks-Smith likes eggs and tomatoes. Hemingway is an apple man. Or seems to be. It is early to tell. He is five hours into his first day, and I ask how he is getting along. Hemingway says, "These women in Harlem are driving me nuts, but the Jews in Brooklyn will be worse." Across his dark face flies a quick, sarcastic smile. "How *you* doing?" he asks me.

"Fine. I am a pepper seller who long ago missed his calling."

"You like peppers?"

"I have come to crave them. When I go home, I take a sackful with me, and slice them, and fill a big iron skillet to the gunwales—and when they're done I eat them all myself."

"Cool."

"These tomatoes come from a remote corner of Afghanistan," Derryck Brooks-Smith is saying to some hapless client. "They will send you into ecstasy." She is young and appears to believe him, but she may be in ecstasy already. Brooks-Smith is a physical masterpiece. He wears running shorts. Under a blue T-shirt, his breasts bulge. His calves and thighs are ribbed with muscle. His biceps are smooth brown loaves. His hair is short and for the most part black, here and there brindled with gray. His face is fine-featured, smile disarming. He continues about the tomatoes: "The smaller ones are from Hunza, a little country in the Himalayas. The people of Hunza attribute their longevity to these tomatoes. Yes, three pounds for a dollar. They also attribute their longevity to yogurt and a friendly family. I like your dress. It fits you well."

Brooks-Smith teaches at John Marshall Intermediate School, in Brooklyn. "A nice white name in a black neighborhood," he once remarked. He was referring to the name of the school, but he could as well have meant his own. He was born in the British West Indies. His family moved to New York in 1950, when he was ten. He has a master's degree from City University. "It is exciting for me to be up here in Harlem, among my own people," he has told me over the scale. "Many of them are from the South. They talk about Georgia, about South Carolina. They have a feeling for the farm a lot of people in the city don't have." He quotes Rimbaud to his customers. He fills up the sky for them with the "permanganate sunsets" of Henry Miller. He instructs them in nutrition. He lectures on architecture in a manner that makes them conclude correctly that he is talking about them. They bring him things. Books, mainly. Cards of salutation and farewell, anticipating his return to the school. "Peace, brother, may you always get back the true kindness you give." The message is handwritten. The card and its envelope are four feet wide. A woman in her eighties who is a Jehovah's Witness hands him a book, her purpose to immortalize his soul. She will miss him. He has always given her a little more than good weight. "I love old people," he says when she departs. "We have a lot to learn from them."

"This is where it is, man. This is where it is!" says a basketball player, shouldering through the crowd toward the eggplants and tomatoes, onions and pears. He is well on his way to three metres in height, and his friend is taller still. They wear red shorts with blue stripes and black-and-white Adidas shoes. The one who knows where it is picks up seven or eight onions, each the size of a baseball, and holds them all in one hand. He palms an eggplant and it disappears. "Man," he goes on, "since these farmers came here I don't hardly eat meat no more."

Now comes a uniformed racing cyclist—All-Sports Day at the Greenmarket. He is slender, trained, more or less thirty, and he seems to be on furlough from the Tour de France. He looks expensive in his yellow racing gloves, his green racing shoes. Partly walking, partly gliding, he straddles his machine. He leans over and carefully chooses peppers, apparently preferring the fire-engine-red ones. Brooks-Smith whispers to me, "That bicycle frame is a Carlton, made in England. It's worth at least five hundred dollars. They're rare. They're not made much anymore."

"That will be one dollar, please," I say to the cyclist, and he pays me with a food stamp.

Woman says, "What is this stuff on these peaches?"

"It's called fuzz."

"It was on your peaches last week, too."

"We don't take it off. When you buy peaches in the store, the fuzz has been rubbed off."

"Well, I never."

"You never saw peach fuzz before? You're kidding."

"I don't like that fuzz. It makes me itchy. How much are the tomatoes?"

"Three pounds for a dollar."

"Give me three pounds. Tomatoes don't have fuzz."

"I'm a bachelor. Give me a pound of plums." The man is tall, is wearing a brown suit, and appears to be nearing seventy. "They're only for me, I don't need more," he explains. "I'm a bachelor. I don't like the word 'bachelor.' I'm really a widower. A bachelor sounds like a playboy."

"Thirty-five cents, please. Who's next?"

"Will somebody lend me a dollar so I can get some brandy and act like a civilized human for a change?" We see very few drunks. This one wears plaid trousers, a green blazer, an open-collared print shirt. He has not so much as feigned interest in the peppers but is asking directly for money. "This is my birthday," he continues. "Happy birthday, Gus. My mother and father are dead. If they were alive, I'd kick the hell out of them. They got me into this bag. For twenty years, I shined shoes outside the Empire State Building. And now I'm here, a bum. I need to borrow a dollar. Happy birthday, Gus."

SLADE, OPPOSITE, is taking a break. He sits on an upturned tall narrow basket, with his head curled into his shoulder. Like a sleeping bird, he has drifted away. I need a break, too—some relief from the computations, the chaotic pulsations of the needle on the scale.

"Two and a quarter pounds at three pounds for a dollar comes to, let's see, seventy-five cents. Five and a half pounds at three for a dollar twenty-five, call it two and a quarter. That's three dollars."

"Even?"

"Even."

"Y'all going up every week. Y'all going to be richer than hell."

"How much are the nectarines?"

"Weigh these, please."

Turn. Put the fruit in the pan. Calculate. Turn again. Spin the plastic bag. Knot the top. Hand it over. Change a bill.

"You take food stamps?"

"Yes, but I can't give you change."

"How much are the green beans pounds for a dollar and with you in a minute next one—please."

I take off my money apron, give it to Rich, and drift around the market. I compare prices with the Van Houtens. I talk cows with Joe Hlatky. We are from the same part of New Jersey, and he once worked for the Walker-Gordon dairy, in Plainsboro, with its Rotolactor merry-go-round milking platform. Hlatky is a big, stolid man with a shock of blond hair not as neatly prepared as his wife's, which has been professionally reorganized as a gold hive. They work together, selling their sweet white corn and crimson tomatoes—not for nothing is it called the Garden State. Hlatky's twenty-one-year-old daughter, Juanita, often sells with him, too. She is a large-boned, strongly built, large-busted blonde like her mother. Hlatky says that he and his family are comfortable here in Harlem, feeling always, among other things, the appreciative good will of the people. I remember Minerva Coleman telling me that when the farmers came into Harlem the first Tuesday they were "a little nervous—but after that they were O.K." She went on to say, "You can tell when people don't feel quite secure. But now they come in here and go about their business and they don't pay nobody no mind. They like the people here better than anywhere else. I don't know why. I would assume they'd get ripped off a little bit—but not too much." And now Hlatky, standing on 137th Street weighing tomatoes, says again how much he likes this market, and adds that he feels safer here than he does in other parts of the city. He says, "I'll tell you the most dangerous place we sell at. The roughest part of the city we go to is Union Square." So rough, he confides, that when he goes there, on Saturdays, he takes along an iron pipe.

Hlatky today has supplemented his homegrown New Jersey vegetables with peaches from a neighbor in California. They are wrapped in individual tissues. They are packed and presented in a fine wooden box. He bought them at a wholesale market. Robert Lewis, assistant director of the Greenmarket, happens along and sees the peaches. Lewis is a regional planner about to receive an advanced degree from the University of Pennsylvania, a gentle person, slight of build, a little round of shoulder, with a bandanna around his throat, a daypack on his back, steel-rimmed spectacles—all of which contribute to an impression of amiable, academic frailty. He says to big Joe Hlatky, "Get those peaches out of sight!"

With an iron pipe, a single tap on the forehead could send Lewis to heaven twice. Hlatky respects him, though, and is grateful to him, too, for the existence of the market. Hlatky says he will sell off these peaches, with a promise not to bring more—never again to bring to a Greenmarket so much as a single box of wholesale fruit.

"The peaches are from California," says Lewis. "They must go back on the truck."

Hlatky casts aspersions up one side of 137th Street and down the other. Has Lewis noticed Slade's beans, Hodgson's onions, Van Houten's lettuce, Sekulovski's entire load? He says he feels unfairly singled out. He knows, though, that without Lewis and Barry Benepe, who created and developed the Greenmarket, the Hlatky farm in New Jersey would be even more marginal than it is now. ("Here you can make double what you make wholesale. If I sold my stuff in a wholesale market, I couldn't begin to exist.") And while Lewis and Benepe might lack a certain shrewdness with regard to the origin of beans, they contribute an essential that no farmer could provide: a sophisticated knowledge of the city.

One does not just drive across a bridge with a load of summer squash, look around for a vacant lot, and create a farmers' market in New York. Tape of every color is in the way:

(33)

community boards, zoning committees, local merchants, City Hall. In order to set up even one open-air market—not to mention five or six—it was necessary to persuade, and in many cases to struggle against, nine city agencies, which Benepe describes in aggregate as "an octopus without a head; pull off one tentacle and another has a grip." Benepe is an architect who has worked as a planner not only for the city government but also in Orange County, watching the orchards disappear. When he conceived of the Greenmarket, in 1974, it seemed "a natural answer to a twofold problem": loss of farm-land in the metropolitan area and a lack of "fresh, decent food" in the city. Moreover, farmers selling produce from their trucks would start conversations, help resuscitate neigh-borhoods, brighten the aesthetic of the troubled town. "It seemed too obvious to ignore," Benepe says. "But most ob-vious things do get ignored." Benepe, like Lewis, is a native of the city. Son of an importer of linen, he studied art history at Williams College (1950) and went on to M.I.T. His dress and appearance remain youthful. To the Greenmarket office, on Fortieth Street, he wears brown denim highwaters, polo shirts, and suède Wallabees. He has long sandy graying hair, a lithe frame, a flat stomach. He rides a bicycle around town. He has a steady gaze, pale-blue eyes. He knows where City Hall is. He once worked for the Housing and Redevelopment Board. To start the Greenmarket, he knew which doors to knock on, and why they would not open. He approached the Real Estate Department. "They seemed to think I wanted to rip them off." He affiliated the project with the Council on the Environment of New York City in order to be eligible to receive foundation funds. He tried the Vinmont Foundation, the Richmond Foundation, the Fund for the City of New York, the America the Beautiful Fund. Finally, the J. M. Kaplan Fund said it would match anything he raised elsewhere. He went back to the others, and enough came through. Of the Greenmarket's overall cost—forty-two thousand dollars in 1977—the farmers, renting space, pay a third.

Lewis, twenty years younger, was a colleague of Benepe in Benepe's urban-planning firm, and helped him start the market. They searched for sites where farmers would be welcome, where neighborhoods would be particularly benefitted, where local fruit-and-vegetable stores were unlikely to open fire. Lewis to a large extent recruited the farmers. He sought advice from Cornell and Rutgers, and wrote to county agents, and interviewed people whose names the agents supplied. He went to roadside-marketing conferences, to farmers' associations, to wholesale outlets. Under his generally disarranged locks, his undefeated shrug, Lewis has a deep and patient intelligence that tends to linger over any matter or problem that comes within its scrutiny. If he is ready to rebuke the farmers (for selling West Coast peaches), he is also ready to listen, without limit, to their numerous problems and even more numerous complaints. Day by day, market to market, he is a most evident link between the farmers and the city. He binds them to it, interprets it for them. Son of a New York University professor, he has no idea what shoe-peg corn is, but he was born in Brooklyn Jewish Hospital, grew up in Crown Heights, and has a sense of neighborhoods, of urban ways, that reaches from Flatbush to the hem of Yonkers. He is not much frightened by Harlem or intimidated by Fifty-ninth Street. He is a city man, and, more important, he is an emeritus city kid.

After staring up the street for a while, Hlatky puts the peaches back on the truck.

"Cigarette lighters! Cigarette lighters!"

The Zippo man did not grow his produce down home. "Cigarette lighters!" Never mind where they're from. They're fifty per cent off and selling fast. While Lewis goes after the Zippo man—effecting an at best temporary expulsion—I return to my peppers.

"Give me two, please. Just two. I ain't got nobody with me. I live by myself. I throw food in the pot. I stick a fork in it. When it gets soft, I eat it."

"Lysol! Lysol!"

A man has come along selling Lysol. He offers cans to Rich Hodgson and, at the same time, to a woman to whom Rich is selling apples. One result of the Greenmarket's considerable success is the attraction it presents to street hucksters, not the Sabrett's-hot-dog sort of street venders, who are licensed by the city, but itinerant merchants of the most mercurial kind. Some conceal things under their jackets. They are readily identifiable because their arms hang straight, as whose would not with five pounds of watches on either wrist? They sell anything—ski hats, tooled-leather belts, turquoise rings, inflatable airplanes. They spread blankets on the sidewalk and sprinkle them with jewelry. Man comes by now selling his dog. They always try to sell to the farmers, who are possibly better customers than the customers. A guy came up to me once in Brooklyn and offered me a case of hot mangoes. I assume they were hot. What other temperature could they be when the case-lot price was two dollars? Another day in Brooklyn, a man pulled up to the curb in an old Chevrolet sedan, opened the trunk, and began selling Finnish porgies. Cleaning them, he spilled their innards into a bucket and their scales fell like snow on the street.

As to nowhere else, though, such people are attracted to

137th Street. All day they come by, selling coconuts, guavas, and terminal-market cucumbers out of carts from the A. & P. "Crabs! Crabs!" The crab man has bright-red boiled blue crabs. Three for a dollar, they dangle from strings. Now a man arrives with a rolling clothes rack crammed with sweaters and pants. He wants eighteen dollars for a two-piece ensemble. "No, thanks," a woman tells him. "I don't want to go to jail." She turns to the peppers and glances up at me, saying, "If a cop came around the corner they'd drop that stuff and run." Now a young man and woman in turtlenecks and Earth shoes wheel up a grocery cart full of comic books, cotton hats, incense, and tube socks. He has a premature paunch. Her eyes are dreamy and the lids are slow. She leans on him in a noodly manner. She looks half asleep, while he looks half awake, as if they were passing each other in the middle of a long journey. "Tube socks! Incense! Tube socks!" The man fixes his attention on Rich. "It's going to get—I'm telling you—*cold* on that farm, man." The socks are still in the manufacturer's package, marked a dollar ninety-five a pair. "Cold, man, I'm telling you. Here's six pairs for five dollars." Sold.

Minerva Coleman, who has been watching, stares after the couple as they go. "That must have been a Long Island girl," she says. "A Harlem girl would know I'd break her ass."

There was a firehouse across the street once. It was razed, and a vest-pocket park is there now, smoothly paved, with a chain-link fence, three strands of barbed wire, and a fan-shaped basketball backboard that (most weeks) has a net. When I am not turned toward the scale, and while I wait for customers to fill their plastic bags, I often watch the games across the street. Some of the boys who play there move like light, their gestures rehearsed, adroit. They go both ways, hit well from the outside. The game they play, almost to the exclusion of any other game, begins from the outside.

Say five, in all, are playing. One starts things off with a set from outside.

"How much are the peppers?"

"Three pounds for a dollar."

"Pick me out three pounds. I'll be back after I get some corn."

"Where are your beans? What happened to your beans today?"

The shooter hits five straight from twenty feet. He is a pure shooter. Now he misses. He and the four others go for the rebound. The one who gets the ball is now on his own to try to score, while everyone else tries to stop him. He dribbles right, into the one-on-four. He stops. Jumps. Shoots. Misses.

"Weigh these, please."

"Weigh mine, please."

Another player grabs the ball. Now *he* makes his moves, trying to score against the four others. The ball pulsates in his hands. His legs are flexed. His feet do not stir. He picks his moment, leaps, arches his back (ball behind his head), scores. The ball is handed to him. He goes outside and shoots an unguarded set. He hits. He shoots another. He misses. Someone else gets the rebound. Now it is four against *that* player as he tries to drive and score. He misses. The player who gets the rebound now faces the four others. . . .

"Mister, will you weigh these peppers? Do you want to sell them to me or not?"

"Sorry. Three and a half pounds. Take them for a dollar." Who wants to make change?

After a reverse pivot that is fluid beyond his years, the kid with the ball scores. He walks to the outside. He takes a free set. Swish. He hits again.

"Weigh these, please."

The shooter misses. The rebound goes high. All five are after it. The boy who grabs it turns and faces the mob.

We see the same game all over the city. Always, the player with the ball is alone, the isolated shooter, the incubating star—versus everyone else on the court. There is never a pass, a screen, a pick, a roll, a two-on-two, a two-on-three, a three-on-two, a teammate. I turn with some peppers and rattle the scale.

Bartley Bryt comes by and says a cop caught a thief who was ripping off Sekulovski. Bryt is young and white, in blue-jeans, Pumas, and a rugger shirt. He is doing a summer job, helping administer the market. He is slim, good-looking, with a shock of light-brown hair—Dalton School, 1977.

I ask him how old the thief was.

"About forty-five," says Bryt. "The only elderly person I've ever seen stealing here. When there's trouble here, it's usually from kids, but there's not much trouble, because the community feeling is so great here. People are so nice to you. Where I live, people go in and turn on their air-conditioners and that's it."

"Where do you live?"

"Seventy-fifth Street between Park and Lexington."

"How much are the cucumbers?"

"Eight for a dollar."

"Give me some ham knuckles, too."

(39)

"No ham knuckles."

"I was here earlier and there was ham knuckles here."

"Not at this truck, ham knuckles."

"Bobby Van Houten has ham knuckles."

"Yeah. He's killing us."

"Look at all those people at his truck. They're ten deep."

"He'll gross five thousand dollars today if he takes home a cent."

"He buys the stuff at a slaughterhouse."

"I'd like to see those pigs he talks about."

"If he raises pigs, I raise bananas."

The Van Houtens, next to us, are working from a truck with an eighteen-foot box. There is no larger vehicle here. To secure their choice position—on the corner, at the mouth of the street—they arrived at four in the morning on the first Harlem Tuesday. Wherever you are at the start, you remain for the summer. The Van Houtens are nothing if not aggressive. With their high-piled fruit-and-vegetable displays and sixteen hundred pounds of ham hocks, hog jowls, and additional pig products coming out of a cooler on the truck, they are frenetically busy. Of the five people working there, four are named Van Houten. Like the Hodgsons', their operation is a family conglomerate. Behind the peaches and peppers is Jim Van Houten, stocky, cheerful, nervous, with a big lick of dark brown hair shading a round, thoughtful face. He is a Master of Business Administration (Cornell University). His wife, Sue Ellen, is close to the cabbage. She brings paperbacks for lulls in the glut. Kay Van Houten, Jim's mother, is dark-haired, trim, youthful, and small. Tomatoes, peppers, jowls alike, she works tirelessly at the scales, the all-day conversion of weight to cash, which she accumulates in a steel box in the cab of the truck. Her other son, Bobby, while selling at least as much as anyone else, periodically leaps onto the truck, lights his pipe, heaves out produce, jumps off the truck, builds and rebuilds high displays, lights his pipe, and moves up and down behind the tables exhorting, encouraging, assisting, scolding, spreading the contagion that seems to impel him, his need to get the best of the bazaar. Bobby has pale-blue eyes. He has patrician high cheekbones, turn-of-the-century sideburns, the heroic good looks of an archaic star. He is obviously the boss—the field boss, anyway, his father being the corporate mastermind, the absentee trucklord.

"They have a big place out in Pennsylvania."

"They *say* they have a big place out in Pennsylvania."

"Yeah. I happen to know they run a fruit stand in Rockland County."

"They buy their stuff wholesale and bring it from the stand."

"Bobby is a truck driver, not a farmer. He makes long hauls in big rigs."

"I seen him at Hunts Point."

"Look at the stuff on their truck—all those brand-new cartons of Lake Ontario celery."

"They got lettuce from upstate, too."

"Florida cabbages."

"Long Island potatoes."

"Pennsylvania my ass."

"You know the name of their place? It's called Van Houten's Hunts Point Farms."

The Van Houtens last year spent ten thousand dollars on seeds. Their place—near Orangeville, Pennsylvania—is on a tributary of the Susquehanna River, about a hundred and fifty miles west of New York. They rent a couple of hundred neighboring acres as well, so they have about five hundred under cultivation. They work not just busily but feverishly—from dawn some distance into dark—with little time and probably less inclination to contemplate the scenery they are helping to preserve. Their farm is among the intervales where the Poconos and the Alleghenies reach toward one another in the central Appalachian uplift. Their terrain is like rising bread against backdrops of long, low mountains. These Pennsylvania ridges, steep-sided and flat-topped, run on for tens and even hundreds of miles. Knob Mountain, the nearest to the Van Houtens, stands high above the farm, its slopes mainly wooded but open, too, with fairways of upland pasture. There are red covered bridges, nut-colored unpainted barns, narrow crown roads among corn shocks in the autumn—pheasant land. It is a strangely mottled country, where, not many miles to the east, you can make your way in brilliant sunshine across long vistas of standing grain—pastures full of Guernseys, barns full of milk—all the while approaching a high plateau on which there is stationary cloud. When you go up there and out of the warm countryside you enter a spitting fog and before long come into the slippery streets of a small corroding city where atmospheric acids are eating the J. C. Penney and the town common is a huge anthracitic pit. Not much seems to link these plateau towns with the needlepoint-sampler valleys that surround them—not much except, perhaps, the pheasant. The bird is curious and goes up there, too—pecks at the edges of the pit. On a coal-town street, I killed one with my car one day when I went out with Bob Lewis to visit the Van Houtens. The right front fender broke its neck and little else. I tossed it into the back seat and dressed it later at home, expecting pea coal to come out of its gizzard but discovering instead the pebbles of the valley. Stuffed with bread, raisins, and Green-market onions, it was as succulent a bird as ever climbed a hill.

The Van Houtens' packinghouse is a white barn in a state of picturesque dilapidation. The farmhouse is brick, square, solid, and Dutch, with a windowed cupola at the apex of a pyramidal roof. It is surrounded by heavy oaks and maples, and a hundred acres of field corn are visible from the kitchen. Bobby's parents have a place nearby, while he lives in the farmhouse with his wife, Anne, who is a schoolteacher, and their four young children, including twins. He was wearing the same threadbare jeans and faded denim shirt he wears in New York, his belt buckle roughly a pound of steel, on which raised letters said "FIELD BOSS." We cruised in his pickup, climbed steep roadless hills, and crossed bottomlands crowded with cabbage—savoy cabbage, with its spinachlike cobbled leaves. Cucumbers, broccoli, collards, cauliflower, canta-loupes, eggplant, peppers, lettuce—Van Houten's "Hunts Point" Farms. "Yeah," said Bobby. "The good Lord made twenty-four hours in a day and seven days in a week, and we work every bit of it. We spray with parathion. We spend forty thousand a year for fertilizer and chemicals, and another two thousand for the chopper that spreads the chemicals. Para-thion is deadly, but in three days it's dissipated. It will never take the place of DDT. It's not as safe, either. You can drink DDT straight. It won't hurt you. During the war, Italian pris-oners were sprayed with DDT. No one ever died from it. The government hurt us bad when they took away the DDT."

There was a stock pond and a fenced-in woodlot, with pigs and cows among the hemlocks, cherries, and pines. Pigs were squealing and fighting for position around an Agway feeder. We leaned on the fence and watched. "Field-corn prices are dropping every week, and the futures are worse," said Bobby, with a suck and a puff and a dash of flame. He uses a steel cylindrical lighter that shoots a foot-long tongue of gas. "So right now it pays to put the field corn through the pigs. If the price goes up, it won't pay. Pigs go well behind cows. They run together. Pigs will eat what the cows won't eat. A third of corn goes through a cow. Pigs thrive on that stuff." Burlap bags soaked in crankcase oil were wrapped around the trunks of trees. After the pigs rub up against the trees the oil that coats them discourages lice. In a lean-to deep in the woodlot rested a pig three times the size of any of the other pigs. "The truck must have missed that one," Bobby said. "And more than once. Some of them hide in the woods when the truck comes. We have up to a hundred and fifty here at any one time. We send off about twenty a week. The slaughterhouse gives us extra jowls and knuckles for the New York market. No one around here eats that stuff. You'd be surprised what they do eat, though. When the testicles are sliced off, the more farmer farmers take them in and cook them. I throw them away." Standing nearby was a Mercedes-Benz diesel fifty-ton refrigeration unit, keeping cool the knuckles, jowls, spareribs, sausage, baloney, and smoked neck bones that within a few hours would be transferred to the truck for Harlem.

Van Houten Farms is a heavy supplier for Mrs. Smith's Pies, of Pottstown, Pennsylvania, where Mrs. Smith bakes ten thousand pumpkin pies an hour and uses Van Houten Boston marrow squash. They are grown by the no-till method. Just plant the seeds and let the field go—sixty-five acres, two thousand tons of squash, big orange bombs hidden under thatches of weed.

"Did you ever see ketchup *before* it went into a bottle?" Bobby said, turning into a field of tomatoes grown for the kitchens of Chef Boy-ar-dee. They appeared to have been harvested by migrant sauropods who had ripped whole vines from the soil and thrashed the tomatoes free. Hundreds of thousands—crushed and split—were now ready for delivery. On arrival at the plant they would be unloaded with a high-pressure hose—tomato slurry. We went up on a dome of channery shale, hundreds of feet above the surrounding terrain, where tomatoes grew wider than the spread of a man's hand, almost to the size of curling stones. The ground was so steep that, to hold the soil, rows of hay and sod were interspersed with the vines. While the low-ground tomatoes were on the way to Boy-ar-dee, these would be rolling toward Harlem.

The Van Houtens sell to Boy-ar-dee for three cents a pound. The tomatoes they take to Harlem return ten times that. They sell tomatoes at Hunts Point, too—for less than half of what they get in the Greenmarket. "Lots of times we don't make money selling wholesale. When corn goes at Hunts Point for two-seventy-five a box, there's nothing left for us." From big canneries to city sidewalks, they sell at every type of outlet. They have to—to dispense their considerable production. And, as one would imagine, their roadside stand is not a card table. Rather, it is a fair-sized store. It is close to the New York-New Jersey line, less than twenty miles north of the George Washington Bridge. "It attracts the carriage trade," Bobby said. "Cadillacs, Lincolns, Jaguars. We pay a hundred and seventy dollars a week in taxes there, and the customers are bitches. One Tuesday in Harlem, we had six salespeople working the counter. *Each* of the six grossed as much as the roadside stand for that day—and four people were working the stand. I'd rather wait on those people in Harlem anyway.

I'd rather wait on them for ten hours than on our affluent trade at the stand for ten minutes. If I had my choice I'd take a market every day solid black. Second choice I'd take the Spanish, last of all the whites. They're a solid pain in the ass. They ask if something has sodium nitrite. Well, to preserve something, the only alternative is embalming fluid. Some woman gets out of a Lincoln Continental and peels back an ear of corn. 'Oooo, a worm!' she says. 'Do you use chemicals on this corn?' And I say, 'Lady, you can't have it both ways.' The people in Harlem appreciate our being there. We sell cabbage three heads for a dollar there. Three heads for a dollar is a good deal for those people and a good deal for us. They rarely complain. They tell you how nice the tomatoes are, how nice the sweet corn is. It gives you a nice feeling at the end of the day."

The Van Houtens are, as Bobby says it, "Blauvelt Holland Dutch," yielding only twenty years' seniority to Henry Hudson himself. Gerrit Hendricksen Blauvelt was their seminal patroon. His sons were part of a syndicate that bought the Tappan Patent, west of the Tappan Zee. "Oh, yeah, we're S.A.R., C.A.R., D.A.R. Both my mother and father are Blauvelts. I'm Blauvelts fourteen ways. The Van Houtens didn't come over until 1670. The house I grew up in was built in 1731." The original address was Muddy Brook, New York, a name that was changed a century ago—in an early example of suburban semantics—to Pearl River.

When Bobby was growing up, the family ran a dairy farm in Pearl River that is now three fathoms deep—a reservoir owned by the Hackensack Water Company. In 1953, when he was in kindergarten, he and Jim put up a table beside the road and sold vegetables from the family garden. With the money they took in, they bought their first TV. They planted a larger garden the next year, and bought an automatic washing machine for their mother. Four years later, they built the present stand. In the late sixties came the reservoir. "Dad and I were not going to be storekeepers. We didn't want to grow things on a few acres for window dressing and bring in all the rest— like most roadside stands." From Albany to Delaware, they searched for a farm, and, answering an ad, found the one in Pennsylvania. In the big woodlot where the pigs now hide were thirty-eight oaks, each with a girth of eight to ten feet, and coveted by cabinetmakers. These oaks were older than the nation—O.A.R. Fortunately, the previous farmer had repeatedly refused to sell them. As a result, the farm was in a position to make a payment on itself. The Van Houtens sold the trees.

Bobby, out of Pearl River High School, did not go on to college. "What could it teach me?" His extraordinarily integrated knowledge of what was coming to be called agribusiness would develop empirically on the farm, and his passion for the driving of behemoth trucks would develop on the road. Twenty-six hours here, thirty-three there, he often takes field corn from Orangeville to sell to cattlemen in Florida, and something in him lives for those journeys. "I know every route number going to and around the South, and that's worth something. It may not be worth much, but it's worth as much as Greek mythology." Once, in a big tandem-axle twin-screw sleeper-cab tractor-trailer, he started alone out of Vero Beach with twenty-five tons of Indian River oranges, and thirty-six hours and no pills later he delivered the fruit in Toronto. The air there was twenty below zero and he was still in his Florida shirtsleeves. He had supported his stamina with "sixteen gal-

(47)

lons of coffee." He feels sheer contempt toward all the young drivers on pills.

Hanging around Hunts Point over the years, Bobby developed considerable admiration for the savoir-faire of a certain broker there. He once observed him taking on a buyer to whom he had sold rotting peppers. There had been a layer of good ones on the top. Now the buyer was back in a rage, and the broker was rising to the situation. Speaking with disarming and convincing candor, he succeeded in calming the man down. Then he sold him another load of peppers. As these, too, went out of the terminal, they were split and seamy but covered with a healthy green-pepper veneer. Bobby said, "You're crazy. You're really crazy. That guy will kill you."

"Bobby, you don't understand," said the broker. "Think about it. And tell me a better way to get that man back here tomorrow."

"Yeah, this is some business," Bobby said, finishing the story. "We have friends in New Jersey, and they hope we'll have a cyclone, or a flood. We hope they'll have a hurricane. Things like that drive the prices up for the lucky ones. Every year has its own difficulties. In 1972, we had a dry, dry summer. We irrigate from two creeks, and they were running very low. We took a bulldozer and dammed both of them—ended them right here. People downstream all said it was the driest year they'd ever seen."

We went into the farmhouse for dinner with Bobby's wife, Anne, and his father, James, who has the air of a contented President retired on a farm in Pennsylvania—a big man with a baby's grin, a tan scalp, protruding ears, a swift staccato manner of speech. Like Hodgson *père*, though, he runs the place, prepares the trucks for Bobby's trips to town. "Your market there in Harlem, now, your colored want a good heavy yellow corn," he observed, and went on to say that among the various outlets for their produce the Greenmarket, by a wide margin, is in every way the best. Anne set turkey before us and gravy, stuffing, and single tomato slices that overlapped their plates. "It's too good to be true," she said. "The Greenmarket is too good to be true." Before sitting down herself, she added a buttery-crusted peach pie that was above two inches thick. "Something will spoil it," she went on. "I know it will. It's just too good to be true."

"It's a land of plenty," Bobby said.

"It's a land of too much," said his father.

Monday evenings Bobby is loaded and away by nine. Over the mountains and through the Water Gap he runs four hours to Pearl River, where he sleeps two hours in the cab. Jim, who lives nearby, meets him at three, and they unload produce for the stand. Then they load on onions, potatoes, fruit—the things they will sell in the city that they don't grow on the farm. By four-thirty, Bobby is away for Harlem. By six he is selling hard. Now, in the afternoon, he is still unflaggingly at it—displays descending, his mother and brother beside him, scales rocking gently like boats.

Bartley Bryt brings us the news. Like the rest of us, the Van Houtens keep their cab doors locked, but this afternoon for a short time someone forgot. The door (it was not the outside one but the door on *their* side of the truck) was left unlocked for perhaps fifteen minutes. We are watched more closely than we think, for in that brief lapse someone, somehow—coming possibly from under the truck—reached into the cab and took the steel box there, which contained upward of two thousand dollars. Without detectable changes of expression, the family continues to sell.

Brooklyn, and the pickpocket in the burgundy jacket appears just before noon. Melissa Mousseau recognizes him much as if he were an old customer and points him out to Bob Lewis, who follows him from truck to truck. Aware of Lewis, he leaves the market. By two, he will have made another run. A woman with deep-auburn hair and pale, nervous hands clumsily attracts the attention of a customer whose large white purse she is rifling. Until a moment ago, the customer was occupied with the choosing of apples and peppers, but now she shouts out, "Hey, what are you doing? Your hand is in my purse. What are you doing?" The auburn-haired woman not only has her hand in the purse but most of her arm as well. She withdraws it, and with intense absorption begins to finger the peppers. "How much are the peppers? Mister, give me some of these!" she says, looking up at me with a gypsy's dark, starburst eyes. "Three pounds for a dollar," I tell her, with a swift glance around for Lewis or a cop. When I look back, the pickpocket is gone. Other faces have filled in—people unconcernedly examining the fruit. The woman with the white purse has returned her attention to the apples. She merely seems annoyed. Lewis once sent word around from truck to truck that we should regularly announce in loud voices that pickpockets were present in the market, but none of the farmers complied. Hodgson shrugged and said, "Why distract the customers?" Possibly Fifty-ninth Street is the New York Pickpocket Academy. Half a dozen scores have been made there in a day. I once looked up and saw a well-dressed gentleman under a gray fedora being kicked and kicked again by a man in a green polo shirt. He kicked him in the calves. He kicked him in the thighs. He kicked him in the gluteal bulge. He kicked him from the middle of the market out to the edge, and he kicked him into the street. "Get your ass out of here!" shouted the booter, redundantly. Turning back toward the market, he addressed the curious. "Pickpocket," he explained. The dip did not press charges.

People switch shopping carts from time to time. They make off with a loaded one and leave an empty cart behind. Crime on such levels is a part of the background here, something in the urban air, so many parts per million. The condition is accepted with a resignation that approaches nonchalance. The Van Houtens' loss was extraordinary but theirs was by no means the only cash box that has been stolen. We lost one once in Brooklyn, with something like two hundred dollars. For various reasons, suspicion immediately attached itself to a part-time employee who was selling with us and probably handed the box in a bag to a confederate. The previous Wednesday, he had been working for another farmer, who discharged him for dishonesty. Now, just after our cash box disappeared, he began saying, and repeating, in an excited voice, "It's real, man. It's real. We don't like it but that's reality—reality, man—and there is nothing we can do." Rich felt there *was* something he could do. He said, "You're fired."

Politely, the man inquired if he could know the reason for his dismissal.

"Sure," Rich said. "I don't trust you."

"That's cool, man, cool," said our ex-employee. He took off his apron and was gone.

Most thievery is petty and is on the other side of the tables. As Rich describes it, "Brooklyn, Fifty-ninth Street, people rip off stuff everywhere. You just expect it. An old man comes along and puts a dozen eggs in a bag. Women choosing peaches steal one for every one they buy—a peach for me, a peach for you. What can you do? You stand there and watch. When they take too many, you complain. I watched a guy one day taking nectarines. He would put one in a plastic bag, then one in a pocket, then one in a pile on the ground. After he did that half a dozen times, he had me weigh the bag."

"This isn't England," Barry Benepe informed us once, "and a lot of people are pretty dishonest."

Now, in Brooklyn, a heavyset woman well past the middle of life is sobbing pitifully, flailing her arms in despair. She is sitting on a bench in the middle of the market. She is wearing a print dress, a wide-brimmed straw hat. Between sobs, she presents in a heavy Russian accent the reason for her distress. She was buying green beans from Don Keller, and when she was about to pay him she discovered that someone had opened her handbag—even while it was on her arm, she said—and had removed several books of food stamps, a telephone bill, and eighty dollars in cash. Lewis, in his daypack, stands over her and tells her he is sorry. He says, "This sort of thing will happen wherever there's a crowd."

Another customer breaks in to scold Lewis, saying, "This is the biggest rip-off place in Brooklyn. Two of my friends were pickpocketed here last week and I had to give them carfare home."

Lewis puts a hand on his forehead and, after a pensive moment, says, "That was very kind of you."

The Russian woman is shrieking now. Lewis attends her

like a working dentist. "It's all right. It will be O.K. It may not be as bad as you think." He remarks that he would call the police if he thought there was something they could do.

Jeffrey Mack, eight years old, has been listening to all this, and he now says, "I see a cop."

Jeffrey has an eye for cops that no one else seems to share. (A squad car came here for him one morning and took him off to face a truant officer. Seeing his fright, a Pacific Street prostitute got into the car and rode with him.)

"Where, Jeffrey?"

"There." Jeffrey lifts an arm and points.

"Where?"

"There." He points again—at trucks, farmers, a falafel man.

"I don't see a policeman," Lewis says to him. "If you see one, Jeffrey, go and get him."

Jeffrey goes, and comes back with an off-duty 78th Precinct cop who is wearing a white apron and has been selling fruits and vegetables in the market. The officer speaks sternly to the crying woman. "Your name?"

"Catherine Barta."

"Address?"

"Eighty-five Eastern Parkway."

Every Wednesday, she walks a mile or so to the Greenmarket. She has lived in Brooklyn close to half her life, the rest of it in the Ukraine. Heading back to his vegetables, the officer observes that there is nothing he can do.

Out from behind her tables comes Joan Benack, the baker, of Rocky Acres Farm, Milan, New York—a small woman with a high, thin voice. Leaving her tropical carrot bread, her zucchini bread, her anadama bread, her beer bread, she goes around with a borrowed hat collecting money from the farmers for Catherine Barta. Bills stuff the hat, size 7—the money of Alvina Frey and John Labanowski and Cleather Slade and Rich Hodgson and Bob Engle, who has seen it come and go. He was a broker for Merrill Lynch before the stock market imploded, and now he is a blond-bearded farmer in a basketball shirt selling apples that he grows in Clintondale, New York. Don Keller offers a dozen eggs, and one by one the farmers come out from their trucks to fill Mrs. Barta's shopping cart with beans and zucchini, apples, eggplants, tomatoes, peppers, and corn. As a result, her wails and sobs grow louder.

A man who gave Rich Hodgson a ten-dollar bill for a ninety-five-cent box of brown eggs asks Rich to give the ten back after Rich has handed him nine dollars and five cents, explaining that he has some smaller bills that he wants to exchange for a twenty. Rich hands him the ten. Into Rich's palm he counts out five ones, a five, and the ten for a twenty and goes away satisfied, as he has every reason to be, having conned Rich out of nine dollars, five cents, and a box of brown eggs. Rich smiles at his foolishness, shrugs, and sells some cheese. If cash were equanimity, he would never lose a cent. One day, a gang of kids began taking Don Keller's vegetables and throwing them at the Hodgson truck. Anders Thueson threw an apple at the kids, who then picked up rocks. Thueson reached into the back of the truck and came up with a machete. While Hodgson told him to put it away, pant legs went up, switchblades came into view. Part of the gang bombarded the truck with debris from a nearby roof. Any indication of panic might have been disastrous. Hodgson packed deliberately, and drove away.

Todd Jameson, who comes in with his brother Dan from

Farmingdale, New Jersey, weighed some squash one day, and put it in a brown bag. He set the package down while he weighed something else. Then, reaching for the squash, he picked up an identical bag that happened to contain fifty dollars in rolled coins. He handed it to the customer who had asked for the squash. Too late, Todd discovered the mistake. A couple of hours later, though, the customer—"I'll never forget him as long as I live, the white hair, the glasses, the ruddy face"—came back. He said, "Hey, this isn't squash. I didn't ask for money, I asked for squash." Whenever that man comes to market, the Jamesons give him a bag full of food. "You see, where I come from, that would never, never happen," Todd explains. "If I made a mistake like that in Farmingdale, no one—no one—would come back with fifty dollars' worth of change."

Dusk comes down without further crime in Brooklyn, and the farmers are packing to go. John Labanowski—short, compact, with a beer in his hand—is expounding on his day. "The white people are educating the colored on the use of beet greens," he reports. "A colored woman was telling me today, 'Cut the tops off,' and a white woman spoke up and said, 'Hold it,' and told the colored woman, 'You're throwing the best part away.' They go on talking, and pretty soon the colored woman is saying, 'I'm seventy-three on Monday,' and the white says, 'I don't believe a word you say.' You want to know why I come in here? I come in here for fun. For profit, of course, but for relaxation, too. I like being here with these people. They say the city is a rat race, but they've got it backwards. The farm is what gets to be a rat race. You should come out and see what I—" He is interrupted by the reappearance in the market of Catherine Barta, who went home long ago and has now returned, her eyes hidden by her wide-brimmed hat, her shopping cart full beside her. On the kitchen table, at 85 Eastern Parkway, she found her telephone bill, her stamps, and her cash. She has come back to the farmers with their food and money.

WEST OF THE SUBURBS, thirty and more miles from Manhattan, the New Jersey–New York border terrain is precipitous and glaciated and—across a considerable area—innocent of high-speed roads. Minor roads run north and south, flanking the walls of hogback ridges—Pochuck Mountain, Bearfort Mountain, Wawayanda Mountain—but the only route that travels westward with any suggestion of efficiency is the Appalachian Trail. The landscape is remarkably similar to Vermont's: small clearings, striated outcroppings, bouldery fields; rail fences under hard maples; angular roads, not well marked, with wooden signs; wild junipers signalling, as they do, penurious soil; unfenced cemeteries on treeless hillsides; conflagrationary colors in the autumn woods. Moving among such scenes, climbing, descending, losing the way and turning back—remarking how similar to rural New England all this is—one sooner or later tops a rise where the comparison in an instant blinks out. Some distance below, and reaching as far as the eye can conveniently see, is a surface perfectly flat, and not merely flat but also level, and not only level but black as carbon. There are half a dozen such phenomena in this region, each as startling to come upon as the last. Across their smooth expanses, distant hills look like shorelines, the edges of obsidian lakes. The black surfaces were, indeed, once fluid and blue—lakes that stood for many centuries where north-flowing streams were blocked by this or that digital terminus of the retreating Laurentide glacier. Streamborne silt and black organic muck gradually replaced the water—prognosticating Lake Mead, Lake Powell, Lake Sakakawea, and the Lake of the Ozarks some years hence when they have filled in solid behind their dams. The surface of the mucklands (as they are called) is not altogether firm. It will support a five-inch globe onion. For that matter, it will support a tractor—but it is not nearly dense enough to hold up a house. There are only a few sheds on the wide flats. People live on "islands," once and present islands, knobs that break through the black surface just as they did when it was blue. Pine Island, New York, is a town in a black-dirt sea—the largest and most productive muckland of them all. Maple Island, Merritts Island, Big Island, Black Walnut Island are spaced across it as well, and their clustered houses resemble small European farming communities. The fields surrounding them seem European, too, for the acreages of black dirt are ruled off in small, familial segments, like vineyards in Valencia or the Côte d'Or. No fences, no hedgerows interrupt the vista or separate one farmer from another. Plots abut. The vegetables that come out of this rich organic soil are in their way as special as wines: tall celeries, moist beets, iceberg lettuce as crisp as new money, soft Boston salad lettuce, broccoli, cauliflower, carrots—and, above all, onions. What the beluga is to caviar the muckland is to the onion. Millions upon millions of onions are grown in the black dirt. Early flat onions. Hybrid onions. Red Globe, White Globe, Yellow Globe onions. Buccaneer, Bronze Age, Benny's Red Onions. Tokyo Long White Bunching Onions. Harvestmore, Ebenezer, Nutmeg Onions. Yellow sweet Spanish late mild onions. Everywhere you go and everywhere you look are bags and boxes and bushels of onions. Pine Island, where the crop is warehoused, is Onionapolis. The hot days are dry on the muckland. After leaving it, in the evening, farmers sometimes go hopping from island to island, have a beer or two at the Meadow Tavern, and two to four at Mike's Tavern, and four to eight at Leo's Tavern in order to be ready for the Red Onion, a sort of staging area, or base camp, as good a place as any to prepare an all-out assault on the Jolly Onion.

Onion boxes, in this early-autumn harvest season, are in random stacks across the level plain. All day long, harvesting rigs move slowly among them like floating dredges, scooping the powdery soil, "pulling onions." John Labanowski has been pulling onions for twenty days now, stirred toward delirium by the fine black dust, the hammering sun, the asynchronous cacophony of his odd machine. The lower end of a steel conveyor belt, which is angled toward the ground like a stairway, moves forward through the soft earth and nuzzles under the onions. The conveyor consists of runglike rods set apart so that dirt can fall through, but not as far apart as the diameter of an onion. Tops and all, the onions ride uphill. The tops are brittle and dry. Bolted to the rig is a fan that could fly a Jenny. It blows off the tops and scatters them downwind. Clean now, appearing just as they will in a market, the onions reach the top of the conveyor, turn a corner, and roll down a chute. Andy Labanowski, John's uncle, is sitting on a cantilevered seat shoving crates into place beneath the downpour of onions. Roughly four hundred and fifty will fill a crate—in nine seconds. The crates are wooden and heavy. Their loaded weight is eighty pounds apiece. With his left hand, Andy begins to ease one (on rollers) off the harvester, and with his right hand he moves another one below the falling onions. Empty crates are piled on the harvester almost to the point of toppling, and John feeds them down to Andy while the whole grotesque contrivance is kept in motion by John's father, John Labanowski, who sits out in front on a steel-padded tractor—taciturn, enigmatic, in his visored cap and tinted glasses—and advances the enterprise at ten to the minus seven miles per hour. There are thunderheads along the border of the sky, but even if they were directly above us we could not hear the rumbling. Three separate engines power the rig. We are well into the afternoon now, four of us working this Orange County clipper ship. Our skins are as black as the four of spades. There are white doughnuts around the eyes. Old John has the look of a coal miner moments out of the shaft. His brother, Andy—spare, dark-eyed, gregarious—is courting sunstroke under a Budweiser hat that has turned black. Young John, also called Yash, came to work in high-top leather boots, gray twill trousers, monkey-fist gloves, a blue porkpie hat, and a pink T-shirt—all of which now are solid black. He turns away from a gust of dirt. "You can get blowed out," he says. "Winds blow fine dirt so hard it sometimes cuts the tops. But don't worry. This dirt will never kill you. My father's sixty-three and he's still going."

A stone jams the conveyor, and John the elder stops the tractor, gets off, picks up a wrench, and crushes the stone. When Polish farmers first cleared the muckland, stones were hauled in and dumped on the soil to help it support the weight of horses. There are fifty Labanowskis in the valley now. Their cousins the Osczepinskis—who also go to Greenmarket —farm here, too. The harvester moves on. Its weight shakes the earth. The tenth part of an acre vibrates around us like a quaking bog. There are cracks in the dry muck—crevasses of a sort—that will go as much as six feet deep. Onions by the hundred are lost in the cracks. The soil is so rich it will burn. Now and then a farmer flicks a cigarette off his rig and starts a ground fire. Old John, who smokes, has put out three such fires on his fifty acres this summer. Blazing black dirt is not easily controlled. In 1964, there was a fire in which a couple of thousand acres of soil burned. The fire crossed many property lines. It was harvest time, and crated onions were stacked across the plain. Fifteen million onions roasted. The fallout quickened appetites in Greece. "There were big winds. You couldn't go nowheres evenings. The air was too thick to see." A tractor blew up. The fire engines of many towns and a firefighting helicopter converged upon the muckland without significant effect. The fire lasted more than a week, and went out under long heavy rains.

John's father, John, flies in chartered aircraft to spy on onions elsewhere in the state. He is the Francis Gary Powers of the Labanowskis. If black-dirt farmers know the stages of the harvest in competitive counties, they can decide whether to wait or pull. Labanowski and his wife and two neighbors hire a twin-engine plane at the airfield that was Stewart Air Force Base, and, taking off over Hodgson's Brussels sprouts, head north by northwest—to Canandaigua, Canastota, Batavia, Elba, Fulton, Oswego. They land in some places and snoop by car. They fly low over other checkpoints and bulbous destinations.

Lurching onward. It is now my turn to align the boxes under the thundering onionfall. One small timing error and two hundred onions crash in your lap, spew out over the ground. I somehow lose a foot between two rollers, and nearly crack an ankle. "I guess that's dangerous," I remark, recovering the foot.

"On a farm, everything is dangerous," says Yash.

After thirty minutes of filling boxes, my arms feel as if they have gone eighteen innings each. I scarcely notice, though, under the dictates of the action, the complete concentration on the shifting of the crates, the hypnotic effect—veiling everything else in this black-surfaced hill-bordered surreally level world—of the cascade of golden onions. Onions. Onions. Multilayered, multilevelled, ovate, imbricated, white-fleshed, orange-scaled onions. Native to Asia. Aromatic when bruised. When my turn is over and a break comes for me, I am so crazed with lust for these bulbous herbs—these enlarged, compressed buds—that I run to an unharvested row and pull from the earth a one-pound onion, rip off the membranous bulb coat, bare the flesh, and sink my teeth through leaf after leaf after savory mouth-needling sweet-sharp water-bearing leaf to the flowering stalk that is the center and the secret of the onion. Yash at the end of the day will give me three hundred pounds of onions to take home, and well past the fall they will stand in their sacks in a corner of the kitchen—the pluperfect preservers of sweet, fresh moisture—holding in winter the rains of summer.

We quit in early evening, having filled two thousand crates with a hundred and fifty thousand pounds of onions, which would bring thirty thousand dollars at Greenmarket prices if only so many could move there. They will bring about eight thousand dollars at the current (and not attractive) wholesale price. They are five per cent of the Labanowski harvest. In the family's packinghouse on Big Island is a tall refrigerator filled to capacity with beer and surrounded by onion crates full of empty cans. We open sixteen cans to smooth off the day. Beer running down our arms streaks them white. We sit on onion crates with the building between us and the falling sun, and we look out over the black lake to forested hills called Mount Adam and Mount Eve. "Yeah, it gets to be a rat race here," says Yash. "In the city, sometimes, I slam things and screech at the customers. I don't know why. We've made a lot of friends there, you know. I sort of favor Brooklyn. The colored go for the big beets there. The whites go for the small beets. I don't know why. Everybody wants the Boston lettuce. I say, 'If I'd known you wanted to buy it this bad, I'd of grew a whole acre for you.' They like to bargain in Brooklyn. My cabbage is fifty cents a head, and they say they want three for a dollar. Tomatoes they watch the scale. I give them two pounds always for a pound and a half. Fifty-ninth Street? That's like high class. At Fifty-ninth Street, I get people with gloves."

FIFTY-NINTH STREET in the rain, and—despite the awning— the apples and peppers are wet.

"Is there a towel?" a customer asks. She wears a white hat, no gloves.

"Excuse me?"

"A towel. Water weighs something, you know."

I give her three and a third pounds for three. "There you are, madam. I weighed your water."

I remember asking Derryck Brooks-Smith, before I'd ever been here, to describe the Fifty-ninth Street Greenmarket for me, and he said, "White people. *Mucho* white people—or ones passing for white. Be careful with nickels and dimes. People are more careful there than in any other market. Sixty per cent of them are richies, and people who are really making it, and upper middle class, but when you weigh something you have to defend what you say. They'll ask you, 'Why is this a dollar-ten, and not a dollar-five?' They are—shall we say?—a little tight."

Brown bags are breaking open, corn and potatoes spilling into mud. Nonetheless, as midday approaches, the crowd becomes ever more dense and compressed, moving between parallel rows of farmers in complex slow currents.

"Amazing!" I remark across the table. "So many people out in the rain."

"It's this or the supermarket," says a tall woman in a transparent coat, handing me a sack of pears.

"Two pounds even, at three for a dollar twenty-five—that's eighty-five cents, please."

"Twice forty-two is eighty-four."

"Eighty-four, then." Out of one wet dollar. My apron is filled with wet bills. When a twenty comes along, five minutes are required to change it.

"How much are the tomatoes?"

"Three pounds for a dollar."

"How much are the apples?"

"Three pounds for a dollar. It says so there on the sign."

"They are McIntoshes, are they not?"

"Yes, they are."

"Why are they called McIntoshes?"

"After Charles Macintosh (1766–1843), who invented their waterproof skin."

"I'm finally discovering what real vegetables smell like."

"I never knew lima beans came in a pod."

"These beans, they don't snap."

"My bean hasn't snapped in years."

"Where is your lettuce? I'll take a head of lettuce."

"We don't have any lettuce. Try the Labanowskis, across the way."

The rain is not hurting their beautiful lettuce, and Yash is soaked to the skin. In salute, he lifts a Budweiser. People are formed around his truck in scrums. They press in from all sides, bent over, pushing hard, and now and again a head of lettuce flies out to the side. Between beers, the Labanowskis munch carrots. They pick up heads of lettuce and bite into them as if they were large green apples.

"If I had to stay on the farm seven days a week I'd go crazy!" shouts Yash, over the crowd.

"I'd say he went some time ago," mutters a man choosing peppers in a London Fog.

Across the sky immediately to the north of us run the improbable cables of the Roosevelt Island tramway, and from time to time a gondola appears, floating up and eastward, or slowly descending, suspended, increasing the sense of carnival in the scene that lies below. The Greenmarket occupies a quarter of an acre running from Fifty-ninth Street to Fifty-eighth along Second Avenue, bordered with fence-climbing vines and trees of heaven. The lot is rented from the city for a dollar a year. Not long ago it contained a row of shops and restaurants, and upstairs apartments—all of which were wiped out in the name of a fresh approach to the Queensboro Bridge. The approach road has not been built, but tall cooperatives have risen overhead—thirty-six floors and up-ward, with balconies sprocketing their sides and swimming pools deep in their kidneys. One building has a Rolls-Royce agency on the ground floor. The Greenmarket's obvious popularity at this address is not altogether welcomed by the people of the big co-ops, and through their community board they and others of the upper East Side have imposed some severe if not Draconian rules. No cider by the glass. No brownies by the square. No bread. No jam. No jelly. No houseplants. No balloons. No banners. No music (the market attracts enough riffraff as it is). No market, in fact, in the early or late season —an articulated suspicion that everything ever sold here has not been grown, as claimed, on regional farms.

"How many acres do you have up there?"

"A hundred and twenty."

"And how many chickens?"

"Forty thousand."

"Forty thousand chickens?"

"Four times ten to the fourth."

"Are they running loose?"

"They are not running anywhere."

"What do you feed them?"

"Grain products, plant-protein products, animal-protein products, processed grain by-products, dehydrated alfalfa meal with Ethoxyquin added as a preservative, ground limestone, salt, calcium iodate . . ." Prepared for the question, I am reading from a card. "Cobalt carbonate, copper oxide, copper sulfate, iron sulfate, manganous oxide, zinc oxide, methionine hydroxy analogue calcium, Vitamin A supplement, D-activated animal sterol, niacin, calcium pantothenate, riboflavin supplement, Vitamin B-12 supplement, menadione dimethylpyrimidinol bisulfite, Vitamin E supplement, and folic acid."

"Just as I suspected. And how fresh are the eggs?"

Derryck Brooks-Smith—working Saturday, off from school —speaks up to answer. "They were laid, to be perfectly frank, two days ago or one day ago but not this morning."

"Oh. You call yourself a farmer. The eggs should be fresh."

"They *are* fresh. The yolks will stand up and yell at you. The average egg in a supermarket is three weeks away from the hen."

Brooks-Smith sells two dozen jumbos to a black man with seven bracelets on each wrist, hair in ringlets, and what appears to be about six pounds of tin around his neck. An occasional star comes in here, a face shot out of the midnight tube, and people also arrive in Lincolns, which they park in the Kinney next door. For the most part, though, they are everyday eye-shadowed urban Americans. A dog is in the market. Male. He is not loose. He is leashed. He is, nonetheless, in the market, and a woman makes strong complaint. "Put up a sign! Keep them out! A person's legs are too precious!" she screams.

She has gained the attention of Bob Lewis. "This woman is referring to the fact that we don't really allow dogs in here," Lewis says quietly to the dog's owner.

"She is crazy, too," says the owner, whose dog is six inches high.

The rain has ended and shafts of bright sun have broken through, with the result that mists are rising. An elderly woman tells me she walked a mile to be here. A big bald man in a button-down shirt is drinking beer from a one-quart can. The can is in a brown bag. "The heaviest consumption of beer in the world is in Belgium," he informs us. "Belgium is one place where I believe I could get in trouble." He buys six pounds of apples and an ear of corn. There is a short man before us now in lemon-lime-cherry-and-grape striped trousers and a shirt in bourbon, burgundy, and crème-de-menthe squares. He explains to a neighbor how to bake an eggplant. "Insert holes in it," he tells her, "or the thing will explode."

Man in a Harley-Davidson T-shirt over a gravid half-mast paunch. He wants the telephone number of the community board so he can call and complain that the farmers here are not permitted to sell plants. The number is 679-2287, and Bob Lewis writes it, crossing the stems of the sevens.

Harley-Davidson: "That's a *seven*?"

"That's the way they write sevens in Europe."

"This isn't Europe. This is America. We've got too many Europeans here. And Spanish. What we need is more Americans, not Spanish. They came here—these animals—and won't learn English."

"Honey! Honey here!" shouts Brooks-Smith. (We have no honey. We never sell honey.)

"Eggs! Eggs! Get your eggs here!" shouts the honey man, across the way.

There is a rhythm in the movement of the crowd, in the stopping, the selecting, the moving on—the time unconsciously budgeted to assess one farm against another, to convict a tomato, to choose a peach. The seller comes to feel the rate of flow, and—for all the small remarks, the meeting of eyes—to feel as well the seclusion of anonymity that comes with the money aprons and the hanging scales. Rich Hodgson —handing them their blue free plums. They don't know he skis in Utah. Melissa Mousseau—changing a twenty for a bag of pears. They don't know that she goes, too. Hemingway and Thueson, the athletes, have heard more encouraging sounds from other crowds. "If you charge for three pounds, give me three full pounds and not two pounds and fifteen ounces, boy."

By a blue Chevrolet panel truck, opposite us, the crowd's rate of flow is perceptibly arrested. The displays there are smaller than most, the list of items shorter. Some of the prices are higher. The zucchini is fifty cents a pound. The corn, the tomatoes, the green beans, the squash are not *all* superior to their counterparts around the market, and certainly not to ours. So why, then, does the crowd almost crystallize when they come to Alvina Frey? They don't know anything about her except her address (Chad's Farm, Mahwah, New Jersey), if they happen to notice it on the truck, but they can easily sense a consistent standard, a kind of personal signature, in the colors and textures before her.

"What the small farmer offers is fresher, more selected material," Alvina has said. "The small farmer throws away the bad stuff. If my produce is better than some people's, I'll charge more for it. Some of the other guys say I'm Fifth Avenue. I don't care."

She is trim and attractive, petite, with intensity in her narrow, gentle face, and gold earrings that swing and flash. Her hair is short and has flecks of gray in it. Her skin is richly tan, her eyes a bright pale blue. She wears tennis shoes and light-blue denims with bell bottoms and a striped cardigan that looks soft and expensive. At first glance she seems so Short Hills that one wonders whether she is playing, and whether she, as some others have done, starts from home empty and collects her goods on the way to market—hand-me-down potatoes, Hunts Point pears. From years in the sun, though, there are deep radial lines around her eyes. And now, toward the end of the season, her hands are rough, callused, cracked, her fingers like small bananas. Her nails are split, and the skin that surrounds them is dark with terrarian stains.

She is very busy, and pressed for time, selling. But she takes time to educate, too. She tells people not to be impressed by fat cucumbers. The long thin ones have fewer seeds. To the universal question "Is the corn fresh?" she says, "You can tell for yourself." She reaches for an ear and holds it upside down. If the stem at the break is a damp, pale green, the corn has been off the stalk less than a day. After about twenty-four hours, the stem turns white and chalky, opaque. With more time, it turns various shades of brown. The stem at the break of the ear in her hand is damp, pale green.

"Are the beans fresh?"

"Eat one. If you can eat it and it's juicy and not stringy, it's fresh."

People may also sense when they linger close around Alvina Frey that she is—perhaps a little more than anyone else here—what the Greenmarket is about. Not far from the city, she works a long-established farm that, before the Greenmarket, was on its way to being cut up and sold. While the Hodgsons look for new ground and the Van Houtens have found it, Alvina is all but desperate to hold the farm she has, which her grandmother farmed before her. Her grandmother, in fact, cleared the land. The grandmother's name was Alwine Pelz, and she was born on a farm in Saxony in the eighteen-sixties, emigrating as an adult to New Jersey. Her husband was a loom mechanic, and he found a job in a Paterson mill while she looked through the country for a farm. Fifteen miles northeast of Paterson, in the township of Ho-Ho-Kus, she bought fifty-five acres, close by the New York State line. To irrigate her crops, she dug a well, and walled it with fieldstone, topped by four stone columns and a pagoda roof. With her husband's help, she then constructed a fieldstone barn. "She did what she knew how to do, my grandmother—she farmed.

When my grandfather went to the mills in Paterson, he took her tomatoes, corn, beans, potatoes, beets—you name it—to the Island Market and sold them there. He went down with his horse and wagon. He didn't have a truck until the late twenties. My grandmother grew strawberries, too—two or three acres of them—and she had apples. She made cider, and I know damned well that during Prohibition she made hooch. She worked every day out in the fields until six months before she died. She was ninety-one years old. She farmed with horses. She never went in for anything mechanized. Neither did I, at first. Toward the end, when stuff grows high, you can't get in with a tractor. I had horses until fifteen years ago. About the only mechanical thing my grandmother ever had was the cider mill. It was steam-driven and made an awful racket. The ones that lived over the hill, they used to complain."

Her nearest neighbors are no longer over the hill. They are on the hill, around the hill, in the hill. The farm is on an old, blacktopped crown road that has become a suburban street, with a Little League field, swimming pools, trim lawns, and mini-wheelbarrows a foot high that have house numbers on their sides. The well is still there, however—its masonry tight, its water serving the farm. The stone barn is a high and beautiful structure that is now covered, like a superannuated college, with ivy. The countryside Alvina remembers from her girlhood had many truck farms, dairy farms, separating what have become contiguous towns: a future that the New Jersey State Highway Department began to sketch in the nineteen-thirties, when it created what is now Route 17, a north-south bifurcation of Bergen County, its purpose being to bring the Catskills closer to the city. Alvina remembers the new road running through garden country with rich dark earth full of carrots, radishes, and beets. All of what is now Paramus—of what is now a levitated Levittown with houses checkered to the curve of the earth—was celeryland and lettuceland. Where Okonite and Minolta are now, Alvina's father, Frank Pelz, had a farm of his own. The day the new road opened he went down it with a load of cabbages. The truck body was not bolted on well, and the load shook loose—heads all over the road. Route 17 has come to be called a "butcher boulevard," and when heads roll on it now they are more likely to be human. Alvina is safe enough at six in the morning as the Chad's Farm truck moves south toward the city past the Olds-Toyota and the Swiss Chalet, past the Tiffany Diner and Pay Less Building Supply, past steak houses the size of high schools. Castle Auto Truck Parts (turrets, battlements). Car Crazy Eddie. The Value House. The Cottage Beautiful. McDonald's, Burger King, Shatzi's Hofbrauhaus (Bavarian half-timber). John Barleycorn's Restaurant. The Golden Plough (a barn full of steak and lobsters). The Jade Fountain ("Chinese-Polynesian"). Nasser Aftab's House of Carpets. When Route 17 opened, New Jersey had twenty-nine thousand farms. Today there are seventy-nine hundred. Only forty-eight are left in all of Bergen County, and one is Alvina Frey's.

After her grandmother was gone and her father, too, Alvina worked the place with her first husband, Chad Chodorowski, and for some years they sold all their produce wholesale, mainly in Paterson. Eventually they built a roadside stand. The day it opened, in 1968, Chad suffered a heart attack. A year later, he died. Alvina's grandmother had had ten children, most of whom helped her with the farm. Alvina has no children. She has reduced the acreage under cultivation to

(71)

thirty-eight, and works it generally alone, with part-time help in the fields and in the stand. Her husband, Ed Frey, assists to some extent, but he is an excavator with a full-time business of his own, and while she is digging furrows he digs sewers and graves. "I love to see stuff grow. When it doesn't do well I could cry," she says. "But I don't like herbicide. The last time I used it was in tomatoes. I use as little chemical as I possibly can."

People who come regularly to the Greenmarket often bring things to Alvina. At Fifty-ninth Street, an elderly woman appears weekly with a container of orange juice for her. When there is no juice, Alvina sucks on the ice with which John Labanowski chills his beer. People take pictures of her. They invite her up for coffee. "I got one customer here at Fifty-ninth Street who's a drinker, male—a damned good-looking distinguished man, even if he drinks. He once brought me a hard-boiled egg in clear gelatin. Some kind of French dish. You don't like it, but you have to eat it." She receives weekly reports from a man who once bought a gourd. Following her directions, he cut holes in it and hung it out a twentieth-story window. A bird came to live in his gourd.

"I love the city—meeting different people, learning that all the things you learn about the city are not true. I see more people in the two markets I come to—Brooklyn and Fifty-ninth Street—than I do in several weeks in Mahwah at the stand. I wouldn't quit this for nothing in the world. The people are wonderful, and the market means a lot to them. They don't want anything to screw it up so we won't come in anymore."

A short time ago, Chad's Farm was drifting down a long and steady economic decline. In the wholesale markets, the middleman, in her opinion, wanted too much. A couple of years ago, a half bushel of tomatoes brought as much as four dollars and fifty cents. Now it brings five dollars, a difference that fails to compensate for the inflating costs of gasoline, fertilizer, utilities, containers, and dust. "I'm too small for Hunts Point and too big to make a living only out of a roadside stand. There was four of us—farmers—on my road once. When Johnny Werling went out of business he was forty. He finally had to get a job. That's rough—to farm all your life and then have to get a job. That's where I was headed when the Greenmarket came along. The Greenmarket is a godsend. Next year, I'd like to do different. I'd like to rent out my stand and come into the city every day."

THE
ATLANTIC
GENERATING
STATION

THE ATLANTIC GENERATING STATION was first imagined early one morning in 1969 by a man in Westfield, New Jersey, who happened at the moment to be taking a shower before dressing and going to work. His name was Richard Eckert. He was a Public Service Electric & Gas Company engineer, fairly high in the corporate tree. A large part of his job was to seek out new sites for power plants—an assignment that had once, in a less complicated era, called for a person who could look at a map and find a river. Now difficulties had thickened to a point near desperation, and plant siting required scientific and diplomatic talents undreamed of in the age of the pluming smokestack and the good five-cent cigar. Apparently needed as well, by now, was a leap of the imagination, for New Jersey was not only among the smallest of the fifty states, it was also the most densely populated, and nearly all appropriate sites for any kind of power plant, fossil or nuclear, had been chosen and used. Environmentalists and intervenors were phalanxed upon the sites that remained, and the environmentalists and intervenors seemed to be multiplying even more rapidly than the

(77)

population at large. In the absence of new plants, demand for power would before long exceed supply. Then, when New Jersey went brown, New Jersey would serve as an indicator to the rest of the country that the rest of the country was going to go brown, too, because the problem was a universal one and was only somewhat more immediate in the superconcentrated, megalopolitan, residential-industrial-transportational corridor between Philadelphia and New York. If New Jersey's problem was to be solved, Public Service would have to solve it, for the company's territory included eighty per cent of the state's people. A power plant needed plenty of space and plenty of cooling water—five hundred acres of ground and a million gallons a minute. The state's interior rivers were small. The utility had nowhere to go. The compact human warren it served—containing, in some places, forty-five thousand people per square mile—was hemmed in between Pennsylvania and the open Atlantic.

Those were the terms of the dilemma constantly on Eckert's mind, and it was the last part—the Atlantic—that became arrested there for a moment that morning in 1969, opening to him a form of solution. Standing wet, naked, and soapy in his shower, he envisioned a huge nuclear-power plant, as prodigious as any yet built on land, mounted on an immense hull, floating on the sea. There was certainly enough room on the ocean, and, heaven knew, enough water. Other advantages suggested themselves as well. To construct a nuclear-power plant at a specific site on land, something like thirty-five hundred skilled workers had to be sought out, hired, and assembled. They had become nomads of the times, moving from state to state, reactor to reactor—stainless-steel welders, for the most part, of a class so high that they were hard to find.

With the proliferation of the nuclear-power industry, they would become scarcer still, as would nuclear engineers and designers, of whom there might soon not be enough to go on making unique designs to fit the conditions of new sites. If all these people were to build floating power plants, however, the situation would reverse itself. The personnel would stay in one place, and the plants would travel. An assembly line could be set up somewhere, and a permanent work force could settle in around it, to manufacture plants and ship them out. With standardization, the cost of making a nuclear-power plant would decline, and the margin for errors of all kinds would narrow. Start to finish, the amount of time required to build a nuclear plant might be reduced by several years. Moreover, a floating plant would go up and down with the tides. Its water-sucking orifices would remain in a constant position with respect to the surface of the sea and not have to adjust to sudden and sometimes considerable changes in the water level—a problem inevitable at river sites. Eckert ate his breakfast and told his wife, Joan, that he wanted to launch nuclear-power plants as, in effect, ships on the ocean.

"There you go again," she said.

Eckert was not quite forty at the time. A lean man, amiable, slightly bald, he did not by appearance in any way suggest the fearsome, two-dimensional, fictive American businessman with reinforcing rods in his jaws, emerging from some dark, polluted labyrinth to hand out the wages of fear. Eckert was a man given to gray suits, gray socks, black shoes, white shirts, and Paisley ties. He commuted to Newark and liked to sail with his children on New Jersey estuaries and bays. He was a New Jersey native, a lifelong resident, born and raised in Plainfield, with a boyhood behind him of New

Jersey saltwater vacations. In an anonymous way, he would soon be the Antichrist to several hundred thousand people along the barrier beaches of the state. Yet he was one of them. And he had not invented the electric toothpick or the electric scalpel or the aluminum beer can or central air-conditioning or the six-thousand-watt sauna, or any of the other hardware, large and small, vital or vulgar, that had helped to make a necessity of something that had not existed—not in commercial form—a century before. All those people on the beach had, in a sense, given Eckert his job, and his job was to find sites and then build nuclear-power plants, and now he was imagining one in the ocean, for the plain reason that there was nowhere else to build it.

In Newark, at the Public Service Company's principal office, Eckert's idea readily acquired buoyancy of its own. Utilities are renowned for their conservatism, but this one was not in a position to watch and wait. In Eckert's words, it had to "keep searching for any exotic idea that would improve and sustain the breed." Public Service was already giving large annual sums to support university research in the control of thermonuclear fusion. And now it unblinkingly agreed that Eckert and his staff should explore the concept of the oceanborne nuclear plant, and spend enough time and money to answer the primary question: Is there any reason, technically, that it won't work?

There were fragments of precedent. In 1929, when Tacoma, Washington, temporarily ran out of power, the aircraft carrier Lexington went down Puget Sound, hove to, and fed electric current to the stricken city. Ships were used as power plants during the Second World War, when they were sometimes equipped as mobile, diesel-fuelled generating stations. By

1969, of course, submarines and certain surface vessels had for some years been using nuclear reactors to make the heat to make the steam to drive them, and there was even one example of a ship that contained a nuclear reactor intended primarily for the production of electricity. Operated by the United States Army, it had been anchored since October of 1968 in Gatun Lake, there to cope with a bizarre situation in the Panama Canal. The lake supplied water both to the locks of the canal and to the hydroelectric plant that made the power that enabled the locks to operate. Every time a ship went through the locks, fifty-two million gallons of water irretrievably left the lake, and millions more fell to the hydroelectric plant. The lake, as an integral segment of the canal system, also had to float ships, and during the dry season the surface often went down to a critical level at which there might be water enough to bring ships in but not enough to float them once they got there. The result was a heavy curtailment of traffic in the canal—until the Sturgis, a Liberty ship with a new pressurized-water reactor in it, came into the lake and began to supplement the Panama Canal power system with enough electricity to save, for use in the locks, twenty-three billion gallons of water a month, an amount sufficient for the transit of four hundred and forty ships.

Compared with the watt resource that Public Service was about to develop, though, the stories of the Lexington and the Sturgis would be mere curiosities in the history of electrical power on the sea. The Sturgis's reactor was rated at ten megawatts of electricity. The Atlantic Generating Station would send ashore, through cables buried in the seabed, a net electrical output of twenty-three hundred megawatts. As discussion and research went forward, it was decided that the power would come from two plants, identical, floating side by side—so that, for refuelling and other purposes, half the generating station could go on operating while the other half was shut down.

Eckert and others—notably Muzaffer Kehnemuyi, a Turk who had received a master's degree in civil engineering from the University of Illinois in 1948 and would eventually, under Eckert, be the project manager—travelled the United States in search of answers to basic questions. They never encountered the irrefutable negative that would have ended the project for technical reasons, and meanwhile, in their gropings, they gradually discovered the dimensions and characteristics of what they planned to build. For example, they learned that no shipyard in the United States had a slipway wider than a hundred and forty feet, so a floating nuclear plant would either have to be very long, like the Cunard Queens, or have to be built in components, on several separate hulls—a reactor here, a turbine there. Public Service at first considered the component way but later decided that a new shipyard would have to be built to construct hulls that were nearly square—four hundred feet long and three hundred and seventy-eight feet wide. A breakwater would be needed to protect the hulls from the assaults of waves, which could come from any direction, so the breakwater should surround the floating plants. For its shape, a rectangle was considered first, but, as Eckert put it, "a square corner in the ocean doesn't last," and the shape that evolved was penannular—a kind of atoll, with a great curve convex to the east and the open sea, a straight wall on the landward side, and openings for the passage of boats that would bring, among other things, assemblies of fresh nuclear fuel. The curved segment alone would be from end to end three thousand feet, and it would be built in sloping form, like an earthfill dam, the whole structure rising from the sea-floor like a pyramid.

WHEN CHEOPS undertook to build the Great Pyramid, nearly thirty centuries before Christ, he brought into being, where nothing had been but sands of the desert, a labor market, of sorts, that lasted thirty years, employing, on the average, a hundred thousand people. In 1971, within the halls of Public Service, the Atlantic Generating Station was pronounced feasible. From segments of the nuclear, industrial, consultative, and academic worlds, people in expanding numbers began to be drawn into a project still so nebulous that not even a specific site had been chosen—beyond the understanding that it would be some miles off the Jersey coast, in the undeveloped sea. Costs were underwritten on the immediate level by Public Service, of course, but eventually they were absorbed by the pharaoh himself—a collective name for people in New Jersey who pay electricity bills. Construction of the breakwater alone would take four years and four million man-hours, but numerous endeavors of far-reaching complexity had to be initiated first. Westinghouse had put several dozen people to work on the concept; General Electric had a team, too—preparing to make eventual bids for the reactor contract. Public Service had also tried to arouse the interest of Babcock & Wilcox and Combustion Engineering, the two other makers of conventional light-water reactors, but they had said, in effect, "Nothing doing. We are too small for this one. We'll have to stand by and let someone else do it first." Shipyards from Massachusetts to Texas were approached, and presentations were made in Washington to some thirty-five federal agencies, among them the National Oceanic and Atmospheric Administration, the Federal Aviation Administration, the Federal Power Commission, the Coast Guard, the Army Corps of Engineers, the Environmental Protection Agency, and, of course, the Atomic Energy Commission—any of which, having licensing power over one or another aspect of the project, could kill it. Reaction in Washington was favorable. The agencies, in their turn, and a whole list of analogous units of the state government set people to work preparing to contribute their part when the time came for hearings.

Most remarkable, though, was the kind of money that came spilling out of the pharaoh as a result of the environmental movement. Where once someone might have sized up the wind drift and then sited the plant, it was now necessary for scientists of multiple and overlapping disciplines to describe the New Jersey coast and adjacent seas probably in more detail than had ever been contemplated by anyone. It was a bonanza for the scientific community. Research grants that had once been copious from the federal government had dwindled considerably, causing panics in universities, and now, thanks to the friends of the earth, money was flowing from the corporate world for everything from core-borings in the bed of the ocean to exhaustive studies of pelagic life. Ichthyological Associates, a group formed at Cornell, was engaged by Public Service, and set up a branch laboratory in Absecon, near Atlantic City, to study all species of regional marine life, to establish a baseline description of the ecological environment, and to keep on gathering data for many years—all through construction and into the era of electrical production—in order to record the effects of such things as the breakwater, the cooling system, and the thermal-discharge plume on every form of life from phytoplankton to the biggest of fish, and to suggest to the plant's designers modifications that might reduce detrimental effects. Similarly, a group of physical oceanographers was brought to New Jersey to establish a baseline on tides, waves, currents, wind. A group of seismologists and geologists was commissioned to study, among other things, foundation conditions of the ocean floor, geological structures, regional earthquake history. An earthquake broke windows in Asbury Park on June 1, 1927. The earthquake of October 9, 1871, whose epicenter was near Wilmington, Delaware, delivered what for this area was the most intense earth shock in historical times. The New York City earthquakes of 1884 and 1737 were less intense but on the same order of magnitude. With a proton magnetometer, the geologists began aeromagnetic surveys to develop a general view of the region's geological structure. To profile the seabed, they cruised around in boats using seismic instruments —high-resolution boomers, high-resolution sparkers. Deep borings into the bottom showed almost a mile of miscellaneous clays and sands resting on rock that had been where it was for at least two hundred million years. Earthquake risk, small as it was, would affect only the breakwater anyway, because the generating station, being afloat, would be decoupled from the earth. The only seismic effect that could reach the floating hulls would be a tsunami. The largest tsunami ever recorded locally had been originated by an earthquake off the Iberian coast and had been less than a foot high when it reached New Jersey.

Analyses of seventy-nine constituents of New Jersey ocean

water were done by chemists from Rutgers. Meteorologists were commissioned to make detailed portraits of New Jersey's coastal temperatures, humidity, precipitation, fogs, thunderstorms, tornado potentialities, and "probable maximum hurricanes." Hydrologists were brought in to make thermal studies to establish isotherms for varying tide and current conditions. Because cables would someday have to come out of the water and traverse land in order to bring power from the ocean to the people, general ecologists were commissioned to begin field studies that would eventually consider every tree, every bird, every animal—literally, every mouse—that might in any way be disturbed: white-footed mouse, meadow jumping mouse, house mouse, pine vole, Norway rat, short-tailed shrew, least shrew, semipalmated sandpiper, American widgeon, horned grebe, Atlantic white cedar, pitch pine, rabbitfoot clover, many hundreds of other species.

As more and more people became involved and information grew like dunes, the prime movers back in the Electric Engineering Department, in Newark, were increasingly encouraged. The ocean now seemed to be not just the only remaining place to go but in some respects the best place to be. To dissipate the plant's waste heat, the ocean, technically, was the world's best heat sink. Floating nuclear plants could be moved from place to place, if desired, to meet immediate needs. Engineering uniformity would bring such rewards that one day it would make sense to float plants even to sites on rivers. This, of course, could be done with any sort of power station—nuclear or fossil—but one advantage in choosing fission reactors as the heat source was that each one of them would eliminate the need to burn twelve million barrels of oil a year. "Others are waiting and watching," Kehnemuyi said.

"Once everyone is assured that we are going to get licensed, they are all going to come and jump into the water with us."

Two or three miles from land, rising and falling with the swells, the Atlantic Generating Station could be the first tentative step toward the submarine countries imagined by Glenn Seaborg, who, when he was chairman of the Atomic Energy Commission, published a book called *Man and Atom*, in which were described whole colonies of people, utterly disjunct from the rest of the race, living under vast plastic domes on the floor of the deep ocean. Each colony was built around a reactor doing the work of the sun.

A schedule was eventually framed whereby the first nuclear unit of the Atlantic Generating Station would be floated into place in the spring of 1985, the second in 1987. Construction of the breakwater would begin at least four years earlier. As seen even from conflicting points of view, the floating nuclear plant could make a considerable contribution to the developing fate of mankind. The Great Pyramid, for its part, had been built in order to contain through the ages nothing more important than Cheops the Builder.

ECKERT, KEHNEMUYI, and the others would have liked to choose a site as far away from shore as possible in order to use the horizon as an aesthetic screen between the floating power plant and the people of the beach communities. There would be value in the precedent, for when substantial parts of continents were necklaced with nuclear plants, it would clearly be preferable that the plants be as inconspicuous as possible. "Out of sight, out of mind," Eckert said. There were difficul-

(87)

ties, though, in going out of sight. For one thing, the highest parts of the Atlantic Generating Station's two plants—the summits of the containment domes over the reactors—would be a hundred and ninety feet above the water. The rough formula for the relationship between sight lines and the curve of the earth is that the square root of the observer's altitude in feet will equal the number of miles over flat land or water between the observer and the horizon. A person lying on a beach nine feet above sea level can see three miles across the water before hulls begin to be lost to view. The Atlantic Generating Station, to be out of sight from the beach, would have to be some fourteen miles at sea.

The calculated maximum practical depth for normal seas around a floating nuclear plant proved to be about seventy feet—a purely economic limitation, imposed by the great size and cost of the necessary breakwater. Off the East Coast of the United States, the continental shelf is broad, reaching out seventy or eighty miles, sloping gently. And off much of New Jersey it is possible to go out fourteen miles and still be in seventy feet of water or less. The water is international, though, and murky with maritime law. The mere suggestion of such a site was enough to make tremors under the State Department. Governments were trying to reach new understandings in this field, but for the time being no distance would be secure that was greater than the traditional and conservative three miles. The minimum depth required was forty feet, because the big hulls would draw thirty-two. The site also had to be reasonably near an inlet, so that vessels ferrying people and supplies from a shore facility could dock in calm water. The site had to be away from established shipping lanes. The breakwater, of course, had to have something geologically firm to rest on. And there had to be a right-of-way on shore where the transmission line, after emerging from the seabed, could continue inland.

Nine possible sites were chosen. The northernmost was off Long Branch—less than twenty miles from New York. The southernmost was off the Cape May peninsula. All were suitable, and nine generating stations might one day float at them, but now the utility had much room in which to be particularly selective. Cape May—a hundred and forty miles from Newark —seemed a little too far away. On the other hand, waters three miles offshore gradually deepen toward the New York Bight, not prohibitively but enough to add to the cost of the breakwater. A very good site off Forked River was somewhat incommoded by a nuclear-power plant that already happened to be in operation on the mainland there. Choices soon diminished to two. One was off Harvey Cedars, on Long Beach Island, a resort that attracts, among other people, basketball coaches with loud voices, and they may have got up from the bench and shouted the utility away. Public Service, in any case, decided that it preferred not to choose a site directly in the view of summer homes, so Harvey Cedars was crossed off, and what remained as the final choice was a position eleven miles northeast of Atlantic City and two and eight-tenths miles from Little Egg Inlet and Great Bay—thirty-nine degrees, twenty-eight minutes north latitude; seventy-four degrees, fifteen minutes west longitude. Seven fathoms was the depth of the ocean there. Just seaward of the site was an extensive sand hill whose summit was less than thirty feet below the ocean's surface. Geologists quickly acupunctured the hill with stakes to see if, over time, it was moving. A couple of miles away, toward shore, there had once been an island that had supported houses, stores, streets, and picket fences, and was now visible only at low tide. The submarine sand ridge appeared to be stable, however, for it had been recorded on charts a century old. The ridge would serve in big storms as a kind of breakwater for the breakwater—redundant engineering through the cooperative efforts of man and God.

In time, there would appear on a table in Eckert's office a triptych photograph of broad white sands and blue sea—a panorama that had been shot from the shore, looking toward the site. The foreground was patterned with wind ripples, bird tracks, and waving grass. In the middle distance was a thin white line of breaking waves. Beyond them was the sea. Given one glance, that was about all the picture included, but close observation would reveal on the horizon what appeared to be a pair of distant buttes, nearly lost under the sky. The work of an artist, of an architect, of an airbrush, this was the Atlantic Generating Station, *in situ*, veiled in summer haze.

PUBLIC SERVICE felt that it was doing quite enough pioneering in the marine aspects of the project and did not wish to be in any sense experimental with the nuclear components. The company wanted "state-of-the-art" reactors. Westinghouse was chosen to supply them, and Westinghouse, which had never been asked to build a ship before, sought help from Tenneco, an industrial conglomerate that owned the Newport News Shipbuilding & Dry Dock Company, the largest shipyard in the United States. Westinghouse and Tenneco (which has since dropped out of the partnership) formed a third company, naming it Offshore Power Systems, and bought an estuarine island near Jacksonville, there to manufacture floating nuclear plants at the eventual rate of—it was hoped—four a year. The Florida Audubon Society tried to go to court in defense of the island but was rebuffed. Offshore Power Systems then began to dig an assembly line—a broad canal, about four hundred and fifty feet wide, penetrating the center of the island and ending in a slipway that would release new hulls to the water. In shops on the surrounding acreage, the nuclear and turbine-generator components would be built in very large segments, then crane-lifted to the assembly line and set in place. The crane alone would cost thirteen million dollars. A whole nuclear plant—to go—would cost about three hundred and seventy-five million. It would displace a hundred and fifty thousand deadweight tons. Richard Eckert and Muzaffer Kehnemuyi vowed that when Atlantic Generating Station Unit 1 finally travelled up the coast they would be aboard. The trip would take about ten days, passing Georgia's Golden Isles and the island Kuwait has bought off South Carolina, rounding Cape Hatteras, traversing the wrecks of a thousand ships. An insurance syndicate would underwrite the trip. Setting a premium for such a voyage calls for, if nothing else, wit. The premium would be somewhere between five and ten million dollars. "When that first unit leaves Jacksonville, I'm going to be on it," Eckert said. "Because if it goes down at sea I'm going down with it."

A HARBOR BREAKWATER at East London, on the Wild Coast of South Africa, was rendered ineffective by a storm in 1963. The armor, as the outer layer of a breakwater's material is called, consisted of blocks of solid concrete, each weighing forty tons. East London's breakwater had been weakened by rough seas some years earlier, and now the storm of 1963 tore off sixty per cent of the armor. Eric M. Merrifield, East London's harbor engineer, wondered whether that would have happened if the armor had not been solid—had not been designed to accept on one plane in one moment the great force of the ocean. He decided to reconstruct the breakwater with porous armor, and in doing so he invented a momentous novelty in harbor engineering.

The idea was to cover the breakwater with objects of branching shape—like children's jacks—that would engage with one another, clinging together while absorbing and dissipating the power of waves. There had been similar attempts. The French had tried a four-legged concrete form, a tetrapod, and it had worked well enough but had required an expensive preciseness in construction, because each one had to be carefully set in place in relation to others. Merrifield wanted something that could almost literally be sprinkled on the breakwater core. Eventually, he thought of *dolosse*.

Dolosse—the singular is *dolos*—were crude toys that had been used by South African white children since the eighteen-thirties, when they acquired them from tribal children in the course of the eponymous trek, the overland march of the *voortrekkers* from the Cape Colony to the Transvaal. A *dolos* was the knucklebone of a goat or a sheep, and might be described as a corruption of the letter "H" with one leg turned ninety degrees. The game that had been played with *dolosse* by *voortrekker* children, and by South African children ever since, was called knucklebone. As crude toys, *dolosse* were also thought of as imaginary oxen. Witch doctors had used them as instruments of magic power. Merrifield replicated them on a grand scale in concrete, making *dolosse* that weighed twenty tons apiece, and with these he armored his breakwater. When high seas hit them, the water all but disappeared—no slaps like thunder, no geysers in the air. The revised breakwater seemed to blot up the waves after breaking them into thousands of pieces.

According to plan, the ocean floor at the site of the Atlantic Generating Station would be dredged—graded, more or less —and then huge concrete caissons would be floated to the site, lined up like boxcars going around a curve, and sunk to the bottom. The caissons would be filled with sand and gravel, and then, both above the caissons and seaward of them, a hill of rock would be built that would emerge sixty-four feet into the air above mean low water and slope on down into the sea to toe the bottom three hundred feet from the inner perimeter. Many thousands of *dolosse*—in varying sizes, but typically weighing forty tons apiece—would be used as armor. On the landward side and parallel to the coast, the straight breakwater would consist of filled caissons, armored with *dolosse* only at the ends. The straight section would complete the atoll. Caissons could be removed in order to float nuclear plants in or out.

Like the plants themselves, the breakwater was truly, as the Atomic Energy Commission described it, a "unique and first-of-its-kind" undertaking. A list was made of all hard-rock quarries from western Pennsylvania to northern Maine. Big pieces of hills would be cracked apart. Some of the rocks of the inner armor would be so large that each would ride alone, under chains, on a big flatbed truck from quarry to seaport. Then—Egyptian journey—it would ride in a barge down the coast. Meanwhile, in southern New Jersey, on Delaware Bay, a concrete yard would cast *dolosse* with armspreads of twenty feet and place them a few at a time on barges, to be tugged slowly around the Cape May peninsula and up the long fetch to the site—eighteen thousand *dolosse*. In all, more than five million tons of material would be compiled over an area of a hundred acres. The Dravo Corporation, of Pittsburgh, bid two hundred million dollars and got the job.

ON THE SAND PLAINS of the continental shelf, a foreign object that comes to rest, even if it is as small as an automobile tire, will tend to concentrate fish. Automobiles themselves have been dumped into the sea by commercial and charter fishermen as points to return to for future good days. First attracted to such objects are the organisms on which fish feed. Then come the fish. In the ocean off Murrells Inlet, South Carolina, a great mass of rock was piled up some years ago, and it attracted various fish species in concentrations ranging from three hundred times to eighteen hundred times their frequency in nearby waters. The spot was named Paradise Artificial Reef. If an entrepreneur building such a place were to contrive to warm some of the adjacent water, many more fish would be attracted. Some would stay longer in the autumn before heading south. Some would not bother to migrate at all. Bluefishing and bass fishing might become winter sports. Small boats by the hundred would converge the year round.

The Public Service Electric & Gas Company's breakwater atoll off New Jersey would become a stupendous artificial fishing reef—its armoring *dolosse* an ichthyological magnet, with warmth guaranteed to the adjacent water by two nuclear reactors creating a thermal plume. The *dolosse* would grow lush with algae, invertebrates, barnacles, mussels. Sea bass would establish residence, and so would sculpin, skates, porgies, flukes, whitings, hakes, rock crabs, starfish, blackfish, lobsters. Lobsters are numerous in New Jersey but have to hunt around for places to hide, and for that purpose the labyrinthine hollows among the *dolosse* would outdo the granites of Maine. Lobsters would come to live there by the tens of thousands. In the words of David Thomas, the project director of Ichthyological Associates' New Jersey Marine Ecological Study, "There would be more fish and shellfish in that area than in any other square mile in the Atlantic Ocean."

Certain questions had to be considered, though. While cooling themselves, the floating nuclear plants would suck in more than two million gallons of seawater per minute. Screens would cover the ingress. What would happen to fish drawn toward the screens? What kinds of fish would they be? At what speed should the water be sucked in? What should be the size of the mesh? Phytoplankton, zooplankton, larval fish, and other small creatures would go through the screens and through the plant. What percentage would die? The water would increase in temperature seventeen degrees. Biocides would be injected into it to keep the plumbing clean. After four minutes, the water would be returned to the ocean. At discharge, how fast should it come out, and at what level? Would fish die in the thermal plume?

In 1972, when the final site selection was made, the marine biologists of Ichthyological Associates, who had long since become part of the project in a more general way, marked off a grid of sixty square miles and began what their founder,

Edward Raney, described as "the best-financed, the most intense study that's ever been done of a limited area in the ocean." Raney, emeritus professor of zoology at Cornell and an authority on the striped bass, the bluefish, and the American shad, had previously set up other studies attempting to counsel the designers of nuclear plants and to save the lives of fish. Very few fish have actually been killed by the heated water emerging from power plants. They die instead from the lack of it—as they have, for example, at Forked River, in New Jersey, when, in winter, the nuclear plant there temporarily shut down. Many thousands of fish that would have been farther south but had been attracted to the warm effluent of the power plant died in the suddenly cold water. Such an event would be most unlikely at the Atlantic Generating Station, since one reactor would always be kept running. The tons of fish that died a few years ago at the nuclear station at Indian Point, New York, were attracted into channels that had been built to conduct water from the edge of the Hudson River to the Consolidated Edison Company's intake screens. The fish went into the channels, apparently, because they liked the shelter and they liked the feel of the flow of the indrawn water. They would turn and face it, and swim against it, and keep on swimming in place until they were so tired they could not swim out. They then went up against the screens and died. Consolidated Edison moved the screens out to the river. The fish kill would not have happened if the behavior of fish had been taken into account in the initial design.

Raney and his ichthyologists significantly influenced certain basic design choices for the Atlantic Generating Station, and refinements would no doubt come along with the continuing study. In tanks, they tested the swimming speed and swimming strength of various species. They recommended that the water-intake velocity be kept below a foot per second. This would require six screens per plant, each fourteen feet wide and twenty-seven feet deep. The ichthyologists also recommended that the heated water be discharged rapidly, since a jet of water would repel fish. Such a jet—sent out through pipes in the breakwater—would create a mixing area of about two acres, in which temperatures would range from seventeen to five degrees above the temperature of the surrounding seas before the water spread out as a thermal plume. Experiments with fish of varying species had shown that a rise of five degrees, in any season, would be well below "the thermal point at which the locomotory activity becomes disorganized and the animals lose their ability to escape from conditions that will cause their deaths." Because currents of the littoral drift, whether they were moving northeast or southwest, almost always ran parallel to the coast, Ichthyological Associates suggested that there be two openings in the breakwater atoll, that they be lined up with the currents, and that no obstructions float between. It was this suggestion that resulted in the penannular shape of the breakwater. Fish having a difficult time at one opening could slide back with the current and go out the other. On the rare occasions when no current was moving and the sea was calm, water would be sucked in toward the plants from both openings in the atoll, but at less than a foot per second—not enough to trap a fish. Gossip went around the nuclear-safety circuit that in the design of the Atlantic Generating Station fish were getting even more consideration than human beings.

Meanwhile, the two or three dozen people in the employ of Ichthyological Associates who were conducting the New Jersey Marine Ecological Study continued to scrape the bottom for benthic samples, to trawl systematically for demersal fishes, and to compile intricate records of species by age, by season caught, by temperature, by weather, and by hour of the day. Early one morning, Valiant II, a chartered fishing boat out of Leeds Point, traversed the plant site dragging a twenty-five-foot semi-balloon trawl. Four miles or so to the northwest, on the lower stretches of Long Beach Island, stood the water towers of Holgate and Beach Haven. The one tower was green, the other orange, and from the perspective of the site they looked like loaded golf tees. Eleven miles to the southwest was the skyline of Atlantic City, rising tall, suggesting Manhattan to an eye that moved no closer. On a summer day at the site, many dozens of small fishing boats would have crowded the foreground, but now, in winter, three clam dredges were the only neighbors the ichthyologists had. Scooping tons of big surf clams—some for Snow's, some for Howard Johnson's—the clammers moved slowly. Thick smoke from their exhausts braided above them and formed a black plume that reached from the three-mile limit to the Holgate tower. For fifteen minutes, Valiant II, moving at two knots, had been collecting a benthic sample, beginning the trawl just to landward of the submarine sand hill. (On Valiant II's Simrad depth recorder, graphite tracings showed the position of the ridge, rising from minus forty feet to minus twenty-eight and descending again to minus forty-three at the site.) A winch turned, and long ropes that trailed behind the ship were hauled in. Trawl doors came aboard first—their purpose was to keep the mouth of the net seventeen feet wide—and then the net itself. It had a fine-mesh inner liner for stopping larvae and post-larval fishes. Young men wearing rubber gloves, rubber boots, and rubber overalls lifted the net and spilled hundreds of creatures into a galvanized tub and onto the deck around it. A surf clam. Moon snails. Pipefish. Little skates. Sand shrimp. Winter flounder. Longhorn sculpin. Eelpout. Atlantic herring. Spotted hake. Red hake. A five-pound cod. In a couple of years of such hauls, this was the first cod. New Jersey cod are usually associated with wrecks. They prefer, in any case, to stay a good many miles offshore. This one was dropped into a large jar that contained ten per cent formalin and ninety per cent seawater, slits having been made in its skin so the formalin could get into the flesh beneath.

Kneeling on the deck, griping, the young men began a meticulous count of specimens and species—and now and again offered comments.

"Jesus, what a big haul."

" 'Jesus' is right."

"Yeah."

"Look at all that hake."

Red hake, when small, live inside scallop shells with scallops, they said. The scallops somehow know that their shellmates are red hake. If fish of another species try to get in, the scallops kick them out.

The teeth of the eelpout were green.

"From eating sand dollars, which are covered with algae."

Codium, a grasslike material, was copious on the deck.

"It's only been around here ten or fifteen years. It has air pockets in it. It grows on clams, rocks them loose, and floats them to the surface."

The bodies of conger-eel larvae were transparent, with eyes —black dots—bulging at one end. Through the young windowpane flounders one could see the grain of the wood of the deck.

"Windowpane flounders eat a lot of mysid shrimp."

"Summer flounders are left-eyed. Winter flounders are right-eyed."

"We look at their scales—see how fast they're growing. Look at their stomachs—see what they've been eating."

"Look. A god-damned anchovy."

"They're important in the diets of weakfish and bluefish."

"Herring time. Four. Eight. Twelve . . ."

"My grandfather smokes them."

There were forty-two herring, each about fourteen inches long.

"Butterfish. Silversides. Sand lances."

The sand lances had both the length and the diameter of standard pencils.

"We once brought in a twenty-two-pound striped bass and found a quart of sand lances in its stomach."

Don Danila was working on a master's degree there on the deck with Rich Smith and Gerry Miller. As they sorted and counted, they spoke data to Chuck Milstein, the assistant project leader. A trim and light-figured man with a blue knitted cap, blue-tinted glasses, rubber overalls, and a clip-board, Milstein recorded numbers of specimens, numbers of species, the total weight of each species, along with the depth, temperature, salinity, and dissolved-oxygen content of the water the fish had come from. The day was calm, partly cloudy, under a cool sun. The air temperature was forty-seven degrees. The sea's temperature was forty, and it varied only half a degree throughout the water column, from the surface to the bottom.

Seven stations were a day's trawling. Between counts, while the net was in the water, the ichthyologists sat in the Valiant II's cabin and read the newspaper—the *National Fisherman*.

Or they checked instruments. Or they threw a secchi disc into the ocean to measure turbidity. White, heavy, attached to a line knotted at one-foot intervals, it sank, and when it disappeared from view its depth in feet was recorded.

"Ten feet."

"Not very clear."

"It's getting ready for a plankton bloom, that's why."

"When phytoplankton is blooming, you can smell it. The ocean smells dank."

"When plankton is concentrated in the net, it smells sweet, like cucumbers."

"A thousand pounds of phytoplankton can support a hundred pounds of zooplankton. A hundred pounds of zooplankton can support ten pounds of small predators. Ten pounds of small predators can support one pound of large predator—in other words, a striped bass."

On other trips, on other days, they would tend their lobster pots; they would tag striped bass; they would make gillnetting runs and pelagic trawls. They once caught so many lion's-mane jellyfish they could not haul the net in. Jellyfish might be something of a problem going up against the screens, for jellyfish cannot fight a foot-per-second current.

Summer trawls had yielded, typically, sea robins, dogfish and other sharks, scup, perch, menhaden. Menhaden were the most numerous fish of the region. A school of them might weigh sixteen tons. Sixteen tons of menhaden could be a problem against the screens. A massive impingement of menhaden could shut the plant down.

Over the years, about a hundred and fifty fish species had been collected. Sturgeon. Goosefish. Fluke. Squid. Rays—including a twenty-five-pound spiny butterfly ray, out of its place, which is the deep ocean. Sea snails—a rare fish in this area. All were kept in jars on the shelves of a fish library behind the group's lab, which had once been a private home, in Absecon. When a count was finished on the deck of Valiant II, only a certain number of fish were kept for the library. The others were thrown back over the side.

Northern fish and tropical fish were migrants to the area— for example, barracuda. The summer of 1973 had brought warm seas and the highest temperature ever recorded in the surf at Atlantic City—eighty-three degrees. Tropical fish rarely seen in New Jersey waters came into the trawling nets: bigeyes, lookdowns, goatfish, pompano.

Jay Chamblin, a medical parasitologist who was now doing zooplankton studies for Ichthyological Associates, was aboard. "In one haul of the net, eighty thousand gallons are filtered," he observed. "More than two million gallons per minute are supposed to go through the cooling system of each reactor. You can begin to see the problem." Through the cooling system would go the eggs and larvae of many fish, and the phytoplankton they feed on. The plant might kill millions of organisms, but it was hard to say what the impact would be on the total population, because populations explode.

Chamblin, pleasant and subtle, had a lean and ecological look. He lived in Beach Haven, the nearest community to the site. He saw a fly, caught it in one hand, and stared at it in fascination. "I think this may be the first fly of the spring," he said. Mischievously, he added, "Look at its small abdomen. At first, I thought it was one of those radioactive flies with abnormally small abdomens they find around nuclear plants and don't talk about very much."

As a group, Ichthyological Associates prefer to stay out of

discussions about radiation. All nuclear plants emit certain radioactive isotopes—such as iodine 131 and tritium—both in gases that go into the air and in discharged cooling water. In the Atomic Energy Commission's *Survey of Unique Technical Features of the Floating Nuclear Power Plant Concept,* it had been noted that "individuals who fish near the plant and its breakwater may be exposed both to the radiation from the liquid effluent and to the accumulated radioactivity in the fish that they catch." The survey continued, "The potentially significant radiation dose from fish ingestion and from fishing and boating near the plant will have to be evaluated at each proposed site. The problem could be similar to that at a lakeside nuclear power plant, although it may be more severe if the breakwater becomes a site for accumulation of radionuclides that can be taken up by edible marine organisms." The amount of radiation, in any case, would be small, the A.E.C. said. As around any land-based plant, it would be "a small fraction of the population dose attributable to the natural radiation background." Or, as one Public Service consultant later put it, "the radiation content of the plant's discharge water will actually be less per unit volume than that present in an ordinary can of beer." Ichthyological Associates' director, Edward Raney, testifying before the New Jersey State Assembly's Committee on Air, Water Pollution, and Public Health, had forthrightly said, "Radioactivity has nothing to do with fish. This is not in my field of expertise, but . . . I can assure you that the fish you eat from out there will be no different than the fish you get anywhere else."

Now, on Valiant II, Chamblin said, "No one in the lab is a proponent of nuclear energy. The staff is wary of fission."

It was marine biology, in the context of what Milstein

called a "wide-scale ecological project," that had attracted them to the job—a chance to advance their knowledge and their degrees with what amounted to a grant from Public Service.

"We have no constraints on what we do," Milstein said.

Chamblin said, "We know more and more about what we are destroying."

Milstein said, "Some companies would insist that all findings be kept in-house. Public Service actually disseminates the information. And our reports are not sanitized before they are published. To do the job adequately, we try to avoid getting into the nuclear-safety discussion generally. Let me say this, though: if this were an oil rig going in, we wouldn't want to work here."

ON ANOTHER WINTER DAY, more raw and windy, a research vessel called Sea Quest went out through the inlet and on into confused and choppy water to tend what the Atlantic Generating Station's full-time oceanographers referred to as "the farm." In the immediate acreage of the site they had planted some hundreds of instruments at varying depths. Wave riders rested on the sea. Spherical, tied to long lines, they could ride any wave from trough to crest. They knew where they were in feet from the bottom, and they broadcast their movements to recorders ashore, which, in turn, provided numbers to computers. Wind instruments were bolted to a toroidal buoy. Dominating the farm was a tower that rose sixteen to twenty feet above the ocean surface and stood on a tripod of heavy steel pipes. It stood in thirty-eight feet of water, and its pilings went down fifty-five feet into the seabed. A few months before, a once-in-forty-years wave had completely overtopped the tower, causing damage but not destruction. Instruments excluded, the tower had cost more than a hundred thousand dollars. It had been put there by the Environmental Equipment Division of E.G.&G. International, Public Service's oceanographic consultants. Instruments clung to it like mollusks—an anemometer, a bubbler tide gauge, a barnacle collector, an orthogonal current meter, a tank for red dye.

The purpose was to construct a hydrographic profile through many seasons over a broad ocean grid—to predict the effect that the sea would have on the generating station and to predict the effect that the generating station would have on the sea, most notably in the outspreading thermal plume. Many of the instruments were powered with batteries. Some contained 16-mm. cameras. All needed regular attention on a rotating schedule. Divers in wet suits stood prepared on Sea Quest's deck, their legs braced against pitch and roll—bare flesh showing between their rubber pants and rubber shirts.

"Is it cold in those things?"

"You're damned right it's cold."

Green spray came across the cockpit coaming. The divers jumped into the ocean. Treading water, they inspected wave riders. Going below, they brought up a nine-hundred-pound railroad wheel with current meters and temperature recorders strung along a chain behind it. Remaining on deck were John Cooper, the chief oceanographer on the project, and his boss, Ralph Eldridge, the program manager for E.G.&G. Eldridge —partly bald, middle-aged, quick with words—was by training a meteorologist. He described Cooper as a wet oceanographer, explaining that a wet oceanographer works in literal touch with the sea, while a dry one sits at a desk and uses data. Cooper was a heavyset man, still youthful, with tortoiseshell glasses, which were now flaky with salt. His hair was stringy, brine-soaked. He had a warm, disarming smile. He said he had been at the Woods Hole Oceanographic Institution, on Cape Cod, for nine years before signing on for this project. At Woods Hole, when he was there, no one had been doing shallow-water oceanography. "After the Second World War, they all went into deep water," he said. "It was easier. Now, with the environmental movement, they have been coming inshore. It's good. People are very much interested in what we are doing here, just from the oceanographic point of view."

They were finding out where the water came from, he said. Water from the New York Bight, for example, apparently moved south in gyres—great vortices ten miles in diameter, rolling down the coast. They mixed, gradually, with waters of the continental shelf. One could tell where water had come from by its temperature and salinity. Mediterranean water, for instance, is thirteen degrees centigrade, and its salinity is thirty-seven parts per thousand. Moving into the Atlantic, it sinks. Wherever it goes, it keeps its Mediterranean characteristics for years. Look deep enough and you can find it in the Caribbean. Typical ocean salinity is thirty-five parts per thousand. The water from the New York Bight can be as low as twenty-nine. On this part of the continental shelf, Cooper said, the characteristic salinity was thirty-two. Using such facts, one could determine where water had come from and pretty much where it was going. Oceanographers used to think that when water had settled somewhere it would stay down and old for centuries. That was not necessarily true. The Atomic Energy Commission, making such an assumption, had once dumped radioactive wastes in the Gulf of Mexico, only to discover that the water was much younger than people had thought.

These were boundary conditions here—two and eight-tenths miles offshore, near an inlet, near the surface, near the bottom. It was neither deep nor estuarine water. It was "a never-never region," Cooper said, where some waves were feeling the bottom and others were not. Winds, predominantly, were what created the local currents. Years ago, Vagn Walfrid Ekman, the great Swedish oceanographer, had written a book on wind-drift currents, and that was about all that E.G.&G. had to refer to beyond its own accumulating data. The prevailing current here ran southwest. About a fifth of the time, it turned around and flowed northeast. When it did, considerable upwelling occurred just seaward of the site, and that, said Cooper, contradicted everything he had previously learned. ("Classically, you learn that upwelling takes place in deep water and is then advected in.") Taking all things together—wind stresses, shallow-water waves, upwelling, the variability of current systems, interreaction of air and sea—the oceanographers had as their goal to reach an understanding of mixing processes in near-coastal areas, this one in particular. Water masses were being created here which would then flow somewhere else. In a decade or so, they were to begin to carry the effluent of a Westinghouse reactor.

When the oceanographers were not checking fixed instruments, Eldridge put in, they sometimes chased drogues for as much as ten hours, simulating a tracking of the thermal plume. Drogues were floats that consisted of intersecting planes designed to be equally affected from any direction by the push of current. Often, here, it was a two-layer ocean. While the littoral drift moved southwest in the lower fathoms, wind-drift currents made tangents above. So E.G.&G. had developed two kinds of drogue—surface and subsurface—and the oceanographers often chased sixteen at a time.

Or they might drop five hundred cc.s of rhodomine-B into the sea at the site and watch as a plume the color of Mercurochrome began to drift. As the plume matured, it would turn into what Cooper described as a "rotating swastika"—spinning along the coast, or toward land, or toward the open sea. As the dye diffused, the eye could continue to see it until the solution was as weak as two parts per billion. A fluorometer on Sea Quest could see four times as well as that.

To an extent much greater than had been true with the ichthyologists, the oceanographic people seemed dedicated to the success of the utility's project. They said that indeed they were. "We try to keep our thinking reasonably germane to what we're trying to do out here," Eldridge said. "We feel no conflict with the interests of Public Service Electric & Gas." Cooper, for his part, said he felt that his commitment was fifty per cent to oceanographic study and fifty per cent to the utility. Cooper and Eldridge both said they thought the concept of ocean-floating nuclear plants was sound and sensible. Eldridge said, "My first reactions were 'What a hell of a place to put a plant! Can't they think of a better place than the ocean? Why put a nuclear plant in such a hostile environment?' But after I got into it I changed my mind. We all did. And everyone in my group here is a professional environmentalist—not a cocktail environmentalist, self-appointed. Regulations are nebulous for this site and this concept. The work we do will help establish regulations for future floating plants."

More spray had dried on Cooper's glasses, but he did not seem to notice. "Seventy million cubic metres per second goes by in the Gulf Stream," he said. "To me, the real brass ring is trying to figure out how to grab it. Take one per cent of the energy of the Gulf Stream and you've done it. That's it. All you'll ever need. The problem is solved. Of course, I don't know how you'd do it."

THE DESIGN LIFE of the floating nuclear plants would be forty years. What if a storm so great that it would happen only once in a million years should come along during that time? The million-year storm would be a hurricane about eighty miles in diameter, moving with an advance speed of fifty knots, with sustained winds blowing at something like a hundred and fifty miles an hour, and with gusts far higher than that. Such a hurricane coming into the vicinity of the plant site would surge the surface of the ocean to a point beyond which it could be surged no more. The level of the sea would be lifted there about nineteen feet—a figure governed by the bathymetry, or depth and configuration, of the bottom. And what if the million-year storm should happen to come at a time of highest astronomical tide, which would be six feet—twice the normal daily variation? Now the water depth—forty plus nineteen plus six—would be up to sixty-five feet, the most prodigious water column that could ever stand at the selected site, two and eight-tenths miles off Little Egg Inlet. Never mind that a large percentage of southern New Jersey would now be under water. Atlantic City would be drowned outright. Vineland would be Venice. The hills of the Pine Barrens would be islands in the flood. What would happen to the floating nuclear plants? And what would happen if at the height of such a storm a three-hundred-thousand-ton supertanker—the largest that could float in these waters with its tanks discharged—were to stray off course and at sixteen knots crash head on into the breakwater? What if the supertanker rammed its prow into one of the gaps left open for the benefit of fish?

The Atomic Energy Commission wished to know the answers to these questions. For that matter, the A.E.C. wished to know what would happen if a supertanker hit the breakwater on a dead-calm day. Intentions were that the floating nuclear plants would be in "safe shut-down condition" during the "probable maximum hurricane" (the once-in-a-million-years storm), but what about the once-in-a-hundred-years storm, when the ocean surface was up sixteen feet and forty-foot waves were breaking? Could the plants continue to make fissions, steam, and electricity safely under such conditions? Could the hundred-year storm be the maximum "operating-basis storm"? The A.E.C. required that information, too.

At the Stevens Institute of Technology, in Hoboken, in 1972, a crude model breakwater made of wood, chicken wire, and pebbles was put in a tank and hit with the scaled equivalent of fifty-foot waves. The idea was that green water should never overtop the breakwater, and thus, for twenty-five thousand dollars or so, Public Service learned how high to build it. More advanced tests of model nuclear plants and a model breakwater were made at the Army Corps of Engineers Waterways Experiment Station, in Vicksburg, Mississippi. Certain basics about the configuration of the breakwater were determined there—the angles of its slopes, the appropriate weight for the armoring *dolosse*. (In an early test, the million-year storm knocked a few *dolosse* off the breakwater.) Such tests gave answers only for components, though, and ultimately nothing less than a total model would do—a model of the bathymetry of the entire region of the chosen site, with a model ocean upon it, and a model nuclear generating station floating there, surrounded by a breakwater made of stone and sand and *dolosse*. A suitable scale would be one to sixty-four. Within two thousand miles of Newark, there was only one test basin large enough to contain such a design. Europeans were far ahead of Americans in such coastal-engineering facilities. The Dutch, for example, could have placed a suitable piece of New Jersey's ocean in a corner of their laboratory at Delft. The one sufficiently ample facility in the United States was at the University of Florida, in Gainesville, where a coastal-and-oceanographic-engineering laboratory had been built to house extensive working models of Florida bays, inlets, estuaries, and beaches—whose erosion was worth preventing, because it could produce concomitant erosion in the treasuries of the state.

Kehnemuyi took me there one day in 1975. As we approached the building, on the edge of the university campus, he commented that the European, particularly Dutch, laboratories of this type were more numerous because "in this world we do what we need to do, and they live with water." And now, he said, New Jersey was in a predicament analogous to Holland's. The structure we entered was steel-walled and might have been a gymnasium. Its "model slab" was close to twelve thousand square feet in size (roughly four basketball courts), and had been molded to the bathymetry of the New Jersey seabed. Almost a foot of water covered the entire basin—a level scaled to the water column as it would be during a once-in-a-hundred-years storm. Floating in the center of the room were two squarish hulls supporting scaled nuclear-power plants, and these were surrounded by an atoll breakwater complete from caissons to *dolosse*. Eighteen thousand *dolosse* would be required for the breakwater in the sea, so eighteen thousand *dolosse*—precisely configured, made to scale—covered the breakwater here. Electrical wires from the model power plants went up to a central ganglion suspended from the ceiling and then ran over to a control room, where electronic equipment could absorb the findings of a hundred and twenty instruments that profiled, among other things, hull pressures, mooring forces, and six degrees of freedom of motion: pitch, yaw, roll, heave, surge, and sway. Afloat in a sheltered corner of the basin was a supertanker about eighteen feet long. "All that is missing are fish," Kehnemuyi said. "We don't know how to one-sixty-fourth a fish." Across one end of the basin was a wave generator—a set of a hundred paddles on a cam—repetitively shoving toward the breakwater waves of the once-in-a-hundred-years storm. The waves were seven or eight inches high. Scaled up, they would have been forty-footers—great, booming rollers—and they simply went into the *dolosse* like ripples licking the edge of a pond, while the nuclear plants themselves, steady in the atoll, pitched and rolled to a degree imperceptible to the eye. The degree was less than one. The generating station could operate with impunity in the midst of tremendous seas, Kehnemuyi observed. "I'm sure you could design a floating nuclear plant that would take ten or fifteen degrees of roll and pitch, but you would have to change systems inside them. Our design maximum is three degrees, and at three degrees everything that would be in a land-based plant would operate O.K. on the sea."

Stone beaches absorbed the waves at the far end. There was no apparent backwash, or "reflection." A desk and a chair stood surreally in the ocean, landward of the plant, the better for the test director to make notes in proximity to the model. His name was Robert Dean, and he was a University of Florida professor, physical oceanographer, civil engineer—a tall, slender man with dark-rimmed glasses, a black mustache, and an extraordinary affection for water. On his days off, he liked nothing more than to dive into one or another of Florida's limestone sinks, scuba gear on his back, and swim upstream into the total darkness of an underground river, carrying a light and seeing albino crayfish that had no functioning eyes. He had found stone knives from the Ice Age, when the water table was lower and such caverns were dry. He had to watch his oxygen supply closely, and turn back when it was not quite half gone. And now he strode through the ocean in long rubber boots, and pointed to other boots for us to put on, but said to be careful, because not long ago a visitor from the Atomic Energy Commission had pulled on one of those boots and there had been a snake in it.

We walked through the ocean to the plants and the breakwater. They were built on a turntable, so that waves could approach from any angle. In a typical winter storm, Dean said, when eighteen-foot waves would be hitting the breakwater, they would merely ripple around its base and look like swells. So the tests had indicated. In a two- or three-year storm —the biggest storm to come along in such a period—the plants would pitch and roll about a quarter of one degree.

The model ocean was fresh water, but the density difference—salt water is two and a half per cent denser than fresh water—had been calculated into every part of the model. The plants themselves were just platforms of wood and steel covered with calibrated weights and plumbed to deliver thermal discharge. A large boiler on one side of the room provided the "nuclear" heat. Also off to one side were two glistening white Styrofoam shells that had been sculptured in the shape of the ultimate power plants. Purely cosmetic, they could be placed over the weighted platforms to impress a camera.

Certain harbors sometimes have problems with a phenomenon known as resonance, wherein waves that might be, say, two feet high on the outside build up energy within the harbor until waves in there stand ten feet high or higher. The harbor at Marina del Rey, in California, has this problem, and so does Los Angeles-Long Beach. Such harbors are energy traps. The most notable one in the world is Capetown. Under certain conditions of incoming wind and wave, resonance builds up there to such an extent that ships snap their hawsers. Resonance seems to be a function of, more than anything else, the periods of the waves. Various A.E.C. consultants, including one from Capetown, had worried about resonance within the New Jersey atoll, so the Gainesville lab had created waves of widely differing size and periodicity in an attempt to get a real chop going within the breakwater. The biggest stir they could create was one-quarter the size of the waves outside, and they concluded that the Atlantic Generating Station would have no difficulty with resonance.

The formula for the tallest wave that can stand in a given swatch of relatively shallow sea is seventy-eight hundredths of the depth of the water it moves through. If the ocean is sixty-five feet deep, as it would be during a superhurricane at the site off New Jersey, the largest wave that could stand there would be a forty-eight-footer. Anything larger would have broken before it got there. "So we are not interested in the hundred-foot wave," Kehnemuyi said. "It would never get to us. A wave feels the bottom, feels any object. The bathymetry is not an absolute ramp. When the wave feels that there is an object in front of it, it breaks. A forty-eight-foot wave would be almost impossible, but we test for it. We also feel that the storm that would produce it is not credible, but we make the storm."

The most punishing of waves come at fifteen-second intervals. To imitate such waves on a one-to-sixty-four scale, it is necessary—according to the laws of hydraulic modelling—to divide the desired interval between the waves by the square root of the scale, which in this case is eight. So the waves in Gainesville generally pound the breakwater eight times as fast as they would in the ocean. Cameras film them at eight times normal film speed. When the pictures are projected on a screen at normal speed, the waves fragment and shoot spray in the air exactly as they would in the ocean. Public Service's films are something to see, with probable-maximum-hurricane waves, in Ektachrome, sending white water over the top of the breakwater, but never a sheet of green. The supertanker has been filmed, too, hitting the breakwater from every angle at sixteen knots, with the ocean surface up to the big-hurricane levels. A supertanker crash is anticlimactic. After a minor crunch, the ship stops dead. The bows do not buckle. Instead, they form a nest in the *dolosse*. When the ship is removed, the breakwater heals itself, as *dolosse* fall into the nest.

Peter C. H. Pritchard, vice-president of the Florida Audubon Society, appeared unexpectedly in the model basin, waded out from shore, and began to beard Kehnemuyi about the safety of nuclear-power plants, floating or otherwise. He said he wanted to make clear, first, that he had no patience with people who deplore power plants while freehandedly consuming the power they produce. He said he recognized the complexity of the utilities' problem. But still he was worried about loss-of-coolant accidents, core meltdowns, and breaches of containment walls—accidents that could release to the air and the sea much more radioactivity than there was in the bombs of Hiroshima and Nagasaki.

Kehnemuyi said that the company was doing tests for core meltdowns—seeing, by computer more than by tank testing, what might happen if a core got into the water. "But we categorically and very emphatically feel that this is a paper exercise," he said. "Such a thing will never happen. Studies are showing that the chances of a reactor's having a major accident are one in a billion years—reactors are that carefully and that redundantly designed. Let me assure you, our company would not put a penny into this sort of project if we thought such a thing could happen."

Pritchard—young, handsome, tall—stood there towering above the floating nuclear plants and looking doubtful. As it happened, he had been born in Belfast and educated at Oxford. He was the author of a book called *Turtles of the World*. Kehnemuyi—stocky, with short-cropped graying hair and shining brown eyes—had grown up in Istanbul, where his father was an importer of fine stationery. And now here they were, paths crossed, a Turk educated in Illinois and an Irishman from Oxford, standing in an artificial ocean in Florida and joining the issue of a floating nuclear plant off the coast of New Jersey and aspects of it that conceivably could concern the world.

The power station floating beside them was still the only thing of its kind, of any size, anywhere—and would be for some time to come. Years had passed since it had been conceived. Not so much as a pail of gravel had yet been placed in the authentic ocean.

Public Service and Offshore Power Systems would first have to obtain construction and operating permits. From the A.E.C.—now split into two government agencies—they had received only "generic approval." Opposition had formed among the beach communities ("S.O.S., Save Our Seas"), and the Atlantic County Citizens' Council on the Environment had petitioned to intervene. Hearings would be held at every level, and the fate of the project depended on the outcome of each hearing. Public Service had already put tens of millions of dollars into the project. Opponents complained that so much committed money might serve unfairly as leverage toward the granting of permits. The company, for its part, complained that the United States was "approaching an unworkable system" when so much had to be spent on a concept merely to prepare it for the hearing stage.

The company people were, if nothing else, prepared. They knew how many planes flew over the site—two hundred and fifty a day. They had mapped the location of every major well within a twenty-mile radius. They knew how many people were likely to be living within fifty miles of the site in the year 2020. They knew the exact distance—eleven and two-tenths miles—from the site to the nearest dairy cow. They had published an *Environmental Report—Construction Permit Stage,* which weighed twenty-two pounds and contained fifteen hundred pages. And now—roughly halfway toward their goal—they had come to the isthmus of the hourglass, where everything could, quite conceivably, stop.

Like bulbs around a mirror, floating nuclear plants might one day edge the seas. People who thought the concept was madness still had much time in which to say so. People who thought the concept was among the best of possible alternatives could present their case as well. More than fifty construction and operating permits were absolutely required. So far, not one had been issued.

In December 1978, Public Service put off its order for the two Atlantic power plants, explaining that rising rates and conservation of electricity had reduced the annual increase in demand for the company's product, with the result that new generating sites would not be needed, after all, for the remainder of this century. To float large-scale nuclear-power plants on the surface of the sea was apparently an idea whose time had not yet come—at any rate, in New Jersey. One might think that the idea would be more remote than ever in the aftermath of Three Mile Island, the nuclear plant on the Susquehanna that in the early spring of 1979 seemed to be preparing to relocate itself on the banks of the Yangtze River. But Offshore Power Systems, the manufacturer, continues to advance the licensing process, and hopes to put eight floating nuclear plants into production as soon as a license is granted by the Nuclear Regulatory Commission.

THE
PINBALL
PHILOSOPHY

New York City, March 1975

J. ANTHONY LUKAS is a world-class pinball player who, between tilts, does some free-lance writing. In our city, he is
No. ½. That is to say, he is one of two players who share pinball preeminence—two players whose special skills within the
sport are so multiple and varied that they defy comparative
analysis. The other star is Tom Buckley, of the *Times*. Pinball
people tend to gravitate toward Lukas or Buckley. Lukas is a
Lukasite. He respects Buckley, but he sees himself as the
whole figure, the number "1." His machine is a Bally. Public
pinball has been illegal in New York for many decades, but
private ownership is permitted, and Lukas plays, for the most
part, at home.

Lukas lives in an old mansion, a city landmark, on West
Seventy-sixth Street. The machine is in his living room, under
a high, elegant ceiling, near an archway to rooms beyond.
Bally is the Rolls-Royce of pinball, he explains as he snaps a
ball into action. It rockets into the ellipse at the top of the

playfield. It ricochets four times before beginning its descent. Lukas likes a four-bounce hold in the ellipse—to set things up for a long ball. There is something faintly, and perhaps consciously, nefarious about Lukas, who is an aristocratic, olive-skinned, Andalusian sort of man, with deep eyes in dark wells. As the butts of his hands pound the corners of his machine, one can imagine him cheating at polo. "It's a wrist game," he says, tremoring the Bally, helping the steel ball to bounce six times off the top thumper-bumper and, each time, go back up a slot to the ellipse—an awesome economy of fresh beginnings. "Strong wrists are really all you want to use. The term for what I am doing is 'reinforcing.'" His voice, rich and dense, pours out like cigarette smoke filtered through a New England prep school. "There are certain basics to remember," he says. "Above all, don't flail with the flipper. You *carry* the ball in the direction you want it to go. You can almost cradle the ball on the flipper. And always hit the slingshot hard. That's the slingshot there—where the rubber is stretched between bumpers. Reinforce it hard. And never—never—drift toward the free-ball gate." Lukas reinforces the machine just as the ball hits the slingshot. The rebound comes off with blurring speed, striking bumpers, causing gongs to ring and lights to flash. Under his hands, the chrome on the frame has long since worn away.

Lukas points out that one of the beauties of his Bally is that it is asymmetrical. Early pinball machines had symmetrical playfields—symmetrical thumper-bumpers—but in time they became free-form, such as this one, with its field laid out not just for structure but also for surprise. Lukas works in this room—stacks of manuscript on shelves and tables. He has been working for many months on a book that will weigh five pounds. It will be called *Nightmare: The Dark Side of the Nixon Years*—a congenially chosen title, implying that there was a bright side.* The pinball machine is Lukas's collaborator. "When a paragraph just won't go," he says, "and I begin to say to myself, 'I can't make this work,' I get up and play the machine. I score in a high range. Then I go back to the type-writer a new man. I have beat the machine. Therefore I can beat the paragraph." He once won a Pulitzer Prize.

The steel ball rolls into the "death channel"—Lukas's term for a long alley down the left side—and drops out of sight off the low end of the playfield, finished.

"I have thought of analogies between Watergate and pin-ball. Everything is connected. Bumpers. Rebounds. You light lights and score. Chuck Colson is involved in almost every aspect of the Watergate story: the dirty tricks, the coverup, the laundered money—all connected. How hard you hit off the thumper-bumper depends on how hard you hit off the sling-shot depends on how well you work the corners. In a sense, pinball is a reflection of the complexity of the subject I am writing about. Bear in mind, I take this with considerable tongue-in-cheek."

With another ball, he ignites an aurora on the scoreboard. During the ball's complex, prolonged descent, he continues to set forth the pinball philosophy. "More seriously, the game does give you a sense of controlling things in a way that in life you can't do. And there is risk in it, too. The ball flies into the ellipse, into the playfield—full of opportunities. But there's

* Lukas ultimately decided to be less congenial, and changed the title to *Nightmare: The Underside of the Nixon Years* (Viking Press, 1976).

always the death channel—the run-out slot. There are rewards, prizes, coming off the thumper-bumper. The ball crazily bounces from danger to opportunity and back to danger. You need reassurance in life that in taking risks you will triumph, and pinball gives you that reaffirmation. Life is a risky game, but you can beat it."

Unfortunately, Lukas has a sick flipper. At the low end of the playfield, two flippers guard the run-out slot, but one waggles like a broken wing, pathetic, unable to function, to fling the ball uphill for renewed rewards. The ball, instead, slides by the crippled flipper and drops from view.

Lukas opens the machine. He lifts the entire playfield, which is hinged at the back, and props it up on a steel arm, like the lid of a grand piano. Revealed below is a neat, arresting world that includes spring-loaded hole kickers, contact switches, target switches, slingshot assemblies, the score-motor unit, the electric anti-cheat, three thumper-bumper relays, the top rebound relay, the key-gate assembly ("the key gate will keep you out of the death channel"), the free-ball-gate assembly, and—not least—the one-and-a-quarter-amp slo-blo. To one side, something that resembles a plumb bob hangs suspended within a metal ring. If the bob moves too far out of plumb, it touches the ring. Tilt. The game is dead.

Lukas is not an electrician. All he can do is massage the flipper's switch assembly, which does not respond—not even with a shock. He has about had it with this machine. One cannot collaborate with a sick flipper. The queasy truth comes over him: no pinball, no paragraphs. So he hurries downstairs and into a taxi, telling the driver to go to Tenth

Avenue in the low Forties—a pocket of the city known as Coin Row.

EN ROUTE, Lukas reflects on his long history in the game— New York, Cambridge, Paris—and his relationships with specific machines ("they're like wives"). When he was the *Times'* man in the Congo, in the early sixties, the post was considered a position of hardship, so he was periodically sent to Paris for rest and rehabilitation, which he got playing pinball in a Left Bank brasserie. He had perfected his style as an undergraduate at Harvard, sharing a machine at the *Crimson* with David Halberstam ("Halberstam is aggressive at everything he does, and he was very good"). Lukas's father was a Manhattan attorney. Lukas's mother died when he was eight. He grew up, for the most part, in a New England community—Putney, Vermont—where he went to pre-prep and prep school. Putney was "straitlaced," "very high-minded," "a life away from the maelstrom"— potters' wheels, no pinball. Lukas craved "liberation," and developed a yearning for what he imagined as low life, and so did his schoolmate Christopher Lehmann-Haupt. Together, one weekend, they dipped as low as they knew how. They went to New York. And they went to two movies! They went to shooting galleries! They went to a flea circus! They played every coin-operated machine they could find— and they stayed up until after dawn! All this was pretty low, but not low enough, for that was the spring of 1951, and still beyond reach—out there past the fingertips of Tantalus—was pinball, the ban on which had been emphatically reinforced a few years earlier by Fiorello H. LaGuardia, who saw pinball as a gambling device corruptive of the city's youth. To Lukas, pinball symbolized all the time-wasting and ne'er-do-welling that puritan Putney did not. In result, he mastered the game. He says, "It puts me in touch with a world in which I never lived. I am attracted to pinball for its seediness, its slightly disreputable reputation."

On Coin Row, Lukas knows just where he is going, and without a sidewise glance passes storefronts bearing names like The World of Pinball Amusement ("SALES—REPAIR") and Manhattan Coin Machine ("PARTS—SUPPLIES"). He heads directly for the Mike Munves Corporation, 577 Tenth Avenue, the New York pinball exchange, oldest house (1912) on the row. Inside is Ralph Hotkins, in double-breasted blazer—broker in pinball machines. The place is more warehouse than store, and around Hotkins, and up-stairs above him, are rank upon rank of Gottliebs, Wil-liamses, Ballys, Playmatics—every name in the game, including forty-year-old antique completely mechanical machines, ten balls for a nickel, the type that Mayor La-Guardia himself destroyed with an axe. Hotkins—a pros-perous man, touched with humor, not hurting for girth—got his start in cigarette machines in the thirties, moved up to jukeboxes, and then, in 1945, while LaGuardia was still mayor, to game machines. He had two daughters, and he brought them up on pinball. They were in the shop almost every afternoon after school, and all day Saturday. One daughter now has a Ph.D. in English literature and the other a Ph.D. in political science. So much for the Little Flower. In this era of open massage and off-track betting, Hotkins has expected the ban to lift, but the courts,

strangely, continue to uphold it.* Meanwhile, his customers
—most of whom are technically "private"—include Wall
Street brokerage houses where investors shoot free pinball
under the ticker, Seventh Avenue dress houses that wish to
keep their buyers amused, the Circus Circus peepshow em-
porium on West Forty-second Street, many salesrooms,
many showrooms, and J. Anthony Lukas.

"Yes, Mr. Lukas. What can we do for you?"

Lukas greets Hotkins and then runs balls through a few
selected machines. Lukas attempts to deal with Hotkins, but
Hotkins wants Lukas's machine and a hundred and fifty dollars. Lukas would rather fix his flipper. He asks for George
Cedeño, master technician, who makes house calls and often
travels as far as Massachusetts to fix a pinball machine.
Cedeño—blue work smock, white shoes, burgundy trousers,
silver hair—makes a date with Lukas.

LUKAS STARTS FOR HOME but, crossing Forty-second Street,
decides on pure whim to have a look at Circus Circus, where
he has never been. Circus Circus is, after all, just four blocks
away. The stroll is pleasant in the afternoon sunlight, to and
through Times Square, under the marquees of pornographic
movies—*Valley of the Nymphs, The Danish Sandwich, The
Organ Trail.* Circus Circus ("GIRLS! GIRLS! GIRLS! LIVE EXOTIC
MODELS") is close to Sixth Avenue and consists, principally,
of a front room and a back room. Prices are a quarter a peep
in the back room and a quarter to play (two games) in the

* And they did so until 1976, when pinball at last became legal.

front. The game room is dim, and Lukas, entering, sees little at first but the flashing scoreboards of five machines. Four of them—a Bally, a Williams, two Gottliebs—flash slowly, reporting inexperienced play, but the fifth, the one in the middle, is exploding with light and sound. The player causing all this is hunched over, concentrating—in his arms and his hands a choreography of talent. Lukas's eyes adjust to the light. Then he reaches for his holster. The man on the hot machine, busy keeping statistics of his practice, is Tom Buckley.

"Tom."

"Tone."

"How is the machine?"

"Better than yours, Tone. You don't realize what a lemon you have."

"I love my Bally."

"The Bally is the Corvair of pinball machines. I don't even care for the art on the back-glass. Williams and Gottlieb are the best. Bally is nowhere."

Buckley, slightly older than Lukas, has a spectacled and professorial look. He wears a double-breasted blazer, a buff turtleneck. He lives on York Avenue now. He came out of Beechhurst, Queens, and learned his pinball in the Army—in Wrightstown, New Jersey; in Kansas City. He was stationed in an office building in Kansas City, and he moved up through the pinball ranks from beginner to virtuoso on a machine in a Katz drugstore.

Lukas and Buckley begin to play. Best of five games. Five balls a game. Alternate shots. The machine is a Williams Fun-Fest, and Buckley points out that it is "classic," because it is symmetrical. Each kick-out well and thumper-bumper is a mirror of another. The slingshots are dual. On this machine, a level of forty thousand points is where the sun sets and the stars come out. Buckley, describing his own style as "guts pinball," has a first-game score of forty-four thousand three hundred and ten. While Lukas plays his fifth ball, Buckley becomes avuncular. "Careful, Tony. You might think you're in an up-post position, but if you let it slide a little you're in a down-post position and you're finished." Buckley's advice is generous indeed. Lukas—forty-eight thousand eight hundred and seventy—wins the first game.

It is Buckley's manner to lean into the machine from three feet out. His whole body, steeply inclined, tics as he reinforces. In the second game, he scores fifty thousand one hundred and sixty. Lukas's address is like a fencer's *en garde*. He stands close to the machine, with one foot projecting under it. His chin is high. Buckley tells him, "You're playing nice, average pinball, Tony." And Lukas's response is fifty-seven thousand nine hundred and fifty points. He leads Buckley, two games to none.

"I'm ashamed," Buckley confesses. And as he leans—palms pounding—into the third game, he reminds himself, "Concentration, Tom. Concentration is everything."

Lukas notes aloud that Buckley is "full of empty rhetoric." But Lukas, in Game 3, fires one ball straight into the death channel and can deliver only thirty-five thousand points. Buckley wins with forty. Perhaps Lukas feels rushed. He prefers to play a more deliberate, cogitative game. At home, between shots, in the middle of a game, he will go to the kitchen for a beer and return to study the situation. Buckley, for his part, seems anxious, and with good reason: one mistake now and it's all over. In the fourth game, Lukas lights up forty-three thousand and fifty points; but Buckley's fifth ball, just before it dies, hits forty-four thousand two hundred and sixty. Games are two all, with one to go. Buckley takes a deep breath, and says, "You're a competitor, Tony. Your flipper action is bad, but you're a real competitor."

Game 5 under way. They are pummelling the machine. They are heavy on the corners but light on the flippers, and the scoreboard is reacting like a storm at sea. With three balls down, both are in the thirty-thousand range. Buckley, going unorthodox, plays his fourth ball with one foot off the floor, and raises his score to forty-five thousand points—more than he scored in winning the two previous games. He smiles. He is on his way in, flaring, with still another ball to play. Now Lukas snaps his fourth ball into the ellipse. It moves down and around the board, hitting slingshots and flippers and rising again and again to high ground to begin additional scoring runs. It hits sunburst caps and hole kickers, swinging targets and bonus gates. Minute upon minute, it stays in play. It will not die.

When the ball finally slips between flippers and off the play-field, Lukas has registered eighty-three thousand two hundred points. And he still has one ball to go.

Buckley turns into a Lukasite. As Lukas plays his fifth ball, Buckley cheers. "Atta way! Atta way, babes!" He goes on cheering until Lukas peaks out at ninety-four thousand one hundred and seventy.

"That was superb. And there's no luck in it," Buckley says. "It's as good a score as I've seen."

Lukas takes a cool final look around Circus Circus. "Buckley has a way of tracking down the secret joys of the city," he says, and then he is gone.

Still shaking his head in wonder, Buckley starts a last, solo game. His arms move mechanically, groovedly, reinforcing. His flipper timing is offhandedly flawless. He scores a hundred thousand two hundred points. But Lukas is out of sight.

THE
KEEL OF
LAKE
DICKEY

WE HAVE BEEN out here four days now and rain has been falling three. The rain appears to be ending. Breaks of blue are opening in the sky. Sunlight is coming through, and a wind is rising.

I was not prepared for the St. John River, did not anticipate its size. I saw it as a narrow trail flowing north, twisting through balsam and spruce—a small and intimate forest river, something like the Allagash, which is not many miles away. The river I imagined would have been river enough, but the real one, the actual St. John, is awesome and surprising. How could it, unaltered, be here still in the northeastern United States? There is nothing intimate about it. Cities could be standing beside it. It's a big river.

I call to the next canoe. "How wide is it now, Sam?" I asked him that yesterday, and he said it was eight chains, he guessed, there, approaching Seven Islands. Sam—Sam Warren—is a timber cruiser up here, and when he looks through the woods or across the river he thinks in chains. When he is cruising—walking by compass through the forest—he never wears raingear, and he wears none now. He has been paddling three days soaking wet, and he doesn't seem to mind. The air temperature is fifty degrees. He has cruised the woods at minus thirty. He says he thinks the river is ten chains wide now—six hundred and sixty feet.

We are a bend or two below the Priestly Rapid, and we can see more than a mile ahead before the river turns from view. Bank to bank, the current is running fast. It is May 28th. The ice went out about a month ago. We have seen remnant snow in shadowed places on the edges of the river. The hardwoods are just budding, and they are scattered among the conifers, so the riverine hills are bright and dark green, streaked with the white stems of canoe birch. The river is potable, God knows, for it rises here in the Maine woods, and almost nothing stands near it except hundreds of millions of trees. The only structures we have seen were three logging bridges and a few cabins—one in use by a game warden, another the fishing camp of a timber-management company, the others, for the most part, roofless and moldering.

John Kauffmann, in the stern of a red Royalex canoe, has come from Alaska to go down the St. John. We are four canoes and eight people. Kauffmann has been here before. He is the author of a book on Eastern rivers and, in part of his time, is a professional canoe traveller—a planner with the National Park Service, going out from his office, in Anchorage, to study, from water level, wilderness rivers that might one day be part of the national-park system. A big man, tall, he has finished pushing fifty. He wears a dark, broad-brimmed hat. Twenty years in the National Park Service—he looks like a smoked bear. Here, there, he has seen a lot of rivers.

"What rivers remind you of this one, John?"

Kauffmann thinks awhile, paddling. "Oh, I don't know. I guess there's some flavor of it in the upper Androscoggin," he says, and he lets it go at that for a hundred yards. "It has more presence than the Penobscot," he adds. "It's not a second-string, minor waterway—and it's not another Allagash, close as it is. Its dimensions are so much grander. Just look at it. It has stature, character. It's a majestic, noble river. It's something like the upper Hudson, but not much. I am groping for comparisons, but I can't think of a river like this one—not in the United States. It's a wild river, not a scenic river in the Shenandoah sense. Or the Connecticut or Housatonic Valleys. You have reminiscences of it in the Delaware, high up, and even, in a way, in the Kobuk—but you can't compare a taiga river to a Maine river. This one is unique. It's like some rivers in eastern Canada, but of our rivers it is unto itself. It's the St. John."

Time soon to put things away and look over the Big Black Rapid. Ahead we hear the coal-chute white-water sound, even though the wind is blowing stiffly behind us in squalls. Running before them, we fairly scud downriver. We pull over and, from the left bank, study the rapid. It is not a particularly long one. In on the left, out on the right appears to be the driest way to do it. One does not have to be a limnologist to see that.

One does not have to be cocky, either. Any rapid can be trouble—bad luck, bad guesses—and, looking at this one, I feel adrenalin run. Twenty years ago, on a fairly cold October day, Kauffmann and I turned over in a gorge of the upper Delaware, having gone there in a time of near flood, and we washed down at least a mile before we were able to get the canoe out of the big, chocolate river. I'm sure we will never be fools enough to do that again, but, together and separately, we have had canoes capsize under us in less dangerous places. So a little adrenalin runs. The rapid is beautiful, bouldery, and bending—the forest rising steeply from the two sides. It is called the Big Black Rapid because it is near the mouth of the Big Black River, which flows into the St. John a mile downstream. There is nothing black about the rapid. It is blue and mostly white, running over big rocks and ledges, with standing waves on long diagonals, like ranges of hills. The wind is so stiff now it is tearing spray off the tops of the waves. The rapid curves left, then right. If I thought I had one chance in ten of going into the river, I wouldn't run the rapid. I would line it—let the canoe down slowly on ropes—or carry around it. If I do get a thrill out of missing a rock and flying along on racing water, that is not what I came for. The rapid is only a part of the river—of a hundred and some miles of this trip and this part of the St. John—and the highest pleasure I can derive from running it is to get from the beginning to the end of the stretch of white water with canoe and cargo sound and, if possible, dry. This is a canoe trip, not a rodeo. When the Canadian *voyageurs*, in the eighteenth and nineteenth centuries, came to rapids in their bark canoes, they did not seek out the deepest souse holes and the highest standing waves. With their four-ton cargoes of furs, they looked for the *fil d'eau* —the safest, surest route through the rapid. For us, just being out here—in this country, on this river—is the purpose of the journey, and not shooting like spears to hit God knows what and where. A test of courage is not the point—not my point, anyway. I have too little courage to waste any on a test. In our own fashion, with our own bulging gear lashed into the four canoes, we had better think like the *voyageurs*.

The plan is that I will lead (paddling an eighteen-foot

Grumman), with Mike Moody. John Kauffmann will follow, with Tom Cabot. Lev and Dick Byrd, in their fifteen-foot Grumman, will go next. And Dick Saltonstall, with Sam Warren, in a big E. M. White canoe with mahogany gunwales, will sweep.

We shove off. One by one, the four canoes describe an easygoing, bobbing S down the rapid. The Byrds hit a rock and add a deep, tympanic bass to the contralto of the rapid, but they do not stick (as aluminum canoes too often will). No one else comes even close to buying the river. At the foot of the rapid, the aggregate water in all the canoes is maybe five or ten quarts.

"I've poled up worse rapids than that one," says Tom Cabot.

No one doubts him. Tom wrote the first of the Appalachian Mountain Club's New England canoeing guides. Also, with others, he designed the Grumman canoe.

I have been remembering all day that less than two weeks ago a canoer died in the river—in, as I thought I had understood it, the Big Black Rapid. Looking back up the steps of white water, ordered and unmenacing, I mention it. "I just don't see how anyone could have died here—could have had such an accident in this place. What do you suppose happened?"

"It didn't happen here," Saltonstall says. "This is the Big *Black* Rapid. It happened forty miles below here, just above Dickey, in the Big Rapid."

LAST NIGHT, I slept nine hours, rain thunking on the tent. Each night out here has been much the same. At home, I am lucky if I get five. Preoccupations there chase each other around and around, the strong ones fighting for the lead; and at three-thirty or four I get up and read, preferring the single track in the book to the whirling dozens in the brain. It's a chronic—or, at least, consistent—annoyance, and nights almost without exception are the same for me until I come to the woods, stretch out on the ground, and sleep nine hours.

We were brought in by air—in three float planes from Greenville, at the foot of Moosehead Lake. I was in the third plane. In the air, the two in front seemed to hang without motion, pontoons pendent—canoes tied to the pontoons. In the shallows of Moosehead we could see clearly the rocks of the bottom. There were whitecaps over the deeps. Off to the right, with more altitude, we saw Allagash Mountain, Caucomgomoc Lake, Chesuncook Lake, the West Branch of the Penobscot River, and, beyond all, the Katahdin massif, aglint with ice and snow. Moving north-northwest, we flew about sixty miles over streams and forest, and set down at the south end of Baker Lake, downstream a few miles from the string of ponds that are the headwaters of the St. John River.

I had never before taxied in an airplane up to a campsite, and when the last plane was gone I felt as if the towns and cities behind were somehow just over the trees, and I felt, too, a certain dismay with myself for not having worked my way out here with a paddle in my hands. Given all that, I thought it would take at least a day for things to simplify, for the checklist of current concerns to reduce itself sufficiently to lengthen sleep—but it took less time than the sun used going down. None of this is a matter of exercise. I get almost as much of that at home as here. Physical labor as a bringer of sleep doesn't seem to do much for me. But the woods do, where thoughts of weather, of food, and of the day's journey so dominate the mind that everything else subsides. The rise and fall of temperature and of wind, the beginning and the end of rain matter here in a way that is irrelevant elsewhere. With the right gear, it is a pleasure to live with the weather, to wait for sun and feel the cool of rain, to watch the sky with absorption and speculation, to guess at the meaning of succeeding events. I hate feeling miserably wet and cold. But with boots, heavy wool socks, rain pants, rain parka, and a wide-brimmed hat I have been dry and warm through all the downpours, on and off the river.

Saltonstall calls himself "a mail-order freak." He says I am one, too. His desk at home is piled deep with catalogues from the premier woods-equipment houses of the land: L. L. Bean, of Freeport, Maine; Eddie Bauer, of Seattle; Recreational Equipment, of Seattle; Synergy Works and Sierra Designs, of Berkeley and Oakland; Moor & Mountain, of Andover, Massachusetts; Eastern Mountain Sports, of Peterborough, New Hampshire; Herter's, of Mitchell, South Dakota; Kirkham's AAA Tent & Awning, Salt Lake City; the Great World of Ecology Sports, West Simsbury, Connecticut—and on down to the surface of the desk, a foot below. We had scarcely hit the beach at Baker Lake when he and I had an equipment shootout, which he seemed to think he was winning. He put up his new tent, an ice-blue JanSport with glass wands and a three-quarter-length fly, the whole affair a subtle compromise —in breathing and impermeable nylons—between the statistical probabilities of incoming water and air. Round, repulsive, mycophane, it appeared to be a model of the Houston Astrodome, its ceiling four feet high. I put up my tent, a tall pavilion in traditional canvas, by Eureka, of Binghamton,

New York, with a six-foot-six-inch ceiling—instant Camelot. (John Kauffmann meanwhile removed from his pack two small bags that contained enough onionskin nylon to cover an Alp. On a framework of slender aluminum rods he then constructed a villa. He offhandedly mentioned that his architect had been Barry Bishop, of the south col of Mt. Everest, and that Bishop's name for the tent was Bishop's Ultimate. Lighting his pipe, Kauffmann sat down in his foyer and watched Saltonstall and me with apparent amusement.) Saltonstall got out his Uncle Sam's Canoe Bags, sold by Moor & Mountain—rubber, government surplus, and supposedly waterproof. He handed one to me, saying he was sure I would need it, less for the rain than for the river. He also got out his new twenty-five-cup, porcelain-enamelled Old-Fashioned Coffee Pot, dark blue with white spatters, and his new wide-mesh Allagash Dishwasher's Bag—both from the Great World of Ecology Sports. In the logging camps of the Maine woods, utensils were put in bags and shaken dry. I flicked chips into the fire with my Buck knife, an instrument of such hard steel that the manufacturer agrees to have it back for sharpening whenever necessary throughout the owner's life. Saltonstall drew attention to the sewn-in tumpline on his new Duluth pack, from Gokey, of St. Paul. I then took from a canvas bag my new thirteen-inch reflector oven, from L. L. Bean, and set it, shining, at his feet.

Saltonstall has a minor speech impediment. He cannot say "L. L. Bean." Nor can he say the variants "Bean" and "Bean's." Instead, he refers to the place as "Leon's." Saltonstall, in Maine, is more seasoned than seasonal. He is not a native, but neither is he—and this is the point—a summer parvenu. He grew up near Boston and now lives in Virginia, but he owns a house and several hundred acres on a lake in Lincoln County, Maine, and he intends to settle there before long for the rest of his life. He is a sailor and has cruised the Maine Coast since his youth. He is a writer, and the title of his most recent book is *Maine Pilgrimage*. People of his ilk—old Maine hands from other states—seek ways of distinguishing themselves from run-of-the-summer tourists, and one curious way is not to admit to patronizing L. L. Bean.

Among outdoor-equipment suppliers in the United States, Bean's is more or less the source pond—a business begun in 1912, when the Maine Hunting Shoe was developed by a noted woodsman, Leon Leonwood Bean. Boots with leather tops and rubber bottoms, they are of considerable utility in the quagmires of the north woods, and Bean's still sells them— eighty-eight thousand pairs a year. Bean's-boots simulacra are in the mail-order catalogues of nearly all the other outdoor suppliers in the country. Adding item after item over the years, Bean, who died in 1967, built a national reputation. In recent times, the company has further expanded, somewhat disturbingly, to become a kind of balsam-scented department store, but, for all its Japanese pot holders and Seventh Avenue jumpers, it still has truly serviceable woods equipment in sufficient variety to hold position in the field. If you travel in bush Alaska, you find Bean's catalogues in cabin after cabin there, and Bean's boots and garments on the people. Most transactions are by mail, but the home store, in Freeport, in Cumberland County, is open twenty-four hours a day seven days a week. I know people who have gone shopping at Bean's at four o'clock in the morning and have reported themselves to have been by no means the only customers there. The store is a rampant mutation of New England connective architecture—

an awkward, naïve building, seeming to consist of many wooden boxes stacked atop one another and held together by steel exterior trusses. There is nothing naïve about the cash register. Sometimes it is necessary to go off to the woods for indefinite periods to recover from a visit to Bean's. John Kauffmann and I have stopped there at nine in the morning, fanned out for boots, mink oil, monoculars, folding scissors, Sven saws, fishing gear, wool shirts, met at noon by the windproof-match bin, gone out to lunch (lobsters—four—on the wharf at South Freeport), and returned to Bean's for a good part of the afternoon. Saltonstall, in his travels, makes regular visits to Bean's and, among trusted friends, is not too shy to admit it.

"Dick, where did you get that canoe-repair kit?"

"Leon's."

"What do you think of this Sierra Designs jacket?"

"I guess I like Leon's a little better."

Going to Leon's, though, is second-best to buying from Leon by mail, for a mail-order freak on the Saltonstall level needs to savor merchandise in his imagination in a way that is impossible in a store. Mailorderphrenia will not happen to just anyone. It requires a yeasty imagination. Long zip gaiters, bacon ironers, folding buckets seem more magical to Saltonstall on the printed page than ever they could in a store. The mail-order freak also prefers not to deal with hortatory clerks and the pressures of commercial time. He wants his decision to arrive at leisure. He does not want to cave in before a sales pad. So he hits the mails.

Tom Cabot, of Boston, is, in Maine, more seasoned by far than Saltonstall. On the way into Maine for this trip, Cabot's car broke down in Freeport, and he called to tell Saltonstall that he would be a little late. Saltonstall understood, and told the rest of us that Cabot had stopped at Leon's. Cabot, when he arrived, emphatically denied the charge.

Now, in that first campsite, on Baker Lake, Saltonstall opened one of three pack baskets and removed a jug of wine, a ten-pound slab of steak, and an earthenware crock full of perking sourdough, its lid secured in a web of cord. He had organized the trip—done all the planning, and the chartering of planes—and now he was laying out his credentials as guide. Professional guides still work in Maine, but the day has passed when canoers, by custom, would not go into the woods without them. The guides of old did all the cooking and, often, all the paddling. Their customers were known as "sports." Saltonstall was hardly going to be paddling us down the river, but around the fire from the start we have been his sports. He is a skillful cook and a master builder of fireplaces, not to mention fires, and he seems by inclination to want to take charge of things over the heat. He is a tall man, thirty-eight, with a handsome, round, ceramic face, and curly hair and Wedgwood-blue eyes—a bit of a woods dude, with his straw hat, his Glen-plaid shirt, and his Sierra Club cup hooked onto his belt. He once worked as a reporter in the Pacific Northwest and Alaska, and he once taught sailing at the United States Naval Academy. One can do worse than be a Saltonstall sport. He is surely as hardworking as any guide the woods have known. He has also dedicated himself to the interests of this terrain, and he has put this trip together to expand his knowledge of it, and ours. The St. John is Maine's remotest river, and it is essentially unknown, somewhat mysterious, even to the people of Maine. In Congress each year, a debate takes place about the fate of the St. John, and whether the Army

Corps of Engineers can or cannot have another year's funds for the advancement of a project that would backflood the river from a dam at Dickey, the first village one encounters after going downriver through the woods. Almost no one in Congress has ever seen the St. John—least of all from water level, in the woods. Only two people in the Corps of Engineers have canoed the river. There is a conservationist coalition called the Friends of the St. John, few of whose members have seen the river, either.

Wine, steak, and to bed at nine. At midnight, some of us got up for a while and got out of our tents to stare at the full moon. The night was cold for this time in spring. No clouds. No wind. Millions of stars spread over the sky. We could blow our breath at them and cloud them for an instant before they came back bright as before. Slowly, the shadow of the earth began to move across the moon. We watched the shadow grow, and sipped bourbon or drank chocolate. The temperature fell to the high thirties. Lev Byrd had on nothing but a cotton sweatshirt that said "Property of D H A" (Harvard Department of Athletics). He had played hockey there (1972-73-74) and was a star at it, and between practices he must have slept on the ice. At any rate, while I was shivering in a down jacket and a Scottish sweater he seemed unaffected—as well might a grandson of Richard E. Byrd. The shadow continued to cover the moon until just a small brightness, like a spot of yolk, remained; and then that, too, was gone. In the crystal sky, the moon was totally eclipsed, and appeared to be hanging there in parchment. When the last of its bright light was cut off, millions and millions of additional stars seemed to come falling into the sky. The Milky Way became as white as a river. Sam Warren said skies were like that up here on clear, moonless nights in winter. With the passing of the shadow and the return of the light, the stars of lesser magnitude evanesced as quickly as they had come into view. The air was down to freezing now. In the morning, there was frost over the ground, mist curling up from the lake, and ice solid in our cups.

SPILLING OUT OF BAKER LAKE, the St. John runs white for five miles in light and uncomplicated rapids, for the most part unobstructed by protruding rock: regular waves, gentle bends. Most rivers are toughest near the source, but the St. John, as it gathers itself together and develops from a forest stream into a big river, presents a kind of introductory course in white-water canoeing, beginning with easy runs, then featuring long days of well-spaced scholastic examples (a rock here with a good practice eddy, a chute there well illustrating the formation and nature of the standing wave), and then offering two or three days of assembled and more difficult rapids that culminate with the Big Rapid itself, the final exam. The first five miles out of Baker Lake were gone too quickly—the canoes flying along.

The river grew strikingly as tributaries came in—Turner Brook, Brailey Brook—and was a ten-lane turnpike by the end of the day, just below the confluence of its Baker and Southwest branches. The upper St. John drains an immense watershed—more than two thousand square miles—with a high proportion of streams to ponds. Water drains quickly here after it falls or ice melts. A day comes in the spring when the river's frozen surface, which has been solid four or five months, breaks into giant floes, and they begin to move downstream. Weighing many tons, they grind and screech and, in bends of the river, jam up until backrising water explodes them free. Downriver move hills of avalanchine ice, pale green, crashing, tumbling, tearing the banks, splitting the sunlight into rainbows. Great pieces skid off the edges and come to rest on the forest floor. All the way down, we have seen trees, high above the river, with sapwood glistening, big blazes of bark having been torn away by the ice. The temperature of the river now is forty-six degrees—cold still, but on the way to summer. Cold enough to hold down the catch of trout, which do not really get with it until the water warms to fifty-five degrees. Two-thirds of the St. John's annual runoff occurs in April and May. In summer, the rapids are bony, and the water is so shallow over some stretches of rock and gravel that canoers have to frog their canoes—walk in the water beside them. The St. John is hardly an intermittent stream, but it is more like one than any other river in Maine. After its high season, it is a small river in a large bed. Such is the natural year of a river—an unusual pattern now, because there are so few natural rivers. The St. John is the only Maine river of any size that has not been dammed. From its highest source—First St. John Pond, above Baker Lake—the St. John goes free for two hundred miles, until it breaks out into Canada, where it has been both dammed and, in places, polluted on its way through New Brunswick to the sea. It ends, incidentally, with a flourish, a remembrance of its upper waters—a phenomenal rapid. The phenomenon is that the rapid turns around and thunders back toward the source. The white water flows alternately in two directions—down with the river and up with the tide. In June of 1604, on the day of the feast of John the Baptist, Samuel de Champlain and the Sieur de Monts sailed into the river mouth on the voyage of discovery. They could have named it the Reversible River. Instead, they called it St. John.

We are sharing the St. John with many other canoes, and the river, to say the least, can accommodate them—ample campsites all the way. At first in a hot and blistering sun and then in the cool, steady rain, we have done as little as nine miles in a day and as much as twenty-seven. We have been eating even faster than we have been paddling—M&M's, cashews, raisins, peanuts, prunes, apricots, soybeans, sunflower seeds, hardtack, peanut butter, devilled ham, strawberry jam, and, in the campsites, sourdough pancakes, biscuits, raisin bread, gingerbread, eggs, bacon, and six or seven varieties of freeze-dried cud. Getting out of the rain, we had lunch one day (near the Ledge Rapid) on the porch of an old ranger cabin that, while still standing, was gradually settling into the forest in an attractive way. Its walls—peeled logs, notched and overlapping—were covered with a thin green film of moss. The roof, dark brown, was of arm-length cedar splits, and now, in its last seasons, had become a garden, with moss growing on it, and British soldiers (bright-red tiny lichens), and, most prominently, a sapling birch. The tree had somehow established roots in the cedar splits, and it had a trunk two inches thick reaching up to a parasol of new green leaves. It was a lovely scene—the old, long-abandoned cabin, with its colors of Harris tweed, melting into the forest on that damp day. I looked at some notes in a register there. "Liked the blackflies, gnats, and three bull moose. J. P. Hemmings, C. B. Metzler, New York, N.Y. 8-24-72." (The flies and gnats drive the moose to the river; in our cool May weather, no insects have hatched.) "Beautiful water and rain. One cow moose and two calves. Some deer and plenty of rocks. Bernard Prue. 6-17-74." There were no winter notes, but Saltonstall said that people do sometimes make their way to the St. John River in winter—in snowmobiles, God apparently willing. Saltonstall refers to such people as "toads" and gives their home town as "Toadville." He says he knows one toad who bought an antique sleigh so he could haul it behind his snowmobile.

We rotate from canoe to canoe, and I moved on from the ranger cabin with Dick Byrd. He told me that he was still a small child in 1957 when his grandfather the Admiral died but that he remembered him as a great old guy who supplied him with penny candy—and demanded the pennies in return. Once a year, Admiral Byrd dressed up as a spook and tried, without much success, to scare the hell out of Dickie. Now twenty-five, Dick is red-headed and strongly built, and has a quick sense of humor. Like his brother Lev, he is recently out of Harvard, and he is enrolled in the forestry school of the University of Maine. He told me that his father and mother had long ago been divorced, and that as a result he had been particularly close through his youth to his other grandfather, Leverett Saltonstall, who is Dick Saltonstall's uncle. Sam Warren, as it happens, is Saltonstall's brother-in-law. When Saltonstall goes on a canoe trip, he likes to load it up with clan.

We camped that night at Nine Mile Bridge, so named because it is nine miles above Seven Islands, so named by someone who may not have been able to count the thirteen islands in the river there. Our tents at Nine Mile were strung out like a tribal parliament on smooth grass under big birches and white pines—all on a bluff near a spring. The grass had once been the lawn of a young warden, Curly Hamlin, and his wife, Helen, who lived at Nine Mile, winter and summer, in the nineteen-thirties, soon after the logging bridge was constructed. In *Nine Mile Bridge*, a book published in 1945, Helen left behind her a rich and simple record of life in isolation in the woods. Their cabin was made of unsplit logs, and its door was scarcely five feet high. There was plenty of room inside, though—a big kitchen, a big living room with a bulldog stove—and they passed the long winter belting each other with pillows and eating four meals a day. Their only companions were a team of huskies and other dogs that Curly used on his forays against crime, covering many hundreds of square miles of deep snow and forest in his twelve-foot racing sled. Illegal trappers were his quarry, and he arrested few, but he made his presence known—tossed traps away and left a calling card, of all things, where trappers would return. Just by being there in the woods, he kept the number of poachers down. On his days off, he fixed his equipment or stretched out on his back and studied the rafters for traversing mice. He had a gun in his hand. When a mouse put its nose out, he fired. In summer, he specialized in houseflies, giving them rides through the roof on bullets. The Hamlins' furniture was laced with rawhide, and they made incense of the bark of quaking aspen. They also used aspen bark to worm the dogs. Trout swarmed the river and its tributary streams. To fish for togue, the Hamlins went up to Chemquassabamticook Lake. They were careful to keep fish out of contact with their canoe, because a bear that smells fish on a canoe will destroy it, imagining that fish are somehow inside. The Nine Mile Bridge was part steel, and in deep cold it hummed—set up a mournful wailing in the winter night, interfering with sleep at forty below.

There would be half an inch of beautiful, lacy frost on the windowpanes, and a red-hot fire had to be kept burning all night. Forty degrees below zero sounds cold. It is cold—a dry suffocating cold. The coldest I ever experienced was fifty-four below, when I had to breathe through a woolen scarf. But I would rather see forty below in Aroostook County than ten below near the seacoast where a damp wind cuts through woolen clothes as though they were gauze.

Helen Hamlin remembered the ice going out as early as March and as late as the tenth of May. After ice-out, the Hamlins travelled the rivers, shot the rapids, went down the St. John, and—once—went up the Allagash in the middle of the night. ("It's a funny sensation not to see the rough places until you're in them and feel the canoe rocking in the swells.")

The Allagash River—Allagash means hemlock bark—is tranquil and quiet compared to the St. John River. The land is flat, and there are channels through rocky and rough places. The river is so controlled by logging dams that it no longer pounds furiously down the waterways, a characteristic that gave it its reputation.

Each quarter mile of the upper St. John River produces whitewater, and few men have run Big Black Rapids at its highest pitch. The river is wild and rocky, practically untouched by the hand of man, and still in its natural, boisterous state. It is unhampered by logging dams, and the water level rises and falls with every slight rainfall or spell of dry weather.

Life in the woods was eventful enough, and seldom drove them "woods queer." When they did go out—to the border and across to Québecois towns or down the big river to the village of Allagash and the town of Fort Kent—their sudden immersion in society was not wholly agreeable. "I could never shake off the feeling," Helen wrote, "that the world was crowded and that people were odd."

The big wall of ice in 1970 was too much for Nine Mile Bridge, and only its piers stand in the river now. The Hamlins' cabin is a heap of splintered, twisted logs and rubble, behind where it once stood. A ponderous machine has come along and crushed it, ramming it as debris into a small ravine.

We were up at six in the morning at Nine Mile Bridge, and were soon eating trout for breakfast—trout and freeze-dried eggs, mixing in our stomachs the sublime and the ridiculous. The flesh of the trout was firm and as pink as salmon's. Every hatchery trout I've ever eaten was as white as halibut. These, through their lifetimes, had fed on nymphs in the river. The rain was light, after falling heavily through the night. The Uncle Sam's Canoe Bag that Saltonstall gave me is authentically waterproof. I keep in it my change of clothes—the things I care most to keep dry—and in the night, in the interest of sleeping space, I toss it out in the rain, because not a drop will penetrate the bag. The morning temperature was fifty-three, the sky was gray, and the air felt raw. We had come into Sam's terrain now—the one million seven hundred thousand acres managed by the Seven Islands Land Company, his employer. Somewhere in the distance we heard an engine, and we looked questioningly at Sam.

"Skidder," he said.

The skidder, which vaguely resembles a pair of tractors coupled together and is flexible in its motions through the forest, replaced the horse not long ago as the means of "twitching" a tree (lugging it through the woods) from the cutter to the truck. Skidders do the job remarkably well, but they have an unsavory reputation for tearing up the ground and beginning an all too swift process of erosion.

"How far away, Sam?"

"It's hard to tell. On a clear day, you can hear a skidder for sixty miles." Sam is dark-haired and ruddy, and heavyset, like a football lineman, which he once was, and he has a sober manner that is belied by his quickness to laugh. With his shirt soaking wet, as always, and rain pebbling his glasses, he went on, "The forest industry is slow to catch on to things. The chain saw, for example, was invented in the late nineteenth century. It got into general use in the north Maine woods in the late nineteen-forties. We are already thinking, though, of getting new machinery to replace the skidder. Small tractors, maybe. Or we may try aerial logging."

The company virtually never clear-cuts land, he said—only in strips, occasionally, to remove "decaying old stuff." On the whole, it takes trees selectively—about three hundred and fifty thousand cords a year—cutting annually on about thirty thousand of its million seven hundred thousand acres. The logging crews, who are independent contractors, go where the timber manager tells them to, and the timber manager is Sam, cruising the woods with his prisms and his angle gauges, pausing in selected spots to do variable plot samplings, boring into trees for core samples, and emerging with a sense of just how much wood is where and how ready it is for the saw. Yanked from the woods of late and set at a desk in Bangor, he has been trying to put into a computer a total inventory of Seven Islands' land, including not only the timber but the ponds, lakes, streams, and rivers, too, because hunters, fishermen, and canoe people will come whether the company likes it or not, so they have to be "managed" along with the trees.

All this has given Sam a perspective of his own in the group in which he is now travelling. The rest of us, to one extent or another, are wilderness romantics—tipsy on the drafts of Mudjekeewis, the West Wind. "I don't want to take anything from the feeling you may have," Sam has said. "But this is not wilderness. Every square foot of this country is managed land."

"Yes," I said, "but what you are managing is wilderness."

Sam said that could be, but he had trouble seeing things that way when the forest was his place of work. He said, moreover, that he thought it a shame that the law setting up the Allagash Wilderness Waterway had specified that a strip of woods reaching four hundred to eight hundred feet back from the water must be left permanently uncut. "The wood there is like pick-up-sticks," he told me. "It's just rotting timber, and in its decay it is using oxygen at the same rate oxygen is being produced. The wood should be cut. The way Seven Islands handles streams, ponds, and lakes—we leave plenty of standing trees; we don't cut steep banks; we make it a point to be careful. If you cut too heavily, you slow down your total rate of growth. A tree is unique in that it is the machine as well as the product. The tree makes the fibre. So you want to cut it when the machine becomes inefficient, and have it replaced by a faster-growing or younger tree. You get the tree when it slows down. Trees that we're not cutting are *dying*. You want to get the fibre as it grows."

The St. John in Maine is a wild river because timber companies have owned its surroundings for upward of a hundred and fifty years—a fact that can be taken, or not, as ironic.

I asked Sam how he felt about the Dickey dam.

He shook his head in dismay. "Trees renew themselves," he said. "Destroying something forever is unnerving."

NINE MILES FROM NINE MILE, we moved out of a corridor of confining, high-wall, riverine forest and into a great range of open space, with long river views, and big islands, and long lateral views across fields of grass to hills distant from the river. This was Seven Islands—sweeping, isolated, abandoned. Far up a slope beyond the left bank stood five log cabins, roofless but with walls intact. We walked up there to those dark cabins, elevated and sombre on the plains of grass, and I almost expected to walk through a door and see dead soldiers, their rifles awry, their necks bent as if, in vigil, they had fallen asleep. No soldiers. Only porcupine skeletons inside the cabins, and the drumming, like distant artillery, of grouse in the near woods. The horses that once worked the forest with the loggers were fed from these fields and others like them, dispersed along the rivers—the Penobscot, the Kennebec, the Allagash, the St. John. More or less by squatters' rights, Seven Islands was a French settlement. Québecois farmers came and cleared the land, and, in their custom, piled all the rocks in the center of the fields, not building walls of them, as New Englanders would do. There were, in any case, no neighbors to fence out. The rocks, of course, remain—a great loaf of them, six feet high and sixty feet long, a memorial to Seven Islands' vanished lumberjacks and a cairn to French Canada.

We spent the rest of the day at Seven Islands, fishing, looking around—in light rain that stopped and started all afternoon. We joined a couple of other campers there—Richard Barringer and Herbert Hartman, who, together, happened to be Maine's Bureau of Public Lands. They had a big twenty-foot, exquisite, forty-year-old wood-and-canvas E. M. White canoe, and in it they were looking over terrain to which they might lay claim. They shared their lunch with us—a bit of cheese, some cucumbers, raw potatoes, a bowl of fiddleheads, an expansive drop of wine.

Maine is half of New England, and half of Maine is un-organized. The state is completely divided into something like a thousand townships, and only four hundred and forty of them have—so far in history—been settled and incorporated as towns. Almost all the others are nameless—carry only numbers and letters in squares that dominate the official map. T 16 R 9. T 16 R 10. Township Sixteen, Range Nine. Township Sixteen, Range Ten. There are as many of these as there are Kennebunks and Arundels. And most of the unorganized townships are in the north woods. A township is twenty-two thousand acres, and by constitutional provision a thousand acres of each township is public land, reserved for parsonages, churches, and schools in the nonexistent towns. Land and timber companies own the woods, own hundreds of unorganized townships, but what about the so-called public lots? In aggregate, the state has claim to some four hundred thousand acres in the unorganized townships. In recent times, the state legislature passed a bill that (never mind the parsonages in Maine's unborn cities) allowed the public lots to "float"—by decreeing, in effect, that it would be all right if deals were made whereby any number of public lots could be assembled in one place, creating a large hunk of permanent public land. Hartman and Barringer had been dubbed the Bureau of Public Lands and were sent out to scout the best places to be claimed for the state. Trading off with the timber people, they had already acquired half a dozen swatches of terrain, including Gero Island, on Chesuncook Lake; Little Squaw Mountain, on Moosehead Lake; and the margins of Holeb Pond, on the Moose River. Inevitably, they were contemplating Seven Islands and other sections of the banks of the St. John.

Barringer—wiry, athletic, in a wool shirt and a battered red hat—appeared to have been left over from a log drive that had long since gone down the river. Before taking his job in Augusta, though, he had taught economics at Harvard. Hartman, son and grandson of Bowdoin professors, was an emeritus grad student who had spent many summers and autumns as a full-time north-woods guide. He said that when he gave up trying to write his doctoral thesis—on pre-Islamic Bedouin poetry—he had become for a time a beaver trapper near Jackman (one of the few organized townships in the north Maine woods). Like Barringer, Hartman was in his thirties. He was a tall man with narrowly set, quizzical eyes behind steel-rimmed glasses, and he had a lot of talent around a canoe. He had a black-spruce setting pole, full of spring and glistening with boiled linseed oil, and with it he could move his big twenty-footer at a handsome clip upstream, even against a stiff current. Standing in the stern, the twelve-foot pole in his hands, he looked like a gondolier, with the difference that he was jabbing his pole against the bottom of the pure St. John and not sculling the cess of Venice. To move the canoe, he reached forward, set the pole (point on the bottom), and then seemed to climb it like a gymnast on a rope. Sometimes—waxing fancy—he twirled it, end over end, on the recovery. To correct his course, he now and again poled behind his back. He said that when searching the woods for a new pole it was important always to cut a dead one, because green wood will dry out and check. In his guiding days, he used to tell his sports that he would never cut a pole on which a moose had not urinated.

"Why?"

"Because you have to tell people stories to keep them amused."

Poking around the six plus seven islands (I went with them as they explored), Hartman dropped anchor occasionally, picked up a bamboo rod with an English reel, and began to massage the air with sixty feet of line. From either bank, everywhere on the river, small brooks spit nutrients into the St. John, and trout will wait there like bums for a handout. Hartman drew streamers across the mouths of these brooks and provoked strikes despite the cold.

Hartman said there was among guides an age-old practice that would always help a sport feel better about his fishing. Sooner or later, inept as he may be, the sport will catch a fish. The guide nets the fish. Placing a shoulder between the fish and the sport, the guide works studiously, apparently to extricate the hook. What he is really doing is stuffing buckshot down the trout's throat. The guide, all the while, much admires the fish. "Yes, sir, that's a fish, that is *quite* a fish." The fish, ultimately, is weighed. Three pounds. "Ay-uh, well, I guess so, quite a fish." When it's time for the guide to clean the fish, he slips the shot back into his pocket.

"Did *you* ever know anybody who did that, Herb?"

"Oh, well, I guess so."

Hartman said that guides liked to coat the bottom of a canoe with dark shellac, so it would look to a fish like a floating log. He said, too, that it was characteristic of guides to assimilate the manner of the sports they worked for—becoming quite high-nosed, like butlers and chauffeurs. Guides' fishing equipment escalated accordingly, and they spent large chunks of their pay for tackle like the sports'—English reels, for example, and bamboo rods. Hartman's mentor was an old guide named Myron Smart, from Milo, and Hartman remembered his saying, "Out in the woods, you live different, and you do different. You know, I've been in the woods all my life, and I think I get more enjoyment out of the trips than the sports."

In a bogan near the campsite, we stopped to pick fiddleheads—enough for all ten of us for supper. A bogan is a pocket of still water projecting from a river. In other parts of New England, the term is "logan." A fiddlehead is the new leaf of certain ferns—ostrich ferns, cinnamon ferns, hay-scented ferns, evergreen wood ferns. When the leaf first develops, it is coiled like the head of a violin, and, in this young state, is crunchy in texture, sweet in flavor, bland, and succulent—incredibly delicious. We drew up the canoe and loped through the woods, excited by the colonies of ferns. The fern tops are fiddleheads for several days. It is a maxim of the woods that blackflies do not appear and trout are reluctant to bite until the fiddleheads are gone. We have seen damned few trout and no blackflies. When blackflies hatch, said Hartman, he repels them with fly dope—a mixture of citronella, pennyroyal, and tar. It makes him smell like a new driveway. Sometimes, fighting blackflies or mosquitoes, Hartman builds a fire in a bucket, throws green grass into it, and sets the bucket upwind. And no-see-ums, the all but invisible insects that mass on the skin and eat it as if they were acid—what does he do about them?

"I use Vicks Vaporub," he said. "It's the only thing that works."

We saw two beaver swimming in the bogan, cutting long wakes across the still water. On shore, we found the scat of fox and bear.

It rained all night at Seven Islands—heavily and steadily—but tapered in the early morning to drizzle and mist. Hartman was up at four-thirty, in the first light, in a sleeveless undershirt, beneath a balsam, shaving. The air temperature was forty-eight degrees. In the low light and mists of that early morning, Seven Islands was even more beautiful than it had been the afternoon and evening before. The bottoms of clouds were touching the plains of grass. I thought of all the water that had fallen in the night, and of the engineered flood that would stop the river. Seven Islands, not far from the head of Lake Dickey, would at times be under fifteen feet of water. At other times, as the dam made its electricity and coped with the river's irregular contributions of water, the surface of the lake would go down as much as forty vertical feet, and Seven Islands would then emerge, like the engulfed cathedral, coated with mud.

After a breakfast of trout and fresh hot raisin bread, we moved on downstream to Priestly Bridge, a loggers' crossing —part bridge, part gravel causeway. Barringer and Hartman had to leave the river there, as they had planned, although they would have liked to stay—would have liked to go with us through the Big Black Rapid. Barringer explained that Maine is "a banana republic" and they had to hurry back to Augusta to see if their bureau was still there.

The spring ice had not been kind to the causeway. The big floes had plowed into it and carried hundreds of tons of it some distance downriver. A bulldozer had been hauled in on the logging road to reclaim the gravel from the river, and the bulldozer was there now, downstream, gathering the gravel spillage and slowly hunkering it upstream. Back and forth the dozer grunted. The dozer belched, coughed, and wheezed. In what was now approaching a hundred miles of the St. John, the only inhabited cabin we had seen was a warden's near Baker Lake, and the only person we had seen (other than travellers in canoes) was a man in a bulldozer in the middle of the river.

SIX MILES BELOW the Big Black Rapid, we stop for the night on a grassy ledge that was once a logging road—cut into a steep hillside, twenty feet above the river. Down the hillside we tumble rocks and build a fireplace. Building the fire itself takes longer, in part because the rain has returned and—for dinnertime—is inconveniently heavy, and in part because I do a hurried and slovenly job of putting the fire together. With added shavings, added bark, and a lot of blowing, I eventually have a blaze that can shrug off the falling water. The Byrds and Mike Moody set up a rig of flying tarps—wide sheets of blue nylon held high with saplings and rope. Moody departs for the mouth of a brook. A year out of Nasson College, in Springvale, Maine, he apparently got his degree in fly-fishing, for he stays at it six, seven hours a day. The fireplace, hissing away, is just outside the shelter of the tarps, and we are now clustered inside—six of us, anyway—variously sipping gin, rum, and bourbon, and watching Saltonstall boil water. In all the mail-order catalogues in Saltonstall's collection, there is nothing approaching rum in the rain. Certainly, gin has good loft and weather repellence. But this rum—a hundred and fifty-one proof—is watertight.

The St. John, framed in spruce, with big rock ledges protruding, bends from view a mile down, and Saltonstall—never too wet to sell the river—says the scene reminds him of anchorages on the Maine coast, of fjordlike bays that penetrate the islands there. He says, "Don't you think so, Tom?"

Tom Cabot—who is a connoisseur of maritime islands and has many Maine ones in his private collection, who has slept in hundreds of Maine anchorages in his yawl, Avelinda—does not seem to be under the illusion that he is looking out from the shelter of the blue tarpaulins through the smoke of our fire at a piece of Penobscot Bay. He nods agreement, though, and smiles, and toasts the river with a gesture of his cup.

In the morning, big rips of blue appear in the eastbound clouds. On the river again, Tom is with me, and we are bound for Chimenticook Stream. A bend or two, and Sam Warren sees a yearling moose. He gets out of his canoe and goes after it, on a dead run up the riverbank. He learns that he is slower than the moose. He wanted to ride it. We have seen otters, ospreys, black ducks, mergansers, loons. No bears. There is ice this morning in the river—small chunks from big pieces on the bank, near trees with shredded bark. It is sixty hours to June.

"How many chains now, Sam?"

"Oh, fifteen, at least, I'd guess."

A thousand feet. Wide enough, surely, for four canoes. But gradually we string out in a long tandem—out of earshot, and even out of sight. Tom tells me about March, 1923, when he was twenty-five years old and shipped three canoes (wood-and-canvas) to the Quaboag River, in central Massachusetts. With five others, he planned to go eighty miles in a day and a half—down the Quaboag to the Chicopee and down the Chicopee to the Connecticut and down the Connecticut to Hartford. The water seemed fast enough to make that possible. Perhaps it was, but Tom and his friends would never know. In the first twenty miles, they totalled the three canoes. One broke completely in half. The two others came through irreparable, while Cabot and company, hanging on to the gunwales, washed down among cakes of ice. Somehow, all this inspired Cabot's affection, and he wrote an article for the journal of the Appalachian Mountain Club on the joys of white-water canoeing. It helped build interest in the nascent sport, and it led as well to Tom's collaboration (with John Phillips) on *Quick Water and Smooth*, the first guidebook to New England canoeing. Because northern Maine was the professionals' exclusive terrain, northern Maine was not included. This is Tom's first look at the St. John River.

Tom is about five feet ten, a trim and athletic man, with dark eyebrows, weathery skin, and a prominent nose in a somewhat narrow face. He wears black rubber nautical boots; an old, thin down jacket; a perky white hat with a blue-and-yellow band. His rucksack, stencilled "т. d. CABOT," must be fifty years old. His paddle is maple and is dark and scarred. He strokes steadily and smoothly as he talks, telling one story after another, and, conserving himself, he does not dig up the river. Statistically, he is old and decrepit. He's seventy-eight, and he has had several operations for abdominal cancer. But he looks sixty and acts forty, and to the question "How could an old man like that go down a wild river anytime, let alone when ice is still on the ground?" the answer seems to be that

Tom's infirmities may have crossed his body but may never cross his mind.

With Julius Caesar and Chief Crazy Horse, Tom is one of few people whose names have appeared in the line index to Bartlett's *Familiar Quotations.* The familiar quotation, of course, is what John Bossidy sardonically said in giving a toast, in Boston, at the 1910 midwinter dinner for the alumni of the College of the Holy Cross. He said:

> *And this is good old Boston,*
> *The home of the bean and the cod,*
> *Where the Lowells talk only to Cabots*
> *And the Cabots talk only to God.*

Bossidy was paraphrasing. Five years earlier, on an analogous occasion, a member of the Harvard Class of 1880 had said:

> *Here's to old Massachusetts,*
> *The home of the sacred cod,*
> *Where the Adamses vote for Douglas,*
> *And the Cabots walk with God.*

Tom Cabot, who has been everything from a Harvard Overseer to Director of International Security Affairs in the Department of State, will walk and talk with anybody. Especially talk. Listening to him is like listening to a ballgame on the radio, and in the canoe he makes the hours fly. He tells of an expedition he once led to the Sierra Nevada de Santa Marta, in Colombia, the highest coastal mountain mass in the world, and of a day in 1927 when he climbed Mt. Katahdin on skis. He was the first person (and possibly the last) ever to do that. He often mentions Harvard and his wife, Virginia, to each of whom he has been married for more than fifty years.

Qualified to be at least a dozen kinds of snob, he appears to be only one kind: in the way that English people refer to "red-brick" and "glass" universities, he talks about "freshwater colleges" in the U.S.A. He was once, briefly and unhappily, president of the United Fruit Company. (Saltonstall says that Tom "refused to bribe the Costa Ricans, and the bananas never got out on time.") But primarily he worked in his family's business, the making of carbon black. He is an engineer, and aggressive, and he developed and internationalized the company so that it became the world's foremost in its field. Made from aromatic petroleum residuals, carbon black is used to color things black, including printer's ink, but mainly it goes into rubber tires. Carbon black is about a third, by weight, of every tire that rolls on the roads.

"So why are you telling *me* all this, Tom? You're a Cabot. You're supposed to talk only to God."

Tom grins, and tells me what his father, Godfrey Lowell Cabot, used to say when asked that question. A look of shock and horror would come over old Cabot's face, and, backing away, he would say, "But I thought you *were* God."

We stop for the day near the mouth of Chimenticook Stream, setting up our tents on the edge of what was once a logging camp. A few clearings are all that remain, and some big logs that form a kind of sitting-frame around our fireplace. This was the settlement of the Castonian lumberjacks, reputed to have been the toughest, wildest, unruliest on the river, their axes, their crosscuts, and even their cabins long since obviated by the chain saw, the truck, the skidder. Chimenticook Stream is wide and fast—is in itself a river—and is white with high turbulence from bank to bank, pouring down from the west and into the St. John. I wade out into the mouth to fish, and in five minutes have a trout on the line. Fifteen minutes later, I have another, and tomorrow's breakfast is gaining weight. Unfortunately, though, my legs are numb, and I can no longer feel the river bottom through my shoes. I drop a thermometer into Chimenticook—forty-three degrees. It is apparently not too cold for these remarkable trout, but it's too cold for me, and I retreat to the campfire.

The air grows colder, too, falling into the thirties, and we build up the fire. We'll be shooting the Big Rapid tomorrow, and the thought of it comes to mind from time to time. The person who died there twelve days ago was an airman from Loring Air Force Base, which is in Limestone, Maine, about eighty miles east of the river. He was twenty-one years old and happened to be a native of Maine. With three other airmen, he rented a twenty-foot Grumman canoe, and all four —two too many for safety—were in it on the river. They had no life jackets (which are required by state law). When the canoe turned over, near the head of the Big Rapid, all four left it and tried to swim to safety—a literally fatal error. There is almost no reason to leave a canoe when it overturns, and there are any number of reasons to stay with it, the first of which is that it floats. It's a life raft. If it is pointed downstream—as it should be, so it has a more favorable mean free path through the boulders—the swimmers should place themselves on either side of the upstream end and wash on down to calm water. If the canoe is across the current and resists being turned around, then the swimmers should cling to the upstream side—a terribly important matter to remember, because when a canoe happens to press a person into a rock and pin a person there, it does so with a force of some ten thousand pounds.

John Kauffmann, knocking his pipe on one of the big logs,

pulls his field jacket up closer about his neck. He is disturbed by the death in the river, and dismayed by the foolishness that caused it. If four people get into a canoe and break every rule of sense and practice, and one of them dies, canoeing in general takes a loss. Some people think that anyone who goes down a white river is a suicidal fool—even if the rapids, as here, are far between. Kauffmann is not a white-water competitor—a wild-water or slalom racer. He is a canoe traveller —analogous to a cross-country skier—but he knows what the racers do and how they do it, and to learn their techniques he has been to school. "What we're trying to do with the white water on this trip is to get through it," he says. "A rapid is a problem, and we solve it. But we are not really involved with the white water. If you want to understand it, you have to get in there and wrestle with it, deal with it on its own terms, literally immerse yourself in it, as the racers do. That is the best training for this kind of tripping, because if you have it you know what white water is. The person who can most peacefully walk down the streets of New York is someone who has a black belt in karate. Under wilderness conditions, you just don't shoot a rapid unless you are certain of success. The primary rule in wilderness is: When in doubt, carry. Sometimes you misjudge. There's an eye for white water—like the eye in any other sport—and if you are away from rivers for a time you can lose your eye. From shore, standing waves can look smaller than they actually are. After a few rapids, you warm up, and your eye comes back. In the first place, though, you have to know what you're looking at. You must know what an eddy is. There is one below every ledge and behind every rock—with water flowing gently upstream—but look out for souse holes. I just don't understand the hydraulics of the souse hole. You must know how to make an eddy turn. It's easy to do, but you have to learn it. The eddy is your emergency landing field. You spin into it—through the eddy wall. If the bowman turns too soon and leans upstream, you dump. You can also go into the eddy with a back ferry. Once you're in the eddy, the canoe just nuzzles up to the rock and sits there, as still as if it were on a pond. Another major rule is: Never lean upstream. You lean upstream and the gunwale lowers, and then the rapid gets its paws on the upstream gunwale and pulls it down. Skiers learn to lean away from the mountain. In standard, open canoes like ours, you have to hit an adroit compromise between paddling too hard and not paddling hard enough. If you paddle too soft, the standing waves will rock you and may roll you over. If you paddle too hard, you may take in a lot of water. Remember: there is a critical limit to the amount of water you can take in. You have to stop and bail or dump the water. Or you'll just eat the river. So drive—but don't drive in too deeply. Talk a lot to each other. It helps things go right. Sometimes the deepest water, the main chance, is too damned rough. Say you've got heavy water. You've got big waves in there. You've got buddhas. You back-ferry. Face forty-five degrees off the direction of the current and paddle backward. You move sideways, across the current, like a ferry, and you avoid that vacuum pull that tends to drag you into the heaviest water. These skills should be practiced and practiced, like shooting baskets. Every one of these skills is applicable to saving your canoe and your cargo and getting through with a whole skin. You don't have to be a slalom racer, but if you immerse yourself for a while in the white-water sport you get to know some hydraulics and you get to know what the river can do not only against you but for you. Those white-water people really know what they are doing."

Tom Cabot says he thinks he'll go through the Big Rapid with John Kauffmann. He has the dibs, and rightly so. He doesn't know that John Kauffmann owns an old aluminum canoe that looks like foil in which a turkey has been roasted.

TOWARD FIVE IN THE MORNING, there is a veil of mist from sky to river and in it hangs the moon. Half gone now, gradually eclipsing itself, it tells us how long we have travelled. Half a moon.

Breakfast at six. Strong tea. "Sheep dip" was what the lumberjacks called their tea. We need it. The air is just above the freeze point. We do not eat light. Trout. Fried potatoes. Sourdough pancakes. Big red boiled "logging berries"—the lumberjacks' term for beans.

Tom Cabot returns from a walk in the woods. "I just saw a cow moose," he says. "I looked up, and there was the ass of a moose."

By nine, the sky is blue around big clouds. The day looks good on the river. Easing through the morning, we drop ten miles—Schoolhouse Rapid, Fox Brook Rapid, Poplar Island Rapid—and hunt around for a place to have lunch. For Saltonstall, as guide, any old sandspit will not do. He looks over a brook mouth fringed with alders, crinkles his nose, and keeps paddling.

"Why didn't we stop there?"

"He didn't think it was aesthetic enough, and, being an aesthete, he thought we had better move on," Cabot explains.

Tom is part aesthete, part Wall Street, and he can take his scenic settings or leave them alone. He knows both sides of the wilderness argument, and he is not always with nature in its debate with man. He has seen Lake Powell in Utah, the result of the dam in Glen Canyon, and while he knows what was lost in Glen Canyon, he is (for reasons of public recreation) not sorry the lake exists. Glen Canyon is sometimes brought into discussions about the St. John, because Glen Canyon was remote and few people knew it was there until it wasn't there anymore.

Saltonstall finally picks a luncheon site under three big white pines—symbols of Maine, the Pine Tree State. There were far-reaching stands of them here once, throughout the north Maine woods. They were cut for the masts of navies. These above us are among the few left. Old-growth eastern white pine, they're up there a hundred feet—their kind the tallest trees in Eastern America. If the lake fills over this point in the riverbed, these pines will reach up like masts from a shipwreck, and even their skysail branches will be twenty-five fathoms down.

The Big Rapid is three miles below. We move toward it—all crews the same as for the Big Black Rapid—with everything trebly lashed. Moody and I have the eighteen-foot Grumman, and have again been designated by the guide to go first. If we find trouble, our problem will suggest alternatives to the others. We are the refectory slaves, testing the food of kings.

The four canoes stop on the left bank, and we study the rapid. It does not look forbidding or, for the most part, fierce. It will not be like crossing a turnpike on foot. It is a garden of good choices. Overwhelmingly, it is a spectacular stretch of river—big and white for a full mile before, continuing white, it bends from view. The river narrows here by about a third, pressed between banks of rock, but it is still hundreds of feet wide—big boulders, big submarine ledges, big holes, big pillows, big waves, big chutes, big eddies. Big Rapid. About two-thirds of a mile down, on the left shore, a lone birch leans crazily toward the river. Below the birch, there appears to be a bankside eddy. Shouting above the sound of the rapid, we form our plan. Moody and I are to get into that eddy, and bail, and wait there for everybody else.

"Are you ready?"

"What did you say?"

"All set?"

"Yes, it's lovely here. Possibly we could stop here for another lunch."

"Get going, you sarcastic bastard."

"See you there."

And so we're in it. We make choices, and so does the river. We shout a lot, above the roar. Words coordinate the canoe. My eye is certainly off the mark. I underestimated the haystacks. They are about as ponderous as, for this loaded canoe, they can safely be. I look steeply down at Moody in the bottoms of the troughs. But the route we picked—generally to the left, with some moves toward the center, skirting ledges— is, as Kauffmann would say, solving the problem. We are not playing with the Big Rapid. We are tiptoeing in and hoping it won't wake up. Under the slanting birch, we swing into the eddy and stop. Two. Three. Four. Everybody home, and we bail many quarts.

The river now bends almost ninety degrees to the right, and we can see around the bend to another anchorage, under an isolated maple with an ovate crown.

The run this time is more difficult—the bow kicking high into the air and returning to the surface in awkward slaps. We dig for momentum, sidestep rocks, but not nimbly, for the canoe is sluggish with shipped water. Anxious to get into the calm below the maple, I try a chute that is just about as wide as the beam of the canoe. It's a stupid and almost unsuccessful move, and I get out of the canoe and climb up on a boulder to wave the others around the chute.

We bail a few gallons. Everybody is dry. We relax and joke and look down the rest of the rapid. Less than a mile below we can see flat, and much wider, water. We're so full of ourselves now it's as if we were already there. We do and do not want to be there, for after the end of the rapid the run is smooth and short to Allagash and the end of the wilderness river. The St. John after that is another river—a borderland, farmland, potatoland river—and then a Canadian, developed river, and not what we think of when we think of the St. John. So we look back upstream, at the whiteness of the river here in big display, coming out of a hundred miles of forest.

A canoe appears, bouncing in the waves. Half a mile above us, it rolls over and begins to wash down. Tom Cabot grabs a rope and runs up the bank, jumping from ledge to boulder, boulder to ledge. Everybody follows, but as we get nearer to the capsized canoe we realize there is nothing we can do. It is near the middle of the rapid. We can't throw a rope two hundred feet. The two paddlers are afloat and are hanging on, but the canoe—a fifteen-foot Grumman—is broadside to the current and they are on the downstream side. They are missing rocks, fortunately, but they are apparently oblivious of the danger of being caught between a rock and the canoe. We shout at the top of our lungs, "Get on the other side! Get on the upstream side!" But they don't look around. They can't hear us.

We watch them helplessly, and we return to our canoes. Because the water in the river is little more than ten degrees above freezing, the two in the river could have a greater problem with cold than with rock. When they reach our level, Kauffmann and Cabot move into the rapid in their canoe, Moody and I in ours. Cabot throws them a rope. One of them appears to be shaking but assures us that he is all right. Back-paddling, we wash along with them until the force of the rapid begins to decline, and then we haul in tandem and bring them and their canoe ashore.

One is tall, bearded, and, so it seems, physically unaffected. Relief is the last thing he is about to feel. It has apparently not crossed his mind that the river could have kept him. Instead, he shows fury, frustration, disappointment—like an athlete who has had his big chance and blown it. All the way to the north woods he has come, and has paddled a hundred miles downriver to dump in the Big Rapid, and, kneeling by his canoe, he pounds fist into palm in disgust, saying, "Damn! Damn! Oh, God damn!"

The other paddler is short and thin, and is shaking deeply from cold. He minimizes it, tries to be nonchalant, but does not seem disappointed to be standing on the bank. His T-shirt is dark gray, and above the left breast are small black letters—"YALE."

Tom Cabot questions him about the shirt, asking if it means that he's a student there.

"Yes. I'm there now."

"And how far along are you?"

"I'm '78."

Over Tom's face comes a small-world smile, and he says, "How about that! I'm seventy-eight, too."

WE MOVE DOWN the wide, placid, but still powerfully flowing river, and around a big island to Dickey. Looked at from our point of view, it is the beginning of the constructed world; approached the other way—to the end of U.S. 1 and then to the end of Maine 161—it is the utter end of the line. It's a hamlet, miscellaneously spread up the river slopes: frame houses, house trailers, overturned automobiles, general store, a single gas pump (Shell), over which hangs a giant rack of antlers—bull moose. Under wet laundry strung on someone's porch sits a snowmobile. There's a skidder on a lawn. The river draws us downstream, and Dickey recedes from view.

With low ground on the right and steep-rising forest to the left, we go down the final corridor, three miles or so of straightness, and come to the many-islanded mouth of the Allagash River. The Allagash rushes into the St. John, chopping the current, dumping nutrients into the big river, like all the other feeder streams. On the largest island—Gardner—we end our trip. Allagash, Maine, even smaller than Dickey, is across the way. We pitch our tents on high ground, facing back upriver —a view through the channels among the islands and on up the long wooded passage we have just come through. The river is framed in hills, the one on the right rising steeply some eight hundred feet above the St. John, the one on the left set back a mile from the river across the low, marshy ground at the end of the Allagash. The scene is a big one, but nothing of the size of what the imagination now superimposes on it. Outlined in the air between the hills and above the rivers is the crestline of Dickey Dam. It is more than three hundred feet above us, and it reaches from hill to hill. The dam is two miles wide. It plugs the St. John. It seals the Allagash marshland. Smaller than Oroville, bigger than Aswan, it is the twelfth-largest dam on earth. It contains what were once Aroostook mountains (Township Fifteen, Range Nine), blasted to shards and reassembled here. Its long downstream slope—the classic profile of the earth-fill dam—moves up before us to the crest. If we could put our canoes on our backs and portage up that slope, we'd see fifteen miles of whitecaps in the wind—a surging sea, but just a bay of Lake Dickey, whose main body, bending around a point to the left, reaches fifty-seven miles over the improved St. John. Paddles dipping, we fly the Big Rapid at three hundred feet, and, where the native trout have departed, we fish—thirty-five fathoms above Chimenticook Stream—for stocked Confederate bass. Chimenticook Bay is a five-mile reach, and Big Black Bay is thirty. In all, the lake bottom includes some ninety thousand acres of stumps, and, because Lake Dickey is one to three miles wide and no bridge is contemplated or economically feasible, two hundred thousand acres of standing timber are isolated from the rest of Maine. The lake fills up in spring, and the water is mined for power during the rest of the year, gradually revealing—along three hundred and fifty miles of shore—thirty thousand acres of mud. From the dam, and through the St. John-Allagash north Maine woods, runs a transmission line, continuing for four hundred and fifty miles, to southern New England, and carrying seven hundred and twenty-five megawatts of electricity for two and a half hours a day. That's all. That is the purpose of the Dickey dam. It is a soupçon, but anything more would drain the lake.

Many decades ago, the United States and Canada considered developing a tidal electric power source in Passamaquoddy Bay. It seemed a pretty good idea—pump-storage, with the tide as pump—but its daily output would be so erratic that another source would be needed to smooth out the curve of power. A conventional dam could do this, on the upper St. John. The Passamaquoddy project was eventually abandoned, but it had put the St. John dam in the book of public works, and dams are not recorded there in delible ink. For some years, though, few people were much interested in spending hundreds of millions of dollars for so small an amount of electricity—for a "peaking power" dam that could supply its power only during roughly a third of each day's peaking time. With the oil embargo of 1973, the situation changed, and the so-called Dickey and Lincoln School Lakes Multiple Purpose Project came back into the conversation. (To even out the flow from the big dam's irregular releases, a small dam would have to be built as well, a few miles downstream, at a place called Lincoln School.) New England power is largely derived from oil—seventy million barrels a year—and the dam at Dickey would save a million and a half barrels each year. Never mind that it would give New England roughly one per cent of its electricity. Never mind that it would almost surely cost, in the end, a billion dollars. It would provide pollution-free, Arab-free, indigenous New England power. The Corps of Engineers came through with a handsome benefit-to-cost ratio, indicating the shrewd Yankee good sense of building the dam, with computations based on a three-and-a-quarter-per-cent interest rate and zero future inflation. Additional cogent arguments were conjured as well—including flood control for villages downriver (dikes, built for a small fraction of the cost of the dam, would do), an upwelling of employment in the depressed environs of Dickey (never mind that the employment would be gone in a few years, when the construction jobs had vanished and a few people with clipboards had come from somewhere else to run the dam). It was felt, finally, that Maine, a state of two thousand lakes, needed a new one for summer recreation, and in the benefit-to-cost computations the recreational value of Lake Dickey was set at one million two hundred and fifty thousand dollars, while, on the other side of the ledger, the St. John River in its natural state was assigned no value at all.

Panic about the Arabs brought all this on, but deeper than the panic is an apparent belief that it is the right of people to have all the electric power they can afford to buy, with the subsidiary right of squandering it when and how they please and of buying it at the same rate at any time of day. We throw away more power than a Dickey Dam could ever give us, by ten times ten times ten. We throw it away in kilowatt-years. And anyone who would do that would throw away a river.

John Kauffmann, packing up his gear, winces in the direction of the damsite and says of Lake Dickey that it would be "like an artificial mountain in the Rockies." He says that he thinks there are plenty of technical arguments sufficient to prove the foolishness of the building of the dam but that in this case one point is really enough: "It would be a sin to murder that beautiful river." Tom Cabot, in his carbon-black boots, says he sees no benefit that would justify the cost.

Each year, of late, when the public-works-appropriations bill has rolled out on the floor of Congress, Congress has taken a vote on the St. John. Before the energy crisis, when the environmental movement was still going forward, the vote went against the dam, but since then the vote has gone the other way, getting up a few hundred thousand dollars here, a million there, to move the Corps through its studies toward the days of construction. The vote on construction funds—the vote to settle it all—looks to be in the offing for the nineteen-eighties. The St. John, it is said, was traded for the Allagash, at the time that the Allagash was preserved in legislation. If so, it was an uneven trade. When the guides of the Allagash take their vacations, they load their canoes and go down the St. John.

BRIGADE
DE CUISINE

THE FIFTH-BEST MEAL I have ever sat down to was at a sort of farmhouse-inn that is neither farm nor inn, in the region of New York City. The fourth-best was at the same place—on a winter evening when the Eiswein afterward was good by the fire and the snow had not stopped falling for the day. The third-best meal I've ever had was centered upon some smoked whiting and pale mustard sauce followed by a saltimbocca, at the same place, on a night when the air of summer was oppressive with humidity but the interior of the old building was cool and musty under a slowly turning paddle fan. When things come up so well, culinary superlatives are hard to resist, and the best and second-best meals I have ever had anywhere (including the starry citadels of rural and metropolitan France) were also under that roof—emanations of flavor expressed in pork and coriander, hazelnut breadings, smoked-roe mousses, and aïoli. The list of occasions could go deeper, and if it were complete enough it might number twenty or thirty before the scene would shift—perhaps to the fields of Les Baux or the streets of Lyons. The cook who has been responsible for such pleasure on this side of the Atlantic was trained on the other side, in kitchens in various places on the Continent, notably in Switzerland, and including Spain, where he grew up in a lavish and celebrated Andalusian hotel that was managed by his father. His father was Austrian, but his mother was English, and so, from the age of eight, he was sent to be educated in Great Britain. As a result, he is in manner, speech, and appearance irremediably English. He has an Oxbridge accent and a Debrettian flourish of names—not one of which he will allow me to divulge. His customers tend to become his friends, and I had been a friend of his for something like five years before I thought to ask him if I could sit in his kitchen and take notes. He said it would be all right, but with the condition that I not—in any piece of writing—use the name of the restaurant, or his name, or the nickname of his wife, Anne, who is not known as Anne and is always called by her nickname. We further agreed that I would not even mention the state in which they live and work, or describe in much detail the land- and waterscapes around them, let alone record what is written over the door of the nearest post office, which is, as it happens, more than five miles and less than a hundred from the triangle formed by La Grenouille, Lutèce, and Le Cygne.

The man's right knee is callused from kneeling before his stove. He would like to see his work described. He would like to be known for what he does, but in this time, in this country, his position is awkward, for he prefers being a person to becoming a personality; his wish to be acknowledged is exceeded by his wish not to be celebrated, and he could savor recognition only if he could have it without publicity. He works alone, with Anne (who makes desserts and serves as hostess, bartender, *sommelière*). In a great restaurant of Europe, the team in the kitchen will be led by the *gros bonnet*, and under him a *saucier*, an *entremettier*, a *potagiste*, a *rôtisseur*, a *grillardin*, a *friturier*, a *garde-manger*, and any number of *commis* running around with important missions, urgent things to do. Here—with Anne excepted, as *la pâtissière-en-chef*—this one man is in himself the entire *brigade de cuisine*. It is his nature not just to prefer but to need to work alone, and he knows that if his property were invaded and his doors were crowded up with people who had read of him in some enamelled magazine he could not properly feed them all. "There is no way to get qualified help," he explains. "You'd have to import kids from Switzerland. If you did, you'd lose control. The quality would go down the drain." In the *haute cuisine* restaurants of New York, kitchens are often small, and, typically, "five ill-educated people will be working there under extreme pressure, and they don't get along," he says. "Working alone, you don't have interaction with other people. This is a form of luxury."

Sometimes, at the height of an evening there are two customers in his dining room. His capacity is fifty-five, and he draws that number from time to time, but more often he will cook for less than forty. His work is never static. Shopping locally to see what is available today, reading, testing, adding to or subtracting from a basic repertory of roughly six hundred appetizers and entrées, he waits until three in the afternoon to write out what he will offer at night—three because he needs a little time to run to the store for whatever he may have forgotten. He has never stuffed a mushroom the same way twice. Like a pot-au-feu, his salad dressing alters slightly from day to day. There is a couple who have routinely come to his dining room twice a week for many years—they have spent more than fifteen thousand dollars there—and in all that time he has never failed to have on his menu at least one dish they have not been offered before. "I don't know if they're aware of this," he has told me. "We owe it to them, because of the frequency of their visits. They keep us on our toes."

In the evening, when his dining room is filling and he is busy in the rhythm of his work, he will (apparently unconsciously) say aloud over the food, and repeat, the names of the people for whom he is cooking. A bridge-toll collector. A plumber. A city schoolteacher. A state senator—who comes from another state. With light-edged contempt, he refers to his neighborhood as *Daily News* country. There are two or three mobsters among his clientele. They are fat, he reports, and they order their vegetables "family style." There is a couple who regularly drive a hundred and twenty miles for dinner and drive home again the same night. There is a nurse from Bellevue who goes berserk in the presence of Anne's meringue tortes and ultra-chocolate steamed mousse cakes, orders every dessert available, and has to be carted back to Bellevue. There is an international tennis star who parks his car so close against the front door that everyone else has to sidle around it. Inside, only the proprietors seem to know who the tennis star is. The center of attention, and the subject of a good deal of table talk, is the unseen man in the kitchen.

"Usually when you go out to dinner, the social event revolves around the people you are eating with and not the people who prepared the food. Soon after we started going there, he appeared by our table and wanted to know how something was—a shrimp al pesto he was trying for the first time. We have been there about once a month for nine years and he has never disappointed us."

"He's better than any restaurant I've eaten in in New York."

"He's a shy, compulsive, neurotic artist."

"He could never expand. He is a legitimate perfectionist who would find anyone else's work inferior to his own. No one would meet his standards. *He* doesn't meet his standards. Sometimes when I try to compliment him he refuses the compliment."

"I see him as one of the last of the great individualists, very happy in his kitchen, with his illegal plants out back. If he were to become prominent, his individualism would be damaged, and he knows that."

In part, the philosophy of this kitchen rests on deep resources of eggs, cream, and butter, shinbone marrow, boiled pig skins, and polysaturated pâtés of rich country meat. "Deny yourself nothing!" is the motto of one of the regulars of the dining room, who is trim and fit and—although he is executive vice-president in charge of public information at one of the modern giants of the so-called media—regards his relationship with the chef as a deep and sacred secret. "The place is not chic," he goes on. "It is no Southampton-type oasis. The people there are nondescript. In fact, that place is the only realizable fantasy I have ever had. The fantasy is that there exists a small restaurant in the sticks, with marvellous food, run by civilized, funny, delightful people who have read every book and seen every movie and become your good friends—and almost no one else knows about them. I used to fantasize such people. Now I know them. They exist. And the last thing in the world they would want is fame that is associated with hype and overpublicity. They are educated, sensitive, intelligent. Their art is what comes out of the kitchen. I'm sure he wants his work appreciated, but he doesn't want visitors coming to his hideaway for purposes of seeing the freak—the guy out in the woods who is making three-star meals. He would like to be appreciated for the right reasons—like an author who wants to be writing instead of going on TV talk shows. He is delighted when someone finds him, but wary, too. I think one proof of his sincerity is that he could raise his prices but he doesn't. He could advertise, but he doesn't. Somehow, that would be making too much of a commercial venture out of his work. It is inconceivable to imagine how his business could be run to make less money."

The chef is an athletically proportioned man of middle height—a swimmer, a spear fisherman. One day when he was thirteen he was picking apples in a tree between North Oxford and St. Giles and he fell out of the tree onto a bamboo garden stake. It impaled his cheek at the left corner of his mouth. His good looks are enhanced, if anything, by the scar that remains from this accident. He has dark hair, quick brown eyes, and a swiftly rising laugh. Anne is tall, finely featured, attractive, and blond. Each has eaten a little too well, but neither is falling-down fat. They work too hard. She works in a long ponytail, a cotton plaid shirt, unfaded dungarees, he in old shirts with the sleeves rolled up, rips and holes across the chest. His trousers are generally worn through at the knees. There are patches, sutures of heavy thread. His Herman boots are old and furred and breaking down. He pulls out a handkerchief and it is full of holes. "I don't mind spending money on something that is going to be eventually refundable," he explains. "A house, for example. But not a handkerchief." Most of the time, he cooks under a blue terry-cloth sailor hat, the brim of which is drawn down, like his hair, over his ears.

He was working with a Fulton Market octopus one morning, removing its beak, when he happened to remark on his affection for the name Otto.

"I like Otto," he said. "I think Otto is a sensational name. It's a name you would have to live up to, a challenging name. It suggests aloneness. It suggests bullheaded, Prussian, inflexible pomposity. Someone called Otto would be at least slightly pompous. Intolerant. Impatient. Otto."

Anne said, "He has written his autobiography in that name."

"I like Otto," he said again. "Why don't you call me Otto?"

I said, "Fine, Otto. I'll call you Otto."

Otto stepped outdoors, where he set the unbeaked octopus on a wide wooden plank. "Otto," he repeated, with savor. And he picked up an apple bough, a heavy stick about as long as his arm, and began to club the flesh of the octopus. "Otto," he said again, moving from one tentacle to the next. "I like that very much." Smash. "You do this to break down the fibres." Steadily, he pounded on. In time, he said, "Max is a good name, too—a sort of no-nonsense, straightforward name. Otto sounds humorless, and I don't think I'm humorless."

"Fine, Max. I'll call you Max."

"I like the way Max looks," he said. "It looks wonderful written on paper. You have the imagery of 'maximum,' too. And all the Maximilians." He struck the octopus another blow with the apple bough. "However," he went on, "I prefer Otto. Otto is autocratic. One word leads to another."

He carried the octopus inside. He said he has a cousin in the Florida Keys who puts octopuses in his driveway and then drives over them. "It's just to break down the fibres. I don't know what happens. I just know that it works." He went into the restaurant bar and took down from a wall an August Sander photograph of an anonymous German chef, a heavy man in a white coat of laboratory length over pin-striped trousers and highly polished shoes. The subject's ears were small, the head a large and almost perfect sphere. On the upper lip, an aggressive mustache was concentrated like a grenade. The man was almost browless, his neck was too thick to permit a double chin, and his tiny black eyes— perhaps by the impertinence of the photographer—were opened wide. In his hammy hands were a bowl and a wooden-handled whip. "This pig-faced guy is a real Otto," said the chef. "When our customers ask who that is in the picture we say he is our founder."

As we returned to the kitchen, I thought about the chef's actual name, which, like the man's demeanor, like the man himself in nearly all his moods, is gentle and unaggressive—an all but dulcet name, ameliorative and smooth, a name like Randal or Malcolm or Neal or Duncan or Hugh or Alan or John. For all that, if he wished to call himself Otto, Otto he would be.

Anne said, "He is less pompous than when I met him."

"Never let it boil," said Otto, lowering the octopus into a pot. "It mustn't boil. It should just simmer."

Nine o'clock in a spring morning and with a big square-headed mallet he is pounding a loin of pork. He has been up for three hours and has made school lunches for the two of his children who are still at home, boned some chicken, peeled potatoes, peeled onions, chopped shallots, shucked mussels, made coffee, swept the kitchen, made stock with the head of a twenty-pound grouper, and emptied outside a pail of scraps for the geese. His way of making coffee is to line a colander with a linen napkin and drip the coffee through the napkin. He ate a breakfast of leftovers—gâteau Saint-Honoré, Nesselrode cream-rum-chestnut mousse. He said, "I always eat dessert for breakfast. That's the only time I like it. For the rest of the day, if I'm working, I don't eat. It's wonderful not to eat if you're in a hurry. It speeds you up."

Anne works late and sleeps late. Otto goes to bed when his cooking is done and is up, much of the year, before dawn. Even at 6 A.M., he is so pressed with things to do that he often feels there is no time to shave. Into the school lunches today went small pork cutlets. He said, "I really don't believe in letting children eat the food served at school. Hot dogs. Baloney. Filth like that." His children carry roast chicken, veal, various forms of fish instead. At home, at the inn, they cook their own meals and eat more or less at random. The family business being what it is, the family almost never sits down at a table together. Sometimes the children, with friends, have dinner in the restaurant. Otto says, "They dress as if they're going to a disco, contemptibly wearing their collars outside their jackets, which is worse than wearing a blazer patch." He charges them half price.

The pork loin flattens, becomes like a crêpe. He dips the mallet in water. "All the cookbooks tell you to pound meat between pieces of waxed paper," he remarks. "And that is sheer nonsense." He is preparing a dish he recently invented, involving a mutation of a favored marinade. Long ago he learned to soak boned chicken breasts in yogurt and lemon juice with green peppercorns, salt, garlic, and the seeds and leaves of coriander, all of which led to a flavor so appealing to him that what he calls chicken coriander settled deep into his repertory. In a general way, he has what he describes as "a predilection for stuffing, for things with surprises inside," and so, eventually, he found himself wondering, "Maybe you could translate a marinade into a stuffing. You could pound a pork loin thin and fold it like an envelope over a mixture of cream cheese, fresh coriander leaves, lemon juice, and green peppercorns. Then you'd chill it, and set it, and later bread it. Sauté it a bit, then bake it. It should have a beguiling taste."

Picking up a knife now, he extends his fingers beyond the handle to pinch the blade. He rocks his wrist, and condenses a pile of parsley. There are calluses on his fingers where they pinch the blade. "The great thing is the *mise en place*," he says. "You get your things together. You get ready to cook. You chop your parsley, peel your onions, do shallots, make the hollandaise, make demi-glace sauce, and so forth." He does most of this in the center of the room, a step from the stove, at a long, narrow table that sags like a hammock. He works on two slabs of butcher block, and around them accumulate small tubs, bowls, and jars full of herbs and herb butters, stocks and sauces, grated cheeses. A bottle of apple-jack stands nearby for use in pâtés, and a No. 10 can full of kosher salt, which he dips into all day and tosses about by hand. Everything he measures he measures only with his eyes. How does he know how much to use? "I just know what is going to make things taste good," he says.

"Even with garlic, for example?"

"In garlicky dishes, you can hardly use too much—as long as you don't burn it."

He nibbles some parsley, wipes the block. On his shoulder is a hand towel, and with it he polishes his working surfaces as if he were polishing cars. He wipes the edge of the stove. He wipes the lips of pots. After he sautés something, he wipes out the interior of the pan. All day long the cloth keeps coming off the shoulder—or out of a rear pocket when it has migrated there—and as it grows foul it is frequently replaced. Like a quarterback, a golfer, a dentist, he would be unnerved without his towel.

When he finishes a patch of work—stops pounding loin of pork, completes a forcemeat for quenelles—he neatly puts the product away. Moving on to some new material, he carries it to a working surface, and cuts or separates or pours out just what he needs, and then returns the matrix—to the refrigerator, or wherever it came from—*before* he begins the new preparation. If he did not do this, he would risk chaos. His day will grow in frenzy and may eventually come a bit unstuck, but even in the whirl of the height of the evening he never fails to replace a source before he works on the substance.

He has a Vulcan gas stove with two ovens, a broiler, and six burners. Every time he turns it on he has to use a match. He keeps matches in a McDonald's French-fry packet nailed to a post. He saves the wooden sticks to use again as tapers. "We're really cheap," he confesses. "We wash our Reynolds Wrap and use it again."

His evolving salad dressing is stored in whiskey bottles and is topped up a few times a week with oil, egg yolk, wine, tarragon, marjoram, chervil, salt, pepper, chives, garlic, parsley, onions, scallion tops, vinegar, mustard seed—and almost anything but sugar. The thought of sugar in salad dressing disgusts him, although he knows it will sell salad dressing. He blends in some lightly boiled potatoes. They homogenize the dressing, he says, emulsify it, hold it together.

There is no top on the blender. Otto and Anne cover it with their hands—sometimes with a napkin. The blender is old and bandaged with tape. They have an electric mixer. "It's the worst-engineered thing I've ever seen. It spits ingredients into the air." To facilitate their preparations they have no other appliances. There is not even an electric dishwasher, just a three-tub stainless deep sink where Anne washes dishes in the dead of night, except on weekends, when a high-school student comes in to help. Three plugs stop the sink. A sign on the wall above says, "HANG PLUGS HERE. THIS IS A PROPHYLAXIS AGAINST DEMENTIA NERVOSA. PLEASE!" No rotisserie. No microwave. No Cuisinart in any form. "We're not anti-technology. We're just anti-junk," said Otto one morning. "There's no reason to be anti all 'labor-saving' things—just from sheer perversity to be against them—but, as it happens, there is nothing a Cuisinart can do that I can't do as quickly. And after using a Cuisinart I would have to clean it. Steak tartare cut with a knife has a better texture than it does if it comes out of a Cuisinart. The Germans call it Schabefleisch. For that matter, it is easier to cut hamburger meat than to make it in any kind of machine. If you grind it, you then have to clean the grinder." I asked him to make me a hamburger. He removed from the refrigerator the hundredth part of a ton of beef, sliced off a portion, put the rest of the meat back in the cooler, and returned to his working block, where his wrist began to flutter heavily, and in thirty seconds he had disassembled the chunk of beef and rearranged it as an oval patty. He ate some of the meat as he worked. Fast as it all happened, the cutting was done in three phases. He began with a one-handed rocking motion, and then held down the point of the knife with his left hand while pumping the handle with his right. He ended with a chopping motion, as if the knife were a hatchet. As he made the patty, he did not compact it crudely in his hands like a snowball. He tapped it together with the flat of the knife. The knife was Swiss (*hachoir* size), the blade vanadium stainless steel. "It's a lot of bull not to use stainless," he said. "If you know how to sharpen a knife, you can sharpen a stainless knife. You can't use a carbon knife to cut anything that has acid in it. If you cut anything acid with a carbon knife, it develops big black splotches. The splotches flavor the food." From under the stove he pulled a damaged iron skillet. Something that looked like a large bite was missing from the rim. He cooked the hamburger, turning it, touching it, turning it again and again, using the knife as a spatula. One morning he made fresh pork sausage for me the same way—mixing into the patty the salt, thyme, pepper, and coriander that are the essences of the flavor of sausage. The awakening aroma was vigorous and new. He tasted the raw pork as he went along. He said sausagemakers do that routinely. He observed that if one does need to make use of a meat grinder it is a good idea to put chunks of the meat into a freezer for twenty minutes beforehand. This in some way—he has no idea why— greatly reduces the stringiness that will often clog a grinder.

The kitchen has the dimensions of a fair-sized living room, and the refrigerator is a multi-doored affair that fills one end from wall to wall. The kitchen at a New York frog pond would not be half as large. (A frog pond, in Otto's vernacular, is any French restaurant, but particularly the finest and Frenchest of the supraduodenal boutiques.) Otto much admires André Soltner, chef of Lutèce, for removing (after he took over the ownership of the restaurant) some of his dining space in order to expand the kitchen. In Otto's kitchen, there is room for an old brass-studded leather Spanish chair. There is a television set, a big Grundig Majestic radio. On spacious high shelves are the chef's unending agents of flavor—his angelica seeds, his sorrel jam, his twenty-seven-dollar pelures de truffes, his valerian root, his Ann Page filberts, his Sun-Maid currants, and a thousand other things. Holding a deep, half-filled pan below my nose, he says, "This is rendered beef fat. We render all our pork and beef fat. It is extraordinarily unhealthy, but smell it. It smells of roast beef. Cooked in this, French-fried potatoes taste nutty and have a thick crust. The Belgians do all their *frites* like that. You can burn yourself badly, of course. I wouldn't want a large deep-fat fryer here. I'm too accident-prone. I burn myself all the time. The awful thing about burning is that you always burn yourself on a useful part of the hand." On a windowsill in the kitchen he grows *Aloe vera*, and tends it with affection, a handsome plant with its lanceolate, serrate, basal leaves. When he burns himself, he takes a leaf of aloe and slices it from the side, as if he were filleting a small green fish. He presses the leaf's interior against the burn, and holds it there with a bandage. "That takes the burn right away."

Outside, in his kitchen garden, Otto grows asparagus, eggplant, chili peppers, bell peppers, tomatoes, cucumbers, potatoes, spinach, zucchini, and chard. He also grows chervil, fennel, parsley, horseradish, basil, chives, marjoram, arugula, and tarragon, among other herbs. He freezes his herbs, he dries his herbs, and he aspirates the "h." He knows how to pronounce "Hertford," "Hereford," "Hampshire," and "herbs." He went to school in Oxford. Chervil, he says, is as potent to smoke as marijuana. "Black agaric is growing by the house, but I have not yet plucked up the courage to eat it. I grow my own garlic because the aroma is so much stronger when fresh. Garlic, fresh, throws a long cast through the kitchen."

The garden is not much affected by the shade of a condemned elm, where morels grow. Seashells in deep profusion —clam shells, oyster shells, conch shells, mussel shells—make tabby of the surrounding ground. Hold a conch to your ear. You can almost hear the sea. There are dogwoods, maples, white and Scotch pines, junipers, and dying apple trees beside the long drive that leads to the front door. The building is tall and proportional, not offensively ungainly, three stories, white, with many windows and a red tin roof. It glows at night at the end of its lane, and in daylight stands aloof in a field of tall grass, which is silvery brown after an autumn frost—fox grass. The place was a commune once, a boarding house, a summer hotel. There were two red barns. The communists burned up one for firewood. Otto's geese nest in the other. When Otto and I went in there once, he said, "It's a myth that geese are so dangerous. They don't bite hard." Wanting to show me some eggs in an embankment of down, he shoved aside a nesting goose. She struck, ineffectively, at the tough skin of his hand. I thought I'd like to see what that felt like, so I extended a hand of my own toward the head of the goose. She struck and struck again. She savaged my hand. She raised a pulpy red welt. Otto's geese patrol the grounds. Sixteen of them march up and down the driveway. "Geese once protected the Roman capitol," he says. "If something alarms these, they will make a commotion. But not during working hours." He used to kill and serve his domestic geese, but the flock has grown too old. He raised ducks and chickens, too. "Eating grubs and insects, the odd bit of corn, they tasted infinitely better." But he gave that up in surrender to the pressures on his time. He cautions you to beware the dog. Oh, no, not Zulu—not the shaggy black fun-loving Tibetan mastiff.

Beware Fofa, the bitter little brown-and-white spaniel with beagley undertones—Fofa, half cocked, with the soprano bark and the heavy bite.

Behind the inn are a can-and-bottle dump, rusting fragments of dead machinery, lengths of snow fencing, an automobile radiator, used lumber, two iron bathtubs, three mattresses, a rubble of used cinder blocks. There is little time to tidy what the dark paints out. The chef, who is not always ebullient, does not seem to care much anyway. "One of my great disadvantages is that I grew up in Spain in a luxury hotel with lots of servants," he will say. "I'll never be able to live as well as that, no matter how much money I make. It sort of crushes one's ambitions." He lives where sewer lines run up against winter wheatland and arms of forest interrupt the march of towns. There are heavy concentrations of wild deer. A man up the road sells mutton to hunters to take home as venison. On Otto's property, a clear stream flows into a good-sized pond. Water falls over its dam. He makes quenelles sometimes with pickerel from the pond. He makes quenelles, too, with whiting and other ocean fish and with a combination of shrimp and veal. "The veal binds them together and makes them very fluffy. My quenelles are much better than any quenelles you actually get anywhere. I don't know why. My quenelles have spring." To drink the pond or to share with the geese the scraps of Otto's profession, raccoons appear, and skunks, opossums—every creature of the woods, including one whose name would blow all this away. Otto will kill such creatures only to eat them. He has a Havahart trap in which he catches skunks. He takes the trap down the road to where some "perfectly contemptible" neighbors live, and releases the skunks there. He and Anne pick blueberries and wild grapes.

They gather dandelions for salads, and blackberries for cobblers and pies. He has cooked, and served to customers, stinging nettles and the fiddleheads of ferns. He gathers sheep sorrel for soups and salads. He once served creamed cardoons. In a lake not far away, he dives for crayfish, collecting them from under boulders and ledges. "The sauces you can make with their heads are unbelievable." He has shot and served rabbits and squirrels (Brunswick stew). He shot a raccoon and attempted a sort of coon au vin but considered the dish a failure. Sometimes there are wood ducks and wild geese in the pond. Over the land at dusk, woodcocks swoop and plummet, sometimes into the oven. Otto eats thrushes and blackbirds ("Delicious") but does not serve them. He would like to raise and serve kid, but he could not bring himself to kill one. He feels it would be "like killing a kitten." And, for all his youth in Spanish kitchens, he says he could not bring himself to take the life of a suckling pig. When, however, the odd pheasant happens through his fields of grass, he is not the least bit reluctant to go through the steps necessary to roast it for twenty minutes and then flame it with cognac and put out the fire with madeira. Disjointed, the pheasant next enters a heavy clay crock and is covered over with slices of goose liver and peelings of truffle. "Then I nap it with a fairly strong game gravy, really a demi-glace of game, made with rabbits. I hang them a bit, let them get a little high." He adds more sliced goose liver and truffles; then he covers the crock with its heavy lid and glues it down tight with a dough of egg white, water, and flour. He sets the pot in a bain-marie, and puts the whole rig into a very hot oven—for less than half an hour. The contents are ready when the dough turns brown. Pheasant Souvaroff. It was in the *Spezialrezepte der Französische Küche,* one of his textbooks when he was in Basel.

OTTO ROUTINELY DUSTS meat with white pepper "to lock in the freshness." Its taste seems unaffected. "It loses nothing," he says. "Bacteria don't like to eat their way through pepper any more than you would." Since he told me that, I have gone off on canoe trips with the meat in my pack basket dusted with pepper. The meat lasts for days. Otto doesn't camp. He once came down with pneumonia after sleeping a night on the ground.

When he makes béarnaise, he uses green peppercorns, preferring the stronger taste. When he makes bordelaise, he uses pork rinds, boiled until tender, in preference to marrow. He does almost everything, as he phrases it, *"à ma façon."* As a result of a tale often told by English friends of his parents, he is a particular admirer of a parvenu member of the peerage whose eccentric and umbrageous reputation had caused his applications to be rejected by any number of London and provincial clubs. At the helm of a yacht, he appeared one year at the Royal Regatta flying a pennant lettered "MOBYC," which, he was by no means reluctant to explain, was the simple heraldry of My Own Bloody Yacht Club. "I do things MOBW—my own bloody way," says Otto. "I should write that —or 'à ma façon'—on the menu after every dish."

The unfortunate peer. He may never have tasted English marrowbones roasted after being sealed with flour. "A very clubby thing they are, marrowbones, done that way," says Otto. "The ends are closed hermetically, with dough. When the bone is roasted, you remove the crust and eat the marrow with a spoon. They serve that at the best clubs—of which I also am not a member."

In his affection for marrowbones, he collects veal shanks—slowly, one at a time as they arrest his eye—and they pile up like cordwood in the freezer for about three months. He pan-fries them in butter and olive oil. He sautés his bouquet garni. He then braises the lot in stock, tomato purée, herbs, and wine. And when he has the sauce in place and the bones on plates and ready to serve, he dusts them with fine-chopped lemon peel, parsley, and garlic. "It's called gremolata," he says, "and that is what makes the osso bucco explode." Not absolutely everything is, or needs to be, *à ma façon*. That one, unaltered, is from the *Joy of Cooking*.

In a roasting pan with hickory chips he is smoking shad roe. He will make a shad-roe mousse. "But it's not really a mousse. It's more like a butter. A form of pâté." He is struggling to name it because he has not made it before. He buys his hickory chips at the sporting-goods store—three dollars a pound—if he is pressed. He knows a carpenter, some distance away, who gives them to him for nothing. He smokes shrimp, trout, turkey breasts, and whiting, and turns pork loin into Canadian bacon. After twenty minutes with the chips, seven fresh rainbow trout will come out of the pan at what he considers acceptable (and I find remarkable) levels of taste and texture. He prefers the trout he smokes outside. He has a semi-dugout igloo made of earth and block, full of tunnels and traps, in which he cold-smokes trout for twenty-four hours. The wood is from his dying apple trees. He gets up to tend the smoker two or three times in the night. The principal difference between the twenty minutes inside and the twenty-four hours

outside is that the resulting flesh is not opaque, it is translu-
cent. When he smokes salmon out there, it takes thirty-six
hours. He sometimes gives ducks a little outdoor smoke before
he roasts them in the oven. "If I ever perfect cold-smoking,"
he says, "I'm going to smoke swordfish. It is fantastic. It turns
pink, like a rose."

He rocks a knife through some scallions, hauls a grouper
out of storage and begins to reduce it to fillets. He eats some
scallions and, slipping a hand into the refrigerator, pops a
couple of shrimp and two or three fresh scallops. "Fresh scallops stink like boiling cabbage for a while," he remarks.
"These no longer stink. They breathe. They freshen themselves and come clean. Here are some I put away last night in
lime juice with pepper flakes and red onion. Try one. Beautiful, isn't it? Seviche. I just make stuff and keep making stuff
through the day until I've got enough. Then I sit down and
write it out."

Anne enters the room, her first appearance of the morning
—hunting shirt, dungarees, long hair akimbo. "Every spring I
go mad. I am subject to the same swirling forces that pull the
crocuses out of the ground," she reveals. "It is because I retain
fluids."

Her husband seems to agree. He says, "She is subject to the
same forces that govern the tides."

The forces have spread her hair to form a spectacular
golden Afro, beaming outward from a physiognomic sun. She
removes Otto's hat. It has become too grubby for her to look
at in this part of the morning. He makes no struggle, but he is
not completely assembled without his terry-cloth hat. He never
eats aspirin. If he has a headache, he fills a plastic Baggie with
ice, places it on his head, and pulls down around his temples

the brim of his terry-cloth hat. Anne has much to do. She will make a mocha meringue. Then a gâteau victoire au chocolat. But for the moment she is only holding her head. She says, "I can't do anything until my head is clear."

I ask how long that might be, and she says, "It's almost clear."

Anne is Latvian and was six when she left the country. Her American-accented English contains no trace of those six years (that I, at any rate, can discern). Her predominant memories of Riga are of food—wide bowls full of caviar, mountained platters of crayfish, smoked lampreys served under crystal chandeliers at banquets in her home. In an album is a photograph of Anne's mother all in white satin among sprays of lilies and roses bending attentively toward a bunting-covered drape-folded canopied bassinet—the day of the christening of Anna Rozmarja. Anna Rozmarja Grauds.

Otto sums it up. "They were rich," he says. "I mean, they were rich rich."

"When I was a little girl, I was swathed in ermine and mink. I don't have a need for it now. It's been done."

"Her family had flocks of money, many ships. It was one of the First Families of Latvia, which is like being one of the First Families of Scranton."

"When the Germans took over the house, they allowed us to live on the top floor."

Words rise quickly in Anne's mind, but in speaking them she often hesitates and stumbles, and most of what she says comes slowly. "When the Russians were after us, we had to hide in the country. I remember the cows and the river and the food. Latvia is rich in milk and cheese and eggs. Even in the war no one was hungry. When we were escaping, we stayed at a farm where there were hams and wheels of cheese and things."

"Was that far from Riga?"

"In LLLatvia, nnnnnnothing is far from Riga."

Tilsit was not far from Riga, and Tilsit was not even in Latvia. Otto's grandfather was an architect in Tilsit. One day, the architect saw an advertisement in a newspaper in which sums of money were mentioned in connection with the connubial availability of a young woman in Salzburg. "Her brother placed the ad, and this chap came down from Tilsit and married her," Otto recounts. "It was the only way she could attract a man. She was quite plain."

"She was a handsome woman," Anne informs him.

Otto says, "She was about as handsome as Eleanor Roosevelt. She was a violent Nazi, that grandmother."

Her husband, at any rate, was excoriated by his family for "promiscuous marrying into the proletariat." Her son, Otto's father, went to *Gymnasium* in Salzburg and was later trained in hotels in Berlin and Munich. By 1936, when he was asked to be manager of the Reina Cristina, in Algeciras, he had been married, in England. The Mediterranean and Iberian Hotels Company, Ltd., an English concern, wanted someone they could trust who could also get on with the Germans. Otto's father carried a German passport during the Second World War.

Otto was born in Buckinghamshire, in July, 1938, and was taken home on a Japanese ship. Food was scarce in Spain for many years thereafter—to the ends of, and beyond, two wars. Gypsies, near starving, came to the hotel, asked for food, performed circus stunts as a way of paying, and then ate less than they were given. Asked why they would ignore food set before them, they said that if they ate a great deal they would soon be hungrier than they would be if they ate little. When Otto was nine, he discovered a boy in a persimmon tree on the hotel grounds stealing fruit. Otto happened to be carrying an air rifle. Pointing it, he ordered the boy to descend. On the ground, the boy "broke for it," and began to climb a garden wall. Otto threw a brick and knocked him down. Proudly, he reported the achievement to his parents. His father cracked him over the head. Otto saw the boy as a thief; his father saw the boy as someone so hungry that he had to steal—and therefore it was proper to let him steal.

"You must remember," Anne will say of her husband, "that he learned early what food really is. He knows what it is to be without it. He has a grasp of the sanctity of food. That is his base. He finds delight just in seeing his ingredients. He goes on to luxury after that. Remember, too, that he ate awful meals endlessly—for years. He was in school in England after the war."

Tutored from the age of three, Otto was sent to Britain a year after the German surrender—to Tre-Arddur House School, on Tre-Arddur Bay, in North Wales, a place that, according to him, "specialized in ridding industrialists' sons of their accents, boys from Yorkshire and Lancashire." Otto spoke Spanish, French, and German, and virtually no English, so he had several accents that were targeted for destruction, too. He was called Dago or Greaser, because he came from "Franco Spain." When he was caught in this or that misdemeanor, the headmaster, gnashing craggily, told him not to "use your Spanish tricks" at Tre-Arddur. "My character was deformed there." Otto's tone is more factual than bitter. "I was a happy kid before then, and I became a morose loner.

Eventually, when I was invited to join things, I realized I no longer needed to join." The headmaster whipped the boy for his miserable handwriting. On the rugger field, the headmaster caned anyone who funked a tackle. "We won a lot of rugger matches. I was a hooker—in, you know, the center of the scrum." The Tre-Arddur year had its fine moments. The assistant headmaster fished in Scotland and brought back enough salmon to feed everyone in school.

Otto lived for the long vacs in Spain, for the big sardines on sticks over beach fires, the limpets, the wild asparagus, the fishing, and the catch of red mullet baked on fig leaves and tile. The Reina Cristina was lush beyond thought with its fountains and pools under bougainvillea, its date palms and tangerines, its Islamic arcades and English gardens. "You would have to be a Saudi sheikh to live that life again." English colonials, Andalusians, Murcians, titled and rich, "the whole of the south of Spain knew each other very well, they were very cliquey, and when they came to Gibraltar to clothe their women in English finery they stayed at the Reina Cristina." Above them all stood Otto's father, six feet five inches, thin and regal, actually a dominant figure among the sherry people and the rest of his distinguished guests. Guy Williams (Williams & Humbert), the Gonzalezes, the Palominos, the Osbornes, the Domecqs. "My father was, you know, *amigo íntimo* with all of them." Having four hundred employees, he was as well a figure of first importance in back-street Algeciras. He and a cork company were the principal employers in the town. He had his standards. He never hired a former altar boy. He felt that altar boys were contaminated by priests. He was scrupulously sensitive to the needs and natures of his staff. When Otto called the chef's son a *mariquita azúcar*, his father made him write a calligraphically perfect note of apology. On a tour of countries to the north, the family went out of its way to stop in Lourdes, because the Reina Cristina's housekeeper had mentioned that she would like some holy water with which to cure her black dog, which had come down with terminal mange. Approaching home through dry hundred-degree heat on the brown plains of the Iberian plateau, Otto and his younger brother suffered so with thirst that they drank the holy water. Their father filled the bottle from a tap, gave it to the housekeeper, and the dog was cured. The boys were thrashed about once a week—their mother's riding crop, their father's hand. There was no cruelty in it, merely custom. Otto calls his parents "permissive," and cites his father's reaction to his experiments with hash. Otto had an underwater-diving companion named Pepe el Moro who would sniff kif before diving in order to clear his sinuses and increase the depth of the dives. Otto sniffed, too. When his father learned that his son was using narcotics, he said only, "Stop that. It's unhealthy." When the *cuadrillas* were in town, the great matadors stayed at the Reina Cristina. Otto as a child knew Belmonte, and later Litri, Ordoñez, Miguelín. Their craft so appealed to him that he knew every moment of their ritual, from the praying in the chapel to the profiling over the sword. In the album is a snapshot of Otto with Ernest Hemingway on the veranda outside the Cristina's bar. Otto marvels at "the incredible patience" Hemingway displayed toward "a callow youth" in his teens. Otto's family had a farm in the mountains with an irrigation system that he still thinks of as nothing less than lyrical—its pools and rivulets descending among terraced beds of kitchen plants. His father also managed the Hotel Reina Victoria, in Ronda. Otto would go there on horseback, the more to be involved in the beautiful country—the Serranía de Ronda—and he paid for all his needs with Chesterfield cigarettes. He went slowly when he went back to school.

His mother's parents lived in Oxford, and he moved on from Tre-Arddur to St. Edward's because St. Edward's was there. It was a distinguished public school, distinguished for having been repugnant to young Laurence Olivier some decades before. Otto was hungry there, not caring for the food. With his air rifle, he killed sparrows and thrushes in his grand-parents' garden and roasted them on spits over open fires. In his form, he won the St. Edward's general-knowledge prize in all the years he was there. He was very fond of his grand-parents. His grandfather was J. O. Boving, an engineer known for a proposal to harness the Severn bore. He gave his grandson a copy of the Boving family tree, which is fruited, for the most part, with farmers. Its mighty trunk, emerging from the soil, has cracked to pieces a Corinthian temple, thus implying the family's durability relative to the artifacts of the earth. Anne, absorbed, now looks up from the picture. She says, "Most of my family should hang from a tree."

She pours cream from a cup into a bowl, and the cream is so thick that it clings to the cupside like mayonnaise. In bottles, it will not pour at all. To have such cream, she drives many miles each week to a farm in another state. Between layers of pecan cake, she is about to establish three concentric circles of royale chocolate and whipped cream. She has turned to this project after finishing another, in which a layer of meringued hazelnut was covered with a second story of hazelnut Bavarian cream that was in turn covered, top and sides, by a half-inch layer of chocolate cake that had been formed upon an overturned pie plate. Atop this structure was a penthouse confected of chocolate, butter, egg yolks, and brandy. "It looks simple, but it takes so bloody long," she said as she finished. "To admit you eat something like that, these days, is almost like confessing to incest. I was a size twelve before I met Otto. Now I'm size eighteen." Her height saves her. One might well say that she is grand, but she could not be described as fat. Her husband, for his part, works sixteen hours a day, is in constant motion, professes to eat almost nothing, and should be quite slim. By his account, "a couple of cucumbers" is about all he consumes in a day. Somehow, though, he has acquired at least twenty-five pounds that he would like to do without.

Now and again, he will stop to hold a pastry sleeve for her or hammer a dented cake pan back into form, but in the main they work separately, and rapidly, at spaced stations of the table, he slicing some salmon, completing a brioche to enclose it, she making puff paste, or a cake from yogurt cheese. (It takes a couple of days to drip, through cloth, the whey out of a gallon of yogurt. The yield is a quart of cheese.) She makes two, three, four, even five new desserts in a day. A light almond dacquoise is—as much as anything—the standard, the set piece, from which her work takes off on its travels through the stars. The dacquoise resembles cake and puts up a slight crunchy resistance before it effects a melting disappearance between tongue and palate and a swift transduction through the bloodstream to alight in the brain as a poem.

OTTO LICKS SHAD-ROE PÂTÉ from a rubber scraper, wipes clean his working surfaces, and carries to the refrigerator a sour-cream aggregate of curried Moroccan lentils, tasting a spoonful as he puts them away. He leaves the kitchen. Time to drive who knows how many miles for supermarket shopping. Behind the wheel and rolling north, he says, "Supermarkets occasionally have fresher stuff than you can buy anywhere else." He is more or less forced to shop retail anyway. He feeds two hundred people a week, not enough to warrant wholesale buying if he is going to offer a virtually different menu every night—if he is going to shop, as he does, opportunistically, and "just make things," willy-nilly, through a free-lance working day. If he happens to see scallops the size of filets mignons, he will take them home, grill them, and serve them under sauce béarnaise. He knows a certain ShopRite that is "wonderful for brains, sweetbreads, and chicken," and the Grand Unions of his region are supplied now and then with amazingly fine beef. He reads the ads. He makes his rounds. He walks through a supermarket, sees some good shell steaks on display, and tosses fifty pounds of them in small packages into his cart. He drives eighty miles for Westphalian ham. He drives an upper-middle-aged eight-cylinder Dodge, a car so overpowered it is no good on ice. The family call it their "off-the-road vehicle." They had a Volkswagen bus once. Otto is a competent driver but easily bored and tending toward sleep. One day, with him snoozing and safely belted, the bus rolled over three times and spilled green crawling lobsters onto the road. To avoid the irritation of a summons, Otto gave the lobsters to the cops. On the dashboard of the Dodge now are two plastic packets of malt vinegar from Arthur Treacher's Fish & Chips. "I like junk food," Otto declares. "Treacher's chips are awful. They don't seem real. They seem to be made of mashed potatoes. But the fish is good. Actually, it is great."

"Define 'great.'"

"Specifically, the batter is delicious and the fish is acceptable. The fish is white and moist. It has no flaw. The batter is very clever. Water, flour, baking powder, a bit of cornmeal —we think it's like a churro batter. The texture is just wonderful—crunchy and crisp. You don't concentrate on taste but on texture. What a horrible thing to say about food! They have plastic packets of sauce tartare there, too. You suck it out. It's degenerate." He will go big distances for a McDonald's Egg McMuffin. "It's a triumph," he explains. "It's inspired. With melted cheese instead of hollandaise, it is eggs Benedict for the masses. I don't know why it wasn't thought of long ago." If you ask for a doggie bag in Otto's dining room, your pheasant Souvaroff or your grilled squid rings in aïoli sauce are returned to the table in a polystyrene container that first held an Egg McMuffin. (Otto is generous to a fault, and the unwary amateur can eat his way into a stupor.) His professed affection for junk food is pretty much used up on Arthur Treacher and the Egg McMuffin. Other examples are few and faint. "I've had a Big Mac. Over the years, I've had a Big Mac four times. Once, when I was quite hungry, it was good." He enjoys the sort of anisette Italian sausages that are sold in hard rolls from old white vans. He has never crossed the threshold of a Colonel Sanders. Fried chicken is one of his favorite things on earth. He soaks lean chicken overnight in milk, and fries it in pure raging lard.

Soft drinks?

He shakes his head, but reconsiders. "Oh," he says, "I'll drink a Tab if I have a headache."

Coffee?

"No. Very little. Six or seven cups a day, no more. And twenty cups of tea." He also guzzles vichy by the quart.

Beer?

"Only on Saturday night. A six-pack, after work."

Wine?

"When we go out. Not often at home."

Booze?

"I've been known to drink four or five pink gins. Gin and Angostura. If it weren't for my work, I could drink all the time. You simply can't cook and drink. You cut yourself and burn yourself. You lose your edge. You can't do it and drink. Impossible."

"Faulkner drank. One of his relatives is supposed to have asked him, 'Bill, are you drunk when you write those stories?' And Faulkner said, 'Not always.'"

"Oh," says Otto, "Evelyn Waugh has a very good line on drinking. One evening during the war, his commanding general said to him, 'Waugh, you're making a spectacle of yourself. I must ask you to stop.' And Waugh—he was the rich man's John O'Hara—he said, 'Surely, sir, you can't expect me to change the habits of a lifetime to accommodate your whim.'"

Once, when we were out on the road like this, Otto said he often wished he could keep on going—to destinations more exotic than the Grand Union. He was not altogether content with this region. He had dreams of San Antonio. He thought about Key West. He said he felt a need for "new momentum," felt "imprisoned in the economics" of the present inn. Waitresses had netted as much from the business as he and Anne combined. In a year, several thousand dollars were going for heat alone, and even more to insure the ungainly wooden building. After he had paid the oil company and the insurance company, what was left was less than he could earn by doing unskilled labor. He said that in Algeciras there was one fire engine and it performed two functions. It put out fires in the cork factory and it watered the ring at corridas. Homes and restaurants did not burn. They were made of fieldstone and mortar. Otto would like to construct a new building half underground, heated and powered by the sun, and with such a high percentage of masonry in its materials that it would be virtually fireproof—a restaurant where heating bills and fire insurance are covered by hors d'oeuvres.

At an A. & P. he picks up bibb and ruby lettuce, at the ShopRite potatoes and brains. "The A. & P. have wonderful produce. Sometimes. And they always have bibb lettuce." The next stop is in a mall parking lot, between a Rite Aid Pharmacy and a K Mart, in the shadow of a Great American. "The fruit in here is terrible," says Otto as he picks out the Great American's six best pears. Moving his cart along, he collects five pounds of bean curd, some bean sprouts, and a couple of dozen Japanese midget eggplants. "Bean curd is the cow of the Orient," he says. "It has many of the same nutrients as milk. Look there. Eggroll wrappers. When you can buy bean curd and eggroll wrappers in a supermarket in a town like this there's some sort of quiet revolution going on." He sees and excitedly handles five packages of lovely big leeks. "Hey, I'm glad I came! I'll make leeks vinaigrette, certainly, and leek soup. When the Welsh come to play rugger at Twickenham, they have leeks in their lapels. If you cut off the roots of leeks and plant them, they grow. That will appeal to your Scottish sense of thrift." Scallions. Onions. Outsize artichokes. Endive. Escarole: "It's slippery. It's meaty. It's got everything!" Parsley root: "Hey, great! Here, eat one. I put it in with parsley for flavoring, but mainly I just eat it raw, eat it all myself. It's too

(2 1 1)

good for the customers." A parsley root in its appearance suggests a stunted and misshapen albino carrot. It has the texture of an apple and the taste of parsley. "It's good sliced in soup. Or grated in a salad." He takes a bottle of ReaLemon from a shelf, saying, "Ever smelled this? It smells like skunk." By a forest of bottles of Frothee creamy head for cocktails, he stops, picks one up, and reads the label, finding there a form of glycol that he identifies as a substance used in brake fluids. Two pounds of bacon. Thirteen and a half pounds of fresh ham. Seven and a half pounds of veal. Veal kidneys. Veal hearts. Eleven half pound packages of sweetbreads go into the cart. There is a gap in the tilting mirrors behind the meat, and a butcher's startled face is framed there. "That's all the sweetbreads we have," he says. "That's all there is."

That may be all there is in this tank town. It hardly bothers Otto. For all his rampant eclecticism—and the wide demands of his French-based, Continentally expanded, and sometimes Asian varietal fare—he knows where the resources of his trade are virtually unlimited. Mondays, when the inn is dark, he leaves his Herman boots in his bedroom—his terry-cloth hat, his seam-split dungarees—and in a dark-blue suit like a Barclays banker he heads for New York City. "In a few square blocks of this town are more consumer goods than in the whole of Soviet Russia," he remarked one time as he walked up Ninth Avenue and into the Salumeria Manganaro, where he bought a pound of taleggio ("It's like a soft fontina") and was pleased to find white truffles. "They're from Piedmont. Grate them on pasta and they make it explode." At Fresh Fish (498 Ninth), he bought river shrimp from Bangladesh weighing up to a quarter of a pound each. He bought sausage flavored with provolone and parsley at Giovanni Esposito (500), and at Bosco Brothers (520) he stopped to admire but not to purchase a pyramid of pigs' testicles, which he said were delicious in salad. "Texas strawberries, you know. They're wonderful. They're every bit as good as sweetbreads. Boil them tender. Dry them. Dredge them in flour. Pan-fry them." At Simitsis International Groceries & Meat (529), he bought a big hunk of citron in a room full of open bins of loose pasta, of big bags and buckets full of nuts and peppers, of great open cannisters of spices and sacks full of cornmeal, hominy grits, new pink beans, pigeon peas, split peas, red lentils, semolina, fava beans, buckwheat kasha, pearl barley, Roman beans, mung beans. "This place is fabulous. If I had a restaurant in New York—oh, boy! New York has everything you could possibly want in food. If you look hard enough, you'll find it all." At Citarella (2135 Broadway, at Seventy-fifth), he admired but did not buy a twenty-pound skate. He had walked the thirty-five blocks from Simitsis to Citarella. He prefers to walk when he's in town. I have seen him on the street with a full side of smoked salmon, wrapped in a towel, tied to a suitcase like a tennis racquet. If Anne is with him, he rides. "You poach skate and serve it with capers and black butter," he said. "It's a wonderful fish, completely underrated. I shot a big electric one in the Caymans." Citarella had flounder roe for eighty-five cents a pound. "You pay four dollars a pound for shad roe," said Otto. "Flounder roe is every bit as good. Shad roe has the name." He stopped for tea, ordering two cups, which he drank simultaneously. At Zabar's (Eightieth and Broadway), he bought thin slices of white-and-burgundy Volpi ham. "It's from St. Louis and it's as good as the best jamón serrano." At Japanese Food Land (Ninety-ninth and Broadway), he bought a couple of pounds of bean

(2 1 3)

threads and four ounces of black fungus. On the sidewalks and having a snack, he ate twelve dried bananas. "That's, actually, nothing," he remarked. "I once et thirty-six sparrows in a bar in Spain. Gorriones, you know—spitted and roasted."

He tried to prove to himself not long ago that with United States ingredients he could duplicate the taste of chorizo, a hard Spanish sausage. He had to throw a good part of it away, because he failed to pack it tight enough and "fur grew inside." Casa Moneo, on Fourteenth Street between Seventh and Eighth, "is the best place for chorizos," he says. "They're made in Newark. They're as good as you can get in Spain."

He also buys chorizos at La Marqueta—a series of concession stalls housed below the railroad tracks on Park Avenue in Spanish Harlem. Chorizos. Jamón serrano. Giant green bananas—four for a dollar. Dried Irish moss. Linseed. Custard apples. "When they're very ripe they get slightly fermented. Mmm." He will buy a couple of pounds of ginger, a bunch of fresh coriander, a couple of pounds of unbleached, unpolished rice—letting go the dried crayfish and the green peanuts, the Congo oil and the pots of rue, letting go the various essences, which are in bottles labelled in Spanish: Essence of Disinvolvement, Essence of Envy and Hate. Breadfruit. Loin goat chops. "OHIO STATE UNIVERSITY" shopping bags. "Goat is milk-white when it's young. I don't want to get into an argument with these people, but that is not kid, it's lamb." Seeing a tray of pigs' tongues, he calls them "beautiful." And high-piled pigs' ears: "You slice them thin."

He drops in at the Bridge Kitchenware Corporation, 212 East Fifty-second Street, nods at Fred Bridge, and says, "I'm looking for a whip for crème fouettée. I have never seen one in America that's any good." Bridge hasn't either. Bridge has overcome the problem, however, by having a supply of stainless ones made for him in France. Otto looks over several as if he were choosing a new squash racquet. "Perfect," he says, eventually, to Bridge. "Very beautiful. Flexible." He buys a quenelle scoop. Rummaging in the back of the store, he picks up a tin sieve. A clerk frankly tells him not to take it because it is no good. "That's why I want it," he says. "I've never seen one that was any good. The best of them won't last six months." He asks for parchment paper. To "make stuff *en papillote*," he sometimes uses, instead of parchment, narrow bags from liquor stores. "Tied at each end and oiled, they are perfect *en papillote* bags, as long as the paper has not been recycled. You can't make things *en papillote* in recycled paper because of the chemicals involved. Some restaurants use aluminum foil for *en papillote*. Contemptible."

He has lieutenants—certain fish merchants from his general neighborhood—who shop for him at the Fulton Market. But often enough he goes there himself, his body, at 4 A.M., feeling what he calls the *resaca*—"when the tide goes out and leaves the dry sand." He loves this world of rubber boots and bonfires, wet pavement and cracked ice, and just to enter it—to catch the bright eye of a fresh red snapper—is enough to cause his tides to rise. "There is no soul behind that eye," he says. "That is why shooting fish is such fun." Under the great illuminated sheds he checks everything (every aisle, bin, and stall), moving among the hills of porgies and the swordfish laid out like logs of copper beech, the sudden liveliness in his own eyes tempered only by the contrast he feels between the nonchalance of this New York scene and the careful constructions of the Algeciras wholesale fish market, where "they display the food with a lot more love."

"You never know what is going to be good. You have to look at everything," he says, and he looks at bushels of mussels, a ton of squid, bay scallops still in their shells. "Make sure they're not Maine mussels," he remarks, almost to himself. "If they are, forget it. Maine mussels are very clean, but they're small and awfully tough. You just want the big squid. The New Jersey squid." He looks at a crate of lobsters. They are dragons—up into their salad years—and three of them fill the crate, their heads seeming to rest on claws the size of pillows. "People think they're dragons because they look like dragons, but they're called that because they are caught in dragnets," he says, picking one up and turning it over, then the second, and the third. The third lobster has many hundreds of green pellets clinging like burrs to its ventral plates. "Eggs. They're better than caviar," says Otto. "They're so crunchy and so fresh-tasting—with lemon juice, and just enough bland vegetable oil to make them shine. You remove them from the lobster with a comb."

Baskets of urchins disappoint him. "See all the white spots? The freckles? See how the spines are flat? If the spines are standing, the creature is very much alive." For many months, he and his legates have been on the watch for urchins that are up to his standards. They must be very much alive because their roe, which is what he wants, is so rich and fragile that it soon goes bad.

He views with equal scorn a table of thin fresh herrings. He serves herring fillets in February, and this is not February. "That's the only time of year when we can get big fat herrings. They're sensational then, maybe a day or two out of the sea. You have et bottled herring, have you? Awful. Herring, or salmon, in sour cream. They don't use crème fraîche. They

(216)

use a sauce with dubious taste but with better keeping quali-
ties." Otto never prepares herring the same way twice, but his
goal is the same if his ingredients are not. He uses, say, vinegar and dill with peppercorns and onions, and his goal is to
give the herring "a taste so clean it's lovely."

He feels the slender flanks of sand lances, and he says,
"You dredge them with flour, drop them into deep fat, and
eat them like French fries." He presses the columnar flank
of a swordfish, pleased to have it back in the market. He
quotes Ted Williams. It is Williams' opinion that the surest
way to save the Atlantic salmon is to declare the species full of
mercury and spread the false word. "Swordfish is a bummer in
the freezer," Otto says. "But there are all sorts of fish you *can*
freeze. Shrimp are better frozen properly on a ship than carried for days to market unfrozen. In properly frozen shrimp
there's never a hint of ammonia. Scallops freeze well, too—
and crabmeat, octopus, striped bass, flounder, conch, tilefish,
grouper. Red snapper frozen is no good. It gets watery, water-
logged. A soft-fleshed fish like a sea trout is no good frozen.
Freezing tuna or bluefish precipitates the oily taste. No frozen
fish is better than fresh, but well-frozen fish is better than fish a
week old."

Groupers—weighing thirty, forty pounds—face him in a
row, like used cars. "You can split those big heads," he says.
"Dredge them in flour and pan-fry them. Then you just pick at
them—take the cheeks, the tongue."

There are conger eels the size of big Southern rattlesnakes.
"With those I make jellied eel, cooked first with parsley, white
wine, and onions. Almost no one orders it. I eat it myself."

As he quits the market, he ritually buys a pile of smoked
chub, their skins loose and golden. "Smoked chub are so

good," he says. "They just melt like butter. You can eat half a dozen quite happily on the way home in the car."

LUNCHTIME IN THE KITCHEN AND OTTO, who never eats a meal when working, offers me an artichoke and some veal with wild mushrooms and Portuguese sauce. "The best veal is not young but nearest to beef," he says, malleting and dusting the slice before him. "Heavy veal—older veal—is easier to work with, and it looks healthier. Do you know what Provimi is? It's an artificial milk feeding that more or less bleaches veal on the hoof. Keeps it from turning pink. Ugh." He has been trimming romaine and chicory, and he puts the trimmings into a pot and steams them until they collapse. With a sprinkling of parmesan, they whet the palate. "I never throw anything away," he says, "unless it's been paid for." He picks up a handful of hot greens and shoves them into his mouth.

"English people are less conscious of utensils than Americans are," says Anne.

He replies, "That is because you can't buy your hands."

" 'Eating food with a knife and fork is like making love through an interpreter,' " she goes on. "Somebody wrote that. I can't remember who."

Lunches have been good in the kitchen—Otto's fast foods, in his fashion, selected not to slow up his routine.

Veal and Westphalian ham dusted with marjoram and wrapped around big fried croutons. He pan-fries them on a skewer and deglazes the juices with wine to make a full-bodied, gelatinous gravy.

Sautéed squares of lemon sole, with Swiss chard and anchovies which he tosses in a frying pan, holding the handle with both hands as he flings the chard and anchovies into the air.

Smoked whiting, seviche, cucumbers, and Vouvray.

Octopus al amarillo, with saffron, onions, potato, parsley, garlic, and wine—a peasant Spanish dish he has been eating all his life. "It's the sort of thing the maids would make at home for me after I'd been clamming, or caught an octopus or an eel or any fish with firm flesh."

Fried bread with tomato, garlic, and oil. "It's working-class food. The Spanish servants made that for me, too. It was comparable to a white child's being fed by slaves in the South. I learned from the Spaniards to stay away from expensive oil. It is said that the finest olive oil has the lightest color, and that is as great a myth as the maple-syrup myth. Dark, Grade B maple syrup has more flavor than Grade A. This is good green oil. Expensive oil is jejune and very pale."

He made a crêpe one day, filling it with spinach and shrimp. "You can put anything in a crêpe and sell it," he confided.

I asked if he had eaten at La Crêpe.

"Once," he said.

"And how was it?"

"We liked the cider."

One noon he handed me a very large bean curd grilled like a steak and standing in a soy-based sauce with ginger, vinegar, and scallions; another noon, shad roe. Cooks vulcanize shad roe. This, however, was light and springy and all but underdone. "Why not undercook everything?" Otto said. "That way, if you need to you can cook it some more."

Directly from the sea I brought some mackerel one day, and we built an applewood fire outside. For the occasion, he quickly assembled a small cinder-block fireplace, and at the finish he kicked the hot blocks apart so he could get the mackerel right down on the fire and "burn" it, giving it what he called "a good Spanish smell"—the smell of wood smoke in broiled flesh.

Alex comes into the kitchen now, home from school under a tumble of hair—amazingly tall for an eighth-grader and as mature in manner as appearance. He moves lightly through the room on big feet, amusement indelible in the corners of his mouth. "Jesus saves," he remarks. His father's look suggests approaching aircraft. His father is preparing leeks. Alex circles the kitchen, and, as he goes out, says, "Moses invests." Anne was divorced. The three older children are hers. Alex is theirs. For his most recent birthday he was given raw fish and a Roman coin—mackerel sushi, octopus sushi, fluke sushi, shrimp sushi, and salmon sushi, followed by a boiled lobster. "Lobster is delicious raw but not for a little boy," says Otto. Two boys and two (college) girls—they work for their parents from time to time as waiters. When Alex was learning to take orders, a customer—an old family friend—asked him for a chocolate-covered frog. Intently, the grandson of the late distinguished manager of the Reina Cristina of Andalusia wrote down, "1 chocolate frog." He thought it was a drink.

Otto puts away his marinating leeks, makes some wine-butter-cream-and-parsley sauce, tastes the sauce, and tosses a lump of crabmeat to the cat. Alex returns to the kitchen and pours himself some milk. His father, putting the sauce away, tells him, "If Moses had brains, he would have landed in Saudi Arabia."

Fish man calls—one of the emissaries to the Fulton Market —giving news that electrifies Otto. Anne is in another room.

After putting down the phone, he shouts exultantly to her, "I've got sea urchins from Maine! Greg says they're perfect. We'll eat them raw." It would appear that the urchins are too good for the customers. "If they're truly fresh, they should be eaten raw," he goes on. "On the other hand, I could make a fish ragout with urchin-roe sauce. I've never tried that. The roe is pungent stuff, but a little of it would make the ragout sauce subtle—with cream, butter, fish fumet, and reduced white wine." His mind keeps turning, pausing over this or that possibility, and in his generosity he is obviously expanding his thoughts to include the clientele. "Perhaps I'll take some urchin egg and spread it on fish and broil it. It gives a lobster taste. Yes. Also, I'll make an urchin mayonnaise." He has not seen the creatures yet. He may be forging ahead of himself. While he stands here and plans and dreams, what if their spines are falling like pick-up-sticks? He answers the question with a rattling-fast trip in the Dodge, and when he comes back he is carrying a basket of *Strongylocentrotus drobachiensis* in the flush of life, spotless, glistening, their spines erect—tiny little porcupines frightened green. Anne and Otto begin to crack them open and remove with spoons the golden-orange ovaries and testes collectively known as roe. The open urchins are passed like cups of wine. The roe looks and tastes something like scrambled egg, but no comparison with another food can really suggest the flavor. It is the flavor of sea-urchin roe, light and pleasantly aromatic, with the freshness of a whitecap on the sea. Anne, removing it, says, "This is a religious experience." And, since one does not gorge on urchin roe, they turn soon from feeding themselves to filling a jar for use with dinner.

From a high shelf at one end of the kitchen, where cookbooks and culled magazines run fifteen feet from wall to wall, Otto pulls his copy of the *Joy of Cooking*. He looks in it to see what it has to say about sea-urchin roe, and is surprised to find no recipe. So he turns to Elizabeth David, there being no culinary writer for whom he has more respect, and also to A. J. McClane's *Encyclopedia of Fish Cookery*. The *Joy of Cooking* is rumpled, swollen, split, bent, frayed, and bandaged, its evident employment matched on the bookshelf only by Auguste Escoffier's *Le Guide Culinaire*, which belonged to Otto's father and in appearance is even more exhausted. "You cannot live without the *Joy of Cooking*," Anne remarks. "It is not great and complex, but it is diverse and basic. It is a book that will translate other books. We have fifty books and more, but if we have a problem we go to the *Joy of Cooking*."

"There is nothing fake or pretentious in it," her husband says.

"It is America's touchstone."

"It tells you how to skin a squirrel."

"Beyond the basic information, basic recipes, you might be surprised how much it includes. It tells you everything from how to poach eggs to how to prepare a raccoon."

"It is very good on bread, and even has a breakdown on grains."

"It tells you how to make a Sacher torte."

"It tells you how to do live snails, how to build a smoker, how to cook octopus, how to prepare a possum, how to make rouille sauce. Put rouille sauce in bouillabaisse and it explodes. Rouille sauce is not in Larousse. But you'll find it in the *Joy of Cooking*."

Otto reaches for his Pellaprat—Henri-Paul Pellaprat, *Modern French Culinary Art*—and it comes off the shelf in half volumes. During a marital-professional fracas, Anne once took hold of the Pellaprat and Otto did, too, and each tugged in a warlike direction. The Pellaprat, in its photographic and textual elegance, deals with the roe of the sturgeon and the roe of the shad but not with the roe of the urchin. Otto flips randomly at the book and lays it open to page 291, where there is a color photograph of Russian coulibiac of salmon, incorporating sturgeon marrow with egg and salmon, en brioche—a sort of czarist eggroll, this one pictured with generous slices off the loaf, latticed trimmings crusty brown. "Mine does not look as good as that, but it tastes better," he says. One of the books that have been with him since his days as a cook-apprentice is Gringoire and Saulnier's *Le Répertoire de la Cuisine*, which is a work analogous to the *World Bibliography of Bibliographies*. It is, in effect, a menu of menus—listing, for example, three hundred ways to do sole. Humbling even to someone with a continually changing repertory of six hundred dishes, it is a catalogue of everything that God's personal chef might be expected to know.

After St. Edward's, Otto went to hotel schools in Germany and Switzerland and worked for a time in Madrid. He says his father had brainwashed him into wanting to become a hotel manager, but after a brief education in accounting and reception, and even briefer experiences with electricians and plumbers, he could see that his interests were wholly in the kitchen. In the kitchen of the Euler, in Basel, he was systematically taught every aspect of cooking in a basic procedure that lasted a year. Given two kilos of butter, twenty-four egg yolks, and "a wire whisk the size of a ball bat," he attempted to create a pond of hollandaise. It curdled. Conversely, he was told to make eighty omelettes one at a time. In that way, he would learn. Augean jobs were deliberately assigned to him, tasks of almost unbearable tedium—immense bales of spinach to trim alone—in the expectation that he would muster a chef's endurance or quit. He went to school in Lausanne as well, and worked at Vittel, in the Vosges, and at the Ritz in Madrid, where he was used most often as a bartender because he was multilingual. In the restaurants there, he developed a sense that staff should dine well. "The help should always eat what the guests eat. If they don't, they'll steal off the plates. When I worked in Madrid, we were always stealing off the plates. What was meant to be four slices was two when it got to the table." Subsequently, he cooked at the Reina Cristina and also worked as a waiter at the Rock Hotel, in Gibraltar. He was fired from that job after the headwaiter, responding to a bell for ice, found him enjoying a drink with Margaret Leighton and Laurence Harvey. Otto may wash his aluminum foil, but he has a prodigal's sense of the highest, best uses of money. At a ship chandler's in Gibraltar, he would buy a couple of pounds of caviar—at thirty dollars a pound—and go off with friends and "just eat it."

His father was dying, and Otto was helping him with his last project, the development of a small restaurant overlooking the Bay of Gibraltar. After the funeral, in 1959, he went to England. He had received a call-up notice, and he cooked for a time at a Wimpy Bar in Oxford before reporting to Perth, in Scotland, for training with the Black Watch. He became a commissioned officer in counterintelligence, functioning mainly from Berlin. "I wouldn't have minded staying in the Army, to tell you the truth. I had a wonderful time in the Army. I liked the power of leadership. I found it intoxicating."

"Then why did you come out?"

"I didn't have an independent income."

Finca el Bornizo, his family's place in the mountains, had been remodelled as a small resort that could handle twenty guests. Otto cooked for them. In winter, the only vegetables available to him were chard, carrots, and celery. He had to serve chard, carrots, and celery twice a day and be extremely inventive. For a short time, he sold real estate on the east coast near Valencia, and there developed his knowledge of paella and his regard for parellada, for huge roasted scallions, for toasted-hazelnut sauce. His love of mussels dates from that experience, too—an affection that has been enriched in the United States by the high cost of clams. Returning to Andalusia, he met a Latvian named Gunars J. Grauds, who had spent enough time in America to imagine the vast fortune that might come to the developer of a chain of Spanish motels. His loss leader was the Rio Grande, at Kilometre 116 on the road from Algeciras to Málaga, and Otto cooked for him there. Otto thought that Gunars' wife bore an extremely close resemblance to Rita Hayworth—and that, specifically, is why he took the job. When Gunars' sister appeared in the country, Otto forgot Rita Hayworth.

Set into the wall above the fireplace in their American farmhouse-inn is an enamelled Spanish tile on which appears St. Paul's cryptic advice *"Mejor es casarse que abrasarse"* ("It is better to marry than to burn"). The fireplace is in the room where the customers sit and have their apéritifs while they wait for a message from the kitchen that it is time to go to table for dinner. I remember from the first moment I walked into it the compact and offhand rural European character and feeling of that room. With its nonchalant miscellany of detail, it was beyond the margins of formal design, but it was too pleasurable merely to have been flung together and too thematic not to imply a tale. There was a pair of bullfight prints—one called "La Lidia" and the other a depiction of a *desencajonamiento*—and protruding sharp-horned from the wall between these pictures was the head of a fighting bull. The animal had been raised on the *dehesa* of Pepe Alvarez and killed in the ring with a sword. Crossed Spanish swords had been hung above the fire. All around the room were wrought-iron Spanish sconces with small amber bulbs. There was a three-hundred-year-old map of the Danube, a two-hundred-year-old map of "Magna Britannia." There were hand-carved cabinets. There were tall wicker chairs, Queen Anne chairs, and Spanish brass-studded leather chairs in groups on a red tile floor. I eventually learned that many of these things had come down through the chef's family—to America from England via Spain. There were heavy red curtains on brass rods. The ceiling slanted upward in the mansard manner, with boards of tongue and groove. The silent paddle fan hung down between exposed checked beams. Staring back at the bull were the small glass eyes of a taxidermal fox—just its head and neck, on a plaque—and near it were photographs made in Alaska of dog foxes and vixens. A poster in one corner said "Extinct is forever" and presented line drawings of vanishing and vanished creatures—Cape lion (1860), quagga (1883), Labrador duck (1875), solenodon, snow leopard, northern kit fox.

Summoned to dinner, one moved through a dark drafty hall decorated with a cigarette machine, coat hooks, two watercolors of foxes by Ralph Thompson, and plaster-cast reproductions of six Manhattan gargoyles. The dining room, curtained red, suggested a small loft held up by hand-hewn posts and beams, and was lined with starburst sconces around heavy tables of Spanish walnut, with woven placemats and fresh flowers. The floor sloped remarkably enough to tip one's sober balance, and the direction in which it sloped was toward the kitchen. A glass of wine needed to be chocked or it would slide off a table and crash. At one end of the room was a Flemish oak chest seven feet tall with insets of ebony. On its top were an empty magnum of Château Margaux, a copper cask that had once held the chef's father's preferred sherries, and (a taxidermal masterpiece) a whole red fox. The great chest, like so much else in these rooms which had come down from forebears, helped produce a sense of generations, a deep familial atmosphere. Yet there was nothing, of course, nothing whatsoever, that had come from Latvia.

Anne's father, owner of ships, was also the captain of a ship, and when he was ordered to leave his country he stayed on his ship. Russians boarded the ship and took him away. The family heard later that he had died in a Soviet hospital. Anne says, though, that "people from Latvia who died in Russia did not die in hospitals." As a child, hidden in the countryside, she was told never to say her name to anyone. "Don't say your name or they'll come and get you." She was not to play with other children. If anyone were to ask if her family owned property, she must remember to say no. To this day, she recoils inwardly when someone asks her name. When she goes to town to shop, there are implications of poverty in her clothes. "It's because they'll come and get me," she says, and then adds, "I don't really believe that. Things are not quite that bad. I'm odd, but I'm not crazy. Nothing bad ever happened to me. I was just a normal refugee. But as a result of it all you know forever that everything that is peaceful and beautiful and runs on time isn't there. What is there—just lurking there—is disorder."

By November, 1944, the Germans had been driven into the

west of the country and the Russians were assuming control. It was a time for attempting to escape. Against a red night sky, an ambulance moved Anne, her mother, her grandmother, and others from one farm to another and to the coast. A dory took some twenty people to a fishing boat. Anne wore a green taffeta dress. Gold coins had been stitched into her underwear. The family had more to their name than a few gold coins—if they could get to it. They had funds in a bank in England, a ship or two in America. A German submarine surfaced in the night and approached the fishing boat. In their panic, the party heaved chests of silver into the Baltic. The Germans let them go. Off Gotland, a man went ashore in a barrel and arranged for the group to stay in the refugee center there. They spent Christmas in Gotland, and what Anne remembers primarily is the smell of ginger cookies. "All my life, I've been obsessed with food." After Christmas, they crossed to the Swedish mainland. They spent a year there, in "this fairyland of food, of open sandwiches and the smell of baking in the air." Age seven, she moved to England. Postwar England. "Watered-down oatmeal. Baked beans and spaghetti on toast. I threw up. There was one egg a week. I lived on Ovaltine." For all the drama of her escape from Latvia, the war did not make its deepest impression on her until it was over and she was in England, where she saw, for example, pictures of a bombed-out school, walls half gone, hallways in rubble, coatracks "with all the little coats hanging there." She lived in the Dominions Hotel looking out on Hyde Park, and watched from her window "English ladies walking their Pekinese" when she was not "chained to a little desk," learning English from a tutor. She could read and write Latvian. She was forced to learn English in one year. "I was taught English mercilessly. A child is not a person in England. 'You will learn English,' they said. 'You *will* learn English.' " She learned. She learned to stammer.

Like so many people with similar obstructions, she has a beautifully textured sense of language. She is not just at home in English. She is in vigorous charge of the language that stops her tongue. She will have difficulty trusting a recipe that says that something should be "thinly sliced" or "coarsely chopped" or that egg whites should be "stiffly beaten."

There was a family ship that had sought asylum in the West and had been in the service of the United States government when it was torpedoed and sunk by the Germans. Insurance money came out of it like bubbles. That money made it possible for Anne and her mother to move to America. She had two older brothers. In the war, Gunars had been in the Wehrmacht and Vilnis in the United States Army. Anne was educated in New York, Pennsylvania, and Switzerland, and grew to be a tall and arrestingly attractive woman. In 1956, she married a career officer in the American paratroops. Separating from him in the nineteen-sixties, she moved with her children to Spain. Gunars was there, building a sort of Andalusian Howard Johnson's at Kilometre 116 on the road from Algeciras to Málaga. She was a more than able cook, and as a gesture of affection soon after she arrived she began making Latvian borscht for her brother. The *gros bonnet* of the motel came walking into the kitchen. He grasped at once what was happening and began to offer what she recalls as "cryptic criticisms." He was English, and polished, and not unpleasantly arrogant, a Harrovian sort of Lady Margaret Boat Club chap with a lyrical sense of flavor, a man with a dulcet name and a generally analogous manner who wished he had been christened Otto. He said, "You're using beef and you should be using duck bones. That's not proper at all."

"We began arguing," Anne says, finishing the story. "We began arguing, and have been arguing ever since."

He, at the moment, is assembling the *mise en place* for his paella and she is making trifle—slices of génoise with fresh peaches, fresh sliced strawberries, sherry, blackberry brandy, apple wine, and custard cream. They came to live in the United States, she says, because she chose it as the country where her children should be educated.

Otto says, "I think that was a mistake."

He had motives of his own. He was prepared to leave Spain, in no small part because he felt that anything he might accomplish would be done with his father's reputation behind him. His affection for his father notwithstanding, he had no desire to become that sort of alloy. New Mexico seemed the obvious place to go, and they went there, and took an extensive look, and found it "ugly" and "not remotely Spanish—it would take five years to get to love it." So they settled in *Daily News* country and became professional partners, with the understanding that he is *el mandamás*—he who gives orders.

"I can cook every bit as well as he can, but I couldn't make so many meals under pressure," she says. "I can make elaborate seafood mousses and sauces, but I complete one item in four hours. His ability to juggle things in his head in the course of an evening is amazing, and that is the difference between a chef and a cook. He makes appetizers, entrées, more appetizers—overlapping in time—and he keeps it all in order for as many as fifty-five people, and brings it all off by himself. You have to have that before everything else. Being a good chef is functionally less aesthetic than mechanical. You either have the aesthetic or you don't. Then, you have to have the timing—the actual feeling of what needs more cooking and what needs less cooking, varying times for each type of fish, and so forth. If he is cooking eight different things, and each takes a different amount of time, he has all that, always, ordered in his head."

"Women do not make good chefs because you have to juggle too much in your head," Otto adds. Anne abruptly looks up from her work and regards him as if he had just sprinkled powdered cloves over a pike mousse. "A person who is easily rattled can't do it," he goes on. "You've got to be unflappable."

I nibble some smoked whiting and return my gaze from Otto to Anne.

"Careful," she tells him. "You're on dangerous ground."

To accommodate the paella, he lifts from a shelf a huge iron skillet, diameter of a manhole cover, and says, "Women are not cooks for the same reason they're not backhoe operators. Imagine a woman trying to lift this. On a Saturday night I lose five pounds."

"Careful!" Anne repeats. "You don't know what you're saying."

"Certainly I know what I'm saying. A third reason women aren't chefs is that kitchen workers, by and large, are Nazis. Super rednecks. They were taken out of school at fourteen. They have no ethical sense or standards. They're the sort of people who would not tolerate working for a woman."

"We are both extremely opinionated," Anne says.

Otto may be *el mandamás*, but their relationship is complicated by marriage, and, as he describes it, "in her role as wife she does not give unquestioning obedience." When their opinions collide, she has been known to pick up a wine glass, hold

(2 3 1)

its stem between two fingers high above the tile floor, and open the fingers. She has picked up water glasses and sent them smashing into the kitchen wall. He once threw a shot glass that hit her toe. It has been my inadvertent role, in my visits over the past year, to suppress to some extent these customary events. Thus I have altered, in however minor a measure, the routines I have come to observe. As his usual day accelerates toward dinnertime, the chef's working rhythms become increasingly intense, increasingly kinetic, and finally all but automatic. His experience becomes his action. He just cruises, functioning by conditioned response. "You cook unconsciously," he says. "You know what you're going to do and you do it. When problems come along, your brain spits out the answer." With a working, eating journalist sitting on a stool not far from the stove—pecking facts, pecking bits of salmon cured in salt and saltpetre with dill and sour cream—the chef is more or less obliged to think and to answer questions, with the result that he stops to consider what he is doing, and this makes the doing all the more difficult, as if he were a surgeon on television tying knots with one hand. His volatility is inhibited, too. On days when I am here, I am some sort of weather front that holds back the buildup of his afternoon storm. At least that is what Anne tells me. And he nods, and grins. It's true. In the presence of the media he throws fewer bottles and glasses. The sin, stink, and brimstone go out of his language. I have not once seen him crack an egg over Anne's head, as he confesses to doing from time to time. Nor have I seen *her* heaving duck scraps on the floor. "Duck scraps" is their term for the garbage they save for the geese. In crescendo situations, she will dump duck scraps on the kitchen floor, then clean them up, feeling better. "Communication, relationships, interaction, baloney," Anne says. "You only live with yourself. You are only in your own head. You *govern* your reactions to others. Throwing things, breaking things, you are keeping your own house in order."

Occasionally the storms of the kitchen roll on into the evening. Once, in a real line squall, Anne shouted into Otto's face: "Will . . . you . . . calm . . . down! The . . . customers . . . will . . . hear . . . you!"

Otto thundered back: "I don't give a bloody damn *what* the customers hear!"

The door to the kitchen swung open. "I heard that," said a customer, poking his head a short way into the room.

Anne's mother lived with them for a time. One day she was present when they were fighting in the kitchen. Anne told her to leave. She refused, saying, "I want to watch the divorce." Anne filled a pitcher with water and advised her mother that she would pour it all over her if she did not go to her room. Mother stayed put. Anne upended the pitcher.

There is nothing Anne and Otto will agree about more readily than that the tensions of the kitchen are mere blips in their routine—unavoidable, and possibly important. More than once they have ended up together on the kitchen floor, hugging their Tibetan mastiff. Take hold of his paw and he moans.

NAP TIME and, before retiring, Otto runs down to the nearest Grand Union for his last-minute shopping, saying, as the electric eyes recognize him, "This is a terrifically expensive store. You only buy the minimum." With a list in his hand, he buys

(2 3 3)

lemons, strawberries, apples, walnuts, romaine, parmesan, chocolate, and chicory. As he hurries past the meat, his eye is stopped by twelve pounds of irresistible rib-eye beef, and he puts that in his cart, too. "It's on the menu for those wretched people who live in developments up the road," he says. "I'll make a bordelaise."

Otto the Neighbor contributes his share of covered dishes to the suppers of churches he does not attend, but he sees very little of the people who live around him, in part because he prefers it that way and in part because he works so much that he has no time to repair his rail fences let alone put his foot up and talk. Neighbors for the most part ignore him and he ignores them, except when young Almquist from up the road comes through on his snowmobile and Otto outshouts the thing for making shrapnel of his nap. After working nine hours or so, he needs serenity and rest to get himself ready for the payoff zone of his day. Often he doesn't sleep but just reads for two hours in bed—books somewhat more than periodicals, fiction more than fact. (He reads after work each night until he falls asleep.) His other diversions are few, and are analogously solo. When he skin-dives, he likes to go alone. He describes squash as "a good game—you can play it alone." But he seldom plays games. His two primary diversions are reading and restaurants. "He eats as well as he cooks," Anne says. "I love to eat out with him." Anyone would. Anyone who could recognize him on a city sidewalk— with his Savile Row look and his carelessly flying hair—would do well to drop all other plans and shadow him whither he goes. Say he happens to be walking along Madison Avenue in the general purlieu of Altman's. Stay back. Be polite. Respect his treasured privacy. Stay across the street if possible, but by all means keep him in sight. Stand by as he browses windows and goes into wet-suit stores. When he comes out, and crosses Thirty-fourth Street, make the light. If he goes into, say, Salta in Bocca, linger two minutes outside. Now go in, too. With luck, you will be seated at a table near him. Listen. Watch. At any rate, contrive to learn what he orders. He orders spiedino. You order spiedino—slivers of prosciutto cotto and moz-zarella with capers and anchovy sauce in a casing of sautéed fragrant bread. He orders a bottle of Verdicchio. You order a bottle of Verdicchio. He orders paglia e fieno, a green-and-white straw-and-hay pasta in a silky butter-cream-and-parme-san sauce. Precisely what you wanted for lunch.

Otto, on such occasions, picks up ideas. He duplicates at home what he eats in town. Coming upon a dish he has never seen, he pulls it apart and looks it over. "Sometimes you say, 'Ah, I can duplicate that.' Other times you know you'd never be able to do it. There are flavors that are hard to decipher. It's easier, of course, to tell what's in something raw than in something cooked. I cribbed pork hocks from the Veau d'Or —you know, pieds de porc. Pieds de porc are usually in vinaigrette sauce, but these were slightly crisp on top and saturated with a gravy that made your lips stick together. It was a strong gravy. It had a good sharp mustardy taste—a very rich demi-glace sauce with a lot of good French mustard in it. We serve that every so often."

"What do you call it on your menu?"

"Braised pigs' knuckles."

At Kitcho, on Forty-sixth Street, he first ate soba—cold green Japanese buckwheat noodles dipped in sauce. He went home, got out his buckwheat, and made soba. Many years ago, after a visit to Charley O's, on Forty-eighth Street, he

Xeroxed their soused shrimp—cooking shrimp in pickling spice and then making a marinade of the sauce they were cooked in, adding onion, garlic, and sherry. He likes to go to The Siamese Garden, on Fifty-third Street, where he regards the clientele as "seedy State Department types—you half expect a hand grenade to come rolling your way." He once tried a shrimp roll there that created effects he found agreeable and novel, so he pulled the thing apart, went home, and made something almost identical, using Chinese cabbage, ginger, onion, Alaska midget shrimp, lemon grass, and fermented-fishhead sauce. Impressed by a chef at Peng's, on Forty-fourth Street, who turned chopped shrimp into spheres of flavor and air, Otto bought a basket of quahogs at the Fulton Market, took them home, ground them up, combined them with flour and beaten egg white, a touch of hot sauce, vinegar, onion powder, salt, and pepper, and dropped the mixture by the spoonful into hot olive oil. The spoonfuls bloomed. He serves them as "clam puffs." Otto's appreciation of Japanese food is enhanced in the American milieu, because in a general way he thinks that our Japanese restaurants are "straightforward—their materials are obviously fresh," and he cannot say as much for the commercial conveyance of some other national cuisines. To illustrate, he flips open *Chef* magazine and quickly finds an ad for Trufflettes. "The unique artificial truffle with real truffle flavor keeps indefinitely under refrigeration," says the text. "Perfect for decoration. Won't melt even if boiled. Perfect black inside and out." Tossing aside the magazine, Otto says, "That's what almost the whole food industry is—what can be got away with rather than what can be done. That's why we go to Japanese restaurants."

Otto is the wave of the past. This is the age of the microwave and the mass-produced entrée, and while he is working at his daily preparations the chefs of other inns are watching the clock in their morning classes in college. Under the stately shade of credit cards, freezer-bodied "reefer" trucks pull up at country inns with chicken Kiev, veal cordon bleu, crêpes à la reine, and rock-frozen "Cornish" hens stuffed with a mixture of wild rice and mushrooms soaked in cognac. Such deliveries, of course, are made in cities, too—clams Casino by the case, crab imperial, coquilles Saint-Jacques, crêpes de la mer, crêpes cannelloni, quiche Lorraine, filets of beef Wellington. Otto has often heard that the best maker of instant entrées is Idle Wild Farm, of Pomfret Center, Connecticut, a division of Idle Wild Foods, of Worcester, Massachusetts. Driving through northeastern Connecticut one time, I stopped in at Idle Wild Farm to watch its cooks at work. There was no identifying sign, no proclamation of the marvel of the presence of such an operation in the oak-and-maple countryside thirty miles west of Providence. Set back from a narrow tertiary road was a ranch house that had been converted to an office, and attached to it was a spread-out mustard-colored building—not Gulden's yellow, it should be said, but Dijon gold. The kitchen inside was vast and immaculate, windowless, brightly illuminated in close approximation to daylight. Cooks, assemblers—two hundred in all—were working there. Down the center of the room ran a broad conveyor belt on which completed products—chicken breasts cordon bleu, shrimp-lobster-and-crabmeat Newburg—moved slowly toward, and ultimately disappeared within, a horizontal stainless-steel cylinder that was aswirl in cold fog and resembled an Atlas missile. This was Cryotransfer 36 II. In the course of a day, it takes in some five to ten thousand appetizers and entrées, sprays them with liquid nitrogen at three hundred and twenty degrees below zero, and, seven minutes later, emits from its far end food so frozen it could scratch granite. A succession of living goldfish once went into Cryotransfer 36 II. They came out resembling jewelry. Only the big ones died. When a fishbowl filled with water restored them to room temperature, the little ones swam as before. Coming in from either side to the central conveyor were twenty-five tributary conveyors, each attended by a team in blue, preparing a different item. There was a manicotti conveyor, a chicken-breast-cordon-bleu conveyor, a beef-Wellington conveyor. The cooking teams were under instructions to stop and wash their hands every hour. The room had been disinfected with chlorine. There was food for hospitals and airlines as well as for couples in candlelight, and beside one of the tributary conveyors sat a young woman making omelettes. With an ice-cream scoop she reached into a large steel tub that contained thawed whole eggs that had been mixed with carrageenan to become a bright-yellow custard. The carrageenan would help the omelettes stand up. After lifting a scoopful of the egg mixture some twelve to fourteen inches above the moving conveyor belt, the young woman rolled her wrist. Splat, the yellow custard landed on the belt and spread out much like a flapjack, its dimensions programmed exactly by the height of the free fall, the density of the egg custard, and the volume of the scoop. Metronomically the cook repeated the process, and in rows of three the yellow discs moved away from her and into an infrared oven. She smiled. There is no cafeteria at Idle Wild Farm. The cooks eat lunch from vending machines, or they bring brown bags. Emerging from the oven, the omelettes were not permitted to go on to the central conveyor. Cryotransfer 36 II would shatter them like glass. With other delicate products—crêpes cannelloni, crêpes de la mer—they went to a room where air was gently circulating at twenty below zero.

Beside another tributary conveyor, a woman held a pair of scissors in one hand while she weighed breasts of chicken with the other. The breasts were boned, skinned, and glistening— material clean enough and fresh enough to be eaten raw—and they weighed more or less five ounces apiece. More or less was not the way of this kitchen. The chicken in an Idle Wild Farm chicken breast cordon bleu must weigh precisely five ounces. The scissors took care of that. Add a little, snip a little, from chicken to chicken. Add pre-portioned ham and cheese. There was a separate cook for each addition, and an automatic shower of egg batter, and a machine to coat the product with breading. Another scale weighed the assembled breast—seven ounces.

This was the farm where a retired promoter named Jacques Makowsky crossed Cornish gamecocks with Plymouth Rock chickens to develop what he decided to call the Rock Cornish Game Hen. Makowsky is gone and so are the chickens. The farm buys them from Maine to Delmarva and in upstate New York. The old "kill line" is now the Formula Room, where spices and sauces are mixed in tubs, but the senior entrée on Idle Wild's list is still the Rock Cornish hen stuffed with wild rice. The general manager now is Dieter H. Buehler, Chevalier du Tastevin, who, in the thirteen years before he came to Connecticut, fed a hundred and fifty million meals to the passengers of Trans World Airlines, as its dining director. His degree is from Cornell. His memberships include the Beefeater Club and the Chaîne des Rôtisseurs. Tall and polished, amiable, verbal, in a pin-striped shirt and a striped tie, he walked through the kitchen like an executive seraph walking on a cloud, for he was knee-deep in drifting mists of nitrogen as he said that by 1982 the typical American family would be eating fifty per cent of its meals in restaurants of one type or another, and cooks were simply not going to exist to handle this demand. It was the mission of Idle Wild Farm to usher the world appropriately into the era of "the kitchenless kitchen."

I had told him something about Otto. "For how many years will that sort of person be around?" he said. "With changing life styles, who wants to spend his life in a kitchen? Who wants to work in a kitchen fifteen hours a day and seven days a week? We are filling a need. We are here to improve the quality of the existence of people like your friend, to help them not to have to work fifteen hours a day but still maintain a high standard in their operations, with food they are proud to serve."

After such advances in the art, the French could not be far behind. And, indeed, there is a new shop in Paris called the Comptoir Gourmand, where the celebrated chef Michel Guérard—who has earned three Michelin stars at his restaurant in Gascony—sells frozen entrées for six or eight dollars a brick: trout-with-mushrooms poached and frozen, fish terrine with watercress sauce, cryogenic calf's-tongue pot-au-feu.

"At Idle Wild Farm, we do things in small batches, with a lot of love and care and special handling," Buehler went on. "In the more modern restaurants, there are minimal kitchen facilities. Menus are limited. They run a broiler and they roast prime ribs, but the staff is basically unskilled. The staff is college kids. Don't ask a college kid to do a cordon bleu. We help the operator to better utilize his time, and with our appetizers and entrées there is never a disaster on a chef's bad night."

The big reefers that go out from Idle Wild Farm are headed for regional distributors, such as Berkshire Frosted Foods, in Pittsfield, Massachusetts; Pocono Produce, in Stroudsburg, Pennsylvania; Smith, Richardson & Conroy, in Miami; and A. Peltz & Sons, in New York City. From the distributors, restaurants order Kievs for their customers and lasagna to feed the help. One can buy Idle Wild products retail at Hammacher Schlemmer, on Fifty-seventh Street, thickly packed in dry ice. The instructions are abecedarian. Anyone who knows how to tell time can turn out veal cordon bleu or crêpes à la reine. There is no "slack." The product goes directly from the freezer to the oven—so many minutes at four hundred degrees. There are adjusted instructions for conventional ovens, convection ovens, microwave ovens, infrared ovens, deep fryers. "One thing that holds us apart from other people is that we can make anything at all on a custom-processed basis," Buehler said. "There's a fifty-case minimum—two thousand pieces. That's a production run."

We were joined by Jacques Noé, Idle Wild's executive chef, who spends most of his time working out new dishes. Noé was born in Asnières, one bend down the river from Paris, and he worked in Parisian restaurants and was trained in kitchens in France and Switzerland. He has been in America more than twenty years, mainly in Boston, working in restaurants and as a teacher in a cooking school. Handsome and blue-eyed, with a light-brown mustache, he spoke with the sort of suave French voice that, in English, seems to be emerging from a purring cat. That morning, as it happened, he had been working on a coulibiac of ocean bass, which was not a true coulibiac, he explained, because the recipe called for phyllo dough instead of a brioche. In fact, he was testing the recipe with scrod. He had a sample ready for submission to a customer. With few exceptions, he hastened to say, the dishes prepared at Idle Wild Farm do not deviate from the descriptions one can read of those dishes in *Larousse Gastronomique*. We stopped to observe a team assembling individual filets of beef Wellington. The puff pastry was in squares like handkerchiefs. In tall racks beside the conveyor were thick slices of filet mignon charred and appetizing as a result of a trip through the "automatic searer." Actually, they were raw within and frozen solid. Freezing the meat beforehand prevents blood from leaking out during the assembly process. In *Larousse* you would hardly expect to find something called Wellington, and indeed you do not, but, Noé explained, it is orthodox to accompany the meat either with some liver pâté or with duxelles ("a kind of mushroom hash"). "Liver pâté in this country is not very well accepted," he said, and therefore an ounce of duxelles was being placed on each filet. To absorb moisture during thaw, bread crumbs were sprinkled on the meat, too, and then it was turned over while the puff pastry was folded around it in a manner known as butcher wrap. So that steam would escape during cooking, it was one woman's job to poke a hole in the pastry with her pinky. Next came a wash of egg and milk in vital proportions, for the egg and milk would help the puff pastry become a rich and ceramic brown. If the proportions were awry, the crust could go black before the beef inside had thawed. "We save labor, save time in the kitchen," said the chef. "What we make for restaurants we send out of here raw and ready for people to put in the oven. We don't save a lot of time if we cook it for them." The act of removing a frozen entrée from a freezer and putting it into an oven is known as "restoration."

"Do you miss working in restaurants?" I asked him.

"Oh, yes. Yes."

"Why?"

"I miss the excitement. I don't miss the six days a week and the long hours and the holidays. They were not my holidays. But I miss . . . In a restaurant, you never know what to expect. I miss the pressure, the challenge. I love a big crisis."

When I described to Otto that visit in Connecticut, he said, "Those people are pandering to chefless kitchens. Eventually, American restaurants will buy almost all of their materials that way, and they will be limited to a set number of dishes. On the other hand, a frozen entrée, well made, gives people a hint of what could be possible. It's something like what Maurice Girodias, of the Olympia Press, said about pornography: 'It gets people to read who otherwise wouldn't read.' "

He paused. His thought shifted. "The chefs at the big frog ponds have more than enough pride not to use something they haven't had a hand in," he continued. "They want their signature on the dish. But they're not above compromise. They're not above using frozen turbot and frozen Dover sole. Dover sole comes into this country frozen, and anyone who says it isn't frozen is a liar. The frog ponds always have it." His expressions of apparent contempt for this ethnic group should not be misinterpreted as distaste for French cuisine. It is, rather, distaste for the manner in which French cuisine is sometimes derived in America. He is not shy to spend his minimum wages in the ne-plus-expense-account restaurants of the city, and when he is in one his nostrils filter out the scent of money. The prices don't ruin his dinner. Nor do prices create in him, as they seem to in some people, a favorable prejudice. Milieus, for the most part, don't interest him, either. His con-

(2 4 3)

centration is on the table. Waiters are contemptible until they prove that they are not. "The less the waiter can afford the meal, the more hostile he's going to be." Otto once tried to correct a captain's pronunciation of "Montrachet." He said, "Both 't's are silent."

The captain said, "No. One pronounces the first 't.' "

"Are you French-Canadian?" said Otto.

He regards restaurant owners generally as "a shabby lot." They overcook their country inns in order to collect fire insurance—that sort of shabbiness—and, in the city, "if Jackie Onassis is coming they bump you." He calls that "shameful," and says, "A reservation is a contract." He admires The Four Seasons—the splendiferous show aside—because he thinks The Four Seasons does things well "and in an enlightened, honest fashion." With his shoes off under the table there, he is clearly relaxed and happy, addressing his pike-and-salmon pâté, his sweetbreads-and-spinach, his asparagus maltaise. In Lutèce, he keeps his shoes on, out of respect, perhaps, for the proprietor-chef but scarcely for the elegance of the clientele and least of all for the funereal snobs with pencils and pads who carry the food from the kitchen. There is a man seated at the next table in bulging dungarees. Otto likes very much the mousseline de brochet et écrevisses. "It's hard work," he says. "Hard to keep hot. Hard to serve. The pike has to be boned. Then it's thrown in with eggs and cream and condiments and bread panada in a Robot Coupe—a commercial Cuisinart." He tastes from other plates on his table—a bit of pâté en croûte et terrines ("it's O.K.—just O.K."), and pèlerines à la méridionale ("Very good, not overcooked—*al dente*"). He is not awed by André Soltner, in the kitchen—at least not to the extent that he has been awed by Japanese. "The turbot is delicious, very fresh, perfectly cooked," he says of another of Soltner's entrées—turbot de Dieppe poché, hollandaise. "My guess is it was frozen,* which is the only kind you can buy, unless it is flown over. It's probably Holland turbot— three dollars a pound with the head on, and the head is a third of the fish. No doubt it swam past Dieppe. Turbot is easy to cook. You can't make much of a mistake." Lutèce's sole farcie Elzévir, on the other hand, does not seem to him very fresh. "It isn't pristine," he says. "It has a fishy taste. Oh, yes, it's Dover sole. It has the firm texture. You can do things with it you can't do with American flounder. Stuff it. Roll it. Make paupiettes. Dover sole is crunchy. It has a bite to it." He examines Lutèce's coquelet à la crème aux morilles. "It's juicy and good," he says. "It isn't squab. It's Cornish hen, you know—Frank Perdue. There has been a certain sacrifice here of quality for volume. Prices are higher. Rents are higher. I mean, the guy's a businessman." And what man of business would not have on his menu ris de veau financière? Sampling, Otto finds its pastry light and crisp but the sauce too reduced and not distinguished. "If you et it, your beard and your mustache would congeal together," he says to me. "The sweetbreads themselves are white. No fibre. Delicious. There should be truffles in the financière garnish. Financière means money, riches. We could do without the olives. A financière garnish has ground mushrooms, kidneys, cockscombs, and small chicken-forcemeat quenelles. Do you see any cockscombs? If you can make something better than the correct way—I mean, objectively better—then go ahead and do it. But be careful if you're a French restaurant in New York and are

* Otto guessed wrong.

charging a fortune. If you're supposed to have truffles or morels or cockscombs and you cheat—that's reprehensible. We'll let him off on the cockscombs, but he could have gone to a kosher butcher. His prices are not chicken feed. When he is asking two or three hundred dollars to give four people their dinner, he should go by the book. Right?"

THE CUSTOMERS ARE UNAWARE of Otto's bell. It rings in the kitchen when they step on a mat in the vestibule, and it produces in him a sense of dimming houselights, a conditioned adrenal twitch. Just by the way they trip the bell, they sometimes tell him who they are. The tennis star is on the list tonight (a long-footed, insistent ring) and the bridge-toll collector (brief and unassuming) and the couple who come here twice a week (a mixed staccato). "We'll have forty people— some nice people, quite a few decent people," Otto says. He reserves his compliments for less than half his clientele. "Many people who eat here seem to appreciate it," he continues. "They're thankful. And they are what has kept me going. Thirty per cent are excellent eaters. Ten per cent are fun to talk to. Five per cent know about food and really enjoy it. To them we can sell pretty much anything, because there is some trust. I've served cod-roe salad with roundels of roe. The people who tried it loved it, but in general it didn't go. It was just too unfamiliar. Remember, however, what P. Lorillard said: 'The quickest way to failure is to try to please everybody.' "

He is cooking a steak for Anne. She battles anemia—and prepares for her evenings—with thick shells of sirloin. He has trimmed off a slice or two for himself, raw, and another for

Mercedes, the cat. "All I've had to eat today is some tea and a bit of cucumber," he claims. "It's wonderful not to eat if you're in a hurry. It speeds you up." His way of not eating comes to roughly eight thousand calories a day. The steak is searing in a ribbed iron skillet. How can he tell, without cutting in, just when the colors are what he wants inside?

"Just by touching it," he says. "You can tell exactly." He quarters some scallops and splits the long legs of Alaskan crabs—last-minute preparations. "The customers are sometimes afraid to order steak because they think they should have something fancier," he goes on. "So I tart it up with bordelaise. Or béarnaise. That way, it's got a bit of sophistication. If they want it 'well done,' I'm pretty uncompromising. I just don't do it 'well done.' To cook it that way is such a shame."

The ovens are set at four hundred degrees, where they will stay unless he becomes unusually busy, in which case he needs four-fifty. Anne, dressed for business, wears a white-and-black polka-dot jacket over a floor-length black dress. Her hair is swept back and knotted in a bun. She says of her husband, "He is safe in here doing the work he loves, here in the purity of his little inner sanctum. To me it is a different operation. I'm up front with the people. I have to listen to urologists and bulldozer operators telling me things about food. After eleven years, your opinion of the public is low. I used to think anyone eating reasonably well-prepared food will know he's eating it, but I move through the dining room sometimes and it's depressing. For some people, we could just as well open a can. They are so used to artificial flavors that when you give them actual food they don't know what it is. They look at fresh whipped cream with suspicion."

(247)

Otto says, "The only kind they've seen has come out of an aerosol can. To show them what it actually is, I go into the dining room and whip the cream there."

People ask for ketchup, and they put it on fillet of sole Florentine, on scallops in garlic butter.

"They ask, 'What's fresh this evening?' or 'Are these good?' "

"If it wasn't good, we wouldn't serve it. They complain that veal chops are tough, because they've never had good, firm veal. They want to know if the wines are good. We chose them."

"A great many people think anyone who owns a restaurant is crooked. So their attitude is that we are dishonest and are trying to put something over on them and they have to be very swift in order to catch us. They've read somewhere that manta rays are cut up and sold as scallops. So they ask us if our scallops are ray."

A woman once asked for Chivas on the rocks. Anne went into the pantry and poured Chivas on the rocks, and when time came to ask about another, the woman said, "Not here."

"Why?"

"That was not Chivas."

"Oh, but it was. We don't do that sort of thing."

"A restaurant can't stay in business if it doesn't cheat."

"You get out of here!" Anne screamed. "You get out of here and you *never* come back!"

The woman ran for her car. "I was shaking," Anne recalls. "I shook for a couple of days. I have a rule of thumb. Never trust anyone who drives a Cadillac."

There is a printed menu—a short list of items that do not require long preparation, are always on hand, and "don't scare people," such as grilled rib-eye steak, grilled lamb kidneys and sausage, shrimp in ajillo sauce, and émincé of veal zurichois—sautéed veal strips with wine, cream, and scallions. There are three soups, home-smoked trout, snails, marinated mushrooms. "People want a menu in their hands," Otto says. "They want to eat boring things. They actually want to eat stodgy stuff. Marinated mushrooms, you know, are for nowhere people. I serve baked potatoes so often because I'm tired of people saying I'm too cheap to serve them. They bitch if you give them something else." He makes Swedish-fried potatoes, which are cut in ganglion strings and cooked in very hot fat, where they enmesh in a filament mass that comes up golden and crisp. Yet the nurdier clients want foil. They don't want golden-brown Brillo pads. "They want potatoes cooked in an oven in foil," Otto says. "If the potatoes are in foil, that's gourmet."

"When did you last serve a potato in aluminum foil?"

"Never."

"Why not?"

"They're not baked potatoes. They're steamed. Mind you, if the customers were uniformly objectionable there would be no joy at all. Many of our customers are open-minded people. We have served octopus and snails successfully since the day we started. There is, in fact, less Mickey Mouse about Americans than anyone else I've ever dealt with—French, German, Spanish, English. Basically, the Americans are more secure."

Tina, his waitress, arrives—trim, dark-haired, petite. She studies Otto's written list of extras and asks him to explain what she doesn't understand—as does Cam, his waiter, young and Filmland handsome, with a cadet's vertical spine, and bright-blond hair. Cam is in high school and is Anne's son.

The bell sounds, long in the foot, and sounds soon again, sporadic and sharp. Otto's working surfaces are as clean and prepared as athletic fields, surrounded by the *mise en place*. He takes his towel from his shoulder and nervously wipes them cleaner. He has regained his blue terry-cloth hat. It sits on the back of his head. His sleeves are rolled. Tina goes out with the list.

Half a dozen customers are waiting in the wicker chairs under the head of the fighting bull and the chart of the endangered species. Some are looking at the printed menu. Some have not picked it up. She greets the first group and reads the list. "These are tonight's extras," she says. "For appetizers:

> RUSSIAN COULIBIAC OF SALMON
> SMOKED SHAD-ROE PÂTÉ MOUSSE
> QUENELLES OF VEAL AND SHRIMPS
> STUFFED CLAMS
> LEEKS VINAIGRETTE
> MUSSELS À LA POULETTE
> OCTOPUS SALAD.

And the entrees:

> BREADED PORK LOIN CORIANDER
> PAELLA À LA MARINERA
> OSSO BUCCO
> SAUTÉED SCALLOPS AL PESTO
> SAUTÉED CHICKEN BREASTS WITH
>   APPLE-CIDER SAUCE
> BROILED FILLET OF GROUPER
>   OURSINADE."

Someone in the party says, "Imagine all that out here in the sticks!"

The host, an old customer from the Upper West Side, says, "This is not the sticks. This is the apex of the civilized world."

Tina, in response to questions, explains "oursinade," "coulibiac," and "à la poulette," and reads out the list again. Otto has learned never to write "marjoram" on his extras list. People hear it as "margarine." Oleomarjoram. When he made sweetbreads with veal-forcemeat quenelles, various customers said the horsemeat was very good, and Otto has never used the word "forcemeat" on his extras list again.

Tina returns to the kitchen. "One clam, one coulibiac, one octopus, one mousse, two pork loins, one osso, one grouper," she says, presenting the order also in writing.

More footsteps on the bell. From my stool near the stove, I say to the chef, "Good luck."

He says, "I'll go into the chapel and pray."

He has dripped melted butter through a hole in the roof of the golden-brown coulibiac. Now he cuts an inch-thick slice. The interior is white and yellow and reddish-orange. "I'll make a lot of money out of this one," he says. "The materials, per serving, are not expensive. The more work you do, the more money you make. There's no profit in a shrimp cocktail."

Moving rapidly from worktable to stove to refrigerator, he shelves the coulibiac, shoves clams into an oven, and fetches a bowl of octopus. He eats some octopus. "Crunchy," he says. "That's how it should be. If you cook octopus until it's tender, all the buds come off. I've never made it this way before. This is based on a picadillo salad, which is as *andaluz* as gazpacho. You see? Here is a completely new dish, and they go along with it." He serves it on a bed of romaine with a light tartar sauce, which he made when he got up from his nap.

The stuffed clams are not ground up, as stuffed clams almost always are. Nor are they served in shells. They are whole, and collected in a ramekin, and submerged in a matrix consisting of onions, bread crumbs, garlic, marjoram, olive oil, butter, a drop of hot sauce, and some chopped curly lettuce, "which is very stringy, gives it consistency, puts some weave into it." He started cooking clams in this fashion as a way of using up old bread. His bread contains a thirteen-to-one ratio of unbleached flour to rye, and when it is old it is durable. It makes what he calls "good tough bread crumbs that hold up." When it is fresh, its aroma alone would melt butter. He does not make it every day because he and Anne eat so much of it they endanger their health. Other days, they give their customers commercial French bread they themselves scarcely touch.

He removes from the oven a ramekin of clams, gouges one out with a finger, and offers it to me. It is light and springy and aburst with flavor. "I think they're the best stuffed clams around," he says, sculpting over the cavity he has made in the dish and putting it back in the oven so the heat will erase his theft. With reference to the people who are waiting for the clams, he says to Tina, "They can go in now," and she goes out to shepherd them to their seats. He builds on a plate a buttery mound of shad-roe pâté mousse, garnishes it with a bit of cress, and puts it on a tray with the octopus, the salmon, and the clams, saying, "I think that people should eat at my convenience, not that I should cook at their convenience. *Pour savoir manger, il faut savoir attendre.* If people have any common sense, they will subordinate themselves to the cook's wishes. In any event, here, they go into the dining room when I am ready." The four appetizers on the tray are as attractive to the eye as they are to the nose and will be to the palate.

They are informal, a little offhand, arranged with enough artistry to imply care but not so much as to suggest that the care was squandered on cosmetics. A year or so ago, on the first evening I spent with Otto in his kitchen, he turned to me at this moment and said, "I want to make a point. There is something that happens to food when it goes from the kitchen to the dining room. It looks better in there, because it is in a dining room. A metamorphosis takes place."

The second order has come in, and the assembly of its appetizers will coincide with the timing of the first entrées. The bell rings. The pattern of the night compounds. Grouper fillet, in a skin of flour, is searing in a skillet. He flips it, flips it back. He turns things in skillets not once but many times. He is using a knife as a spatula. He is not contemptuous of spatulas. A knife is more often in his hand. He lacks time to switch instruments. He is a chef, not a dentist. He removes the skillet from the flame. He brushes the grouper with a purée of urchin roe, oil, and fish fumet, and he sets the pan in the oven.

"How long are you going to leave that in there?"

"I don't know. I have no idea. Until it's cooked. Five minutes probably. More or less."

Tina enters, saying, "Octopus, mussels, onion soup." Anne is behind her, saying, "The Siegels are ready when you are." She has a small silver frog in her hand, a gift from a customer. There are other presents as well—a bottle of Château Haut-Brion, a tin of caviar, an authentic Habana cigar. Otto rolls the cigar in Saran Wrap and stores it in the cooler. He will smoke anything. There are customers who have brought him joints. The presents tonight have such loft because his people have discovered what many of them feared—that Otto is selling the inn. In a short time, he and Anne will be gone. After eleven years, they have sought and found release from the heating-oil company they have in effect been working for, the insurance company that has collected their rewards. Their buyer and successor is an experienced New York waiter.

Seven-fifteen, and before the chef now are five sets of orders. Seventeen appetizers. Seventeen entrées. The Vulcan seems to be functioning on its own. Below the high blue flames of six surface burners, there is a shutting and opening, opening and shutting, slamming percussion of doors, with sudden veils of escaping steam and puffs of brown cloud. "It's the pork loin. It's got to be a little burnt to taste right." Of some grouper in the other oven the reverse is true—in its fragile urchin purée. He pulls it out and looks it over, touches it, smells it. "Delicate," he says. "It almost smells like egg." The surface of the fish is mustard brown. He has opened the door a dozen times to watch that color develop. We sample the grouper before letting it go to the customer. The sea-urchin flavor seems to me to be the sort that is so modest you have to chase after it. Otto has his own vocabulary. With apparent pleasure, he compares the flavor to iodine.

He continuously touches and tastes the food. He pinches it. He taps it. He licks and nibbles it. He tastes every part of every dish as he puts it together and the whole when it is done. He wipes and wipes again the front edge of the stove, wipes his block surfaces, washes his hands. He moves about his kitchen with athletic stamina. When the pressure is highest, he runs. "It's like having a hobby that pays you," he says. "I actually enjoy this, thank God."

"Two quenelles, one seviche, conch chowder, two paellas, two ossos."

A quarter to eight, and the china is rattling. Pot lids are

(254)

spinning on the floor. The oven is up to four-fifty. Otto is moving so fast his work has become a collage of itself, as—all in a minute—he pours out lime juice, eats a handful of seviche, tosses veal into a skillet, and hunts through wild mushrooms for deposits of grit. Chaos cannot get at him in the depths of composition. Those are finished compositions going out through the door—the mottled brown envelopes of pork loin, the drape-fold saucing of the poached quenelles. He is not only cooking. He works on all the levels of the kitchen. He sections the bread. He cuts and apportions desserts. He slices open the baked potatoes. "See. They are nice and floury," he says. "Conservatives order baked potatoes. Liberals ask for rice." He smacks his forehead. "Oh, Christ Almighty, I forgot the rice." Moving to correct one error, he makes another. He nicks a mocha meringue. Anne, passing through, stops to help. She shaves chocolate above the meringue, and the dark concealing snow drifts over the field of beige. "The most important thing to learn is how to rescue," she says.

"The most important thing to learn is to go slowly," says Otto. "There is a wonderful Spanish expression: 'Dress slowly. We're in a hurry.' If you remember that, you slow up, and you make less mistakes."

"Do you serve mistakes?"

"I'm not going to eat my errors, not if they taste good. An error that tastes good is a 'classic mistake.' A 'classic mistake' is a discovery. That's how I learned to put sapsago cheese into al-pesto sauce. I put it in by mistake." Sapsago is a green Swiss that smells like a farm. It is good for grating, "for flavoring anything," he says. "Quiche. Vegetable soup."

"Where do you get it?"

"Macy's."

Unless someone specifically asks for vegetables, he serves none with entrées. "I generally have, if nothing else, carrots, celery, Brussels sprouts, and artichoke hearts around, and I often have ratatouille as an appetizer, but I'm damned if I'm going to give away vegetables when people just leave them on the table. If they want vegetables, all they have to do is order them."

Someone asks for sour cream, and, as it happens, there is none in the house. Otto somehow feels he should have it, and so, for a single customer, he takes time to pour fresh thick cream into a bowl and whip it with a whisk, adding salt and vinegar. As the mixture stiffens, it takes on with remarkable exactness the texture of sour cream. He cuts up a scallion, mixes it in, and serves this patrician substitute to the unsuspecting stranger.

He licks his thumbs. "Wild mushrooms give veal sauce a meaty flavor," he says, finishing an osso bucco. He walks to the sink with an iron skillet, eating the remainder of the sauce. The predominant color of the osso bucco is cordovan, and it is pearled with shining marrow.

He cuts raw pork and eats some, too. He tosses a piece to Mercedes. "This cat eats more in a day than the average Indian eats in a year," he says. The cat nonetheless is skinny and sour. Otto himself eats so much meat that he occasionally turns vegetarian to give himself a cure. He doesn't work in June, and just by taking it easy he loses thirty pounds.

Otto's broiler has at times failed him, and on these occasions, to help finish certain dishes, he has used a propane torch. Crossing the ocean long ago on the S.S. Constitution, he saw baked Alaska beautifully browned, and he wondered how that was done. He went to the galley, where a chef was "baking" the meringue by playing over its surface the flame of a portable torch. "That was my first acquaintance with American know-how, which seems to be declining," he remarks, tossing pork-cutlet gravy in a big iron skillet with such vigor that it spills into a surface burner and flames leap two feet high. "Ever see a gas-stove repairman? They have no eyebrows."

Eight-twenty-five, and six are waiting, in the thirteenth hour of his working day. He puts herb butter into godets with mussels, and, arranging two plates of scallops al pesto, eats a generous fraction of the scallops. "O.K. O.K. Small and springy."

Anne enters. "Mr. Almquist says we have been good neighbors and wants us to know he will miss us," she tells him.

"I wish I could return the compliment," says Otto.

He bites one end of a huge boiled leek. Its center shoots out the other end. He drops a little saffron in the blender, adds water, and lets the mixture churn for many minutes as the color changes, grows, from flax to jonquil to canary to high lemon chrome. He mixes it with chicken stock and undercooked rice. A purist would do a whole paella at once, but Otto thinks rice comes up too crunchy that way and the *puristas* can go back to La Costa Brava. In a big iron skillet in sizzling oil, he half cooks scallops, mussels, shrimps, and floured grouper. In a pot with stock, he has tomatoes, bell peppers, peas, and bites of crab. Bringing the pot to a boil, he empties it into the skillet, and puts the skillet in the oven. Five minutes go by. "I forgot garlic!" he cries out, and rapidly dices a dozen fresh buds that throw a long cast through the room. "This you can do something about," he says, opening the oven and tossing in the garlic. "What's awful is when you forget to put sugar in the caramel custard." The chef is not inherently impressed with paellas, retaining in his prejudice an Andalusian coolness to this triumph of Valencian peasants. So he overcompensates. Arranging the mussels like symmetrical black petals against a field that is pink, red, yellow, and orange, he achieves a paella that is beautiful to see. "Kitchens in New York are so small they could not possibly cook to order many things on a busy night," he remarks, eating what is left of the rice in the pan.

Anne comes in again. "The Hubers are ready when you are," she says, also informing him that to keep herself going she will need some mashed potatoes. He mashes her potatoes. She takes away with her as well a ball of butter that is equal in volume to an Acushnet Titleist. Otto glances significantly at the butter. Retreating toward the pantry, she says over her shoulder, "I weigh less than two hundred pounds."

Searing grouper, he brushes it with urchin roe while ambidextrously reaching into an adjacent skillet to turn over a steak without the help of a utensil. He presses the steak with his fingers. He kicks the mastiff out of the kitchen. A third iron skillet stands empty over high blue flame. To see where the heat is, he places the palm of his hand flat on the bottom of the pan. He is in no great hurry to pull the hand away. "You never know where the hot areas are," he says. "They're never in the same place. They move around the pan." After melting butter, he sets a floured breast of chicken in the hot part of the pan.

Tina requests rice, which is being finished in the broiler. Otto reaches in and rests a hand on the rice. He says it is almost ready. Some years ago, he had a waitress who regularly wore miniskirts. He would ask her to stand on high stools to reach for out-of-the-way spice. "It's O.K. now," he tells Tina. "Take the Hubers in."

Tripping over a pan that he left on the floor, he spills a large quantity of al-pesto sauce (butter, basil, olive oil, parmesan, sapsago, and hazelnuts), and as he cleans it up he synopsizes aloud the plot of a novel in which a pet dog becomes a woman's lover and later causes an accident fatal to her husband.

Tina comes back to the kitchen, saying, "The Hubers would like to take a minute longer."

Otto gives this some thought, and he consents.

OTTO IS ASLEEP NOW. He drank some beer and made his bows and smoked his gift cigar, and then he took his leave, soon after work. With many of his customers, his appearance at their table at the end of their meal has become routine to the point of obligation. He seems not to mind. In all other ways he may avoid the light, but in these moments he seeks—and he says it in so many words—evidence that he has made people happy. Those customers he looks upon with favor he thinks of also as friends, and he will even invite them to "come around on Sunday" for lunch when the restaurant is dark. He is confident that he can go almost anywhere in the region and the sort of business he wants will follow. "And why wouldn't it?" he says. "All my friends will know where I am." He seems equally secure in his chosen anonymity, feeling certain that— far from being likely to betray him—his friends will see themselves as his cabal.

He accepted the compliments of the tennis star tonight

(smoked shad-roe pâté mousse, paella à la marinera). The tennis star brought him poinsettias. In 1973, the tennis star bet Otto a bottle of Dom Pérignon that Bobby Riggs would "beat the ass off that broad." When Billie Jean King was gelding Riggs, she was winning champagne for Otto. He talked Roman coins tonight with a man who comes regularly from a town seventy miles to the west (quenelles of veal and shrimps, breaded pork loin coriander). Otto advised him to read Robert Graves' translation of Suetonius. The customer had the book in his car. There was an Austrian—a stranger to the inn—who fought with the British at Tobruk (Russian coulibiac of salmon, osso bucco). Grateful for his praise, Otto joked with him in German.

Now the inn is quiet, Anne up and working while her family sleeps. She says she believes in guardian angels. She says her good luck is so pervasive that she pulls into gas stations and has flat tires there. She had luck today. When the sea urchins came, she had made enough trifle and baked enough cake to cover her desserts. She works on urchins now—cracking, scooping, separating out the roe. The column of gold is rising in the jar. She says of their move to another place that they are not going far, not far from New York, no telling where. "He has to feel comfortable. I trust in his paranoia to tell us where to go. What is certain is that we'll be between nowhere and no place, and things will be the same. For all those people who want flames and white gloves, there will be no flames or white gloves. What we have is simple food. Simple food if it is good is great. If you understand that, you understand him."

Her hair has come out of its knot, and a long strand crosses one eye. She puts down her work, dries her hands, and runs them backward from her temples. She speaks on, slowly. "You may have grasped this, but I don't know him very well. If you're close to a screen you can't see through it. He doesn't know me, either. We're just together. People are unknowable. They show you what they want you to see. He is a very honest person. Basically. In his bones. And that is what the food is all about. He is so good with flavor because he looks for arrows to point to the essence of the material. His tastes are very fresh and bouncy. He has honor, idealism, a lack of guile. I don't know how he puts them together. I don't know his likes and dislikes. I can't even buy him a birthday present. He has intelligence. He has education. He has character. He has integrity. He applies all these to this manual task. His hands follow what he is."

Modern
Factor
Analysis

Harry H. Harman

Modern Factor Analysis

Third Edition Revised

The
University of
Chicago
Press

Chicago and
London

Harry H. Harman's interests, training and broad experience cover the fields of mathematics, statistics, and psychology, with emphasis on computer utilization. He is the author of numerous articles and contributions to books, and co-author, with Karl J. Holzinger, of *Factor Analysis* (1941). Formerly principal scientist at the System Development Corporation in California, he is now senior research psychologist and director, Developmental Research Division, Educational Testing Service, Princeton, New Jersey.

The University of Chicago Press, Chicago 60637
The University of Chicago Press, Ltd., London
© 1960, 1967, 1976 by The University of Chicago

Library of Congress Cataloging in Publication Data

Harman, Harry Horace, 1913–
    Modern factor analysis.

    Bibliography: p.
    Includes indexes.
    1.   Factor analysis.   I.   Title.
QA278.5.H38   1976   519.5′3   75-22267
ISBN 0-226-31652-1

To my wife, Rose

Contents

Contents

Contents

Preface to Third Edition

While extremely pleased with the favorable responses from the readers of *Modern Factor Analysis,* I am equally appreciative of the constructive criticisms and suggestions I have received for the improvement of this book. They have had their influence in shaping the new edition, which is intended to improve the presentation of the basic material that remains essentially unchanged and to introduce new material in the clearest manner.

To carry out these objectives, two new chapters have been introduced and considerable revision of the structure and content of many of the other chapters were done in order to reflect the changed emphasis in several of the factor methods. The revisions were accomplished within the general framework established in earlier editions—major parts covering the foundations of factor analysis, direct methods, derived solutions, factor measurements, problem material, and a comprehensive bibliography—but with drastic changes in every one of these areas.

The new material covers some direct methods of analysis, namely, canonical factor analysis, image factor analysis, and alpha factor analysis; and offers an expanded treatment of the problem of relationships among factors from different analyses, including "matching" of factors and "Procrustes" rotations. Also, new sections have been introduced to cover questions on the types of correlations that are appropriate for factor analysis, general classes of orthogonal and oblique transformations not previously covered, and a comparison of methods for estimating factor scores. Six additional sections contain major additions or revisions. In all, eight of the sixteen chapters contain new material.

All material from the second edition that is retained has been edited and revised for the third edition. Some thirteen sections of the second edition have been combined, shortened, or deleted. Much of this rearrangement was necessitated by the elimination of practically all hand calculations that had occupied considerable space in the earlier editions. However, such details as are necessary to clarify some concepts and procedures have been retained. Thus, by deleting some procedures and tightening others, the new material could be introduced with only a slight increase in the overall length of the revised text.

The manner of presenting some material was changed in order to enhance communication with the reader. To make matrix notation more consistent, several major changes in mathematical notation were introduced in the second edition. Similarly, in the present edition, a few additional changes were made to make the symbology of factor analysis as clear and consistent as possible. The use of illustrating figures to help the reader visualize the problem of factorization has, from the first, been employed throughout the text; but in the revised text the first instances occur much earlier. Also, there had been a gross omission from the list of illustrative examples in the previous editions of this book, namely, the classical box problem of Thurstone. In making amends, the treatment of the problem in this edition goes far beyond Thurstone's original work, and it is hoped that the student will find it enlightening and the researcher will find it useful for testing new ideas in factor analysis.

The bibliography has been completely revised and updated, so that it now contains upwards of 600 references, about half of which are new since the second edition. Also, a major change has been introduced in the manner of citation in the text—from numerical style to author-date. The bibliography, of course, contains all the references cited in the text. In addition, as an aid to the serious researcher, it contains a comprehensive listing of the theoretical works in factor analysis that provide the basis or support for the developments in the text and a guide to new developments in the field. It was designed to serve as a guide to the researcher even for topics not covered—or touched on very lightly—in the text, as for example, three-mode factor analysis, higher-order factors, or the use of correlations between persons or other alternative forms of factor analysis.

This book does not profess to be a research work; it is a distillation into textbook and reference format of research findings, consisting of theoretical and computing developments. In particular, an important objective of this text is to provide a foundation for the proper understanding and use of factor analysis (including computer programs) in the analysis and interpretation of multivariate data.

The author has drawn upon many published researches to enhance the text, and the acknowledgments made in the two previous editions are implied once again. In addition, three reviews were especially helpful to the author: Andersen (1968) suggested some basic organization changes; Braverman (1972) recommended reduced emphasis on older methods and hand calculations; Pennell (1973) urged that certain new topics be included.

My professional associations at Educational Testing Service have been invaluable in helping me to keep informed about new developments in theory and computing procedures relevant to factor analysis, and for this I wish to thank the staff of ETS. In particular, I am greatly indebted to Samuel Messick for the encouragement and support that facilitated this work. Also, I am grateful to Bary G. Wingersky for the stimulation provided by the incisive discussions with him on philosophical, theoretical, and practical computing problems.

I wish to thank C. Brooke Gruenberg for her contribution to the changeover to the new style and for typing the bibliography, as well as for her help on the index.

I am grateful to Doris Conway for her assistance on all aspects of preparing the revised manuscript.

The University of Chicago Press has been most cooperative and helpful during all the years of our association. I greatly appreciate this and I want to thank them for the excellent manner in which they have handled the editorial and technical aspects of production of this book.

Most importantly, I am especially pleased to express my deepest thanks to my wife, Rose, for her encouragement, guidance, and patience during the many years spent on the several editions of this work.

Preface to the
First and Second Editions

Modern Factor Analysis reflects the progress made in the nineteen years since my publication with Professor Karl J. Holzinger of *Factor Analysis,* and includes the advances that have taken place in the computing art. Many new concepts and procedures have been developed in these years while some unwieldy methods are now obsolete.

A revised edition of Holzinger and Harman's *Factor Analysis* might have appeared several years ago were it not for the untimely death of Dr. Holzinger in 1954. We were just laying the groundwork for the revision of our original work, and were anticipating the actual start in the late summer of that year, following his appointment as visiting professor at the University of California at Berkeley. In addition to the deep personal loss, Dr. Holzinger's death ended a professional partnership of twenty years which the writer held in highest esteem.

In the light of the vast and broad advances that have occurred in factor analysis due largely to the advent of electronic computers, a revision alone would have been insufficient to include the new material covered in the present text. Among the more important features of *Modern Factor Analysis* are the following: (1) the treatment of "simple structure" concepts and methods, usually associated with the Thurstone school of factor analysis; (2) the introduction of analytical methods of rotation to desired final solutions; (3) the use of high-speed electronic computers in factor analysis; (4) the use of the square root method for desk calculator operations; (5) the introduction of statistical tests of hypotheses in factor analysis; (6) the presentation of problems and exercises, and answers to go with them; and (7) the very extensive, pertinent bibliography on the theory and methods of factor analysis. This book is intended to serve as a reference treatise on factor analysis in the current stage of advancement of the subject. Furthermore, it is hoped that its utility as a text book

---

Prefaces to the first two editions of *Modern Factor Analysis* were combined and condensed to produce the preface which appears here.

will be enhanced by the many problems and exercises, as well as the computing algorithms and summaries of concepts and notation.

The text is organized into five major parts, covering the foundation of factor analysis, direct methods, derived solutions, some special topics, and problem material. The six chapters of part I provide the historical background and basic notions of factor analysis, introducing the fundamental mathematics necessary for a proper understanding of the subject, and concluding with an enumeration and general description of the principal forms of factor solutions. Part II develops several of these methods directly from the observed data (the correlations among the variables). This is accomplished in five chapters where computing procedures and illustrative examples are presented as well as the theoretical developments. The notion of derived solutions is introduced in part III. Then follows an elaboration of the simple structure principles, the distinction between primary and reference coordinate systems, and the analytical methods of arriving at either orthogonal or oblique multiple-factor solutions from some arbitrary initial solution. Part IV is devoted to the problem of measuring the factors in terms of the variables.

Following the text proper there are several additional items. In part V a large group of problems and exercises not only provides useful material for classroom use, but is intended to support and supplement the formal presentation. Of the statistical tables presented in the Appendix, some are standard and are provided simply for the convenience of the reader while some are unique to factor analysis. The Bibliography has been carefully culled from the vast literature to include only those specific papers and treatises that are relevant to the theory and methods of factor analysis. A myriad of applications has purposefully been excluded. Finally, a very detailed Index is included.

Throughout the text the theoretical developments are elucidated both by the detailed computing procedures and the numerical illustrations. The particular content area of these data has no special significance since they are employed merely to exemplify the techniques. For this reason, many of the numerical examples that were first employed by Holzinger and Harman, and have since become classics in the literature, are used in *Modern Factor Analysis* to illustrate the new techniques and make possible comparisons with the old.

Between the publication of the first and second editions of this text, factor analysis made considerable progress in several directions. Continued research has led to new techniques for coping with long-standing problems in factor analysis as well as for pushing into areas previously unexplored. Largely responsible were the advances made in electronic computers and their associated programs. Not only have the computers suggested new avenues of research, but because of their greater availability and at reduced costs, factor analysis has been applied in many new areas and by many new workers. All this is reflected in the revised edition, but always with emphasis on the methodological aspects rather than the applications.

Important changes were introduced as a direct result of the impact of computers: certain classical methods of factor analysis are now obsolete. For example, the centroid method, for all its historical interest and importance, is a technique that has given way to the more mathematically sound principal-factor method made possible by the modern-day computer. By the same token, hand-computing techniques assume less importance in the present computer era, but their study has considerable heuristic value. In general, an eclectic approach is still favored in the book, but more attention is paid to the present-day relevance of the various methods and recommendations are made among the several alternatives.

While factor analysis was created and developed largely by psychologists, its usefulness as a statistical tool has much broader implications. It is in the latter sense that the subject is presented in this text. Psychological data are used for illustrative purposes, but no attempt is made to formulate new psychological theories. This book is intended to provide the student with the basis for a clear understanding of the concepts and techniques of factor analysis. He is then in a position to employ factor analysis as a statistical tool in developing theories in psychology or other disciplines.

Mathematical language is employed in order to present a precise, unambiguous picture—not for the sake of mere elegance, nor even for rigorous proof. Some proofs are given, some roughly indicated, some omitted entirely. Primarily, the work is an exposition and not a formal mathematical development. However, the mathematical language represents careful selection and is precise. It is the author's firm belief that a little effort on the part of the reader to grasp and to follow the notation will yield immeasurable rewards in understanding the subject.

I have been very gratified with the reception of *Modern Factor Analysis* over the past years. During this time I have listened intently to reviewers, correspondents, and colleagues. The revised edition takes cognizance of such suggestions and criticisms—improving, it is hoped, the presentation of the original material—and also introduces much new material.

I gratefully render due homage to the many individuals whose published researches have been drawn upon for the enrichment of these pages. I wish it were possible in every instance to assign credit where it is due, but in any event, I want to avoid claiming credit to myself for any development first made by another. It is a particular pleasure for me to acknowledge my debt to both Professor Holzinger and Professor Thurstone for my early development in the field of factor analysis.

Of course many of my thoughts on the foundation and basic mode of presenting the factor problem were incorporated in my joint work with Dr. Holzinger. I am indebted to the University of Chicago Press for permission to use portions of such work which first appeared in Holzinger and Harman, *Factor Analysis*.

Permission from John Wiley and Sons, Inc., to reprint material from my chapter, "Factor Analysis," in *Mathematical Methods for Digital Computers*, edited by Anthony Ralston and Herbert S. Wilf, is gratefully acknowledged. I am indebted to Professor Sir Ronald A. Fisher, F.R.S., Cambridge, and to Dr. Frank Yates, F.R.S., Rothamsted, also to Messrs. Oliver & Boyd Ltd., Edinburgh, for permission to reprint Table D in the Appendix, taken from their book *Statistical Tables for Biological, Agricultural and Medical Research*.

Portions of the manuscript have been read, and helpful suggestions made, by Dr. Edith S. Jay and Dr. John M. Leiman. Invaluable assistance was provided by Mr. Leonard W. Staugas in the application of electronic computers to the solution of many problems in the text. The drafting of the illustrations is largely due to Mr. Toshio Odano. Mr. Wayne H. Jones offered critical assistance and wise counsel on many occasions during the final preparation of this book. All of the foregoing were my colleagues at the System Development Corporation, and to each one I acknowledge indebtedness and deep appreciation.

I had the benefit of consultation with Professor John B. Carroll, Harvard University, Professor Henry F. Kaiser, University of Illinois, and Dr. David R. Saunders, Educational Testing Service, in regard to the analytical methods for the multiple-factor solution. In addition, Professor Kaiser gave me a critical appraisal of the first drafts of these chapters, and arranged for the calculation of several complex problems on the Illiac. Professor Carroll also read these chapters and provided me with the computer programs and his draft of the oblimin methods as soon as they were available in late 1958. It is a pleasure to acknowledge appreciation for this generous assistance.

Dr. Ardie Lubin, Walter Reed Army Institute of Research, provided stimulation and encouragement at the initiation of the work. While I may not have written the text along the lines of compact matrix algebra and precise statistical terms as Dr. Lubin would have liked to see it, nonetheless I am grateful for the many incisive discussions with him.

In the development of the second edition, I especially want to extend my thanks to Professor Robert I. Jennrich and my son, Alvin J. Harman, both of whom suggested a more consistent use of matrix notation and critically reviewed portions of the revised manuscript. Also, Dr. Jennrich made available to me draft copies of his paper and computer program, upon which the direct oblimin method is based.

In the attempt to keep up to date on the new developments in factor analysis, I have been aided materially by the stimulating and provocative discussions of the Factor Analysis Work Group, sponsored in part by the U.S. Office of Naval Research, during 1962–66. The regular members at the semiannual meetings of this group included L. R. Tucker, chairman, R. Bargmann, H. H. Harman, C. W. Harris, P. Horst, L. G. Humphreys, H. F. Kaiser, W. Meredith, and C. Wrigley, and visitors at specific meetings included L. Guttman, K. Jöreskog, and A. Madansky.

My sincere thanks are due Mr. Harry A. Liff for suggesting that the present work be undertaken and for his constant encouragement during the last two years of preparation of the manuscript.

Finally, I owe a special debt of gratitude to Margot von Mendelssohn for her tireless assistance in all phases of the preparation of the first edition and for her continued help in updating the bibliography and in the preparation of the manuscript for the second edition.

List of Illustrations

Guide to Notation

The text is organized to assist the reader in quickly locating any topic or displayed material. All items are tied to the chapter number. The primary subdivisions of chapters are sections—printed in boldface type and consisting of chapter number, period, and serial number of section within chapter, e.g., **10.4** for the fourth section in chapter 10. The mathematical equations, tables, and figures are similarly numbered within each chapter, but in ordinary type and with the equation number enclosed in parentheses. Examples of these are: equation (11.6), Table 11.2, Figure 5.1. In referring to a table or figure, the identifying word is always employed; but since equations are distinguished by parentheses, frequently the equation number is given without the words "equation" or "formula." References are given in author-date style: citations in the text are by name and year (in parentheses); the bibliography is in alphabetical order and year.

Definitions and symbols are introduced as necessary to clarify the presentation. For convenience, the locations of the principal sources of notation are indicated in the following table.

SUMMARIES OF NOTATION

Item	Page	Description
Eq. (2.20)	20	Symbols for composition of variance
Sec. **3.2**	34	Definitions of determinants and matrices
Sec. **3.2**, par. **8**	36	Notation for vectors, matrices, and determinants
Table 3.2	46	Square root method for calculating inverse of a matrix
Table 4.1	69	Geometric concepts
Table 6.1	108	Summary of factor methods
Eq. (7.8)	118	Set-theory notations
Table 10.1	201	Notation for matrices in statistical estimation of factor weights
Table 12.6	275	Notation in oblique solutions
Table 14.1	301	Concepts and notation for analytical multiple-factor solutions
Table 15.1	337	Concepts and notation for factor comparisons
Table 16.1	364	Notation for matrices frequently used

Part I

Foundations of Factor Analysis

1 Introduction

1.1. *Brief History of Factor Analysis*

Factor analysis is a branch of statistical science, but because of its development and extensive use in psychology the technique itself is often mistakenly considered as psychological theory. The method came into being specifically to provide mathematical models for the explanation of psychological theories of human ability and behavior. Among the more famous of such theories are those proposed by Spearman, Burt, Kelley, Thurstone, Holzinger, and Thomson.

The origin of factor analysis is generally ascribed to Charles Spearman. His monumental work in developing a psychological theory involving a single general factor and a number of specific factors goes back to 1904 when his paper "General Intelligence, Objectively Determined and Measured" was published in the *American Journal of Psychology*. Of course, his 1904 investigation was only the beginning of his work in developing the Two-Factor Theory, and his early work is not explicitly in terms of "factors." Perhaps a more crucial article, certainly insofar as the statistical aspects are concerned, is the paper by Karl Pearson (1901) in which he sets forth "the method of principal axes." Nevertheless, Spearman, who devoted the remaining forty years of his life to the development of factor analysis, is regarded as the father of the subject.

A considerable amount of work on the psychological theories and mathematical foundations of factor analysis followed in the next twenty years. The principal contributors during this period included Charles Spearman, Cyril Burt, Karl Pearson, Godfrey H. Thomson, J. C. Maxwell Garnett, and Karl Holzinger; the topics receiving the greatest attention were attempts to prove or disprove the existence of general ability, the study of sampling errors of tetrad differences, and computational methods for a single general factor which included the fundamental formula of the centroid method. An expository account of the early history of factor analysis in psychological research, from a British perspective, is given by Burt (1966).

The early modern period, including the bulk of the active and published controversy on factor analysis, came after 1925, with a real spurt of activity in the 1930s. By this time it had become quite apparent that Spearman's Two-Factor Theory was not always adequate to describe a battery of psychological tests. So group factors found their way into factor analysis; although the experimenters, at first, were very reluctant to admit such deviation from the basic theory and restricted the group factors to as small a number as possible. What actually happened was that the *theory* of a general and specific factors in Spearman's original form was superseded by theories of many group factors, but the early *method* continued to be employed to determine these many factors. Then it naturally followed that some workers explored the possibility of extracting several factors directly from a matrix of correlations among tests, and thus arose the concept of multiple-factor analysis in the work of Garnett (1919).

While the actual term may be attributed to L. L. Thurstone, and while he undoubtedly has done most to popularize the method of multiple-factor analysis, he certainly was not the first to take exception to Spearman's Two-Factor Theory and was not the first to develop a theory of many factors. It is not even the centroid method of analysis (see sec. **8.8**) for which Thurstone deserves a place of prominence in factor analysis. The centroid method is clearly admitted by Thurstone to be a computational compromise for the principal-factor method. The truly remarkable contribution of Thurstone was the generalization of Spearman's tetrad-difference criterion to the *rank* of the correlation matrix as the basis for determining the number of common factors (see **4.10** and chap. 5). He saw that a zero tetrad-difference corresponded to the vanishing of a second-order determinant, and extended this notion to the vanishing of higher order determinants as the condition for more than a single factor. The matrix formulation of the problem has greatly facilitated further advances in factor analysis.

The mathematical techniques inherent in factor analysis certainly are not limited to psychological applications. The principal concern of factor analysis is the resolution of a set of variables linearly in terms of (usually) a small number of categories or "factors." This resolution can be accomplished by the analysis of the correlations among the variables. A satisfactory solution will yield factors which convey all the essential information of the original set of variables. Thus, the chief aim is to attain scientific parsimony or economy of description.

As will become evident in the course of this text, a given matrix of correlations can be factored in an infinite number of ways. (It is not entirely clear whether this well-known fact was truly appreciated in the earlier days of factor analysis; and if, in fact, the failure to recognize this mathematical truism may not have been the cause of the many controversies regarding the "true," the "best," or the "invariant" solution for a set of variables.) When an infinite number of equally accurate solutions are available, the question arises: How shall a choice be made among these possibilities? The preferred types of factor solutions are determined on the basis of two general principles: (1) statistical simplicity, and (2) scientific meaningfulness. In turn, each of these requires interpretation, and each has been applied variously to yield several distinct schools of factor analysts.

If one were to make a choice entirely upon statistical considerations, a rather natural approach would be to represent the original set of variables in terms of a number of factors, determined in sequence so that at each successive stage the factor would account for a maximum of the variance. This statistically optimal solution—the method of principal axes discussed in chapter 8—was first proposed by Pearson at the turn of the century, and in the 1930s Hotelling provided the full development of the method. While this procedure is perfectly straightforward, it entails a very considerable amount of computation, and was impractical for a matrix of order 10 or greater in the days before the high-speed electronic computer.

Another choice based upon statistical considerations is the centroid method. As indicated above, this method was introduced only as a computational expedient when it was apparent that the principal-factor method was too laborious. All that can be said for the centroid method is that it produces without much arithmetic one of many possible sets of axes which account for the variance in a manner approximating the optimal situation of the principal axes.

The end product of these methods—principal or centroid—would not be acceptable to subject-matter specialists. In particular, psychologists have introduced various theories in the hope of arriving at a form of solution which would be meaningful, unique, and apply equally well to intelligence, personality, physical measurements, and any other variables with which they might be concerned. Holzinger's Bi-Factor Theory and Thurstone's Simple Structure Theory are in this class. On the other hand, Thomson's Sampling Theory (1951, chaps. 3 and 20) is primarily a psychological theory of the mind. There is no preferred factor method that leads uniquely to a solution on grounds of psychological significance (see **6.2** and **11.4**). If scientific meaningfulness rather than a mathematical standard is imposed, then the judgment of the investigator must be invoked. The progress that has been made toward objective solutions to this problem is presented in chapters 13, 14, and 15.

As pointed out above, a principal objective of factor analysis is to attain a parsimonious description of observed data. This aim should not be construed to mean that factor analysis necessarily attempts to discover the "fundamental" or "basic" categories in a given field of investigation such as psychology. It might be desirable to base such an analysis upon a set of variables which measures all possible mental aspects of a given population as completely and accurately as possible. Even in such a case, however, the factors would not be completely fundamental because of the omission of important measures which were not yet devised. While the goal of complete description cannot be reached theoretically, it may be approached practically in a limited field of investigation where a relatively small number of variables is considered exhaustive. In all cases, however, factor analysis does give a simple interpretation of a given body of data and thus affords a fundamental description of the particular set of variables analyzed.

The essential purpose of factor analysis has been well expressed by Kelley (1940, p. 120): "There is no search for timeless, spaceless, populationless truth in factor analysis; rather, it represents a simple, straightforward problem of description in several dimensions of a definite group functioning in definite manners, and he who assumes to read more remote verities into the factorial outcome is certainly doomed to disappointment." This statement was made at a time when factor analysis was perceived as a kind of mystique among many psychologists. Now such admonition is hardly necessary—it is generally conceded that, traditionally, factor analysis serves primarily as an exploratory device. The investigator certainly may have some ideas about the interrelations among a set of manifest variables and the probable latent variables (factors) that might appear, but is prepared to find unexpected factors on occasion.

The methodology of this text—"exploratory" factor analysis—may be useful in formulating theories in the behavioral and social sciences, but the "analytical tools" (including factor analysis) should not be confused with the "science." As an exploratory tool (among others), factor analysis can be used to verify or modify theories through new experiments and new data subjected to fresh analyses for purposes of clarifying or polishing previous formulations. By contrast, "confirmatory" factor analysis may be used to check or test a preconceived or given hypothesis about the structure of empirical data. One aspect of the latter approach is treated in **15.5**. For some of the original development of confirmatory factor analysis see Bock and Bargmann (1966) and Jöreskog (1969b), and for a detailed summary see Muliak (1972, pp. 361–401).

1.2. *Applications of Factor Analysis*

The application of factor-analysis techniques has been chiefly in the field of psychology. This limitation has no foundation other than the fact that it had its origin in psychology and that accounts of the subject have tended to be ". . . so bound up with the psychological conception of mental factors that an ordinary statistician has difficulty in seeing it in a proper setting in relation to the general body of statistical method" (Kendall and Babington-Smith 1950, p. 60). One objective of this book is to correct this situation.

The methods of factor analysis may lead to some theory suggested by the form of the solution, and conversely one may formulate a theory and verify it by an appropriate form of factorial solution. The latter approach is illustrated by Spearman's theory *"all branches of intellectual activity have in common one fundamental function (or group of functions) whereas the remaining or specific elements of the activity seem in every case to be wholly different from that in all others"* (Spearman 1904, p. 202). He showed that if certain relationships (the tetrads defined in **5.3**) exist among the correlations, all the variables can be resolved into linear expressions involving only one general factor and an additional factor unique to each variable. These relationships furnish the statistical verification of the "Two-Factor Theory." If a set of psychological variables yields correlation coefficients which do not satisfy the preceding relationships, then a more complex theory may be postulated. This may require several common factors in the statistical description of the variables.

One of the earliest proposals for broadening the psychological uses of factor analysis (Kelley 1940b) involves a method for attaining the greatest social utility while at the same time preserving individual liberties and rights. Then during World War II, with the large-scale testing, classification, and assignment problems, factor analysis was employed widely throughout the several branches of the military services of the United States. Psychologists, of course, have continued to develop and exploit the technique to the present day.

Many psychologists have engaged in extensive testing programs, employing factor analysis to determine a relatively small number of tests to describe the human mind as completely as possible. The usual approach includes the factor analysis of a large battery of tests in order to identify a few common factors. Then the tests which best measure these factors, or, preferably, revised tests based upon these, may be selected as direct measures of the "factors of mind." However, only to the extent to which psychologists agree that the tests selected are the "right tests" can they be said to be actual measures of the factors. Such "factor tests" should be of a "pure" nature, differing widely from one another so as to cover the entire range of mental activity. Several major studies have been undertaken to identify factors from large sets of tests. Among the early studies of this type are the Spearman-Holzinger unitary trait investigation (Holzinger 1936) and Thurstone's primary mental abilities study (Thurstone 1938b). More recent broad attempts to identify and classify psychological factors include a general structure of intellect (Guilford 1956), a major study of personality (Cattell, Eber, and Tatsuoka 1970), a structure of concept attainment abilities (Harris and Harris 1973), a theory of individuality (Royce 1973), and a guide to factor-referenced cognitive tests and temperament scales (Harman et al. 1975). Of course, applications of factor analysis to the identification of specific psychological factors in a particular investigation are very numerous and the reader is referred to such journals as *Behavioral Science, British Journal of Mathematical and Statistical Psychology, Educational and Psychological Measurement,* and *Multivariate Behavioral Research.* (Articles reporting factor analytical results of applied studies are no longer published in *Psychometrika.*)

Applications of factor analysis in fields other than psychology have become very popular since 1950, along with the ready accessibility of the computer. These fields include such varied disciplines as meteorology and medicine, political science and taxonomy, archaeology and economics, sociology and regional science. Also, there are many individual studies that are difficult to assign to a particular discipline. While it is not the intent here to go into any detail on the many areas of application of factor analysis, it may be of some interest to note some of the newer ones. A sampling from more than two hundred such studies that the author has been collecting will give some idea of the breadth of applications.

Economics: Evaluating the performance of systems (Burch 1972); Investment decisions under uncertainty (Farrar 1962); Latent structure of security price changes (King 1964); Economic equation systems employing principal components (Kloek and Mennes 1960).

Medicine: Studies in allergy (Andrews 1948); Cardiovascular studies (Cady et al. 1961, 1964; Christian, Kropf, and Kurth 1964; Cureton and Sterling 1964; Horan, Flowers, and Brody 1964); Analyses of the electrocardiogram and the electroencephalogram (Scher, Young, and Meredith 1960; Elmgren and Löwenhard 1969); Diagnosis and classification (Overall and Williams 1961; Overall and Hollister 1964; Petrinow and Hardyck 1964).

Physical sciences: Factor analysis of heavy-mineral data (Imbrie and van Andel 1964); Geological maps (Krumbein and Imbrie 1963); Predictions in meteorology (Aubert, Lund, and Thomasell 1959).

Political science and sociology: Relationships between social and political variables and GNP (Adelman and Morris 1966); Studies of the Supreme Court and the

General Assembly (Schubert 1962; Alker 1964); Dimensions of nations (Rummel, Sawyer, Guetzkow, and Tanter 1968; Tanter 1964); A study of international fellows (Gullahorn 1967); Analyses of sociometric data (Macrae 1960; Peterson, Komorita, and Quay 1964).

Regional science: Structure and economic development of urban areas (Berry 1961, 1962; Berry and Rees 1969; Gittus 1964; Hattori, Kagaya, and Inanaga 1960; Schnorre 1961; Kilchenmann 1970); Dimensions of American local governments (Burns and Harman 1966; Wood 1961).

Taxonomic applications: Classification system for psychological reports (Borko 1965); Biological classification (Rohlf 1965; Rohlf and Sokal 1962; Sokal 1956; Sokal and Sneath 1963); Classification of yeasts (Harman 1972).

Miscellaneous applications: Analytical techniques in archaeology (Redman 1973); Assessments of buildings by architects and nonarchitects (Canter and Wools 1970); Study of lightplane accidents (Gregg and Pearson 1961); Man-machine systems and human engineering (Sackman and Munson 1964; Topmiller 1964); Acoustics and communication (Voiers 1964; Westley and Jacobson 1962).

Unlike the field of psychology, in which theory has been primary and the factor analytic model has been used to test and modify such theory, the application of factor analysis in the areas noted has been exploratory, almost exclusively, in the hope of bringing order out of the relationships among the many variables that could now be investigated with the aid of the computer. A caution to the practitioner is in order here; there is no substitute for understanding, at least in principle, what is going on in the analysis of a body of data if the objective is to draw meaningful conclusions in a particular field of application. The applied scientist does not have to be an expert in the methodology of factor analysis, but should not expect the computer to make the important decisions that may be necessary in drawing inferences from the computer output either for practical action or for formulation of scientific theory or its revision. Such a person should request computer output and study it for certain expectations and leads on deviations or aberrations from the expected for possible modifications or extensions of preconceived order or structure.

While the present text is concerned primarily with the exposition of various procedures in factor analysis, numerous examples are employed for illustrative purposes. Some examples are hypothetical, but most of them are taken from psychology and the social sciences. These examples serve to clarify the theoretical treatment only, not to exhibit the practical usefulness of factor analysis.

1.3. *Scientific Explanation and Choice*

Factor analysis, like all statistics, is a branch of applied mathematics. Thus, it is used as a tool in the empirical sciences. In dealing with observed data, of course, there are inherent discrepancies. One of the objectives of statistical theory is to provide a scientific law, or mathematical model, to explain the underlying behavior of the data. Some simple examples include: (1) a linear regression for the prediction of school success from three entrance examinations; (2) a mathematical curve, such as the normal distribution or one of the Pearson family of curves, for the explanation of an observed frequency distribution; (3) a chi-square test of significance for the independence of such classifications as "treated or not treated with a certain serum," and "cured or not cured." Such laws make allowance for random variations of the observed data from the theoretically expected values. It is conceivable that any one of several, quite different, mathematical models may provide an equally good fit or explanation of a set of data.

In general, science is concerned with the establishment of laws regarding the behavior of empirical events or elements in the particular field. Such laws—usually expressed as mathematical functions—serve to relate the knowledge about the known elements and to provide reliable predictions about future elements. The standard procedure in developing a scientific theory involves the formulation of a mathematical law on the basis of some observations (with discrepancies), followed by the verification of the particular mathematical model with new observations. For any problem in an applied science there may be a number of mathematical theories which explain the phenomena in a satisfactory manner. A misunderstanding of the relationship between a mathematical model and observed data is frequently encountered. When a theory has been successfully employed in explaining a set of data, there is a tendency to accept this law as the only correct one for explaining the observations.

> Furthermore, it is sometimes inferred that nature behaves in precisely the way which the mathematics indicates. As a matter of fact, nature never does behave in this way, and there are *always more mathematical theories than one* whose results depart from a given set of data by less than the errors of observation.
>
> . . . .
>
> The danger is always when a theory has been found to be convenient and effective over a long period of time, that people begin to think that nature herself behaves precisely in the way which is indicated by the theory. This is never the case, and the belief that it is so may close our minds to other possible theories and be a serious impedience to progress in the development of our interpretations of the world around us (Bliss 1933, pp. 472, 477, author's italics).

The above observations apply equally well in different fields. One of the simplest cases arises in the problem of surveying a small tract of land. For this purpose either of two mathematical theories, plane or spherical trigonometry, may be applied. Thus, in surveying a city lot the result by either theory would be equally satisfactory, and the engineer would prefer the plane theory because of its greater simplicity. In this instance, however, there is no doubt as to the greater accuracy of the spherical theory since the earth is essentially spherical.

In the field of astronomy there are two common theories describing the solar system. The Ptolemaic and Copernican theories, with suitable modification of the former, describe the motions of the planets with equal accuracy. "There is really no advantage for either of these theories as compared with the other, as far as their adaptability to explain numerically the facts of the solar system is concerned. The Copernican theory is, however, much the simpler geometrically and mathematically. For this reason it has been adapted and developed until astronomers can predict coming celestial events with most surprising accuracy" (Bliss 1933, pp. 477–8).

Even the subject of geometry, which might seem to depend on a unique mathematical theory, can be described by means of many different theories. Thus, the physical configurations in a plane can be interpreted in the light of Euclidean geometry, Riemannian geometry, or various other types of non-Euclidean geometry. Therefore, the applied science of geometry can have several alternative theories as its basis.

As in the foregoing illustrations there are different models, or forms of solution, which may arise in the factorial analysis of a particular set of data. The usefulness of factor analysis as a scientific tool has been questioned by some workers because of this indeterminacy. It should be evident, however, that this is tantamount to indicting all applied sciences because they do not depend upon unique theories.

Since the beginning of this century, psychologists and statisticians have developed several types of factorial solutions. The proponent of each system of analysis has urged its suitability for the interpretation of psychological data. The strong feelings and emotions that characterized one period in the development of factor analysis have been described wittily by Cureton (1939, p. 287):

> Factor theory may be defined as a mathematical rationalization. A factor-analyst is an individual with a peculiar obsession regarding the nature of mental ability or personality. By the application of higher mathematics to wishful thinking, he always proves that his original fixed idea or compulsion was right or necessary. In the process he usually proves that all other factor-analysts are dangerously insane, and that the only salvation for them is to undergo his own brand of analysis in order that the true essence of their several maladies may be discovered. Since they never submit to this indignity, he classes them all as hopeless cases, and searches about for some branch of mathematics which none of them is likely to have studied in order to prove that their incurability is not only necessary but also sufficient.

The heated and inspired controversies about the "best" method of factor analysis are over—Charles Spearman (1863–1945), L. L. Thurstone (1887–1955), Karl J. Holzinger (1893–1954) have all passed from the scene. It is not a personal controversy that is implied here, but rather the strong conviction of each individual who had devoted a major part of his life to the development of a particular school of thought in factor analysis. The many papers that appeared during the thirties and forties urging "this method" rather than "that method" had their place in the growth of the subject. However, with a fuller understanding of the salient features of each method, and with the increased efficiency of computations, the differences among the various methods no longer loom so ominously, and the followers of a particular approach are much more tolerant of the adherents of an alternative scheme.

It should be evident that the different factorial methods correspond to the different mathematical theories in the explanation of a particular scientific problem. Several preferred forms of solution are enumerated (see chap. 6), before the detailed presentation of the factor analysis theory and computing procedures. From such statements of the salient features of the preferred types, the researcher may weigh the advantages and limitations of any particular solution for his particular data.

It is the sincere hope of the author that the present book will provide a better understanding of apparently competing methods of factor analysis. By bringing the several methods under proper focus, an unbiased decision regarding the appropriateness of any one of them should be possible.

2   Factor Analysis Model

2.1. *Introduction*

As noted in the preceding section, one of the first tasks confronting anyone who is concerned with the analysis of a body of observed data is the formulation of some kind of theoretical statistical model. Sometimes this fundamental step is overlooked or only tacitly implied. In any event, a particular model must be acknowledged if any inference is to be made about the observed data. Of course, there are many different models for observed data depending on the purpose of the analysis. Because of the inherent desire of scientists to explain observed phenomena in terms of elegant (i.e., simple) theories, and because the mathematical development might otherwise become frightfully complex, a linear model is frequently assumed. That is a basic assumption made throughout this book. The generalizations that might ensue from the removal of the linear constraint are indicated by Bartlett (1953), McDonald (1967), and Wood (1964).

The fundamental statistical concepts and notation required in factor analysis are set forth in **2.2**. This is followed by the linear models employed in factor analysis. The variance composition of a variable, attributable to the different types of factors postulated in the model, is presented in **2.4**. Again, some of the basic terms are delineated and clearly defined. The factor problem is then presented in **2.5**, where the elements to be determined by the analysis are identified. Some comments on the type of correlations used in factor analysis are presented in **2.6**. Then the degree of fit of the factor model to the observed data is considered in **2.7**, and the indeterminacy of factor solutions is explained in **2.8**. Finally, in **2.9** many of the preceding concepts are put in much more compact form by the use of matrix notation.

2.2. *Basic Statistics*

A statistical study typically involves a group of individuals with some common attributes. The term "individual" is used here in a generic sense to stand for such objects or entities as persons, census tracts, businesses, etc. Measurements made on such individuals, or attributes of these entities, are designated simply as *variables*.

11

Throughout this text the letter N is used for the total number of individuals, and the letter n for the number of variables. A particular variable is denoted by X_j, or simply j, which may be any one of the n variables: $1, 2, 3, \ldots, n$. The index i is employed to designate any one of the N individuals: $1, 2, 3, \ldots, N$. Then, the value of a variable X_j for individual i is represented by X_{ji}, the order of the subscripts being of importance. A particular X_{ji} is called an *observed value* which is measured from an arbitrary origin and by an arbitrary unit.

It is customary in statistical literature to employ Greek letters to denote population parameters (and hypothetical or latent variables) and corresponding Latin letters to indicate simple observations of these variables. Also, to indicate a sample *estimate* of a population parameter, the latter symbol is modified by placing a caret (^) over it. To the extent that it is convenient, and does not violate long established practice in factor analysis, such notation will be followed in this text.

Some simple statistical concepts are presented here for ready reference. Frequent use is made of the sum of the N values for a variable X_j, namely:

$$(2.1) \qquad \sum_{i=1}^{N} X_{ji} \quad \text{or} \quad \sum X_{ji},$$

where, in the second expression, the summation is understood to be over all values of the variable. This convention for the summation with respect to the number of observations of a particular variable will be observed throughout the text. Furthermore, the index i will be reserved explicitly to refer to the individuals, that is, for the range 1 to N.

For a sample of N observations, the *mean* of any variable is defined by

$$(2.2) \qquad \overline{X}_j = \sum X_{ji}/N.$$

The n population means would be designated μ_j if they were required in any theoretical development. The observed values of the variables may be transformed to more convenient form by fixing the origin and the unit of measurement. When the origin is placed at the sample mean, a particular value

$$(2.3) \qquad x_{ji} = X_{ji} - \overline{X}_j$$

is called a *deviate*.

The *sample* variance[1] of variable X_j is defined by

$$(2.4) \qquad s_j^2 = \sum x_{ji}^2/N.$$

The population variances are denoted by σ_j^2. Now, taking the sample standard deviation as the unit of measurement, the *standard deviate* of variable j for individual i is given by

$$(2.5) \qquad z_{ji} = x_{ji}/s_j.$$

---

[1]It should be noted that the sample value of the variance is a biased estimate of the population variance from a normal distribution, but multiplication by $N/(N-1)$ makes it unbiased.

The set of all values z_{ji} ($i = 1, 2, \ldots, N$) is called a variable z_j in *standard form*. Obviously the variance of z_j is unity. It will be found convenient in the later development to define the *small standard deviate* as

$$z_{ji}^* = z_{ji}/\sqrt{N}.$$

For any two variables j and k the sample *covariance* is defined by

$$(2.6) \qquad s_{jk} = \sum x_{ji}x_{ki}/N,$$

and the corresponding population parameter is designated σ_{jk}. The *correlation coefficient* in the universe is ρ_{jk} and in the sample is defined by

$$(2.7) \qquad r_{jk} = s_{jk}/s_j s_k = \sum x_{ji}x_{ki}\Big/\sqrt{\sum x_{ji}^2 \sum x_{ki}^2} = \sum z_{ji}z_{ki}/N = \sum z_{ji}^* z_{ki}^*.$$

The correlations among all the variables of a study are usually computed as the initial step in a factor analysis.

In order to provide concrete illustrations of some of the basic statistics, a very simple numerical example is now introduced. The same example will be used throughout the text to demonstrate the various features of factor analysis. Only $N = 12$ individuals and $n = 5$ variables are considered in order to bring out all aspects of factor analysis, while at the same time keeping the computation at a minimum. While artificial data might have been contrived to yield exact mathematical solutions, it was deemed more advisable to use objective, fallible data, even though most of the standards regarding experimental design, sampling, and reliability are obviously ignored. So, while the data are "real," the results are not intended to have any real substantive value but merely to illustrate the methods, and perhaps to provide a convenient numerical problem for checking of computer programs.

With this understanding, the data in Table 2.1 were taken (not entirely arbitrarily) from a study of the Los Angeles Standard Metropolitan Statistical Area. The twelve individuals used in the example are census tracts—small areal subdivisions of Los Angeles. A full-scale factor analysis of sixty-seven variables (in percentage form rather than actual values to allow for greater comparability) and 1,169 census tracts is reported by Burns and Harman (1968). The study was designed to include groups of variables involving population, employment, income, and housing characteristics, and these are represented in the little example. From the raw data, the correlations among the five variables were computed as the initial step toward subsequent factor analysis work. These correlations are shown in Table 2.2.[2] While the calculation of the correlations is singled out as a separate step, it is done so only for ease of presentation. Nowadays, when large electronic computers are quite readily available for factor analysis work, the determination of the correlations is a trivial step in the computer process going from the raw data to the final solution. As this example is used again and again in the text, the thread will be picked up from the correlations to the next phase and subsequent ones.

[2]The only reason for showing five decimal places (as output from a computer) is to provide a means for checking numerical calculations.

Table 2.1

Raw Data for Five Socio-Economic Variables

Individual (Tract No.) i	Variable				
	Total Popula-tion 1	Median School Years 2	Total Employ-ment 3	Misc. Professional Services 4	Median Value House 5
1 (1439)	5,700	12.8	2,500	270	25,000
2 (2078)	1,000	10.9	600	10	10,000
3 (2408)	3,400	8.8	1,000	10	9,000
4 (2621)	3,800	13.6	1,700	140	25,000
5 (7007)	4,000	12.8	1,600	140	25,000
6 (5312)	8,200	8.3	2,600	60	12,000
7 (6032)	1,200	11.4	400	10	16,000
8 (6206)	9,100	11.5	3,300	60	14,000
9 (4037)	9,900	12.5	3,400	180	18,000
10 (4605)	9,600	13.7	3,600	390	25,000
11 (5323)	9,600	9.6	3,300	80	12,000
12 (5416)	9,400	11.4	4,000	100	13,000
Mean	6,242	11.4	2,333	121	17,000
Standard deviation	3,440	1.8	1,241	115	6,368

Table 2.2

Correlations among Five Socio-Economic Variables

Variable j	1	2	3	4	5
1. Total population	1.00000	.00975	.97245	.43887	.02241
2. Median school years	.00975	1.00000	.15428	.69141	.86307
3. Total employment	.97245	.15428	1.00000	.51472	.12193
4. Misc. profess. services	.43887	.69141	.51472	1.00000	.77765
5. Median value house	.02241	.86307	.12193	.77765	1.00000

2.3. *Linear Models*

It is the object of factor analysis to represent a variable z_j in terms of several underlying *factors*, or hypothetical constructs. The simplest mathematical model for describing a variable in terms of several others is a linear one, and that is the form of representation employed here. However, there are still several alternatives within the linear framework, depending on the objective of the analysis. A distinction between two objectives can be made immediately, namely: (1) to extract the maximum variance; and (2) to "best" reproduce the observed correlations.

An empirical method for the reduction of a large body of data so that a maximum of the variance is extracted was first proposed by Karl Pearson (1901) and fully developed as the method of *principal components*, or *component analysis*, by Harold

14

Hotelling (1933). The model for component analysis is simply:

$$(2.8) \qquad z_j = a_{j1}F_1 + a_{j2}F_2 + \cdots + a_{jn}F_n \qquad (j = 1, 2, \cdots, n),$$

where each of the n observed variables is described linearly in terms of n new uncorrelated components $F_1, F_2, \cdots, F_n$. An important property of this method, insofar as the summarization of data is concerned, is that each component, in turn, makes a maximum contribution to the sum of the variances of the n variables. For a practical problem only a few components may be retained, especially if they account for a large percentage of the total variance. However, all the components are required to reproduce the correlations among the variables.

In contrast to the maximum variance approach, the *traditional*, or *classical factor analysis* model is designed to maximally reproduce the correlations (various methods for accomplishing this are the subject of a large portion of this book). The basic factor analysis model may be put in the form:

$$(2.9) \qquad z_j = a_{j1}F_1 + a_{j2}F_2 + \cdots + a_{jm}F_m + u_jY_j \qquad (j = 1, 2, \cdots, n),$$

where each of the n observed variables is described linearly in terms of m (usually much smaller than n) *common factors* and a *unique factor*. The common factors account for the correlations among the variables, while each unique factor accounts for the remaining variance (including error) of that variable. The coefficients of the factors are frequently referred to as "loadings."

To call attention to the fact that the expression (2.9) is a mathematical model of the observed variable, it is sometimes designated by $\hat{z}_j$. For simplicity the "hat" will usually be omitted in the theoretical expression for the variable. Furthermore, if one wanted to be precise, as regards statistical notation, the symbols for the factors and their coefficients should be Greek letters since they are in the nature of population parameters and can only be inferred from the observed data. However, the notation of (2.9) is so well established in the factor analysis literature[3] that it was demed wiser not to change it. Of course, the a's and F's are generally used symbols and imply no relationships between the two models (2.8) and (2.9).

The classical factor analysis model (2.9) may be written explicitly for the value of variable j for individual i as follows:

$$(2.10) \qquad z_{ji} = \sum_{p=1}^{m} a_{jp}F_{pi} + u_jY_{ji} \qquad (i = 1, 2, \cdots, N; j = 1, 2, \cdots, n).$$

In this expression F_{pi} is the value of a common factor p for an individual i, and each of the m terms $a_{jp}F_{pi}$ represents the contribution of the corresponding factor to the linear composite, while u_jY_{ji} is the "residual error" in the theoretical representation of the observed measurement z_{ji}.

Without any loss of generality, it can be assumed that the F's and Y's have zero means and unit variances, since they are unknown in practice. Furthermore, the n unique factors are supposed to be independent of one another and also independent of the m common factors. In model (2.9) the F's are considered statistical variates or

---

[3] The only exception occurs in the mathematical-statistical contributions to factor analysis.

random variables, defined by a probability density function which, for certain purposes, is taken to be normal. When the factors are assumed to be independent normal variates, it follows that the z's have a multivariate normal distribution (discussed further in chap. 10).

While the statement of the factor analysis model in (2.10) makes explicit the values of the factors, usually they must be estimated indirectly, as explained in chapter 16. There is another model which overtly is like (2.10), but with the important difference that the factor values F_{pi} are treated as parameters to be estimated directly, along with the factor loadings. It appears to have certain desirable features, but also many unresolved problems. This model, which is investigated by Anderson and Rubin (1956), Whittle (1952), and Jöreskog (1963) will not be developed in this text. However, some of the methods presented in chapter 11 involve the theoretical values of the factors themselves in the course of getting the factor loadings.

The model of primary interest is (2.9), with the basic problem of factor analysis being the estimation of the nm loadings of the common factors. Various methods are available for accomplishing this and are developed in detail in the chapters following the foundations set forth in part I. Throughout this text, the variables are standardized and the correlations among them are employed in the calculations of the factor loadings. Some attempts have been made to estimate the factor loadings directly from the observed values of the variables rather than their covariances or correlations—for example, Holzinger (1944), Saunders (1950), Whittle (1952), Young (1941)—but such procedures are not considered here. It should be apparent that the factor analysis model bears a strong resemblance to that of regression analysis insofar as a variable is described as a linear combination of another set of variables plus a residual. However, in regression analysis the set of independent variables are observable while in factor analysis they are hypothetical constructs which can only be estimated from the observed data. Finally, the factors themselves are estimated in a subsequent stage of the analysis (see chap. 16).

A look at some numerical results may be useful in providing a general appreciation for the two basic models; a fuller understanding, of course, must await the orderly development of many concepts. For the five socio-economic variables, a components analysis according to model (2.8) produces for the "median school years" variable, say,

$$z_2 = .767P_1 - .545P_2 + .319P_3 + .112P_4 - .022P_5,$$

with similar equations for the other four variables (see Table 8.1). The five principal components are designated by P's instead of F's. While the full analysis leads to five principal components, almost any investigator would be satisfied with the analysis into only the first two components since they account for more than 93 percent of the total variance. Nonetheless, that is not the same as a classical factor analysis, according to model (2.9), into two common factors. In the latter case, the second variable of the example is described as follows:

$$z_2 = .701F_1 - .522F_2 + .486Y_2,$$

with equations for the other four variables being similar, involving the same two common factors (F_1 and F_2) but a different unique factor in each case (see Table 9.1).

16

For this simple problem the actual differences between the two models, insofar as the coefficients of the first two principal components and the two common factors are concerned, may appear to be trivial; and indeed they are. What is important to note is that, in the first instance, the model describes an observed variable entirely in terms of principal components (even if only two are retained for practical reasons); while in the second instance, the theoretical model calls for two different types of factors (the two common factors among all the variables and the five unique factors, one for each of the variables). To provide an intuitive feeling for the results of a factor analysis, the five variables are represented by points in the plane of the two common factors F_1 and F_2 in Figure 2.1. Also indicated here is how the variables might be interpreted

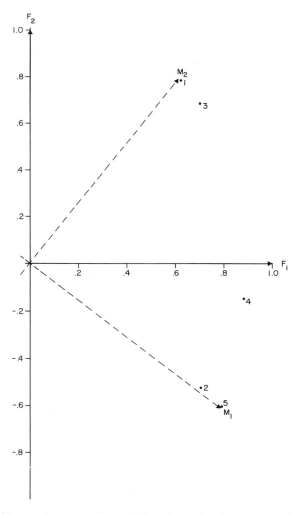

Fɪɢ. 2.1—Five socio-economic variables shown in the common factor space

in terms of two alternative factors M_1 and M_2, which might be more meaningful in the socio-economic study, even though it was not designed as a "true" study but only serves as a numerical illustration of the methodology.

2.4.   *Composition of Variance*

The variance of a variable may be expressed in terms of the factors according to the model of the preceding section. Thus, applying the definition (2.4) to the model (2.10) of z_j yields:

$$s_j^2 = \sum z_{ji}^2/N = \sum_{p=1}^{m} a_{jp}^2 \left(\sum F_{pi}^2/N \right) + u_j^2 \sum Y_{ji}^2/N$$

$$+ 2 \sum_{p<q=1}^{m} a_{jp}a_{jq} \left(\sum F_{pi}F_{qi}/N \right) + 2u_j \sum_{p=1}^{m} a_{jp} \left(\sum F_{pi}Y_{ji}/N \right),$$

where, it will be remembered, the sums without an indicated index are on i from 1 to N. Now, since the variance of a variable in standard form is equal to unity, and all variables (including the factors) are assumed to be in standard form for any sample, the last equation may be written

(2.11) $$s_j^2 = 1 = \sum_{p=1}^{m} a_{jp}^2 + u_j^2 + 2 \sum_{p<q=1}^{m} a_{jp}a_{jq} r_{F_p F_q} + 2u_j \sum_{p=1}^{m} a_{jp} r_{F_p Y_j}.$$

The unique factors are always uncorrelated with the common factors, and if the common factors are uncorrelated[4] among themselves, then the expression (2.11) simplifies to

(2.12) $$s_j^2 = 1 = a_{j1}^2 + a_{j2}^2 + \cdots + a_{jm}^2 + u_j^2.$$

The terms on the right represent the portions of the unit variance of z_j ascribable to the respective factors. For example, a_{j2}^2 is the contribution of the factor F_2 to the variance of z_j. The *total contribution* of a factor F_p to the variance of all the variables is defined to be

(2.13) $$V_p = \sum_{j=1}^{n} a_{jp}^2 \qquad (p = 1, 2, \cdots, m),$$

and the total contribution of all the common factors to the total variance of all the variables is given by

(2.14) $$V = \sum_{p=1}^{m} V_p.$$

The ratio V/n is sometimes employed as an indicator of the completeness of the factor analysis.

[4]The case of correlated factors is treated in detail in chaps. 12 and 14.

From the composition of the total unit variance as expressed by (2.12), two important concepts in factor analysis follow: (1) the *communality* of a variable z_j, which is given by the sum of the squares of the common-factor coefficients, viz.,

$$(2.15) \qquad h_j^2 = a_{j1}^2 + a_{j2}^2 + \cdots + a_{jm}^2 \qquad (j = 1, 2, \cdots, n),$$

and (2) the *uniqueness*, which is the contribution of the unique factor. The latter indicates the extent to which the common factors fail to account for the total unit variance of the variable. Sometimes it is convenient to separate the uniqueness of a variable into two portions of variance—that due to the particular selection of variables in the study and that due to unreliability of measurement. If additional variables were added to a given set, their correlations with the original variables might necessitate the postulation of further common factors. However, any such potential linkages of a given variable can only be expressed as a portion of its uniqueness in the study with the original set of variables. This portion of the uniqueness is termed the *specificity* of the variable. The remaining portion, due to imperfections of measurement, is the *error variance* or *unreliability* of the variable. The complement of the error variance is sometimes called the "reliability" of the variable. In psychology, this systematic component of the variable (as distinguished from error components) is usually measured by the correlation between two separate administrations of the same test, or parallel forms of the test. Two such representations of a variable may be denoted z_j and z_J, and their correlation r_{jJ} is then the measure of the reliability of the variable.

When the unique factors are decomposed into the two types described above, the linear model (2.9) for any variable may be written in the form

$$(2.16) \qquad z_j = a_{j1} F_1 + a_{j2} F_2 + \cdots + a_{jm} F_m + b_j S_j + e_j E_j \qquad (j = 1, 2, \cdots, n).$$

Here S_j and E_j are the *specific* and *error factors*, respectively, and b_j and e_j their coefficients. Since the specific and error factors are uncorrelated, the following relationship between the uniqueness and its component parts is immediately found:

$$(2.17) \qquad u_j^2 = b_j^2 + e_j^2.$$

Hence, the total variance may be expressed in the following alternative way:

$$(2.18) \qquad s_j^2 = 1 = h_j^2 + u_j^2 = h_j^2 + b_j^2 + e_j^2.$$

Thus, the total variance of a variable may be said to be made up of the communality (attributable to the F's) and the uniqueness; or alternatively, the total variance is made up of the communality, the specificity (attributable to the S's), and the unreliability (attributable to the E's).

By factorial methods the communality h_j^2 and the uniqueness u_j^2 of each variable in a set are obtained. The uniqueness of each variable may then be split into the specificity and unreliability, but this is independent of the factorial solution. If the reliability r_{jJ} of a variable z_j is known (it may be obtained by experimental methods), then the error variance may be obtained by means of the equation

$$e_j^2 = 1 - r_{jJ}.$$

Then, knowing the unreliability, the specificity follows from (2.17), viz.,

$$b_j^2 = u_j^2 - e_j^2,$$

where the uniqueness u_j^2 is known from the factorial solution. Since the reliability is the complement of the unreliability e_j^2, it follows from (2.18) that

$$r_{jJ} = h_j^2 + b_j^2$$

and hence:

(2.19)
$$h_j^2 = r_{jJ} - b_j^2 \leqq r_{jJ}.$$

In other words, the communality of any variable is less than or equal to the reliability of the variable, and equals the reliability only when the specificity vanishes.

Employing the model (2.16) for the expression of a variable z_j in terms of factors, the composition of variance of such a variable (in decreasing order of magnitude, generally) is given by:

(2.20)

Total variance	(1) $= h_j^2 + b_j^2 + e_j^2$	$= h_j^2 + u_j^2,$	
Reliability	$(r_{jJ}) = h_j^2 + b_j^2$	$= 1 - e_j^2,$	
Communality	$(h_j^2) = h_j^2$	$= 1 - u_j^2,$	
Uniqueness	$(u_j^2) = b_j^2 + e_j^2$	$= 1 - h_j^2,$	
Specificity	$(b_j^2) = b_j^2$	$= u_j^2 - e_j^2,$	
Error variance	$(e_j^2) = e_j^2$	$= 1 - r_{jJ}.$	

An index of *completeness of factorization* may be expressed in the form:

(2.21)
$$C_j = 100 h_j^2/(h_j^2 + b_j^2) = 100 \text{ communality/reliability}.$$

This index shows the percentage of the reliability variance of a variable accounted for by the common factors. The index C_j is always less than 100 and approaches 100 only when the specificity b_j^2 vanishes. Obviously the analysis for determining the coefficients a_{jp} should not be carried to the point where no specificity is present when dealing with a finite set of variables.

Some workers may not care to assume specific or even error factors as indicated by (2.16). Then the factors S_j and E_j are not postulated, and the number of common factors m may be less than, or equal to, the number of variables n. However, the hypothesis of factors indicated by (2.16) appears tenable even for variables which appear to describe a set of objects very completely and with great precision.

2.5.   *Factor Patterns and Structures*

Having described the composition of variables in terms of factors, it is now possible to consider in broad outline the objectives of a factor analysis of data. For a set of n variables, the linear model (2.9) expressing any variable z_j in terms of m common factors and its unique factor may be written in a slightly expanded form as follows:

$$z_1 = a_{11}F_1 + a_{12}F_2 + \cdots + a_{1m}F_m + u_1 Y_1$$

(2.22)
$$z_2 = a_{21}F_1 + a_{22}F_2 + \cdots + a_{2m}F_m \qquad\qquad + u_2 Y_2$$

$$\cdots \cdots \cdots \cdots \cdots \cdots \cdots \cdots \cdots \cdots \cdots$$

$$z_n = a_{n1}F_1 + a_{n2}F_2 + \cdots + a_{nm}F_m \qquad\qquad\qquad + u_n Y_n.$$

Such a set of equations is called a *factor pattern*, or more briefly, *pattern*. For simplicity a pattern may be presented in tabular form in which only the coefficients of the factors are listed, with the factor designations at the head of the columns. Sometimes a table including only the coefficients of the common factors may be referred to as the pattern. In a pattern (2.22), the common factors F_p ($p = 1, 2, \cdots, m$) may be either correlated or uncorrelated, but the unique factors Y_j ($j = 1, 2, \cdots, n$) are always assumed to be uncorrelated among themselves and with all common factors. In the linear description of a particular variable, the actual number of common factors involved may be less than m, some of the coefficients being zero. The number of common factors involved in the description of a variable is called its *complexity*.

Factor analysis yields not only patterns but also correlations between the variables and the factors. A table of such correlations is called a *factor structure*, or merely a *structure*. Both a structure and a pattern are necessary in order to furnish a complete solution. The functional relationships between the elements of a structure and the coefficients of a pattern will now be shown.

Multiplying any one of equations (2.22) by the respective factors, summing over the number of observations N, and dividing by N, produces

$$r_{z_jF_1} = a_{j1} \qquad + a_{j2}r_{F_1F_2} + \cdots + a_{jp}r_{F_1F_p} + \cdots + a_{jm}r_{F_1F_m},$$

$$\cdots \cdots \cdots \cdots \cdots \cdots \cdots \cdots \cdots \cdots \cdots \cdots$$

(2.23)
$$r_{z_jF_p} = a_{j1}r_{F_pF_1} + a_{j2}r_{F_pF_2} + \cdots + a_{jp} \qquad + \cdots + a_{jm}r_{F_pF_m},$$

$$\cdots \cdots \cdots \cdots \cdots \cdots \cdots \cdots \cdots \cdots \cdots \cdots$$

$$r_{z_jF_m} = a_{j1}r_{F_mF_1} + a_{j2}r_{F_mF_2} + \cdots + a_{jp}r_{F_mF_p} + \cdots + a_{jm},$$

and

(2.24)
$$r_{z_jY_j} = u_j.$$

Equation (2.24) shows that the correlations with the unique factors (the elements $r_{z_jY_j}$ of a factor structure) are always identical with the coefficients of the unique factors in the pattern. When no confusion can arise, the table of correlations of variables with common factors only, i.e., the table of $r_{z_jF_p}$, will be referred to as the factor structure.

While it might appear that equations (2.23) are to be used to evaluate the structure elements, more frequently these equations are used to obtain the values of the pattern coefficients when the correlations between variables and factors and the correlations among the factors themselves are known. Formally, (2.23) may be considered as n sets of m linear equations in the unknown a_{jp} ($j = 1, \cdots, n; p = 1, \cdots, m$), with the left-hand members as known quantities. It is then possible to solve these systems of equations for the unknown coefficients a_{jp}. Computing procedures for such formal solutions are developed in chapter 3 and applied in chapter 12, while the entire part ii is devoted to the direct analyses for the factor patterns.

From equations (2.23) it is apparent that the elements $r_{z_jF_p}$ of a structure are generally different from the coefficients a_{jp} of a pattern. In case the common factors F_p are uncorrelated, that is, $r_{F_pF_q} = 0$ $(p \neq q)$, then equations (2.23) reduce to

$$(2.25) \qquad\qquad r_{z_jF_p} = a_{jp} \qquad (j = 1, 2, \cdots, n; \; p = 1, 2, \cdots, m)$$

Thus, *only in the case of uncorrelated factors are the elements of a structure identical with the corresponding coefficients of a pattern.* In an analysis involving uncorrelated factors, a complete solution is furnished merely by a factor pattern inasmuch as the correlations of the variables with the factors are given by the respective coefficients.

As already indicated, both structure and pattern should be produced in making a complete factor analysis. The structure reveals the correlations of variables and factors—the data variables with which we presumably are familiar and the hypothetical constructs (factors) that we wish to understand—and hence are useful for the identification or naming of the factors. The structure values are also required for subsequent estimates of factor scores (see chap. 16). The pattern shows the linear composition of variables in terms of factors in the form of regression equations. It may also be used for reproducing the correlations between variables to determine the adequacy of the solution, which is discussed in **2.7**. In comparing different systems of factors for a given set of variables, again patterns are useful.

Another set of empirical data (Mullen 1939) are now introduced and will be employed throughout this text. These consist of eight physical measures on 305 girls from seven to seventeen years of age. These eight variables were selected from a much larger set because they appeared to fall into two distinct groups. Thus, it can be seen from their correlations in Table 2.3 that the first four variables are measures of "lankiness" while the last four are measures of "stockiness." This fact is brought out clearly in Figure 2.2.

Table 2.3

Correlations Among Eight Physical Variables for 305 Girls

Variable	1	2	3	4	5	6	7	8
1. Height	—	—	—	—	—	—	—	—
2. Arm span	.846	—	—	—	—	—	—	—
3. Length of forearm	.805	.881	—	—	—	—	—	—
4. Length of lower leg	.859	.826	.801	—	—	—	—	—
5. Weight	.473	.376	.380	.436	—	—	—	—
6. Bitrochanteric diameter	.398	.326	.319	.329	.762	—	—	—
7. Chest girth	.301	.277	.237	.327	.730	.583	—	—
8. Chest width	.382	.415	.345	.365	.629	.577	.539	—

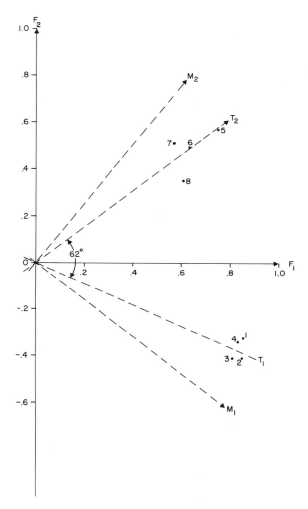

F_IG. 2.2—Factor analyses (orthogonal and oblique) of eight physical variables

The factor analysis of these data is shown both in terms of uncorrelated factors (M_1 and M_2) and in terms of correlated factors (T_1 and T_2). In the former case, the complete solution for the first variable is

$$z_1 = .879M_1 + .272M_2 + .403Y_1$$

with expressions similar to this for the remaining seven variables (see Table 13.5), and where it is understood that the correlation between M_1 and M_2 is zero. In the solution involving correlated factors, the first equation of the factor pattern is

$$z_1 = .883T_1 + .065T_2 + .403Y_1$$

23

while the correlations of z_1 with the two common factors are .914 and .481, respectively, and the correlation between these factors is .471. From this correlation between the factors it can be determined that the reference axes, representing the factors, are separated by an angle of 62°. Of course, similar equations of the factor pattern for the other seven variables are available (see Table 14.9), and the correlations of the variables with the factors are computed from these data for the factor structure.

From inspection of Figure 2.2 it is evident that the eight physical variables can very effectively be described in terms of two factors. As a matter of fact, it is almost too simple an example. Even though deliberate selection of variables for a well-designed study is certainly recommended, such clear-cut delineation cannot ordinarily be expected.

2.6.   *Underlying Correlations*

A few remarks may be in order about the type of correlations that should be used in a factor analysis. The observed correlation matrix is generally presumed to contain product-moment correlations. An assumption of normality is not made. However, the increase in interpretive possibilities stemming from the assumption of a bivariate normal distribution make such an assumption desirable very often (Binder 1959). A fuller discussion is presented by Carroll (1961) of the descriptive use of correlation coefficients and the added interpretive value of assumed statistical models, as well as problems of manifest and latent relationships between variables.

An especially pertinent question arises when dealing with dichotomous data. Strictly speaking, factor analysis requires that the correlations be of the product-moment type even in this case. Of course, the correlation from a fourfold table for two dichotomous variables is a product-moment correlation between the two variables, each of which has two point values. Such a measure is sometimes called "coefficient of association" or "fourfold point correlation" or "phi coefficient." By any of these names it is still a product-moment correlation.

There are other measures of association between two dichotomous variables that are not product-moment correlations. The most common one is the tetrachoric correlation. This assumes an underlying bivariate normal distribution for the two variables. However, all that is known is the number or proportion of cases above and below a point of cut that dichotomizes the variables. Such an assumption is quite reasonable for many psychological variables, especially cognitive traits. The mathematical theory is available and the computation of tetrachoric correlations can readily be done on modern-day computers. However, the corresponding theory and formulas for the calculation of the tetrachoric correlation for every possible pair from a set of n variables that have a multivariate normal distribution has not yet been developed. Therefore, while it is relatively easy to calculate tetrachoric correlations, if an entire matrix were determined under the assumption of bivariate normal distribution of a pair of variables at a time (rather than from a multivariate normal assumption), there is no assurance that the matrix will be consistent. In other words, a matrix of tetrachoric correlations may not be proper for factor analysis.

For most of the exposition in this text, no assumptions are made about the statistical distributions of the variables. More precisely, the correlations among the variables for a given sample are treated as if they were the true correlations in the population, ignoring statistical variation. Alternatively, various procedures are developed which operate on the correlations among a set of variables to produce solutions in the sense of model (2.9), accepting these correlations as mathematical rather than statistical entities. However, when questions of statistical inference arise—regarding the number of common factors or the significance of factor loadings—then specific assumptions on the distribution functions of the factors and the observed variables are introduced (see chaps. 9 and 10).

2.7. *Statistical Fit of the Factor Model*

In the preceding sections a model was developed as the mathematical theory underlying the observed data. This model—the set of equations (2.22)—makes the assumption that the variables are composed linearly of the factors. In what sense does a set of factors explain the relationships among the variables? That is the subject of the present section.

The observed correlations among the variables constitute the primary data. What happens to the correlation between two variables which are approximated by the linear model? If, in general, such correlations derived from the factor model are little different from the observed correlations, the model is said to fit the empirical data well; otherwise, the approximation is poor and the hypothesis should be altered. The correlation between two variables may be reproduced from the factor pattern (2.22) by the following procedure: multiply any two such equations, sum over the number of individuals N, and divide by N. Remembering that the factors are in standard form, the correlation between variables z_j and z_k ($j, k = 1, 2, \cdots, n$) can be expressed as follows:

$$(2.26) \quad \begin{cases} \hat{r}_{jk} = a_{j1}a_{k1} + a_{j2}a_{k2} + a_{j3}a_{k3} + \cdots + a_{jm}a_{km} \\ \quad + (a_{j1}a_{k2} + a_{k1}a_{j2})r_{F_1 F_2} + \cdots + (a_{j1}a_{km} + a_{k1}a_{jm})r_{F_1 F_m} \\ \quad + (a_{j2}a_{k3} + a_{k2}a_{j3})r_{F_2 F_3} + \cdots + (a_{j2}a_{km} + a_{k2}a_{jm})r_{F_2 F_m} \\ \quad + \cdots + a_{j1}u_k r_{F_1 Y_k} + a_{k1}u_j r_{F_1 Y_j} + \cdots + a_{jm}u_k r_{F_m Y_k} \\ \quad + a_{km}u_j r_{F_m Y_j} + u_j u_k r_{Y_j Y_k}, \end{cases}$$

where the *reproduced correlation* (computed from the pattern) is written $\hat{r}_{jk}$ to distinguish it from the observed correlation r_{jk}. This distinction is made throughout the text.

The unique factors have been assumed to be uncorrelated with the common factors and among themselves, hence $r_{F_p Y_j} = r_{F_p Y_k} = r_{Y_j Y_k} = 0$. If the common factors are uncorrelated, equation (2.26) simplifies still further. The correlations $r_{F_p F_q}$ ($p \neq q$; $p, q = 1, 2, \cdots, m$) are then zero, and everything below the first line of the equation vanishes. For the case of uncorrelated common factors, the correlation between any two variables is reproduced from the factor pattern by an equation of the following form:

$$(2.27) \quad \hat{r}_{jk} = a_{j1}a_{k1} + a_{j2}a_{k2} + \cdots + a_{jm}a_{km} \quad (j \neq k; \; j, k = 1, 2, \cdots, n).$$

This expression is merely the sum of the products of corresponding pattern coefficients of the two variables correlated. Of course, the self correlation of a variable is unity. The factor analysis model preserves this property through the unique factor for each variable. Thus, the reproduced self correlation for variable j can be obtained from (2.26) by setting $k = j$, and again assuming uncorrelated factors, it can readily be seen that its value is simply the sum of the communality and the uniqueness of the variable.

Now that the distinction between the observed and the reproduced correlations has been made, what should be the extent of their agreement? The correlations reproduced by the factor pattern, as given most generally in (2.26) or for the case of uncorrelated factors in (2.27), should not agree exactly with the observed correlations because allowance must be made for sampling and experimental errors. It is a commonly accepted scientific principle that a theoretical law should be simpler than the observed data upon which it is based, and hence discrepancies between the law and the data are to be expected. In the case of factor analysis, functions (the correlations $\hat{r}_{jk}$) of the assumed linear composition of variables should be expected to vary somewhat from the observed values.

After a factor pattern has been obtained, its adequacy as a description of the variables is determined from the extent to which it explains the correlations among the variables. This is done by forming the reproduced correlations from the pattern and subtracting them from the corresponding observed correlations. The resulting differences are known as *residual correlations*, and are defined by

$$(2.28) \quad \bar{r}_{jk} = r_{jk} - \hat{r}_{jk},$$

where r_{jk} is the observed correlation and $\hat{r}_{jk}$ is the correlation reproduced from the pattern. In case the common factors are uncorrelated, the residuals then reduce to the form:

$$(2.29) \quad \bar{r}_{jk} = r_{jk} - (a_{j1}a_{k1} + a_{j2}a_{k2} + \cdots + a_{jm}a_{km}).$$

The question then arises as to how nearly the correlations reproduced from a factor pattern should fit the observed ones.[5] The agreement may be judged by the size and distribution of the residuals $\bar{r}_{jk}$. The magnitude of the residuals should, of course, be approximately zero. When all common factors have been removed in forming the residuals, then no further linkages between variables exist. It might, therefore, be expected that the distribution of residuals would be similar to that of a zero correlation in a sample of equal size. The standard error of such a zero correlation is given by the formula

$$\sigma_{r=0} = 1/\sqrt{N - 1},$$

---

[5] A simple standard for "when to stop factoring" has not been developed. This problem is discussed in chaps. 8, 9, and 10.

and, since N is usually large, a standard for judging adequacy of fit may be taken to be:

$$(2.30) \qquad\qquad \sigma_{\bar{r}} \leqq 1/\sqrt{N},$$

where $\sigma_{\bar{r}}$ is the standard deviation of the series of residuals. This standard is a crude one since it depends only on the size of the sample, whereas the briefest reflection would suggest that the size of residuals must depend also on other characteristics, especially the number of variables.

On the basis of the size of the sample alone, the following conclusions from the criterion (2.30) may be drawn. If $\sigma_{\bar{r}}$ is appreciably greater than $1/\sqrt{N}$, it may be concluded that there are further significant linkages between variables, and a modification of the form of solution is required. In case $\sigma_{\bar{r}}$ is considerably less than $1/\sqrt{N}$, it would appear that unjustified linkages between variables have been included in the solution. When the standard deviation of the residuals is just below that of a zero correlation, the solution may be regarded as acceptable in the light of the above standard. This simple statistical test was recommended more than forty years ago (Kelley 1935, p. 12; Thurstone 1935, p. 147). More exact statistical tests are discussed in chapters 9 and 10.

2.8.   *Indeterminacy of Factor Solutions*

In any scientific field the observed phenomena can be described in a great variety of ways which are mutually consistent. The choice of a particular interpretation must then depend upon its utility. The arbitrariness or indeterminacy, which has been recognized by philosophers of science for a long time, is put succinctly by F. R. Moulton (1939, p. 484):

> . . . . every set of phenomena can be interpreted consistently in various ways, in fact, in infinitely many ways. It is our privilege to choose among the possible interpretations the ones that appear to us most satisfactory, whatever may be the reasons for our choice. If scientists would remember that various equally consistent interpretations of every set of observational data can be made, they would be much less dogmatic than they often are, and their beliefs in a possible ultimate finality of scientific theories would vanish.

The factor problem, likewise, is indeterminate in the sense that, given the correlations of a set of variables, the coefficients of a factor pattern are not uniquely determined. That is, systems of orthogonal, or uncorrelated, factors may be chosen, *consistent with the observed correlations*, in an infinity of ways. This property has been known by mathematicians and statisticians from the time they had become interested in factor analysis, and one of the first formal demonstrations was given by Hotelling (1933) for the case of principal components. A more general proof was given by Anderson and Rubin (1956).

In essence, the indeterminacy in the model—the factor loadings a_{jp} are not unique— arises from the fact that a solution determines the m-dimensional space containing the common factors, but it does not determine the basis or frame of reference or the exact position of these factors. The indeterminacy occurs at two stages: in getting an (arbitrary) solution which satisfies the model in a statistical sense, and in getting the solution in a form most amenable to interpretation. In general the computational methods do not yield unique values for the factor loadings, an exception being the principal-factor solution (chap. 8). However, any solution may be put in a "canonical form" (see **8.7**). The indeterminacy at the second stage still exists (see part III). After a factor solution has been found that fits the empirical data (to within a given degree of accuracy), it may be transformed or "rotated" to another solution (fitting the data equally well) which may have greater meaning to investigators in a particular field.

The indeterminacy of the factor model has several ramifications and raises some related issues. If the variables are not expressed uniquely in terms of the factors, what is meant by factor measurements or scores for the individuals? This is taken up in chapter 16. Again, if the factor pattern is not unique for a given sample of individuals and variables, what can be said about the factors obtained for two different samples of individuals or tests? Some discussion of such problems is presented in chapter 15. For a fuller treatment the serious student is referred to Ledermann (1938), Guttman (1955), Heermann (1966), Mulaik (1972, pp. 327–60), Schonemann and Wang (1972), and Meyer (1973).

2.9.   *Factor Model in Matrix Notation*[6]

Before leaving the general overview of factor analysis, it is desirable to set forth the ideas developed earlier in this chapter in compact matrix notation. The advantages go beyond mere simplification; frequently, certain properties and proofs can be derived by the use of matrix language which might otherwise be hidden from view. In this section some of the fundamental properties of factor patterns and structures are put in matrix form, while in subsequent chapters many of the methods of factor analysis are developed by the use of matrix algebra.

First, some of the very basic concepts involved in factor analysis will be expressed in matrix notation. The n variables of a study may be designated by a column vector, as follows:

$$(2.31) \qquad \mathbf{z} = \begin{bmatrix} z_1 \\ z_2 \\ \cdot \\ \cdot \\ \cdot \\ \cdot \\ z_n \end{bmatrix}$$

---

[6]The reader who wishes a review of the basic concepts of matrix algebra may want to turn to chap. 3 before reading this section.

while the complete set of N values for each of the n variables will be represented by the $n \times N$ matrix:

$$(2.32) \qquad \mathbf{Z} = \begin{bmatrix} z^*_{11} & z^*_{12} & \cdots & z^*_{1N} \\ z^*_{21} & z^*_{22} & \cdots & z^*_{2N} \\ \cdot & \cdot & \cdot & \cdot \\ z^*_{n1} & z^*_{n2} & \cdots & z^*_{nN} \end{bmatrix},$$

where small standard deviates are used to avoid the need for division by N in the subsequent matrix manipulations. Similarly, the factors may be represented as follows:

$$(2.33) \qquad \mathbf{f} = \begin{bmatrix} F_1 \\ \cdot \\ \cdot \\ \cdot \\ F_m \end{bmatrix}, \quad \mathbf{F} = \begin{bmatrix} F_{11} & F_{12} & \cdots & F_{1N} \\ \cdot & \cdot & \cdots & \cdot \\ F_{m1} & F_{m2} & \cdots & F_{mN} \end{bmatrix}.$$

$$\mathbf{y} = \begin{bmatrix} Y_1 \\ \cdot \\ \cdot \\ \cdot \\ Y_n \end{bmatrix}, \quad \mathbf{Y} = \begin{bmatrix} Y_{11} & Y_{12} & \cdots & Y_{1N} \\ \cdot & \cdot & \cdots & \cdot \\ Y_{n1} & Y_{n2} & \cdots & Y_{nN} \end{bmatrix}.$$

The coefficients of the factors in a factor pattern may be represented by the following matrix:

$$(2.34) \qquad \mathbf{M} = \begin{bmatrix} a_{11} & a_{12} & \cdots & a_{1m} & u_1 & 0 & \cdots & 0 \\ a_{21} & a_{22} & \cdots & a_{2m} & 0 & u_2 & \cdots & 0 \\ \cdot & \cdot & \cdots & \cdot & \cdot & \cdot & \cdots & \cdot \\ a_{n1} & a_{n2} & \cdots & a_{nm} & 0 & 0 & \cdots & u_n \end{bmatrix} = (\mathbf{A}|\mathbf{U}),$$

wherein the total pattern matrix $\mathbf{M}$ is made up of the matrix $\mathbf{A}$ of common-factor coefficients and the diagonal matrix $\mathbf{U}$ of unique-factor coefficients. Usually the matrix $\mathbf{A}$ is referred to as the *pattern matrix*. It should be noted that the algebraic signs of all the entries in any column of a pattern matrix $\mathbf{A}$ may be reversed (i.e., reflecting the direction of the factor) without affecting the reproduced correlations. In general, the elements a_{jp} of the matrix $\mathbf{A}$ are to be considered as coefficients in an oblique-factor pattern, i.e., a pattern based upon correlated factors. In the course of a factor analysis, sometimes both an (initial) orthogonal pattern $\mathbf{A}$ and a (final) oblique pattern $\mathbf{P}$ are determined. When there are two distinct pattern matrices in the same context, then it is necessary to use distinguishing notation.

Employing the foregoing definitions, the factor pattern (2.22) may be written:

$$(2.35) \qquad \mathbf{z} = (\mathbf{A}|\mathbf{U})\{\mathbf{f}|\mathbf{y}\} = \mathbf{Af} + \mathbf{Uy} = \mathbf{c} + \mathbf{e}$$

where

$$(2.36) \qquad\qquad \mathbf{c} = \mathbf{Af} \quad \text{and} \quad \mathbf{e} = \mathbf{Uy}$$

represent the common parts and the unique parts of the observable variables $\mathbf{z}$, respectively. Because the common factor portion of a factor pattern is often of primary interest, it is designated by $\mathbf{z}$ as a matter of tradition; when a distinction must be made the vector $\mathbf{c}$ will be employed for the common parts.

In addition to a pattern, a factor analysis also yields a structure, i.e., a table of correlations of the variables with the factors (the latter being identical with the pattern only if the common factors are uncorrelated). Of course, the correlations of the variables with the unique factors are identical with the unique factor coefficients according to (2.24), and the diagonal matrix of these values has been designated $\mathbf{U}$. Now, defining the correlations with the common factors by

$$(2.37) \qquad\qquad s_{jp} = r_{z_j F_p}, \qquad (j = 1, 2, \cdots, n; \quad p = 1, 2, \cdots, m)$$

the factor structure may be represented by:

$$(2.38) \qquad\qquad \mathbf{S} = \begin{bmatrix} s_{11} & s_{12} & \cdots & s_{1m} \\ s_{21} & s_{22} & \cdots & s_{2m} \\ \cdot & \cdot & \cdots & \cdot \\ s_{n1} & s_{n2} & \cdots & s_{nm} \end{bmatrix}.$$

The notation for the elements of a factor structure should not be confused with the definition (2.6) of a sample covariance. The context will make it perfectly clear which is implied.

Having expressed a pattern and a structure of a given factor analysis in matrix form, it is possible to develop certain relationships between them. As the first step toward this end, consider the factor pattern (2.36) written explicitly for the N entities, namely,

$$(2.39) \qquad\qquad \mathbf{Z} = \mathbf{AF},$$

and postmultiply both sides of this expression by the transpose of the matrix of factor values to obtain:

$$(2.40) \qquad\qquad \mathbf{ZF'} = \mathbf{A(FF')}.$$

The left-hand member of this equation simplifies as follows:

$$(2.41) \qquad\qquad \mathbf{ZF'} = \mathbf{S},$$

since each element is a correlation coefficient according to the basic definition (2.7). The expression within the parentheses in the right-hand member of (2.40) is also a matrix of correlation coefficients—among the factors—since all the factors may be assumed to be appropriately standardized. This matrix of correlations among the common factors is defined by

$$(2.42) \qquad \mathbf{\Phi} = \mathbf{FF'} = \begin{bmatrix} 1 & r_{F_1 F_2} & \cdots & r_{F_1 F_m} \\ r_{F_2 F_1} & 1 & \cdots & r_{F_2 F_m} \\ \cdot & \cdot & \cdot & \cdot \\ r_{F_m F_1} & r_{F_m F_2} & \cdots & 1 \end{bmatrix}.$$

Upon substituting (2.41) and (2.42) into (2.40), the latter expression reduces to:

$$(2.43) \qquad \mathbf{S} = \mathbf{A\Phi}.$$

This is the fundamental relationship between a factor pattern **A** and a factor structure **S**—the structure matrix is equal to the pattern matrix postmultiplied by the matrix of correlations among the factors. From this relationship it is clear that if the factors are uncorrelated (i.e., **Φ** is an identity matrix), the elements of the structure are equal to the corresponding elements of the pattern. The explicit expression for the pattern matrix can be obtained from (2.43) by postmultiplying both sides by **Φ**$^{-1}$. The result is

$$(2.44) \qquad \mathbf{A} = \mathbf{S\Phi}^{-1}.$$

It is possible to express the matrix $\hat{\mathbf{R}}$ of reproduced correlations (with communalities in the diagonal) in several alternative forms, employing the foregoing relationship between a pattern and a structure. By definition, the matrix of observed correlations is given by

$$(2.45) \qquad \mathbf{R} = \mathbf{ZZ'},$$

where it is understood that the variables have been standardized in such a manner (i.e., small standard deviates) so that division by N is not required. If (2.39) is substituted into this equation, and the observed correlation matrix is replaced by the matrix of reproduced correlations, there results:[7]

$$(2.46) \qquad \hat{\mathbf{R}} = \mathbf{AFF'A'} = \mathbf{A\Phi A'},$$

where the last equality follows from (2.42). Another formula, in terms of the structure instead of the pattern, can be obtained by substituting the value of **A** from (2.44) into (2.46), namely:

$$(2.47) \qquad \hat{\mathbf{R}} = \mathbf{S\Phi}^{-1}\mathbf{S'}.$$

Sometimes it is desirable to consider the reproduced correlation matrix with ones in the diagonal, i.e., adding the uniqueness u_j^2 to the communality h_j^2 of each variable. This matrix is represented by $(\hat{\mathbf{R}} + \mathbf{U}^2)$, and equation (2.46) becomes:

$$(2.48) \qquad (\hat{\mathbf{R}} + \mathbf{U}^2) = \mathbf{M} \begin{pmatrix} \mathbf{\Phi} & \mathbf{O} \\ \mathbf{O} & \mathbf{I} \end{pmatrix} \mathbf{M'},$$

[7]In replacing observed by "theoretical" correlations, the tacit assumption is made that the residuals vanish. To avoid additional symbolism, **R** is employed sometimes for both matrices, but it should be clear when it is determined empirically (from the observed data) and when it is determined theoretically (from the factor model).

in which the composite square matrix (of order $m + n$) includes the identity matrix (of order n) of correlations among the unique factors as well as the correlation matrix (of order m) among the common factors.

From the relationship between a pattern and a structure, alternative formulas can be derived which obviate the explicit use of the matrix $\mathbf{\Phi}$. Thus, substituting (2.43) into (2.46) produces

$$(2.49) \qquad\qquad \hat{\mathbf{R}} = \mathbf{SA'} = \mathbf{AS'},$$

since $\mathbf{\Phi}$ is symmetric.

Of course, when the factors are uncorrelated, the matrix $\mathbf{\Phi}$ reduces to an identity matrix and formula (2.46) simplifies to the following expression for the reproduced correlations:

$$(2.50) \qquad\qquad \hat{\mathbf{R}} = \mathbf{AA'}.$$

This equation has been called "the fundamental factor theorem" (Thurstone 1935, p. 70).

An important observation can be made at this point. The factor problem is concerned with fitting a set of data (the observed correlations) with a model—the factor pattern (2.22), or (2.35) in matrix notation. Under the assumption of such a pattern, the correlations are reproduced by means of the common-factor coefficients alone, as may be seen from (2.50).[8] For the reproduced correlation matrix $\hat{\mathbf{R}}$ to be an appropriate fit to the observed correlation matrix $\mathbf{R}$, the diagonal elements must also be reproduced from the common-factor portion of the pattern. Thus, if numbers approximating the communalities are put in the diagonal of the matrix of observed correlations, the factor solution will involve both common and unique factors and the foregoing formulas will appropriately reproduce all the elements comparable to the observed data. On the other hand, if unities are placed in the principal diagonal of the observed correlation matrix then the factor solution must necessarily involve *only* common factors in order for equation (2.50) to reproduce the unities. In this case no provision is made for unique factors, implying the component analysis model (2.8). If such values between communalities and unities as the reliabilities are employed, then the factor solution would involve common and error factors, but the specificity would be included in the "common-factor" variance. From these considerations it should be clear that the *values put in the diagonal of the observed correlation matrix determine what portions of the unit variances are factored into common factors.*

---

[8]In the discussion of this paragraph, there is no loss in generality to assume that the factors are uncorrelated.

3 Matrix Concepts Essential to Factor Analysis

3.1. *Introduction*

The solution of systems of linear equations provided the impetus for the development of the theory of determinants, and from the latter grew the theory of matrices. In modern mathematical thinking it is generally accepted that "the idea of matrix precedes that of determinant." Furthermore, it is now recognized that the importance of the concept of determinant is over-rated. While determinants are quite useful, systems of equations certainly can be solved efficiently without them. Also, the bulk of the mathematical theory of matrices can be developed without the explicit use of determinants. Nonetheless, because of historical precedent that has been established, the basic concepts of determinants are enumerated before matrices and introduced in **3.2**.

Many problems arising in applied mathematics can be formulated in terms of systems of linear equations. While this fact has long been recognized, the advent of high-speed digital electronic computers has provided a special impetus to the problem of solving a system of linear equations and the associated problem of finding the eigenvalues of a matrix (see chap. 8). Considerable research in these areas has been conducted in recent years, and there are many excellent expositions of the theory and numerical methods especially amenable to high-speed computers. Examples of such works include the reports of the National Bureau of Standards, Faddeev (1963), and White (1958).

Many phases of factor analysis involve the solution of a set of simultaneous linear equations, either explicitly or implied in the work. While it is assumed that the reader will have access to a high speed computer for his factor analytic work, to give him a feel for some of the intermediate calculations, a general method for solving a small set of equations with a desk calculator is presented in **3.3**, and applied to the calculation of the inverse of a matrix in **3.4**.

3.2.   *Basic Concepts of Determinants and Matrices*

For a full and proper understanding of factor analysis it is almost imperative that the student have a basic knowledge of matrix algebra. In the development of the text, it is presupposed that the reader has had some exposure to this subject. The aim of this section is to assist him in recalling this knowledge, and to make the fundamental definitions and theorems on matrices immediately available.[1] For purposes of reference, the classical or more traditional notation and properties of determinants as well as matrices are presented.

1. Definition of a determinant of order 2.—A sum of product terms, with alternating algebraic signs, frequently occurs in mathematical work and has been given a special name and notation. For example, the expression

$$ad - bc$$

is denoted by the symbol

$$\begin{vmatrix} a & b \\ c & d \end{vmatrix},$$

which is called a *determinant of the second order*, since it contains two rows and two columns.

2. Definition of a determinant of order 3.—The symbol

$$\begin{vmatrix} a_1 & b_1 & c_1 \\ a_2 & b_2 & c_2 \\ a_3 & b_3 & c_3 \end{vmatrix}$$

is called a *determinant of the third order* and stands for

$$a_1 b_2 c_3 - a_1 b_3 c_2 + a_2 b_3 c_1 - a_2 b_1 c_3 + a_3 b_1 c_2 - a_3 b_2 c_1.$$

The nine numbers $a_1, \cdots, c_3$ are called the *elements* of the determinant. In the symbol these elements lie in three (horizontal) *rows* and also in three (vertical) *columns*. For example, a_3, b_3, c_3 are the elements of the third row, while the three b's are the elements of the second column. The diagonal from the upper left-hand corner to the lower right-hand corner is called the *principal diagonal*.

3. Definition of a determinant of order n.—A determinant of the nth order is defined by:

$$(3.1) \qquad \det A = \begin{vmatrix} a_{11} & a_{12} & \cdots & a_{1n} \\ a_{21} & a_{22} & \cdots & a_{2n} \\ \cdot & \cdot & \cdots & \cdot \cdot \\ a_{n1} & a_{n2} & \cdots & a_{nn} \end{vmatrix},$$

---

[1]For detailed treatment of these subjects the reader is referred to such excellent texts as Graybill (1969), Hadley (1961), and Paige and Swift (1961).

where the n^2 elements are denoted by a's with two subscripts, the first representing the number of the row and the second the number of the column in which the element appears. By definition the determinant A stands for the sum of $n!$ terms, each of which is (apart from sign) the product of n elements, one and only one from each column, and one and only one from each row. The algebraic signs are determined most easily by the method of expanding the determinant which is explained in **5** below.

4. Minors and cofactors.—The determinant of order $n - 1$ obtained by striking out the row and column crossing at a given element of a determinant of order n is called the *minor* of that element. Thus, corresponding to the element a_{jk}, in the jth row and the kth column of the determinant A, there exists the minor M_{jk} which is obtained upon crossing out the given row and column. Frequently there is occasion to consider not this minor M_{jk} but the *cofactor* A_{jk} of a_{jk} defined by

(3.2) $$A_{jk} = (-1)^{j+k} M_{jk}.$$

The algebraic signs attached to the minors to obtain the corresponding cofactors are alternately $+$ and $-$, as indicated by the following diagram which is associated with the elements of a determinant:

$$\begin{array}{cccc} + & - & + & - \\ - & + & - & + \\ + & - & + & - \\ - & + & - & + \end{array}$$

5. Expansion of a determinant.—Any determinant A may be expanded according to the elements of any row j:

(3.3) $$\det A = \sum_{k=1}^{n} a_{jk} A_{jk} \qquad (j = 1, 2, \cdots, n),$$

or, in terms of any column k:

(3.4) $$\det A = \sum_{j=1}^{n} a_{jk} A_{jk} \qquad (k = 1, 2, \cdots, n).$$

Thus, for the third-order determinant

$$\det A = \begin{vmatrix} a_{11} & a_{12} & a_{13} \\ a_{21} & a_{22} & a_{23} \\ a_{31} & a_{32} & a_{33} \end{vmatrix},$$

the expansion according to the elements of the second column becomes, according to (3.4) with $k = 2$:

$$\begin{aligned} \det A &= a_{12} A_{12} & + a_{22} A_{22} & + a_{32} A_{32} \\ &= -a_{12} M_{12} & + a_{22} M_{22} & - a_{32} M_{32} \\ &= -a_{12}(a_{21}a_{33} - a_{31}a_{23}) + a_{22}(a_{11}a_{33} - a_{31}a_{13}) - a_{32}(a_{11}a_{23} - a_{21}a_{13}), \end{aligned}$$

which, upon rearranging of terms, may be written as follows:

$$\det A = a_{11}a_{22}a_{33} + a_{12}a_{23}a_{31} + a_{13}a_{32}a_{21} - a_{13}a_{22}a_{31} - a_{23}a_{32}a_{11} - a_{33}a_{21}a_{12}.$$

By successively applying the foregoing method, a determinant of any order eventually can be reduced to the explicit expansion of determinants of the second order.

6. Definition of a matrix.—A system of mn numbers a_{jk} arranged in a rectangular array of m rows and n columns is called an $m \times n$ *matrix*. If $m = n$, the array is called a square matrix of order n. A matrix will be represented by any of the following:

(3.5)
$$\mathbf{A} = (a_{jk}) = \begin{bmatrix} a_{11} & a_{12} & \cdots & a_{1n} \\ a_{21} & a_{22} & \cdots & a_{2n} \\ \cdot & \cdot & \cdots & \cdot \\ a_{m1} & a_{m2} & \cdots & a_{mn} \end{bmatrix},$$

7. Definition of a vector.—Two special instances of a matrix occur frequently, namely, a single row or a single column. Any such array of $1 \times n$ or $n \times 1$ elements is called a *vector*, or more specifically, a *row vector* or a *column vector*, respectively. Simple examples of a row vector are the notations (x, y) and (x, y, z) for points in a plane and in space, the elements of these vectors being the coordinates of the points. Similarly, the coordinates of a point in space might be represented by a column vector in any one of the forms:

$$\mathbf{x} = \begin{bmatrix} x_1 \\ x_2 \\ x_3 \end{bmatrix} = \{x_1 \ x_2 \ x_3\},$$

where the last expression may be used to conserve space.

8. Notation for vectors, matrices, and determinants.—It should be noted that even when a matrix is square it is not a determinant. A determinant whose elements are real numbers, represents a real number, while a matrix does not have a value in the ordinary sense. The difference between a square matrix and a determinant is clearly seen upon interchanging the rows and columns; the determinant has the same value, but the matrix is generally different from the original one.

Throughout this text, capital **boldface** letters are used to denote matrices other than row or column vectors, while lower case **boldface** letters are used for vectors. A determinant, when represented by a single letter, is printed in *italic* (usually preceded by "det"). The determinant of a matrix $\mathbf{A}$ (see **10** below) is indicated by $|\mathbf{A}|$.

9. Transpose of a matrix.—A matrix which is derived from another by interchanging the rows and columns is called the *transpose* of the original *matrix*. Thus, if

$$\mathbf{A} = \begin{bmatrix} a_{11} & a_{12} & a_{13} \\ a_{21} & a_{22} & a_{23} \\ a_{31} & a_{32} & a_{33} \end{bmatrix},$$

then the transpose of **A** is the matrix

$$\mathbf{A'} = \begin{bmatrix} a_{11} & a_{21} & a_{31} \\ a_{12} & a_{22} & a_{32} \\ a_{13} & a_{23} & a_{33} \end{bmatrix}.$$

The prime notation for the transpose is followed throughout the text. The transpose of a row vector is a column vector, and vice versa. Thus, in the example of **7** above, the transpose of the column vector **x** is the row vector $\mathbf{x'} = (x_1 \ x_2 \ x_3)$.

10. Determinants of a matrix.—Although square matrices and determinants are wholly different things, it is possible to form from the elements of a square matrix a determinant which is called the *determinant of the matrix*. The notation employed is bold-face type for the matrix and vertical lines for the determinant of the matrix. Thus the determinant of a square matrix **A** is denoted by |**A**|. Other determinants, of lower order, can be formed from any rectangular matrix by striking out certain rows and columns. For many problems it is important to know the order of the highest non-vanishing determinant of a matrix.

11. Rank of a matrix.—A matrix **A** is said to be of *rank r* if it contains at least one *r*-rowed determinant which is not zero, whereas all determinants of **A** of order higher than *r* are zero. In other words, the rank of a matrix is the order of the largest non-vanishing determinant.

By the rank of a determinant is meant the rank of its matrix.

12. Singular matrix.—A square matrix is said to be *singular* if its determinant is zero. Otherwise, it is called *nonsingular*.

13. Matrix equations.—Any two matrices **A** and **B** are said to be equal if and only if every element of **A** is equal to the corresponding element of **B**. Thus, if $\mathbf{A} = (a_{jk})$ and $\mathbf{B} = (b_{jk})$ then the equation

$$\mathbf{A} = \mathbf{B}$$

implies that $a_{jk} = b_{jk}$ for every j and k. Thus it is evident that a single matrix equation stands for as many algebraic equations as there are elements in either of the matrices which are equated.

14. Symmetric matrix.—A matrix **A** is *symmetric* if and only if it is equal to its transpose **A'**. In other words, the matrix $\mathbf{A} = (a_{jk})$ is symmetric in case it remains unaltered by the interchange of its rows and columns, i.e.,

$$a_{jk} = a_{kj} \qquad\qquad (j, k = 1, 2, \cdots, n).$$

The following is an example of a symmetric matrix:

$$\begin{bmatrix} .78 & -.16 & .23 & .04 \\ -.16 & .59 & -.34 & -.21 \\ .23 & -.34 & .86 & .40 \\ .04 & -.21 & .40 & .65 \end{bmatrix}.$$

All correlation matrices are symmetric.

15. Gramian matrix.—A matrix of special interest to factor analysis is frequently referred to in psychological literature as a "Gramian" matrix, or a matrix with Gramian properties. These properties include symmetry and positive semidefiniteness. The symmetric characteristic of a matrix is defined in **14** above. A matrix is said to be *positive semidefinite* if all its principal minors are greater than or equal to zero.[2] All correlation matrices with unities in the principal diagonal are Gramian matrices (see Theorem 4.5); and communality estimates as replacements for the diagonal values are considered "proper" only if the Gramian properties are preserved (see chap. 5).

16. Sum or difference of matrices.—The sum (or difference) of two matrices each of m rows and n columns is defined to be an $m \times n$ matrix each of whose elements is the sum (or difference) of the corresponding elements of the given matrices. All the laws of ordinary algebra hold for the addition or subtraction of matrices.

17. Multiplication of matrices.—The element in the jth row and the kth column of the product of a matrix **A** with n columns by a matrix **B** with n rows is the sum of the products of the successive elements of the jth row of **A** by the corresponding elements of the kth column of **B**.

For example, if

$$
\mathbf{A} = \begin{bmatrix} a_{11} & a_{12} & a_{13} \\ a_{21} & a_{22} & a_{23} \end{bmatrix}, \qquad \mathbf{B} = \begin{bmatrix} b_{11} & b_{12} \\ b_{21} & b_{22} \\ b_{31} & b_{32} \end{bmatrix},
$$

then the product **C** of these matrices is

$$
\mathbf{C} = \mathbf{A} \cdot \mathbf{B} = \begin{bmatrix} a_{11}b_{11} + a_{12}b_{21} + a_{13}b_{31} & a_{11}b_{12} + a_{12}b_{22} + a_{13}b_{32} \\ a_{21}b_{11} + a_{22}b_{21} + a_{23}b_{31} & a_{21}b_{12} + a_{22}b_{22} + a_{23}b_{32} \end{bmatrix}.
$$

It should be noted that in this *row-by-column multiplication* of matrices the number of columns in the first matrix must be equal to the number of rows in the second. The product matrix then contains the number of rows of the first matrix and the number of columns of the second. Thus, in the example, the product of the 2×3 matrix by the 3×2 matrix is a 2×2 matrix. This may be conveniently noted by writing the order of each matrix as superscripts, namely,

$$
\mathbf{A}^{2 \times 3} \cdot \mathbf{B}^{3 \times 2} = \mathbf{C}^{2 \times 2}.
$$

In general,

(3.6)
$$
\mathbf{A}^{m \times n} \cdot \mathbf{B}^{n \times s} = \mathbf{C}^{m \times s},
$$

that is, the product of an $m \times n$ matrix by an $n \times s$ matrix is an $m \times s$ matrix.

Multiplication of matrices is not commutative in general, that is,

(3.7)
$$
\mathbf{AB} \neq \mathbf{BA}.
$$

[2]In Thurstone (1947, p. 10), these conditions are inadvertently ascribed to a *positive definite* matrix instead of a *positive semidefinite* matrix. Only if all the principal minors of a matrix are greater than zero (none equal to zero) is the matrix said to be positive definite.

Thus, in the example above the product $\mathbf{C} = \mathbf{AB}$ certainly is different from the product

$$\mathbf{D} = \mathbf{BA} = \begin{bmatrix} b_{11}a_{11} + b_{12}a_{21} & b_{11}a_{12} + b_{12}a_{22} & b_{11}a_{13} + b_{12}a_{23} \\ b_{21}a_{11} + b_{22}a_{21} & b_{21}a_{12} + b_{22}a_{22} & b_{21}a_{13} + b_{22}a_{23} \\ b_{31}a_{11} + b_{32}a_{21} & b_{31}a_{12} + b_{32}a_{22} & b_{31}a_{13} + b_{32}a_{23} \end{bmatrix}.$$

Hence it is important to specify in what order matrices are multiplied. In the product **AB** the matrix **B** is said to be *premultiplied* by the matrix **A**, or **A** is *postmultiplied* by **B**.

18. Alternative rules for matrix multiplication.—In the course of numerical computations it is sometimes more expeditious to multiply two matrices by some other rule than the conventional row-by-column. Following is a listing of all the permutations for given matrices **A** and **B**:

(3.8)
$$\begin{aligned} &\textbf{AB} \quad \text{means row-by-column multiplication of } \textbf{A} \text{ and } \textbf{B}; \\ &\textbf{AB}' \quad \text{means row-by-row multiplication of } \textbf{A} \text{ and } \textbf{B}; \\ &\textbf{A}'\textbf{B} \quad \text{means column-by-column multiplication of } \textbf{A} \text{ and } \textbf{B}; \\ &\textbf{A}'\textbf{B}' \quad \text{means column-by-row multiplication of } \textbf{A} \text{ and } \textbf{B}. \end{aligned}$$

19. Inner product of two vectors.—The "inner product" or "dot product" of two vectors is defined to be the sum of the products of pairs of corresponding numbers in the two vectors. Thus, if the two vectors are $\mathbf{a} = (a_1\ a_2\ a_3)$ and $\mathbf{b} = (b_1\ b_2\ b_3)$, their inner product is given by

(3.9)
$$\mathbf{a} \cdot \mathbf{b}' = a_1 b_1 + a_2 b_2 + a_3 b_3.$$

20. Scalars.—In order to distinguish the ordinary quantities of algebra (i.e., real and complex numbers) from matrices, the former are called *scalars* and will here be designated in italics. The product of a matrix **A** by a scalar k ($k\mathbf{A}$ or $\mathbf{A}k$) is defined to be the matrix each of whose elements is k times the corresponding element of **A**. All the laws of ordinary algebra hold for the multiplication of matrices by scalars.

21. Diagonal and scalar matrices.—A matrix in which the diagonal elements do not all vanish and all remaining elements are zero is called a *diagonal matrix*. A special instance of such a matrix is one in which all the elements of the diagonal are identical; it is then called a *scalar matrix*. If a scalar matrix

$$\mathbf{K} = \begin{bmatrix} k & 0 & \cdots & 0 \\ 0 & k & \cdots & 0 \\ \cdot & \cdot & \cdots & \cdot \\ \cdot & \cdot & \cdots & \cdot \\ 0 & 0 & \cdots & k \end{bmatrix}$$

is premultiplied or postmultiplied by any matrix **A** of the same order as **K**, the following relationships become evident:

(3.10)
$$\mathbf{KA} = \mathbf{AK} = k\mathbf{A}.$$

In particular, the matrix

(3.11)
$$\mathbf{I} = \begin{bmatrix} 1 & 0 & \cdots & 0 \\ 0 & 1 & \cdots & 0 \\ \cdot & \cdot & \cdots & \cdot \\ \cdot & \cdot & \cdots & \cdot \\ 0 & 0 & \cdots & 1 \end{bmatrix}$$

is called the *identity matrix*, and it has the property that, if $\mathbf{A}$ is any matrix whatever,

(3.12) $\mathbf{IA} = \mathbf{AI} = \mathbf{A}.$

It is evident that, in matrix algebra, all scalar matrices may be replaced by the corresponding scalars and, conversely, that all scalars may be considered as standing for the corresponding scalar matrices. The identity matrix $\mathbf{I}$ corresponds to unity in ordinary algebra, and hence in products of matrices the factor $\mathbf{I}$ may be suppressed.

22. Inverse matrix.—If a square matrix

$$\mathbf{A} = \begin{bmatrix} a_{11} & a_{12} & \cdots & a_{1n} \\ a_{21} & a_{22} & \cdots & a_{2n} \\ \cdot & \cdot & \cdots & \cdot \\ a_{n1} & a_{n2} & \cdots & a_{nn} \end{bmatrix}$$

is nonsingular, i.e., $|\mathbf{A}| \neq 0$, then there exists another matrix

(3.13) $\mathbf{A}^{-1} = 1/|\mathbf{A}| \begin{bmatrix} A_{11} & A_{21} & \cdots & A_{n1} \\ A_{12} & A_{22} & \cdots & A_{n2} \\ \cdot & \cdot & \cdots & \cdot \\ A_{1n} & A_{2n} & \cdots & A_{nn} \end{bmatrix} = \begin{bmatrix} a^{11} & a^{21} & \cdots & a^{n1} \\ a^{12} & a^{22} & \cdots & a^{n2} \\ \cdot & \cdot & \cdots & \cdot \\ a^{1n} & a^{2n} & \cdots & a^{nn} \end{bmatrix}$

in which A_{kj} denote the cofactors of the elements of $\mathbf{A}$, and the matrix of these cofactors (with $1/|\mathbf{A}|$ factored out) is called the *adjoint* of matrix $\mathbf{A}$. The matrix $\mathbf{A}^{-1}$, with elements denoted by a^{jk}, is called the *inverse* of $\mathbf{A}$ and is itself a nonsingular matrix which has the property

(3.14) $\mathbf{AA}^{-1} = \mathbf{A}^{-1}\mathbf{A} = \mathbf{I}.$

It should be noted that the rows and columns of cofactors in the adjoint matrix are interchanged, i.e., the element A_{kj} in the jth row and k^{th} column of the adjoint of $\mathbf{A}$ is the cofactor of the element a_{kj} in the kth row and j^{th} column of $\mathbf{A}$.

23. Theorems on transpose and inverse of products of matrices.—The transpose of a product of matrices is equal to the product of their transposes taken in reverse order. Thus,

(3.15) $(\mathbf{ABC})' = \mathbf{C}'\mathbf{B}'\mathbf{A}'.$

The inverse of a product of matrices is the product of their inverses taken in reverse order. For example,

$$(\textbf{ABC})^{-1} = \textbf{C}^{-1}\textbf{B}^{-1}\textbf{A}^{-1}.$$

(3.16)

24. Orthogonal matrix.—A square matrix **A** (of real elements) is said to be orthogonal if and only if

$$\textbf{A}^{-1} = \textbf{A}'.$$

(3.17)

From this definition, it follows that an orthogonal matrix has the property $\textbf{A}'\textbf{A} = \textbf{I}$ and that the determinant of an orthogonal matrix is plus or minus one. Also, the inverse (as well as the transpose) of an orthogonal matrix is itself an orthogonal matrix.

3.3. *Solution of Systems of Linear Equations*

In general, a system of n linear equations in n unknowns can be solved by means of determinants. While the determinantal method may have some undisputed theoretical advantages, a more economical procedure is desired, especially when dealing with a large number of variables. The systems of equations which appear in factor analysis have symmetric matrices of coefficients and so lend themselves to special methods of solution. Gauss's method of substitution[3] produces a routine scheme for the solution of such a set of equations, including a complete check on the arithmetical work (see, for example, Dwyer 1951).

While it is not an objective of this text to go into elaborate hand methods of computation in the present age of readily available programmed computers, there are occasions when manual procedures can enable the student to grasp a better understanding and may point the way to effective use of the computer. An alternative to the method of substitution is the "square root method." Not only is this method more expedient for solving a symmetric set of equations, but it is especially useful in obtaining the inverse matrix in solving problems in statistics. For these reasons, the square root method will be described in general terms and illustrated with a simple problem involving least-squares prediction. For simplicity, suppose a dependent variable z_4 is to be predicted from three independent variables by means of the regression equation:

$$z_4 = \beta_1 z_1 + \beta_2 z_2 + \beta_3 z_3,$$

where the β's are to be determined. The normal equations in this case are:

$$r_{11}\beta_1 + r_{12}\beta_2 + r_{13}\beta_3 = r_{14},$$
$$r_{21}\beta_1 + r_{22}\beta_2 + r_{23}\beta_3 = r_{24},$$
$$r_{31}\beta_1 + r_{32}\beta_2 + r_{33}\beta_3 = r_{34},$$

(3.18)

[3]This method is referred to as the "Doolittle Solution" in many textbooks on statistics. Convenient forms for the solution of a set of normal equations, arising in the problem of curve-fitting, were devised by M. H. Doolittle and presented in Wright and Hayford (1906, pp. 101–24).

where, of course, $r_{jj} = 1$ and the conditions for symmetry $r_{jk} = r_{kj}$ are satisfied for $j, k = 1, 2, 3$. The system of equations (3.18) is to be solved for the three unknown β's in terms of the known correlations. Suppose the numerical values of the correlations have been provided, so that the system of equations becomes:

$$1.000\beta_1 + .693\beta_2 + .216\beta_3 = .571,$$

(3.19) $$.693\beta_1 + 1.000\beta_2 + .295\beta_3 = .691,$$

$$.216\beta_1 + .295\beta_2 + 1.000\beta_3 = .456.$$

In Table 3.1 computing procedures are presented for the solution of a general system of equations (3.18), and illustrated with the numerical data of (3.19). The step-by-step procedure, immediately following, is readily extended to any number of variables.

Step 1.   Enter the intercorrelations among the independent variables and their correlations with the dependent variable on the first three lines of the worksheet.

Table 3.1

The Square Root Method

Line	Independent Variables			Dependent Variable	Total	Check
	z_1	z_2	z_3	z_4		
			Schematic			
1	r_{11}	r_{12}	r_{13}	r_{14}	t_1	r'_{14}
2	*	r_{22}	r_{23}	r_{24}	t_2	r'_{24}
3	*	*	r_{33}	r_{34}	t_3	r'_{34}
4	s_{11}	s_{12}	s_{13}	s_{14}	s_{1t}	s'_{1t}
5		$s_{22.1}$	$s_{23.1}$	$s_{24.1}$	$s_{2t.1}$	$s'_{2t.1}$
6			$s_{33.12}$	$s_{34.12}$	$s_{3t.12}$	$s'_{3t.12}$
7	β_1	β_2	β_3		$R^2_{4.123}$	$R_{4.123}$
			Illustration			
1	1.000	.693	.216	.571	2.480	.571
2	*	1.000	.295	.691	2.679	.691
3	*	*	1.000	.456	1.967	.456
4	1.000	.693	.216	.571	2.480	2.480
5		.721	.202	.410	1.332	1.333
6			.955	.262	1.217	1.217
7	.171	.492	.274		.563	.750

* Terms below the diagonal of a symmetric matrix are deleted for simplicity. Terms below the diagonal of the "square root" matrix are actually zero, and are simply omitted.

Step 2. Obtain the sums by rows, i.e.,

(3.20)
$$t_j = \sum_{k=1}^{4} r_{jk}. \qquad (j = 1, 2, 3)$$

Note: entries in "Check" column for lines 1, 2, 3 are described in Step 10.

Step 3. The actual square root process is begun by using r_{11} as a pivot to get the first element in line 4 simply by

(3.21₁)
$$s_{11} = \sqrt{r_{11}},$$

and the remaining elements by the formula:

(3.21₂)
$$s_{1k} = r_{1k}/s_{11}. \qquad (k > 1)$$

Note: Since $r_{11} = 1$, the elements of line 4 are equal, respectively, to the elements of line 1.

Step 4. The calculation in the "Total" column of line 4 is carried out as for any other column, yielding s_{1t}. This value should agree, except for rounding errors, with the sum s'_{1t} ("Check" column) of all elements computed in Step 3.

Step 5. The formulas for the elements of line 5 are:

(3.22)
$$s_{22 \cdot 1} = \sqrt{r_{22} - s_{12}^2},$$
$$s_{2k \cdot 1} = (r_{2k} - s_{1k}s_{12})/s_{22 \cdot 1}. \qquad (k > 2)$$

Step 6. Check line 5 by comparing the calculated value, $s_{2t \cdot 1}$, with the row sum, $s'_{2t \cdot 1}$.

Step 7. The formulas for the elements of line 6 are:

(3.23)
$$s_{33 \cdot (2)} = \sqrt{r_{33} - s_{13}^2 - s_{23 \cdot 1}^2},$$
$$s_{3k \cdot (2)} = (r_{3k} - s_{1k}s_{13} - s_{2k \cdot 1}s_{23 \cdot 1})/s_{33 \cdot (2)}, \qquad (k > 3)$$

where the notation $s_{3k \cdot (2)}$ is used instead of the specific $s_{3k \cdot 12}$ to suggest an easy generalization when the number of variables already eliminated is more than 2.

Step 8. Apply row sum check to line 6.

Step 9. The values of the regression coefficients are obtained by application of the following formulas (back solution):

(3.24)
$$\beta_3 = s_{34 \cdot 12}/s_{33 \cdot 12},$$
$$\beta_2 = (s_{24 \cdot 1} - s_{23 \cdot 1}\beta_3)/s_{22 \cdot 1},$$
$$\beta_1 = (s_{14} - s_{13}\beta_3 - s_{12}\beta_2)/s_{11}.$$

Step 10. A check on the entire computations can be made by substituting the regression coefficients into the normal equations (3.18). The results are designated by r'_{14}, r'_{24}, r'_{34} and should agree (except for rounding errors) with the original correlations of independent with dependent variables.

Step 11. The multiple correlation coefficient can be computed by use of the usual formula involving the β's and r's, viz.,

$$(3.25) \qquad R^2_{4 \cdot 123} = \beta_1 r_{14} + \beta_2 r_{24} + \beta_3 r_{34}.$$

From the formal solution of the three-variable problem it can be verified that

$$(3.26) \qquad \begin{bmatrix} r_{11} & r_{12} & r_{13} \\ r_{21} & r_{22} & r_{23} \\ r_{31} & r_{32} & r_{33} \end{bmatrix} = \begin{bmatrix} s_{11} & 0 & 0 \\ s_{12} & s_{22 \cdot 1} & 0 \\ s_{13} & s_{23 \cdot 1} & s_{33 \cdot 12} \end{bmatrix} \begin{bmatrix} s_{11} & s_{12} & s_{13} \\ 0 & s_{22 \cdot 1} & s_{23 \cdot 1} \\ 0 & 0 & s_{33 \cdot 12} \end{bmatrix}$$

More generally, the square root method can be formulated in matrix notation, as follows:

$$(3.27) \qquad \mathbf{R} = \mathbf{S}'\mathbf{S},$$

whence the term "square root of a matrix" is seen to correspond to the ordinary square root of an algebraic expression. The identity of equation (3.27) with the fundamental theorem of factor analysis, equation (2.50), clearly indicates why factor analysts independently discovered the square root method, although it was referred to by various names (see **6.3**). In other words, the square root method applied to a matrix **R** yields a matrix **S** such that premultiplication by its transpose (i.e., column-by-column multiplication of **S** by itself) reproduces the matrix **R**. It is convenient at times, to refer to the "square root operation," by which is meant $(\mathbf{S}')^{-1}$, since $(\mathbf{S}')^{-1}$ operating (premultiplying) on **R** produces **S**. Then the square root operation can be applied to other matrices than the basic one from which it is derived.

At times it is more convenient to arrange the work in adjacent vertical sections rather than in horizontal blocks. This is especially true if there are a large number of variables to which the square root operation is to be applied.

While the square root method may be applied to any symmetric matrix, some difficulties will be encountered if the matrix is not positive definite; then certain of the diagonal elements may turn out to be zero or negative, and the process may degenerate or lead to imaginary numbers. When working with a correlation matrix (with unities in the diagonal), the square root method will proceed without any complications. However, when the diagonal values are replaced by communalities (less than or at most equal to one), then special considerations must be made to obtain the "real" portions of the solution (see **6.3**).

3.4.   *Calculation of the Inverse of a Matrix*

There are many situations in factor analysis where the inverse of a matrix is either required explicitly, or, if it were readily available, could lead to simplification in the work. One example is in regard to the estimation of communality, which is treated in chapter 5. A lower bound to the communality is the squared multiple correlation of a variable with the remaining variables, and the calculation of these multiple corre-lations is expedited by use of the inverse of the correlation matrix. Another example involves the calculation of a factor pattern from a factor structure for an oblique solution (see **11.5**, **12.4**, and chap. 14), in which the inverse of the matrix of factor correlations simplifies the task. The inverse of the matrix of factor correlations may also be used in estimating a small number of factors by the method of **16.5**. All of these examples point to the usefulness of an efficient means for determining the inverse of a given matrix.

While the inverse of a matrix is defined in **3.2**, paragraph **22**, such a mathematical statement does not provide a practical means for its calculation with numerical data. The methods for solving systems of linear equations can be employed in getting the inverse of a matrix. The procedure can be demonstrated with the simple problem of deriving the inverse of the following matrix of correlations among three variables:

$$\mathbf{R} = \begin{bmatrix} 1 & r_{12} & r_{13} \\ r_{21} & 1 & r_{23} \\ r_{31} & r_{32} & 1 \end{bmatrix}.$$

The property (3.14), that the product of a matrix by its inverse is an identity matrix, may be put in the form:

$$(3.28) \qquad \begin{bmatrix} 1 & r_{12} & r_{13} \\ r_{21} & 1 & r_{23} \\ r_{31} & r_{32} & 1 \end{bmatrix} \begin{bmatrix} r^{11} & r^{21} & r^{31} \\ r^{12} & r^{22} & r^{32} \\ r^{13} & r^{23} & r^{33} \end{bmatrix} = \begin{bmatrix} 1 & 0 & 0 \\ 0 & 1 & 0 \\ 0 & 0 & 1 \end{bmatrix}$$

where the elements of the inverse matrix $\mathbf{R}^{-1}$ are denoted as in (3.13). The problem is to determine the elements of the inverse matrix from the known correlations.

Upon carrying out the matrix multiplication indicated in the left-hand member of (3.28), and setting each resulting element equal to the corresponding element of the identity matrix on the right it will be noted that each set of three equations involves the same matrix of coefficients, the correlation matrix $\mathbf{R}$. Hence, the work can be so organized that the solution for all the r^{kj}'s can be made simultaneously by the method described in **3.3**.

To illustrate the procedure, a matrix of correlations of six hypothetical variables will be inverted. This is accomplished in Table 3.2, where general instructions are given and the work is outlined in schematic form as well as the actual calculation for the numerical example. The square root operation is applied both to the correlation matrix $\mathbf{R}$ and to the identity matrix, yielding $\mathbf{S}$ and $(\mathbf{S}')^{-1}$, respectively. Then, when the latter is premultiplied by $\mathbf{S}^{-1}$ the result is the inverse of the original matrix $\mathbf{R}$. The proof of the last result follows simply by taking the inverses of both sides of equation (3.27):

$$(3.29) \qquad \mathbf{R}^{-1} = \mathbf{S}^{-1}(\mathbf{S}')^{-1}.$$

Table 3.2

Calculation of the Inverse of a Matrix: Square Root Method

Instructions	Schematic		Numerical Example												
Original matrices	**R**	**I**	1.00	.72	.75	.49	.42	.28	1	0	0	0	0	0
			*	1.00	.78	.42	.36	.24		1	0	0	0	0
			*	*	1.00	.35	.30	.20			1	0	0	0
			*	*	*	1.00	.42	.28				1	0	0
			*	*	*	*	1.00	.24					1	0
			*	*	*	*	*	1.00						1
Square root operation (**S′**)⁻¹	**S**	(**S′**)⁻¹	1.00	.72	.75	.49	.42	.28	1.00	0	0	0	0	0
				.69	.35	.10	.08	.06	−1.04	1.45	0	0	0	0
					.56	−.09	−.08	−.06	−.69	−.91	1.79	0	0	0
						.86	.23	.15	−.52	−.26	.19	1.16	0	0
							.87	.09	−.31	−.15	.11	−.31	1.15	0
								.94	−.16	−.09	.07	−.16	−.11	1.06
Column-by-column multiplication by (**S′**)⁻¹, i.e., premultiplication by **S**⁻¹	**R**⁻¹ (Result is **I**, except for rounding errors—may be left blank)		2.95	−.68	−1.38	−.48	−.34	−.17						
			*	3.02	−1.68	−.24	−.16	−.10						
			*	*	3.26	.18	.12	.08						
			*	*	*	1.47	−.34	−.17						
			*	*	*	*	1.33	−.12						
			*	*	*	*	*	1.13						

*See footnote to Table 3.1.

4   Geometric Concepts Essential to Factor Analysis

4.1. *Introduction*

The understanding of factor analysis methods is enhanced by the use of geometry to supplement and extend the algebraic and matrix ideas. The geometric foundation developed in this chapter furnishes a basis for subsequent analysis and comparison of methods. Since the number of variables subjected to a factor analysis usually is quite numerous, and since the dimension of the geometric space will be found to be intimately related to this number, the geometry of concern will be "higher dimensional".

After a very brief exposition of the nature of higher dimensional geometry, a coordinate system is introduced, so that the succeeding development can be made analytically. Then, in **4.4**, the notion of linear dependence is developed, which paves the way for one of the fundamental theorems of factor analysis. Before the application of these geometric ideas to the factor problem is made, certain necessary formulas for distance and angle are developed in **4.5** and **4.7** for rectangular coordinates and, in **4.8** for general coordinates. The formulas in terms of general coordinates are included so that a geometric interpretation of oblique forms of factorial solutions may be made. The theory of orthogonal transformations, presented in **4.6**, forms the basis upon which some actual analyses are obtained in later chapters.

In **4.9** a variable is interpreted as a point, or a vector, in higher dimensional space. The standard deviation of the variable then becomes a distance, and the correlation between two variables is the cosine of the angle between the two vectors representing the variables. The direct application of the geometric theorems to the fundamental problems of factor analysis is made in the final section. There it is shown that the dimension of the smallest space which contains the vectors representing a given set of variables is equal to the rank of the matrix of correlations with communalities in the diagonals.

4.2. *Geometry of N Dimensions*

The concept of higher dimensions is arrived at by geometric and algebraic means. The notions of point, line, and plane may be generalized to higher dimensional objects, and extended geometric interpretations of algebraic relationships may be given. The deductions made in the higher dimensional spaces are based upon the analogous theory in three-dimensional space.

The basic axioms (see Sommerville 1958) for Euclidean geometry may be assumed and such modifications made as are necessary to insure that the space has a sufficiently high dimensionality. The point, straight line, and plane are taken as undefined elements, and later corresponding elements of higher dimensional space may be defined in terms of these.

Starting with four given non-coplanar points, all the points, lines, and planes can be obtained which constitute a three-dimensional space. The space, or manifold, determined by these points is essentially ordinary space of three dimensions. All that is necessary is to postulate that there is at least one point *not* in the three-dimensional space to generate a four-space. The three-dimensional region does not now constitute the whole of space but merely a subspace of the space of four dimensions. The three-dimensional region is called a *hyperplane* lying in the four-space, analogous to a plane lying in a three-space. A hyperplane in a space of four dimensions is determined by four non-coplanar points, a point and a plane, or by two skew lines.

Some of the elementary geometric properties of the elements in a three- and four-dimensional projective[1] space may now be enumerated. In a three-dimensional space two planes intersect in a line; a line cuts a plane in a point; and any three planes have a point in common, while four planes do not in general have a point in common. In a four-dimensional space two hyperplanes intersect in a plane, three hyperplanes intersect in a line, and four in a point, while five do not in general have any point in common; a hyperplane cuts a plane in a line, and a line in a point; two planes have in general only one point in common, and a plane and a line in general have no point in common.

The notion of dimensionality may be viewed in another manner. A point in a line is said to have one degree of freedom (of motion); in a plane, two; and in ordinary space, three. The point being taken as element, a line is said to be of one dimension; a plane, two; and ordinary space, three. These spaces are called *linear spaces*, or *flat spaces*, i.e., a plane is a *two-flat* and ordinary space is a *three-flat*. An $(N-1)$-flat in an N-space will be called a *hyperplane*. The linear spaces point, line, plane, three-flat, $\cdots$, hyperplane, N-flat are manifolds determined by one, two, three, four, $\cdots$, N, $N+1$ points,[2] respectively, and having zero, one, two, three, $\cdots$, $N-1$, N dimensions.

4.3.   *Cartesian Coordinate System*

The geometric ideas are found to be most useful and easily formulated when they are given analytic representation. A point P may thus be represented by the *vector* $(x_1, x_2, \cdots, x_N)$. Each x_i is a real number, and all N numbers may be called a *system*

---

[1]In assuming a projective space, the discussion is simplified by avoiding the special cases of parallel elements.

[2]It is understood that the set of p points, which determine a $(p-1)$-flat, do not lie in a $(p-2)$-flat.

or *N-tuple*. By a "point" is meant simply one of the undefined elements of the space which is characterized by a given set of axioms, so that a set of points is really an arbitrary set of any whatever elements. On the other hand, the *N*-tuple $(x_1, x_2, \cdots, x_N)$ may be called an "arithmetic point." A correspondence between a set of "geometric points" and a set of "arithmetic points" is called a *coordinate system*.[3] The numbers, $x_1, x_2, \cdots, x_N$, which constitute the representation of *P*, are called the coordinates of *P*. For purposes of factor analysis, the distinction between a "geometric" and the corresponding "arithmetic" point is not essential, and the word "point" will be used for either one. The notation $P:(x_i)$ will frequently be used to designate the point and its coordinates.

An *N*-dimensional Euclidean space is assumed, and in this space a non-homogeneous *Cartesian coordinate system* is set up. The points $O:(0, 0, \cdots, 0)$, and $E_1:(1, 0, \cdots, 0)$, $E_2:(0, 1, 0, \cdots, 0)$, $\cdots$, $E_N:(0, \cdots, 0, 1)$ are called the origin and unit points, respectively. The *N* lines Ox_i $(i = 1, 2, \cdots, N)$, each passing through the origin and one of the unit points, are the *coordinate axes*. The *N* hyperplanes[4] $\pi_i = Ox_1 x_2 \cdots)x_i(\cdots x_N$, each passing through *O* and containing $N - 1$ axes are the *coordinate hyperplanes*. A hyperplane π_i is said to be "opposite" to the axis Ox_i. The *coordinates* $(x_1, x_2, \cdots, x_N)$ of any point *P* are equal, respectively, to its distances from each coordinate hyperplane measured along a line parallel to the opposite axis; or, in other words, the distance cut off on each axis by a hyperplane parallel to the respective opposite coordinate hyperplane. For example, the coordinate x_1 is equal to the distance (denoted by x_1) cut off on the Ox_1 axis by a hyperplane parallel to the coordinate hyperplane π_1.

4.4. *Linear Dependence*

The *N*-tuple $(x_1, x_2, \cdots, x_N)$, which represents a point *P*, may be considered as a vector which joins the origin *O* to the point *P*. Such a vector is sometimes called a "radius vector." Two fundamental operations in vector algebra are multiplication by a number and addition of vectors. More precisely, if *P* is a point represented by the vector $(x_1, {}_2, \cdots, x_N)$ and *c* is any number, then according to **3.2**, paragraph **20**, *cP* is the point

$$(cx_1, cx_2, \cdots, cx_N).$$

Also, according to **3.2**, paragraph **16**, if $P_1:(x_{11}, x_{12}, \cdots, x_{1N})$ and $P_2:(x_{21}, x_{22}, \cdots, x_{2N})$ are two points,[5] then $P_1 + P_2$ is the point

$$(x_{11} + x_{21}, x_{12} + x_{22}, \cdots, x_{1N} + x_{2N}).$$

---

[3]The coordinate systems introduced in this volume always produce a one-to-one correspondence between the geometric and arithmetic points. This restriction may be removed, however. A correspondence may carry each point *P* into a set of arithmetic points, as, for example, in a *homogeneous coordinate system*.

[4]The inverted parentheses are used in the designation of any hyperplane to indicate the omitted coordinate axis.

[5]The double subscript notation is used on the coordinates in order to distinguish the points. Thus x_{qi} designates the *i*th coordinate of the point P_q.

In general, any linear combination of m points, $P_1:(x_{11}, x_{12}, \cdot\cdot\cdot, x_{1N}), \cdot\cdot\cdot, P_m:$ $(x_{m1}, x_{m2}, \cdot\cdot\cdot, x_{mN})$, may be defined by combining the two previous operations, as follows:

$$t_1 P_1 + t_2 P_2 + \cdot\cdot\cdot + t_m P_m,$$

where the t's are any numbers. By taking varying values of the t's, different linear combinations of the original m points can be obtained. Any one of these new points may be denoted[6] $P(t)$ or $P(t_1, t_2, \cdot\cdot\cdot, t_m)$, with coordinates given by

(4.1)
$$x_i = \sum_{q=1}^{m} t_q x_{qi} \qquad (i = 1, 2, \cdot\cdot\cdot, N),$$

and is said to be *linearly dependent* on the original points $P_1, P_2, \cdot\cdot\cdot, P_m$. Each coordinate x_i of a point $P(t)$ is expressed as a linear combination of the corresponding coordinates $x_{1i}, x_{2i}, \cdot\cdot\cdot, x_{mi}$ of the m points $P_1, P_2, \cdot\cdot\cdot, P_m$. Perhaps the linear dependence of any new points on the m original points can be visualized better from the following expanded matrix equivalent of (4.1):

(4.2)
$$(x_1\ x_2\ \cdot\cdot\cdot\ x_N) = (t_1\ t_2\ \cdot\cdot\cdot\ t_m) \begin{bmatrix} x_{11} & x_{12} & \cdot\cdot\cdot & x_{1N} \\ x_{21} & x_{22} & \cdot\cdot\cdot & x_{2N} \\ \cdot & \cdot & \cdot\cdot\cdot & \cdot \\ x_{m1} & x_{m2} & \cdot\cdot\cdot & x_{mN} \end{bmatrix}.$$

To clarify the foregoing ideas, consider the special case of $N = 3$ and two points $P_1:(x_{11}, x_{12}, x_{13})$ and $P_2:(x_{21}, x_{22}, x_{23})$. All the points $P(t)$ which are linearly dependent on the points P_1 and P_2 are given by the following coordinates:

$$P(t_1, t_2): \quad \begin{aligned} x_1 &= t_1 x_{11} + t_2 x_{21} \\ x_2 &= t_1 x_{12} + t_2 x_{22} \\ x_3 &= t_1 x_{13} + t_2 x_{23} \end{aligned}$$

for any whatever values of t_1 and t_2. For particular values of t_1 and t_2, the first coordinate of $P(t)$ is a linear combination of the first coordinates of P_1 and P_2; the second coordinate is the same linear combination of the second ones; and the third coordinate is again the same linear combination of the third ones. For example, if the coordinates of P_1 are (1, 3, 4) and those of P_2 are (2, 1, 5) and $t_1 = 1, t_2 = 2$, then $P(t)$ is given by the coordinates $x_1 = 5, x_2 = 5, x_3 = 14$.

The preceding description of linear dependence can be made, alternatively, by giving a direct definition of *linear independence*. Thus, a set of points $P_1, \cdot\cdot\cdot, P_m$ is linearly independent if the N conditions

(4.3)
$$\sum_{q=1}^{m} t_q x_{qi} = 0 \qquad (i = 1, 2, \cdot\cdot\cdot, N)$$

---

[6]The symbol $P(t)$, or $P(t_1, t_2, \cdot\cdot\cdot, t_m)$, is the conventional function notation which is to be read, "P is a function of t (in this case, a set of t's), or P is a function of $t_1, t_2, \cdot\cdot\cdot, t_m$." On the other hand, $P:(x_i)$ is the notation for a point P with coordinates x_i.

imply that $t_1 = t_2 = \cdots = t_m = 0$. This can readily be shown to be consistent with the definition (4.1). For, if one of the coefficients were different from zero, say $t_1 \neq 0$, then (4.3) could be written in the form

$$x_{1i} = -\frac{t_2}{t_1}x_{2i} - \frac{t_3}{t_1}x_{3i} - \cdots - \frac{t_m}{t_1}x_{mi};$$

and, according to (4.1), the point P_1 would be one of the points $P(t)$ which is linearly dependent on the points $P_2, P_3, \cdots, P_m$. Having a positive definition of independence, the definition of linear dependence is given by its negation, that is, a set of m points is linearly dependent if the conditions (4.3) hold for the coefficients not all zero.

When a set of points is given, it may be of interest to know how many of them are linearly independent. Let $P_1:(x_{11}, x_{12}, \cdots, x_{1N})$, $P_2:(x_{21}, x_{22}, \cdots, x_{2N})$, $\cdots$, $P_n:(x_{n1}, x_{n2}, \cdots, x_{nN})$ be any set of n points. Either all these points coincide with the origin or at least one of them, say P_1, is independent. Of the remaining points, either they will all depend upon P_1 or at least one of them, say P_2, will be independent of P_1. Proceeding in this way an independent set of points, say $P_1, P_2, \cdots, P_m$, will be obtained upon which all the points $P_1, P_2, \cdots, P_n$ will be linearly dependent. A criterion for determining m may be obtained by means of the matrix

$$\mathbf{X} = (x_{ji}) = \begin{bmatrix} x_{11} & x_{12} & x_{13} & \cdots & x_{1N} \\ x_{21} & x_{22} & x_{23} & \cdots & x_{2N} \\ x_{31} & x_{32} & x_{33} & \cdots & x_{3N} \\ \cdots & \cdots & \cdots & \cdots & \cdots \\ x_{n1} & x_{n2} & x_{n3} & \cdots & x_{nN} \end{bmatrix},$$

whose rows are the n points in N space. An important result for linear dependence of points, and which will be utilized later to determine the number of common factors necessary to describe a set of variables, may be stated as:

THEOREM 4.1. *If m is the rank of the matrix* $\mathbf{X}$, *the points* $P_1, P_2, \cdots, P_n$ *are all dependent upon m of them, which are themselves independent.*

The proof of this theorem may be split into two parts. First consider the case where $n \leqq N$. By hypothesis the matrix $\mathbf{X}$ is of rank m, so that without loss of generality it may be assumed that the determinant

$$D = \begin{vmatrix} x_{11} & x_{12} & \cdots & x_{1m} \\ x_{21} & x_{22} & \cdots & x_{2m} \\ \cdots & \cdots & \cdots & \cdots \\ x_{m1} & x_{m2} & \cdots & x_{mm} \end{vmatrix}$$

is different from zero. If $m = n$ the set of equations

$$\sum_{k=1}^{n} x_{kj}t_k = 0 \qquad (j = 1, 2, \cdots, n)$$

have the unique solution $t_1 = t_2 = \cdots = t_n = 0$, since $D \neq 0$. Then, according to the definition (4.3), the points $P_1, P_2, \cdots, P_n$ are linearly independent. If $m < n$ the points $P_1, P_2, \cdots, P_m$ may be shown to be independent by the preceding argument. This establishes the last part of the theorem.

Now to show that all n points are dependent upon these, form a new matrix by annexing a row and column to the matrix of D as follows:

$$\Delta = \begin{bmatrix} x_{11} & x_{12} & \cdots & x_{1m} & x_{1i} \\ x_{21} & x_{22} & \cdots & x_{2m} & x_{2i} \\ \cdot & \cdot & \cdot \cdot \cdot & \cdot & \cdot \cdot \\ x_{m1} & x_{m2} & \cdots & x_{mm} & x_{mi} \\ x_{p1} & x_{p2} & \cdots & x_{pm} & x_{pi} \end{bmatrix},$$

where $p = m + 1, \cdots, n$ and i is arbitrary. The determinant of this matrix, when expanded according to the elements of the last column, becomes

(4.4) $$|\Delta| = x_{1i}D_{1i} + x_{2i}D_{2i} + \cdots + x_{mi}D_{mi} + x_{pi}D,$$

where $D_{1i}, D_{2i}, \cdots, D_{mi}$ are the cofactors of $x_{1i}, x_{2i}, \cdots, x_{mi}$, respectively, and D is the cofactor of the last element x_{pi}. This expression vanishes, for, if $i \leq m$, two columns then have equal elements; and, if $i > m$, it vanishes, since the rank of $\mathbf{X}$ is m and every $(m + 1)$-order minor vanishes. The solution for x_{pi} from the expression (4.4) set equal to zero is

(4.5) $$x_{pi} = \sum_{q=1}^{m} t_q x_{qi} \qquad (p = m + 1, \cdots, n),$$

where the constants

(4.6) $$t_q = -\frac{D_{qi}}{D}$$

do not depend on the elements $x_{1i}, x_{2i}, \cdots, x_{mi}, x_{pi}$. It follows from definition (4.1) that the points P_p, whose coordinates are given in (4.5), are linearly dependent on the points $P_1, P_2, \cdots, P_m$, which are themselves independent.

While the situation would not arise in ordinary application of factor analysis, to complete the proof of the theorem consider the remaining case when $n > N$. In this case the points $P_j : (x_{j1}, x_{j2}, \cdots, x_{jN}, 0, \cdots, 0)$ are in a space of n dimensions. Then the foregoing argument can be applied to obtain the relation (4.5), and thus the theorem is established for all values of n.

The meaning of Theorem 4.1 may be demonstrated with the very simple example of the three points:

$$\begin{bmatrix} 1 & 3 & 4 \\ 2 & 1 & 5 \\ 5 & 5 & 14 \end{bmatrix}.$$

This matrix is seen to be of rank two because the third-order determinant is zero while a second-order determinant can be found which is different from zero. According to the theorem, since the matrix is of rank two, the three points are dependent upon two of them, which are themselves independent—a fact that was known about these particular points from the way the third point was constructed as the sum of the first point and twice the second.

Subspaces of the *N*-space may now be given analytical representation. If $P_1, P_2, \cdots, P_k$ are *k* linearly independent points, the set of all points linearly dependent on them is called a *linear k-space* and is defined by the equations

$$(4.7) \qquad\qquad x_i = \sum_{j=1}^{k} t_j x_{ji} \qquad\qquad (i = 1, 2, \cdots, N),$$

where the *t*'s are a set of *k* parameters, and for each set of values $(t_1, t_2, \cdots, t_k)$ there is a corresponding point of the linear *k*-space. Any one of the original *k* linearly independent points is, of course, given by definition (4.7); for example, P_2 is given by $t_2 = 1$ and $t_1 = t_3 = \cdots = t_k = 0$. The *k* points $P_1, P_2, \cdots, P_k$ are said to determine the linear *k*-space. A linear 1-space consists of all points whose coordinates are proportional to those of a given point $P_1:(x_{11}, x_{12}, \cdots, x_{1N})$, and may be called a line through the origin. Its equations are given by

$$(4.8) \qquad\qquad x_i = t_1 x_{1i} \qquad\qquad (i = 1, 2, \cdots, N).$$

In an *N*-space, these are a set of *N parametric equations* of a line through the origin, where t_1 is known as the parameter.

In a plane, a linear 1-space consists of all points proportional to a given point, say $P_1:(x_{11}, x_{12})$, and passing through the origin. Its parametric equations are:

$$(4.9) \qquad\qquad \begin{aligned} x_1 &= t_1 x_{11}, \\ x_2 &= t_1 x_{12}. \end{aligned}$$

Or course, this pair of equations reduces to the more elementary expression of a straight line through the origin:

$$(4.9') \qquad\qquad y = bx$$

where *y* is the ordinate x_2, *x* is the abscissa x_1, and *b* is the slope x_{12}/x_{11}, derived from the given point P_1.

The transitive law for linear dependence may now be indicated. All points linearly dependent on *m* points $P_1, \cdots, P_m$ in a linear *k*-space are contained in that *k*-space. The coordinates of the *m* points are given by equations of the form (4.7), and any point linearly dependent on $P_1, \cdots, P_m$ is then obviously dependent on $P_1, \cdots, P_k$.

Furthermore, if the points $P_1, \cdots, P_k$ determine a linear *k*-space, there is no other linear *k*-space containing these points. A linear *k*-space is thus determined by any set of *k* independent points contained in it, and a linear *k*-space does not contain a set of *l* independent points, where $l > k$. For, by definition (4.1), it is implied that any *k* points in a set of l independent points are themselves independent, and hence determine a linear k-space contained in the larger set. Theorem 4.1 may then be stated as follows:

THEOREM 4.2. *If m is the rank of the matrix* $\mathbf{X}$, *the points* $P_1, P_2, \cdots, P_n$ *are all contained in a linear m-space but not in a linear μ-space, where $\mu < m$.*

A geometric interpretation of linear dependence can now be given. The m vectors $P_q : (x_{q1}, x_{q2}, \cdots, x_{qN})$, $(q = 1, 2, \cdots, m)$, employed in the definition (4.1), determine an m-dimensional subspace of the original N-space, and if $OP_1, OP_2, \cdots, OP_m$ are taken as the coordinate axes, then $t_1, t_2, \cdots, t_m$ in (4.1) are the coordinates x_i of $P(t)$.

A set of m vectors is said to *span* an n-space if every vector in this space can be expressed as a linear combination of the m given vectors. An important consideration is the smallest number of vectors which will span the space, and this turns out to be equal to the dimension of the space provided these vectors are linearly independent. Thus, any system of m linearly independent vectors spans an entire m-space and forms a *basis* for that space. An example of a basis is the set of unit vectors along the coordinate axes. A basis for a space certainly is not unique. As a matter of fact, there are an infinite number of bases for a given space (see Faddeev and Faddeeva 1963, pp. 37–38). This, in essence, is the indeterminacy of the factor problem. The choice of a particular basis, sometimes referred to as the "rotation" problem of factor analysis, is the subject of part III of this text.

A linear k-space, as defined by equations (4.7), always contains the origin, since the origin is linearly dependent on any set of points. The notion of subspaces of the N-dimensional space may be generalized to spaces which do not include the origin. For this purpose, a *translation* of coordinates,

$$(4.10) \qquad\qquad y_i = x_i + c_i,$$

is defined. Then any set of points which corresponds, under a translation, to a linear k-space may be called a *flat k-space*, or merely a k-*flat*. As noted in **4.2**, a 0-flat is a single point; a 1-flat is a straight line; a 2-flat is a plane; and an $(N - 1)$-flat is a hyperplane.

4.5.   *Distance Formulas in Rectangular Coordinates*

When the coordinate axes are mutually orthogonal, i.e., at right angles to one another, the reference system set up in **4.3** is called a *rectangular Cartesian system*. Some elementary formulas in *rectangular* coordinates are presented in this section.

For any two vectors or points $P_1 : (x_{11}, x_{12}, \cdots, x_{1N})$ and $P_2 : (x_{21}; x_{22}, \cdots, x_{2N})$, their *scalar product* (or *inner* or *dot* product) as defined in **3.2**, paragraph **19** is given by:

$$(4.11) \qquad\qquad P_1 \cdot P_2 = \sum x_{1i} x_{2i},$$

where the summation with respect to i is understood. The *norm* of P_1 is defined as the positive square root of the inner product of P_1 with itself, that is,

$$(4.12) \qquad\qquad N(P) = \sqrt{P_1 \cdot P_1} = \sqrt{\sum x_{1i}^2};$$

and the *distance* between P_1 and P_2 is defined by

(4.13)
$$D(P_1 P_2) = N(P_1 - P_2) = \sqrt{\sum (x_{1i} - x_{2i})^2}.$$

It is readily seen that the norm of a point is the distance from the origin to the point, that is, $N(P) = D(OP)$. The distance function satisfies the following familiar conditions of elementary geometry:

(4.14)
$$\begin{cases} D(P_1 P_1) = O, \\ D(P_1 P_2) > O \text{ if } P_1 \neq P_2, \\ D(P_1 P_2) = D(P_2 P_1), \\ D(P_1 P_2) + D(P_2 P_3) \geqq D(P_1 P_3). \end{cases}$$

The first three of these relations are obvious. The fourth, however, requires some proof. It may be noted that distances are invariant under translations. Thus if two points P_1, P_2 are translated into two points P_1', P_2', then $D(P_1 P_2) = D(P_1' P_2')$, which may be verified by applying (4.10). The fourth formula of (4.14) will therefore be unaltered if the points P_1, P_2, and P_3 are transformed by a translation which carries P_2 into the origin. Then, by (4.12) and (4.13), the inequality of (4.14) becomes

(4.15)
$$\sqrt{\sum x_{1i}^2} + \sqrt{\sum x_{3i}^2} \geqq \sqrt{\sum (x_{1i} - x_{3i})^2},$$

which may be verified algebraically.

Now the equality occurs in (4.15) if, and only if,

$$x_{3i} = -t_1 x_{1i} \qquad (i = 1, 2, \cdots, N),$$

where t_1 is a positive constant. These equations are of the form (4.8) and so represent a straight line through the origin with the points P_1 and P_3 on opposite sides of the origin. Hence, equality occurs in the fourth relations of (4.14) if, and only if, the coordinates of P_1, P_2, and P_3 are related by equations of the form

(4.16)
$$A(x_{1i} - x_{2i}) + B(x_{3i} - x_{2i}) = 0,$$

where A and B are constants of like sign and not both zero. If the condition (4.16) is satisfied, and if $P_1 \neq P_2$ and $P_2 \neq P_3$, then P_2 is said to lie *between* P_1 and P_3.

4.6. *Orthogonal Transformations*

Of special interest to factor analysis are some theorems of elementary geometry which have to do with transformations which leave distances invariant. Such transformations, in which any point $P_1:(x_{1i})$ is carried into $Q_1:(y_{1i})$ and $P_2:(x_{2i})$ is carried into $Q_2:(y_{2i})$, have the following property

(4.17)
$$\sum (x_{1i} - x_{2i})^2 = \sum (y_{1i} - y_{2i})^2.$$

From the condition that a point P_2 is between two others, P_1 and P_3, if, and only if,

$$D(P_1P_2) + D(P_2P_3) = D(P_1P_3),$$

it follows that a transformation which leaves distances unaltered carries straight lines into straight lines. Now, by a fundamental theorem of geometry,[7] the transformation is linear, that is, of the form

(4.18)
$$y_{ji} = \sum_{k=1}^{N} \alpha_{ik} x_{jk} + c_i \qquad (i = 1, 2, \cdots, N; \ j = 1, 2, 3, \cdots).$$

Upon substituting the values of y_{1i} and y_{2i} from (4.18), equation (4.17) becomes

(4.19)
$$\sum_{i=1}^{N} (x_{1i} - x_{2i})^2 = \sum_{i=1}^{N} \left[\sum_{k=1}^{N} \alpha_{ik}(x_{1k} - x_{2k}) \right]^2.$$

It now remains to find the conditions which the α's must satisfy in order that (4.19) should hold, and then the most general transformation which preserves distance will be specified. The right-hand side of (4.19) can be written as follows:

(4.20)
$$\sum_{i=1}^{N} \sum_{k=1}^{N} \sum_{l=1}^{N} \alpha_{ik}\alpha_{il}(x_{1k} - x_{2k})(x_{1l} - x_{2l}).$$

Hence, equation (4.19) is satisfied when

(4.21)
$$\sum \alpha_{ik}\alpha_{il} = \delta_{kl},$$

where δ_{kl} is the Kronecker delta which is equal to unity if $k = l$ and equal to zero if $k \neq l$. Any linear homogeneous transformation,

(4.22)
$$y_{ji} = \sum_{k=1}^{N} \alpha_{ik} x_{jk},$$

whose coefficients satisfy (4.21) is called *orthogonal*, and its matrix an *orthogonal matrix*. The following theorem has thus been established:

THEOREM 4.3. *The distance between any two points is an invariant under a general rigid motion, that is, an orthogonal transformation followed by a translation.*

The concept of an orthogonal transformation can be expressed most clearly in matrix notation. To this end, let the sets of initial coordinates and final coordinates in the N-space be represented by rows of the following matrices:

$$\mathbf{X} = \begin{bmatrix} x_{11} & x_{12} & \cdots & x_{1N} \\ x_{21} & x_{22} & \cdots & x_{2N} \\ \cdot & \cdot & \cdots & \cdot \\ \cdot & \cdot & \cdots & \cdot \end{bmatrix} \quad \text{and} \quad \mathbf{Y} = \begin{bmatrix} y_{11} & y_{12} & \cdots & y_{1N} \\ y_{21} & y_{22} & \cdots & y_{2N} \\ \cdot & \cdot & \cdots & \cdot \\ \cdot & \cdot & \cdots & \cdot \end{bmatrix}.$$

[7] The theorem states that *any nonsingular transformation of an N-space into itself is linear if it carries straight lines into straight lines.* For a proof of this theorem see Veblen and Whitehead (1932, pp. 12–15).

Then, if

$$T = \begin{bmatrix} \alpha_{11} & \alpha_{12} & \cdots & \alpha_{1N} \\ \alpha_{21} & \alpha_{22} & \cdots & \alpha_{2N} \\ \cdot\cdot & \cdot & \cdot\cdot\cdot & \cdot\cdot \\ \alpha_{N1} & \alpha_{N2} & \cdots & \alpha_{NN} \end{bmatrix},$$

the transformation (4.22) becomes:

(4.23)
$$Y = XT'.$$

The transformation matrix **T** is said to be orthogonal if and only if (see **3.2** paragraph **24**):

(4.24)
$$T'T = I.$$

In other words, the conditions (4.21) that the coefficients α_{ik} must satisfy in order that the transformation (4.22) be orthogonal imply an identity matrix. It also follows that a matrix **T** is an orthogonal matrix if it satisfies the condition (4.24).

4.7. *Angular Separation between Two Lines*

Other geometric ideas that are useful in factor analysis center around the notion of the angle between two lines. The only characteristic of a point is its position, as given by its coordinates in a frame of reference. A line is ordinarily distinguished not by coordinates but by its inclinations to the respective coordinate axes. The angles which a line OP makes with the axes, i.e., $\theta_i = \angle POx_i$, are called the *direction angles* of the line, and their cosines are called *direction cosines*. If the norm $N(P)$, i.e., the distance $D(OP)$, is denoted by ρ, then the direction cosines are given by

(4.25)
$$\lambda_i = \cos\theta_i = x_i/\rho \qquad\qquad (i = 1, 2, \cdots, N).$$

By (4.12),

$$\rho^2 = \sum x_i^2,$$

and substituting the value of x_i from (4.25), gives

(4.26)
$$\sum \lambda_i^2 = \sum \cos^2\theta_i = 1.$$

This property, that the sum of the squares of the direction cosines of a line in N-space is equal to unity, is a direct extension of the one in ordinary space.

The parametric equations of a line through the origin O and a fixed point $P_1 : (x_{1i})$ are given by (4.8). The coordinates of any point $P : (x_i)$ on a line through the origin with the direction cosines λ_i are given by (4.25). When ρ is taken as a parametric variable along the line, the N equations (4.25) can be regarded as the equations of the line, which may be written

$$\rho = \frac{x_i}{\lambda_i} \qquad\qquad (i = 1, 2, \cdots, N).$$

Upon equating the N expressions for ρ, the following $N - 1$ equations arise:

(4.27)
$$\frac{x_1}{\lambda_1} = \frac{x_2}{\lambda_2} = \cdots = \frac{x_N}{\lambda_N}.$$

If $P:(x_1, x_2, \cdots, x_N)$ is taken as a variable point on the line, (4.27) can be regarded as the equations of the line.

By means of a translation, of the form (4.10), the equations of a line AP through an arbitrarily fixed point $A:(a_1, a_2, \cdots, a_N)$ and with the direction cosines λ_i are transformed from (4.27) to

(4.28)
$$\frac{x_1 - a_1}{\lambda_1} = \frac{x_2 - a_2}{\lambda_2} = \cdots = \frac{x_N - a_N}{\lambda_N}.$$

Moreover, if

(4.29)
$$\lambda_i = bl_i \qquad\qquad (i = 1, 2, \cdots, N),$$

where b is a constant different from zero, the equations of the line AP may be written in the form

(4.30)
$$\frac{x_1 - a_1}{l_1} = \frac{x_2 - a_2}{l_2} = \cdots = \frac{x_N - a_N}{l_N},$$

where the l_i are not now equal to, but only proportional to, the direction cosines. The numbers l_i are called *direction numbers* of the line.

The actual direction cosines of a line can readily be obtained from the numbers proportional to them. For, squaring both sides of (4.29) and summing for i, this equation becomes

$$b^2 \sum l_i^2 = \sum \lambda_i^2 = 1,$$

where the last equality follows from (4.26). Then the constant of proportionality is

$$b = \frac{1}{\sqrt{\sum l_i^2}},$$

and the direction cosines are given by

(4.31)
$$\lambda_i = \frac{l_i}{\sqrt{\sum l_i^2}}.$$

Hence (4.30) may be taken as the general form of the $(N - 1)$ equations of a line in N-space.

The coordinates of any point $P:(x_i)$ on a line through $A:(a_i)$ with direction numbers l_i are

(4.32)
$$x_i = a_i + tl_i \qquad\qquad (i = 1, 2, \cdots, N),$$

where t is the common value in (4.30). Equations (4.32) may be regarded as a system of parametric equations of a line through a fixed point. The distance $D(AP)$ along the line from the fixed point A to any position of the variable point P is

58

$$D(AP) = \sqrt{\sum (x_i - a_i)^2} = t\sqrt{\sum l_i^2},$$

so that,

(4.33)
$$t = \frac{D(AP)}{\sqrt{\sum l_i^2}}.$$

It is thus evident that the parameter t in equations (4.32) is proportional to the distance from the fixed point to a variable point on the line and is equal to this distance when the equations of the line are given in terms of the direction cosines.

Now a formula for the cosine of the angle between two lines in N-space may be derived. When two lines meet in a point,[8] a plane can be drawn through the point

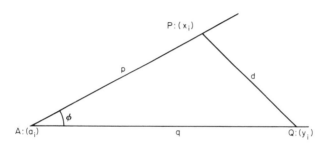

FIG. 4.1.—Angle between two lines

containing the two lines, and their inclination can be obtained from the trigonometric properties of a triangle in the plane. Let the two lines through $A:(a_i)$ be represented by the equations

(4.34)
$$\frac{x_1 - a_1}{\lambda_1} = \frac{x_2 - a_2}{\lambda_2} = \cdots = \frac{x_N - a_N}{\lambda_N},$$

$$\frac{y_1 - a_1}{\mu_1} = \frac{y_2 - a_2}{\mu_2} = \cdots = \frac{y_N - a_N}{\mu_N},$$

where the x_i and y_i are the coordinates of the variable points on the lines, and the λ_i and μ_i are the direction cosines of the lines. On the first line take any point P at a distance p from A; on the second line take any point Q at a distance q from A; and connect the points P and Q with a line, which necessarily lies in the plane. The points and lines are plotted in the plane of the two given lines in Figure 4.1.

Let ϕ = angle PAQ and let $d = D(PQ)$, then the law of cosines applied to the triangle PAQ gives

(4.35)
$$d^2 = p^2 + q^2 - 2pq \cos \phi.$$

[8]If the lines do not meet in a point, the angle between the lines may be defined as the angle which one of the lines makes with a line parallel to the second, which intersects the first line.

The distance d is also given by formula (4.13), in which, according to (4.32), the coordinates of P are $x_i = a_i + p\lambda_i$ and those of Q are $y_i = a_i + q\mu_i$, so that

$$\begin{aligned}
d^2 &= \sum (x_i - y_i)^2 = \sum (p\lambda_i - q\mu_i)^2, \\
&= p^2 \sum \lambda_i^2 + q^2 \sum \mu_i^2 - 2pq \sum \lambda_i\mu_i, \\
&= p^2 + q^2 - 2pq \sum \lambda_i\mu_i,
\end{aligned}$$

(4.36)

since $\sum \lambda_i^2 = \sum \mu_i^2 = 1$ by (4.26). When the terms of (4.36) are identified with the corresponding ones of (4.35), the following result is obtained:

(4.37)
$$\cos \phi = \sum \lambda_i\mu_i.$$

Thus the cosine of the angle of separation of two lines is given by the sum of the products of corresponding direction cosines of the lines, i.e., the scalar product of the vectors $(\lambda_1, \lambda_2, \cdots, \lambda_N)$ and $(\mu_1, \mu_2, \cdots, \mu_N)$.

By means of formula (4.37) another expression for the scalar product of two vectors or points may be written in place of (4.11). The coordinates of the two points $P_1:(x_{1i})$ and $P_2:(x_{2i})$ may be expressed as follows:

$$x_{1i} = \rho_1\lambda_{1i}, \qquad x_{2i} = \rho_2\lambda_{2i} \qquad (i = 1, 2, \cdots, N),$$

where ρ_1, ρ_2 are the respective distances from the origin to the points, and $\lambda_{1i}, \lambda_{2i}$ are the direction cosines of the lines OP_1 and OP_2. Then, substituting these values in (4.11), there arises

$$P_1 \cdot P_2 = \sum x_{1i}x_{2i} = \rho_1\rho_2 \sum \lambda_{1i}\lambda_{2i},$$

which, according to (4.37), reduces to

(4.38)
$$P_1 \cdot P_2 = \rho_1\rho_2\cos \phi_{12},$$

where ϕ_{12} is the angle P_1OP_2. Formula (4.38) states that the scalar product of two vectors is the product of the lengths of the vectors by the cosine of their angular separation. This is very often taken as the definition of the scalar product.

4.8.   *Distance and Angle in General Cartesian Coordinates*

In sections **4.5** and **4.7** formulas for distance and angle are presented in terms of rectangular coordinates. Now the restriction that the coordinate axes are mutually orthogonal will be removed, and more general formulas obtained. The formulas for distance and angle will then be in terms of general Cartesian coordinates and will simplify to the preceding ones when the angles between all pairs of reference axes are taken as 90°.

The general Cartesian coordinate system contains N reference axes Ox_i which may make any angles with one another. Then the angle between the x_i and x_k axes may be designated $\theta_{ik}(i, k = 1, 2, \cdots, N)$. As may be expected, the formulas for distance and angle in terms of general Cartesian coordinates will involve the inclinations of the reference axes.

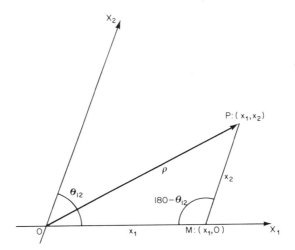

FIG. 4.2.—Distance from origin to a point in general coordinates

Formulas for the distance function in general coordinates will first be given. In the plane the square of the length of the radius vector OP is readily found to be

$$\rho^2 = [D(OP)]^2 = x_1^2 + x_2^2 - 2x_1 x_2 \cos(180° - \theta_{12}) = x_1^2 + x_2^2 + 2x_1 x_2 \cos \theta_{12}.$$

This formula follows immediately on applying the law of cosines to the triangle POM, indicated in Figure 4.2. By induction, it can be shown that in N-space the distance ρ from the origin O to an arbitrary point $P:(x_1, x_2, \cdots, x_N)$ is given by

(4.39)
$$\rho = \sqrt{\sum\sum x_i x_k \cos \theta_{ik}},$$

where $\sum\sum$ indicates summation for i and k from 1 to N. This convention for the double summation will be employed throughout this section. Similarly, the distance between any two points

$$P_1:(x_{11}, x_{12}, \cdots, x_{1N}) \quad \text{and} \quad P_2:(x_{21}, x_{22}, \cdots, x_{2N})$$

may be shown to be given by the following formula:

(4.40)
$$D(P_1 P_2) = \sqrt{\sum\sum (x_{1i} - x_{2i})(x_{1k} - x_{2k}) \cos \theta_{ik}}.$$

The relations (4.39) and (4.40) reduce to the corresponding formulas (4.12) and (4.13) for distance in rectangular coordinates, inasmuch as $\cos \theta_{ik} = 0$ for every $i \neq k$.

There will now be given several properties of a line in terms of more general (not necessarily rectangular) coordinates. The direction of a line OP is determined by the ratios of the coordinates of an arbitrary point $P:(x_1, x_2, \cdots, x_N)$ on the line to the length $\rho = D(OP)$ from the origin to the point. These ratios, denoted by $\lambda_i = x_i/\rho$, are called the *direction ratios* of the line OP. Then if the coordinates of P are expressed in the form

(4.41)
$$x_i = \rho\lambda_i \quad \text{or} \quad x_k = \rho\lambda_k,$$

and substituted in (4.39), there results

$$(4.42) \qquad \sum \sum \lambda_i \lambda_k \cos \theta_{ik} = 1.$$

The direction ratios become the direction cosines of a line when a general Cartesian coordinate system is specialized to a rectangular one. Then formula (4.42) reduces to (4.26).

An expression for the angle between two lines, in general coordinates, can now be deduced. For simplicity, let the two lines pass through the origin and be distinguished by the direction ratios λ_i, μ_i $(i = 1, 2, \cdots, N)$, respectively. Select a point $P:(x_i)$ on the first line, and a point $Q:(y_i)$ on the second line, and let $p = D(OP), q = D(OQ)$, $d = D(PQ)$, and $\phi =$ angle POQ. Then

$$d^2 = p^2 + q^2 - 2pq \cos \phi.$$

But d is also given by (4.40), in which the coordinates of P are $x_i = p\lambda_i$ and those of Q are $y_i = q\mu_i$, so that after these values are substituted, the formula becomes

$$d^2 = p^2 + q^2 - 2pq \sum \sum \lambda_i \mu_k \cos \theta_{ik}.$$

By equating the two expressions for the square of the distance, the following formula for the angle between two lines is obtained:

$$(4.43) \qquad \cos \phi = \sum \sum \lambda_i \mu_k \cos \theta_{ik}.$$

This formula reduces to (4.37) when the axes make right angles with one another.

4.9. *Geometric Interpretation of Correlation*

In this and the following section there will be presented a number of applications of the preceding geometric ideas to the factor problem. The raw data are the values of n variables for each of N individuals. When the variables are in standard form, the matrix of such values:

$$\mathbf{Z} = (z_{ji}) = \begin{bmatrix} z_{11} & z_{12} & \cdots & z_{1N} \\ z_{21} & z_{22} & \cdots & z_{2N} \\ \cdot & \cdot & \cdot\cdot\cdot & \cdot\cdot \\ z_{n1} & z_{n2} & \cdots & z_{nN} \end{bmatrix},$$

may be interpreted as containing (by rows) the rectangular Cartesian coordinates of n points z_j $(j = 1, 2, \cdots, n)$ in an N-space. Similar interpretation can be made of the elements in the matrix $\mathbf{X} = (x_{ji})$ of deviate values.

The length of the radius vector to a point x_j, according to formula (4.12), is

$$(4.44) \qquad \rho_j = \sqrt{\sum x_{ji}^2}.$$

According to definition (2.4), however, this expression simplifies as follows:

$$(4.45) \qquad \rho_j = \sqrt{N} s_j.$$

The standard deviation of a variable may thus be interpreted as being proportional to the distance from the origin to the point representing the variable, the constant of proportionality being $1/\sqrt{N}$.

By way of geometric representation of a set of values of two variables, x_j and x_k, it is customary to think of the x_{ji} and the x_{ki} as the coordinates of N points (x_{j1}, x_{k1}), $(x_{j2}, x_{k2}), \cdots, (x_{jN}, x_{kN})$ in the plane $x_j O x_k$. This plot of points is called a *scatter diagram*; and, by means of this representation, a better understanding of the relations involved in the definition (2.7) of a coefficient of correlation can be obtained. In general, for n variables this will be referred to as the *point representation*.

Even more important in some respects is a geometric representation not by N points in a plane (for two variables) but by two points in an N-space. The two variables are then represented by the vectors $\mathbf{x}_j : (x_{j1}, x_{j2}, \cdots, x_{jN})$ and $\mathbf{x}_k : (x_{k1}, x_{k2}, \cdots, x_{kN})$. Such a configuration for n variables will be called the *vector representation*.

The interpretation of the n rows of matrix $\mathbf{Z}$ as the coordinates of n points in an N-space is the vector representation of the variables. On the other hand, the same numbers in the matrix $\mathbf{Z}$ may be read in sets by columns to give N points in an n-space. In the latter case there will be a swarm of N points in the point representation of the n variables. While both concepts are employed in factor analysis, somewhat greater use is made of the notion of n vectors to represent the variables in a space corresponding to the N individuals.

If the direction cosines of these vectors are denoted by λ_{ji} and λ_{ki}, respectively, then by (4.25),

$$(4.46) \qquad \lambda_{ji} = \frac{x_{ji}}{\rho_j}, \qquad \lambda_{ki} = \frac{x_{ki}}{\rho_k} \qquad (i = 1, 2, \cdots, N),$$

where $\rho_j = D(Ox_j)$ and $\rho_k = D(Ox_k)$. Inserting these values in formula (4.37), it becomes

$$(4.47) \qquad \cos \phi_{jk} = \sum \lambda_{ji} \lambda_{ki} = \frac{\sum x_{ji} x_{ki}}{\rho_j \rho_k},$$

where ϕ_{jk} is the angle of separation of the two lines. Then $\cos \phi_{jk}$ may be interpreted as the scalar product of the vectors x_j and x_k divided by the product of the lengths of these vectors. Upon substituting the values for ρ_j and ρ_k from (4.45), formula (4.47) reduces to:

$$(4.48) \qquad \cos \phi_{jk} = \frac{\sum x_{ji} x_{ki}}{N s_j s_k} = r_{jk} \qquad (j, k = 1, 2, \cdots, n).$$

The coefficient of correlation between two variables (measured as deviates from their respective means) is the cosine of the angle between their vectors in N-space.

While the raw data of a study are the values of the variables, whether they are in arbitrary units or standardized, such data are usually reduced to correlation coefficients among the variables before a factor analysis is made. For this reason, it is important to put some of the preceding geometric notions in terms of the correlation matrix $\mathbf{R}$ instead of the matrix of standard deviates $\mathbf{Z}$. In particular, it is desirable to have an interpretation of Theorem 4.2 in terms of the correlation matrix. To this end, the following is required first:

THEOREM 4.4. *The rank of the product of a matrix by its transpose is equal to the rank of the matrix.*

The proof follows immediately from another theorem (Hadley 1961, p. 138), which states that the rank of the product of any two matrices is less than or equal to the minimum of the rank of either one. Since the two matrices under consideration in Theorem 4.4 are transposes of one another, and have the same rank, the rank of the product is equal to this common rank.

The product of the matrix $\mathbf{Z}$ by its transpose $\mathbf{Z}'$ is equal to the correlation matrix $\mathbf{R}$ multiplied by the scalar N, viz.,

$$(4.49) \qquad\qquad \mathbf{ZZ}' = N\mathbf{R},$$

corresponding to (2.45) but in which the scalar N appears because the variables were not assumed to be small standard deviates. Since the theorem is concerned only with the ranks of the matrices, the non-zero factor N is irrelevant to it. With this understanding, the theorem may be restated as follows: If m is the rank of matrix $\mathbf{Z}$, then the rank of $\mathbf{R} = \mathbf{ZZ}'$ is equal to m. In other words, the rank of the correlation matrix is equal to the rank of the matrix of observed values.

A more powerful relationship between these two matrices (and also between the reproduced correlation matrix and the factor matrix) is the following:

THEOREM 4.5. *If $\mathbf{Z}$ is an n by N matrix of rank m, with real elements, then $\mathbf{ZZ}' = \mathbf{R}$ is a positive semidefinite real symmetric matrix (Gramian) of rank m.*[9]

4.10.   *Common-Factor Space*

The geometric notions introduced in this chapter make it possible to determine the minimum number of common factors necessary to describe a set of variables in the sense of equations (2.22). According to Theorem 4.2, the n points whose coordinates are given in the matrix $\mathbf{Z}$ are all contained in a linear m-space, where m is the rank of the matrix. In other words, the n vectors can be described in terms of m reference vectors. Furthermore, since the rank of the correlation matrix $\mathbf{R}$ is equal to the rank of the matrix of standardized values $\mathbf{Z}$ (according to Theorem 4.4), any property of the variables which is inferred only from the rank of the latter matrix may be stated in terms of the correlation matrix. It therefore follows from Theorem 4.2 that *the n variables can be expressed as linear functions of not less than m factors, where m is the rank of the correlation matrix.*

In the case of the component analysis model (2.8), the correlation matrix contains ones in the diagonal and its rank usually is n. The variables would then be describable in terms of not less than n factors.

If it is desired to describe the n variables in terms of fewer than n common factors, a pattern of the form (2.22) may be postulated. From such a pattern the correlations are reproduced so as to approximate the observed correlations, but with commu-

[9]For proof see Albert (1941, p. 65).

nalities in place of 1's in the diagonal. Such a theoretical correlation matrix $\hat{\mathbf{R}}$ (of rank m) would yield a factor solution $\mathbf{A}$ in terms of m common factors that satisfies the fundamental factor theorem (2.50). By the preceding argument, the number of common factors in the pattern, m, is equal to the rank of the reproduced correlation matrix. This is the smallest number of factors that will account for the intercorrelations. Stated geometrically, the smallest space containing the n points is a flat m-space. Such a space will be referred to as the *common-factor space*. For purposes of reference the above ideas may be recapitulated in the following:

THEOREM 4.6. *If m is the rank of the reproduced correlation matrix then the smallest number of linearly independent factors which will account for the correlations is m, or, the common-factor space is of m dimensions.*

Of course, the matrix $\hat{\mathbf{R}}$ is not known in advance—only the observed correlation matrix $\mathbf{R}$ is given. What is often done, in practice, is to analyze the observed correlation matrix but with (estimates of) communalities in the diagonal. Such a *reduced correlation matrix* is, in effect, a mixture of the empirical and theoretical correlation matrices—the actual observed correlations off the diagonal and communalities in place of the 1's on the diagonal. The rank of the reproduced (or theoretical) correlation matrix $\hat{\mathbf{R}}$ is m according to the model specified, but there is no assurance that this would also be the rank of the reduced correlation matrix as here defined. As a matter of fact it more likely would be n, as in the case of the full correlation matrix $\mathbf{R}$ (with 1's in the diagonal). Nonetheless, practitioners analyze the reduced correlation matrix *as if* it were the matrix of reproduced correlations, tacitly assuming that the observed correlations are reasonable approximations for the theoretical ones, and that the rank can be assumed to be m.

It should be emphasized that while the dimension of the common-factor space can be determined by any of several methods (see part II), such solutions do not provide unique positions of the factors. Any m linearly independent factors form a basis of the common-factor space, and, as noted before, the selection of a particular basis is considered in part iii.

In order to clarify the preceding ideas, the three important spaces will be reviewed. For any variable z_j the system $(z_{j1}, z_{j2}, \cdots, z_{jN})$ of N real numbers may be considered as the rectangular Cartesian coordinates of a point in an N-dimensional space. By means of this vector representation, the configuration of two variables is merely two dimensional, i.e., in a plane, although it has to be regarded as imbedded in an N-space. In general, the configuration of n vectors may be regarded as in an n-dimensional space which is imbedded in the original N-space. For purposes of factor analysis, this space may be reduced further, to the m-space which will contain the n vectors, as indicated in Theorem 4.6.

Before giving the final interpretation of the vectors representing the variables in the common-factor space, the geometric meaning of the linear expressions (2.9) which include unique as well as common factors will be indicated. The n vectors may then be considered in the total-factor space of the m common factors and n unique factors. The vector representation of any variable in this space is given by

$$\hat{z}_j : (a_{j1}, a_{j2}, \cdots, a_{jm}, 0, \cdots, 0, u_j, 0, \cdots, 0),$$

where the hat is employed to indicate the linear model (2.9) for the observed variable z_j. The first m coordinates are with respect to the common-factor axes, and the last n coordinates, consisting of only one value different from zero, are with respect to the unique-factor axes. For simplicity let it be assumed that the common factors are mutually orthogonal, and, as usual, the unique factors are orthogonal to all factors. Then the norm, or length, of such a vector, according to (4.12), is

$$(4.50) \qquad N(\hat{z}_j) = \sqrt{a_{j1}^2 + \cdots + a_{jm}^2 + u_j^2} = 1.$$

In other words, each of the vectors representing the variables in the total factor space is of unit length. The direction cosines of such a vector in this space are simply the coordinates of the end point. The cosine of the angle of inclination ($\hat{\phi}_{jk}$) of two such vectors, $\hat{z}_j$ and $\hat{z}_k$, then becomes

$$(4.51) \qquad \cos \hat{\phi}_{jk} = \sum_{p=1}^{m+n} \lambda_{jp} \lambda_{kp} = \sum_{p=1}^{m} a_{jp} a_{kp} = \hat{r}_{jk},$$

where λ_{jp} and λ_{kp} denote the sets of direction cosines of $\hat{z}_j$ and $\hat{z}_k$, respectively. Equation (4.51) shows that the reproduced correlation for any two variables is the cosine of the angle between their vectors in the total-factor space. The reproduced correlation $\hat{r}_{jk}$ will approximate the observed correlation r_{jk} to the extent that the mathematical models of the variables are adequate.

Now the final interpretation of the variables as vectors in the common-factor space can be made. The orthogonal projections of the n vectors from the total-factor space into the common-factor space of m dimensions are defined to be the vectors representing the variables in this subspace. Such a vector may be denoted by a tilde ($\tilde{\ }$) or curl over the symbol for the variable, namely,

$$\tilde{z}_j : (a_{j1}, a_{j2}, \cdots, a_{jm}).$$

This representation was previously introduced as the vector **c** in (2.35) and (2.36) to emphasize the common parts of the variables. The coordinates of the end point of this vector are the same as the first m coordinates in the total-factor space. This property holds even if the common-factor axes are oblique, provided only that the unique-factor axes are orthogonal to the common-factor space. It will again be assumed for simplicity that the common factors are uncorrelated.

A projected vector in the m-space is usually of smaller magnitude than the corresponding vector in the total-factor space, being of the same length only if the variable has no unique variance. Likewise, the angles between pairs of vectors in the common-factor space are smaller and, consequently, their cosines larger. The length of a vector $\tilde{z}_j$ in this space is given by

$$(4.52) \qquad N(\tilde{z}_j) = \sqrt{a_{j1}^2 + a_{j2}^2 + \cdots + a_{jm}^2} = h_j,$$

that is, the square root of the communality h_j^2 of the variable. The direction cosines of any two vectors $\tilde{z}_j$ and $\tilde{z}_k$ in the common-factor space are given by

$$(4.53) \qquad \tilde{\lambda}_{jp} = a_{jp}/h_j, \qquad \tilde{\lambda}_{kp} = a_{kp}/h_k \qquad (p = 1, 2, \cdots, m).$$

Putting these values into (4.37), the cosine of the angle of inclination of these vectors becomes

$$(4.54) \qquad \cos \tilde{\phi}_{jk} = \sum_{p=1}^{m} \tilde{\lambda}_{jp} \tilde{\lambda}_{kp} = \sum_{p=1}^{m} a_{jp} a_{kp} \Big/ h_j h_k.$$

It is obvious that this expression is generally larger than that given by (4.51), being equal to it only when $h_j h_k = 1$. Hence the angles between vectors in the common-factor space are smaller than the corresponding angles in the total-factor space.

The problem of interpreting a reproduced correlation $\hat{r}_{jk}$ geometrically can be treated in the common-factor space. It is evident from (4.51) and (4.54) that

$$(4.55) \qquad \tilde{r}_{jk} = \cos \tilde{\phi}_{jk} = \hat{r}_{jk}/h_j h_k.$$

The cosine of the angle of separation of two vectors representing variables in the common-factor space may be referred to as the correlation corrected for uniqueness. In other words, the expression (4.55) would be the value of the reproduced correlation between j and k if these variables were free from unique variance. Solving (4.55) explicitly for the reproduced correlation, there results

$$(4.56) \qquad \hat{r}_{jk} = h_j h_k \cos \tilde{\phi}_{jk} = h_j h_k \tilde{r}_{jk}.$$

Thus, by formula (4.38), the reproduced correlation between two variables is given by the scalar product of their vectors in the common-factor space. Of course, the observed correlation r_{jk} differs from the value given in (4.56), unless the residual is exactly zero.

Many concepts useful in factor analysis have been developed and given geometric interpretation in this chapter. In order to summarize these ideas, and to make them readily available for future reference, they are recapitulated in Table 4.1.

A simple illustration of the foregoing ideas is given for the case of only two factors. The common-factor space is of two dimensions, and the two (uncorrelated) factors F_1 and F_2 are represented in Figure 4.3 by unit vectors separated by a right angle. Each variable z_j of a set can be described in terms of the two common factors and a unique factor. The linear expressions for two such variables may be written as follows:

$$\hat{z}_1 = a_{11} F_1 + a_{12} F_2 + u_1 Y_1 + 0 \cdot Y_2,$$
$$\hat{z}_2 = a_{21} F_1 + a_{22} F_2 + 0 \cdot Y_1 + u_2 Y_2.$$

The geometric representation of these linear expressions for the original variables can be made in the total-factor space of four dimensions, defined by the two common factors and the two unique factors. In this space the vectors representing $\hat{z}_1$ and $\hat{z}_2$ are of unit length, and their correlation is given by

$$\hat{r}_{12} = a_{11} a_{21} + a_{12} a_{22}.$$

Such essential information about the variables as the correlations can be obtained from the consideration of the common-factor space. The projections of the two vectors $\hat{z}_1$ and $\hat{z}_2$ into this space are indicated in Figure 4.3 by $\tilde{z}_1$ and $\tilde{z}_2$, respectively, and may be written analytically in the form

$$\tilde{z}_1 = a_{11}F_1 + a_{12}F_2,$$

$$\tilde{z}_2 = a_{21}F_1 + a_{22}F_2.$$

The lengths of these vectors are given by the square roots of their communalities, i.e.,

$$D(O\tilde{z}_1) = \sqrt{a_{11}^2 + a_{12}^2} = \sqrt{h_1^2},$$

$$D(O\tilde{z}_2) = \sqrt{a_{21}^2 + a_{22}^2} = \sqrt{h_2^2}.$$

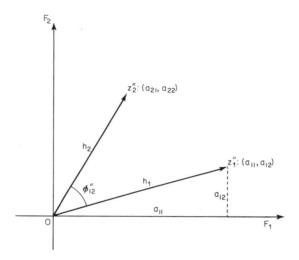

FIG. 4.3.—Common-factor space of two dimensions

The cosine of the angle ($\tilde{\phi}_{12}$) separating these vectors is given by

$$\cos \tilde{\phi}_{12} = \frac{a_{11}}{h_1} \cdot \frac{a_{21}}{h_2} + \frac{a_{12}}{h_1} \cdot \frac{a_{22}}{h_2} = \frac{1}{h_1 h_2}(a_{11}a_{21} + a_{12}a_{22}),$$

or

$$\hat{r}_{12} = h_1 h_2 \cos \tilde{\phi}_{12}.$$

This formula shows that the reproduced correlation of two variables is given by the product of the lengths of the two vectors by the cosine of their angle of separation in the common-factor space.

In the foregoing discussion it was necessary to employ distinct notation to clearly represent elements in the different spaces. Since it would be rather clumsy to retain the "hats" and "curls" in the remainder of this volume, they will be dropped when no confusion can arise as to the particular space involved.

Table 4.1

Concepts Stemming from Vector Representation of Variables

(N = number of individuals; n = number of variables; m = number of common factors)

Concept	Sample Space			Total-Factor Space	Common-Factor Space
	Variables in Deviate Form	Variables in Standard Form	Variable Space		
Number of dimensions	N	N	n	$n + m$	m
Variables $(j = 1, 2, \cdots, n)$	x_j	z_j		$\hat{z}_j = a_{j1}F_1 + \cdots + a_{jm}F_m + u_jY_j$	$\tilde{z}_j = a_{j1}F_1 + \cdots + a_{jm}F_m$
Coordinates $(i = 1, \cdots, N;$ $p = 1, \cdots, m)$	x_{ji}	z_{ji}		a_{jp}, u_j	a_{jp}
Length of radius vector	$\rho_j = \sqrt{N}s_j$	$\rho_j = \sqrt{N}$		$\hat{\rho}_j = N(\hat{z}_j) = 1$	$\tilde{\rho}_j = N(\tilde{z}_j)$ $= h_j$
Direction cosines of vector corresponding to variable j	$\lambda_{ji} = \dfrac{x_{ji}}{\rho_j}$	$\lambda_{ji} = \dfrac{z_{ji}}{\sqrt{N}}$		$\lambda_{jp} = a_{jp},$ $\lambda_j = u_j$ $\lambda_k = 0$ for $k \neq j$ $(k = 1, \cdots, n)$	$\tilde{\lambda}_{jp} = \dfrac{a_{jp}}{h_j}$
Angle between variables j and k	θ_{jk}	θ_{jk}		$\hat{\theta}_{jk}$	$\tilde{\theta}_{jk}$
Cosine of angle	$\cos \theta_{jk}$ $= \sum_i \lambda_{ji}\lambda_{ki}$ $= \dfrac{\sum_i x_{ji}x_{ki}}{Ns_js_k}$ $= r_{jk}$	$\cos \theta_{jk}$ $= \sum_i \lambda_{ji}\lambda_{ki}$ $= \dfrac{\sum_i z_{ji}z_{ki}}{N}$ $= r_{jk}$		$\cos \hat{\theta}_{jk}$ $= \sum_{p=1}^{m+n} \lambda_{jp}\lambda_{kp}$ $= \sum_{p=1}^{m} a_{jp}a_{kp}$ $= \hat{r}_{jk}$	$\cos \tilde{\theta}_{jk}$ $= \sum_{p=1}^{m} \tilde{\lambda}_{jp}\tilde{\lambda}_{kp}$ $= \dfrac{\sum_{p=1}^{m} a_{jp}a_{kp}}{h_jh_k}$ $= \tilde{r}_{jk}$
Correlation between variables j and k	r_{jk}	r_{jk}		$\hat{r}_{jk} = \sum_{p=1}^{m} a_{jp}a_{kp}$	$\tilde{r}_{jk} = h_jh_k\tilde{r}_{jk}$

5   The Problem of Communality

5.1. *Introduction*

From basic mathematical theory it is known that a matrix of real numbers that is symmetric and is dominated by the principal diagonal is positive semi-definite (i.e., Gramian) with the important property of having all of its eigenvalues (see chap. 8) as positive numbers or zero. Since a correlation matrix is symmetric with unities in the principal diagonal and fractional numbers between -1 and $+1$ off the diagonal, it satisfies all these conditions and all of its eigenvalues must be positive or zero. This implies that the number of common factors would be equal to the order n of the correlation matrix except for the possible zero cases. Of course, when the diagonal of 1's in the correlation matrix is altered—replaced by communality estimates—such a reduced correlation matrix will not be Gramian in general.

The essential problem of factor analysis—manifested by a set of linear equations (2.22) describing the variables in terms of new constructs (factors)—is to find a theoretical matrix $\hat{\mathbf{R}}$, with lower rank than the matrix $\mathbf{R}$ of observed correlations, for which the off-diagonal residuals can be attributed to sampling errors. If such a matrix $\hat{\mathbf{R}}$ can be found, with the rank $m < n$, a solution $\mathbf{A}$ may have considerable scientific value. The various methods of factor analysis seek such a "best fitting" theoretical matrix through the analysis of the observed correlation matrix $\mathbf{R}$ with certain assumptions about its rank or the communalities.

In the preceding chapter it was shown that the dimension of the common-factor space is equal to the rank of the reproduced correlation matrix. The rank of this matrix is effected by the particular values in the principal diagonal, and it will also be recalled from **2.9** that the portions of the variances to be factored are determined by these diagonal elements. When unities are employed, i.e., assuming the component analysis model (2.8), the resulting descriptions of the n variables are in terms of n (rarely fewer) common factors. With the classical factor analysis model (2.9), the communalities are the basic quantities to be analyzed. Herein lies the trouble—there is no *a priori* knowledge of the values of the communalities. Either the rank of the correlation matrix or its diagonal values must be known, or approximated, in order to obtain a factor solution. According to Theorem 4.6, if the rank of the reproduced correlation matrix is known (or can be assumed) to be *m*, then the common-factor space is of *m*-dimensions. Several procedures for getting factor solutions make suitable approximations of the number of common factors (with more or less refined statistical tests of the adequacy of the assumed *m*). Other procedures require some estimates of the communalities, i.e., the diagonal values of the correlation matrix rather than its rank. The latter approach is employed in the principal-factor method and the centroid method, treated in chapter 8, as preliminary multiple-factor solutions (which may subsequently be transformed to more desirable solutions by the methods of part III). A problem that has been plaguing factor analysts since the beginning of the multiple factor approaches is the question of how to determine suitable approximations to "communality."

The general problem of communality is approached through the following considerations: (1) the conditions that the correlation coefficients must satisfy in order for their matrix to have a given rank; (2) the determination of communality under the assumption of the rank of the correlation matrix; (3) the theoretical solution for communality; (4) the estimation of communality without prior knowledge of the rank; (5) a simple example in which a factor solution is obtained directly, once the communalities of the variables have been determined. The first of these items is covered in Sections **5.2** and **5.3**, while the determination of communality using assumed rank is developed and illustrated in **5.4**. The theoretical considerations are presented in **5.5**, and followed by practical methods with examples in **5.6**. Finally, in **5.7**, a hypothetical example is employed to bring together the notions of communality and the factor model developed in the preceding chapters.

5.2.   *Determination of the Common-Factor Space*

The discussion of the common-factor space in **4.10** indicated how its dimension *m* was determined from the assumed factor model as the rank of its resultant theoretical correlation matrix. Conversely, it was suggested that the observed correlation matrix **R** might be analyzed into a factor matrix **A** of reduced rank by first changing its diagonal of 1's to communalities. Such a reduced correlation matrix may be represented by:

$$\mathbf{R} = \begin{bmatrix} h_1^2 & r_{12} & r_{13} & \cdots & r_{1n} \\ r_{21} & h_2^2 & r_{23} & \cdots & r_{2n} \\ r_{31} & r_{32} & h_3^2 & \cdots & r_{3n} \\ \cdot & \cdot & \cdot & \cdots & \cdot \\ r_{n1} & r_{n2} & r_{n3} & \cdots & h_n^2 \end{bmatrix},$$

where **R** is employed, just as for the full matrix with 1's in the diagonal, only to avoid additional symbolism. Of course, in practice the reduced matrix **R** will differ from the reproduced matrix **R̂** to the extent that the residuals are not precisely zero. However, the statistical variations are ignored in the following mathematical development of conditions that the correlations must satisfy in order that the rank of this matrix can be reduced from n by a suitable choice of the communalities for a given set of observed correlations. The number of linearly independent conditions that the unknown communalities h_j^2 must satisfy in order that the matrix **R** shall be of rank m can be determined by means of the following theorem (for proof see Dickson 1930, p. 79).

THEOREM 5.1. *The rank of the symmetric matrix* **R** *is m if an m-rowed principal minor* **R**$_{mm}$ *is not zero and if zero is the value of every principal minor obtained by annexing to* **R**$_{mm}$ *one row and the same column of* **R**, *and also of every principal minor obtained by annexing two rows and the same two columns.*

The number of conditions imposed on the communalities can be found by formal application of the procedure set forth in this theorem. There are n rows in **R** and m in the nonvanishing principal minor **R**$_{mm}$. This leaves $(n - m)$ rows which may be annexed, one at a time, to **R**$_{mm}$, or $(n - m)$ determinants which must vanish. The $(n - m)$ rows may be added two at a time in $\binom{n - m}{2}$ ways to **R**$_{mm}$, giving $(n - m)$ $(n - m - 1)/2$ additional determinants which must vanish. Hence the total number of independent conditions (i.e., the number of minors set equal to zero) that the communalities must satisfy in order that **R** be of rank m is[1]

$$(5.1) \quad \nu_m = (n - m) + (n - m)(n - m - 1)/2 = (n - m)(n - m + 1)/2.$$

In general, the ν_m equations have solutions $h_1^2, h_2^2, \cdots, h_n^2$ only if the number of unknowns is greater than or equal to this number of conditions. If the number of unknowns is less than the number of equations, then the coefficients in the equations (the correlations) must satisfy certain relations in order that the number of independent conditions for the unknowns may be reduced to the number of unknowns, i.e., in order that the equations be consistent. The fact that there is a match between the number of unknowns and the number of equations does not, in itself, guarantee that the equations (which may be quite complex) are solvable.

First, however, let it be assumed that the correlations are arbitrary values, in the sense that no constraints exist among them. Then the set of conditions can be satisfied only if they are no greater in number than the unknowns, viz.,

$$(5.2) \qquad\qquad n \geqq \nu_m.$$

The last inequality may be written in the following equivalent form:

$$(5.3) \qquad \phi(m) = \nu_m - n = [m^2 - (2n + 1)m + n(n - 2)]/2 \leqq 0.$$

---

[1]The proof given here is incomplete in the sense that the ν_m equations have not been shown to be linearly independent, i.e., that none of them follows from the others. Walter Lederman (1937) arrives at the same number of conditions for the n unknown communalities, although by a different argument, and offers a proof of the linear independence of these equations.

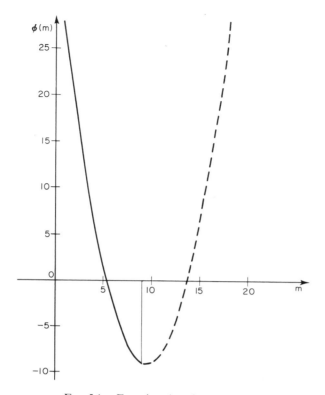

FIG. 5.1.—Function $\phi(m)$ for $n = 9$

Setting the quadratic $\phi(m)$ equal to zero and solving for m, the two roots are given by

$$(5.4) \qquad m = \left[(2n + 1) \pm \sqrt{8n + 1}\right]/2.$$

It can readily be shown that the plot of the quadratic function $\phi(m)$, for any fixed value of n, is a parabola which opens up vertically. A typical member of this family of parabolas is shown in Figure 5.1 for the case of $n = 9$. While the complete mathematical function is depicted in this figure, only the left part of the curve up to the point where $m = n$ has any interpretive value for factor analysis. In general the curve crosses the m-axis at the two points whose abscissas are given in (5.4), and hence $\phi(m) \leq 0$ for values of m between these extremes. The rank of the correlation matrix, with unknown communalities and arbitrary correlations, may thus be reduced to the value m, which is given by

$$(5.5) \qquad \left[(2n + 1) + \sqrt{8n + 1}\right]/2 \geq m \geq \left[(2n + 1) - \sqrt{8n + 1}\right]/2.$$

The smallest possible value for m is then the smallest integer greater than or equal to the value in the right-hand member of (5.5). In Table 5.1 there is listed the smallest rank that can be attained for a matrix of a given order, up to $n = 15$, when the correlations are assumed to be quite arbitrary.

Table 5.1

Minimum Rank under Assumption of Independent Correlations

n	2	3	4	5	6	7	8	9	10	11	12	13	14	15
m	1	1	2	3	3	4	5	6	6	7	8	9	10	10

Generally, the observed correlations from statistical variables cannot be considered as arbitrary or independent. The inequality in (5.2) may then be reversed, that is, the number of unknowns may be less than the number of conditions which they must satisfy. The unknown communalities are then "overdetermined" in the sense that the larger number of equations may not be consistent. In order for a solution to exist, the coefficients in the equations must satisfy at least $\phi(m)$ relations. The differences $\phi(m) = (v_m - n)$, that is, the number of conditions that the correlations must satisfy so that a matrix of order n can be reduced to rank m, are given in Table 5.2.

The lower left-hand corner of the table has no entries because the rank cannot exceed the order of a matrix. A negative value represents a larger number of unknowns

Table 5.2

Number of Linearly Independent Conditions on the Correlations: $\phi(m)$

m \ n	2	3	4	5	6	7	8	9	10	11	12	n
1	-1	0	2	5	9	14	20	27	35	44	54	$\binom{n-1}{2} - 1 = \dfrac{n(n-3)}{2}$
2	-2	-2	-1	1	4	8	13	19	26	34	43	$\binom{n-2}{2} - 2 = \dfrac{n(n-5)}{2} + 1$
3		-3	-3	-2	0	3	7	12	18	25	33	$\binom{n-3}{2} - 3 = \dfrac{n(n-7)}{2} + 3$
4			-4	-4	-3	-1	2	6	11	17	24	$\binom{n-4}{2} - 4 = \dfrac{n(n-9)}{2} + 6$
5				-5	-5	-4	-2	1	5	10	16	$\binom{n-5}{2} - 5 = \dfrac{n(n-11)}{2} + 10$
6					-6	-6	-5	-3	0	4	9	$\binom{n-6}{2} - 6 = \dfrac{n(n-13)}{2} + 15$
m												$\binom{n-m}{2} - m = \dfrac{n(n-2m-1)}{2} + \binom{m}{2}$

than conditions, so that there is an infinite number of solutions in such a case, the general solution involving $(n - v_m)$ arbitrary parameters. A zero value represents the case of as many unknowns as equations. For a given number of variables, n, a negative or zero entry indicates the rank m which the correlation matrix can attain without any restrictions on the correlations. In these cases the inequality (5.2) is satisfied, and the conditions on the communalities are met under the assumption that the correlations are independent variables. The value of m for the first negative or zero entry, reading down a column of Table 5.2, corresponds to the value of m, for the same n, in Table 5.1.

Of course, there would be little gained in parsimony of thought if the correlations in a study were indeed independent and required as many factors as indicated in Table 5.1. In a factor study the investigator usually selects the variables on some hypothesis of an underlying order, and the correlations cannot be expected to be independent. The relationships that exist among them lead to a rank of the correlation matrix lower than its order, if appropriate values are inserted in the principal diagonal. In the next section specific mathematical conditions are indicated which guarantee that the common-factor space is of one and two dimensions. In subsequent sections approximate methods are presented for the determination of higher dimensional common-factor spaces.

5.3. *Conditions for Reduced Rank of Correlation Matrix*

The number of independent relationships that must exist among the correlations in order that the rank shall be lower than the minimum in (5.5) is given by the positive values in Table 5.2. Thus for $n = 3$, no relationships are necessary to attain rank one; that is, three variables can always be described in terms of one common factor. Four variables, however, cannot be described by just one factor unless their intercorrelations satisfy two (independent) conditions. These well-known conditions (Spearman 1927) are the vanishing of the *tetrads*, namely,

(5.6)
$$\begin{cases} r_{12}r_{34} - r_{14}r_{23} = 0, \\ r_{13}r_{24} - r_{14}r_{23} = 0. \end{cases}$$

It may be well to indicate how the conditions (5.6) are arrived at when $n = 4$ and $m = 1$, so that the method of generalization will be more evident. When there are just four variables, the reduced matrix of correlations is simply

$$\mathbf{R} = \begin{bmatrix} h_1^2 & r_{12} & r_{13} & r_{14} \\ r_{21} & h_2^2 & r_{23} & r_{24} \\ r_{31} & r_{32} & h_3^2 & r_{34} \\ r_{41} & r_{42} & r_{43} & h_4^2 \end{bmatrix}$$

This matrix will be of rank one if all second-order minors vanish. By selecting appropriate minors—involving one row and column intersecting in the desired communality, and the other row and column different from each other—several linear equations result for the solution of each of the communalities. Thus, h_1^2 is given by any one of the following three equations:

$$\begin{vmatrix} h_1^2 & r_{13} \\ r_{21} & r_{23} \end{vmatrix} = 0, \qquad \begin{vmatrix} h_1^2 & r_{14} \\ r_{21} & r_{24} \end{vmatrix} = 0, \qquad \begin{vmatrix} h_1^2 & r_{14} \\ r_{31} & r_{34} \end{vmatrix} = 0,$$

or

$$(5.7) \qquad h_1^2 = r_{12}r_{13}/r_{23} = r_{12}r_{14}/r_{24} = r_{13}r_{14}/r_{34}.$$

On eliminating h_1^2, the two equations (5.6) arise. The three separate solutions (5.7) for h_1^2 are consistent if the conditions (5.6) are satisfied.

Referring to Table 5.2 again, it is seen that five relationships must exist among the correlations of five variables if they are to be described in terms of only one common factor. From their correlation matrix, with unknown communalities in the principal diagonal, several linear equations for the solution of each of the communalities can be obtained by setting appropriate second-order minors equal to zero. The first communality, for example, is given by any one of the six equations:

$$(5.8) \quad h_1^2 = r_{12}r_{13}/r_{23} = r_{12}r_{14}/r_{24} = r_{12}r_{15}/r_{25} = r_{13}r_{14}/r_{34} = r_{13}r_{15}/r_{35} = r_{14}r_{15}/r_{45}.$$

The five conditions that must be satisfied to assure a unique value of h_1^2 may be put in the equivalent form:

$$(5.9) \quad \begin{cases} r_{13}r_{24} - r_{14}r_{23} = 0, \\ r_{13}r_{25} - r_{15}r_{23} = 0, \\ r_{12}r_{34} - r_{14}r_{23} = 0, \\ r_{12}r_{35} - r_{15}r_{23} = 0, \\ r_{13}r_{45} - r_{14}r_{35} = 0. \end{cases}$$

Any other conditions must be linearly dependent on the above equations. Thus if instead of obtaining the solutions for h_1^2, those for h_2^2 were obtained, the resulting five conditions could then be shown to be dependent on the foregoing relations (see ex. 7).

In general, a set of n variables is contained in a one-dimensional common-factor space if $n(n-3)/2$ relationships exist among their correlations, according to the last entry on the first line of Table 5.2. These conditions, whatever form they take, are equivalent to the following set:

$$(5.10) \quad \frac{r_{12}r_{13}}{r_{23}} = \frac{r_{12}r_{14}}{r_{24}} = \cdots = \frac{r_{12}r_{1n}}{r_{2n}} = \frac{r_{13}r_{14}}{r_{34}}$$
$$= \cdots = \frac{r_{13}r_{1n}}{r_{3n}} = \cdots = \frac{r_{1,n-1}r_{1n}}{r_{n-1,n}}.$$

For any variable z_e, a term of the form

$$(5.11) \qquad t_{jk} = \frac{r_{ej}r_{ek}}{r_{jk}} \qquad \begin{pmatrix} e,j,k = 1,2,\cdots,n \\ e \neq j \neq k \end{pmatrix}$$

76

is called a *triad*. When the matrix of correlations is of rank one then the communality of variable z_e is given by any one of the triads (5.11). It is readily seen that there are $\binom{n-1}{2}$ triads in (5.10), or (subtracting one from this number), $n(n-3)/2$ equations of condition for one general factor among n variables.

The number of conditions of the form (5.10) to determine whether a matrix is of rank one is considerably less than the number of tetrads. Every four variables give rise to three tetrads so that the total number of different tetrads for n variables is

$$(5.12) \qquad 3\binom{n}{4} = \frac{n(n-1)(n-2)(n-3)}{8}.$$

The difference between this number and the number of triad conditions is

$$(5.13) \qquad \left[\frac{n(n-3)}{2}\right] \cdot \left[\frac{n(n-3)-2}{4}\right].$$

To indicate the magnitude of this number, suppose $n = 15$. The total number of tetrads is 4,095, while the number of triad conditions (5.10) is only 90. In other words, the labor of computing the conditions (5.10) is only about one-fortieth of that of computing the tetrads, for fifteen variables. For a large number of variables the economy of labor becomes more pronounced.

The necessary conditions for a matrix of correlations to attain rank two will next be considered. For five variables it is a well-known fact that one relationship must exist, namely, the following *pentad criterion* (first obtained by Kelley 1935):

$$(5.14) \quad \left\{ \begin{aligned} & r_{12}r_{23}r_{34}r_{45}r_{51} - r_{12}r_{23}r_{35}r_{41}r_{54} - r_{12}r_{24}r_{35}r_{43}r_{51} \\ & + r_{12}r_{24}r_{31}r_{45}r_{53} + r_{12}r_{25}r_{34}r_{41}r_{53} - r_{12}r_{25}r_{31}r_{43}r_{54} \\ & - r_{13}r_{24}r_{35}r_{41}r_{52} + r_{13}r_{25}r_{34}r_{42}r_{51} + r_{14}r_{23}r_{31}r_{45}r_{52} \\ & - r_{14}r_{25}r_{32}r_{43}r_{51} - r_{15}r_{23}r_{31}r_{42}r_{54} + r_{15}r_{24}r_{32}r_{41}r_{53} = 0. \end{aligned} \right.$$

This condition can be derived in a manner similar to the preceding. The correlation matrix for the five variables must have every third-order minor equal to zero if it is to be of rank two. By selecting appropriate minors, several linear equations for the solution of each of the communalities and hence the conditions for consistency can be obtained. Accordingly, for h_1^2 the following two determinants are employed:

$$\begin{vmatrix} h_1^2 & r_{13} & r_{15} \\ r_{21} & r_{23} & r_{25} \\ r_{41} & r_{43} & r_{45} \end{vmatrix} = 0, \qquad \begin{vmatrix} h_1^2 & r_{14} & r_{15} \\ r_{21} & r_{24} & r_{25} \\ r_{31} & r_{34} & r_{35} \end{vmatrix} = 0.$$

The two solutions for h_1^2 are obtained and equated to get the following single consistency condition:

$$(5.15) \quad \left\{ \begin{aligned} & [r_{24}r_{35} - r_{25}r_{34}][r_{21}(r_{13}r_{45} - r_{15}r_{43}) - r_{41}(r_{13}r_{25} - r_{15}r_{23})] \\ & \quad - [r_{23}r_{45} - r_{25}r_{43}][r_{21}(r_{14}r_{35} - r_{15}r_{34}) - r_{31}(r_{14}r_{25} - r_{15}r_{24})] = 0. \end{aligned} \right.$$

If the correlations of five variables satisfy (5.15), or the equivalent condition (5.14), then five communalities can be determined to make the rank of the correlation matrix equal to two, i.e., the five variables can be described in terms of two common factors.

According to Table 5.2, the correlations among six variables must satisfy four independent conditions in order for their correlation matrix to attain rank two. It will be convenient to define the following:

$$(5.16) \qquad |h_1^2\, r_{ab}\, r_{cd}| = \begin{vmatrix} h_1^2 & r_{1b} & r_{1d} \\ r_{a1} & r_{ab} & r_{ad} \\ r_{c1} & r_{cb} & r_{cd} \end{vmatrix},$$

that is, a representation of a determinant by the elements of the principal diagonal.

In order that a 6×6 matrix be of rank two, every third-order minor must vanish. Five such determinants (each involving the first row and column but otherwise unique rows and columns) are set equal to zero, as follows:

$$|h_1^2\, r_{23}\, r_{45}| = |h_1^2\, r_{23}\, r_{46}| = |h_1^2\, r_{23}\, r_{56}| = |h_1^2\, r_{24}\, r_{56}| = |h_1^2\, r_{34}\, r_{56}| = 0.$$

The solutions for h_1^2 from these five equations follow:

$$(5.17) \qquad \begin{cases} h_1^2 = \dfrac{r_{21}|r_{13}\, r_{45}| - r_{41}|r_{13}\, r_{25}|}{|r_{23}\, r_{45}|}, \\[2mm] h_1^2 = \dfrac{r_{21}|r_{13}\, r_{46}| - r_{41}|r_{13}\, r_{26}|}{|r_{23}\, r_{46}|}, \\[2mm] h_1^2 = \dfrac{r_{21}|r_{13}\, r_{56}| - r_{51}|r_{13}\, r_{26}|}{|r_{23}\, r_{56}|}, \\[2mm] h_1^2 = \dfrac{r_{21}|r_{14}\, r_{56}| - r_{51}|r_{14}\, r_{26}|}{|r_{24}\, r_{56}|}, \\[2mm] h_1^2 = \dfrac{r_{31}|r_{14}\, r_{56}| - r_{51}|r_{14}\, r_{36}|}{|r_{34}\, r_{56}|}. \end{cases}$$

Upon eliminating h_1^2, the four conditions which the correlations must satisfy are obtained. The equality of the right-hand members of equations (5.17) are the necessary conditions for six variables to be describable in terms of two common factors.

This process can be continued for any number of variables. The positive entries for $m = 2$ in Table 5.2 give the number of conditions that must exist among the correlations for a set of n variables to be describable in terms of only two common factors. In general, the correlations among n variables must satisfy $(n^2 - 5n + 2)/2$ conditions in order that their matrix shall be of rank two. These conditions may be obtained by eliminating any communality h_e^2 from $(n^2 - 5n + 4)/2$ equations of the form

$$(5.18) \qquad h_e^2 = \frac{r_{ae}|r_{eb}\, r_{cd}| - r_{ce}|r_{eb}\, r_{ad}|}{|r_{ab}\, r_{cd}|} \qquad \begin{pmatrix} e, a, b, c, d = 1, 2, \cdots, n \\ e \neq a \neq b \neq c \neq d \end{pmatrix}.$$

It will be noted that many more conditions than the number indicated in Table 5.2 can be written for n variables by means of the foregoing procedure. Corresponding to any four indices in the denominator of (5.18) there is a third-order determinant of the form (5.16) which is to be set equal to zero for the calculation of a particular communality h_e^2. The total number of possible denominators, and hence, third-order determinants, for the calculation of the communalities would seem to be enormous. Fortunately, however, this number is considerably reduced owing to the symmetry of the correlation matrix and certain properties of second-order determinants.

Thus, of the twenty-four possible evaluations of a particular communality from the permutations of the four indices selected for the denominator in (5.18), only two determinations need be considered. The total number of third-order determinants which must vanish, for the rank of the $n \times n$ correlation matrix to be two, becomes:

$$2\binom{n-1}{4} = (n-1)!/12(n-5)!$$

The number of conditions which arise upon equating the evaluations of a communality from these determinants is in excess of that indicated in Table 5.2 for $n > 5$. Although all these values of a particular communality must necessarily be equal (statistically) if the rank is two, these conditions are not all independent. The use of the large set of conditions furnishes a check on the rank. In practice, however, it will be found sufficiently accurate to equate a smaller number of evaluations of communality for each variable of a set, as illustrated in the following section.

The procedure of this section can be generalized to obtain the necessary conditions for any correlation matrix $\mathbf{R}$ to be of rank m. In such case every $(m+1)$-order minor must vanish. When m is greater than two the work of computing determinants of the fourth or higher order becomes so laborious that no explicit conditions corresponding to the tetrads or pentad criterion have been worked out. While it is of theoretical interest to note from Table 5.2 the number of conditions that must be satisfied by sets of variables for their correlation matrices to attain reduced rank, they cannot be put to practical use beyond an expected rank of two.

5.4. *Determination of Communality from Approximate Rank*

The problem of determining communalities classically has been put in the form: How much can the rank of the nth order correlation matrix be reduced by a suitable choice of diagonal values (communalities)? If m is the rank of the reproduced correlation matrix then m is the smallest number of common factors necessary to account for the intercorrelations (Theorem 4.6); and if m can be reduced by the choice of communalities, then the number of required factors can be reduced and greater parsimony achieved.[2]

The concern in this section is with the calculation of communalities when some

---

[2]As pointed out by Lederman (1937), even when the rank of the correlation matrix is fixed the communalities may not be uniquely determined.

approximation to the rank of the reduced correlation matrix can be made. Such assumptions about the rank are also made in two methods of factor analysis (see chaps. 9 and 10); not, however, for purposes of computing communalities directly but rather as requirements of the particular methods, with the communalities coming out as a by-product. For the problem at hand, the reduced correlation matrix may be expressed in the form

$$(5.19) \qquad\qquad \mathbf{R} = \mathbf{R}_o + \mathbf{H}^2$$

where $\mathbf{R}_o$ is the nth order correlation matrix but with diagonal elements all zero, and $\mathbf{H}^2$ is a diagonal matrix whose elements h_j^2 (the communalities) are to be determined. The algebraic problem to be solved is the determination of $\mathbf{H}^2$ such that $\mathbf{R}$ will have the minimum rank μ.

A more restrictive aspect of this problem, and the one of greatest interest to factor analysts, is the determination of "rank" when only off-diagonal elements of $\mathbf{R}$ are permitted in the minors. In other words, consider the "rank" to be m if the largest order of a non-vanishing minor of $\mathbf{R}_o$ is obtained by a selection of m of its rows and m *different* columns. This value m has been called the *ideal rank* by Albert (1944a), who obtained an algebraic solution for the communality problem for the case where $\mu = m$. In another paper (Albert 1944b) he proves that the solution produces unique communalities. Of course, in considering only minors with off-diagonal elements of $\mathbf{R}$, it follows that a fundamental condition underlying Albert's conclusions is that

$$(5.20) \qquad\qquad m < \frac{n}{2}.$$

Now, this exact mathematical condition will almost certainly never be met with empirical data. Thus, while Albert provides an exact algebraic solution for the communalities when the ideal rank is known and is less than $n/2$, it is a solution in theory only.

The idea of determining the communalities from the known rank of the correlation matrix can be exploited even when the rank is not known precisely. By approximating the rank of the matrix, the unknown communalities may be computed from the conditions imposed on the correlations to attain such rank, as indicated in the last section. A rough estimate of the rank of the correlation matrix is given by the number of distinct groups of variables. Of course, this is not a mathematically defined concept, but in any empirical study the investigator will have some idea of the grouping of variables—either from the descriptive content of the variables or from a preliminary study of the correlations themselves. A simple statistic on the grouping of variables (the "coefficient of belonging") is presented in **7.4**. In any event, once the rank is approximated, the method of the preceding section may be applied to check whether the correlations satisfy the necessary conditions for the assumed rank. If the conditions are satisfied then the communalities are given by the explicit formulas (5.11) for rank one and (5.18) for rank two, while direct computing formulas for higher rank are not very practical.

The actual process of determining the communalities involves a number of evaluations for each variable under the assumed rank of the matrix. The consistency of such values serves as a check on the rank, and their average is taken as the particular communality. Similar determinations are made for each variable of the set, and the assumed rank must check for all such determinations of communality.

Of course, the correlations need not satisfy the conditions for a given rank exactly with actual data because allowance must be made for chance errors.[3] It is suggested that for rank one all possible triads be written in the calculation of a particular communality. If the variation among these values can reasonably be assigned to chance fluctuations, the mean value may be taken as the communality.

In the case of rank two, all possible expressions (5.18) for the determination of each communality could be considered. Before averaging, however, those based upon insignificant denominators would need to be rejected. The variables yielding insignificant tetrads for the denominator of (5.18) can be identified when the design of the variables is known, and there are but two groups. In such a case each group of variables will approximate rank one, and the tetrads involving three variables of such a group will be insignificant. Knowing the combinations of variables which produce insignificant denominators, it is not necessary to consider the expressions (5.18) which involve them. The denominators should include two variables of each group, considerably reducing the total number of expressions for each communality.

When the rank of a correlation matrix is assumed, and the determination of the communalities is attempted, it may happen that some of the values exceed unity. Of course, such values of the communalities are not permitted, and they indicate that the particular rank assumed is inexact. Before the hypothesis of the specified rank is discarded, however, a number of evaluations of communality should be attempted. If, in general, several consistent values for each communality can be obtained, they should be averaged for the best determination of the communality. The justification for this procedure lies in the fact that the observed correlations are themselves subject to error, and the values to be supplied in the diagonal of the correlation matrix to produce a specified rank can only be expected to satisfy this hypothesis approximately. The final check lies in the agreement of the reproduced correlations from the solution employing these communalities, with the observed correlations. If the final residuals are insignificant, then the choice of the communalities is satisfactory.

Strictly speaking, the considerations in this section apply only when the rank of the correlation matrix is known, and when sampling errors and rounding-off errors in computations are disregarded. In practice, the sampling errors to which the correlation coefficients are subject will cause the correlation matrix generally to have a rank equal to its order. However, it is not the exact mathematical solution of such a matrix that is of interest to a factor analyst. Rather, it is the problem of analyzing the experimentally determined correlation coefficients in such a manner as to make the resulting discrepancies (residuals) insignificant in the statistical sense. Formally, the problem is to find a reproduced correlation matrix $\hat{\mathbf{R}}$ of minimal rank whose elements differ insignificantly from those in the (observed) reduced correlation matrix $\mathbf{R}$. Operationally this begs the question because the determination of the statistical

[3]No sampling error formula is known for the general expression of a communality computed from a higher-order determinant set equal to zero. An approximation to the standard error of a triad was obtained by Holzinger and Harman (1941).

significance of residuals poses problems as great as those inherent in the determination of communalities. Statistical tests for the significance of residuals have been provided by Lawley (1940) and Rao (1955) employing the method of maximum likelihood, and the procedure is given in chapter 10.

To illustrate the foregoing procedure, the set of eight physical variables, introduced in Table 2.3, will be used. Because the variables seem to fall into two groups, rank two is assumed for the correlation matrix. The communality of any variable z_e can be obtained by averaging a number of evaluations (5.18). The calculation of such expressions can be facilitated by systematically considering the four indices, a, b, c, d which determine the denominator of (5.18). In calculating the communality for variable $e = 1$, for example, the indices ab are taken to be 23, 24, and 34 (from the first group of four variables) and the indices cd are taken to be 56, 57, 58, 67, 68, and 78 (from the second group of four variables). When these pairs of variables are considered in every combination, eighteen separate denominators are determined and hence eighteen separate values of h_1^2. While eighteen additional values can be obtained by interchanging the variables in only one of the pairs ab or cd, that was not done since the original values were deemed to be sufficiently consistent. Thus, eighteen evaluations of the communality for each of the eight variables are obtained, and the mean values are taken as their best estimates. The resulting communalities are given in Table 5.3.

No exact standard for judging the consistency of the separate values is available, but the following simple guide may be used. The calculated communality may be regarded as a variance, and the usual formula for the standard error of a variance applied to it, namely,

(5.21)
$$\sigma_{\sigma^2} = \sigma^2 \sqrt{2/N}.$$

If the variations of a set of values for a communality from their mean can be shown to be insignificant by use of formula (5.21), they would also be insignificant by a more accurate test. The standard errors for the eight communalities, as given by the above formula, are presented in Table 5.3. The maximum variation from the mean

Table 5.3

Communalities for Eight Physical Variables

Statistic	h_1^2	h_2^2	h_3^2	h_4^2	h_5^2	h_6^2	h_7^2	h_8^2
Communality	.842	.881	.817	.815	.872	.647	.584	.502
Standard error	.068	.071	.066	.066	.071	.052	.047	.041

of the eighteen separate values for each variable does not exceed 1.5 times the standard error, demonstrating the consistency of these values and justifying the assumed rank and the determination of the communalities.

The direct application of the foregoing method of computing communalities is practical when m is one or two. For a larger number of factors the direct procedure becomes too cumbersome with the use of a desk calculator. While it is conceivable that the direct methods, involving the calculation of determinants of high order, might be feasible on electronic computers, it appears to be more economical to employ special techniques of factor analysis that do not require estimates of communality in advance but produce communalities as by-products (see chaps. 9 and 10).

5.5. *Theoretical Solution for Communality*

Before considering practical means of approximating the communalities, a presentation is made in this section of the theoretical solution to the problem without explicit use of the rank of **R**. Employing the fundamental factor model (2.9) and the notation introduced in **4.10**, any variable z_j can be represented in the total-factor space of m common factors and n unique factors as follows:

$$(5.22) \qquad \hat{z}_j = a_{j1} F_1 + a_{j2} F_2 + \cdots + a_{jm} F_m + u_j Y_j,$$

and in the common-factor space this becomes:

$$(5.23) \qquad \tilde{z}_j = a_{j1} F_1 + a_{j2} F_2 + \cdots + a_{jm} F_m.$$

The correlation between a variable and its "common" part is

$$(5.24) \qquad r_{\hat{z}_j \tilde{z}_j} = \frac{a_{j1}^2 + a_{j2}^2 + \cdots + a_{jm}^2}{N(\hat{z}_j) N(\tilde{z}_j)} = \frac{h_j^2}{1 \cdot h_j} = h_j,$$

where the lengths of the vectors in the total-factor space and in the common-factor space are given in Table 4.1. But the multiple correlation of variable z_j with the linear combination of the m factors (represented by $\tilde{z}_j$) is defined as the simple correlation coefficient between them, namely,

$$(5.25) \qquad R_{z_j \cdot F_1 F_2 \cdots F_m} = r_{z_j \tilde{z}_j}.$$

Then, since $\hat{z}_j$ is the mathematical model of z_j, the expression (5.24) may be put in the form

$$(5.26) \qquad h_j^2 = R_{z_j \cdot F_1 F_2 \cdots F_m}^2,$$

which states that the communality of a variable is equal to the squared multiple correlation of that variable with the common factors.

While this result has been known for a long time (Roff 1936; Dwyer 1939; Guttman 1940), it was not until much later (Kaiser 1956a, 1957; Tryon 1957) that a suggestion was made to adapt it for use in approximating the communalities. Since the $\tilde{z}_j$ as well as the F_p span the common-factor space, it follows from (5.23) and (5.26) that

$$(5.27) \qquad h_j^2 = R_{z_j \cdot \tilde{z}_1 \tilde{z}_2 \cdots \tilde{z}_n}^2.$$

Kaiser (1956a, p. 5) argues that if the n vectors $\tilde{z}_j$ are to lie in the common-factor space of m dimensions, then some of them will be redundant for computing the squared multiple correlation in (5.27). Since it is not necessary to include $\tilde{z}_j$ in the regression equation for h_j^2, this equation becomes

$$(5.28) \qquad h_j^2 = R_{z_j \cdot \tilde{z}_1 \tilde{z}_2 \cdots) \tilde{z}_j (\cdots \tilde{z}_n}^2.$$

This states that the communality of a given variable is given by the squared multiple correlation of that variable on the $n-1$ *common parts* of the remaining variables. The obvious difficulty of this apparent solution is that, in effect, the communalities of the $n-1$ remaining variables must be known in order to compute the squared multiple correlation, i.e., the desired communality. In an attempt to obtain an approximation to the n communalities, Kaiser proposed an iterative procedure for use with an electronic computer. Unfortunately, the process converges only for restricted matrices and he has concluded that the method has ". . . no practical use because of its inability to solve the communality problem for empirical matrices" (1957, p. 10).

There is hope that the iterative approximations to the theoretical solution may yet prove practical. Guttman (1957a) proposes a generalization and improvement of the preliminary procedure suggested above. This method is designed to solve for the diagonal matrix $\mathbf{H}^2$ with proper communalities[4] without requiring *a priori* approximations to the rank of $\mathbf{R}$ nor the extraction of common factors. The final solution is obtained by an iterative process in which trial values $\mathbf{H}_t^2$ eventually converge to the desired matrix of communalities $\mathbf{H}^2$.

It is convenient to designate the successive expressions for the reduced correlation matrix by $\mathbf{R}_t$, so that equation (5.19) becomes

$$(5.29) \qquad\qquad \mathbf{R}_t = \mathbf{R}_o + \mathbf{H}_t^2 \qquad\qquad (t = 1, 2, \cdots)$$

for any approximation $\mathbf{H}_t^2$ to the communalities. The iterative procedure involves the calculation of the inverse of $\mathbf{R}_t$ at each stage; and the diagonal matrix with the principal diagonal of $\mathbf{R}_t^{-1}$ is designated $\mathbf{D}_t$. Then, an entire class of iterative procedures is given (Guttman 1957a, p. 2) by the following recurrence formula:

$$(5.30) \qquad\qquad \mathbf{H}_{t+1}^2 = \mathbf{H}_t^2 - \epsilon \mathbf{D}_t^{-1}, \qquad\qquad (t = 1, 2, \cdots)$$

where ϵ is some positive number. The iterative procedures implied by (5.30) differ from one another according to the choice of ϵ and the initial approximation $\mathbf{H}_t^2$.

The specific iterative process which Kaiser (1956a) employed is (5.30) with $\epsilon = 1$ and $\mathbf{H}_t^2 = \mathbf{I}$. As noted above, this process generally does not converge for empirical data. Guttman (1957a) makes several recommendations, the principal one being to take $\epsilon = \frac{1}{2}$ and $\mathbf{H}_1^2$ as the diagonal matrix of squared multiple correlations of each variable with the $n-1$ remaining variables (further use of this concept is made in **5.6**).

From the preceding discussion it becomes apparent that there is no easy road to a solution of the communality problem. In the following section, several practical avenues are suggested.

5.6. *Estimation of Communality*

Perhaps more space has been devoted to the problem of communality than is warranted by its present-day impact on factorial methods. It had a very important role in the development of factor analysis, especially from the 1930s to the 1950s, but has receded since because of the very efficient alternative methods (see chaps. 9 and 10)

---

[4]As noted in **3.2**, paragraph **15**, communality estimates are considered proper if they preserve the Gramian properties of the correlation matrix.

made possible by the computer. Nonetheless, communalities are still required for the still very popular principal-factor method and its forerunner, the centroid method. For these reasons, along with the need for an historical perspective, the theoretical development of the preceding sections have been presented and some practical methods of estimating communalities will now be given.

Of the many arbitrary estimates of communality, the simplest is the *highest correlation* of a given variable z_j from among its correlations with all the other variables of the given set. This simple procedure has been used by Thurstone and his followers in a large number of studies involving the centroid solution (see **8.8**). They found this simple method of estimating communalities useful for large correlation matrices, but would not recommend it for small numbers of variables.

Another method for approximating the communality of a variable z_j is to employ a *triad*, i.e.,

$$(5.31) \qquad h_j^2 = r_{jk} r_{jl}/r_{kl},$$

where k and l are the two variables which correlate highest with the given variable. It can readily be seen that this formula would have the effect of moderating an extremely high, exceptional correlation. Still another estimate is given by the *average* of all the correlations of a given variable with each of the remaining ones, viz.,

$$(5.32) \qquad h_j^2 = \sum_{k=1}^{n} r_{jk}/(n-1) \qquad\qquad (k \neq j).$$

A more satisfactory procedure for estimating communality follows from **5.4**. The *approximate rank* of the correlation matrix is assumed, making use of the groupings of variables, in order to get suitable estimates of the communality. This method, however, is not very feasible when the rank exceeds two. One simplification of this technique is accomplished by sectioning the correlation matrix into sub-groups of p variables, each approximately of rank one. The *unit-rank estimates* of the communalities may then be calculated by means of the formula:

$$(5.33) \qquad h_j^2 = \frac{1}{\nu} \sum_{k<l=1}^{p} r_{jk} r_{jl}/r_{kl}, \qquad\qquad (k, l \neq j),$$

where $\nu = \binom{p-1}{2}$ is the total number of different triads that can be arranged for the given variable z_j out of the subset of p variables which comprise the section of the correlation matrix of unit rank. This procedure seems much more satisfactory than estimating the communality by a single triad as in (5.31).

It may be convenient to distinguish the foregoing arbitrary estimates of communality, which generally involve only a few correlations, from estimates which are based upon the entire correlation matrix. The latter may be designated as "complete approximations" to communality. Perhaps the simplest procedure that would fall under this heading involves, in essence, the calculation of the *first centroid factor* (see **8.8**). As a start, the highest correlation for each variable is inserted in the principal diagonal of the correlation matrix. Then the estimate of each communality is the ratio of the square of the column sum to the total sum of all the correlations in the matrix, i.e.,

$$(5.34) \qquad h_j^2 = \left(\sum_{k=1}^n r_{jk} \right)^2 \bigg/ \sum_{k=1}^n \sum_{l=1}^n r_{kl},$$

where the self correlation is the highest correlation of the given variable with all other variables. While this formula does employ all correlations in the matrix, it will, nonetheless, tend to give an underestimate of the communality since it results from the employment of only one centroid factor.

A method similar to the preceding, but using the average instead of the highest correlation, leads to the following formula:

$$(5.35) \qquad h_j^2 = [n/(n-1)] \left[\left(\sum_{k=1}^n r_{jk} \right)^2 \bigg/ \sum_{k=1}^n \sum_{l=1}^n r_{kl} \right], \qquad (k \neq j \quad \text{and} \quad k \neq l),$$

in which the diagonal values are actually ignored. This formula employs the square of the coefficient of the *first averoid factor* (Holzinger and Harman 1941). Just as in the case of formula (5.34), so also will formula (5.35) tend to give underestimates of the communalities.

Communality estimates may be calculated by use of the component analysis model (2.8), and then a conventional factor analysis solution in terms of the model (2.9) may be obtained. While this may sound involved, it is actually quite practical with electronic computers. Thus, a correlation matrix (with ones in the diagonal) of order n is analyzed into n principal components and the associated n roots (see chap. 8). It is then assumed that the dimension of the common-factor space is equal to the number of principal components for which the roots are greater than one (Kaiser 1960)—an assumption that is quite plausible since the sum of all n roots is precisely n so that a value of one is merely par and surely if another dimension is to be added it would be desirable to have it account for at least an average contribution. The variance contributed (by this reduced number of principal components) to each variable is taken as the estimate of its communality. Kaiser has used the term "Little Jiffy" for this process of estimating communality and getting a principal-factor solution.

In consideration of the indefiniteness of the communalities—the evasiveness of a fine hypothetical concept—it becomes very attractive to employ some objective measures even though they allegedly are not "communalities." It has been argued, and substantiated by empirical evidence, that it matters little what values are placed in the principal diagonal of the correlation matrix when the number of variables is large (say, $n > 20$). In such a case the actual arithmetic impact of these few diagonal values in relation to the many numbers off the diagonal is so small that the factorial results are not affected very much. Of course, this is a specious argument which would not stand up under a rigorous statistical test were one available. Nonetheless, the desire to employ well-defined, objective measures for the diagonal entries has led to some interesting procedures.

One method for estimating communality which has the semblance of being objective involves *iteration by refactoring*. The operation is initiated with unities or zeros or any other values in the principal diagonal and deciding *a priori* on the number of factors. Typically, such a procedure would involve: (a) the calculation of a principal-factor solution (see chap. 8); (b) the determination of the sum of squares of factor coefficients (for the predetermined number of factors) as new estimates of communality; (c) the calculation of another principal-factor solution; and (d) repeating this process as many times as necessary until the recomputed diagonal values do not change from the preceding set. The same results can now be accomplished more efficiently as a byproduct of the minres method (see chap. 9).

Wrigley (1956) employed such iteration-by-refactoring methods in an excellent empirical study, comparing some fifteen different methods of initial estimation of communality. For five methods of estimation, 100 iterations were made involving very extensive calculations. Although there is no formal proof of the convergence of the iterative process, this study would seem to indicate that it does. Convergence was found to be generally more rapid for low estimates than for high, with unities being especially poor as a starting point for finding the communalities. For work with an electric computer, the squared multiple correlation of each variable with the remaining ones was found to be the best starting point.

The *squared multiple correlation* (*SMC*) of each variable with the remaining $n - 1$ observed variables has much to recommend it as an approximation to communality, quite aside from the foregoing convergence property. Wrigley (1957) suggests that the *SMC*'s be called the "observed communalities" since they, and not the theoretical minimal-rank communalities, measure predictable common variance among the observed correlations. These values are certainly objective and they can be determined uniquely, without iteration, by use of the square root method (see **3.4**) for a small set of variables or by means of an electronic computer for a large set. To obtain the *SMC*'s for all the variables in a set, it is expeditious to calculate the inverse $\mathbf{R}^{-1}$ of the correlation matrix $\mathbf{R}$ (with unities in the diagonal), and then the *SMC* for variable z_j is given by

$$(5.36) \qquad SMC_j = R^2_{j \cdot 12 \cdots)j(\cdots n} = 1 - \frac{1}{r^{jj}},$$

where r^{jj} is the diagonal element in $\mathbf{R}^{-1}$ corresponding to variable z_j. These values are frequently calculated as an incidental step in the computer program for a principal-factor solution (see **8.6**).

The *SMC* has another very important property—it is the lower bound for the communality, i.e.,

$$(5.37) \qquad R^2_{j(n-1)} \leqq h^2_j,$$

where $(n - 1)$ stands for the set of variables excluding z_j. This property was first given by Roff (1936), and explicitly proven by Dwyer (1939). Largely because of this property, Guttman (1956) recommends the *SMC* as the "best possible" estimate of communality. The characteristics that make the *SMC*'s the "best possible" estimates include: (1) actual *equality* in (5.37) for many correlation matrices for which minimum rank m is attained; and (2) the tendency of the *SMC*'s to approach the communalities if the ratio of m to n tends to zero as n approaches infinity.

The insertion of *SMC*'s in the principal diagonal produces a reduced correlation matrix which is not Gramian, in general. While the *SMC*'s are not proper estimates of communality in this sense, they may be employed as lower bounds of the communalities with this recognition of the theoretical impropriety. The Gramian properties of the matrix can be restored by adjusting the off-diagonal values, as proposed by Guttman (1953) in his image theory (for an indication of the relationship between image analysis and principal-factor analysis see **11.3**).

Since some approximation is made to the communalities in conventional factor analysis, there would seem to be an advantage in knowing the direction of the error from the true values. The *SMC*'s are known to be less than (or at most equal to) the communalities. This logical consideration, together with the preceding properties, strongly recommend the *SMC*'s as the most desirable approximations to communalities when suitable computing facilities are available.

An implication of the use of *SMC*'s is that the distinction between common and unique variance as indicated by the factor model (2.9) is a function of the particular variables under consideration rather than any hypothetical domain or universe of variables. Any *SMC* measures variance common to the particular variable and the remaining $n - 1$ variables selected for study, while the communality measures variance common to the variable and the factors resulting from the set of n variables. It should be recognized that in either event, the distinction between common and specific variance is relative to the particular set of variables. The value of communality as the most effective means of reducing the number of factors, is challenged by Wrigley (1957), who concludes: "The principal claim of communalities rests on the fact that they give a better fit than any other diagonal values to the correlations actually observed. The psychological advantages, however, appear to rest with the squared multiple correlations, which measure the proportion of common variance in any particular test selection." It is interesting to note that communalities with the property just mentioned by Wrigley are those determined by the minres solution (see chap. 9).

When factors are extracted one at a time, the diagonal values in each residual correlation matrix may be retained as computed or estimated anew. In general, when one of the "arbitrary approximations" to communality are employed, the values in the principal diagonal of each residual matrix should be re-estimated by the method used originally. For example, when the highest correlation for each variable is taken as its communality, the highest value in each column would again be used for the diagonal entry (in place of the value actually computed) in the matrix of residual correlations with the first factor removed.

On the other hand, when "complete approximations" to communality are employed, the diagonal values are not altered in the succeeding residual matrices. Intead, the factorization is carried to the point where all the diagonal values vanish, except for rounding and sampling errors.

In the past it was quite common to extract one factor at a time and to compute the residual matrix at each stage (e.g., centroid method discussed in **8.8**). Nowadays, with the use of electronic computers, all factors are extracted at one time. Hence it is very important when a method requires estimates of communality (rather than an estimate of the number of common factors), that "complete approximations" be employed.

In order to illustrate the approximation methods, six hypothetical variables are employed and their correlations are given in Table 5.4. Because this is a "textbook example," with no sampling or rounding errors in the data, it is possible to obtain an exact algebraic solution for the communalities from a knowledge of the rank of the correlation matrix. Even a casual observation of the correlations in Table 5.4 indicates a clustering of the first three variables,[5] while the remaining ones correlate no more amongst themselves than with the first three variables. It is then reasonable to assume a rank of two for the correlation matrix, and to test this hypothesis by the method of **5.3**.

Table 5.4

Correlations Among Six Hypothetical Variables

Variable	1	2	3	4	5	6
1						
2	.72					
3	.75	.78				
4	.49	.42	.35			
5	.42	.36	.30	.42		
6	.28	.24	.20	.28	.24	

According to Table 5.2 there are four necessary conditions that the correlations must satisfy in order that the six variables be describable in terms of two common factors. These conditions are arrived at by equating the right-hand members of (5.17). The first three of these expressions are identically equal to .74, while the last two are indeterminate.[6] The necessary conditions among the correlations are satisfied mathematically, and the true rank of the reduced correlation matrix is two. The communality of each of the six variables is obtained by means of equation (5.18), with the several different evaluations for each variable being identical in this hypothetical example. These results are labeled "Actual" in Table 5.5. Following these actual communalities, the different approximations are presented in the successive columns of this table. It is only for heuristic reasons that the several approximations to the communalities are summarized in a single table, rather than to imply any advantage of a particular estimate over another.

The reader is cautioned not to make unwarranted generalizations about the relative merits of the various methods for estimating communality. The only purpose for

[5]The "coefficient of belonging" is 221, according to **7.4**.

[6]This is due to the fact that the tetrads formed from variables 4, 5, 6 and any one of 1, 2, or 3 vanish. As a consequence the minors in the numerators of these expressions also vanish. It is thus apparent that four such variables are describable in terms of only one common factor.

Table 5.5

Communality Estimates for Six Hypothetical Variables

Variable	Actual	Highest r	Triad (5.31)	Average (5.32)	Unit-Rank (5.33)	Centroid (5.34)	Averòid (5.35)	SMC (5.36)
1	.74	.75	.69	.53	.69	.73	.68	.66
2	.72	.78	.75	.50	.75	.68	.61	.66
3	.89	.78	.81	.48	.81	.62	.54	.69
4	.49	.49	.39*	.39	.49	.38	.37	.32
5	.36	.42	.36	.35	.36	.29	.29	.25
6	.16	.28	.16	.25	.16	.14	.14	.12

*Average of the two possible values .29 and .49

exhibiting the different approximations side by side in Table 5.5 is to illustrate the procedures described in the earlier sections. It should be remembered that the data are small in number, artificial, and devoid of sampling errors. While the procedures for computing the several values in Table 5.5 may be instructive, the actual choice of method for approximating communality should be based on the considerations set forth above rather than the apparent superiority of any of the numerical values over the others.

5.7. *Direct Factor Solution*

From the general theory of factor analysis developed so far, it is possible to obtain a factor solution directly, without recourse to the formal procedures treated in the remainder of this text. For a small number of variables a very simple factor model might be appropriate. Then, from a knowledge of the correlations and approximations to the communalities, a complete factor pattern may be determined. In a practical situation, with any sizable number of variables, rather involved mathematical and computational methods are required to get a factor solution.

A direct factor solution for the hypothetical example of the last section will be obtained. As noted above, the correlations in Table 5.4 indicate a strong clustering of the first three variables but not so for the remaining three. A plausible model[7] is presented in Table 5.6, where uncorrelated factors are assumed for convenience.

From the correlations in Table 5.4 and the communalities determined in the last section ("Actual" in Table 5.5), all the coefficients in the factor pattern can be obtained. Since the last three variables involve only one common factor, each of their communalities is merely the square of the coefficient of this factor, i.e.,

$$h_j^2 = a_{jo}^2 \qquad\qquad (j = 4, 5, 6),$$

and hence these factor coefficients are: $a_{40} = .7$, $a_{50} = .6$, and $a_{60} = .4$.

[7]The pattern plan is plausible because the correlations among the variables 1, 2, 3 are higher than those among 4, 5, 6. Such a plan is consistent with the hypothesis that an extra factor should be postulated for a group of variables with higher intercorrelations.

Table 5.6

Factor Pattern Plan*

Variable	F_0	F_1
1	a_{10}	a_{11}
2	a_{20}	a_{21}
3	a_{30}	a_{31}
4	a_{40}	
5	a_{50}	
6	a_{60}	

> * A factor pattern will usually be presented in such a tabular form with the coefficients of the respective factors appearing in the columns headed by the factors.

Next, the coefficients of F_0 for the first three variables can be obtained from the following formula for the reproduced correlations:

$$\hat{r}_{jk} = a_{jo}a_{ko} \qquad (j = 1, 2, 3; \quad k = 4, 5, 6),$$

which is a simplification of (2.27) for the special factor model of Table 5.6. In this formula the a_{ko} are known and if the observed correlations are employed in place of the reproduced correlations, the unknown a_{jo} can be determined. While there are three possible determinations for each j, and an average might ordinarily be taken, the three values are identical in the present case. These coefficients follow:

$$a_{10} = .7, \qquad a_{20} = .6, \qquad a_{30} = .5.$$

Finally, the coefficients of F_1 can be obtained from the following expression:

$$a_{j1} = \sqrt{h_j^2 - a_{jo}^2} \qquad (j = 1, 2, 3),$$

where the communality and the coefficient of F_0 are now known for the first three variables. The resulting coefficients are $a_{11} = .5$, $a_{21} = .6$, and $a_{31} = .8$. The complete factor solution is summarized in Table 5.7.

Table 5.7

Factor Pattern for Six Hypothetical Variables

Variable	F_0	F_1
1	.7	.5
2	.6	.6
3	.5	.8
4	.7	
5	.6	
6	.4	

While it was tacitly assumed that the residuals were precisely zero, some discrepancies between original and reproduced correlations would be expected with empirical data. The extent of agreement between these values is the measure of adequacy of a factor solution, the particular form of the solution being somewhat arbitrary. Thus, in the present example the particular factor model of Table 5.6 was postulated, but some other model might fit the data equally well.[8] Some standards for making a choice among the possible factor solutions are considered in the next chapter.

[8]See, for example, ex. 2, chap. 8.

6   Properties of Different Factor Methods

6.1.   *Introduction*

Before leaving the foundations of factor analysis, a preview of what lies ahead will be presented in this chapter. Some simple, but fundamental, criteria are set forth explicitly; and in the subsequent enumeration of the popular factor models, the extent of adherence to these criteria is indicated in each case. This chapter serves to summarize the most popular factor methods. It gives a brief overview of their properties and the distinguishing characteristics among them, but only schematic solutions are presented; formulas for the computation of the factor coefficients are not given in this chapter. The methods employed in obtaining numerical solutions are developed and illustrated in detail in parts II and III.

As noted several times before, there is a basic indeterminacy in factor analysis—an infinitude of factorizations of a correlation matrix may account for the observed data equally well. The realization of this fact posed a perplexing problem to factor analysts during the rapid growth of the subject in the 1930s and 1940s: How can a factor solution be determined which will be acceptable to other workers? While the principal-factor method (chap. 8) leads to a unique solution in the mathematical sense, at least to psychologists it is not acceptable as the final form. The search for a "psychologically meaningful" solution, which could be obtained by rotation from some arbitrary factorization of the correlation matrix, led Thurstone to formulate the concept of "simple structure" (1935, chap. VI; 1947, chap. XIV), which is discussed in **6.2** under criterion **10**.

Before enumerating some of the principles which have been proposed to objectify the particular choice of factors, a brief review of the problem will be made in geometric terms. As pointed out in chapter 4, the observations on a set of variables can be regarded as determining a number of vectors (corresponding to the variables) in a space equal to the number of subjects. By methods of factor analysis these vectors can generally be contained in a space of smaller dimension than the number of variables. The coordinate axes of this reduced space are the common factors, and the original variables can be expressed linearly in terms of these factors. The determination of this common-factor space is in no way dependent on the particular coordinate frame of reference employed. This arbitrariness is represented geometrically by the infinite number of rotations possible from one set of coordinate axes to another.

For ease of mathematical description, and sometimes to facilitate psychological interpretation, it is common practice to change the frame of reference. In making such a transformation of coordinates it must be remembered that the geometric configuration, e.g., straight line or swarm of points, is left unaltered. The mathematical expressions of formulas describing the geometric configuration may change under transformation, but the configuration itself is invariant.

The *mathematician* usually is concerned with the geometric configuration only, using the frame of reference as a tool, and will prefer one reference system to another if it yields a simpler (and more elegant) expression for his configuration. For example, the elaborate formula consisting of six terms:

(6.1) $$AX^2 + BXY + CY^2 + DX + EY + F = 0$$

represents a geometric configuration (an ellipse if $B^2 - 4AC < 0$) in one (arbitrary) frame of reference, while the expression

(6.2) $$\frac{x^2}{a^2} + \frac{y^2}{b^2} = 1$$

represents *precisely* the same configuration in another (arbitrary) reference frame selected so as to make the equation as simple as possible.

Unlike the mathematician, the *psychologist* frequently concerns himself with the interpretation of the frame of reference, using the configuration of points merely as the vehicle to get to the particular reference axes. Thus, in factor analysis the geometric configuration is a swarm of points, each one representing a test and the density of the points being a function of the correlations among the tests. A frame of reference may be selected for psychological interpretation on the basis of the particular configuration of points but the emphasis in the resulting psychological theory is on the coordinate axes, not the configuration alone.

The criteria listed in **6.2** provide the basis for the selection of the coordinate axes. Depending on how these standards are applied, and whether the empirical data satisfy the conditions, one or another of the solutions enumerated in **6.3** and **6.4** may be obtained. These are referred to as direct solutions since they are obtained by direct calculation from the correlation matrix. In contrast, the multiple-factor solutions introduced in **6.5** are always derived, resulting from a transformation of one of the direct methods of **6.3** or **6.4**. The direct computational methods comprise part ii, and the derived solutions part iii, of this text. Finally, in **6.6** a summary is presented of the assumptions, properties, and characteristics of the different factor methods.

6.2. *Criteria for Choice of Factor Methods*

There are certain assumptions that can be made, and restrictions imposed, that make it possible to describe a given matrix of correlations uniquely in terms of a factorial reference system. However, such a solution is unique only in the sense of the particular criteria; and, selecting other criteria will generally lead to another unique solution. "Unique" is used here merely to denote the fact that any two workers accepting the same criteria and following the same procedures will arrive at an identical result for a given set of data. Some standards, or guides, which assist in defining and delineating the different factor methods are presented in the following paragraphs.

1. Factor model.—A linear model for the variables is assumed. While the principal components, or component analysis, model (2.8) is of some interest, the bulk of the text is concerned with the classical factor analysis model (2.9) or (2.35) in matrix notation.

2. Principle of parsimony.—Following the principle common to all scientific theory, a law or model should be simpler than the data upon which it is based. Thus, the *number of common factors* should be less than the number of variables; and, in the linear description of each variable, the *complexity* should be low.

3. Contributions of factors.—A distinction among different factor solutions may be made on the basis of the contribution (2.13) of each factor to the variances of the variables. One standard may require *decreasing contributions*, i.e., each successive factor contributing a decreasing amount to the total communality. Another standard may require approximately *level contributions* of all factors.

4. Grouping of variables.—In many methods of factor analysis, a notion of the clustering or grouping of the variables is implied. Sometimes the groups are only roughly approximated, as suggested in **5.4** for the purpose of estimating the rank of the correlation matrix. At other times more precise methods are employed for careful assignment of the variables to one group or another. Examples of the latter are the "coefficient of belonging" (see **7.4**), and the method of "cluster analysis" (see Tryon and Bailey 1970).

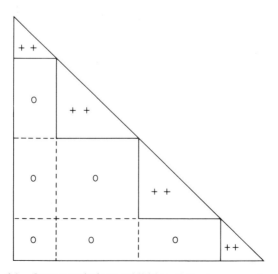

Fig. 6.1.—Intercorrelations exhibiting distinct groups of variables

If the variables of a study are re-numbered so that those that group together are in sequence then the table of intercorrelations may be represented schematically as in Figures 6.1 or 6.2. The plus signs represent correlations, the double plusses indicate even higher correlations among the variables constituting a group, and the zeros mean no correlation. In Figure 6.1 an hypothetical situation is depicted in which there are four well-pronounced groups of variables with no relationships between them. It is extremely unlikely that an empirical matrix of correlations would ever approach this simple form. On the other hand, it is to be expected that a set of relevant variables would be correlated throughout with higher correlations within groups, as indicated in Figure 6.2.

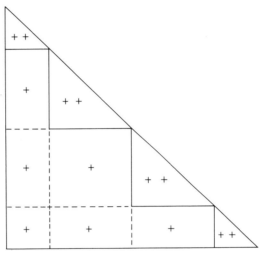

FIG. 6.2.—Intercorrelations showing grouping of variables with relationships between groups

5. Frame of reference.—A choice must be made between an *orthogonal* and an *oblique* reference system, i.e., whether the variables will be described in terms of *uncorrelated* or *correlated* common factors. The observed correlations are fitted equally well by solutions involving factors of either type. Generally it is more convenient to start with an orthogonal solution even if the preferred solution is oblique, arriving at the latter by transformation from the former.

6. Point representation: ellipsoidal fit.—In **4.9** two alternative modes of representing variables geometrically are indicated. It will be recalled that in the point representation there is one point for each of the N individuals, referred to a system of n reference axes—one for each variable. The points which are plotted in this n-space are contained in a common-factor space of only m dimensions (from Theorems 4.4 and 4.6). The loci of the swarm of points of uniform frequency density are, more or less, concentric, similar, and similarly situated m-dimensional ellipsoids, being exactly so for a normally distributed population (Yule and Kendall 1958). It then seems natural to take the principal axes of these ellipsoids as the reference axes, and hence this standard is called *ellipsoidal fit*.

7. Vector representation: linear fit.—In chapter 4 it was shown that the variables may be regarded as vectors in an N-space, and that the correlation between any two is given by the cosine of their angular separation or by the scalar product of their vectors projected into the common-factor space. A group of variables having high intercorrelations is encompassed by a "cone" with a relatively small generating angle. If a *vector* or *reference axis* of the common-factor space is chosen in the midst of this cone, all variables in the group will correlate high with it. The degree of *linear fit* is measured by the extent to which the vectors representing the variables approach the reference axis. By selecting a number of such reference axes, each one passing through a cone of vectors, an oblique solution will generally be obtained.

8. Vector representation: planar fit.—The preceding type of geometric fit also satisfies planar fit in the sense that the vectors lying close to the reference axes will also lie close to the planes of pairs of these axes. In general, the degree of *planar fit* is measured by the proximity of the vectors representing the variables in the common-factor space to such reference planes. Variables which satisfy planar fit need not satisfy linear fit, i.e., their vectors may lie in the plane between the two reference axes without clustering near each one. Thus, greater freedom exists in the choice of the factor axes when reference planes are selected rather than specific reference axes close to clusters of vectors. If a solution can be found in which all vectors lie in one or another of the reference planes, then each variable will involve only two common factors in its linear description.

9. Vector representation: hyperplanar fit.—The two preceding criteria employed either one-spaces or two-spaces to approximate subsets of vectors representing the variables. A natural extension of these ideas is to larger and larger linear spaces—just short of the total space which obviously would offer no simplification. By *hyperplanar fit* in a common-factor space of m dimensions is meant that each vector representing a variable lies in an $(m - 1)$, or smaller, space. When a set of variables satisfies this standard, the complexity of any one of them is less than the total number of common factors. This does not appear as a very stringent criterion, because it is satisfied if each variable is merely of complexity $(m - 1)$ for m common factors. However, the strength of this standard lies in the fact that the hyperplane is the largest permissible space containing each variable. In other words, it is presumed that there will usually be smaller reference spaces which contain certain subgroups of variables. In particular, a vector which lies on a reference axis is contained in that one-space, and the variable it represents has a complexity of one. Similarly, if a vector lies in a reference plane, the variable is of complexity two. It is evident that standards **7** and **8** may be considered as special cases of hyperplanar fit. For, if a set of variables satisfies the criterion of linear fit, or planar fit, it certainly conforms to hyperplanar fit. The converse, of course, is not true generally.

10. Simple structure principles.—The criteria under consideration here are intended to be applied in getting a desired final solution by transformation of a preliminary factor analysis based on some of the preceding criteria. Such derived solutions have been vaguely defined in the past, following some intuitive concepts of "simple structure" proposed by Thurstone. He was among the first to strive for an *objective* definition of this concept and an accompanying objective procedure for a simple structure solution. Since 1935 many individuals have made specific proposals for analytical or semi-analytical procedures for the attainment of simple structure or approximations to it. However, real strides in this direction were not realized until twenty years later. The accomplishments in analytical methods are described in chapters 13 and 14.

Thurstone's original three conditions for simple structure, were as follows (Thurstone 1935, p. 156):

1. Each row of the factor structure should have at least one zero.
2. Each column should have at least *m* zeros (*m* being the total number of common factors).
3. For every pair of columns there should be at least *m* variables whose entries vanish in one column but not in the other.

Later, he gave as a general definition: "If a reference frame can be found such that each test vector is contained in one or more of the . . . coordinate hyperplanes, then the combined frame and configuration is called a *simple structure*" (Thurstone 1947, p. 328). This statement requires only the first condition, namely, that each row of the factor matrix should have at least one zero. The psychological basis for this definition might best be summarized in Thurstone's words: "Just as we take it for granted that the individual differences in visual acuity are not involved in pitch discrimination, so we assume that in intellectual tasks some mental or cortical functions are not involved in every task. This is the principle of 'simple structure' or 'simple configuration' in the underlying order for any given set of attributes" (Thurstone 1947, p. 58).

The other two conditions for simple structure were proposed as insurance that the reference hyperplanes be distinct and overdetermined by the data. Thurstone has since extended the original three conditions to five criteria for the determination of the reference vectors for a simple structure. His criteria (Thurstone 1947, p. 335), in the language of the present text, are as follows:

1. Each row of the factor matrix should have at least one zero.
2. If there are *m* common factors, each column of the factor matrix should have at least *m* zeros.
3. For every pair of columns of the factor matrix there should be several variables whose entries vanish in one column but not in the other.
4. For every pair of columns of the factor matrix, a large proportion of the variables should have vanishing entries in both columns when there are four or more factors.
5. For every pair of columns of the factor matrix there should be only a small number of variables with non-vanishing entries in both columns.

In the foregoing it was tacitly assumed that the factors are uncorrelated, otherwise the term "factor matrix" would be completely ambiguous. The factor pattern and factor structure coincide in an orthogonal solution, so there can be no misunderstanding of the meaning of the "factor matrix" in that event. When the factors are oblique, however, the pattern is distinct from the structure and any reference to the "factor matrix" is vague and can be misleading. This distinction will be developed further in **12.6.** The foregoing principles may lead to either an orthogonal or an oblique derived factor solution. The detailed distinctions are brought out in chapters 12–14. In general, the rotation of axes in order to arrive at simple structure may be viewed as an attempt to reduce the complexity of the variables. The ultimate objective would be a uni-factor solution, in which each variable would be of complexity one. As noted before, an orthogonal uni-factor solution is practically impossible with empirical data, and not very likely even when the factors are permitted to be oblique. Nonetheless, this is the ultimate objective, and it is toward that end that the simple structure principles are proposed.

6.3. *Methods Requiring Estimates of Communalities*

While any matrix of correlations can be factor analyzed so that there is a reasonably close fit to the observed data, such solution may not yield the most desirable frame of reference. Sometimes the solutions answer the needs of the particular investigation; at other times, they serve as preliminary to more meaningful solutions of the type discussed in **6.5.** The solutions enumerated in this and the following section can all be obtained by direct calculation from the correlation matrix. The distinction between the methods in this section and those in **6.4** corresponds to the a priori choice of communalities or the number of common factors—a requirement of the factor model (2.9) as noted in chapter 5. Three methods are considered in this section. Because of the general availability of electronic computers, the *principal-factor* method is most popular today. The *centroid* method hit its peak in the 1930s and 40s, and except for specialized situations is little used now. *Triangular decomposition* is not at all a competing method for a preliminary solution, but it is of interest for its mathematical simplicity and is used in the course of obtaining another form of solution (see **6.4**, par. **3**).

1. Principal-factor method.—The criterion of ellipsoidal fit, as described in **6.2**, paragraph **6**, determines the reference system of the *principal-factor* method. The initial proposal to use the principal axes of the higher-dimensional ellipsoids goes back to Karl Pearson (1901) before the subject of factor analysis was even born. More relevant to the present discussion is the work of Hotelling (1933), who developed the procedures for *component analysis* of the correlation matrix based upon the model (2.8). The principal-factor method follows essentially the same procedures, but operates on the *reduced* correlation matrix (i.e., with estimates of communalities in the diagonal) employing the model (2.9). An important distinction between principal components and principal factors is that the components are immediately expressible in terms of the observed variables while factor measurements can only be arrived at indirectly (see chapter 16). The general appearance and properties of a principal-factor solution will be indicated here, but its mathematical derivation and computing procedures are presented in chapter 8.

When the factors are represented by the principal axes of the ellipsoids, each successive one contributes a decreasing amount to the total communality. In other words, the first principal factor accounts for the maximum possible variance; the second factor accounts for a maximum in the residual space with the first factor removed; the third factor, a maximum in the residual space excluding the first two factors; and so on until the last common factor accounts for whatever communality remains. Assuming that m common factors account for the communality, a principal-factor pattern may be exhibited as follows:

(6.3)
$$\begin{cases} z_1 = a_{11}F_1 + a_{12}F_2 + a_{13}F_3 + \cdots + a_{1m}F_m, \\ z_2 + a_{21}F_1 + a_{22}F_2 + a_{23}F_3 + \cdots + a_{2m}F_m, \\ z_3 = a_{31}F_1 + a_{32}F_2 + a_{33}F_3 + \cdots + a_{3m}F_m, \\ \cdot \quad \cdot \quad \cdot \quad \cdot \quad \cdot \quad \cdot \quad \cdot \quad \cdot \quad \cdot \quad \cdot \quad \cdot \quad \cdot \quad \cdot \\ z_n = a_{n1}F_1 + a_{n2}F_2 + a_{n3}F_3 + \cdots + a_{nm}F_m, \end{cases}$$

from which the unique factors have been omitted. In such a pattern the complexity of each variable is equal to the total number of common factors. The first factor is an ordinary general factor whose coefficients a_{j1} ($j = 1, 2, \cdots, n$) are all positive when the solution is based upon a table of positive correlations. On the other hand, approximately half the coefficients of each of the remaining factors are negative, that is, $F_2, F_3, \cdots, F_m$ are *bipolar factors*.[1] A bipolar factor is not essentially different from any other but is merely one for which several of the variables have significant negative projections. Such variables may be regarded as measuring the negative aspect of the usual type of factor. Thus, if a number of variables identified with "fear" are represented by positive projections, variables with negative projections might be interpreted as measuring "courage." It would appear simpler, however, to regard the factor merely as "fear," and the opposing set of variables as measures of "negative fear." Of course, the signs of all the coefficients of the factor may be changed without altering the adequacy of the solution. Such reversal in the foregoing example would lead to the interpretation of the factor as "courage," and the subgroup of variables with negative coefficients would be regarded as measuring "negative courage." In the illustrations of the text a single name for a bipolar factor is employed. This is consistent with representing any factor by a single continuum.

Obviously a pattern of type (6.3) can reproduce a general table of correlations like that exhibited in Figure 6.2. The solution is thus perfectly satisfactory from a statistical point of view. Although a principal-factor pattern may be more complex than other preferred types, it may sometimes furnish a more convenient representation of a particular set of variables. Since the principal-factor pattern is not restricted to positive coefficients, it can reproduce negative as well as positive correlations. This type of solution may then be applied to any matrix of correlations.

---

[1]This term was introduced by Cyril Burt (1939). In the present text, however, the term is used in a more general sense.

2. Centroid method.—This has been one of the most popular methods in factor analysis, and was often misunderstood and misrepresented. The centroid method of analysis is intended to approximate the results that are obtained with the principal-factor method, but with considerable savings in labor if the calculations are by hand methods. It also attempts to account for as much as possible of the total variance with each successive factor. However, the centroid solution is not unique for a given set of variables nor does it have the other interesting mathematical properties of the principal-factor solution. The appropriate perspective for the centroid method was set by Thurstone (1947, p. 178): "The centroid method of factoring and the centroid solution for the location of the reference axes are to be regarded as a computational compromise, in that they have been found to involve much less labor than the principal-axes solution." Of course, the capability now exists (see **8.5**) for obtaining a principal-factor solution in less than a minute for any correlation matrix up to fifty variables or more.

The general appearance of a centroid solution is indicated by (6.3), just as in the case of the principal-factor solution. For a matrix of positive correlations, the solution contains one general factor and the remaining are bipolar. A centroid solution can also be obtained for a matrix containing negative correlations, but the method becomes somewhat more involved. A full development of the centroid method is presented in **8.8**.

3. Triangular decomposition.—As noted in **3.3**, the square root method may be used to reduce any symmetric matrix to a triangular matrix such that the product by its transpose is equal to the original matrix. This property corresponds to (2.50), the fundamental theorem of factor analysis. In other words, the *triangular decomposition* of a matrix constitutes a factor solution.

As a formal mathematical procedure for the solution of a set of simultaneous linear equations or the reduction of a matrix, the square root method must have been discovered over and over again, and may go back to the time of Gauss. Perhaps the earliest application to the solution of normal equations in least squares theory was made by Commandant A. L. Cholesky of the French Navy around 1915, and published after his death by Commandant Benoit (1924). It was rediscovered by Banachiewicz (1938) and presented as an efficient means for solving a system of linear equations and as a means for calculating determinants and their inverses. The square root method was introduced in the American statistical literature by Dwyer (1944) who emphasized its use in correlation and regression, and who showed the relationship of this method to other methods of linear computation (1951).

Concurrent with this development of the square root method as a means of solving formal mathematical and statistical problems, essentially the same technique was being devised for factor analysis. The method was applied specifically to a correlation matrix by McMahon (1923). Then during the rapid development of factor analysis theory in the 1930s, it was independently developed as the *diagonal method* by Thurstone (1935, p. 78) and as the *solid staircase method* by Holzinger (1935, No. 5). A description of the square root method and its applications to factor analysis was presented by Harman (1954), and an outline of computing procedures is given in **3.3**.

The n variables are described in terms of n (or possibly fewer) new uncorrelated factors, in the following form:

(6.4)
$$\begin{cases} z_1 = a_{11}F_1, \\ z_2 = a_{21}F_1 + a_{22}F_2, \\ z_3 = a_{31}F_1 + a_{32}F_2 + a_{33}F_3, \\ \quad \cdot \quad \cdot \quad \cdot \quad \cdot \quad \cdot \quad \cdot \quad \cdot \quad \cdot \\ z_n = a_{n1}F_1 + a_{n2}F_2 + a_{n3}F_3 + \cdots + a_{nn}F_n. \end{cases}$$

It is evident that a great many variations of this particular form of solution are possible, since any one of the variables may be selected to involve only one factor. For the full correlation matrix (with ones in the diagonal), the triangular decomposition (6.4) would involve all n factors. If the diagonal of the correlation matrix were replaced by communalities, then the reduced correlation matrix would no longer be positive definite and the square root process would lead to imaginary numbers if attempts were made to carry it to n factors.

In practice, interest would lie in only a few factors, especially if they were the most important in some sense. Such a procedure, with an accompanying computer program has been developed by Albert Madansky (1965). The variables are rearranged in such an order that a minimum amount is subtracted from each pivot element, and thus provide the largest possible number for which the square root is taken and which is the denominator for the calculation of all other elements, e.g., (3.22), (3.23). The result is a triangular decomposition $\mathbf{S}$ in which the successive diagonal elements are the maximum possible. The most important factors then come out in sequence. This follows from the following argument: First, the value of the determinant of $\mathbf{R}$ is obtained from (3.27), namely,

(6.5)
$$|\mathbf{R}| = |\mathbf{S}| \cdot |\mathbf{S}'|.$$

Since the determinant of $\mathbf{S}$ is merely the product of its diagonal elements (and similarly for $\mathbf{S}'$), it follows that the product of the squares of all the diagonal elements of $\mathbf{S}$ is equal to the determinant of $\mathbf{R}$. Now, if each of the factors had equal weight, each would contribute an amount equal to the nth root of $|\mathbf{R}|$. Hence, the value of the nth root may be used as a cut-off point for judging the importance of factors, cutting off at the number of factors for which the square of the diagonal exceeds the nth root. In the foregoing discussion, it was tacitly assumed that $\mathbf{R}$ was the full correlation matrix. However, even when communalities are put in the diagonal of the correlation matrix, the procedure for rearranging the order of the variables still assures the determination (of the reduced number) of factors in order of importance.

6.4.   *Methods Requiring Estimate of Number of Common Factors*

As noted at the beginning of **6.3**, all the solutions in that section and the present one are obtained by direct calculation from the correlation matrix. Such solutions may serve in their own rights, or they may be transformed to other desirable forms (see **6.5**). It will be recalled that the solutions enumerated in the last section required some estimates of communalities, while a corresponding requirement for the solutions of the current section is an estimate of the number of common factors. The methods of paragraphs **1**, **2**, and **3** are applicable to any matrix of correlations and may be viewed as alternatives to the principal-factor procedure. The method of paragraph **4** is rather specialized but may have some useful applications. The remaining methods, while properly falling within the scope of this section, are presented primarily for historical reasons.

1. Maximum-likelihood method.—The reference system for the maximum-likelihood method is not determined from the criteria in **6.2**, except for the choice of the classical factor analysis model (2.9). Instead, this method is based on fundamental statistical considerations. It considers explicitly the differences between the correlations among the observed variables and the hypothetical values in the universe from which they were sampled. The first concerted efforts to provide a sound statistical basis for factor analysis were made by Lawley (1940, 1942) when he suggested the use of the "method of maximum likelihood," due to Fisher (1922, 1925), in order to estimate the universe values of the factor loadings from given empirical data. The maximum-likelihood method requires an hypothesis regarding the number of common factors and then, according to such hypothesis, there is derived a factor solution with accompanying communalities. Associated with the method is a test of significance to determine the adequacy of the hypothesis regarding the number of common factors. Chapter 10 is devoted to the maximum-likelihood method, and a variant of it, known as canonical factor analysis, is presented in **11.2**.

While the mathematical development goes back to the early 1940s, the method did not become practical until much later. Even with the electronic computers of the 1950s and early 1960s, it took considerable time to solve the rather complex equations involved in the maximum-likelihood method. Furthermore, convergence of the process cannot always be assured, although there is strong indication that it will do so for most practical needs. In recent years, much work has gone into the development of more efficient algorithms, and together with advances in computer technology, the maximum-likelihood method offers a real viable alternative to the principal-factor method for the preliminary factorization of a correlation matrix.

A maximum-likelihood solution has the same general appearance (6.3) as a principal-factor solution; but it does not have the latter's property of accounting for a maximum amount of variance for a specified number of factors. Also, while a principal-factor solution is unique for a given body of data, a maximum-likelihood solution only determines the common-factor space uniquely. In other words, one maximum-likelihood solution differs from another by a rotation. To remove this inherent indeterminacy, the computing algorithm must provide some side condition which fixes the particular solution.

2. Minres method.—A method of factor analysis which minimizes residuals (hence, the name "minres") was developed (Harman and Jones 1966) not too long ago. Specifically, this method estimates factor loadings in such a way as to make the sum of squares of off-diagonal residuals of the correlation matrix a minimum. In so doing, it literally follows the second objective enumerated in **2.3**, i.e., to "best" reproduce the observed correlations. This is in contrast to the principal-factor method which extracts the maximum variance. Again, however, a minres solution has the same general appearance (6.3) as a principal-factor solution. The minres method is dependent upon an estimate of the number of common factors; the communalities, consistent with this hypothesis, are obtained as by-products of the method. These properties are common to the minres and maximum-likelihood methods.

When one considers that the primary objective of the minres method is identical with the objective of the classical factor analysis approach in general, the question immediately arises why the method was not developed before. The simple answer is that it could not have been accomplished without the power of the modern-day computer. Now that the minres method is a practical procedure it may be preferable to either the principal-factor or the maximum-likelihood methods.

3. Psychometric methods.—The two preceding methods are founded on traditional statistical considerations: maximum-likelihood being based on distributional (multivariate-normal) assumptions; minres on least squares assumptions. By contrast, when the important assumptions deal with the inferences derived from the sample of variables the methods of analysis are sometimes called "psychometric" (scientific content area would be a more general term). Two of these methods—image factor analysis and alpha factor analysis—are described in **11.3** and **11.4**. Neither of these methods requires estimation of communalities; rather, the determination of the number of common factors is an integral part of the procedure. Because the concepts behind these methods and the techniques for their execution are somewhat complex, their explication is deferred to chapter 11.

4. Multiple-group method.—Unlike the preceding methods which serve primarily as preliminary solutions for subsequent "rotation" to the multiple-factor solution, the multiple-group solution usually would be retained as the final form. What it has in common with all the other methods of this section is the requirement that the number of factors be estimated in advance; but it requires estimates of communalities as well. The basic concept in the multiple-group method is that of grouping of variables. Either arbitrary or selected groups of variables provide the basis for the common factors (equal to the number of groups) to be extracted.

The common factors extracted in a single operation can be expected to be oblique to one another. Then the complete analysis should include the factor pattern, the factor structure, and the matrix of correlations among the factors.

5. Early factor models.—Another class of solutions is dependent on a prior decision regarding the number of factors and therefore deserves mention in this section. They are not alternatives for the preceding methods, but are of interest primarily from an historical viewpoint. Their common attribute is the quest for simplicity—in a sense they represent the ultimate in parsimonious description—but unfortunately their attainment can only be expected in very specialized circumstances.

The first, a *uni-factor* solution, certainly must be considered an ideal form hardly to be expected to fit any empirical data. Such a solution satisfies the standard of linear fit, and hence minimum complexity. For the vectors representing the variables to lie exactly on the reference axes, so that each variable would measure but a single factor, implies a matrix of correlations with properties as shown in Figure 6.1 While it is highly unlikely that empirical data would yield an *orthogonal* uni-factor solution, such an *oblique* solution might be approximated.

In the early days of factor analysis, very simple factor models were proposed in defense of certain theories in psychology. Thus, when Charles Spearman (1904, 1927) developed the psychological theory that all intellectual activity consisted of a "general" function and a "specific" function for each element, it conformed to the uni-factor model, albeit in a very limited sense. For in this case *all* the variables of a set are describable in terms of a single common factor, constituting the simplest instance of a uni-factor solution which could arise from a group of variables with correlations depicted by a single triangle in Figure 6.1 and which satisfy the conditions (5.10) for one general factor. Spearman's "Two-factor Theory" was named from the two kinds of factors—general and specific. In recent years, it has been the practice to use the adjectival descriptors of different factor solutions to denote the number (and sometimes the type) of common factors only, it being understood that the factor model (2.9) of common and unique factors apply to all. In this sense, Spearman's *two-factor* solution is a uni-factor or "single-factor" solution, but the old name is retained for historical reasons.

An attempt to meet the inadequacies of the preceding two-factor theory was made by Holzinger (1934–1936) in his proposal of the "Bi-factor Theory." The inadequacies became apparent in the 1930s when the complex psychological test batteries came into being. In developing a broader theory to cope with the greater demand, Holzinger nevertheless was guided by Spearman's earlier work. While he claimed no more for his bi-factor theory than an extension of the two-factor theory, it is in fact an alternative multiple-factor theory as well.

The essence of the *bi-factor* solution is that it includes a general factor in addition to uncorrelated group factors and unique factors. In this way the limitation of the two-factor solution is overcome, i.e., while an orthogonal uni-factor solution can only reproduce a matrix of correlations of the form in Figure 6.1, a bi-factor solution can fit a more general set of correlations as indicated in Figure 6.2. This modification of the uni-factor pattern is tantamount to substituting planar for linear geometric fit. When the vectors of a group of variables lie in a reference plane, each variable measures just two factors. If, furthermore, the vectors lie only in the reference planes formed by a general-factor (F_0) axis and one group-factor axis (none in the planes of two group factors), the configuration can be described as a *pencil of planes* through the F_0 axis.[2]

6.5. *Derived Factor Solutions*

In contrast to the methods of the last two sections, which are calculated directly from a correlation matrix, the solutions considered in the present section can only be

---

[2]In ordinary space geometry a pencil of planes refers to the totality of planes through a line, i.e., all the planes linearly dependent on two distinct planes through the line. In the present setting, however, a pencil of planes in a space of ($m + 1$) dimensions will refer to all the planes through a line which are mutually orthogonal. It is clearly seen that there are m such planes in the pencil through the F_0 axis.

derived from one of the former. Such a transformation is frequently called the "rotation problem" of factor analysis. It is concerned with the problem of choice of the most cogent way of displaying a factor analysis for interpretation. When the rotation is made to accomplish the "simple structure principles" of **6.2**, paragraph **10**, the resulting solution is called *multiple-factor*, a term originated by Thurstone in the 1930s. It is used primarily to distinguish a general type of solution involving *m* common factors without a prior hypothesis regarding the grouping of variables to constitute group factors.

The essential features of a multiple-factor solution include "overlapping" group factors and avoidance of a general factor. By "overlapping" is meant that the several group factors do not involve distinct subsets of variables, i.e., several group factors appear in the description of a variable. Overlapping thus implies complexity of two or more for the variables in a multiple-factor pattern, and hence the prefix "multiple" is employed. Through the overlap of group factors, a table of correlations as in Figure 6.2 can be fit by such a solution.

A multiple-factor solution satisfies the criterion of hyperplanar fit.[3] In analytical terms this means that the complexities of the variables should not exceed $m - 1$, where *m* is the number of common factors. While this is the maximum complexity, it is desirable to obtain a solution in which the description of each variable can be made as simple as possible. Also, in spite of the necessary overlapping of factors, it is desirable to have as many zero coefficients in the columns as possible.

If the multiple-factor solution satisfies the five criteria for simple structure listed in **6.2**, then the graphical plot in the plane of each pair of factors will exhibit the following: (1) many points near the two final factor axes; (2) a large number of points near the origin; and (3) only a small number of points removed from the origin and between the two axes. When the two-dimensional diagrams for all combinations of factors satisfy these three characteristics, Thurstone calls the structure "compelling," and concludes: "In the last analysis it is the appearance of the diagrams that determines, more than any other criterion, which of the hyperplanes of the simple structure are convincing and whether the whole configuration is to be accepted as stable and ready for interpretation" (Thurstone 1947, p. 335). Such diagrams provide the basis for the graphical rotation methods of chapter 12. Various attempts to put the simple structure principles into objective terms are described in chapters 13 and 14, where analytical procedures are given for the multiple-factor solution.

Before leaving the enumeration of the different factor methods, one more should be mentioned. Several statistical techniques are available for fitting a *prescribed factor pattern* (see chap. 15). The object of these procedures is to obtain a multiple-factor type of solution by postulating where the positions of the zeros and large loadings should be in the desired factor pattern, rather than the transformation of the preliminary solution according to certain criteria of simple structure. It should be noted that a bi-factor solution also satisfies a prescribed factor pattern, but its special simplicity and mode of computation sets it apart from the more general treatment. However, a

---

[3]With special reference to psychology, Thurstone has called the factors determined by hyperplanar fit "primary factors," and the corresponding psychological attributes, "primary abilities."

bi-factor solution can be determined as a special case of the general methods for fitting a prescribed factor pattern.

6.6. *Summary of Factor Methods*

More than ten distinct types of factor solutions have been described in this chapter, but they are not equally "preferred" by workers in the field. Some are presented primarily because of their historical significance, some because they meet particular needs, and some because of their general applicability. The first requirement of a factor analysis is for it to adequately explain the interrelationships among many variables. Thus, there should be good statistical fit of the reproduced correlations to the observed correlations. Secondly, after statistical fit is satisfied, it may be desirable to simplify the factorial results and make them more meaningful or interpretable in a particular subject-matter field.

With the general availability of computers, a typical approach followed by many investigators is to obtain a principal-factor (or, unwittingly, a principal-component) solution for an observed correlation matrix, and then transforming it to the varimax multiple-factor solution (see chap. 13). One should not overlook other possibilities, however. The increased capabilities of computers make the maximum-likelihood method more practical than in the past, and it may be preferred to the principal-factor method. Similarly, the minres method may turn out to yield the most desirable initial factorization of a correlation matrix. The multiple-group method may provide a useful final solution or it may also serve as a preliminary factorization for subsequent transformation to the multiple-factor form. For the (transformed) multiple-factor solution there is the choice between orthogonal and oblique factors, and then several alternative methods (see chaps. 13 and 14).

A summary of the different methods is presented in Table 6.1; the assumptions, properties, and characteristics are outlined briefly, and the important distinctions are brought out. It may also serve as a convenient reference source after the detailed development and computing procedures have been studied in the ensuing chapters.

The choice of one form of solution rather than another may take into consideration particular theories of a content area, as well as the standards presented in this chapter. Thus, if in the field of biology, a general growth factor were postulated then a factor analysis of a set of body measurements in the bi-factor form would be appropriate. Examples of well known psychological theories of human abilities are Spearman's Two-factor Theory, Holzinger's Bi-factor Theory, Thomson's Sampling Theory of Ability, and Thurstone's Primary Factor Theory. The factor analysis techniques which were developed in support of some of these theories turned out to have greater applicability than the specific purposes for which they were originally conceived.

An excellent, brief review by Jackson and Messick (1967) traces the development of theoretical conceptualizations of "intelligence" from James McKeen Cattell to J. P. Guilford, paying special attention to the analytical methods devised along the way to test such theories with empirical data. Thus, they touch upon the theoretical work and development of specific measures by Alfred Binet, Lewis Terman, Edward L. Thorndike, and J. P. Guilford and his students, as well as the development of the

Table 6.1

Summary of Different Factor Methods

Method	Chapter where Developed	Factor Model	Principle of Parsimony — Common Factors	Principle of Parsimony — Complexity of Variables	Prior Estimates of — Communality	Prior Estimates of — Number of Factors	Grouping of Variables	Contribution of Factors	Geometric Fit	Distinguishing Characteristics
Principal components	8	(2.8)	n	n	No	No	No	Decreasing	Ellipsoidal	All general factors (bipolar)
Principal-factor	8	(2.9)	m	m	Yes	No	No	Decreasing	Ellipsoidal	
Centroid	**8.8**	(2.9)	m	m	Yes	No	No	Decreasing	Ellipsoidal	
Triangular decomposition*	†	(2.9)	m	1 to m	Yes	No	No	Decreasing	Not appl.	One less var. per factor
Maximum-likelihood Canonical f. a.	10 **11.2**	(2.9)	m	m	No	Yes	No	Decreasing	Not appl.	All general factors (bipolar)
Minres	9	(2.9)	m	m	No	Yes	No	Decreasing	Not appl.	
Image	**11.3**	(2.9)	m	m	No	Yes	No	Decreasing	Not appl.	
Alpha	**11.4**	(2.9)	m	m	No	Yes	No	Decreasing	Not appl.	
Multiple-group	**11.5**	(2.9)	m	1 (approx.)	Yes	Yes	Yes	Level	Linear	Group factors only (oblique solution)
Uni-factor	†	(2.9)	m	1	No	Yes	Yes	Level	Linear	Distinct group factors
Two-factor	**7.2**	(2.9)	1	1	No	Yes	Yes	One large	Linear	One general factor
Bi-factor	**7.5**	(2.9)	$m+1$	2	No	Yes	Yes	One large; others level	Planar	One general and m group factors
Derived: Multiple-factor	12, 13 14	(2.9)	m	1 to $(m-1)$	Depends on preliminary solution		No	Level	Hyper-planar	Overlapping group factors (orthogonal or oblique)

*The entries in the table are for the case of a reduced correlation matrix, i.e., with communalities in the diagonal. The triangular decomposition of the full correlation matrix would, of course, involve n factors.

†These are discussed in the present chapter without further development.

methodological tools by Charles Spearman, Cyril Burt, L. L. Thurstone, and Louis Guttman. Their emphasis is on the "interplay between theoretical and practical considerations in the refinement of assessment techniques."

It should be remembered that when a particular theory is found to be compatible with experimental evidence, it does not follow that nature does in fact behave precisely as stated. No doubt, an alternative theory may be postulated which is also compatible with the data. The mathematical expressions (e.g., the factor patterns) of these theories may be different because of adherence to different criteria. Nonetheless, if both are consistent with the empirical evidence they are equally adequate on statistical grounds, and any preference must be made on other considerations. Certainly, it is wrong to argue that a particular factor solution is incorrect because it appears different than another. Factor analysis, as a statistical technique, yields solutions which are convertible from one to another, and a preference of form must depend upon appropriate content criteria. As in all empirical sciences, several equally satisfactory laws may be usefully employed, although they may be quire different formally.

Part II

**Direct
Factor Analysis
Methods**

7 Early Factor Models and Methods

7.1. *Introduction*

In part I of this text, the foundation and formal groundwork was laid for factor analysis. The direct methods of analysis (in contradistinction to transformation methods) are developed in chapters 7 through 11. Certain techniques which were very useful in the early development of factor analysis are presented in this chapter, followed by more modern and powerful techniques for analyzing any correlation matrix in subsequent chapters. Because of its well-deserved pride of place in factor analysis, Spearman's two-factor solution is treated first.

From the present day perspective it seems only natural that the first approach to factor analysis should have involved the simplest possible model. That is in fact what happened, in 1904, when Spearman formulated a single common factor theory of intellective ability. According to his famous theorem (see sec. **5.3**), when the tetrads vanish every variable can be described in terms of a general factor g and a specific (now called, unique) factor s. The notion of a general factor was carried beyond its actual value as a single common factor which accounted for all the intercorrelations of a particular matrix to a psychological theory that g entered into *all* abilities. Actually, Spearman had cautioned that such a universal law ". . . must acquire a much vaster corroborative basis before we can accept it even as a general principle and apart from its inevitable corrections and limitations" (Spearman 1927, p. 76).

The two-factor solution is developed in **7.2**, and followed in **7.3** by an interesting situation where all the conditions for a single common factor are met but the resulting solution is inappropriate nonetheless. In section **7.4** an index is developed for judging the degree of cohesiveness of variables.

As is all too evident, the two-factor solution is very limited in its application since it implies a correlation matrix of unit rank. Aside from the controversial psychological theory involving a single general factor "g," the method of analysis was inadequate for the correlation matrices resulting from the complex psychological test batteries. Holzinger, who had been one of the chief proponents of Spearman's "two-factor theory," developed the "bi-factor theory" to cover the more complex situations. His bi-factor "theory" of psychological behavior provides for the splitting of Spearman's single general factor into a general and several group factors, so that all variables can be described in terms of a general factor, a group factor, and a unique factor. The analysis of a correlation matrix by the bi-factor method is presented in **7.5**, and illustrated with a twenty-four variable example in **7.6**.

7.2.   *Two-Factor Method*

According to Spearman's fundamental theorem, the necessary and sufficient conditions for a set of n variables to be describable in terms of just one general factor and n unique factors are the vanishing of all tetrads, namely:

$$(7.1) \qquad r_{jk}r_{lm} - r_{lk}r_{jm} = 0 \qquad (j, k, l, m = 1, 2, \cdots, n; \quad j \neq k \neq l \neq m).$$

The number of such conditions increases very rapidly with the size of n, as indicated by (5.12). Actually, not all of these conditions are independent, and as shown in **5.3**, there are $n(n-3)/2$ equations of condition for one general factor among n variables. In the early days of factor analysis sound statistical tests were made before the factor model was accepted. In other words, all tetrad differences were computed from a table of correlations and the median of such a frequency distribution would be compared with its probable error. Formulas for the sampling errors of tetrad differences were developed by Spearman and Holzinger (1925).

The two-factor pattern may be written as follows:

$$(7.2) \qquad z_j = a_{j0}F_0 + u_jY_j \qquad (j = 1, 2, \cdots, n),$$

where F_0 is the general factor and the Y_j are the n unique factors, and again, as in the case of (2.9), the hat on z_j has been dropped for simplicity. When the correlations r_{jk} satisfy the tetrad conditions, or the equivalent conditions (5.10), the pattern (7.2) may be assumed and the coefficients a_{j0} and u_j have to be determined.

The correlations reproduced from the pattern (7.2) are given by

$$(7.3) \qquad \hat{r}_{jk} = a_{j0}a_{k0},$$

and, under the assumption that the residuals vanish, the observed correlations may be written

$$(7.4) \qquad r_{jk} = \hat{r}_{jk} = a_{j0}a_{k0}.$$

In the remainder of this section the reproduced correlations will be replaced by observed correlations. Upon multiplying equation (7.4) by the square of the general-factor coefficient for any variable z_e, and summing over the correlations, there results

$$(7.5) \qquad a_{e0}^2 \sum_{j<k=1}^{n} r_{jk} = \sum_{j<k=1}^{n} r_{ej}r_{ek} \qquad (e \text{ is fixed}; j, k \neq e).$$

The symbol $\sum_{j<k=1}^{n} r_{jk}$ stands for the sum of all the correlations r_{jk}, where j and k each range over the variables $1, 2, \cdots, n$ but subject to the restriction that j is always

less than k. In a symmetric matrix of correlations, this sum is merely the total of all the entries above (or below) the principal diagonal.

Since there is only one common factor, the coefficient of this factor for any variable is merely the square root of the communality of the variable. Hence formula (7.5) may be written explicitly for the square of the coefficient, or the communality, of any variable z_e, as follows:

$$(7.6) \qquad a_{e0}^2 = h_e^2 = \frac{\sum (r_{ej}r_{ek}; j, k = 1, 2, \cdots, n, j, k \neq e, j < k)}{\sum (r_{jk}; j, k = 1, 2, \cdots, n, j, k \neq e, j < k)}.$$

It will be observed that the diagonal elements of the correlation matrix do not enter into formula (7.6). In fact, the formula yields values of the communalities, which theoretically are the diagonal elements preserving the unit rank of the matrix. When the conditions (5.10) are satisfied by the observed correlations a single factor is postulated. The computed diagonal elements must also satisfy these conditions in order that the rank of the reduced correlation matrix be unity.

While formula (7.6) is simple enough, it can be expressed in a more convenient form for computational purposes, namely:

$$(7.7) \qquad a_{e0}^2 = \frac{\left(\sum_{j=1}^{n} r_{ej}\right)^2 - \sum_{j=1}^{n} r_{ej}^2}{2\left(\sum_{j<k=1}^{n} r_{jk} - \sum_{j=1}^{n} r_{ej}\right)} \qquad (e \text{ is fixed, } j \neq e).$$

The adaptability of this formula to machine calculation will be clear from the following restatements of the terms in the formula. If $\mathbf{R}_0$ is the matrix of correlations with the elements in the principal diagonal omitted, then

$$\sum_{j=1}^{n} r_{ej} \text{ is the sum of the correlations in column } e \text{ of } \mathbf{R}_0,$$

$$\sum_{j=1}^{n} r_{ej}^2 \text{ is the sum of squares of the correlations in column } e \text{ of } \mathbf{R}_0,$$

$$\sum_{j<k=1}^{n} r_{jk} \text{ is the sum of all the correlations below the diagonal of } \mathbf{R}_0.$$

An illustrative example will clarify the method of analysis described in this section. The correlations among five variables is presented in Table 7.1. Spearman (1927) used this example to demonstrate the applicability of his "two-factor theory." He computed all the tetrads and found their median to be .013. The probable error of a tetrad difference for a sample of the given size was found to be .011; and from this agreement, Spearman concluded that the observed data were adequately fit by the simple theory. Using the computing formula (7.7), the necessary sums for each variable are recorded in the lower part of Table 7.1, with the general-factor coefficients in the last line of the table.

Table 7.1

Correlations among Five Tests, and Calculation of General Factor Coefficients

Test	1	2	3	4	5
1. Mathematical judgment					
2. Controlled association	.485				
3. Literary interpretation	.400	.397			
4. Selective judgment	.397	.397	.335		
5. Spelling	.295	.247	.275	.195	
Sum: $\sum r_{ej}$	1.577	1.526	1.407	1.324	1.012
Sum of squares: $\sum r_{ej}^2$	.6399	.6115	.5055	.4655	.2617
Denominator of (7.10)	3.692	3.794	4.032	4.198	4.822
a_{e0}^2	.5003	.4526	.3656	.3067	.1581
a_{e0}	.707	.673	.604	.554	.398

7.3. *The Heywood Case*

In the preceding section, the theory and computational methods were described for the solution of a set of variables in terms of a single common factor. As indicated above, the fundamental conditions for such a solution are the vanishing of all tetrads, i.e., all second-order minors (not involving a diagonal element) of the correlation matrix must be zero. It is possible for such conditions to be met (ideal rank, in the sense of **5.4**, being unity), while one of the diagonal elements must be greater than unity in order for the reduced correlation matrix to be of rank one. This apparently startling situation is referred to as the "Heywood" case (Heywood, 1931).

The classical example to illustrate the Heywood case consists of the correlations in Table 7.2. It can be verified readily that all the tetrads vanish, but upon applying formula (7.7) the solution in the middle portion of Table 7.2 results. This solution reproduces the correlations perfectly, but it lacks one basic requirement to be a legitimate solution—the communalities must be positive numbers between 0 and 1. Because one of the communalities is greater than one, this solution is a Heywood case.

Table 7.2

Hypothetical Example Illustrating the Heywood Case

Var.	Correlations					Heywood Solution		Permissible Solution					
	1	2	3	4	5	a_{j0}	h_j^2	a_{j0}	a_{j1}	a_{j2}	a_{j3}	a_{j4}	h_j^2
1						1.05	1.10	.89	.3349	.2170	.1578	.1210	.99
2	.945					.90	.81	.90	.43				.99
3	.840	.720				.80	.64	.80		.59			.99
4	.735	.630	.560			.70	.49	.70			.71		.99
5	.630	.540	.480	.420		.60	.36	.60				.7937	.99

While the ideal rank of the correlation matrix of Table 7.2 is one, the actual rank of the matrix with acceptable numbers in the diagonal certainly exceeds one. If more than one common factor is permitted, an infinitude of solutions is possible in which no communality is greater than one. An example of a solution in terms of five common factors is given in the right-hand portion of Table 7.2. In this case each communality is just under one.

In case the ideal rank is greater than one, but lower than the rank of the reduced correlation matrix unless one of the diagonal values exceeds unity, the resulting solution is referred to as the generalized Heywood case. In all such instances, when a communality greater than one appears, there is pretty clear evidence that the rank of the correlation matrix must be higher than that which produced the Heywood case. Guttman (1954a) proves that there are many cases where the rank of all diagonal-free submatrices of the correlation matrix is small, but the minimum rank which preserves the Gramian properties is nevertheless very large compared with the number of variables. He concludes that merely studying the minors outside the main diagonal is not sufficient for determining communalities or the minimum possible rank.

7.4. *Grouping of Variables*

In the bi-factor method, and some of the subsequent methods of analysis (e.g., **11.5**), a prime consideration is the grouping of variables into subsets. Often, the study will be so designed that three, four, or more variables are of a kind which might measure the same factor. Such a hypothetical design of the variables is tested by the factor analysis, which provides the evidence for retaining or rejecting the original grouping of variables.

When factor analysis is employed as a tool in developing theories of behavior in a particular content field, then hypothetical grouping of variables is usually based upon previous research in which some of the factors have already been identified. The design can then be extended to include other groups of variables used to identify additional factors. In some cases it may be desirable to take a portion of a previous design and add new variables to obtain more refined measures of the factors already identified. The success of such a factor analysis depends in large measure on the skill with which the variables have been selected for the groups.

On the other hand, when factor analysis is used simply as a statistical tool in the simplification and interpretation of a correlation matrix, and grouping of variables is required, then some objective means of getting such groupings from the matrix itself would seem to be indicated. Such a procedure is readily available under the assumption that the variables of a group identifying a factor have higher intercorrelations than with the other variables of the total set. Such an index is designated as the "*B*-coefficient" or "coefficient of belonging" (Holzinger and Harman 1941, p. 24), and is defined as 100 *times the ratio of the average of the intercorrelations among the variables of a group to their average correlation with all remaining variables.*

To distinguish between variables of different groups, the standard set-theory notations can be adapted to the present needs. The primary definitions follow:

(7.8) $\begin{cases} \text{(a) } e \in G_p \text{ means } e \text{ is a variable in the group } G_p. \\ \text{(b) } (z_j; j \in G_p, p = 1, 2, \cdots, m) \text{ denotes the } \textit{system} \text{ of elements } z_j \text{ for all} \\ \quad \text{values of } j \text{ in groups } G_p, \text{ where the range of } p \text{ is indicated. The elements} \\ \quad \text{of the system are first designated, followed by a semicolon, and all the} \\ \quad \text{properties on the elements are to the right of the semicolon.} \\ \text{(c) } \sum (z_{ji}; i = 1, 2, \cdots, N) \text{ means the sum of all the elements in the system} \\ \quad (z_{ji}; i = 1, 2, \cdots, N). \text{ The index } j \text{ is fixed, the summation extending} \\ \quad \text{over } i. \text{ This sum is equivalent to the more conventional form } \sum_{i=1}^{N} z_{ji}. \end{cases}$

It will be found that these definitions aid in clarity and ultimate simplicity in describing much of the following theory.

Employing this notation, the B-coefficient may be expressed as follows:

(7.9) $$B(j) = 100(S/n_S)/(T/n_T), \qquad (j \in G_p, \quad p = 1, 2, \cdots, m)$$

where the variables z_j are said to comprise a group G_p, the sum of intercorrelations among the variables of the group is given by

(7.10) $$S = \sum (r_{jk}; \quad j, k \in G_p, \quad j < k)$$

and the sum of the variables in the group with all remaining variables is given by

(7.11) $$T = \sum (r_{jk}; \quad j \in G_p, \quad j \text{ not in } G_p),$$

while n_S and n_T are the numbers of correlations in the sums S and T, respectively.

The B-coefficients are used to sort the variables on the basis of their intercorrelations. The grouping is begun by selecting the two variables which have the highest correlation. To these is added the variable for which the sum of the correlations with the preceding is highest. This process is continued, always adding a variable which correlates highest with those already in the argument of B, until a sharp drop appears in the value of B. When this occurs, the last variable added is withdrawn from the group. Another variable may be inserted in its place, but, if the drop in B is still large, it should be withdrawn. Thus a group of variables that belong together is determined. Then, excluding the variables that have already been assigned to such a group, the two others which have the highest remaining correlation are selected to start another group. To these variables are added others, exclusive of those that have already been assigned to groups, until a significant drop appears in B, at which stage another group is formed. It is desirable to start each new group with a B-coefficient as large as possible so as to have clearly defined groups. For this purpose it may be necessary to obtain the B-coefficients for more than one pair of variables without completing the groups. The pair yielding the highest B value may then be used to introduce the next group. This process is continued until all variables have been assigned to groups or else do not fit into any group.

If, in the course of determining a group of variables that belong together, the numbers of variables entering into the argument of B is designated by v then

(7.12)
$$n_S = \binom{v}{2} = v(v-1)/2$$

$$n_T = v(n-v)$$

and the basic definition (7.9) of B may be put in the form:

(7.13)
$$B(j) = 200(n-v)S/(v-1)T.$$

While this formula is used in calculating B-coefficients, several auxiliary formulas facilitate the computations. First, another expression for T in place of (7.11) will be found convenient, namely:

(7.14)
$$T = \sum (r_{je}; \quad j \in G_p, \quad e = 1, 2, \cdots, n, \quad j \neq e) - 2S.$$

Since the sums of the correlations of each variable with all others are usually obtained at the start of any analysis, these sums for the variables in the particular group less twice their intercorrelations yield the sum T.

Another aid in the computation of the B-coefficients is the sum of the correlations of the last variable added to the group with the preceding ones. Letting l denote the last variable added to the group, the proposed sum may be written

(7.15)
$$L = \sum (r_{jl}; \quad j \in G_p, \quad j \neq l).$$

If a subscript v is appended to the sums L, S, and T to designate their values for v variables in the argument of B, then successive values of S and T may be obtained by means of the recurrence formulas:

(7.16)
$$S_v = S_{v-1} + L_v$$

and

(7.17)
$$T_v = T_{v-1} + \sum (r_{el}; \quad e = 1, 2, \cdots, n, \quad e \neq l) - 2L_v.$$

Actual computations of B-coefficients are shown later in this chapter, but a word of interpretation is in order here. A value of $B = 100$ means that the average of the intercorrelations of the selected subset is exactly the same as the average correlation of these variables with all the remaining ones. Such variables would not be regarded as "belonging together" any more than they belong with the other variables of the total set. As an arbitrary standard for "belonging together," a group of variables may be required to have a minimum B-coefficient of 130. Actually, there is no sampling error formula for judging the significance of the difference between two successive values of B. Knowledge of the nature of the variables may be of some assistance in deciding whether a drop in B is "significantly" large.

Since the B-coefficient is the ratio of two averages, its properties may be studied by means of them. The average of the intercorrelations of the variables in the group (the numerator of B) tends to decrease as the number of variables in B increases, since the variables are added on the basis of highest correlation with those already in the argument of B. Similarly, the average of the correlations of the variables in the group with all remaining variables (the denominator of B) tends to decrease with an increase in v. The decrease in the numerator is relatively greater, however, than that in the denominator.

To the numerator, which usually consists of a small number of correlations, are added a few additional correlations which are lower in value than the others and thus steadily decrease its value. On the other hand, from the large number of correlations in the denominator a small number of the larger values is taken away. The value of the denominator is decreased, but not so noticeably as that of the numerator. Thus the B-coefficient decreases, in general, as more variables are added to its argument.

An exception to this may occur with the addition of a variable to the subset which has relatively high correlations with the preceding variables but a low sum of correlations with the remaining variables. In this case the decrease in the numerator is relatively smaller than that in the denominator, and B increases. Similar reasoning accounts for the fact that a variable can be rejected from a group because of a large drop in the value of B and then appear in the group later, after several others have been added to the subset.

As the number of variables in the argument of B increases, the decreases in the above averages become less and these averages tend toward stability. A consequence of this is that an actual difference between two successive B values has a greater relative significance as the number of variables v increases.

7.5. *Bi-Factor Method*

A bi-factor solution for n variables, in its simplest form, consists of n linear equations involving one general factor and m group factors (ignoring the unique factors). If the variables are rearranged according to the groups in which they fall, every variable will be expressed in terms of the general factor F_0, and, in addition, the variables in the first group will involve F_1; those in the second group, F_2; and so on to the variables in the last group which will involve F_m. In such a simple model, each of the group factors overlaps with the general factor but not with any of the other group factors. From such a model, the reproduced correlation between any two variables $j \in G_p$ and $k \in G_q$ is given by:

(7.18)
$$
\begin{cases}
\hat{r}_{jk} = \sum (z_{ji} z_{ki}; \quad i = 1, 2, \cdots, N)/N, \\
\quad = \sum ([a_{j0} F_{0i} + a_{jp} F_{pi}][a_{k0} F_{0i} + a_{kq} F_{qi}]; \quad i = 1, 2, \cdots, N)/N, \\
\quad = a_{j0} a_{k0} + a_{j0} a_{kq} r_{F_0 F_q} + a_{jp} a_{k0} r_{F_p F_0} + a_{jp} a_{kq} r_{F_p F_q}, \\
\quad = a_{j0} a_{k0} + a_{jp} a_{kq} r_{F_p F_q},
\end{cases}
$$

where the last equality follows from the fact that the general factor is uncorrelated with the group factors. If the two variables are in different groups, then

(7.19)
$$\hat{r}_{jk} = a_{j0} a_{k0} \qquad (j \in G_p, \quad k \in G_q, \quad p \neq q),$$

but, if they are in the same group, their reproduced correlation becomes

(7.20)
$$\hat{r}_{jk} = a_{j0} a_{k0} + a_{jp} a_{kp} \qquad (j, k \in G_p).$$

The bi-factor solution is obtained by first computing the general factor coefficients and then the coefficients of each of the group factors. Sometimes this is followed by some adjustments to the simple model, as may be suggested by a study of the residuals.

1. General-factor coefficients.—By appropriate choice of variables, a subset can be found such that the conditions for a single common factor are satisfied; and hence the procedure of **7.2** may be applied to get the general-factor coefficients. As a first step the variables are placed into groups, toward which end B-coefficients may be useful. Then, it will be noted that a subset of variables consisting of one each from different groups satisfies the form of the two-factor pattern—there is only a general factor among the variables of such a subset, and a unique factor for each variable.

To indicate how a subset of variables is selected which involves only one common factor, consider three distinct groups G_p, G_q, and G_r, and take one variable from each of them. Such a triplet may be designated (e, j, k), where $e \in G_r$, $j \in G_p$, and $k \in G_q$ and $r \neq p \neq q$. Any one of the many triplets, as the indices take specific values in the different groups, has the property of involving only one common factor. From this property, it follows that the reproduced correlation between any two of these variables is given by (7.19). Next, replace these correlations obtained from the factor pattern by observed correlations[1] and multiply this equation by a_{e0}^2 to get:

$$a_{e0}^2 r_{jk} = (a_{e0}a_{j0})(a_{e0}a_{k0}) = r_{ej}r_{ek} \qquad (e \in G_r, \quad r \neq p \neq q).$$

From this expression a value of the general-factor coefficient for variable z_e can be computed based entirely upon the correlations involving only the particular variables z_j and z_k. To obtain a more reliable evaluation of any general-factor coefficient, sum both sides for all values[2] of j and k which, together with e preserve the property of involving only one common factor. Thus, for any $e \in G_r$ the square of its general-factor coefficient is given by:

$$(7.21) \qquad a_{e0}^2 = \frac{\sum (r_{ej}r_{ek}; \quad j \in G_p, \quad k \in G_q, \quad p < q = 1, 2, \cdots, m, \quad p, q \neq r)}{\sum (r_{jk}; \quad j \in G_p, \quad k \in G_q, \quad p < q = 1, 2, \cdots, m, \quad p, q \neq r)}$$

The formula is comparable to (7.6) for the case where all the variables involve only one common factor.

An important extension of formula (7.21) should be noted. If the pattern plan of a set of variables is of the bi-factor form, but includes a number of variables which measure only the general and no group factors, additional terms can be included in this formula. For any two such variables, together with any other variable e, will involve only one common factor. The summations in (7.21) should extend to all such variables j, k; the only restriction being $j < k$ so that no correlation should be used more than once.

2. Group-factor coefficients.—Before the group-factor coefficients can be computed it is necessary to obtain the residual correlations with the general factor removed.

---

[1] The tacit assumption is that the residuals vanish.

[2] If j and k are merely restricted to be in different groups, and the variables range over all groups, each correlation would appear twice, since $r_{jk} = r_{kj}$. To avoid this, the indices j and k are permitted to range over all groups, namely, $j \in G_p$ and $k \in G_q$ for $p, q = 1, 2, \cdots, m$, but under the condition $p < q$.

Such *general-factor residuals* are defined by

$$(7.22) \qquad \dot{r}_{jk} = r_{jk} - a_{j0}a_{k0} \qquad (j, k = 1, 2, \cdots, n).$$

These residual correlations tend to be of the form shown in Figure 6.1, with the values in the rectangles being approximately zero. The standard error of a residual correlation is indicated in Table A of the Appendix.

In the residual-factor space, the n variables can be described by a uni-factor pattern, i.e., the bi-factor solution may be considered as a uni-factor one with a general factor superimposed. The residual correlations (7.22) for each group of variables, taken alone, should have a matrix of rank one and hence measure only one common factor. While the method of **7.2** can be used for calculating the group-factor coefficients, there will usually be a relatively small number of variables in each group, and it seems more advisable to use the method of triads of **5.3**. By this procedure the group-factor coefficient for any variable $e \in G_p$ is given by

$$(7.23) \ a_{ep}^2 = \frac{1}{v_p} \sum \left(\frac{\dot{r}_{ej}\dot{r}_{ek}}{\dot{r}_{jk}}; \ \ j, k \in G_p, \ \ j < k, \ \ j, k \neq e \right) \qquad (p = 1, 2, \cdots, m),$$

where

$$(7.24) \qquad v_p = \binom{n_p - 1}{2}$$

and n_p is the number of variables in the group G_p.

The complete determination of a bi-factor pattern is possible by means of formulas (7.21) and (7.23). After all the coefficients have been computed, the *final residuals* can be obtained. These are the residuals with all factors removed, namely:

$$(7.25) \qquad \bar{r}_{jk} = \dot{r}_{jk} - a_{jp}a_{kp}.$$

If the variables j and k do not belong to the same group, then $\bar{r}_{jk} = \dot{r}_{jk}$, i.e., the general-factor residuals *are* the final residuals and must not be significantly different from zero. On the other hand, the general-factor residuals for variables within a group must be significant to warrant the postulation of an additional factor among them. Approximate sampling errors of residuals are given in the Appendix.

3. Adjustments.—When it is found that certain residuals between variables of different groups are significant, it may be necessary to modify the simple bi-factor plan. The same is true if certain general-factor residuals within a group are practically zero. Since the bi-factor solution involves the formulation of a mathematical model (the pattern plan) and the calculation of numerical values for this model, it should be possible to establish some measure of "goodness of fit." Rough approximations to the sampling errors for factor coefficients and residuals (indicated in the Appendix) may serve as guides in verifying the appropriateness of a particular factor solution to the given data. Moreover, procedures are now available for fitting a prescribed factor pattern by statistical means (see chapter 15). The prescribed model could, of course, be a bi-factor plan. Before such procedures were available, the practice was to first obtain a simple or pure bi-factor pattern, and then in the course of the analysis certain modifications would be made. A new or revised pattern plan might be suggested from the *B*-coefficients for different subgroups of variables, from the crude tests of significance of residuals, or simply from inspection of the general-factor residuals.

7.6. *Illustrative Example*

In order to illustrate the bi-factor solution, and also for subsequent factorial methods, an empirical set of data will be employed. The particular example consists of twenty-four psychological tests given to 145 seventh and eighth grade school children in a suburb of Chicago, and is largely an outgrowth of the Spearman-Holzinger Unitary Trait Study (Holzinger 1934–1936). The initial data were gathered by Holzinger and Swineford (1939), while applications of these data by Holzinger and Harman (1941), Kaiser (1958), Neuhaus and Wrigley (1954) and others have made this example a classic in factor analysis literature.

The list of the twenty-four variables, their means, standard deviations, and reliability coefficients are given in Table 7.3. Their correlations are presented in Table

Table 7.3

Basic Statistics for Twenty-Four Psychological Tests

Test X_j	Mean $\overline{X}_j$	Standard Deviation s_j	Reliability Coefficient r_{iJ}
1. Visual Perception	29.60	6.90	.756
2. Cubes	24.84	4.50	.568
3. Paper Form Board	15.65	3.07	.544
4. Flags	36.31	8.38	.922
5. General Information	44.92	11.75	.808
6. Paragraph Comprehension	9.95	3.36	.651
7. Sentence Completion	18.79	4.63	.754
8. Word Classification	28.18	5.34	.680
9. Word Meaning	17.24	7.89	.870
10. Addition	90.16	23.60	.952
11. Code	68.41	16.84	.712
12. Counting Dots	109.83	21.04	.937
13. Straight-Curved Capitals	191.81	37.03	.889
14. Word Recognition	176.14	10.72	.648
15. Number Recognition	89.45	7.57	.507
16. Figure Recognition	103.43	6.74	.600
17. Object-Number	7.15	4.57	.725
18. Number-Figure	9.44	4.49	.610
19. Figure-Word	15.24	3.58	.569
20. Deduction	30.38	19.76	.649
21. Numerical Puzzles	14.46	4.82	.784
22. Problem Reasoning	27.73	9.77	.787
23. Series Completion	18.82	9.35	.931
24. Arithmetic Problems	25.83	4.70	.836

Table 7.4

Intercorrelations of Twenty-Four Psychological Tests for 145 Children

Test : j	1	2	3	4	5	6	7	8	9	10	11	12	13	14	15	16	17	18	19	20	21	22	23	24
1	—																							
2	.318	—																						
3	.403	.317	—																					
4	.468	.230	.305	—																				
5	.321	.285	.247	.227	—																			
6	.335	.234	.268	.327	.622	—																		
7	.304	.157	.223	.335	.656	.722	—																	
8	.332	.157	.382	.391	.578	.527	.619	—																
9	.326	.195	.184	.325	.723	.714	.685	.532	—															
10	.116	.057	−.075	.099	.311	.203	.246	.285	.170	—														
11	.308	.150	.091	.110	.344	.353	.232	.300	.280	.484	—													
12	.314	.145	.140	.160	.215	.095	.181	.271	.113	.585	.428	—												
13	.489	.239	.321	.327	.344	.309	.345	.395	.280	.408	.535	.512	—											
14	.125	.103	.177	.066	.280	.292	.236	.252	.260	.172	.350	.131	.195	—										
15	.238	.131	.065	.127	.229	.251	.172	.175	.248	.154	.240	.173	.139	.370	—									
16	.414	.272	.263	.322	.187	.291	.180	.296	.242	.124	.314	.119	.281	.412	.325	—								
17	.176	.005	.177	.187	.208	.273	.228	.255	.274	.289	.362	.278	.194	.341	.345	.324	—							
18	.368	.255	.211	.251	.263	.167	.159	.250	.208	.317	.350	.349	.323	.201	.334	.344	.448	—						
19	.270	.112	.312	.137	.190	.251	.226	.274	.274	.190	.290	.110	.263	.206	.192	.258	.324	.358	—					
20	.365	.292	.297	.339	.398	.435	.451	.427	.446	.173	.202	.246	.241	.302	.272	.388	.262	.301	.167	—				
21	.369	.306	.165	.349	.318	.263	.314	.362	.266	.405	.399	.355	.425	.183	.232	.348	.173	.357	.331	.413	—			
22	.413	.232	.250	.380	.441	.386	.396	.357	.483	.160	.304	.193	.279	.243	.246	.283	.273	.317	.342	.463	.374	—		
23	.474	.348	.383	.335	.435	.431	.405	.501	.504	.262	.251	.350	.382	.242	.256	.360	.287	.272	.303	.509	.451	.503	—	
24	.282	.211	.203	.248	.420	.433	.437	.388	.424	.531	.412	.414	.358	.304	.165	.262	.326	.405	.374	.366	.448	.375	.434	—
$\sum_{c \neq j} r_{jc}$	7.528	4.751	5.309	6.045	8.242	8.182	7.909	8.306	8.156	5.666	7.089	5.877	7.584	5.443	5.079	6.609	6.009	6.808	5.754	7.755	7.606	7.693	8.678	8.220

7.4. In the last row of the latter table is given the sum of the correlations for each variable with all the others. In obtaining such a sum for any variable, all twenty-three entries in its row and column must be added since only half of the symmetric matrix is recorded in the table.

1. B-coefficients.—First, the grouping of variables as described in **7.4** will be illustrated. The analysis into groups is begun by selecting the two tests—5 and 9— which have the highest correlation, namely, $r_{59} = .723$. The value of $B(5, 9)$ is computed by means of formula (7.13) in Table 7.5. The tests j, comprising the argument of B, are for this case z_5 and z_9, and their correlation appears as the value of L and S, since there is only this one correlation in each of the sums. The value T may be obtained by (7.14) using the sums of the correlations from Table 7.4. Then the value of the B-coefficient is

$$B(5, 9) = 200(24 - 2)(.723)/(2 - 1)(14.952) = 213.$$

The form of computation indicated by Table 7.5 will be found very convenient. In addition, the sum L defined in (7.15) and the recurrence formulas (7.16) and (7.17) greatly facilitate the calculation of successive B values.

Following the procedure outlined in **7.4**, all the variables are grouped by means of B-coefficients. The groups G_p ($p = 1, 2, 3, 4, 5$) as determined in Table 7.5, may be defined by

$$G_1 = (1, 2, 3, 4),$$
$$G_2 = (5, 6, 7, 8, 9),$$
$$G_3 = (10, 11, 12, 13),$$
$$G_4 = (14, 15, 16, 17, 18, 19),$$
$$G_5 = (20, 21, 22, 23, 24).$$

The grouping by B-coefficients adheres to the original design of this set of tests because most of these tests had been used in factor experiments before and because the abilities they measured were quite well known. This may not be true in general. In a number of published studies the B-coefficients and the succeeding factor solutions failed to verify some postulated factors.

2. Bi-factor solution.—A simple bi-factor plan of a general factor and five distinct group factors is implied by the grouping of variables, and is subsequently modified as indicated in the course of analysis. In calculating the bi-factor loadings, it is tacitly assumed that all entries in the correlation matrix are positive (small negative values are treated as zeros). The general-factor coefficients are computed by means of formula (7.21), making use of appropriate worksheets to facilitate the numerical work. The loadings on the general factor are in the first column of the body of Table 7.6, which includes the entire bi-factor solution.

The general-factor residuals are computed by (7.22) and are presented below the diagonal in Table 7.7. These residuals should be insignificant except for those within groups, if the grouping of variables is reasonable. In the first four groups, the intra-group residuals are consistently positive and larger than the intergroup values (with the one exception, $\dot{r}_{10,24} = .255$). However, within G_5 there are a number of negative residuals and very small positive ones, indicating that no additional factor is required

125

Table 7.5

Calculation of B-Coefficients

j	v	L	S	$200(n-v)$	T	$(v-1)T$	$B(j) = \dfrac{200(n-v)S}{(v-1)T}$	Notes
(5, 9)	2	.723	.723	4400	14.952	14.952	213	—
(5, 9, 7)	3	1.341	2.064	4200	20.179	40.358	215	—
(5, 9, 7, 6)	4	2.058	4.122	4000	24.245	72.735	227	—
(5, 9, 7, 6, 8)	5	2.256	6.378	3800	28.039	112.156	216	—
(5, 9, 7, 6, 8, 23)	6	2.276	8.654	3600	32.165	160.825	194	(1)
(10, 12)	2	.585	.585	4400	10.373	10.373	248	—
(10, 12, 13)	3	.920	1.505	4200	16.117	32.234	196	(2)
(10, 12, 11)	3	.912	1.497	4200	15.638	31.276	201	(3)
(10, 12, 11, 13)	4	1.455	2.952	4000	20.312	60.936	194	(4)
(10, 12, 11, 13, 24)	5	1.715	4.667	3800	25.102	100.408	177	(5)
(10, 12, 11, 13, 21)	5	1.584	4.536	3800	24.750	99.000	174	(6)
(20, 23)	2	.509	.509	4400	15.415	15.415	145	(7)
(1, 4)	2	.468	.468	4400	12.637	12.637	163	(8)
(1, 4, 3)	3	.708	1.176	4200	16.530	33.060	149	—
(1, 4, 3, 2)	4	.865	2.041	4000	19.551	58.653	139	—
(1, 4, 3, 2, 21)	5	1.189	3.230	3800	24.779	99.116	124	(9)
(17, 18)	2	.448	.448	4400	11.921	11.921	165	—
(17, 18, 19)	3	.682	1.130	4200	16.311	32.622	145	—
(17, 18, 19, 16)	4	.926	2.056	4000	21.068	63.204	130	(10)
(17, 18, 19, 15)	4	.871	2.001	4000	19.648	58.944	136	—
(17, 18, 19, 15, 16)	5	1.251	3.252	3800	23.755	95.020	130	—
(17, 18, 19, 15, 16, 14)	6	1.530	4.782	3600	26.138	130.690	132	—
(17, 18, 19, 15, 16, 14, 24)	7	1.836	6.618	3400	30.686	184.116	122	(11)
(17, 18, 19, 15, 16, 14, 22)	7	1.704	6.486	3400	30.423	182.538	121	(12)
(20, 23)	2	.509	.509	4400	15.415	15.415	145	—
(20, 23, 22)	3	.966	1.475	4200	21.176	42.352	146	—
(20, 23, 22, 21)	4	1.238	2.713	4000	26.306	78.918	138	—
(20, 23, 22, 21, 24)	5	1.623	4.336	3800	31.280	125.120	132	—
(20, 23, 22, 21, 24, 18)	6	1.652	5.988	3600	34.784	173.920	124	(13)
(20, 23, 22, 21, 24, 16)	6	1.641	5.977	3600	34.607	173.035	124	(13)

NOTES ON TABLE 7.5

(1) Test 23 is rejected because of 22 points' drop in B for $v = 6$.

(2) Test 13 is rejected because 52 points' drop in B seems to be too great even for $v = 3$.

(3) Test 11 is retained, although it causes a drop of 47 points in B, because it is of the same general nature as Tests 10 and 12.

(4) Test 13 is retained, although it was previously rejected from the group. After Test 11 was put in the group, Test 13 seemed to belong together with the others, causing a drop of only 7 points in the value of B for $v = 4$.

(5) Test 24 is rejected because of 17 points' drop in B for $v = 5$.

(6) Test 21 is rejected because of 20 points' drop in B for $v = 5$.

(7) Before continuing with the group which starts with Tests 20 and 23, another pair of tests will be tried to see if they yield a value of B greater than 145.

(8) Tests 1 and 4, although having a lower correlation than the pair 20 and 23, produce a higher value of the B-coefficient. Hence the next group is started with Tests 1 and 4.

(9) Test 21 is rejected because of 15 points' drop in B for $v = 5$ and seemingly different nature of Test 21 from Tests 1, 2, 3, and 4.

Table 7.6

Bi-Factor Pattern for Twenty-Four Psychological Tests

Test j	General Deduction B_0	Spatial Relations B_1	Verbal B_2	Perceptual Speed B_3	Recognition B_4	Associative Memory B_5	Doublet D_1	Unique Y_j
1	.589	.484	—	—	—	—	—	.647
2	.357	.285	—	—	—	—	—	.889
3	.401	.479	—	—	—	—	—	.781
4	.463	.317	—	—	—	—	—	.828
5	.582	—	.574	—	—	—	—	.576
6	.575	—	.559	—	—	—	—	.597
7	.534	—	.708	—	—	—	—	.463
8	.624	—	.375	—	—	—	—	.686
9	.560	—	.628	—	—	—	—	.540
10	.388	—	—	.594	—	—	.377	.595
11	.521	—	—	.478	—	—	—	.707
12	.404	—	—	.642	—	—	—	.652
13	.576	—	—	.438	—	—	—	.690
14	.388	—	—	—	.545	—	—	.743
15	.351	—	—	—	.476	—	—	.806
16	.496	—	—	—	.353	—	—	.793
17	.422	—	—	—	.361	.493	—	.670
18	.515	—	—	—	—	.468	—	.718
19	.442	—	—	—	—	.278	—	.853
20	.644	—	—	—	—	—	—	.765
21	.645	—	—	—	—	—	—	.764
22	.644	—	—	—	—	—	—	.765
23	.734	—	—	—	—	—	—	.679
24	.712	—	—	—	—	—	.377	.592
Contribution of factor	6.874	0.645	1.678	1.185	0.779	0.539	0.284	—

for these variables. Hence, the bi-factor plan is modified by eliminating the group factor for G_5, and the general-factor residuals among these variables are taken as the final residuals.

Next, the coefficients of each of the group factors are computed by means of formula (7.23), employing the general-factor residuals (in italics) in Table 7.7. These calculations for the loadings on B_1, B_2, and B_3 are straightforward, and the results are shown in Table 7.6. When the triads in (7.23) were computed for any variable

(10) Test 16 is rejected because of 15 points' drop in B to see if some other test will cause a smaller drop. If some other test cannot be found which causes a smaller drop in B, then Test 16 will be retained in the group at this stage because a drop of 15 points for $v = 4$ does not seem to be definitely significant.

(11) Test 24 is rejected because of 10 points' drop in B for $v = 7$.

(12) Test 22 is rejected because of 11 points' drop in B for $v = 7$.

(13) Tests 18 and 16, although they had previously been allocated to another group, are put into the argument of B along with 20, 21, 22, 23, 24 to see if the latter group of tests must be extended to other tests in the battery. The drop in B in each case, along with the seemingly different nature of Tests 18 and 16, seems to warrant their rejection from this group.

Table 7.7

Residual Correlations*

k \ j	1	2	3	4	5	6	7	8	9	10	11	12	13	14	15	16	17	18	19	20	21	22	23	24
G₁ 1	—	-.030	-.065	.042																				
2	*.108*	—	.037	-.025																				
3	*.167*	*.174*	—	-.033																				
4	*.195*	*.065*	*.119*	—																				
G₂ 5	-.022	.077	.014	-.042	—	-.034	-.061	.000	.037															
6	-.004	.029	.037	.061	*.287*	—	.019	-.042	.041															
7	-.011	-.034	.009	.088	*.345*	*.415*	—	.020	-.059															
8	-.036	-.066	.132	.102	*.215*	*.168*	*.286*	—	-.053															
9	-.004	-.005	-.041	.066	*.397*	*.392*	*.386*	*.183*	—															.117
G₃ 10	-.113	-.082	-.231	-.081	.085	-.020	.039	.043	-.047	—	-.002	.047	-.075											
11	.001	-.036	-.118	-.131	.041	.053	-.046	-.025	-.012	*.282*	—	-.089	.026											
12	.076	.001	-.022	-.027	-.020	-.137	-.035	.019	-.113	*.428*	*.218*	—	-.002											
13	.150	.033	.090	.060	.009	-.022	.037	.036	-.043	*.185*	*.235*	*.279*	—											
G₄ 14	-.104	-.036	.021	.114	.054	.069	.029	.010	.043	.021	.148	-.026	-.028	—	.025	.028	-.020	.000	.000					
15	.031	.006	-.076	.036	.025	.049	-.015	-.044	.051	.018	.057	.031	-.063	*.234*	—	-.017	.025	.000	.000					
16	.122	.095	.064	.092	-.102	.006	-.085	-.014	-.036	-.068	.056	-.081	-.005	*.220*	*.151*	—	-.012	.000	.000					
17	-.073	-.146	.008	-.008	-.038	.030	.003	-.008	.038	.125	.142	.108	-.049	*.177*	*.197*	*.115*	—	.000	.000					
18	.065	.071	.004	.013	-.037	-.129	-.116	-.071	-.080	.117	.082	.141	.026	*.001*	*.153*	*.089*	*.231*	—	.000					
19	.010	-.046	.135	-.068	-.067	-.003	-.010	-.002	.026	.019	.060	-.069	.008	*.035*	*.037*	*.039*	*.137*	*.130*	—					
G₅ 20	-.014	.062	.039	.041	.023	.065	.107	.025	.085	-.077	-.134	-.014	-.130	.052	.046	.069	-.010	-.031	-.118	—	-.002	.048	.036	-.093
21	-.011	.076	-.094	.050	-.057	-.108	-.030	-.040	-.095	.155	.063	.094	.053	-.067	.006	.028	-.099	.025	.046	*-.002*	—	-.041	-.022	-.011
22	-.034	-.002	-.008	.082	.066	.016	.052	-.045	.122	-.090	-.032	-.067	-.092	-.007	.020	-.036	.001	-.015	.057	*.048*	*-.041*	—	.030	-.084
23	.042	.086	.089	.005	.008	.009	.013	.043	.093	-.023	-.131	.053	-.041	-.043	-.002	-.004	-.023	-.106	-.021	*.036*	*-.022*	*.030*	—	-.089
24	-.137	-.043	-.083	-.082	.006	.024	.057	-.056	.025	.255	.041	.126	-.052	.028	-.085	-.091	.026	.038	-.059	*-.093*	*-.011*	*-.084*	*-.089*	—

*The values in italics are not final; they are factored further, and the final residuals corresponding to them appear above the principal diagonal.

in G_4, however, it was found that they varied widely and hence the six variables could not be assumed to measure a single factor. In fact, mere inspection of the general-factor residuals points to a grouping of 14, 15, 16, and 17; another grouping of 17, 18, and 19; and acceptance of the general-factor residuals for 14, 15, and 16 variables. The results of this modification lead to the factor coefficients of B_4 and B_5 in Table 7.6.

Finally, one further adjustment was made for the exceptionally large general-factor residual between variables 10 and 24. A *doublet* (factor through only two variables) is assumed for these variables. As noted in Table 5.2, it takes at least three variables to determine the factor weights for a single factor uniquely, and when there are only two variables their description of a common factor is quite arbitrary. In the example, approximately one standard error was subtracted from the residual before the variance was divided equally between the two variables. The resulting doublet factor coefficients for the variables are shown in Table 7.6.

To complete the linear description of each test in terms of factors there remains the determination of the unique factor coefficients. These are given by

$$u_j = \sqrt{1 - h_j^2},$$

as described in **2.4**. The sums of squares of coefficients of the common factors in Table 7.6 are computed and recorded as the communalities in Table 7.8. The complement of each of these numbers from unity is the uniqueness, which is also recorded in Table 7.8. Then, taking square roots yields the coefficients of the respective unique factors in Table 7.6.

While factorial methods yield the communality and uniqueness of each variable, the latter variance may be split into the specificity and error variance simply from the knowledge of the reliability of the variable. The reliability of each of the twenty-four psychological tests is recorded in Table 7.8, as well as the error variance and specificity which follow from formulas (2.20). In addition to this apportionment of the unit variance of each test, the index of completeness of factorization, as computed by (2.21), is given in the last column of Table 7.8.

It is of interest to judge how well a particular factor solution fits the empirical data. Generally, only crude procedures for "when to stop factoring" are employed (although more rigorous statistical tests are available for certain types of solutions as given in sec. **9.5** and **10.4**). Among the rules employed is the decision, in advance, to analyze up to 50% (or 75%) of the total variance of a battery of tests; or a suitable proportion of the total reliability, leaving room for some specific factors; or, that only factors which include at least 5% (or 2%) of the total variance can have any practical value, in the sense of being identifiable. Other approximate methods may involve some crude standards for the size and distribution of the final residuals.

In a bi-factor solution there is not as much choice of whether to continue factoring or not. The pattern plan predetermines, in a large sense, the proportion of the total variance that will be explained by the analysis. Cognizance of the kind of empirical rules that are used in such a solution as the principal-factor type may also be of benefit in judging the adequacy of a bi-factor solution. Thus, the common-factors of Table 7.6 account for just 50% of the total variance of the twenty-four tests, and

Table 7.8

Apportionment of Test Variances

Test j	Communality h_j^2	Reliability r_{jj}	Uniqueness $u_j^2 = 1 - h_j^2$	Error Variance $e_j^2 = 1 - r_{jj}$	Specificity $b_j^2 = u_j^2 - e_j^2$	Index of Factorization $C_j = 100\dfrac{h_j^2}{r_{jj}}$
1	.581	.756	.419	.244	.175	76.9
2	.209	.568	.791	.432	.359	36.7
3	.390	.544	.610	.456	.154	71.7
4	.315	.922	.685	.078	.607	34.1
5	.668	.808	.332	.192	.140	82.7
6	.643	.651	.357	.349	.008	98.8
7	.786	.754	.214	.246	−.032	104.2
8	.530	.680	.470	.320	.150	77.9
9	.708	.870	.292	.130	.162	81.4
10	.503[a]	.952	.497	.048	.449	52.8
11	.500	.712	.500	.288	.212	70.2
12	.575	.937	.425	.063	.362	61.4
13	.524	.889	.476	.111	.365	58.9
14	.448	.648	.552	.352	.200	69.1
15	.350	.507	.650	.493	.157	69.0
16	.371	.600	.629	.400	.229	61.8
17	.551	.725	.449	.275	.174	76.0
18	.484	.610	.516	.390	.126	79.4
19	.273	.569	.727	.431	.296	47.9
20	.415	.649	.585	.351	.234	63.9
21	.416	.784	.584	.216	.368	53.1
22	.415	.787	.585	.213	.372	52.7
23	.539	.931	.461	.069	.392	57.9
24	.507[b]	.836	.493	.164	.329	60.6

[a] The communality with the doublet D_1 included is .641.
[b] The communality with the doublet D_1 included is .645.

on this basis the solution would not be deemed "over-factored." The doublet D_1 certainly is not identifiable; and B_1, B_4, and B_5 each account for less than 5% (but more than 2%) of the total variance, so that their practical significance may be questioned.

The index C_j of completeness of factorization provides another guide to the adequacy of the solution. The analysis of psychological tests into common factors should not be carried to the point where real specific factors disappear. In the example there is only one value of C_j in excess of 100. It is ignored, as probably due to chance errors either in the factor weights or in the reliability coefficient. If, however, there were several such values for high reliability coefficients, there would be good reason to consider a modification of the factor solution.

In considering the statistical fit of the factor model in **2.7** the standard (2.30) was suggested for judging the agreement of the reproduced correlations with the observed ones. This requires the standard deviation of the final residuals to be less than the standard error of a zero correlation. The frequency distribution of the final residuals is presented in Table 7.9, where the standard deviation is shown to be .0655. Since this value is less than the standard error (.0830) of a zero correlation for a sample of 145 cases, the required condition is satisfied.

3. Factor names.—A few words about the naming of factors may be in order. It will be recalled that the fundamental purpose of factor analysis is to comprehend a large class of phenomena (the values of a set of variables) in terms of a small number of concepts (the factors); and, this description is taken to be a linear function of the factors. In a mathematical or physical theory it may be sufficient to know that twenty-four variables can be described linearly in terms of only six new hypothetical ones—that is usually quite an accomplishment, and it is of little concern as to what the six new variables are called. But in the biological and social sciences—psychology, for example—the practical identification of these new variables (the factors) makes it highly desirable to have them named.

Table 7.9

Frequency Distribution of Final Residuals

Value of Residual	Frequency	Value of Residual	Frequency
.150– .169	3	−.130– −.111	8
.130– .149	5	−.150– −.131	6
.110– .129	6	−.170– −.151	—
.090– .109	8	−.190– −.171	—
.070– .089	12	−.210– −.191	—
.050– .069	25	−.230– −.211	—
.030– .049	33	−.250– −.231	1
.010– .029	30		
−.010– .009	39	Total	276
−.030– −.011	29		
−.050– − 031	29	Mean	−.0004
−.070– −.051	15		
−.090– −.071	17	Standard deviation	.0655
−.110– −.091	10		

The coefficients of a factor pattern indicate the correlations of the variables with the respective factors and furnish the basis for naming them. In the case of oblique factors, to be discussed in later chapters, the structure furnishes the correlations of the variables with the factors, and so it is similarly employed in naming the factors. The investigator is guided by the magnitude of the factor weights in the selection of appropriate names for the factors. The name selected is usually suggested by the nature of the variables having the largest correlations with the factor under consideration. This name should be consistent with the nature of the remaining variables which have low correlations with the factor.

The common factors in the example are named from the pattern given in Table 7.6 and the brief descriptions of the tests. The factor B_0 has positive weights throughout and correlates highest with such deductive tests as Series Completion (23), Woody-McCall Arithmetic (24), Problem Reasoning (22), and Word Classification (8). Hence B_0 might be called a "general deductive factor." This name is consistent with the nature of the remaining variables—those involving a lesser amount of deductive ability have correspondingly smaller factor weights.

The remaining common factors are named from the subgroups of tests which have significant correlations with them. The first group factor is named from the "spatial" subgroup (Tests 1–4), the second from the "verbal" subgroup of tests, and similarly for the remaining factors. The names of the six common factors are indicated in Table 7.6. In addition to the common factors, there is one unique factor for each of the twenty-four tests. If a name were desired for any unique factor, it would be obtained from the description of the particular test. The only unnamed factor is the doublet D_1 involved in Speed of Adding (10) and Woody-McCall Arithmetic (24). This doublet appears to measure "arithmetic speed," which might appear as a more significant factor if more tests of this type were introduced in a battery to experiment for this purpose.

For future work with this factor pattern the doublet will be dropped from consideration, since, as was remarked before, it takes at least three variables to define a factor. The six common factors may be referred to by means of symbols or the descriptive names, which are tentatively assigned for that purpose. The particular name by which a factor is designated, however, should not raise an issue for dispute. If another investigator chooses to call these factors by other names, he is free to do so. The naming of factors is not a problem of factor analysis, which is a branch of statistics, but some descriptive names may be highly desirable in a particular field for purposes of classification.

8

Principal-factor
and Related Methods

8.1. *Introduction*

The principal-factor method is probably the most widely used technique in factor analysis. It was not always that way; the method requires considerable calculations which were much too time-consuming before electronic computers were available. The foundation for "the method of principal axes" was laid at the turn of the century by Karl Pearson (1901). However, it was not until the 1930s that the principal-factor method as we now know it was developed by Hotelling (1933) at the suggestion of Kelley. Subsequently, Kelley (1935) developed an alternative procedure which twenty years later proved to be the most useful one for adaptation to high-speed electronic computers (although the later work was done independently). The first applications of electronic computers to this problem in factor analysis were made by Wrigley and Neuhaus (1952, 1955).

The methods of this chapter are addressed to the first of the two alternative objectives distinguished in **2.3**—to extract the maximum variance from the observed variables. A typical situation where this is useful is in the reduction of a large body of data to a more manageable set. Of greatest interest, of course, are the measurements that vary the most among the individuals. Therefore, if a small number of linear combinations of the original variables can be found which account for most of the variance then considerable parsimony is gained.

Actually, three methods are considered in this chapter. The fundamental method is "component analysis" which is introduced in **8.2**. Then, an adaptation of it—the principal-factor method—is developed in sections **8.3**–**8.5**. Six different sets of data are used in **8.6** to illustrate various features of the principal-factor method. A technique for fixing the coordinate system in a given factor space for *any method* is developed in **8.7** and the relationship to the general principal-factor method is noted. Finally, an approximation to the principal-factor method—the centroid method—is described in **8.8**. This was very popular before computers made the principal-factor method feasible.

8.2.   *Component Analysis*

The method of principal components, or component analysis, is based upon the early work of Pearson (1901) with the specific adaptations to factor analysis suggested by the work of Hotelling (1933). As noted in **6.2**, when the point representation of a set of variables is employed, the loci of uniform frequency density are essentially concentric, similar, and similarly situated ellipsoids. The axes of these ellipsoids correspond to the principal components. The method of component analysis, then, involves the rotation of coordinate axes to a new frame of reference in the total variable space—an orthogonal transformation wherein each of the n original variables is describable in terms of the n new principal components.

An important feature of the new components is that they account, in turn, for a maximum amount of variance of the variables. More specifically, the first principal component is that linear combination of the original variables which contributes a maximum to their total variance; the second principal component, uncorrelated with the first, contributes a maximum to the residual variance; and so on until the total variance is analyzed. The sum of the variances of all n principal components is equal to the sum of the variances of the original variables.

Since the method is so dependent on the total variance of the original variables, it is most suitable when all the variables are measured in the same units. Otherwise, by change of units or other linear transformations of the variables, the ellipsoids could be squeezed or stretched so that their axes (the principal components) would have no special meaning. Hence, it is customary to express the variables in standard form, i.e., to select the unit of measurement for each variable so that its sample variance is one. Then, the analysis is made on the correlation matrix, with the total variance equal to n. For such a matrix (symmetric, positive definite), all n principal components are real and positive.

The formal development of the method of component analysis will not be presented.[1] Instead, the development will be for the factor-analytic adaptation of the method. The important distinction is that the model (2.8) is employed in component analysis as contrasted to the model (2.9) for factor analysis. All the variance of the variables is analyzed in terms of the principal components, while the communality is analyzed in terms of the common factors. Hence, the distinction comes from the amount of variance analyzed—the numbers placed in the diagonal of the correlation matrix. Analysis of the correlation matrix, with ones in the diagonal, leads to principal *components*, while analysis of the correlation matrix with communalities leads to principal *factors*. It will be shown in chapter 16 that the principal components can be expressed simply in terms of the observed variables, while approximation procedures are required for the measurement of factors.

Before the mathematical and computing procedures are presented, it may be of interest to see what the results of a component analysis look like. This is shown in Table 8.1 for the simple numerical example introduced in chapter 2. The main body

---

[1]For detailed discussion of the method of principal components, see the original work of Hotelling (1933) and the treatment by Anderson (1958, chap. 11); and for consideration of statistical inference in component analysis, see Anderson (1963).

Table 8.1

Principal Components for Five Socio-Economic Variables[a]

Variable	P_1	P_2	P_3	P_4	P_5	Variance
1	.5810	.8064	.0276	−.0645	−.0852	1.0000
2	.7671	−.5448	.3193	.1118	−.0216	1.0002
3	.6724	.7260	.1149	−.0072	.0862	.9999
4	.9324	−.1043	−.3078	.1582	.0000	1.0000
5	.7911	−.5582	−.0647	−.2413	.0102	.9999
Variance	2.8733	1.7966	.2148	.1000	.0153	5.0000
Per cent	57.5	35.9	4.3	2.0	0.3	100.0

[a] Again, the only reason for showing the results to so many decimal places is to provide a means for checking numerical calculations.

of the table contains numbers which, when read by columns correspond to the principal components, and when read by rows correspond to the variables. Thus, the entries in the rows are the coefficients of the P's in the linear expressions (2.8) for the z's; they are also the correlations of the variables with the principal components. The direction of a principal component may be reflected, i.e., all entries in a column may be multiplied by -1 without affecting any of the results.

The sums of squares of entries in the rows are the variances of the variables. The variance of each principal component (sum of squares in each column) is shown in the next to last row. The principle of maximum contribution to variance of each successive component is clearly demonstrated. In this example, the first two principal components account for more than 93 per cent of the variance—leading to a reduction in the data that would satisfy the most discerning investigator.

Very often the results of a component analysis and a principal-factor analysis may turn out to be very similar in practical applications. Actually, the factor loadings produced by a component analysis will have the same relative magnitudes (but inflated) as those from any effective method of factor analysis when the communalities for the variables are equal (Rao 1955).

8.3.   *Principal-Factor Method*

While the method of principal components was devised for the model (2.8), Thomson (1934) was the first to apply it to the classical factor analysis model—although, at the time, his application was only to the Spearman two-factor solution. More generally, by the "method of principal factors" is meant the application of the method of principal components to the reduced correlation matrix (i.e., with communalities in place of the ones in the principal diagonal). This is the method that is developed in detail in this and the following two sections.

From the classical factor-analysis model (2.9), the relevant portion for the determination of the common-factor coefficients may be written:

(8.1) $$z_j = a_{j1} F_1 + \cdots + a_{jp} F_p + \cdots + a_{jm} F_m, \qquad (j = 1, 2, \cdots, n)$$

where the unique factor has been omitted, and hence the precise representation should be $\tilde{z}_j$ but the curls are dropped for simplicity. The sum of squares of factor coefficients gives the communality of a particular variable, while any term a_{jp}^2 indicates the contribution of the factor F_p to the communality of z_j. The first stage of the principal-factor method involves the selection of the first-factor coefficients a_{j1} so as to make the sum of the contributions of that factor to the total communality a maximum. This sum is given by

(8.2) $$V_1 = a_{11}^2 + a_{21}^2 + \cdots + a_{n1}^2,$$

and the coefficients a_{j1} must be chosen so as to make V_1 a maximum under the conditions

(8.3) $$r_{jk} = \sum_{p=1}^{m} a_{jp} a_{kp} \qquad (j, k = 1, 2, \cdots, n),$$

where $r_{jk} = r_{kj}$ and r_{jj} is the communality h_j^2 of variable z_j. The conditions (8.3) say that the observed correlations are to be replaced by the reproduced correlations, implying the assumption of zero residuals.

In order to maximize a function of n variables when the variables are connected by an arbitrary number of auxiliary equations, the method of Lagrange multipliers (Apostol 1957, pp. 152–57) is particularly well adapted. This method is employed to maximize V_1, which is a function of the n variables a_{j1} under the $\frac{1}{2} n(n+1)$ conditions (8.3) among all the coefficients a_{jp}. Let

(8.4) $$2T = V_1 - \sum_{j,k=1}^{n} \mu_{jk} r_{jk} = V_1 - \sum_{j,k=1}^{n} \sum_{p=1}^{m} \mu_{jk} a_{jp} a_{kp},$$

where $\mu_{jk} (= \mu_{kj})$ are the Lagrange multipliers. Then set the partial derivative of this new function T with respect to any one of the n variables a_{j1} equal to zero, and similarly put the partial derivative with respect to any of the other coefficients $a_{jp} (p \neq 1)$ equal to zero, obtaining

(8.5) $$\frac{\partial T}{\partial a_{jp}} = \delta_{1p} a_{j1} - \sum_{k=1}^{n} \mu_{jk} a_{kp} = 0 \qquad (p = 1, 2, \cdots, m),$$

where the Kronecker $\delta_{1p} = 1$ if $p = 1$ and $\delta_{1p} = 0$ if $p \neq 1$.

Multiply (8.5) by a_{j1} and sum with respect to j, obtaining

$$\delta_{1p} \sum_{j=1}^{n} a_{j1}^2 - \sum_{j=1}^{n} \sum_{k=1}^{n} \mu_{jk} a_{j1} a_{kp} = 0.$$

Now, the expression $\sum_{j=1}^{n} \mu_{jk} a_{j1}$ is equal to a_{k1} according to (8.5), and, setting $\sum_{j=1}^{n} a_{j1}^2 = \lambda_1$, the last equation may be written as follows:

(8.6) $$\delta_{1p} \lambda_1 - \sum_{k=1}^{n} a_{k1} a_{kp} = 0.$$

136

Upon multiplying (8.6) by a_{jp} and summing for p, this equation becomes

$$a_{j1}\lambda_1 - \sum_{k=1}^{n} a_{k1} \left(\sum_{p=1}^{m} a_{jp} a_{kp} \right) = 0,$$

or, upon applying the conditions (8.3),

$$(8.7) \qquad \sum_{k=1}^{n} r_{jk} a_{k1} - \lambda_1 a_{j1} = 0.$$

The n equations, one for each value of j, represented by the expression (8.7) may be written in full as follows:

$$(8.8) \begin{cases} (h_1^2 - \lambda)a_{11} + & r_{12}a_{21} + & r_{13}a_{31} + \cdots + & r_{1n}a_{n1} = 0, \\ r_{21}a_{11} + (h_2^2 - \lambda)a_{21} + & r_{23}a_{31} + \cdots + & r_{2n}a_{n1} = 0, \\ r_{31}a_{11} + & r_{32}a_{21} + (h_3^2 - \lambda)a_{31} + \cdots + & r_{3n}a_{n1} = 0, \\ \cdot \quad , \\ r_{n1}a_{11} + & r_{n2}a_{21} + & r_{n3}a_{31} + \cdots + (h_n^2 - \lambda)a_{n1} = 0, \end{cases}$$

where the parameter of (8.7) is designated by λ without a subscript.

Thus, the maximization of (8.2) under the conditions (8.3) leads to the system of n equations (8.8) for the solution of the n unknowns a_{j1}. A necessary and sufficient condition for this system of n homogeneous equations to have a nontrivial solution is the vanishing of the determinant of coefficients of the a_{j1} (Hadley 1961, p. 174). This condition may be written:

$$(8.9) \qquad \begin{vmatrix} (h_1^2 - \lambda) & r_{12} & r_{13} & \cdots & r_{1n} \\ r_{21} & (h_2^2 - \lambda) & r_{23} & \cdots & r_{2n} \\ r_{31} & r_{32} & (h_3^2 - \lambda) & \cdots & r_{3n} \\ \cdot & \cdot & \cdot & \cdots & \cdot \\ r_{n1} & r_{n2} & r_{n3} & \cdots & (h_n^2 - \lambda) \end{vmatrix} = 0.$$

If the determinant in (8.9) were expanded it would lead to an n-order polynomial in λ. In expanded form, or in determinantal form, an equation such as (8.9) is known as a *characteristic equation*. Extensive mathematical theory has been developed on the properties of characteristic equations (e.g., Graybill 1969; White 1958; National Bureau of Standards Applied Mathematics Series). For factor analysis, some of the important properties include the fact that all roots are real and that a q-fold multiple root substituted for λ in (8.9) reduces the rank of the determinant to $(n - q)$.

When a simple root of the characteristic equation is substituted for λ in (8.8) a set of homogeneous linear equations of rank $(n - 1)$ is obtained. This set of equations has a family of solutions, all of which are proportional to one particular solution.

From the above analysis, it follows that the factor of proportionality is $\lambda_1 = \sum_{j=1}^{n} a_{j1}^2$.

But this expression is precisely V_1, the quantity which is to be maximized. In other words, V_1 is equal to one of the roots of the characteristic equation (8.9), namely, the largest root λ_1.

The problem of finding the coefficients a_{j1} of the first factor F_1, which will account for as much of the total communality as possible, is then solved. The largest root λ_1 of (8.9) is substituted in (8.8), and any solution $\alpha_{11}, \alpha_{21}, \cdots, \alpha_{n1}$ is obtained. Then, to satisfy the relation (8.2), these values are divided by the square root of the sum of their squares and then multiplied by $\sqrt{\lambda_1}$. The resulting quantities are

$$(8.10) \qquad a_{j1} = \alpha_{j1} \sqrt{\lambda_1} / \sqrt{(\alpha_{11}^2 + \alpha_{21}^2 + \cdots + \alpha_{n1}^2)} \qquad (j = 1, 2, \cdots, n),$$

which are the desired coefficients of F_1 in the factor pattern (8.1).

The roots (λ's) of a characteristic equation (8.9) are called *characteristic roots* (sometimes referred to as "eigenvalues"), or simply the *roots* of the matrix $\mathbf{R}$. The solution to the set of equations (8.8) for a given root leads to a vector (a set of α's) which is defined as a *characteristic vector* (sometimes called an "eigenvector") of the matrix $\mathbf{R}$. The generalized mathematical problem is usually expressed in the form: Find a number λ and an n-dimensional vector $\mathbf{q} \neq \mathbf{O}$ such that

$$(8.11) \qquad \mathbf{Rq} = \lambda\mathbf{q}.$$

Any number λ_p satisfying this equation is a *root* (or *eigenvalue*) of $\mathbf{R}$ and its associated vector $\mathbf{q}_p = \{\alpha_{1p}, \alpha_{2p}, \cdots, \alpha_{np}\}$ is a *characteristic vector* (or *eigenvector*) of $\mathbf{R}$. An eigenvector scaled according to (8.10) is designated $\mathbf{a}_p = \{a_{1p}, a_{2p}, \cdots, a_{np}\}$.

The foregoing expression may be viewed another way. The term $\mathbf{Rq}$ represents a transformation of the vector $\mathbf{q}$, and (8.11) says that this transformed vector is proportional to the original one, with λ the proportionality factor. In general, of course, it is not to be expected that the transformed vector would be proportional to the original one. However, when that is the case then a quantity λ exists such that (8.11) is satisfied. Such a λ must be a root of the characteristic equation (8.9). For each root λ_p the system of equations (8.8) has a non-zero solution $\mathbf{q}_p = \{\alpha_{1p}, \alpha_{2p}, \cdots, \alpha_{np}\}$. Furthermore, the n roots $\lambda_1, \lambda_2 \cdots, \lambda_n$ lead to n vectors $\mathbf{q}_1, \mathbf{q}_2, \cdots, \mathbf{q}_n$ so that (8.11) may be written:

$$(8.12) \qquad \mathbf{R}(\mathbf{q}_1, \mathbf{q}_2, \cdots, \mathbf{q}_n) = (\lambda_1\mathbf{q}_1, \lambda_2\mathbf{q}_2, \cdots, \lambda_n\mathbf{q}_n),$$

or, upon constituting a matrix $\mathbf{Q}$ of the n vectors,

$$(8.13) \qquad \mathbf{RQ} = \mathbf{Q\Lambda},$$

where

$$\mathbf{\Lambda} = \text{diag}(\lambda_1, \lambda_2, \cdots, \lambda_n).$$

When the analysis is in terms of principal components (with unities rather than communalities in the principal diagonal of $\mathbf{R}$), then the vectors in $\mathbf{Q}$ are linearly independent so that their determinant is different from zero and $\mathbf{Q}$ has an inverse. Then from (8.13) it follows that

$$(8.14) \qquad \mathbf{Q}^{-1}\mathbf{RQ} = \mathbf{\Lambda},$$

which brings **R** into diagonal form in which the elements of Λ are the roots and the columns of **Q** are the characteristic vectors. Furthermore, since the correlation matrix is symmetric, i.e., $\mathbf{R} = \mathbf{R}'$, transposing in the expression (8.14) yields:

$$\mathbf{Q}'\mathbf{R}(\mathbf{Q}^{-1})' = \Lambda.$$

From this expression it follows that the rows of $(\mathbf{Q}^{-1})'$ are the characteristic vectors $\mathbf{q}_1, \mathbf{q}_2, \cdots, \mathbf{q}_n$ and that therefore **Q** is *orthogonal*, with the property:

(8.15)
$$\mathbf{QQ}' = \mathbf{I} \quad \text{or} \quad \mathbf{Q}^{-1} = \mathbf{Q}'.$$

Then, for **R** symmetric, (8.14) becomes:

(8.16)
$$\mathbf{Q}'\mathbf{RQ} = \Lambda.$$

This expression—sometimes referred to as the Spectral Theorem (Stewart 1963, pp. 222–24)—says that the matrix **R** of any symmetric (quadratic) form may be diagonalized by means of an orthogonal transformation **Q** and that the resulting elements of Λ and **Q** are real with the n characteristic vectors linearly independent.

When the analysis is in terms of principal factors (based upon estimates of communalities in **R**), then only m (less than n) positive roots and associated real characteristic vectors are obtained. When these are scaled according to (8.10) they are designated by $\mathbf{a}_1, \mathbf{a}_2, \cdots, \mathbf{a}_m$ instead of by **q**'s, and the matrix of these m vectors by **A**. (There are still n elements of each of these column vectors so that **A** is of dimension $n \times m$). While **A** does not have an inverse, the corresponding "orthogonality" property is

(8.17)
$$\mathbf{A}'\mathbf{A} = \Lambda_m = \text{diag}(\lambda_1, \lambda_2, \cdots, \lambda_m),$$

or, in expanded algebraic form:

(8.18)
$$\begin{cases} \sum_{j=1}^{n} a_{jp}^2 = \lambda_p \\ \sum_{j=1}^{n} a_{jp}a_{jq} = 0 \end{cases} \quad (p, q = 1, 2, \cdots, m; \quad p \neq q).$$

It will be noted that (8.6) represents a special instance of the orthogonality property.

The digression in the last four paragraphs gave some of the highlights of the mathematical theory as it pertains to component analysis and to principal-factor analysis. Returning to the formal development, the coefficients a_{j1} of the first factor F_1 were determined in (8.10). Conceptually, it helps to think of the method in terms of one principal factor at a time, even though in practice they are all computed simultaneously. The next problem is to find a factor which will account for a maximum of the residual communality. In order to do this, it is necessary to obtain the first-factor residual correlations. Furthermore, in obtaining still other factors the residual correlations with two, three, $\cdots, (m - 1)$ factors removed are employed, and hence a suitable notation is required. A convenient notation for the residual correlation of r_{jk} with s factors removed is $_s r_{jk}$. Thus, when the first factor has been obtained, the first-factor residuals become

(8.19) $_1r_{jk} = r_{jk} - a_{j1}a_{k1} = a_{j2}a_{k2} + a_{j3}a_{k3} + \cdots + a_{jm}a_{km}.$

More generally, the matrix of the first-factor residuals may be expressed by:

(8.20) $\mathbf{R}_1 = \mathbf{R} - \hat{\mathbf{R}}_1$

where

(8.21) $\hat{\mathbf{R}}_1 = \mathbf{a}_1 \mathbf{a}_1'$

represents the $n \times n$ symmetric matrix of products of first-factor coefficients, i.e., the reproduced correlations from the first factor alone.

In determining the coefficients of the second factor F_2, it is necessary to maximize the quantity

(8.22) $V_2 = a_{12}^2 + a_{22}^2 + \cdots a_{n2}^2,$

which is the sum of the contributions of F_2 to the residual communality. This maximization is subject to the conditions (8.19), which are analogous to the restrictions (8.3) in the case of the first factor. The theory of characteristic equations provides the basis for determining the coefficients of the second and subsequent factors. It is not necessary to carry through an analysis for maximizing the contributions of F_2 to the residual communality. Instead, it will be shown that the required maximum root of $\mathbf{R}_1$ is, in fact, the *second* largest root of the original correlation matrix $\mathbf{R}$.

If $\mathbf{a}_p$ stand for the m characteristic vectors of $\mathbf{R}$ (properly scaled), it can be determined whether they are also characteristic vectors of $\mathbf{R}_1$. Postmultiplying the matrix $\mathbf{R}_1$ by any vector $\mathbf{a}_p$ yields

(8.23) $\mathbf{R}_1 \mathbf{a}_p = (\mathbf{R} - \mathbf{a}_1 \mathbf{a}_1')\mathbf{a}_p$

from the definition (8.20) of the residual matrix. Expanding this expression, and applying (8.11) produces:

(8.24) $\mathbf{R}_1 \mathbf{a}_p = \mathbf{R}\mathbf{a}_p - \mathbf{a}_1 \mathbf{a}_1' \mathbf{a}_p = \lambda_p \mathbf{a}_p - \mathbf{a}_1 \mathbf{a}_1' \mathbf{a}_p.$

Now consider the two cases: $p = 1$ and $p \neq 1$. (a) When $p = 1$, $\mathbf{a}_1' \mathbf{a}_1 = \lambda_1$ according to (8.6), so that the above expression reduces to

(8.25) $\mathbf{R}_1 \mathbf{a}_1 = \mathbf{O}.$

In other words, the characteristic vector corresponding to the largest root λ_1 of $\mathbf{R}$ is also a characteristic vector of $\mathbf{R}_1$ but its associated root in $\mathbf{R}_1$ is zero. (b) When $p \neq 1$, $\mathbf{a}_1' \mathbf{a}_p = \mathbf{O}$ according to (8.6), and expression (8.24) becomes:

(8.26) $\mathbf{R}_1 \mathbf{a}_p = \lambda_p \mathbf{a}_p - a_1 \cdot \mathbf{O} = \lambda_p \mathbf{a}_p,$ $(p \neq 1),$

which says that, except for λ_1, the roots of $\mathbf{R}_1$ are identical with those of $\mathbf{R}$ and their associated vectors are also identical. The expressions (8.25) and (8.26) prove that the characteristic vectors of $\mathbf{R}_1$ are identical with those of $\mathbf{R}$, and that they have corresponding roots except that corresponding to the vector $\mathbf{a}_1$ in $\mathbf{R}_1$ is a zero root in place of the λ_1 in $\mathbf{R}$.

From the foregoing it is clear that the λ_2 of $\mathbf{R}$ is the largest root of $\mathbf{R}_1$. In other words, to obtain the coefficients of the second factor F_2 from the largest root of the residual matrix $\mathbf{R}_1$ it suffices to extract the second largest root of the original matrix $\mathbf{R}$. By the same type of argument, the successive roots and their associated vectors are obtained directly from the original correlation matrix $\mathbf{R}$, until m factors have been extracted.

When unities are placed in the principal diagonal of $\mathbf{R}$ then usually $m = n$. If some numbers less than unities (estimates of communalities) are placed in the diagonal, and the positive semi-definite property of $\mathbf{R}$ is preserved, then m will usually be less than n, and all roots will be real and non negative. However, the reduced correlation matrix $\mathbf{R}$ (i.e., with communality estimates in the diagonal) will not be positive semi-definite in practice, and both positive and negative roots may be expected. Of course, the negative roots, and the associated imaginary vectors, must be extraneous to a practical problem. Even to retain all the real vectors would be an over-factorization because the sum of the positive roots is greater than the original sum of communalities (the negative roots will reduce that sum to the starting value). Since the total communality for the n variables is the trace of the reduced correlation matrix, the factorization process should be stopped when the sum of the roots is equal to this value. The investigator will usually be satisfied with an even smaller number of factors, as indicated in the examples below.

The theoretical development of this section provides the logical basis for the principal-factor method, but it does not furnish an actual means of computation. The direct solution of a characteristic equation (8.9) and sets of linear homogeneous equations (8.8) would entail insuperable algebraic efforts. Practical means of obtaining principal-factor solutions are discussed in the following sections.

8.4. *Additional Theory*

A method of determining the principal axes is developed in this section, based upon two fundamental papers of Hotelling (1933, 1936). While it was devised initially to reduce the labor of hand computation, its theoretical basis is equally suitable for the development of efficient algorithms for present day computers. This method involves an iterative scheme which yields a root of the characteristic equation and the coefficients of the associated factor simultaneously. The roots appear in descending order of magnitude upon successive applications of the method. For this reason the method may be especially suitable in practical situations where n is large but only a few of the largest characteristic roots and the associated factor coefficients are required.

The iterative process is begun by selecting an arbitrary set of n numbers, and transforming them again and again by use of the observed correlations until they converge to the desired coefficients of the first principal factor. As noted in the last section, an operation $\mathbf{R}\mathbf{q}_1$ represents a transformation of the vector $\mathbf{q}_1 = \{\alpha_{11}, \alpha_{21}, \cdots, \alpha_{n1}\}$ into some new vector. Geometrically, this may be thought of as a rotation of a line through the origin (for which the α_{j1} are proportional to the direction cosines) to a new line for which numbers proportional to the direction cosines are in the column vector ($\mathbf{R}\mathbf{q}_1$). In general, the new line will be distinct from the original one. However, when a line remains stationary under such a transformation, then the new vector must be proportional to the original vector as indicated in (8.11). This may be expressed by the matrix equation:

(8.27) $$(\mathbf{R} - \lambda\mathbf{I})\mathbf{q}_1 = \mathbf{O},$$

or, in expanded algebraic form:

$$r_{j1}\alpha_{11} + r_{j2}\alpha_{21} + \cdots + (h_j^2 - \lambda)\alpha_{j1} + \cdots + r_{jn}\alpha_{n1} = 0,$$

remembering that the communality is used in place of the self correlation. As j takes the values 1 to n, it is readily seen that these equations are identical with (8.8). Thus, for any invariant line, the direction cosines are proportional to a solution of (8.8), where λ is a root of the characteristic equation (8.9). Hence it follows that *the invariant lines are the desired principal axes.* It is thus apparent that, if a set of numbers α_{11}, $\alpha_{21}, \cdots, \alpha_{n1}$ can be found which lead to (8.27), the numbers $\mathbf{Rq}_1$ are proportional to the direction cosines of the principal axes. The coefficients of one of the principal factors can be obtained from the latter set of numbers. Furthermore, λ is the sum of the contributions of this factor to the communalities of the variables.

In practice, of course, it cannot be expected that the arbitrary numbers α_{j1} will be so selected as to be proportional to the direction cosines of one of the principal axes. The iterative process then involves the use of the derived numbers $\mathbf{Rq}_1$ as a new set of arbitrary numbers in place of α_{j1}, and the transformation of the new vector $\mathbf{Rq}_1$ becomes $\mathbf{R}(\mathbf{Rq}_1)$. Formal matrix manipulation of this transformation reduces it to:

(8.28) $$\mathbf{R}(\mathbf{Rq}_1) = \mathbf{R}(\lambda\mathbf{q}_1) = \lambda(\mathbf{Rq}_1) = \lambda^2\mathbf{q}_1$$

upon repeated application of (8.27) and factoring out the scalar λ according to **3.2**, paragraph **21**. This transformation effectively does the job of two iterations.

The property exhibited in (8.28) may be generalized to any power, say m, for any vector $\mathbf{q}$, as follows:

(8.29) $$\mathbf{R}^m\mathbf{q} = \lambda^m\mathbf{q}.$$

Then the improvement in the iteration process need not end with the employment of $\mathbf{R}^2$. After doubling the speed of convergence by squaring $\mathbf{R}$, it can be doubled again by squaring $\mathbf{R}^2$, i.e., by multiplying a set of trial values by $\mathbf{R}^4$, and thus the equivalent of four multiplications by $\mathbf{R}$ is obtained. Upon squaring again, a matrix $\mathbf{R}^8$ is obtained, and multiplication by it is equivalent to eight multiplications by $\mathbf{R}$, and so forth to any power of the correlation matrix. This squaring process is continued until the convergence is so rapid that additional matrix squaring is not worth while.

The iterative process is continued until the ratios among the quantities obtained at any stage converge to the corresponding ratios among the coefficients of F_1 to any specified degree of accuracy. The proof of the convergence of these ratios to those of the coefficients a_{j1} of the first principal factor is given by Hotelling (1933, Sec. 4). A convenient procedure is to divide each of the trial values by a fixed one of them, say the largest. Then the next value obtained, corresponding to this number, will be an approximation to the characteristic root λ_1.

The second and remaining principal factors may be determined by the same method, and the convergence can be accelerated by the use of a convenient power of the matrix of residual correlations. It is not necessary, however, to obtain this power of the residual matrix by repeated squarings, as was done in the case of the original matrix of correlations. Instead, the determination already made of the power of **R** and the following algebraic properties of matrices can be employed for this purpose.

In getting the square of the residual matrix algebraically from (8.20), namely:

(8.30)
$$\mathbf{R}_1^2 = \mathbf{R}^2 - 2\mathbf{R}\hat{\mathbf{R}}_1 + \hat{\mathbf{R}}_1^2,$$

it is possible to express the last two terms by quantities already known, so that the actual squaring of $\mathbf{R}_1$ is obviated. Thus, from the definition (8.21) and noting that $\mathbf{a}_1'\mathbf{a}_1 = \lambda_1$ according to (8.17), the last term becomes:

(8.31)
$$\hat{\mathbf{R}}_1^2 = \lambda_1 \hat{\mathbf{R}}_1.$$

Also, from the expression (8.11) for the particular case of the first principal factor (with coefficients $\mathbf{a}_1$) of the correlation matrix **R**, the following relationship

$$\mathbf{R}\mathbf{a}_1 = \lambda_1 \mathbf{a}_1$$

provides the basis for expressing $\mathbf{R}\hat{\mathbf{R}}_1$ in terms of known quantities. Postmultiplying by $\mathbf{a}_1'$ and applying definition (8.21) yields:

(8.32)
$$\mathbf{R}\hat{\mathbf{R}}_1 = \lambda_1 \hat{\mathbf{R}}_1.$$

Upon substituting the known quantities from (8.31) and (8.32) for the terms in (8.30), the square of the residual matrix becomes:

(8.33)
$$\mathbf{R}_1^2 = \mathbf{R}^2 - \lambda_1 \hat{\mathbf{R}}_1.$$

In other words, actual squaring of the residual matrix is not necessary since the square of the correlation matrix and the matrix of products of first-factor coefficients are available.

In similar fashion, it can be shown that for any positive integer e,

(8.34)
$$\mathbf{R}_1^e = \mathbf{R}^e - \lambda_1^{e-1}\hat{\mathbf{R}}_1.$$

Thus the eth power of the residual matrix is expressed in terms of the eth power of the original correlation matrix, obviating actual multiplications of the residual matrix.

From the foregoing development the order of procedure of the iterative scheme may be summarized. Using $\mathbf{R}^e$ as the basis for selecting the set of trial values, this set rapidly yields the values of the first-factor coefficients[2] and the characteristic root λ_1. Furthermore, the value λ_1^e will be determined from the multiplication of the set of trial values by $\mathbf{R}^e$, and λ^{e-1} can be obtained by division. Then multiplying λ^{e-1} by each element of $\hat{\mathbf{R}}_1$ and subtracting from the corresponding element of $\mathbf{R}^e$, the eth power of the residual matrix is obtained. The second-factor coefficients are obtained

---

[2]Burt (1938) points out that to factor a matrix $\mathbf{R}^e$ is equivalent to obtaining a Spearman general factor. This arises from the fact that, with a sufficient number of self-multiplications, any symmetric matrix can be reduced as closely as desired to a matrix of rank one.

from $\mathbf{R}_1$ and $\mathbf{R}_1^e$ in the same manner as the first-factor coefficients are determined from $\mathbf{R}$ and $\mathbf{R}^e$. It may not be necessary to employ the eth power of $\mathbf{R}_1$ in calculating the second-factor coefficients when rapid convergence is evident. Then some lower power of $\mathbf{R}_1$, or $\mathbf{R}_1$ itself, is employed. Further factors are determined similarly until approximately all the communality is analyzed.

8.5. *Outline of Computer Program*

Factor analysis has been troubled in the past with the practical difficulty of requiring an excessive amount of computational work. In the present computer age this is no longer the case. Hence the principal-factor method—with its elegance and precision of mathematical form that was lacking in earlier methods—is a highly desirable form of factorization of a correlation matrix, even though the immediate results may not yield a compelling interpretation. The procedure usually recommended by psychologists is to initiate the analysis of a correlation matrix by means of some arbitrary solution and then rotate it to some (psychologically) more meaningful solution (see part III). Thurstone, the leader and chief proponent of this philosophy, has stated (1947, p. 509): "When the principal-axes solution becomes available with less computational labor, it will, no doubt, be preferred by all students of this subject, and they will start the rotational problem with the principal-factor matrix."

For a problem of the order of magnitude of the twenty-four–variable example of **7.6**, the computational labor is simply prohibitive for the complete principal-factor analysis by hand methods. The time required for the calculation of the first-factor weights, alone, for the twenty-four variables is more than seventy hours (Holzinger and Harman 1941, p. 175). The determination of each additional factor is estimated to require upwards of forty hours. In 1941, Holzinger and Harman recommended that the application of the direct principal-factor method to large sets of variables await the development of appropriate computing machinery. That time has arrived. The principal-factor method can now be considered in its own right as a preferred type of solution, or as an excellent reduction of the correlation matrix which provides a basis for rotation to some other form of solution.

The factor analysis theory of **8.3** leads to a classical problem in mathematics—the determination of the characteristic roots and associated vectors of the reduced correlation matrix **R**. The computation procedures on numerical methods for the solution of systems of linear equations, with the associated problems of matrix inversion and characteristic equations are then available to factor analysis. In the publication *Mathematical Methods for Digital Computers* there is not only a chapter on factor analysis proper (Harman 1960), but Part II on matrices and linear equations has a direct bearing on factor analysis. Modern day computing adaptations of the original work done by Jacobi (1846) more than a century ago has been found very effective in programming the principal-factor method on all present-day electronic computers. The earliest programs written were for the ORDVAC (Wrigley and Neuhaus 1952), the Johnniac (Golub 1955), and the IBM 704 (Sawanobori 1957). Now, very efficient programs for finding the characteristic roots and vectors of symmetric matrices are available for computers throughout the world.

The Jacobi method was the first widely used method for modern computers, but it has been replaced in popularity by a more efficient, and more sophisticated, procedure known as "HOW" for Householder-Ortega-Wilkinson (for a fuller discussion of this method see Ralston 1965 and Wilkinson 1965). This method, in all of its variants, starts out with the procedure (Householder 1958) which reduces a symmetric matrix to a tridiagonal symmetric matrix. The next step involves the determination of the characteristic roots of the tridiagonalized matrix by means of a series of orthogonal rotations such that the resulting matrixes remain tridiagonal (Ortega and Kaiser 1963; Francis 1961, 1962; Bowdler, et al. 1968). The final step in the HOW procedure solves for the characteristic vectors of the tridiagonal matrix directly as a set of simultaneous equations (Wilkinson 1958, 1960).

While the HOW routine is probably the most efficient today, and improvements are being made regularly to speed up the computations, it is not the computer program that will be described here. Instead, because of its historical importance to the development of factor analysis, the basic Jacobi method is presented. It involves the diagonalization of the matrix $\mathbf{R}$ by performing a sequence of orthogonal transformations on it, designed to reduce *one* off-diagonal element to zero at each stage. Each orthogonal transformation is of the form $\mathbf{B}_{jk}\mathbf{R}\mathbf{B}'_{jk}$ where

$$(8.35) \qquad \mathbf{B}_{jk} = \begin{bmatrix} 1 & & & & & & & & & \\ & \cdot & & & & & & & & \\ & & \cdot & & & & & & & \\ & & & \cdot & & & & & & \\ & & & & 1 & & & & & \\ & & & & \cos\theta_{jk} & & -\sin\theta_{jk} & & & \\ & & & & 1 & & & & & \\ & & & & & \cdot & & & & \\ & & & & & & \cdot & & & \\ & & & & \sin\theta_{jk} & & \cos\theta_{jk} & & & \\ & & & & & & 1 & & & \\ & & & & & & & \cdot & & \\ & & & & & & & & \cdot & \\ & & & & & & & & & 1 \end{bmatrix},$$

with the four elements in the intersections of rows and columns j and k as indicated, all other diagonal elements unity, and all other elements zero. The angle of rotation θ_{jk} is chosen so as to transform the element r_{jk} into zero, and is defined by

$$(8.36) \qquad \tan 2\theta_{jk} = \frac{2r_{jk}}{h_j^2 - h_k^2}.$$

When an element is reduced to zero it does not, in general, remain at zero during subsequent transformations. However, the sum of squares of off-diagonal elements is decreased each time by an amount corresponding to $2r_{jk}^2$, and thus Jacobi's method guarantees the convergence of the off-diagonal elements of **R** to zeros (to a designated number of decimal places) with a sufficient number of iterations.

In the process of reducing the original matrix **R** to a diagonal matrix **D**, the off-diagonal elements are considered systematically. Since the original correlations r_{jk} are altered by the transformations (8.35), it would seem more appropriate to designate a general off-diagonal element by d_{jk} and the intermediate derived matrices by **D**'s with suitable subscripts indicated below. Thus, at any stage of a specific transformation directed at reducing one off-diagonal element d_{jk} to zero, the following notation will be employed:

$$(8.37) \qquad\qquad _v\mathbf{D} = \mathbf{B}_{jk(v-1)}\mathbf{DB}_{jk}'$$

where the sequencing of the transformations is derived from:

$$(8.38) \qquad\qquad v = n(j-1) - \frac{j(j+1)}{2} + k$$

in which $j = 1, 2, \cdots, n-1$ and $k = j+1, j+2, \cdots, n$, producing the $n(n-1)/2$ possible pairs (j, k).

At any stage the product of the v individual transformations may be designated

$$(8.39) \qquad\qquad _v\mathbf{B} = \mathbf{B}_{jk} \cdots \mathbf{B}_{13}\mathbf{B}_{12},$$

where v is given by (8.38), and when *all* combinations of j and k have been tried, the product of these transformations in the ith iteration is designated:

$$(8.40) \qquad\qquad \mathbf{B}_i = \mathbf{II}(\mathbf{B}_{jk};\ \ j<k = 1, 2, \cdots, n), \qquad (i = 1, 2, \cdots, \mu).$$

The diagonalizing effect of the ith iteration is given by:

$$(8.41) \qquad\qquad \mathbf{D}_i = \mathbf{B}_i\mathbf{D}_{i-1}\mathbf{B}_i' \qquad\qquad (i = 1, 2, \cdots, \mu).$$

If the product (in the indicated order) of the transformation matrices through the ith iteration is defined by:

$$(8.42) \qquad\qquad \mathbf{P}_i = \mathbf{B}_i\mathbf{B}_{i-1} \cdots \mathbf{B}_2\mathbf{B}_1,$$

then formula (8.41) can be expressed in terms of the original matrix **R** as follows:

$$(8.43) \qquad\qquad \mathbf{D}_i = \mathbf{P}_i\mathbf{R}\mathbf{P}_i'.$$

After a specified number of iterations μ, the solution to the problem will be in the form:

$$(8.44) \qquad\qquad \mathbf{D}_\mu = \mathbf{B}_\mu\mathbf{D}_{\mu-1}\mathbf{B}' = \mathbf{BRB}' = \mathbf{D} = (\delta_{pq}\lambda_p)$$

where

$$(8.45) \qquad\qquad \mathbf{B} = \mathbf{P}_\mu = \mathbf{B}_\mu\mathbf{B}_{\mu-1} \cdots \mathbf{B}_2\mathbf{B}_1.$$

The diagonal elements λ_p of **D** are the characteristic roots of **R**, and the rows of the final transformation matrix **B** contain the corresponding characteristic vectors

$$\boldsymbol{\alpha}'_p = (\alpha_{1p}, \alpha_{2p}, \cdots, \alpha_{np})$$

of **R**. The row vector is shown as the transpose of the column vector previously defined in **8.3**. Since each individual transformation matrix is orthogonal (and hence the product of such matrices is orthogonal), the resulting final matrix **B** is orthogonal and therefore the characteristic vectors are normalized. Then the coefficients of each factor F_p are obtained simply by multiplying the square root of the characteristic root by its associated vector, namely:

(8.46) $$\mathbf{a}_p = \boldsymbol{\alpha}_p \sqrt{\lambda_p}.$$

This formula corresponds to (8.10) in which the first arbitrary eigenvector had to be normalized as well as converted to factor weights.

In general, when the rank m of **R** is equal to its order n, there will be n real non negative roots, and coefficients for n common factors will ensue. If, however, the reduced correlation matrix **R** is positive semi-definite and of rank $m < n$ then there will be $n - m$ zero roots and there will be only m common factors with non zero coefficients. Of course, if the Gramian properties are not satisfied by the reduced correlation matrix, then some of the roots will be negative and the coefficients of the corresponding factors will be imaginary.

An outline of the foregoing procedures for programming a large-scale digital electronic computer is presented in the flowchart of Figure 8.1. The detailed description of each step in this flowchart is as follows:

1. The $n(n + 1)/2$ distinct elements of the reduced correlation matrix **R** are stored by rows, each row starting with its diagonal element. Also stored are the trace $T(\mathbf{R})$, the order of the matrix, n, and the maximum number of iterations, μ (it may be desired to stop the machine after a predetermined number of iterations regardless of the degree of convergence). The matrix **R** also is put in the working location $_\nu\mathbf{D}$ as the initial $_0\mathbf{D}$.

2. The identity matrix is put in the $_\nu\mathbf{B}$ locations as the initial $_0\mathbf{B}$. The counter j is set to 1 and k to 2.

3. The d_{jk} element of $_\nu\mathbf{D}$ (initially, r_{jk} of **R**) is tested to see if it is zero to the specified (ϵ_1) degree of accuracy. If d_{jk} is zero to the degree ϵ_1 proceed to step 7, otherwise to step 4.

4. Compute $\mathbf{B}_{jk}$ as indicated in formula (8.35), using formula (8.36) and well-known trigonometric identities to get the values of the sine and cosine of the transformation angle (employing only algebraic functions of the argument).

5. Compute $_\nu\mathbf{D}$ according to formula (8.37), remembering that $_0\mathbf{D} = \mathbf{R}$.

6. Compute $_\nu\mathbf{B}$ according to formula (8.39), which is equivalent to $_\nu\mathbf{B} = \mathbf{B}_{jk(\nu-1)}\mathbf{B}$, and again, $_0\mathbf{B} = \mathbf{I}$.

7. If k has reached n then all columns have been considered for the particular choice of the row j and the test of step 9 is made. Otherwise proceed to step 8.

8. The index k is increased to continue with the next individual transformation in the particular iteration.

9. If j has not reached $n - 1$ proceed to step 10. When j has reached $n - 1$ then the ith iteration has been completed, i.e., the $\mathbf{B}_i$ of formula (8.40) is the last computed $_\nu\mathbf{B}$ when all combinations of j and k have been considered in

this iteration, and the result of the iteration is $\mathbf{D}_i$. The test of step 11 is then made.

10. The index j is increased to $j + 1$ (with the associated k as $j + 2$) to continue with the next series of individual transformations, involving the elements of the new row, in the particular iteration i.

11. As a check on the preceding calculations, the trace of the resulting matrix $\mathbf{D}_i$ is determined to see that it does not vary from the original value, according to the property:

$$\sum_{j=1}^{n} h_j^2 = T(\mathbf{R}) = T(\mathbf{D}_i) = \sum_{j=1}^{n} \lambda_j.$$

If the test is satisfied go to step 13. Otherwise proceed to step 12.

12. This is a conditional stop. The magnitude of the allowable error ϵ_2 is to be determined by the user of the program. Instructions to the computer operator should include what to do in the event the stop occurs. The instructions may call for certain memory locations to be printed out; or if the user desires, it may even include a continuation of the process after a record is made of the stop.

13. Compute $\mathbf{D}_i\mathbf{P}_i$ and $\mathbf{P}_i\mathbf{R}$, employing the $\mathbf{P}_i$ of formula (8.42) for the product of all the transformation matrices through the ith iteration.

14. Another check is provided by postmultiplying both sides of formula (8.43) by $\mathbf{P}_1$, noting that $\mathbf{P}_i'\mathbf{P}_i = \mathbf{I}$ from the orthogonality property of $\mathbf{P}_i$. If each element of $\mathbf{D}_i\mathbf{P}_i$ agrees with the corresponding element of $\mathbf{P}_i\mathbf{R}$ within the specified (ϵ_3) degree of accuracy, proceed to step 16. Otherwise go to step 15.

15. This conditional stop is treated the same way as step 12.

16. The $\mathbf{D}_i$ and $\mathbf{P}_i$ are retained in temporary storage, being changed as a result of each successive complete iteration.

17. Count the number (c) of off-diagonal elements d_{jk} that are zero within the specified (ϵ_1) degree of accuracy.

18. If all off-diagonal elements are not zero to the degree ϵ_1, go to step 19. Otherwise the process has converged, so proceed to step 20.

19. If the number of iterations i has not reached the maximum number μ, go back to step 2 to initiate the next iteration. Otherwise go to step 20.

20. Since the characteristic vectors appear in the rows of $\mathbf{B}$, and since the factor matrix $\mathbf{A}$ conventionally contains the coefficients of the respective factors in columns, the conversion (8.46) for all the common factors may be expressed by:

$$\mathbf{A} = \mathbf{B}'\mathbf{D}^{1/2}.$$

8.6. *Illustrative Examples*

To demonstrate the feasibility of the principal-factor method, now that computers are generally available, several examples will be given.

1. **Five socio-economic variables.**—First, it should be pointed out that the principal-component solution of Table 8.1 can be obtained on even a relatively slow computer

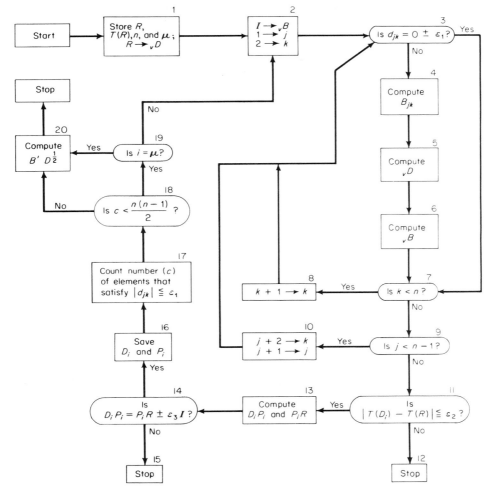

FIG. 8.1—Flowchart for programming the principal-factor method

in a matter of a few seconds. If, instead of ones in the diagonal, SMC's are used as estimates of communality[3] for the reduced correlation matrix the resulting characteristic roots become:

$$2.73429, \quad 1.71607, \quad .03955, \quad -.02452, \quad -.07261,$$

and the solution in terms of two factors is shown in Table 8.2. Of course, since the SMC's are lower bounds for the communalities (see **5.6**), the amount of variance

[3]Most principal-factor computer programs provide an option for the values to go in the diagonal of the correlation matrix, with SMC's as one of the choices; and the desired values are computed as the initial step in the analysis.

Table 8.2

Principal-Factor Solution for Five Socio-Economic Variables
(Communality estimates: SMC's)

Variable	Common Factors[a]			Communality		
	P_1	P_2	Original	Calculated	Difference
1. Total population	.62533	.76621	.96859	.97811	−.00952
2. Median school years	.71417	−.55535	.82227	.81845	.00382
3. Total employment	.71414	.67949	.96918	.97170	−.00252
4. Misc. profess. services	.87979	−.15879	.78572	.79924	−.01352
5. Median value house	.74107	−.57764	.84701	.88285	−.03584
Contribution of factor (V_p)	2.73429	1.71607	4.39277	4.45035	−.05758
Percent of original communality	62.2	39.1	—	101.3	−1.3

[a]The *P*'s in this table and in Table 8.1 are used as generic symbols for principal factors or components, the text making it clear which is implied.

accounted for by these two principal factors (4.450) is less than the 4.670 of the first two principal components. More important, of course, is the fact that the solution in Table 8.2 is for a different model than that in Table 8.1. Even if only the first two principal components are retained, it doesn't make the latter solution equivalent to the former. The models (2.8) and (2.9) make for a fundamental difference in the way the components or the factors are measured (see chapter 16).

Another recommendation for estimates of communality is that determined from all the principal components whose roots are greater than one. From Table 8.1 it can be seen that only the first two components have roots greater than one. The "communalities" of the five variables calculated from these components are:

$$.98783, \quad .88515, \quad .97930, \quad .88023, \quad .93746.$$

If these values are inserted in the diagonal of the correlation matrix, the resulting factorization yields the following roots:

$$2.79652, \quad 1.75496, \quad .10642, \quad .02094, \quad −.00888,$$

and a solution, again in terms of two factors, is obtained which accounts for slightly more of the variance than that shown in Table 8.2. Rather than exhibiting that solution, another solution was obtained by iteration—the preceding communalities were used initially, then replaced by the communalities obtained from the first two factors of the resulting solution, and the process repeated until the communalities agreed to three decimal places on successive trials. This was accomplished in fourteen iterations, with resulting communalities:

$$1.00000, \quad .76687, \quad .95562, \quad .79837, \quad .97142.$$

The principal-factor solution, with these communalities, is shown in Table 8.3.

While there is considerable similarity between the results in Tables 8.2 and 8.3, there are also some differences due to the different choices for the communalities.

Table 8.3

Alternate Principal-Factor Solution for Five Socio-Economic Variables
(Communality estimates: iteration by refactoring)

Variable	Common Factors[a]		Communality
	P_1	P_2	
1. Total population	.622	.785	1.000
2. Median school years	.702	−.524	.767
3. Total employment	.701	.681	.956
4. Misc. profess. services	.882	−.145	.798
5. Median value house	.779	−.604	.971
Contribution of factor (V_p)	2.756	1.740	4.492
Per cent of communality	61.3	38.7	

[a]See Footnote to Table 8.2.

The differences are more apparent in this small problem than they would be if the number of variables were larger; the relative effect of the n diagonal values (out of the total of n^2 elements involved in the calculations) decreases with an increase in n. Before leaving this example, it should be pointed out that the process employed in getting the result of Table 8.3 served as a forerunner for the method of minimum residuals (minres) which is presented in chapter 9. The solution of Table 8.3 may be seen to be very close to the minres solution of Table 9.1.

2. Eight physical variables.—The correlations for this example were introduced in Table 2.3. Estimates of communality were taken from the original study (Mullen 1939), namely:

.854, .897, .833, .783, .870, .687, .521, .579   (trace = 6.024).

Applying the principal-factor method to the reduced correlation matrix, with these values in the diagonal, produced the following characteristic roots:

4.456, 1.513, .130, .059, .033, −.031, −.044, −.092   (trace = 6.024),

and the solution in terms of two factors is given in Table 8.4.

Inasmuch as the problem of factor analysis is to account for the total communality variance, a check on the adequacy of a solution is afforded by the extent to which the sum of the contributions of the factors agrees with the original total communality. In the present example, two common factors account for practically 100 percent of the communality. The percentage contributions of the individual factors are presented in Table 8.4, where the complete principal-factor pattern is exhibited. The coefficients of the first factor are all large and positive, indicating an important general factor of physical growth (G) among these variables. On the other hand, the second factor has loadings of opposite signs for the two subgroups of variables. From the nature of the variables, this bipolar factor might be called "Stockiness." If desired, of course,

Table 8.4

Principal-Factor Pattern for Eight Physical Variables

Variable j	Pattern Coefficients[a]			Communality		
	G	BT	Y_j	Original	Calculated	Difference
1. Height	.858	−.328	.395	.854	.844	.010
2. Arm span	.849	−.414	.328	.897	.892	.005
3. Length of forearm	.810	−.412	.417	.833	.826	.007
4. Length of lower leg	.825	−.339	.452	.783	.796	−.013
5. Weight	.747	.561	.357	.870	.873	−.003
6. Bitrochanteric diameter	.637	.507	.581	.687	.663	.024
7. Chest girth	.561	.488	.669	.521	.553	−.032
8. Chest width	.619	.371	.692	.579	.521	.058
Total	—	—	—	6.024	5.968	.054
Contribution of factor (V_p)	4.455	1.511	—	—	—	—
Percent of total original communality	74.0	25.1	—	—	99.1	.9

[a]Since the reliability of any one of these physical variables is close to unity, the unique factor in each case may be considered as essentially the specific factor. The index of completeness of factorization (2.21) is then approximately 100 times the calculated communality of each variable.

the signs of all the coefficients of this factor may be changed. Then this factor might be labeled "Lankiness."

Whatever name is selected for a bipolar factor, its opposite characteristic should be clearly recognizable. A more fundamental approach is to find a basic term which connotes the entire continuum. For example, a bipolar factor which is named "Heat" (or, "Cold") would have the opposite characteristic "Cold" (or, "Heat"). A name representing both of these characteristics is "Temperature." These two approaches may be indicated schematically as in Figure 8.2.

Inasmuch as "Stockiness" and "Lankiness" are not clearly distinguishable as opposites (according to *a* of Fig. 8.2), neither of these seems to be an appropriate name for the bipolar factor. In an attempt to get a name, of the type *b*, which transcends the specific descriptions of the variables, the term "Body Type" (*BT*) has been adopted. On this continuum, variables describing different body types have projections of opposite sign.

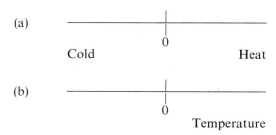

FIG. 8.2—Example of alternative ways of naming a bipolar factor

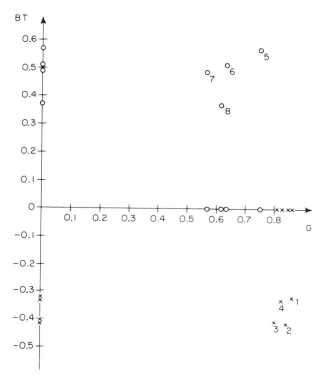

Fig. 8.3—Eight physical variables plotted with respect to two principal-factor axes

The diagram for these eight variables in the plane of the two principal factors is presented in Figure 8.3, the coordinates coming from Table 8.4. The two subgroups of variables lie in the first and fourth quadrants. Hence the projections of all the points form a single cluster on the positive end of the G axis. The projections on the BT axis, on the other hand, fall into two clusters which are widely separated. The projections on the respective axes give the geometric basis for the interpretation of the general and bipolar factors.

3. Eight emotional traits.—Next, an example of eight variables is presented from a field of psychology for which Burt provided the correlations many years ago. He discussed the factorial analysis of emotional traits in another paper (Burt 1939), pointing out the bipolar nature of the resulting factors, but did not actually obtain a principal-factor solution.

The correlations for these traits are given in Table 8.5, including communalities which were estimated from a solution essentially of the bi-factor form. A principal factor analysis disclosed the fact that two common factors adequately accounted for these communalities. The principal-factor pattern is given in Table 8.6.

The first factor may appropriately be called "General emotionality" (G), although the present sample of emotional traits is small. The second factor may be named from

Table 8.5

Intercorrelation of Eight Emotional Variables for
172 Normal Children Aged Nine to Twelve

Variable	1	2	3	4	5	6	7	8
1. Sociability	.94	—	—	—	—	—	—	—
2. Sorrow	.83	.94	—	—	—	—	—	—
3. Tenderness	.81	.87	.89	—	—	—	—	—
4. Joy	.80	.62	.63	.50	—	—	—	—
5. Wonder	.71	.59	.37	.49	.57	—	—	—
6. Disgust	.54	.58	.30	.30	.34	.28	—	—
7. Anger	.53	.44	.12	.28	.55	.38	.63	—
8. Fear	.24	.45	.33	.29	.19	.21	.10	.12

the traits with significant coefficients. As a rough estimate, the standard error of a
factor coefficient may be taken from Table B of the Appendix. Thus, for $N = 172$ and
an average correlation $r = .48$, the standard error is .064 and any coefficient as large
as .20 could certainly be considered significant. The traits with significant coefficients
are anger (.60), wonder (.32), and tenderness (−.51). Since wonder and anger are
indicative of an egocentric personality, and tenderness is indicative of timidity, the
factor characterizing these two opposing emotions may be called "Egocentricity" (E).
If it is desired to change the signs of all the coefficients, then the factor may be called
"Timidity." In Burt's discussion fear and sorrow are classed with tenderness, and in
the present analysis each of these traits has a coefficient of −.14. These values have
some statistical significance and help substantiate the interpretation of the second
factor.

Table 8.6

Principal-Factor Pattern for Eight Emotional Traits

Variable	Common Factors		Communality		
	G	E	Original	Calculated	Difference
1. Sociability	.98	.06	.94	.96	−.02
2. Sorrow	.95	−.14	.94	.92	.02
3. Tenderness	.81	−.51	.89	.92	−.03
4. Joy	.72	−.10	.50	.53	−.03
5. Wonder	.68	.32	.57	.56	.01
6. Disgust	.53	.14	.28	.30	−.02
7. Anger	.52	.60	.63	.63	.00
8. Fear	.35	−.14	.12	.14	−.02
Total	—	—	4.87	4.96	−.09
Contribution of factor (V_p)	4.17	.79	—	—	—
Percent of total original communality	85.6	16.2	—	101.8	−1.8

Before leaving this example, it should be pointed out that an attempt was made to analyze these data with SMC's as communalities, but real computing difficulties were encountered. The most convenient way of getting the squared multiple correlations, according to (5.36), involves the calculation of the inverse of the correlation matrix (of course, the full matrix with ones in the diagonal). While such a matrix must be Gramian (see **3.2**, par. **15**), the value of the determinant of the correlation matrix, produced by the computer, is only .00062. Obviously, the determinant is so close to zero that the inverse of the matrix doesn't exist. When an "inverse" was calculated by the computer (it couldn't tell that the determinant was insignificantly different from zero), most of the diagonal elements were negative, and the corresponding SMC's greater than one. Another way of putting it is to say that the rank of the full correlation matrix is less than eight, and therefore a case of multicollinearity must exist among the eight variables.

4. Eight political variables.—Another example has been selected from a set of political variables in order to illustrate the applicability of the principal-factor method in an entirely different field. The data also furnish a solution in which all the factors, including the first, are of the bipolar form. A set of eight variables was selected from a larger group of seventeen political variables, analyzed by Gosnell and Schmidt (1936). The smaller set includes the variables which are among the best measures of the factors given in Gosnell's solution. A brief description of these variables, measured in 147 Chicago election areas, follows:

1. *Lewis:* Percentage of the total Democratic and Republican vote cast for Lewis
2. *Roosevelt:* Corresponding percentage for Roosevelt
3. *Party voting:* Percentage that the straight-party votes were of the total
4. *Median rental:* Median rental (in dollars)
5. *Homeownership:* Percentage of the total families that own their homes
6. *Unemployment:* Percentage unemployed in 1921 of the gainful workers ten years of age and over
7. *Mobility:* Percentage of total families that have lived less than one year at present address
8. *Education:* Percentage of population, eighteen years and older, which completed more than ten grades of school

The intercorrelations of these variables are given in Table 8.7, in which communalities are also recorded. These communalities were computed by the method of **5.4**.

The principal-factor pattern is presented in Table 8.8. It may be observed that several variables have large negative coefficients for the first factor, in contrast with the positive coefficients found in the preceding solutions. In the present example the first factor, being of the bipolar type, may be named from the nature of the variables in the subsets (1, 2, 3) and (4, 7, 8). The variables of the first subset may be regarded as measures of the "Traditional Democratic Vote" (*TDV*), which is taken as the name of the factor. The variables of the second subset characterize the sociological level of the election areas and seem to be opposite in nature to the "Traditional Democratic Vote." The high weight for variable 6 (Unemployment) is consistent with the foregoing interpretation inasmuch as high unemployment is associated with traditional vote.

155

Table 8.7

Intercorrelations of Eight Political Variables for 147 Election Areas

Variable	1	2	3	4	5	6	7	8
1. Lewis	.52	—	—	—	—	—	—	—
2. Roosevelt	.84	1.00	—	—	—	—	—	—
3. Party Voting	.62	.84	.78	—	—	—	—	—
4. Median Rental	−.53	−.68	−.76	.82	—	—	—	—
5. Homeownership	.03	−.05	.08	−.25	.36	—	—	—
6. Unemployment	.57	.76	.81	−.80	.25	.80	—	—
7. Mobility	−.33	−.35	−.51	.62	−.72	−.58	.63	—
8. Education	−.63	−.73	−.81	.88	−.36	−.84	.68	.97

Table 8.8

Principal-Factor Solution for Eight Political Variables[a]

Variable *j*	Common Factors		Communality		
	TDV	*HP*	Original	Calculated	Difference
1. Lewis	.69	−.28	.52	.55	−.03
2. Roosevelt	.88	−.48	1.00	1.00	.00
3. Party Voting	.87	−.17	.78	.79	−.01
4. Median Rental	−.88	−.09	.82	.78	.04
5. Homeownership	.28	.65	.36	.50	−.14
6. Unemployment	.89	.01	.80	.79	.01
7. Mobility	−.66	−.56	.63	.75	−.12
8. Education	−.96	−.15	.97	.94	.03
Total	—	—	5.88	6.10	−.22
Contribution of factor (V_p)	5.01	1.10	—	—	—
Percent of total original communality	85.2	18.8	—	103.7	−3.7

[a]A principal-factor solution with SMC's as estimates of the communalities produced two factors with contributions of 5.01 and 1.28.

In the case of the second factor, the largest weights appear for variables 5 (Homeownership) and 7 (Mobility), being +.65 and −.56, respectively. Inasmuch as both Homeownership and lack of Mobility are aspects of a single characteristic, the second factor may be termed "Home Permanency" (*HP*). The negative factor weights for the first three variables again appear to verify the naming of this factor. This bipolar factor is conveniently described by a single name because the opposing variables may be considered as measures on a single scale in opposite directions.

5. Twenty-variable box problem.—Another example that is a classic in factor analysis literature (e.g., Harris and Kaiser 1964; Hakstian 1971; Katz and Rohlf 1974) is usually referred to as the "Thurstone Box Problem" and consists of twenty mathematical measurements on a "sample" from a hypothetical population of twenty box

Table 8.9

Raw Data for Population of Boxes

Dimen-sions	Box Type																			
	1	2	3	4	5	6	7	8	9	10	11	12	13	14	15	16	17	18	19	20
x	3	3	3	3	3	4	4	4	4	4	4	4	4	5	5	5	5	5	5	5
y	2	2	3	3	3	2	2	3	3	3	4	4	4	2	2	3	3	4	4	4
z	1	2	1	2	3	1	2	1	2	3	1	2	3	1	2	2	3	1	2	3

types (Thurstone 1940; 1947, pp. 141–44).[4] This problem has been used to demonstrate the recoverability, through factor analytic methods, of an underlying order in the measurements of a set of entities when such an order exists (which is actually the case for these fictitious data).

The boxes are the individuals or entities of a statistical population from which a random sample is assumed to have been selected. Thurstone specified twenty types of boxes in the population, occurring with equal frequency, whose dimensions are shown in Table 8.9. The three "hypothetical" constructs (or factors) are the basic dimensions (x, y, z) of the boxes. Of course, these dimensions are assumed to be latent variables and unknown.

The manifest variables actually constructed for this problem are various functions of the three dimensions (x, y, z) as listed in the stub of Table 8.10. The values of the twenty variables for each box type were computed by applying the mathematical formulas for the different measures to the particular dimensions of the box type. Then the correlations among the measures were computed, as shown in Table 8.10. These correlations are assumed known and may be used to get direct factor analyses and subsequently to determine how successful the factor analytic methods are in reconstructing the underlying physical order of the twenty variables. Although devoid of measurement or sampling errors,[5] this problem certainly is not simple with regard to factorial complexity, as will be seen later (chaps. 13, 14) when attempts are made to get clear-cut simple-structure transformations.

Since the "true" factors have been hypothesized, the correlations of the twenty

[4]The artificial problem of twenty measurements of theoretical boxes should not be confused with the twenty-six measurements actually made of a random collection of thirty boxes (Thurstone 1947, p. 369). Cureton and Mulaik (1971) refer to the latter as "Thurstone's 'invariant' box problem."

[5]To give this problem "a greater degree of realism," Kaiser and Horst (1975) have introduced measurement errors (in the form of random normal deviates), and made the correlation matrix nonsingular. In this text the original intent of Thurstone is maintained, namely, to use these "true" data to test the ability of factor analysis to disclose an underlying order, if it exists, in the data. This purpose is carried out more explicitly here than was possible in Thurstone's time. First, the correlation matrix is shown in Table 8.10, and its characteristic roots, given below, clearly indicate that it is a proper Gramian matrix even though it is singular. Then the "true" factor analysis is presented in Table 8.11—the orthogonal solution can serve as a basis for evaluating direct analyses of the data, while the oblique solution can serve as the target for evaluating rotation methods.

157

Table 8.10

Correlations among Twenty Box Measurements

Variable	1	2	3	4	5	6	7	8	9	10	11	12	13	14	15	16	17	18	19	20
1. x^2	1.000	—	—	—	—	—	—	—	—	—	—	—	—	—	—	—	—	—	—	—
2. y^2	.262	1.000	—	—	—	—	—	—	—	—	—	—	—	—	—	—	—	—	—	—
3. z^2	.098	.247	1.000	—	—	—	—	—	—	—	—	—	—	—	—	—	—	—	—	—
4. xy	.669	.885	.248	1.000	—	—	—	—	—	—	—	—	—	—	—	—	—	—	—	—
5. xz	.487	.304	.894	.477	1.000	—	—	—	—	—	—	—	—	—	—	—	—	—	—	—
6. yz	.190	.606	.904	.561	.859	1.000	—	—	—	—	—	—	—	—	—	—	—	—	—	—
7. $\sqrt{x^2+y^2}$	.859	.712	.207	.942	.515	.459	1.000	—	—	—	—	—	—	—	—	—	—	—	—	—
8. $\sqrt{x^2+z^2}$	.905	.339	.504	.686	.789	.545	.838	1.000	—	—	—	—	—	—	—	—	—	—	—	—
9. $\sqrt{y^2+z^2}$	.231	.878	.668	.787	.657	.887	.632	.488	1.000	—	—	—	—	—	—	—	—	—	—	—
10. $2x+2y$	.779	.805	.236	.980	.508	.519	.988	.780	.720	1.000	—	—	—	—	—	—	—	—	—	—
11. $2x+2z$	.741	.338	.731	.613	.937	.735	.719	.951	.602	.683	1.000	—	—	—	—	—	—	—	—	—
12. $2y+2z$	.216	.773	.795	.701	.771	.960	.567	.527	.979	.644	.683	1.000	—	—	—	—	—	—	—	—
13. $\log x$	.987	.288	.097	.681	.483	.199	.873	.903	.250	.795	.739	.231	1.000	—	—	—	—	—	—	—
14. $\log y$	.213	.978	.299	.853	.329	.635	.672	.317	.902	.773	.338	.805	.237	1.000	—	—	—	—	—	—
15. $\log z$	.104	.198	.949	.213	.891	.864	.185	.493	.620	.206	.734	.763	.101	.246	1.000	—	—	—	—	—
16. xyz	.459	.626	.824	.710	.917	.947	.658	.734	.857	.693	.861	.916	.462	.634	.787	1.000	—	—	—	—
17. $\sqrt{x^2+y^2+z^2}$	.794	.713	.487	.915	.725	.681	.954	.900	.770	.953	.862	.749	.804	.693	.456	.829	1.000	—	—	—
18. e^x	.980	.220	.097	.629	.476	.171	.813	.875	.200	.732	.717	.191	.937	.175	.105	.438	.753	1.000	—	—
19. e^y	.295	.984	.194	.881	.273	.560	.722	.346	.827	.804	.326	.719	.322	.924	.151	.598	.704	.250	1.000	—
20. e^z	.093	.260	.991	.255	.867	.893	.210	.493	.667	.241	.707	.785	.092	.312	.898	.814	.485	.090	.206	1.000
Mean	17.4000	9.6000	4.2000	12.4500	7.8500	5.8500	5.1248	4.5790	3.6126	14.2000	12.0000	9.8000	1.3925	1.0633	0.5519	24.4500	5.5129	78.8052	26.6303	8.9284
Standard deviation	6.2161	4.6733	3.0594	4.4326	3.6507	3.1028	0.8583	0.7956	0.8653	2.4413	2.2804	2.4413	0.1951	0.2700	0.4351	14.6679	0.8988	52.8416	19.0490	6.7503

variables with them can be calculated. The results are shown in the structure matrix **S** in Table 8.11. Also, the correlations among the three additional variables—the factors themselves—are given in the matrix **Φ** at the bottom of the table. It should be noted that this problem invites an oblique solution because Thurstone "assumed that a random collection of boxes would show correlation between the dimensions. A box that is tall is likely to be thick and wide, probably to a greater extent than the correlations which we assumed in the fictitious problem" (Thurstone 1940, p. 227). To round out the oblique solution, the pattern matrix **P** is determined by application of (2.44).

Table 8.11

"True" Factor Analysis of Twenty-Variable Box Problem

Variable j	"Target" Oblique Solution						Orthogonal Solution: **A** (Canonical Form)			Communality h_j^2
	Structure: **S**			Pattern: **P**						
	r_{jx}	r_{jy}	r_{jz}	x	y	z	F_1	F_2	F_3	
1	.997	.239	.103	1.000	−.014	.005	.626	− .667	.396	.994
2	.276	.994	.226	.028	.994	−.028	.774	− .037	− .624	.990
3	.098	.274	.987	− .009	.029	.981	.639	.664	.356	.975
4	.677	.874	.234	.488	.752	−.006	.891	− .331	− .287	.986
5	.487	.318	.904	.399	−.000	.863	.801	.311	.486	.975
6	.195	.624	.896	.008	.423	.788	.835	.523	.041	.972
7	.869	.696	.199	.740	.511	−.006	.864	− .500	− .038	.997
8	.906	.330	.505	.862	.008	.415	.816	− .300	.487	.994
9	.241	.895	.653	− .002	.780	.456	.896	.307	− .315	.996
10	.789	.793	.224	.629	.635	.000	.893	− .422	− .156	1.000
11	.742	.340	.742	.674	−.000	.674	.855	.000	.519	1.000
12	.224	.793	.789	− .000	.635	.629	.893	.422	− .156	1.000
13	.997	.264	.100	.993	.015	−.005	.639	− .669	.371	.994
14	.225	.994	.276	− .028	.994	.028	.774	.038	− .624	.990
15	.103	.223	.987	.009	−.030	.993	.613	.660	.405	.975
16	.462	.634	.816	.295	.386	.689	.924	.264	.137	.943
17	.802	.707	.478	.654	.468	.294	.965	− .241	.071	.995
18	.962	.199	.102	.973	−.050	.016	.588	− .641	.412	.928
19	.309	.960	.175	.075	.960	−.075	.747	− .100	− .603	.931
20	.093	.287	.957	− .017	.053	.945	.631	.645	.324	.919
Factor	Correlations of factors: **Φ**						12.543	4.007	3.002	19.554
x	1.000	.252	.102				Contributions of factors			Total
y		1.000	.252							
z			1.000							

The oblique solution may be said to be the "answer" to Thurstone's box problem. Of course, it must be treated as unknown and the "target" from the vantage point of a researcher who is experimenting with some new procedure in factor analysis (e.g., a new rotation scheme) and wants to test it with the known properties of the box problem.

The orthogonal solution in Table 8.11 is a correct direct factorization of the correlation matrix of Table 8.10. It was simply obtained as the canonical form (see **8.8**) of an orthogonal basis of the oblique solution. This matrix **A** should serve as the "target" in evaluating other direct analyses; but for derived solutions (i.e., oblique transformations) this matrix, rather than Thurstone's centroid solution, should serve as *input* to the procedures, which are then evaluated by how well they recover structure, pattern, and factor correlations.

Another important feature of the box problem is that it justifies the existence of borderline Heywood cases. Specifically, the communalities for variables 10, 11, and 12 are all one. This follows from the fact that these three variables—being perfect linear combinations of x, y and z—form a basis for the original dimensions (i.e., the hypothesized factors). Consequently even for orthogonal factors, the squared multiple correlations of each of these variables with the factors must be one.

Now, returning to the application of the methods developed in this chapter to the box problem, the complete set of characteristic roots was computed for the correlation matrix of Table 8.10, as follows:

12.6149	.0900	.0110	.0000	.0000
4.0369	.0760	.0003	.0000	.0000
2.9813	.0542	.0003	.0000	− .0000
.1155	.0194	.0000	.0000	− .0000

These values clearly show that the correlation matrix is not of full rank—but it is truly positive semi-definite, or Gramian (ignoring the trivial round-off errors of the last two roots). Its rank is probably 9 in the strict mathematical sense, but any rule employed by factor analysts would suggest 3.

In an ordinary application of the principal-factor method some estimates of communalities, such as the squared multiple correlation (SMC) of each variable with the remaining nineteen variables, would be made at this point. Unfortunately, because of the evident instances of multicollinearity among these variables, the correlation matrix must be singular and its inverse cannot be computed to use formula (5.36) for the SMC's. Another approach frequently followed is to take as communality estimates the amount of variance contributed to each of the variables by the number of principal components whose roots are greater than one (this suggestion [Kaiser 1960] was discussed in **5.6**). This was done, but to save space the principal-factor solution will not be exhibited. However, some of its features will be described.

The three characteristic roots, greater than one, of the complete correlation matrix add to 19.6331. The communalities calculated from the corresponding principal components were put in place of the ones to get the reduced correlation matrix. For the latter, the principal-factor method produced eight positive roots and twelve negative roots; the three largest adding to 19.5742. Of course, the sum of all the positive roots (19.7835) and all the negative roots (− .1512) must be the total starting communality, except for round-off errors. Because of the fictitious nature of this problem, the three principal factors not only account for all the starting communality but practically the total variance of the twenty measurements. It would make no sense to try to interpret the principal factors; instead, the success of this problem in demonstrating the recovery of a postulated order (the basic dimensions) should be judged from the derived solutions (Tables 14.13, 14.16, and 15.11) intended to show any inherent structure.

6. Twenty-four psychological tests.—The final illustration is of a fair-sized problem. A problem of this magnitude is commonplace today, but in 1940 it took more than 100 hours to calculate the first two factors by hand methods. Therefore, it was quite an accomplishment to get a complete factorization on the ORDVAC at Aberdeen Proving Grounds in about 40 minutes (in 1952) and on an IBM 704 in about 8 minutes (in 1958). By 1965 this time was cut to about 2 minutes on the IBM 7094, and by 1975 the time has been slashed to less than 8 seconds on such large-scale machines as IBM System/360.

For the correlation matrix of Table 7.4, with unities in the diagonal, the resulting roots of the characteristic equation are given in Table 8.12. This example demonstrates

Table 8.12

Contributions (Roots) of 24 Principal Components for Twenty-Four Psychological Tests

Order	Root	Order	Root	Order	Root	Order	Root
1	8.135	7	.901	13	.533	19	.334
2	2.096	8	.816	14	.509	20	.316
3	1.693	9	.790	15	.477	21	.297
4	1.502	10	.707	16	.390	22	.268
5	1.025	11	.639	17	.382	23	.190
6	.943	12	.543	18	.340	24	.172

that property of characteristic equations which says that all roots are real; and for the case of a positive semi-definite matrix **R**, that all roots are non negative. While all twenty-four eigenvectors were obtained, for economy of space only the first ten principal components are presented in Table 8.13. In addition to the factor weights, the contribution V_p (equivalent to the eigenvalue λ_p) of factor P_p is given at the bottom of each column, along with the percentage that this number represents out of the total variance of twenty-four.

The general characteristics of any principal-factor solution are demonstrated by the data in Table 8.13. First of all, the contributions of the factors to the total variance of the variables (or total communality, when that is being analyzed) decrease with each succeeding factor. This immediately provides a rough statistical guide as to the maximum error that might be introduced by stopping the analysis too soon. If the last factor retained contributes 5% to the total variance, it is known that the next factor, or any succeeding one, will not contribute as much as 5%. Of course, this determination of the effect of each succeeding factor can be judged from the eigenvalues (which are obtained first in the computer) without the actual computation of the factor weights. Another characteristic to be noted is that the first factor has positive loadings for every variable, since (almost) all correlations are positive in the original matrix. For all

Table 8.13

First Ten Principal Components for Twenty-Four Psychological Tests

Test	P_1	P_2	P_3	P_4	P_5	P_6	P_7	P_8	P_9	P_{10}
1	.616	−.005	.428	−.204	−.009	.070	.199	.220	−.153	.156
2	.400	−.079	.400	−.202	.348	.089	−.506	−.024	−.263	−.256
3	.445	−.191	.476	−.106	−.375	.329	−.083	−.356	−.060	.021
4	.510	−.178	.335	−.216	−.010	−.192	.461	.142	.135	−.266
5	.695	−.321	−.335	−.053	.079	.078	−.123	.028	−.232	−.010
6	.690	−.418	−.265	.081	−.008	.124	.001	.129	−.054	−.129
7	.677	−.425	−.355	−.072	−.040	.011	.081	.009	.001	−.091
8	.694	−.243	−.144	−.116	−.141	.119	.158	−.172	.115	−.065
9	.694	−.451	−.291	.080	−.005	−.071	−.009	.117	−.124	.029
10	.474	.542	−.446	−.202	.079	−.085	−.013	−.080	.079	−.099
11	.576	.434	−.210	.034	.002	.301	−.043	.320	−.004	.062
12	.482	.549	−.127	−.340	.099	.039	.158	−.301	−.132	.159
13	.618	.279	.035	−.366	−.075	.364	.130	.175	−.040	.104
14	.448	.093	−.055	.555	.156	.383	−.084	−.126	.262	.056
15	.416	.142	.078	.526	.306	−.057	.126	.072	−.304	.208
16	.534	.091	.392	.327	.171	.172	.081	.128	.297	−.212
17	.488	.276	−.052	.469	−.255	−.107	.248	−.214	−.152	−.137
18	.544	.386	.198	.152	−.104	−.252	−.019	−.003	−.344	−.287
19	.475	.138	.122	.193	−.604	−.139	−.341	.192	.102	.104
20	.643	−.186	.132	.070	.285	−.191	.026	−.294	.176	.057
21	.622	.232	.100	−.202	.174	−.226	−.161	.176	.323	−.000
22	.640	−.146	.110	.056	−.023	−.331	−.045	.131	.022	.368
23	.712	−.105	.150	−.103	.064	−.111	−.081	−.248	.067	.300
24	.673	.196	−.233	−.062	−.097	−.170	−.228	−.119	.154	−.185
V_p	8.137	2.097	1.692	1.501	1.025	.943	.900	.817	.790	.707
$100V_p/24$	33.9	8.7	7.0	6.2	4.3	3.9	3.8	3.4	3.3	2.9

succeeding factors the positive and negative coefficients are about equal in number. Sometimes a principal-factor solution will serve adequately as the final analysis of a correlation matrix, while more often it will be desirable to transform such a solution to a different frame of reference.

Psychologists and other social scientists usually are concerned with the analysis of the total communality rather than the total variance of a given set of variables. The following squared multiple correlations (SMC's), reading from left to right, are taken as estimates of the communalities:

.511 .300 .440 .409 .673 .677 .684 .564 .713 .579 .541 .537
.539 .358 .293 .429 .412 .443 .367 .464 .473 .449 .561 .527

Then the characteristic roots of the reduced correlation matrix (with these values in the diagonal) become:

7.665   .447   .254   .028   −.104   −.199
1.672   .407   .175   −.014   −.127   −.235
1.208   .319   .109   −.048   −.140   −.247
 .920   .305   .046   −.066   −.161   −.269

reading down the columns. It will be seen that thirteen are positive while eleven are negative—a circumstance to be expected when estimates of communalities rather than unities are inserted in the main diagonal of a correlation matrix. Since multiplication by the square root of the eigenvalue is involved in getting the factor weights, eleven of the principal factors are imaginary. For practical interpretation this must mean that the number of relevant factors necessary to describe the total communality (as estimated) of the twenty-four tests certainly must be less than or equal to thirteen. If the analysis is made in terms of all thirteen real factors, the communality (13.555) resulting from this solution will exceed the starting communality (11.943). This follows from the mathematical property that the contributions of the eleven imaginary factors will be negative and will reduce the contributions of the thirteen real factors to the actual amount with which the analysis was started.

The first five eigenvalues account for just about the total starting communality, and it might be argued, therefore, that only these factors have any practical significance. This also fits the criterion (see **5.6**) of retaining a number of factors equal to the number of principal components whose eigenvalues are greater than one. Still another approach to the appropriate number of factors is based on the trend in a plot of all n roots. This is shown in Figure 8.4 for the example. In typical fashion, the size of the roots falls rapidly at first and then tends to straighten out, with small slope, to the last root. This straight portion has been named the *scree* (Cattell 1966) after "the straight line of rubble and boulders which forms at the pitch of sliding stability at the foot of a mountain." From many years of experimentation, including situations in which the true number of substantive factors was known in advance, Cattell "noticed that this scree *invariably* began at the kth latent root when k was the true number of factors" (1966, p. 249). Applying the scree test to the graph in Figure 8.4 it seems to point to five factors, which is also supported by the leveling off of first-order differences after the fifth root.

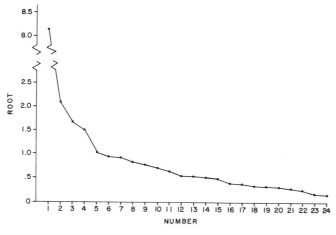

FIG. 8.4—Characteristic roots of **R** for twenty-four psychological tests

It would certainly seem that five factors would provide an adequate model for the description of the interrelationships among the twenty-four tests. As a matter of fact, four factors do almost as good a job, and the greater simplicity might warrant the slight loss in variance. For purposes of reference, all five principal factors are presented in Table 8.14. While psychological interpretations might be made of this solution, the more common practice is to transform it to another frame of reference, eliminating the bipolar factors and causing the variables identifying the factors to be more pronounced (see chaps. 13, 14).

Table 8.14

Principal-Factor Solution for Twenty-Four Psychological Tests
(Communality estimates: SMC's)

Test	Common Factors					Communality	
	P_1	P_2	P_3	P_4	P_5	Original	Calculated
1	.595	−.039	.369	−.184	−.073	.511	.531
2	.374	.026	.270	−.147	.121	.300	.250
3	.433	.115	.396	−.112	−.276	.440	.446
4	.501	.108	.290	−.178	.044	.409	.380
5	.701	.312	−.273	−.050	.003	.673	.666
6	.683	.404	−.213	.067	−.102	.677	.690
7	.676	.412	−.284	−.082	−.046	.684	.716
8	.680	.206	−.088	−.115	−.118	.564	.540
9	.690	.446	−.212	.076	.036	.713	.727
10	.456	−.469	−.446	−.128	.105	.579	.654
11	.589	−.372	−.198	.076	−.185	.541	.565
12	.448	−.491	−.154	−.263	.044	.537	.537
13	.590	−.268	.018	−.300	−.255	.539	.575
14	.435	−.063	−.012	.418	−.057	.358	.371
15	.390	−.102	.055	.362	.101	.293	.307
16	.512	−.098	.325	.259	.006	.429	.444
17	.471	−.212	−.036	.388	−.087	.412	.426
18	.521	−.331	.118	.145	.028	.443	.417
19	.450	−.115	.110	.167	−.178	.367	.287
20	.623	.135	.142	.049	.252	.464	.492
21	.596	−.220	.076	−.140	.204	.473	.471
22	.600	.103	.138	.053	.142	.449	.413
23	.685	.063	.160	−.096	.154	.561	.532
24	.635	−.169	−.192	−.009	.079	.527	.475
V_p	7.665	1.672	1.208	.920	.447	11.943	11.912
$100 V_p / 11.943$	64.2	14.0	10.1	7.7	3.7	100.	99.7

8.7. *Canonical Form*

In this section, a general procedure is suggested for designating a coordinate system in a given factor space with properties closely related to those of the principal-factor method. As is well known (see **2.7**), a factor solution for a correlation matrix usually produces a unique factor space but not a unique set of common-factor loadings (exception being the principal-factor solution). For this reason it is desirable to specify a "canonical" form. Of course, rotation to such form has nothing to do with the "rotation problem" for obtaining a more interpretable solution, which is treated in part III of this text. Rotation to canonical form is merely a means to bring an arbitrary solution to a well-defined form in a mathematical sense. Among other values, it may be useful in resolving the question of the meaning of equivalence of two solutions—they may look different, but if they are truly equivalent, then, when each is brought to canonical form, they will be identical.

The canonical form employed in this text (especially in chaps. 9 and 10) has the property that successive factors account for maximum possible variance in the common-factor space determined by the original solution. This should not be confused with the alternative objective set forth in **2.3** of determining a solution, i.e., the common-factor space, with the property of extracting the maximum variance from the observed variables which has been the primary subject of this chapter.

The canonical form is arrived at in the following manner. Let

$$\mathbf{A} = \text{arbitrary form of factor matrix } (n \times m),$$
$$\mathbf{B} = \text{canonical form of factor matrix } (n \times m),$$
$$\mathbf{T} = \text{orthogonal transformation matrix } (m \times m);$$

then

(8.47)
$$\mathbf{B} = \mathbf{AT}$$

will yield the desired form of the factor solution, and the immediate problem is to determine the matrix $\mathbf{T}$. Premultiplying (8.47) by the transpose of $\mathbf{B}$ produces

(8.48)
$$\mathbf{B'B} = \mathbf{T'A'AT}.$$

Then, setting $\mathbf{\Lambda} = \mathbf{B'B}$ and pre- and postmultiplying by $\mathbf{T}$ and $\mathbf{T'}$, respectively, yields

$$\mathbf{T\Lambda T'} = \mathbf{TT'A'ATT'},$$

which finally reduces to

(8.49)
$$\mathbf{A'A} = \mathbf{T\Lambda T'},$$

since $\mathbf{TT'} = \mathbf{I}$ from the orthogonality property of the transformation matrix (see **4.6**). The expression (8.49) is a special instance of (8.16) for the diagonalization of any symmetric matrix $\mathbf{R}$. By pre- and postmultiplying (8.16) by $\mathbf{Q}$ and $\mathbf{Q'}$, respectively, it becomes

(8.50)
$$\mathbf{R} = \mathbf{Q\Lambda Q'}.$$

The similarity to (8.49) is obvious. It follows that $\mathbf{\Lambda}$ is a diagonal matrix of eigenvalues and the orthogonal transformation $\mathbf{T}$ is the matrix of corresponding eigenvectors of the matrix $\mathbf{A'A}$. Thus, it is only necessary to determine the eigenvectors of an $m \times m$ matrix to obtain the transformation matrix which carries the arbitrary pattern matrix $\mathbf{A}$ into the canonical form $\mathbf{B}$. The general principal-factor computer routines are applicable to this problem.

Of course, the matrix of residuals remains unchanged whether computed from **A** or **B** since, according to (2.50),

$$(8.51) \qquad \hat{\mathbf{R}} = \mathbf{BB}' = \mathbf{ATT}'\mathbf{A}' = \mathbf{AA}',$$

the last equality following from the orthogonality of the transformation matrix. For convenience, after the canonical form of the solution is obtained, it is again designated by **A**, rather than **B**.

8.8. *Centroid Method*

This method of factoring a correlation matrix provided a computational compromise for the principal-factor method before computers were generally available. Now the centroid method is primarily of historical interest. The fundamental formula of the centroid method was first employed by Burt (1917, p. 53), but applied to the problem of determining a single general factor of the Spearman type. The complete centroid method was developed by Thurstone (1931) in conjunction with the analysis of large batteries of psychological tests into several common factors.

The name of the method connotes its close relationship to the mechanical concept of a centroid, or center of gravity. For this reason, the centroid form of analysis can best be described in geometric terms. As noted in **4.10**, the variables may be considered as represented by a set of n vectors which are contained in a space of m dimensions, where m is the number of common factors; and the scalar product of any pair of vectors is the correlation between them, as given in (4.56). The variables may also be considered as represented by the m coordinates of the end points of these vectors with respect to m mutually orthogonal arbitrary reference axes. Since the configuration of the vectors representing the variables completely determines the correlations, the reference system may be rotated without any effect on them. The arbitrary coordinate system may then be rotated so that the centroid point of the set of n points, along with the origin, determines the first axis of reference. Thus it is possible to obtain the projection of each of the vectors, or the coordinate of each variable, on the first axis of reference through the centroid.

Starting with a factor pattern of the usual form (2.22), the correlations are reproduced by means of equation (2.27) when the common factors are uncorrelated. Then, making the assumption that the residuals vanish, the observed correlations may be written

$$(8.52) \qquad r_{jk} = \hat{r}_{jk} = a_{j1}a_{k1} + a_{j2}a_{k2} + \cdots + a_{jm}a_{km} \qquad (j, k = 1, 2, \cdots, n),$$

where m is the number of common factors. The numerical values of a_{jp} ($p = 1, 2, \cdots, m$) are determined by the position of the orthogonal reference axes, since a_{jp} is the pth coordinate of variable z_j.[6] In the arbitrary orthogonal reference system, the m coordinates for each of the n points are as follows:

---

[6]More precisely, this variable should be designated by $\bar{z}_j$ since it is represented in the common-factor space. See **4.10**.

$$P_1 : (a_{11}, a_{12}, \cdots, a_{1p}, \cdots, a_{1m})$$

. . . .

$$P_k : (a_{k1}, a_{k2}, \cdots, a_{kp}, \cdots, a_{km})$$

. . . .

$$P_n : (a_{n1}, a_{n2}, \cdots, a_{np}, \cdots, a_{nm})$$

Any one of the m coordinates of the centroid is the average of the corresponding coordinates of these n points, hence

(8.53) $\text{Centroid:} \left(\dfrac{1}{n} \sum_k a_{k1}, \cdots, \dfrac{1}{n} \sum_k a_{kp}, \cdots, \dfrac{1}{n} \sum_k a_{km} \right),$

where the summation is from 1 to n on the indicated index when the limits are not given specifically.

Now let the frame of reference be so selected that the first axis F_1 passes through the centroid. Then the centroid will have coordinates all zero except the first, i.e.,

(8.54) $$\sum_k a_{k2} = \sum_k a_{k3} = \cdots = \sum_k a_{km} = 0.$$

The m values (8.53) then reduce to

$$\frac{1}{n} \sum_k a_{k1}, 0, 0, \cdots, 0,$$

there being $(m - 1)$ zeros. Since the centroid lies in the first axis, the first coordinate is also the distance of the centroid from the origin.

It is now possible to determine the coefficients of the first centroid factor, i.e., the coordinates a_{j1}, in terms of the observed correlations. Thus, summing (8.52) on k, there results

$$\sum_k r_{jk} = a_{j1} \left(\sum_k a_{k1} \right) + a_{j2} \left(\sum_k a_{k2} \right) + \cdots + a_{jm} \left(\sum_k a_{km} \right),$$

which, on applying (8.54), becomes

(8.55) $$\sum_k r_{jk} = a_{j1} \left(\sum_k a_{k1} \right).$$

Then the sum of all the entries in the correlation matrix is simply

(8.56) $$\sum_j \sum_k r_{jk} = \left(\sum_j a_{j1} \right) \left(\sum_k a_{k1} \right) = \left(\sum_k a_{k1} \right)^2.$$

Now, the square-root of the left side of (8.56) may be substituted for the term in parentheses in (8.55) to yield the following basic centroid formula:

$$(8.57) \qquad a_{j1} = \frac{\sum\limits_{k} r_{jk}}{\sqrt{\sum\limits_{j} \sum\limits_{k} r_{jk}}} = \frac{S_j}{\sqrt{T}} \qquad (j = 1, 2, \cdots, n),$$

where S_j is the sum of all the correlations in column j of the correlation matrix, and T is the total of all the correlations in the matrix, including the diagonal terms in both of these sums. In the above formula, the positive root was selected arbitrarily. Of course, if the negative sign of the radical had been chosen, the coefficients of the factor would all be changed in sign, yielding an equally acceptable factor. Formula (8.57) gives the coefficient of the first centroid factor F_1 for each variable z_j, or the first coordinate for each point representing a variable.

The next step is to get the first-factor residuals, from which the second coordinates are found. Since the residual correlations with one, two, $\cdots$, $(m - 1)$ factors removed are employed in successive stages of the centroid method, the notation introduced in **8.3** is employed again. The first-factor residuals again are given by

$$(8.19) \qquad {}_1 r_{jk} = r_{jk} - a_{j1} a_{k1} = a_{j2} a_{k2} + a_{j3} a_{k3} + \cdots + a_{jm} a_{km}.$$

The residual correlations may be regarded as the scalar products of pairs of residual vectors in a space of $(m - 1)$ dimensions—the dimension of the residual space being equal to the number of terms in the right-hand member of (8.19) or the rank of the matrix of residual correlations, according to Theorem 4.6.

In this residual space, the $(m - 1)$ coordinates for each of the n points may be designated by:

$$ {}_1 P_1 : (a_{12}, a_{13}, \cdots, a_{1p}, \cdots, a_{1m}) $$

$$ \cdot \quad \cdot \quad \cdot \quad \cdot \quad \cdot \quad \cdot \quad \cdot $$

$$ {}_1 P_k : (a_{k2}, a_{k3}, \cdots, a_{kp}, \cdots, a_{km}) $$

$$ \cdot \quad \cdot \quad \cdot \quad \cdot \quad \cdot \quad \cdot \quad \cdot $$

$$ {}_1 P_n : (a_{n2}, a_{n3}, \cdots, a_{np}, \cdots, a_{nm}). $$

The $(m - 1)$ coordinates of the centroid of these n points are

$$ \left(\frac{1}{n} \sum_{k} a_{k2}, \cdots, \frac{1}{n} \sum_{k} a_{kp}, \cdots, \frac{1}{n} \sum_{k} a_{km} \right), $$

which all vanish according to (8.54). Thus the centroid is at the origin in this $(m - 1)$ space, and formula (8.57) cannot be used directly for calculating the values of the second-factor coefficients. It will be noted that in obtaining (8.57) the expression (8.55) was divided by $\sum\limits_{k} a_{k1}$, or n times the distance of the centroid from the origin. It was tacitly assumed that the centroid was not at the origin, for otherwise this division would not have been possible.

The immediate problem, then, is to remove the centroid from the origin in the $(m - 1)$ space, so that the preceding method can again be applied. By means of rotations of certain of the vectors about the origin through 180°—also called *reflections in the origin*—the centroid can be removed from the origin. If the coordinates of a point P_j, representing a variable z_j, are

$$(a_{j1}, a_{j2} \cdot \cdot \cdot, a_{jm}),$$

then the reflected point $- P_j$, with coordinates

$$(-a_{j1}, -a_{j2}, \cdot \cdot \cdot, -a_{jm}),$$

represents the variable $-z_j$. Such a variable corresponds to the original variable measured in the opposite direction.

Now it is evident from (8.52) that to reverse the signs of the coordinates of P_j has the effect of reversing the signs of all the correlations of variable z_j with the remaining ones. Thus the reflection of a variable in the origin is accomplished merely by changing the signs of the correlations of this variable in the correlation matrix. Of course, the same argument holds for the residual $(m - 1)$ space as for the original common-factor space of m dimensions. Hence the reflection of a variable in the residual space is accomplished by changing the signs of the residual correlations for that variable.

In an attempt to determine which variables to reflect, Thurstone (1935, p. 96) suggests that "it is desirable to account for as much as possible of the residual variance by each successive factor." While a rigorous mathematical application of this principle would lead to the principal-factor solution, the centroid procedure is only intended to approximate it. To have the second factor account for as much as possible of the residual variance, the reference axis which represents this factor should pass through a cluster of residual vectors. If there is a clustering of such vectors (i.e., a group of variables having high positive residual correlations), which is balanced by a scattering of vectors on the opposite side of the origin, since the centroid is at the origin, then the second reference axis should be made to pass through this cluster. Thus it would seem that the vectors which scatter, opposite to a cluster, should be reflected so as to fall in with the group. The second centroid coordinates can then be computed as in the first case. In application, those variables which have the greatest number of negative correlations would be reflected first, bringing them into the hemisphere of the cluster. For practical problems, Thurstone (1935, p. 97) suggests reversing "the signs of one trait at a time until the number of negative coefficients in the residual table is less than $n/2$," that is, less than $n/2$ negative signs for any one variable, not the entire table. One need not stop with this, however, for, if it is desired to further "maximize" the variance removed by each successive factor, the reflections of variables may be continued until the sum of the residual correlations for each variable is as large (positively) as possible.

For the remainder of the analytical work it will be convenient to use a symbol to designate whether a point, representing a variable, has been reflected in the origin. Let ϵ_j stand for the algebraic sign of P_j, that is, the point $\epsilon_j P_j$ is $+P_j$ or $-P_j$. If P_j

has not been reflected, ϵ_j is plus, but, if P_j has been reflected, then ϵ_j is minus. Furthermore, ϵ_j may be considered as an algebraic operator defined as follows:

$$\epsilon_j = \begin{cases} +1 \text{ if } z_j \text{ has not been reflected,} \\ -1 \text{ if } z_j \text{ has been reflected.} \end{cases}$$

Then ϵ_j can be attached to the coordinates of P_j, and it can be treated as any other algebraic quantity. Thus, if the first-factor residual correlations after reflection of certain variables are designated by r_{1jk} (in distinction to $_1r_{jk}$ before reflection), then they may be written as follows:

(8.58) $$r_{1jk} = \epsilon_j \epsilon_k (a_{j2} a_{k2} + a_{j3} a_{k3} + \cdots + a_{jm} a_{km}).$$

This result follows immediately from (8.19), where each a_{jp} and a_{kp} was replaced by $\epsilon_j a_{jp}$ and $\epsilon_k a_{kp}$, respectively, and then ϵ_j and ϵ_k were factored out algebraically. If neither z_j nor z_k was reflected, or if both variables were reflected, then $r_{1jk} = {}_1r_{jk}$; but, if only one or the other of z_j and z_k was reflected, then $r_{1jk} = -{}_1r_{jk}$. In other words, $r_{1jk} = \epsilon_j \epsilon_k ({}_1r_{jk})$.

The $(m-1)$ coordinates of the centroid of the n points, after reflection of variables, become:

$$\frac{1}{n} \sum_k \epsilon_k a_{kp} \qquad (p = 2, 3, \cdots, m).$$

Now the system of reference can be rotated about the first axis F_1 so that the second axis F_2 passes through this centroid.[7] Let it be assumed that this has been done, there being no need to change the notation for the coordinates. Then the coordinates of the centroid are

$$\frac{1}{n} \sum_k \epsilon_k a_{k2}, 0, 0, \cdots, 0,$$

since the centroid lies on the F_2 axis. From the values for the last $(m-2)$ coordinates the following useful expressions may be written:

(8.59) $$\sum_k \epsilon_k a_{k3} = \sum_k \epsilon_k a_{k4} = \cdots = \sum_k \epsilon_k a_{km} = 0,$$

corresponding to (8.54) in the case of the first centroid.

Now the projections of the vectors on the second centroid axis can be expressed in terms of the residual correlations. Thus, summing (8.58) for all variables k in a fixed column j of the residual correlation matrix (after reflection of variables) and applying (8.59), there results

$$\sum_k r_{1jk} = \epsilon_j a_{j2} \sum_k \epsilon_k a_{k2}.$$

---

[7]The residual $(m-1)$ space is orthogonal to the first axis of reference F_1. The second axis F_2, i.e., the first one in the $(m-1)$ subspace, may then be rotated to any position in the residual space, and it will be at right angles to F_1.

Then, summing for all columns,

$$\sum_j \sum_k r_{1jk} = \sum_j \epsilon_j a_{j2} \sum_k \epsilon_k a_{k2} = \left(\sum_k \epsilon_k a_{k2}\right)^2.$$

It follows that

$$\epsilon_j a_{j2} = \frac{\sum_k r_{1jk}}{\sqrt{\sum_j \sum_k r_{1jk}}} = \frac{S_{j1}}{\sqrt{T_1}}$$

or, multiplying both sides by ϵ_j,

$$(8.60) \qquad\qquad a_{j2} = \frac{\epsilon_j S_{j1}}{\sqrt{T_1}} \qquad\qquad (j = 1, 2, \cdots, n),$$

where S_{j1} is the sum of all entries in column j of the matrix of first-factor residual correlations and T_1 is the total of all the correlations in this matrix, the signs of all the entries being those after reflection. The ϵ_j indicates that, if the variable z_j was reflected, then the algebraic sign must be changed, but, if the variable was not reflected, then ϵ_j is merely $+1$. In other words, $\epsilon_j S_{j1}$ is the sum of all residual correlations for the unreflected variable z_j with all other variables. Hence, by defining

$$_1 S_j = \epsilon_j S_{j1},$$

formula (8.60) may be put in the form

$$(8.61) \qquad\qquad a_{j2} = \frac{_1 S_j}{\sqrt{T_1}} \qquad\qquad (j = 1, 2, \cdots, n).$$

In this formula the numerator refers to the sum of the residual correlations for the unreflected variable j, while in the denominator T_1 still stands for the sum of all residual correlations after the sign changes. Formula (8.61) gives the coefficients of the second centroid factor F_2 for each variable.

The remaining factor weights can be obtained in a similar manner. To follow the basic principle of accounting for as much as possible of the variances of the variables by each factor, the variables are reflected in the residual subspaces to bring them into clusters. When the sign changes have been made, the centroid of the system of points in the residual space lies somewhere in the cluster of variables, and the next reference axis is selected through this centroid. Each successive centroid axis is at right angles to every one of the preceding axes because the residual space is orthogonal to the space of the centroid axes already established. Upon extracting each centroid factor, the residual correlations are reduced in magnitude, and the rank of each residual matrix is reduced by one, theoretically. The foregoing development was made without any restrictions on the diagonal elements. The number of factors ultimately obtained is dependent upon these diagonal values, leading to the question of "when to stop factoring."

If the simplest of the arbitrary estimates of communality (see **5.6**)—the largest correlation in each column of the correlation matrix—is selected for the diagonal element, then in each subsequent residual matrix the calculated diagonal term is not retained but replaced by the largest residual correlation, regardless of sign, in each column. This procedure does not furnish a standard for determining the number of common factors.

If, instead of modifying the diagonal entries at each stage, the analysis is applied directly, keeping the diagonal terms as calculated, then the number of factors is determined when the original diagonal values have been completely resolved. Only the common factors will be obtained if the correlation matrix contains communalities in the principal diagonal and these values are completely analyzed. In practice, it is recommended that appropriate complete estimates of the communalities, discussed in **5.6**, be employed.

Table 8.15

Centroid Solution for Thirteen Psychological Tests

Test	Common-Factor Coefficients			Communality		
	C_1	C_2	C_3	Original	Calculated	Difference
1	.607	−.060	−.443	.558	.568	−.010
2	.355	.038	−.266	.203	.198	.005
3	.418	.148	−.429	.362	.381	−.019
4	.478	.083	−.287	.314	.318	−.004
5	.729	.257	.244	.646	.657	−.011
6	.707	.354	.167	.641	.653	−.012
7	.721	.367	.257	.750	.721	.029
8	.705	.197	.062	.571	.540	.031
9	.698	.409	.252	.758	.718	.040
10	.455	−.482	.399	.554	.599	−.045
11	.537	−.390	.145	.449	.461	−.012
12	.487	−.553	.033	.531	.544	−.013
13	.674	−.368	−.135	.599	.608	−.009
Total	—	—	—	6.936	6.966	−.030
Contribution of factor (V_p)	4.620	1.392	.954	—	—	—
Percent of total original communality	66.6	20.1	13.8	—	100.4	−0.4

Since electronic computers are generally available, there is no need now to accept a substitute for the principal-factor method. There was a time, in the 1930s and continuing into the 40s and 50s, that the centroid method contributed very importantly to the development of factor analysis. Now there is very little need to go into efficient procedures for applying the centroid method using a desk calculator. However, the results of such calculations will be discussed very briefly for two examples.

The first thirteen of the twenty-four psychological tests, whose correlations are given in Table 7.4, comprise the first example. The communality estimates needed for the centroid method were taken from a bi-factor solution of these tests. The resulting centroid solution for the thirteen psychological tests is presented in Table 8.15 just to show its general form and because this will serve as input to other analyses later.

Table 8.16

Comparison of Variances Resulting from Three Solutions for Twenty-Variable Box Problem

Method	Variance of Factor			Total
	1	2	3	
Principal components	12.615	4.037	2.981	19.633
Principal factors	12.599	4.014	2.962	19.575
Centroid factors	12.570	3.919	3.155	19.644

The second example is the twenty-variable box problem, for which a centroid solution was obtained by Thurstone (1940, p. 225). While it is not repeated here, to save space, it may be of some interest to note how it compares with other methods of this chapter. This is done in Table 8.16. It should be observed that while the centroid method was designed as an approximation for the principal-factor method—a compromise being necessary because it was not feasible to calculate it at the time—the solution by Thurstone had been overfactored. The resulting centroid solution contained six Heywood cases and the total calculated communality of 19.644 is definitely too large. The mathematical maximum amount of variance that can be accounted for with three "factors" is 19.633 so that any factorization other than principal components must yield some lesser amount. Still, it is remarkable how closely Thurstone was able to approximate the computer produced principal-factor solution by his hand methods almost forty years earlier.

9 Minres Method

9.1. Introduction

As noted in chapter 6, a choice must be made of either communality estimates or the dimension of the common-factor space when using the classical factor analysis model (2.9). The methods treated in the preceding chapter involve the assumption of communalities, while the methods in this and the next chapter require the choice of the number of common factors.

The word "minres" is a contraction of "minimum residuals," and represents a method long sought by factor analysts. Now that it is available, it might well replace the principal-factor and the maximum-likelihood methods for initial factorization of a correlation matrix. As noted in **2.3**, one objective of factor analysis is to "best" reproduce the observed correlations. This objective can be traced to Thurstone's statement: "The object of a factor problem is to account for the tests, or their intercorrelations, in terms of a small number of derived variables, the smallest possible number that is consistent with acceptable residual errors" (Thurstone 1947, p. 61). In this chapter, the factor analysis problem as posed by Thurstone is solved by maximally (in the least-squares sense) reproducing the off-diagonal elements of the correlation matrix, and, as a by-product, obtaining communalities consistent with this criterion. The contrast between this objective and that of extracting maximum variance (treated in chap. 8) should be clearly understood.

A brief history leading to the current method and the formal statement of the problem is given in **9.2**. This is followed by the actual development of the method in **9.3**. Special procedures to restrict the derived communalities from exceeding unity are developed in **9.4**. A discussion of statistical tests for the significance of the number of common factors follows in **9.5**. Then a brief outline of the computing procedures is indicated in **9.6**, and numerical illustrations of the minres solution are given in the final section.

9.2.   *Formulation of the Minres Method*

Conceptually, the idea of getting a factor solution by minimizing the residual correlations is an obviously direct approach. The first practical solution, however, was not developed until 1965 (Harman and Jones 1966). The idea certainly is not new—its accomplishment, however, was dependent on the high-speed computer. No doubt it must have crossed the minds of many workers in factor analysis over the years. The first theoretical treatment appeared in 1936, when Eckart and Young (1936, p. 211) noted that "if the least-squares criterion of approximation [of one matrix by another of lower rank] be adopted, this problem has a general solution which is relatively simple in a theoretical sense, though the amount of numerical work involved in applications may be prohibitive." This was followed in the next couple of years by additional theoretical work (Householder and Young 1938; Horst 1937).

More recently, several papers have appeared that seem to bear some relationship to the problem. Whittle (1952) specifically considers the residual sum of squares, but in relation to the principal-component method. Howe seeks an alternative approach to Lawley's maximum-likelihood equations (see chap. 10) and finds that his method—maximizing the determinant of partial correlations—"is approximately equivalent to minimizing the sum of squares of the partial correlations" (Howe 1955, p. 22). Even more germane is the paper by Keller (1962), which is a generalized mathematical treatment skirting the precise problem to which the minres method is addressed.

It should be noted that none of the foregoing papers considers the minimization of off-diagonal residuals—the minimization of the total residual matrix (including diagonal terms) leads to the conventional principal-factor method (see chap. 8). The exclusion of the diagonal elements, although appearing trivial, is of paramount importance. More specifically, as will be amplified below, the diagonal elements of the sample correlation matrix (the communalities) are not fixed but are parameters to be determined along with the factor loadings.

Probably the first attempt to obtain a practical factor solution by minimizing off-diagonal residuals was suggested by Thurstone in 1954 and carried out by Rolf Bargmann and also by Sten Henrysson (see Thurstone 1955, p. 61). More recently, Comrey (1962) independently developed a computing procedure for such a solution. However, these investigators do not tackle the complete problem of determining a factor solution with the property that the sum of squares of residuals between observed and reproduced correlations be a minimum. Instead they consider what might be termed a "stepwise" minimum residual method,[1] obtaining one factor and a residual matrix, which is then the starting point for the factor in the next step; this process is continued until a desired number of factors are extracted. In general, of course, such a solution is different from one obtained under the least-squares criterion for the entire set of factors. There has been one other attempt (Boldt 1964) which is more specifically related to the method treated in this chapter. Boldt poses the problem in

---

[1]It may be of interest to note similar "stepwise" approximations to standard statistical procedures, namely, the determination of the coefficients in multiple regression *successively* rather than *simultaneously* (Gengerelli 1948), and an approximation to a maximum-likelihood factor solution (Bargmann 1963).

essentially the same form and considers solutions by procedures similar to those tried by Harman and Jones (1966, sec. 4).

The minres method assumes the classical factor analysis model (2.9), which is repeated in matrix form as follows:

$$(2.35^{\text{bis}}) \qquad\qquad \mathbf{z} = \mathbf{Af} + \mathbf{Uy}$$

Only the common-factor loadings in the matrix $\mathbf{A} = (a_{jp})$ are the parameters to be estimated. Once such a solution is obtained, the fundamental theorem of factor analysis gives (assuming uncorrelated factors, without loss of generality):

$$(2.50^{\text{bis}}) \qquad\qquad \hat{\mathbf{R}} = \mathbf{AA}',$$

where $\hat{\mathbf{R}}$ is a matrix of reproduced correlations with communalities in the principal diagonal. What is required, then, is to get a "best" fit to the observed correlation matrix $\mathbf{R}$ by the reproduced correlations $\hat{\mathbf{R}}$ employing model (2.35).

A least-squares fit can be obtained either by

$$(9.1) \qquad\qquad \text{fitting } \mathbf{R} \text{ by } (\hat{\mathbf{R}} + \mathbf{U}^2),$$

or by

$$(9.2) \qquad\qquad \text{fitting } (\mathbf{R} - \mathbf{I}) \text{ by } (\hat{\mathbf{R}} - \mathbf{H}^2),$$

where

$$(9.3) \qquad\qquad \mathbf{H}^2 = \mathbf{I} - \mathbf{U}^2 = \text{diag}(\mathbf{AA}')$$

is the diagonal matrix of communalities determined from the solution $\mathbf{A}$. In the case of (9.1), the minimization of residuals of the total matrix leads to the principal-component method (see **8.2**). In the case of (9.2), however, minimizing only the off-diagonal residuals leads to the minres method. This condition may be expressed more precisely by:

$$(9.4) \qquad\qquad \min_{\mathbf{A}} \| [\mathbf{R} - \mathbf{I}] - [\mathbf{AA}' - \text{diag}(\mathbf{AA}')] \|,$$

in which it is emphasized that both $\mathbf{A}$ and $\mathbf{H}^2$ vary. The norm as expressed in (9.4) may be written out algebraically as follows:

$$(9.5) \qquad\qquad f(\mathbf{A}) = \sum_{k=j+1}^{n} \sum_{j=1}^{n-1} \left(r_{jk} - \sum_{p=1}^{m} a_{jp} a_{kp} \right)^2,$$

which is the objective function to be minimized.

It should be noted that this function involves the $n(n-1)/2$ off-diagonal residual correlations which are dependent upon the elements in the factor matrix $\mathbf{A}$. The objective of minres is to minimize the function $f(\mathbf{A})$, for a specified m, by varying the values of the factor loadings. While this function states explicitly the objective of the method and what is to be minimized, its minimal value is not the most effective criterion of the degree of fit of the model to the observed data. That is because the value of the function depends on the number of variables for which the residual correlations are computed. To make it independent of the order of the correlation matrix, the *root-mean-square* deviation is taken as the criterion, namely:

$$(9.6) \qquad rms = \sqrt{2f(\mathbf{A})/n(n-1)}.$$

The diagonal matrix of communalities is obtained as a by-product of the method. It is tacitly assumed, for the moment, that the communality produced for each variable is not greater than one. Actually, if only the condition (9.5) is imposed, an occasional minres solution would be obtained for which a communality would exceed unity. Of course, such a situation must be remedied if the factor analysis is to be acceptable. After developing the basic theory, the side conditions

$$(9.7) \qquad h_j^2 = \sum_{p=1}^{m} a_{jp}^2 \leqq 1 \qquad\qquad (j = 1, 2, \cdots, n)$$

are introduced which restrict the communalities to numbers between zero and one for a minres solution.

9.3. *Minres Procedure*

As noted at the beginning of this chapter, the calculation of a minres solution is so complex that it is feasible only with the aid of an electronic computer. Even then, it can get very costly in computer time unless an efficient algorithm is available. Several mathematical approaches were investigated, and tested empirically on many problems, before the recommended procedure was developed (Harman and Jones 1966). Among the methods explored and discarded was (1) the technique[2] of repeated calculations of a principal-factor matrix $\mathbf{A}$ and its associated communalities $\mathbf{H}^2$ leading to improvements in the objective function f; and (2) several variants of a class of mathematical techniques known as "gradient methods." The latter methods seek an optimal value (maximum or minimum) of a function, iteratively, by proceeding from a trial solution to the next approximation in the direction of maximal change in the function.

While the foregoing methods produced acceptable solutions, they were too time-consuming. Another mathematical method—the Gauss-Seidel process (Whittaker and Robinson 1944, sec. 130)—proved to be much more efficient. This technique is sometimes called a "method of successive displacements" because it is an iterative process in which small changes are made in the variables and the corresponding new variables replace the original ones. It can be applied effectively to the computation of a minres solution. From the basic theorem of factor analysis (2.50), it is evident that if changes or displacements are introduced in only one row of $\mathbf{A}$, the reproduced correlations will be linear functions of these displacements, and the objective function f will be quadratic only.[3] More explicitly, for any row j in $\mathbf{A}$ an increment ϵ_p ($p = 1, 2,$

---

[2]This technique was employed in arriving at the solution of Table 8.3. The corresponding minres solution is given in Table 9.1.

[3]This reduces the computing time considerably below that required in the gradient methods, where fourth-degree polynomials have to be solved (Harman and Jones 1966).

$\cdots, m$) is added to each element:

$$a_{j1} + \epsilon_1, \quad a_{j2} + \epsilon_2, \quad \cdots, \quad a_{jp} + \epsilon_p, \quad \cdots, \quad a_{jm} + \epsilon_m.$$

The new factor loadings may be written in the form:

(9.8) $$b_{jp} = a_{jp} + \epsilon_p \qquad (p = 1, 2, \cdots, m),$$

where the b's are used for clarity; but ultimately, when the final set of factor loadings are obtained they are again designated by a's for simplicity of notation.

Then the reproduced correlations of the fixed variable j with any other variable k is

$$\hat{r}_{jk} = \sum_{p=1}^{m} a_{kp} b_{jp},$$

and the sum of squares of residual correlations with this variable j is given by

(9.9) $$f_j = \sum_{\substack{k=1 \\ k \neq j}}^{n} \left(r_{jk} - \sum_{p=1}^{m} a_{kp} b_{jp} \right)^2 \qquad (j \text{ fixed}).$$

Upon separating out the original factor loading from the incremental change, according to (9.8), the last expression becomes:

(9.10) $$f_j = \sum_{\substack{k=1 \\ k \neq j}}^{n} \left(r_{jk}^* - \sum_{p=1}^{m} a_{kp} \epsilon_p \right)^2, \qquad (j \text{ fixed}),$$

where r_{jk}^* are the original residual correlations of variables k with the fixed variable j (without the incremental changes in its factor loadings), that is,

(9.11) $$r_{jk}^* = r_{jk} - \sum_{p=1}^{m} a_{kp} a_{jp} \qquad (k = 1, 2, \cdots, n; \quad k \neq j).$$

To determine the values of the ϵ's which minimize the objective function f, first take the partial derivatives of (9.10) with respect to each of these, say ϵ_q, as follows:

$$\frac{\partial f_j}{\partial \epsilon_q} = 2 \sum_{\substack{k=1 \\ k \neq j}}^{n} \left(r_{jk}^* - \sum_{p=1}^{m} a_{kp} \epsilon_p \right)(-a_{kq}) \qquad (q = 1, 2, \cdots, m).$$

Then set these expressions equal to zero, and obtain the following implicit equations for the ϵ's:

(9.12) $$\sum_{p=1}^{m} \left(\sum_{\substack{k=1 \\ k \neq j}}^{n} a_{kp} a_{kq} \right) \epsilon_p = \sum_{\substack{k=1 \\ k \neq j}}^{n} r_{jk}^* a_{kq}, \qquad (q = 1, 2, \cdots, m).$$

This may be put in matrix form,

(9.13) $$\epsilon_j \mathbf{A'}_{)j(} \mathbf{A}_{)j(} = \mathbf{r}_j^0 \mathbf{A},$$

where $\epsilon_j = (\epsilon_1, \epsilon_2, \cdots, \epsilon_m)$ is the row vector of incremental changes of the factor loadings for variable j, $\mathbf{A}_{)j(}$ is the factor matrix with the elements in row j replaced by

178

zeros, and $\mathbf{r}_j^0$ is the row vector of residual correlations of variable j with all other variables (and 0 for the self-residual). Then the solution for the displacements to the factor loadings (for a given variable) that will minimize the objective function, is:

$$(9.14) \qquad \boldsymbol{\epsilon}_j = \mathbf{r}_j^0 \, \mathbf{A}(\mathbf{A}'_{)i(}\mathbf{A}_{)i(})^{-1}.$$

The foregoing process is carried out systematically for all variables, in turn. Thus successive approximations of rows of factor loadings are obtained which yield a minimum value for the function f to any desired degree of accuracy. However, there is no guarantee that the resulting matrix of factor loadings will not lead to communalities greater than one. This problem is taken up in the next section.

9.4. *Additional Theory*

When a factor solution leads to the communality of some variable being greater than one, it is referred to as a "Heywood case" (see **7.3**). To constrain the minres method to proper solutions, Harman and Fukuda (1966) developed a mathematical programming procedure in which the final matrix $\mathbf{A}$ is obtained by minimizing (9.5) subject to the conditions (9.7). This is introduced as a modification to the basic computing procedure of the last section only in those instances when a communality exceeds one.

Starting with the computing procedure of **9.3**, the impact on the objective function (9.5) of replacing the a_{jp} (for a fixed variable j) by b_{jp}, as defined in (9.8), is given by (9.9). This function, then, is to be minimized subject to

$$(9.15) \qquad \sum_{p=1}^{m} b_{jp}^2 \leqq 1,$$

i.e., the new values of the factor loadings must satisfy the constraints (9.7) as well. At this stage of the process, the r_{jk} and the a_{kp} are known and only the b_{jp} may vary.

If the minimum of f_j, as defined in (9.9), is obtained at a point $(b_{j1}, b_{j2}, \cdots, b_{jm})$ which belongs to the region defined by (9.15) there is no problem, and no modification is required. If the point does not belong to the region, then the problem gets complicated primarily because of the *inequality* in the side condition. This inequality may be removed by means of the following:

THEOREM 9.1. *If the minimum of f_j is attained at a point outside of the region defined by (9.15), then a minimum of f_j under the constraint (9.15) will be attained at a boundary point of the region, so that the constraint may be replaced by*

$$(9.16) \qquad \sum_{p=1}^{m} b_{jp}^2 = 1.$$

The proof (Harman and Fukuda 1966, pp. 565–68) consists of transforming the quadratic form (9.9)—involving the diagonalization of a symmetric matrix and transformations of the variables b_{jp}—to the simplified expression:

$$(9.17) \qquad f_j = \sum_{p=1}^{m} (x_p - \xi_p)^2 + K$$

and subject to the constraint

(9.18)
$$\sum_{p=1}^{m} \frac{x_p^2}{\lambda_p^2} \leq 1.$$

In these derived expressions, the x_p are functions of the original b_{jp} and are the quantities to be determined; while the λ_p (eigenvalues of an $m \times m$ matrix), the ξ_p, and K are all constants determined from the known r_{jk} and a_{kp} and the intervening transformations. From the simplified form (9.17), it is evident that f_j is the sum of a constant (K) and a square of the distance between a fixed point $(\xi_1, \xi_2, \cdots, \xi_m)$ and a variable point $(x_1, x_2, \cdots, x_m)$ belonging to the region defined by (9.18). Then, minimization of f_j is equivalent to locating a point satisfying (9.18) which is at the minimum distance from the given point $(\xi_1, \xi_2, \cdots, \xi_m)$.

If the given point belongs to the region, i.e.,

(9.19)
$$\frac{\xi_1^2}{\lambda_1^2} + \frac{\xi_2^2}{\lambda_2^2} + \cdots + \frac{\xi_m^2}{\lambda_m^2} \leq 1,$$

then this point itself is the minimizing point, and the solution is

(9.20)
$$x_p = \xi_p \qquad\qquad (p = 1, 2, \cdots, m).$$

On the other hand, if the given point is *outside* the region, i.e.,

(9.21)
$$\frac{\xi_1^2}{\lambda_1^2} + \frac{\xi_2^2}{\lambda_2^2} + \cdots + \frac{\xi_m^2}{\lambda_m^2} > 1,$$

then a point $(x_1, x_2, \cdots, x_m)$ belonging to the region must lie on its boundary in order to be at a minimum distance from the given point. Furthermore, since the x_p/λ_p are obtained by an orthogonal transformation from the original variables, distance is preserved; therefore the point on the boundary of the region can be expressed in terms of the b_{jp} as in (9.16).

Having reduced the side condition to an equality, conventional mathematical methods are applicable to the problem of minimizing the function under the constraint, when the minimum of f_j is attained outside the region (9.15). The proof of Theorem 9.1 provides additional information which facilitates the solution of the problem. First, it shows that when the minimum of f_j is attained in the region (9.15) its value is given by K in (9.17) and the minimizing point is (9.20). More important, for the case of the minimum of f_j being attained outside this region, the foregoing development suggests a much more tractable approach than that originally posed by the problem of minimizing (9.9) under the constraint (9.16). The simplified problem, which follows from (9.17) and (9.18), is to minimize

(9.22)
$$(x_1 - \xi_1)^2 + (x_2 - \xi_2)^2 + \cdots + (x_m - \xi_m)^2$$

under the constraint

(9.23)
$$\frac{x_1^2}{\lambda_1^2} + \frac{x_2^2}{\lambda_2^2} + \cdots + \frac{x_m^2}{\lambda_m^2} = 1.$$

The method of Lagrange's multipliers (as employed in **8.3**) is especially suitable to this problem. This involves the creation of a new function—the function (9.22) minus μ (the Lagrange multiplier) times the function in (9.23)—and setting its partial derivatives with respect to the m variables x_p equal to zero. This leads to the equations

$$x_1 - \xi_1 - \mu\frac{x_1}{\lambda_1^2} = 0$$

(9.24)
$$x_2 - \xi_2 - \mu\frac{x_2}{\lambda_2^2} = 0$$

$$. \quad . \quad . \quad . \quad . \quad .$$

$$x_m - \xi_m - \mu\frac{x_m}{\lambda_m^2} = 0,$$

which, together with (9.23), constitute a set of $(m + 1)$ equations in $(m + 1)$ unknowns $x_1, x_2, \cdots, x_m, \mu$.

The parameter μ can be determined from any one of the equations (9.24), namely,

(9.25)
$$\mu = \frac{\lambda_p^2(x_p - \xi_p)}{x_p} \qquad (p = 1, 2, \cdots, m),$$

and it may be eliminated by setting any one of the m values equal to any other. Thus, each of the subsequent determinations (9.25) may be expressed in terms of the first, i.e.,

$$\lambda_p^2\left(1 - \frac{\xi_p}{x_p}\right) = \lambda_1^2\left(1 - \frac{\xi_1}{x_1}\right),$$

and, solving explicitly for the remaining unknowns x_p in terms of x_1 produces:

(9.26)
$$x_p = \frac{\lambda_p^2\xi_p x_1}{(\lambda_p^2 - \lambda_1^2)x_1 + \lambda_1^2\xi_1} \qquad (p = 2, 3, \cdots, m).$$

Before proceeding to the general solution to the problem of minimizing (9.22) under the constraint (9.23), some special situations should be noted. If $\xi_p = 0$ for any p, then $x_p = 0$ must be a solution in order to minimize the distance, and the terms corresponding to this p may be deleted. Furthermore, it may be assumed that $\xi_p > 0$ for every p. If an ξ_p were negative for any p, it could be replaced by $|\xi_p|$ and the resulting solution x_p replaced by $-x_p$. Therefore it may be assumed that every x_p is positive.

Substitution of the values (9.26) into (9.23) gives rise to a polynomial equation in x_1 of degree $2m$. The direct solution of such an equation can become quite cumbersome, so a numerical method of successive approximations is employed. The basis for it rests on the following:

THEOREM 9.2. *For a given x_1 between 0 and $min(\xi_1, \lambda_1)$, with x_p ($p = 2, 3, \cdots, m - 1$) determined by (9.26) and x_m by (9.23), if*

(9.27)
$$\lambda_m^2\left(1 - \frac{\xi_m}{x_m}\right) \gtrless \lambda_1^2\left(1 - \frac{\xi_1}{x_1}\right),$$

then

(9.28) $x_1 \lesseqgtr x_1^*$,

where x_1^* designates the true solution for x_1.

The proof begins with the fact that x_p is an increasing function of x_1 (the ξ's being assumed positive). Then the two conclusions are reached by the following reasoning: If $x_1 < x_1^*$, then x_p is less than its solution x_p^*, and, consequently x_m determined by (9.23) is larger than its solution x_m^*. Therefore,

$$\lambda_1^2\left(1 - \frac{\xi_1}{x_1}\right) < \lambda_1^2\left(1 - \frac{\xi_1}{x_1^*}\right) = \lambda_m^2\left(1 - \frac{\xi_m}{x_m^*}\right) < \lambda_m^2\left(1 - \frac{\xi_m}{x_m}\right).$$

If $x_1 > x_1^*$, then a similar argument leads to

$$\lambda_1^2\left(1 - \frac{\xi_1}{x_1}\right) > \lambda_m^2\left(1 - \frac{\xi_m}{x_m}\right),$$

completing the proof.

Before leaving the theoretical development of the minres method, certain of its features deserve emphasis. While a principal-factor solution, in general, is not a minres solution, the converse is always true—a minres solution results from application of the principal-factor method with appropriate diagonal entries. A principal-factor solution for a correlation matrix with minres communalities cannot be different from the minres solution that produced those communalities; if it were, both the off-diagonal and the diagonal sums of squares of residuals would be increased—in the former case because the off-diagonal sum is minimized by minres and in the latter case because the diagonal sum is zero for minres. This means that the principal-factor (for the specified communalities) and minres solutions are equivalent. When put in canonical form (see **8.8**) they are identical. In schematic form,

(9.29) $(\mathbf{R} - \mathbf{I} + \mathbf{H}_{\min}^2) \xrightarrow{\text{PFA}} \mathbf{A}_{\min}$

the theorem states that a principal-factor analysis of a correlation matrix with minres communalities produces a minres factor solution. A corollary property is that a principal-factor solution of a correlation matrix with m-factor minres communalities will have a sum of the m largest eigenvalues equal to the sum of the communalities, while the remaining $n - m$ eigenvalues will be positive and negative and add to zero.

Just as a minres solution reproduces itself through PFA, so does a maximum-likelihood solution (see chap. 10), viz.,

(9.30) $(\mathbf{R} - \mathbf{I} + \mathbf{H}_{\text{ML}}^2) \xrightarrow{\text{PFA}} \mathbf{A}_{\text{ML}}.$

Of course, the principal-factor analysis of the correlation matrix with maximum-likelihood communalities is in canonical form, while the original maximum-likelihood solution (from which the communalities were taken) probably is not, and must first be put in that form in order to verify the equivalence. Now, the factor matrix obtained by (9.30) is a least-squares fit to $(\mathbf{R} - \mathbf{I} + \mathbf{H}_{\text{ML}}^2)$ with perfect fit of the diagonal, and must therefore be a minres solution.

9.5.   *Test of Significance for the Number of Factors*

In most of this book the subject of factor analysis is treated essentially in a mathematical fashion accepting the observed data at their face value rather than samples from some universe values. While allusions are made to the "true" values, reproduced correlations are replaced by observed correlations, residuals are assumed to vanish, and the like, nonetheless there is no formal use of statistical estimation theory. It is not intended to disparage the other work, but merely to call attention to the difference between the crude approximate procedures and formal statistical tests.

It should be apparent that factor analysis deals with fallible data—the individual measurements and the correlations among the variables are subject to the vicissitudes of sampling. As a consequence, there is also sampling variation present in the results of a factor analysis. In particular, the judgment concerning the statistical significance of the number (m) of common factors should be based on their contribution to the reproduced correlations as related to the actual sampling variations of these correlations.

The problem of placing factor analysis on a sound statistical foundation has plagued its proponents from the very inception of the theory. In the early days, when the subject was relatively simple, considerable attention was paid to the statistical theory underlying its practical applications. Spearman set forth the conditions for his "Two Factor" theory in appropriate statistical terms, and some work was done on sampling errors of "tetrad difference" (Spearman and Holzinger 1925). In the rapid advance of factor analysis in the 1930s the emphasis was placed on the extension of the method to encompass matrices of correlations which obviously did not form a hierarchy in Spearman's sense. The bulk of the work in this period was devoted to developing computing methods for analysis of a complex battery of psychological tests into multiple factors. In going from a single general factor to many common factors, the statistical questions were complicated manifold, but tended to be overlooked. Of course there were notable exceptions, such as the work of Hotelling (1933).

In the early 1940s the first concerted efforts were made by Lawley (1940, 1942) to provide a statistical basis for the new methods of factor analysis. He suggested the use of the "method of maximum likelihood," due to Fisher (1922, 1925), as the basis for estimating the universe values of the factor loadings from the given empirical data; and for such "efficient" methods of estimation, he provided a statistical test of significance concerning the number of factors required to explain the observed correlation coefficients. These methods are presented in the next chapter.

Prior to the breakthrough in 1940 by Lawley several less fruitful attempts were made to establish statistical tests for the factor analysis model (2.9). Coombs (1941) considered the residual matrix, after any number of factors had been extracted, as containing both common and error variance; and he introduced the notion of "critical value" for that point at which an additional factor would contain error variance overshadowing the common-factor variance. This attempt to determine significant factors was designed specifically for the centroid method, and was dependent upon sign changes of variables and the number of negative entries in the residual matrices. Another attempt, tied to the bi-factor method of analysis, was made by Holzinger and Harman (1941, pp. 122–32). After some laborious manipulations, in the spirit of the earlier work on standard errors of tetrad differences, approximate formulas were derived for the standard error of a residual and for a factor coefficient. These results are shown in Tables A and B of the Appendix. Still another attempt to derive a significance test for the number of common factors was made by Hoel (1939). While he initially developed a test for a principal-component solution, he subsequently modified it for the centroid solution in terms of the factor model (2.9).

Hotelling (1933) was the first to provide a rigorous statistical test for the number of significant factors in a principal-component solution. Later, Bartlett (1950) made further valuable contributions to significance tests. For an analysis into principal components, he presents χ^2 approximations for testing the statistical significance of the unreduced correlation matrix and of the residual roots, i.e., after several of the largest roots have been determined. Bartlett also recommends an adjustment in the χ^2 statistic for the conventional factor analysis model.

Probably the most important theoretical work that can be applied to the minres method was performed by Rippe (1953). Specifically, he developed a large sampling criterion for judging the completeness of factorization. The test is independent of the particular type of factor solution (in contrast to the test of **10.4** which implies maximum-likelihood estimates of the factor loadings). Its basic assumption is that the original variables have a multivariate normal distribution, from which it follows that the correlations have a Wishart distribution (see **10.3**) and the sample values are maximum-likelihood estimates of the population correlations. While Rippe's development is explicitly in terms of the sample covariance matrix, the results are equally applicable to a factor analysis of the sample correlation matrix.

The statistic for testing the significance of m factors, in the notation of the present text, may be put in the form[4]:

$$(9.31) \qquad U_m = N\{\log_e|\mathbf{AA'} + \mathbf{U}^2| - \log_e|\mathbf{R}| + \text{tr}[\mathbf{R}(\mathbf{AA'} + \mathbf{U}^2)^{-1}] - n\},$$

which is asymptotically distributed as χ^2 with degrees of freedom equal to

$$(9.32) \qquad \qquad v = \tfrac{1}{2}[(n - m)^2 + n - m].$$

The test procedure is to reject the hypothesis of m common factors if U_m exceeds the value of χ^2 for the desired significance level; otherwise it would be accepted. Of course, if the hypothesis is rejected an alternate hypothesis of some larger number of factors may be assumed to explain the observed correlations.

It should be noted that the derivation of (9.31) was based upon the sampling variation of the observed correlation matrix $\mathbf{R}$ (and consequently on the sampling variation of the factor matrix $\mathbf{A}$). The variability of the individual correlations is, of course, dependent on the sample size N. Since a correlation matrix would be subject

---

[4]While the multiplying coefficient N is adequate for the gross use suggested in this text, the more accurate value

$$N - 1 - (2n + 5)/6 - 2m/3$$

would be more appropriate if N were not very large (Bartlett 1950, p. 84).

to extreme variation for small samples, it is standard practice to apply factor analysis only to large samples. Hence, the large-sample approximations made in the course of arriving at (9.31) are not really additional constraints on good experimental practice.

The distinction between statistical significance and "practical significance" should be borne in mind. Statistical significance should convey the thought of a technical test with an associated probability level. Inferences about certain numerical values obtained from an empirical study cannot be made in an absolute sense, but must be made in terms of some kind of degree of belief, i.e., in a probabilistic sense. Statistical tests of hypotheses are then described in terms of some arbitrary levels of significance, which are usually expressed as percentages with popular values being 5 and 1 percent. Then, if the difference between the theoretical value of a statistic and its value derived from the observed data were significant at the 1 percent level, one would conclude that the difference was "real," rejecting the null hypothesis of no difference. However, there may be practical considerations which vitiate such a conclusion. There may be real statistical additional information, but it may have no practical importance. Thus, in testing an hypothesis for the number of common factors required to explain the relationships in an observed correlation matrix (based upon a very large sample), the last one or two factors may prove to be highly significant in a statistical sense and still have no practical significance.

Such a formal test as (9.31) should be used only as a general guide to the number of common factors for the practical user of factor analysis. Statistical significance provides an upper limit of the number of factors that might be of practical significance.

On the basis of actual experience, factor analysts have developed crude guides for "when to stop factoring," as indicated in **2.7**. In addition to such crude judgments about the residual matrix (which, incidentally, a number of workers have shown to be remarkably close to the more exact statistical tests), another practical approach has been found to be useful. The proportions of the total variance (or total communality) accounted for by each factor is considered. If, after 75 percent (or 80 percent or 90 percent) of the total variance is accounted for, any additional factor accounts for less than 5 percent (or 2 percent) it would not be retained. Such arbitrary consideration is quite apart from the statistical significance of such an additional factor —it is dropped because the decision was made beforehand that any factor having such small impact on the total variance could hardly have any practical significance.

Through very extensive applications of electronic computers, Kaiser (1960) arrived at a practical basis for finding the number of common factors that are necessary, reliable, and meaningful for the explanation of the correlations among the variables. His recommendation—after considering statistical significance, algebraically necessary conditions, psychometric reliability, and psychological meaningfulness—is that the number of common factors should be equal to the number of eigenvalues greater than one of the correlation matrix (with unities in the diagonal). He has found this number to run from a sixth to about a third of the total number of variables (in the example of Table 8.12 this number is 5 out of 24 variables).

It has been found by a number of workers that empirical tests of significance used by factor analysts frequently lead to about the same results as the more proper statistical tests. The problem of identifiable versus significant factors is aptly summed up by Danford (1953, p. 150): "Perhaps the statistician's complaint about arbitrariness has become a 'smoke-screen,' but practicing statisticians will admit that tests of significance are in many circumstances superfluous to an experienced worker . . . [since] tests of significance may or may not indicate meaningful factors . . . even the 'exact' tests are arbitrary."

9.6. *Computing Procedures*

   The foregoing theoretical development can be adapted to ready calculation on an electronic computer. An abbreviated flowchart for programming the minres method is presented in Figure 9.1. A more detailed description of each step follows.

1. The complete correlation matrix **R** (with ones in the diagonal) is input by rows. Also stored are such parameters as the number of variables, n; the number of factors, m (or a range m_1 to m_2); the maximum number of iterations, t; and the convergence criterion, ϵ (not to be confused with the vector ϵ_j of incremental changes) and the number of cases, N. It is convenient to have the input data printed (possibly for checking purposes).

2. The subroutine for the calculation of the eigenvalues and eigenvectors of a real symmetric matrix is used many times in the course of getting a minres solution. An example of such a subroutine is the flowchart of Figure 8.1 (also see references in **8.5**).

3. At this point the subroutine has calculated and stored the arbitrary factor matrix $\mathbf{A}_0$ with which the minres method is started, consisting of the first m principal components. Actually, the program computes a minres solution for each value of m from m_1 to m_2, but that detail is not shown in the abbreviated flowchart. The initial factor matrix $\mathbf{A}_0$ is printed, along with the communalities for the variables and the variance of each factor.

4. Calculate the incremental changes ϵ_j, which may be done according to (9.14) using step 5. The iteration process is started with the determination of increments for the first variable from the initial factor matrix $\mathbf{A}_0$ and the first row of observed correlations $\mathbf{r}_1^0$.

5. A subroutine for the solution of a system of linear equations.

6. At this point, a new factor matrix $\mathbf{A}_1$ has been determined in which the loadings in the first row have been replaced by the computed values (9.8). This constitutes iteration 1. For each iteration i, a new factor matrix $\mathbf{A}_i$ is determined (the subscript on the **A** represents the iteration number, not the pivot variable).

7. The communality h_j^2 (of the new row of **A**) is tested to see if it is greater than one. If $h_j^2 > 1$ proceed to step 8, otherwise to step 15.

8. The objective function f_j of (9.9) is expressed as a quadratic form $\mathbf{b}'\mathbf{W}\mathbf{b}$, in which **b** is a column vector of the m unknown b_{jp} (j fixed, $p = 1, 2, \cdots, m$), plus a linear expression in these variables and a constant (Harman and Fukuda 1966, sec. 2). The symmetric matrix **W** is determined at this stage.

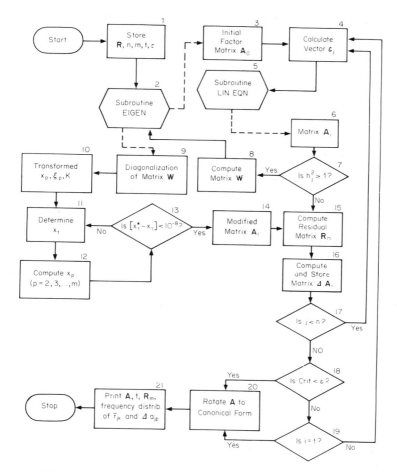

FIG. 9.1–Flowchart for programming the minres method

9. Diagonalization of the matrix **W** is accomplished by means of the subroutine of step 2. According to (8.16), any symmetric matrix may be diagonalized by means of an orthogonal transformation **Q**, given by:

$$\mathbf{Q'WQ} = \Lambda,$$

where Λ is a diagonal matrix with elements $\lambda_1^2, \lambda_2^2, \cdots, \lambda_m^2$ which are the eigenvalues of **W**, and the columns of **Q** are the eigenvectors of **W**.

10. Additional transformations which lead to the derived unknowns x_p as functions of the original b_{jp}, and to the derived constants ξ_p and K as functions of the known r_{jk} and a_{kp}. The result of this step leads to equation (9.17) for the objective function, subject to the condition (9.18).

11. The process pivots on the first unknown x_1 and employs an iterative scheme implied by Theorem 9.2 for the determination of the remaining x's. The following initial value for x_1 seems convenient:

$$x_1^0 = \xi_1 \bigg/ \sqrt{\sum_{p=1}^{m} \left(\frac{\xi_p}{\lambda_p}\right)^2}.$$

12. Compute the remaining x_p ($p = 2, 3, \cdots, m-1$) by use of (9.26) and x_m by use of (9.23).
13. The convergence of x_1 to x_1^*, according to Theorem 9.2, is tested. The loop, steps 11–13, constitutes the distance optimization routine, and the iteration process is continued until x_1 converges to its solution within 10^{-8}.
14. The modified matrix A_i is determined. This completes the modification loop, steps 8–14, to correct for $h_j^2 > 1$.
15. Compute residual matrix (with zeros in diagonal), according to (9.2), from the factor matrix A_i and the original correlation matrix R. The designation R_m merely calls attention to the fact that the residual matrix is based upon m common factors, but the iteration number is omitted for the sake of simplicity.
16. Compute and store the matrix of changes in the factor loadings, from the preceding to the current iteration, for later use.
17. Test to see if each row of the factor matrix has been subjected to the Gauss-Seidel process. The loop from step 4 to step 17, for $j = 1, 2, \cdots, n$, constitutes a major iteration cycle. Thus, in the first major iteration cycle, the successive factor matrices $A_1, A_2, \cdots, A_n$ are determined from the vectors $\epsilon_1, \epsilon_2, \cdots, \epsilon_n$ representing the incremental changes in the loadings for the n variables. Similarly, a set of n factor matrices are determined in each of the major iteration cycles.
18. At the conclusion of each major iteration cycle (i.e., after determining A_{cn}, where $c = 1, 2, 3, \cdots$ is the number of the major iteration cycle), the following convergence criterion is applied:

$$\max_{j,p} |_{(i)}a_{jp} - {}_{(i-1)}a_{jp}| < \epsilon \qquad (j = 1, \cdots, n; \quad p = 1, \cdots, m),$$

where i is the iteration number. This test says that the maximum change in the factor loadings, as stored in step 16, must be less than ϵ. For most problems $\epsilon = .001$ is satisfactory.
19. If the factor loadings have not converged, a test is made to see whether the preset maximum number of iterations has been reached. As a precautionary measure, $t = 1,000$ is recommended (so the process will terminate with $i = cn$, which is the smallest multiple of n exceeding 1,000).
20. When the factor loadings have converged, or the maximum number of iterations reached, the last determined factor matrix is rotated to canonical form (see **8.8**). The subroutine of step 2 is again employed in this process.
21. The output of the program includes the minres factor matrix A; the final

value of the objective function f; the minres criterion *rms*; the matrix of final residuals; and the statistic U_m and the number of degrees of freedom v. Although not shown in the flowchart, the computer program does determine U_m according to (9.31) and the associated number of degrees of freedom. The table lookup of χ^2 for comparison must be done manually.

9.7.   *Illustrative Examples*

Computer programs for the minres method, following the procedure of **9.6**, are generally available (Harman 1975). The method has been very satisfactory, not only in meeting the objective of minimizing the off-diagonal residuals but also in accomplishing this very efficiently. The time required for running a problem on a given computer depends largely on the number of variables (n) and the number of factors (m). Perhaps the best way to give an indication of time estimates is by way of a few illustrations, all on an IBM 360/65. Assuming that the correlations have been computed, and excluding certain other overhead single operations (not iterations), then the time for obtaining a minres solution for a given value of n and m has been found to vary as follows:

Variables	Factors	CPU Time (central processing unit)
$n \leqq 10$	$m = 2, 3$	Up to 3 sec.
$n = 24$	$m = 4$–8	3–30 sec.
$n = 30$	$m = 2$–8	4–50 sec.
$n = 40$	$m = 2$–7	7–50 sec.
$n = 50$	$m = 5$–12	1–2 min.
$n = 77$	$m = 13$–16	4.5–7 min.
$n = 100$	$m = 5$–15	2.5–10 min.

Thus, the method is feasible on modern day fast computers even for very large problems. In general, applied scientists seeking parsimonious descriptions would tend to accept models involving relatively small numbers of factors even for large numbers of variables (especially if these were individual items of tests or public opinion or other survey instruments).

Before considering the individual problems, a general note is in order. It should be apparent that the "best" fit of a model to empirical data, in the sense of the objective function f being a minimum, may not appear very convincing. If the model specifies two factors for a set of 50 variables, it is to be expected that the residuals may be of sizable magnitude, although the sum of squares of off-diagonal residuals has been minimized. All that can be said is that for the given hypothesis, the resulting minres solution best satisfies the least-squares criterion. As regards the actual significance of factors in the statistical sense, the procedure of **9.5** may be applied for large samples.

In any event, for a given hypothesis regarding the number of factors, it is desirable to obtain a stable factor solution. The objective, then, is to set a convergence criterion to guarantee the accuracy of the factor loadings. To be sure that the minres method has stabilized, the maximum change from one iteration to the next of all factor loadings is required to be bounded by some pre-assigned small number, as specified in step 18 of the program flowchart.

1. Five socio-economic variables.—The first illustration is again for the simple numerical example introduced in chapter 2. From the previous experience with this problem, it seems reasonable to assume two common factors. Since the starting point for the minres calculations is an arbitrary factor matrix, the first two principal components are selected for that purpose (this is done automatically by the computer program, once the number of factors m is specified). The computer output gives the solution of Table 9.1, along with the value of the objective function ($f = .00098$), the criterion ($rms = .0099$), and the matrix of residuals. While the latter data may be of

Table 9.1

Minres Solution for Five Socio-Economic Variables
(Two common factors)

Variable j	F_1	F_2	h_j^2
1. Total population	.621	.783	1.000
2. Median school years	.701	−.522	.764
3. Total employment	.702	.683	.958
4. Misc. profess. services	.881	−.144	.797
5. Median value house	.781	−.605	.976
Variance	2.756	1.739	4.495

interest in judging the adequacy of fit, and perhaps for the interpretation of results in a practical application, they are omitted here to conserve space. Also, tests for the statistical significance of the number of common factors are relegated to the problems and exercises for this chapter. It should be evident from Table 9.1 that this problem involved a Heywood case. The first variable required the use of the modification loop (steps 8–14 of the program flowchart) in order to correct for $h_1^2 > 1$.

It is of interest to make certain comparisons of the minres and principal-factor results. Of course, the first two principal components account for more variance (4.670) than any other two factors, but the sum of squares of off-diagonal residuals produced from this initial matrix is not a minimum ($f = .01217$ and $rms = .0348$). For the minres solution of Table 9.1 the objective function was improved considerably. Also, while not designed to maximize variance, the two factors which provide "best" fit to the off-diagonal correlations do account for 90 percent of the total variance in this simple problem.

2. Eight physical variables.—Next, the example of eight physical variables is used, with hypotheses of two and three common factors. The resulting minres solutions are presented in Table 9.2. From a quick glance at the two factor patterns, one would wonder whether there is sufficient justification for the more elaborate model—the fit

Table 9.2

Minres Solutions for Eight Physical Variables
(Two and three common factors)

Variable	Hypothesis: $m = 2$			Hypothesis: $m = 3$			
j	F_1	F_2	h_j^2	F_1	F_2	F_3	h_j^2
1. Height	.856	−.324	.838	.860	−.322	−.160	.868
2. Arm span	.848	−.412	.889	.867	−.432	.242	.998
3. Length of forearm	.808	−.409	.821	.803	−.396	.031	.803
4. Length of lower leg	.831	−.342	.808	.835	−.340	−.163	.839
5. Weight	.750	.571	.889	.751	.583	−.113	.915
6. Bitrochanteric diameter	.631	.492	.640	.626	.492	.019	.635
7. Chest girth	.569	.510	.583	.565	.508	.001	.577
8. Chest width	.607	.351	.492	.611	.362	.182	.537
Variance	4.449	1.510	5.959	4.480	1.533	.158	6.171

of the two-factor solution is indicated by $rms = .0208$, and of the three-factor solution by $rms = .0127$. Also, the latter accounts for 77.1 percent of the total variance, or slightly more than the 74.5 percent accounted for by the former.

A closer look at the solution for $m = 2$ factors provides some additional information that may be useful for other applications of the minres method. If the model were to fit the data precisely, all residuals would vanish—but, of course, this is not to be expected of empirical data. The actual residuals range from −.027 to .044 with a mean of zero to more than four decimal places and a standard deviation of .021. From a practical point of view, the magnitude of the residuals may be considered too small to provide another meaningful factor. However, for adequate statistical explanation of the observed data on 305 cases a third factor may be required. The large sample test of **9.5** can provide an answer to such a question. The statistic (9.31) for the case of two factors becomes $U_2 = 80.0$ where certainly a computer was necessary for the calculations involving the determinants of the matrices of observed and reproduced correlations. The number of degrees of freedom is 21 according to (9.32). It will be found from Table D in the Appendix that for 21 degrees of freedom $\chi^2 = 46.8$ for $P = .001$. This says that the probability of getting a value of χ^2 in excess of 46.8 is only 1 in 1,000, and since the actual value $U_2 = 80.0$ is considerably greater, the hypothesis of $m = 2$ is rejected and it must be assumed that at least three common factors are required for adequate explanation of the observed data.

Next, the statistical test for $m = 3$ can be made. The statistic (9.31) then has the value $U_3 = 26.3$, with 15 degrees of freedom. The corresponding χ^2's are 37.7 for $P = .001$, 30.6 for $P = .01$, and 25.0 for $P = .05$. The hypothesis of three common factors would be rejected at the 5 percent level but would be accepted at the 1 percent level.

The solution with three common factors was used in an empirical investigation of the relationship between minres and maximum-likelihood methods. As noted at the

191

end of section **9.4**, a principal-factor analysis of a correlation matrix with maximum-likelihood communalities produces a maximum-likelihood solution which is equivalent to the original one from which the communalities were taken—yet this solution is a minres solution. According to the conditions for minres and for maximum-likelihood (see **10.3**), the two solutions should be identical only if the communalities are equal. How much the actual communalities for a set of n variables may differ and still produce practically equivalent results is a matter for empirical investigation (so long as it is understood that it is not mathematical equality that is sought). For the current example the following solutions were obtained:

    Maximum-likelihood (arbitrary initial matrix),

    Principal-factor (ML communalities),

    Minres (ML initial matrix), and

    Maximum-likelihood (minres initial matrix).

After the maximum-likelihood solutions were put in canonical form, all four solutions were practically identical. Communalities and contributions of factors differed only in the third decimal place; and individual factor loadings, with only a few exceptions, agreed to within a few units in the third place. The equivalence of these solutions was found in spite of the fact that the 8 communalities range from .5 to 1.0 as can be seen in Table 9.2.

It should be noted, however, that the minres solution found to be equivalent to a maximum-likelihood solution was for a particular local maximum (solution of Table 10.4), while another maximum-likelihood solution (of Table 10.2) differed from it. This problem—local versus global maximum or minimum—is unresolved for either the maximum-likelihood or the minres method. Even when a computing procedure converges there is no assurance that the optimal point (maximum or minimum) is for the entire surface in the multidimensional space or only for a local area. In practical usage, this question may be immaterial as long as a reasonably good solution is obtained.

3. Eight emotional variables.—Another eight-variable example is used for illustration—the eight emotional traits of **8.6**—primarily because of the difficulties encountered in trying to get a principal-factor solution based upon SMC's as communalities. Of course, no such difficulties arose in the minres method because no prior estimates of communalities are required. Instead, the hypothesis of two common factors was assumed (based on the prior experience with this problem), and the resulting minres solution is shown in Table 9.3.

It is interesting to note that the minres solution is very similar to the principal-factor solution of Table 8.6. The most important differences occur for variable 3 (tenderness) for which the minres loadings are somewhat larger and the communality almost one-tenth bigger. The total communality (4.996) produced by the minres method is larger than the estimated communality (4.87) on which the principal-factor analysis was performed. As regards interpretation of results, everything stated about the principal-factor solution in **8.6** applies equally well to the minres solution.

Because of the difficulties with this problem indicated in **8.6**, it was decided to make further explorations with the minres method. If the correlation matrix were indeed singular, what would happen if the minres method were attempted for $m = 3, 4, \cdots, 8$?

Table 9.3

Minres Solution for Eight Emotional Traits
(Two common factors)

Variable j	F_1	F_2	h_j^2
1	.982	.065	.968
2	.935	−.111	.888
3	.833	−.550	.997
4	.720	−.091	.526
5	.676	.330	.566
6	.526	.164	.304
7	.515	.583	.605
8	.355	−.128	.142
Variance	4.176	.820	4.996

If multicollinearity exists among these eight variables, then solutions up to $m = 8$ should not be possible. That is, in fact, what happened. A brief summary of some of the pertinent findings is given in Table 9.4. It can readily be seen that all the correlations (given to two decimal places) are completely explained (mathematically) by the time $m = 6$. Any analysis from that point to $m = 8$ can only be a manipulation of "noise" in the computing system. Actually, the solution of Table 9.3 in terms of two factors still appears to be at the practical level. A solution for $m = 3$ might be considered if one really wanted to get a near perfect fit to the observed correlations.

Table 9.4

Characteristics of Minres Solutions for Eight Emotional Traits
(Two to six common factors)

Number of Factors m	Number of Communalities equal to 1 (to 2 dec.)	Number of Iterations (max = 1000)	*rms*
2	1	56	.0514
3	2	88	.0305
4	4	1,000	.0222
5	4	1,000	.0099
6	7	1,000	.0025

4. Twenty-four psychological tests.—The final illustrations involve a fair-sized problem. To demonstrate the practicability of the minres method, the twenty-four psychological tests (from Table 7.4) were analyzed in terms of 4, 5, and 6 factors.

The average CPU time for these three analyses was 20 seconds. To conserve space, the complete minres solution is shown only for the case of five common factors in

Table 9.5. It should be recalled that a minres solution is in canonical form with the factors appearing in the order of their contribution to the total variance that is analyzed. Therefore, it is relatively easy to make direct comparisons with the corresponding principal factors of Table 8.15. A principal-factor analysis, with reasonably good communality estimates, must come very close to a minres analysis since both methods are of the least-squares variety. In computing the minres solution of Table 9.5

Table 9.5

Minres Solution for Twenty-four Psychological Tests
(Five common factors)

Test j	F_1	F_2	F_3	F_4	F_5	h_j^2
1	.598	.024	.381	−.210	−.086	.555
2	.373	−.035	.261	−.137	.072	.232
3	.421	−.125	.367	−.128	−.119	.358
4	.484	−.112	.258	−.182	.060	.350
5	.686	−.293	−.279	−.044	−.027	.637
6	.688	−.402	−.212	.063	−.140	.703
7	.676	−.407	−.310	−.088	−.029	.728
8	.673	−.194	−.094	−.109	−.038	.513
9	.696	−.445	−.235	.066	.000	.741
10	.473	.541	−.476	−.085	.170	.779
11	.560	.376	−.168	.092	−.271	.565
12	.465	.494	−.125	−.219	.065	.528
13	.614	.306	.028	−.371	−.378	.751
14	.426	.051	.003	.422	−.145	.384
15	.392	.084	.092	.369	.003	.305
16	.512	.075	.346	.251	−.073	.456
17	.465	.195	−.004	.394	−.027	.410
18	.518	.307	.165	.160	.080	.421
19	.443	.093	.102	.137	−.031	.235
20	.621	−.147	.141	.055	.226	.481
21	.596	.210	.080	−.199	.180	.452
22	.613	−.113	.120	.042	.140	.424
23	.692	−.071	.152	−.092	.182	.550
24	.651	.168	−.187	.017	.158	.512
Variance	7.673	1.717	1.233	.948	.498	12.070

some difficulty was encountered. The computer program accepts some starting communalities or else, by default, the process is initiated with 1's in the diagonal of the correlation matrix. Under the default option (probably the worst starting point for this problem), a Heywood case arose for variable 19. The actual figures in Table 9.5 were obtained by starting with SMC's. It is interesting to note that practically identical results were obtained when the process was started with zeros in the diagonal.

While the principal-factor method accounts for the maximum variance for a given number of factors, it cannot account for more variance than originally put in the correlation matrix (i.e., the estimates of the communalities). In the principal-factor solution of Table 8.15, the squared multiple correlations were analyzed. These are known to be lower-bound estimates of the communalities. Therefore, it is not surprising that the minres solution accounts for over 1 percent more than the total communality calculated in the principal-factor solution. The by-product of the minres method—the communalities determined for the specified number of factors—certainly provides the best known approximation to the concept of communality.

In the discussion of this problem in **8.6** it was argued that five factors appeared to be the optimal number and that even four might suffice from a practical vantage point. That served as a guide in this chapter as well. Nonetheless, it is advisable to study the effect of the different number of factors. Without carrying this notion to an extreme, a comparison is made of certain statistics for the choices of four, five, and six factors. Table 9.6 presents such statistics. It should be obvious that as the complexity of the

Table 9.6

Frequency Distributions of Minres Residuals for Twenty-four
Psychological Tests
(Four, five, and six common factors)

Class Interval	Frequency		
	$m = 4$	$m = 5$	$m = 6$
More than .0475	29	21	16
.0425– .0475	9	8	7
.0375– .0425	6	9	5
.0325– .0375	7	7	10
.0275– .0325	16	13	10
.0225– .0275	15	11	11
.0175– .0225	19	13	14
.0125– .0175	13	20	18
.0075– .0125	12	17	18
.0025– .0075	15	17	24
−.0025– .0025	9	14	25
−.0075–−.0025	14	19	18
−.0125–−.0075	12	19	15
−.0175–−.0125	13	11	14
−.0225–−.0175	9	10	14
−.0275–−.0225	12	15	7
−.0325–−.0275	6	8	16
−.0375–−.0325	10	8	8
−.0425–−.0375	10	3	2
−.0475–−.0425	5	5	4
less than −.0475	35	28	20
Total	276	276	276
Mean	−.0000467	−.0000407	−.0000169
S.D.	.04089	.03630	.03186
$f(A)$	.45989	.36303	.27909
rms	.0408	.0361	.0318

model is increased, the fit should be improved. This is evident from the actual frequency distributions and from the summary statistics (means, standard deviations, the objective function, and the root-mean-square deviation). The extent to which the model fits the off-diagonal correlations may be judged not only by the decrease in the objective function as the model increases from four to five to six factors, but also by comparing these values with the corresponding ones for principal-component solutions. Thus, the improvement in the sum of squares of residuals for each hypothesis is given by:

	$f(A)$			rms		
	pc	min	diff.	pc	min	ratio
$m = 4$:	.928	.460	.468	.0580	.0408	1.42
$m = 5$:	.906	.363	.543	.0573	.0361	1.59
$m = 6$:	.837	.279	.558	.0551	.0318	1.73

Thus, while the objective function is smaller for a larger number of factors, whether computed for a principal-component or a minres solution, the difference between the two solutions becomes more pronounced as the number of factors in a model goes up.

Finally, the more precise statistical criterion of **9.5** is applied to test the hypothesis of five common factors. The statistic (9.31) is $U_5 = 207.23$ with $\nu = 190$ degrees of freedom, as given by (9.32), for the sample of $N = 145$ cases. While Table D does not extend to such a large value of ν the probability can be approximated from the normal distribution. This is accomplished by setting

$$z = \sqrt{2\chi^2} - \sqrt{2\nu - 1},$$

treating it as a normal deviate with unit variance, and reading the area under the normal curve from Table C in the Appendix. Then the probability for χ^2 corresponds to the area of a single tail of the normal curve beyond the particular deviate. If a χ^2 equal to U_5 is considered, the normal deviate becomes $z = 0.89$ and

$$P = .50 - .3133 = .1867,$$

where the area from the mean to the deviate is obtained from Table C. This shows the probability of getting a value of χ^2 in excess of that actually obtained is more than 18 in 100, or the probability of getting as bad a fit or worse is almost 1 in 5. Hence the five-factor solution appears to be quite satisfactory.

10   Maximum-likelihood Method

10.1. *Introduction*

Lawley (1940, 1942) made a fundamental contribution to factor analysis by providing a statistical basis for judging the adequacy of the model (2.9), with a specified number of factors, to explain an empirical correlation matrix. His statistical test for the number of common factors is dependent upon a particular type of factor solution, namely, maximum-likelihood estimates of the factor loadings. The amount of computation arising from this method restricted its use to small problems in the 1940s and 1950s. Present-day computers make the maximum-likelihood method feasible.

Because this chapter is concerned with formal statistical theory, a brief summary of some of the basic ideas in statistical estimation is presented in **10.2**. With this foundation, the exposition of the maximum-likelihood method in factor analysis becomes more meaningful and clear. Such a development is given in **10.3**, including the essential mathematics for estimating the factor coefficients. This is followed in **10.4** by an asymptotic χ^2 test of significance for the number of common factors. To assist in an understanding of these ideas the calculation of factor loadings and the test for the number of factors is presented in some detail for the example of eight physical variables in **10.5**. The progress made in computing maximum-likelihood solutions is is discussed and illustrated in **10.6**.

10.2. *Statistical Estimation*

Most of the development in this text has been essentially in terms of *mathematical* methods. While factor analysis methods were applied to sample correlation matrices, the interpretation of results tacitly has been in terms of the population from which the sample presumably was drawn. With the exception of the discussion in **9.5**, little attention has been paid to the *statistical* problems of the uncertainty of conclusions that might be derived from the empirical data. In this chapter, on the contrary, a conscious distinction is made between the intercorrelations of the observed variables and the hypothetical values in the universe from which they were sampled. Then, based on the observed data, estimates are obtained of the universe factor weights, under the assumption of the factor model (2.9), and the statistical significance of such hypotheses is determined.

To help clarify the ensuing methods of analysis, some of the fundamental concepts in statistical estimation are reviewed in this section. First of all, the process of estimation is concerned with making inferences about the values of unknown population parameters from the incomplete data of a sample. Suppose, for example, that the distribution function for a variable x is dependent upon two parameters, θ_1 and θ_2. This is usually represented by $f(x; \theta_1, \theta_2)$, and may be conceived as a distribution function of a single observation x. In contrast, the joint distribution of N (independent) observations $x_1, x_2, \cdots, x_N$ is given by the product of the individual functions, viz.,

$$\prod_{i=1}^{N} f(x_i; \theta_1, \theta_2).$$

When the foregoing is considered as a function of the θ's for fixed x's it is often called the "likelihood function" of the sample, and is denoted by L.

The typical estimation problem involves the determination of numerical values for θ_1 and θ_2 from a random sample of N observations. To estimate the parameters is then tantamount to finding functions of the observations—usually denoted by $\hat{\theta}_1 (x_1, x_2, \cdots, x_N)$ and $\hat{\theta}_2 (x_1, x_2, \cdots, x_N)$—such that the distribution of these functions in repeated samples will concentrate near the true values. Such functions of the sample values are called *estimators*.

Since there are many choices for an estimating function, the following criteria are frequently used in selecting among them:

  1. An estimator $\hat{\theta}$ is said to be *consistent* if it converges (in a probabilistic sense) to the true parameter as the sample increases without limit, i.e.,

$$\lim_{N \to \infty} \hat{\theta} \to \theta$$

  2. An estimator is said to be *efficient* if it has the smallest limiting variance. When an estimator is efficient it is also consistent.
  3. An estimator is said to be *sufficient* if it utilizes all the information in the sample concerning the parameter.
  4. If the expected value of the estimator is the true parameter, i.e.,

$$E(\hat{\theta}) = \theta,$$

then the estimator is *unbiased*. While it is of some advantage to devise an unbiased estimate, it is not a very critical requirement.

The method of maximum likelihood is a well-established and popular statistical procedure for estimating the unknown population parameters because such estimators satisfy the first three of the above standards. Not all parameters have sufficient estimators but if one exists the maximum-likelihood estimator is such a sufficient estimator (Mood and Graybill 1963, p. 185). However, a maximum-likelihood estimator will generally not be unbiased.[1] This method yields values of the estimators which maximize the likelihood function of a sample.

---

[1] By getting the expected value of such an estimator, an unbiased statistic can be derived.

An application of the method of maximum likelihood to a well-known situation may be useful by way of introduction to the more complex problem treated in **10.3**. Consider the normal distribution for the single variable X:

(10.1) $$f(X; \mu, \sigma) = \frac{1}{\sqrt{2\pi}\sigma} e^{-(1/2\sigma^2)(X-\mu)^2}$$

which is dependent upon two parameters, the universe values of the mean and standard deviation. The likelihood function is defined by

(10.2) $$L = \prod_{i=1}^{N} f(X_i; \mu, \sigma),$$

and for the N independent observations takes the form:

(10.3) $$L = \frac{1}{(2\pi)^{N/2}\sigma^N} \exp - \left(\frac{1}{2\sigma^2}\right) \sum_{i=1}^{N} (X_i - \mu)^2.$$

To get the maximum-likelihood estimators of μ and σ it is necessary to maximize the likelihood function L. However, since likelihood functions are products, and many are expressed in terms of exponentials as in the example, it is customary to maximize the logarithm (to the base e) of the likelihood instead. This is done merely to simplify the mathematics because the maximum of the logarithm occurs at the same point as that of the likelihood itself. Proceeding in this manner, the logarithm of the likelihood (10.3) is

(10.4) $$\log L = -\frac{N}{2} \log 2\pi - N \log \sigma - \frac{1}{2\sigma^2} \sum_{i=1}^{N} (X_i - \mu)^2.$$

The maximum of this function of the two variables μ and σ can be obtained by setting its partial derivatives (with respect to each of the variables) equal to zero and solving for them. Thus,

(10.5)
$$\frac{\partial(\log L)}{\partial \mu} = \frac{1}{\sigma^2} \sum_{i=1}^{N} (X_i - \mu) = \frac{1}{\sigma^2}\left(\sum_{i=1}^{N} X_i - N\mu\right),$$

$$\frac{\partial(\log L)}{\partial \sigma} = -\frac{N}{\sigma} + \frac{1}{\sigma^3} \sum_{i=1}^{N} (X_i - \mu)^2,$$

and upon equating these to zero, and solving for μ and σ^2, the following maximum-likelihood estimators are obtained:

(10.6)
$$\hat{\mu} = \frac{1}{N} \sum_{i=1}^{N} X_i = \overline{X}$$

$$\hat{\sigma}^2 = \frac{1}{N} \sum_{i=1}^{N} (X_i - \overline{X})^2.$$

These estimators of the universe μ and σ^2 correspond to the well-known first and second moments of the sample. It should be noted that while the estimator $\hat{\mu}$ is unbiased, the estimator $\hat{\sigma}^2$ is not. Actually, the expected value of this estimator is slightly less than the true parameter, viz.,

$$(10.7) \qquad\qquad E(\hat{\sigma}^2) = \frac{N-1}{N}\sigma^2.$$

In other words, an unbiased estimate of σ^2 (but not the maximum-likelihood estimate) is

$$(10.8) \qquad\qquad \tilde{\sigma}^2 = \frac{1}{N-1}\sum_{i=1}^{N}(X_i - \overline{X})^2.$$

10.3. *Maximum-Likelihood Estimates of Factor Loadings*

Instead of developing mathematical theory for the exact determination of the factor coefficients under such assumptions as those that led to the bi-factor, principal-factor, or minres methods, the present approach is somewhat different. Under the assumption of a given number (m) of common factors, the method of maximum likelihood is applied to get estimators of the universe factor loadings from the sample of N observations on the n tests. Subsequent (see **10.4**) tests of significance can be applied to determine the adequacy of the hypothesis regarding the number of factors. Although the maximum-likelihood principle is relatively simple, the algebraic manipulations are not; therefore the detailed mathematical derivations will be omitted.

First, the model to be used will be stated, together with the assumptions as to distributions. Specifically, the expression (2.9) for a variable in standard form is adopted, more generally, to the case of any variable in its respective unit of measurement, as follows:

$$(10.9) \qquad\qquad x_j = a_{j1}F_1 + a_{j2}F_2 + \cdots + a_{jm}F_m + u_jY_j.$$

Without loss of generality, it may be assumed that the test scores have zero means. It is further assumed that all factors $F_1, F_2, \cdots, F_m, Y_1, Y_2, \cdots, Y_n$ are independent, normally distributed variables with zero means and unit variances. A consequence of this assumption is that the x's have a multivariate normal distribution.

The question of orthogonal or oblique factors is of no consequence here. The statistical estimation problem is concerned explicitly with the prediction of factor loadings for orthogonal factors out of consideration of the mathematical difficulties that would otherwise ensue. Once the (maximum-likelihood) common-factor space is determined, rotation to an oblique frame of reference may be made just as in the case of any other initial solution.

Before proceeding further, it is advisable to employ matrix notation in order to present a complex subject in a compact form. To this end, the necessary basic notation is summarized in Table 10.1

The need for theory on the sampling distributions of statistics of many variables has led to a special branch of mathematical statistics—multivariate statistical analysis. To make the problem tractable in this complex subject, suitable conditions must be introduced. Thus, even the problem of determining the variance of a sample covari-

Table 10.1

Notation for Matrices in Statistical Estimation of Factor Weights

Matrix			Order	Definition
Population	Estimator	Sample		
$\Sigma = (\sigma_{jk})$	$\hat{\Sigma}$	$S = (s_{jk})$	$n \times n$	Covariance matrix
$P = (\rho_{jk})$	$\hat{P}$	$R = (r_{jk})$	$n \times n$	Correlation matrix (unities in diagonal)
$A = (a_{jp})$	$\hat{A}$	—	$n \times m$	Matrix of common-factor coefficients
$U^2 = (u_j^2)$	$\hat{U}^2$	—	$n \times n$	Diagonal matrix of uniquenesses

ance matrix is extremely difficult for samples from an arbitrary distribution. However, under the assumption that the sample comes from a multivariate normal distribution, the actual distribution function of the elements of the covariance matrix can be determined. This remarkable result was first derived by Wishart (1928), and may be expressed as follows:

$$(10.10) \qquad dF = K|\Sigma|^{-\frac{1}{2}(N-1)}|S|^{\frac{1}{2}(N-n-2)} \exp - \frac{N-1}{2} \sum_{j,k=1}^{n} \sigma^{jk} s_{jk} \prod_{j<k=1}^{n} ds_{jk},$$

where K is a constant involving only N and n, and in addition to the determinants of the population and sample covariance matrices, the notation σ^{jk} is employed for the elements of the inverse matrix Σ^{-1} according to **3.2**, paragraph **22**.

Considered as a function of the σ's, the expression (10.10), aside from the product of the differentials, is the likelihood function L of the sample. The remaining task is to find estimates $\hat{A}$ and $\hat{U}^2$ satisfying

$$(10.11) \qquad\qquad \Sigma = AA' + U^2,$$

which maximize L. To this end the logarithm (to the base e) of the likelihood function for Wishart's distribution is first obtained:

$$(10.12) \qquad \log L = -\frac{N-1}{2}\left(\log |\Sigma| + \sum_{j,k=1}^{n} \sigma^{jk} s_{jk}\right) + \text{function independent of } \Sigma.$$

Corresponding to the maximization of L (or its logarithm) is the minimization of the expression,

$$(10.13) \qquad -\frac{2}{N-1}\log L = \log |\Sigma| + \sum_{j,k=1}^{n} \sigma^{jk} s_{jk} + \text{function independent of } \Sigma,$$

which may be more convenient to program.

The next steps consist of finding the partial derivatives of (10.13) with respect to each of the a_{jp} and u_j, ($nm + n$ variables in all), equating these to zero, and solving the resulting equations. Since this process involves extensive algebraic manipulations, only the results will be shown. It is convenient at this point, however, to note that

Lawley (1940) and others have shown that the estimation equations are independent of the scale of measurement of the x's in the sense that the estimated factor loadings for a particular variable are proportional to the standard deviation of that variable. Consequently, the estimation equations for the a's can be expressed in terms of the correlations rather than the covariances. The results, first obtained by Lawley (1940, pp. 66–71), can be put compactly in the following matrix form:

(10.14) $$\hat{\mathbf{P}} = \hat{\mathbf{A}}\hat{\mathbf{A}}' + \hat{\mathbf{U}}^2$$

(10.15) $$\hat{\mathbf{A}} = \hat{\mathbf{P}}\mathbf{R}^{-1}\hat{\mathbf{A}}$$

(10.16) $$\hat{\mathbf{U}}^2 = \mathbf{I} - \text{diag } \hat{\mathbf{A}}\hat{\mathbf{A}}'$$

(10.17) $$\hat{\mathbf{A}}'\mathbf{R}^{-1}\hat{\mathbf{A}} \text{ is diagonal}$$

where $\mathbf{P}$ (capital rho) is the population correlation matrix, $\hat{\mathbf{P}}$ is its estimator, and $\mathbf{R}$ is the corresponding matrix in the sample (of course, with unities in the diagonal). It should be noted that the a's in (10.11) are different from the a's in (10.14), since in the former case the specific units of the several variables are implied while in the latter case the variables are standardized. The same symbols are employed for the elements (and the matrices) in the two cases only for the sake of simplicity. Another point must be mentioned: the condition (10.17) is introduced solely to remove the inherent indeterminacy of $\mathbf{A}$ due to the arbitrariness of rotation. This condition is somewhat analogous to the orthogonality property (8.18) of the principal-factor method; or, to the canonical form described in **8.8** and employed to fix the position of the minres method in **9.6**. The latter condition can certainly be substituted for (10.17).

While equations (10.14) and (10.15), with the conditions (10.16) and (10.17), provide a basis for obtaining maximum-likelihood estimates of the factor loadings, they do entail considerable work, especially to get the inverse of the correlation matrix. The procedure may be simplified by making the assumption that the estimator $\hat{\mathbf{P}}$ is equal to the observed correlation matrix $\mathbf{R}$, so that (10.14) may be written:

(10.18) $$\mathbf{A}\mathbf{A}' + \mathbf{U}^2 = \mathbf{R},$$

where, for simplicity, the caps have been removed from the estimates. Premultiplying both sides of (10.18) by $\mathbf{A}'\mathbf{U}^{-2}$ yields[2]

(10.19) $$(\mathbf{A}'\mathbf{U}^{-2}\mathbf{A} + \mathbf{I})\mathbf{A}' = \mathbf{A}'\mathbf{U}^{-2}\mathbf{R},$$

and defining

(10.20) $$\mathbf{J} = \mathbf{A}'\mathbf{U}^{-2}\mathbf{A}$$

can be put in the form

(10.21) $$(\mathbf{I} + \mathbf{J})\mathbf{A}' = \mathbf{A}'\mathbf{U}^{-2}\mathbf{R}.$$

---

[2]It is tacitly assumed that none of the uniquenesses vanishes.

Finally, this equation can be simplified to

(10.22) $$\mathbf{JA'} = \mathbf{AU}^{-2}\mathbf{R} - \mathbf{A'},$$

which is amenable to an iterative method of solution. Equation (10.22) is employed along with (10.14) and (10.16), but the matrix $\mathbf{J}$ defined in (10.20) is required to be diagonal as an alternate condition to (10.17). The important effect of the simplified procedure is to replace the calculation of the inverse of a matrix of order n by one of order m—a tremendous saving since the number of common factors is usually much smaller than the number of variables.

The iterative method for solving (10.22) for the factor loadings, due to Lawley (1942, p. 181), will now be described in the matrix notation of the present chapter, and illustrated with a numerical example in **10.5**. Since the factor loadings are computed one factor at a time, with succeeding factor weights being dependent on those already determined, it is convenient to designate the separate vectors of the factor-pattern matrix $\mathbf{A}$, viz.,

(10.23) $$\mathbf{A} = (\mathbf{a}_1 \mathbf{a}_2 \cdots \mathbf{a}_m),$$

where any one of the m column vectors is given by

(10.24) $$\mathbf{a}_p = \{a_{1p} a_{2p} \cdots a_{np}\} \qquad (p = 1, 2, \cdots, m).$$

Corresponding to the trial values $\mathbf{a}_p$, the values derived from the iterative process are designated $\mathbf{b}_p$, with $\mathbf{B}$ for the complete pattern matrix and $\mathbf{V}^2$ for the new uniqueness matrix. The iteration equations, exemplified by the following for the case of three factors, are immediately generalizable to any number of factors:

$$\mathbf{b}_1 = (\mathbf{R}\mathbf{U}^{-2}\mathbf{a}_1 - \mathbf{a}_1)/\sqrt{\mathbf{a}_1'\mathbf{U}^{-2}(\mathbf{R}\mathbf{U}^{-2}\mathbf{a}_1 - \mathbf{a}_1)}$$

$$\mathbf{b}_2 = (\mathbf{R}\mathbf{U}^{-2}\mathbf{a}_2 - \mathbf{a}_2 - \mathbf{b}_1\mathbf{b}_1'\mathbf{U}^{-2}\mathbf{a}_2)/\sqrt{\mathbf{a}_2'\mathbf{U}^{-2}(\mathbf{R}\mathbf{U}^{-2}\mathbf{a}_2 - \mathbf{a}_2 - \mathbf{b}_1\mathbf{b}_1'\mathbf{U}^{-2}\mathbf{a}_2)}$$

(10.25) $$\mathbf{b}_3 = (\mathbf{R}\mathbf{U}^{-2}\mathbf{a}_3 - \mathbf{a}_3 - \mathbf{b}_1\mathbf{b}_1'\mathbf{U}^{-2}\mathbf{a}_3 - \mathbf{b}_2\mathbf{b}_2'\mathbf{U}^{-2}\mathbf{a}_3)/$$
$$\sqrt{\mathbf{a}_3'\mathbf{U}^{-2}(\mathbf{R}\mathbf{U}^{-2}\mathbf{a}_3 - \mathbf{a}_3 - \mathbf{b}_1\mathbf{b}_1'\mathbf{U}^{-2}\mathbf{a}_3 - \mathbf{b}_2\mathbf{b}_2'\mathbf{U}^{-2}\mathbf{a}_3)}$$

$$\mathbf{V}^2 = \mathbf{I} - \text{diag } \mathbf{BB'}$$

To avoid further complications in notation, it is suggested that the $\mathbf{b}$'s and $\mathbf{V}$ be replaced by $\mathbf{a}$'s and $\mathbf{U}$ after each iteration before beginning the calculations anew. The computations by equations like (10.25) are repeated again and again until convergence is obtained to the desired degree of accuracy. The final matrix $\mathbf{A}$ contains the maximum-likelihood estimates of the factor loadings for the assumed number of common factors.

A variant of the preceding method was developed and a computer program made available (Harman, 1966). While still based on the assumption (10.18), it does not merely discard the off-diagonal values of $\mathbf{J}$ (in substituting (10.20) for (10.17) as the side condition) but actually diagonalizes this matrix. The essential part of the program can be described as follows:

(10.26)

1. Start with an arbitrary factor matrix $A_{\frac{1}{2}}$ (usually the first m principal components). The reason for the subscript $\frac{1}{2}$ will become clear in the ensuing steps.
2. $U_i^2 = \text{diag } (I - A_{i-\frac{1}{2}}A'_{i-\frac{1}{2}})$, where $i = 1, 2, 3, \cdots$ is the iteration number.
3. $J_{i-\frac{1}{2}} = A'_{i-\frac{1}{2}}U_i^{-2}A_{i-\frac{1}{2}}$, from definition (10.20).
4. $J_i = Q'_i J_{i-\frac{1}{2}} Q_i$, according to (8.16).
5. $A_i = A_{i-\frac{1}{2}}Q_i$, rotation of $A_{i-\frac{1}{2}}$ for which J_i is diagonal.
6. $A_{i+\frac{1}{2}} = (RU_i^{-2} - I)A_i J_i^{-1}$, from (10.22).
7. Test for convergence: $|A_{i+\frac{1}{2}} - A_{i-\frac{1}{2}}| < \epsilon$?

In the foregoing algorithm the subscripts with the $\frac{1}{2}$'s designate intermediate matrices that are employed in the course of a particular iteration, which is represented by a subscript without a $\frac{1}{2}$ in it. The point of departure is step 4 in which the matrix J is diagonalized. This is accomplished, in the ith iteration, by means of the Spectral Theorem (8.16) which states that for Q_i orthogonal (i.e., $Q_i Q'_i = I$), the symmetric matrix $J_{i-\frac{1}{2}}$ is diagonalized by the transformation matrix Q_i so that the new matrix J_i is the diagonal matrix of eigenvalues of $J_{i-\frac{1}{2}}$; and the columns of Q_i are the (normalized) eigenvectors of $J_{i-\frac{1}{2}}$. After the new matrix of factor loadings is obtained, the test for convergence is applied. The loop, steps 2–7, is repeated until the maximum change in the difference of factor loadings is below some specified level (usually $\epsilon = .001$).

Because the maximum-likelihood method has not been proved to converge (and, when it appears to converge it may be only to a relative maximum point), it is wise to apply an additional test. The likelihood function L must increase, of course, or, a negative fraction of it, as in (10.13), must decrease. The difference in this function of the likelihood from one iteration to the next is determined, and if it should fail to go down then there is evidence that the particular maximum point was missed, and the process has proceeded to another "mound." One could back off and try different values for the matrix A in the preceding iteration, or proceed with the new values (for which the likelihood function failed to behave properly) and continue to seek convergence to a new relative maximum.

Still another algorithm and computer program was developed (Hemmerle, 1965) for the maximum-likelihood method in the mid-1960s when this procedure seemed to be very desirable. Hemmerle indicates that in extracting 8 factors from a matrix of order 15 his method is almost five-fold more efficient than the original Lawley iteration scheme described above.

Probably the most important work on the maximum-likelihood method is that of Joreskog (1967a). He has devised a very efficient computational method that converges rapidly, regardless of the values with which the process is started. Furthermore, provision is made for the Heywood case. When the maximization of the likelihood function leads to one or more variables with uniquenesses essentially zero, an adjustment is made for such variables as follows: (1) the principal components of any such variables are obtained; (2) the remaining variables, with the effect of the recalcitrant variables partialed out, are analyzed by the maximum-likelihood method;

(3) the two results are combined to give a complete maximum-likelihood solution for the total set of variables. This procedure is discussed in **10.6**.

10.4.   *Test of Significance for the Number of Factors*

The particular statistical test which is the subject of this section is for the determination of the number of significant common factors. Such a test is needed because implicit in the development of **10.3** is an assumption regarding this number. Fortunately, the problem of testing the hypothesis of a given number of factors has been solved for the case of maximum-likelihood estimates of the factor loadings based upon large samples. The solution rests on a theorem (see Mood and Graybill 1963, p. 301) due to Wilks (1938), which states that -2 times the logarithm of the likelihood ratio[3] is approximately distributed as χ^2 when N is large. This statistic, following Anderson and Rubin (1956, p. 136), may be put in the form,

$$(10.27) \qquad\qquad U_m = -2 \log \lambda = N \log \frac{|\hat{\mathbf{P}}|}{|\mathbf{R}|},$$

with base e for the logarithms. It should be noted that the likelihood ratio λ depends only on the sample observations—the sample correlation matrix and the estimate of the universe correlation matrix under the hypothesis H_0 of m factors. Since the likelihood ratio varies from 0 to 1, the expression in (10.27) increases as λ decreases, approaching infinity as λ approaches zero, and the critical region for U_m is the right-hand tail of the χ^2 distribution. The test procedure, then, is to reject the hypothesis H_0 of m factors if the value of U_m exceeds χ^2 for the desired significance level; otherwise it is accepted. If the hypothesis is rejected, an alternate hypothesis of some larger number of factors may be assumed to explain the observed correlations.

In applying the foregoing test, it is necessary to know the degrees of freedom associated with the χ^2 distribution. This number is the difference between the dimensionalities of the two regions (with respect to the parameters) involved in the likelihood ratio. For the hypothesis H_0 of m common factors, the number of degrees of freedom is given by

$$(10.28) \qquad\qquad v = \tfrac{1}{2}[(n - m)^2 - n - m].$$

For computing purposes, formula (10.27) can be simplified. By formally evaluating the ratio of the two determinants and making a series of approximations (see Lawley 1940, p. 80), this expression can be reduced to

$$(10.29) \qquad\qquad U_m = N \sum_{j<k=1}^{n} \bar{r}_{jk}^2 / u_j^2 u_k^2,$$

---

[3]The likelihood ratio is defined (Mood and Graybill 1963, p. 298) as the quotient of: the maximum of the likelihood function in a specified subspace with respect to the parameters (e.g., the space of the m common factors, with dimension $nm - m[m - 1]/2$); to the maximum of the likelihood function in the total region with respect to the parameters (e.g., the total space of the n variables, with dimension $n[n - 1]/2$).

where, as previously defined, the residuals are given by:

$$\bar{r}_{jk} = r_{jk} - \hat{r}_{jk},$$

and the reproduced correlations $\hat{r}_{jk}$ are the elements of $\hat{\mathbf{P}}$.

For moderate-sized samples, Bartlett (1950, pp. 82, 84) proposes the following multiplying coefficient as more accurate than the N in (10.27):

(10.30) $N - n/3 - 2m/3 - 11/6.$

Such a modification can also be employed in the computing formula (10.29). It should be remembered that the U_m statistic was developed for large-sample tests. While a slight correction for a moderate-size sample may be in order, the coefficient (10.30) cannot make the statistic any more appropriate when N is relatively small. The suggestion in this text is that the tests be employed only for large samples.

The foregoing test makes it possible to determine the statistical significance of the assumed number m of common factors at a given level of confidence. If m^* is the true number of common factors then it is to be expected that by selecting $m \geqq m^*$ a good fit will be obtained, while for $m < m^*$ the fit will be poor. By this is meant that U_m for the former case will be small and for the latter case it will be large. A reasonable procedure is to select a confidence level, say 5%, and take as the estimate of the number of factors the smallest value of m which yields a nonsignificant U_m when compared with χ^2 at this level. Usually one would take sequential values of m, starting with a subjective judgment of the smallest number of factors required, making the test at each stage, and increasing m by one when U_m is significant, until a value of m is reached for which the corresponding U_m is nonsignificant. It should be noted that under the foregoing procedure the exact probability of concluding that $m > m^*$ is not known. However, this joint probability of rejecting the several hypotheses $m = 1, 2, \cdots, m^*$ is less than (or equal to) the probability of rejecting the single hypothesis $m = m^*$, at a given significance level.

The techniques described in this chapter are scientifically sound and powerful. Do they offer a more general guide for factor analysis? There is evidence that the test of significance for the number of common factors has applicability to situations where the maximum-likelihood method is not employed. Thus, if for any factorization the function U_m is computed and found to be insignificant when considered as a χ^2, then the particular factor solution may be assumed to contain at most that number of common factors and have an acceptable pattern of factor loadings. On the other hand, if it is found to be significant, no conclusion can be reached. It might still be true that a maximum-likelihood factorization with the same number of common factors would give an acceptable statistical fit. In other words, the test provides an upper limit for the number of common factors unless the factor loadings are estimated by an efficient method.

Before leaving this test, a comparison with the corresponding test in **9.5** is in order. There, it will be recalled, the statistic (9.31) was developed without specifying efficient estimates of the factor loadings (as in the present case of maximum-likelihood estimates). A consequence of this is that the number of degrees of freedom given by (9.32) is n greater than that given by (10.28). Hence the power[4] of the test in **9.5** is lower than in the present instance.

In addition to the mathematical contributions of Lawley and others, an empirical demonstration of the validity of the test was provided quite early (Henrysson 1950). Working with a table of random numbers from a normal population, Henrysson built 12 samples of 9 variables each containing 200 observations. After computing the variance-covariance matrix for each sample, he proceeded to estimate the factor loadings by the method of maximum likelihood under the assumption of $m = 1$ and to calculate U_1 by (10.29). For 27 degrees of freedom, the 12 values of U_1 ranged from 15.5 to 38.6 with associated χ^2 probabilities from .96 to .07. Assuming the values of P to be distributed rectangularly, the empirical results agree very well with the expected range of .85. Furthermore, upon combining the twelve samples, only one common factor was found to be significant for the explanation of the artificial data, as hypothesized.

10.5. *Computing Procedures*

While it is not expected that the maximum-likelihood method will be employed to estimate factor weights without very powerful computing facilities, nonetheless an outline of the procedure may be very useful as a means of grasping the technique for a small number of variables and factors. In the following outline, the computing procedures are illustrated by means of the example of eight physical variables.

1. **Organization of data.**—The complete correlation matrix (with unities in the diagonal) constitutes the basic data, which, for the example, comes from Table 2.3.

2. **Hypothesis regarding number of common factors** (m).—An assumption regarding the number of common factors must be made at the outset. This hypothesis is made on the basis of all available information, including any previous studies involving the given variables. The eight physical variables have been analyzed by many different methods and different investigators, but always with the same conclusion of two common factors. Hence, the immediate thought was to assume $m = 2$. Maximum-likelihood estimates were obtained under this assumption but a test of this hypothesis showed that at least three factors are statistically significant. Therefore three common factors are assumed in the following calculations.

3. **Initial set of trial values.**—The iterative procedure, which ultimately leads to the maximum-likelihood estimates, is begun with some arbitrary first approximations to the factor loadings. While almost any set of numbers may do, the closer the approximation to the actual weights the faster will the process converge. Usually, some arbitrary factor analysis of the data, employing any of the methods described in earlier chapters, will do for the initial set of trial values.[5] As indicated above, an

---

[4]By the power of a statistical test of an hypothesis is meant the probability that it rejects the alternative hypothesis when that alternative is false. The power is greatest when the probability of an error of the second kind (i.e., accepting a false hypothesis) is least.

[5]An initial minres solution has been found to hasten the convergence process.

Table 10.2

Maximum-Likelihood Estimates of Three Factors for Eight Physical Variables

Line	Instruction	Variable (j)							
		1	2	3	4	5	6	7	8
1	a_{j1}	.894	.896	.866	.871	.656	.554	.490	.551
2	a_{j2}	−.182	−.301	−.291	−.209	.663	.577	.587	.403
3	a_{j3}	−.070	.078	.011	−.101	−.148	−.051	−.292	.592
4	$u_j^2 = 1 - L_1^2 - L_2^2 - L_3^2$	.1627	.1005	.1652	.1875	.1082	.3576	.3301	.1835
5	L_1/L_4	5.495	8.915	5.242	4.645	6.083	1.549	1.484	3.003
6	L_2/L_4	−1.119	−2.995	−1.762	−1.115	6.128	1.614	1.778	2.196
7	L_3/L_4	−.430	.776	.067	−.539	−1.368	−.143	−.885	3.226
8	RL_5	26.326	26.461	25.426	25.662	20.183	17.060	15.316	17.813
9	$L_8 - L_1$	25.432	25.565	24.560	24.791	19.527	16.506	14.826	17.262
10	$a_{j1} = L_9/\sqrt{L_5 \cdot L_9}$	.883	.888	.853	.861	.678	.573	.515	.599
11	RL_6	−1.114	−2.181	−2.172	−1.375	7.226	6.238	6.426	5.255
12	$L_{11} - L_2$	−0.932	−1.880	−1.881	−1.166	6.563	5.661	5.839	4.852
13	$L_{12} - (L_6 \cdot L_{10})L_{10}$	−1.992	−2.946	−2.905	−2.199	5.749	4.973	5.221	4.133
14	$a_{j2} = L_{13}/\sqrt{L_6 \cdot L_{13}}$	−.223	−.330	−.325	−.246	.644	.557	.585	.463
15	RL_7	.079	.559	.310	.031	−.215	.086	−.303	1.790
16	$L_{15} - L_3$	.149	.481	.299	.132	−.067	.137	−.011	1.198
17	$L_{16} - (L_7 \cdot L_{10})L_{10}$	−.177	.153	−.016	−.186	−.318	−.075	−.201	.977
18	$L_{17} - (L_7 \cdot L_{14})L_{14}$	−.185	.142	−.027	−.194	−.296	−.056	−.181	.993
19	$a_{j3} = L_{18}/\sqrt{L_7 \cdot L_{18}}$	−.092	.070	−.013	−.096	−.147	−.028	−.090	.492
20	$u_j^2 = 1 - L_{10}^2 - L_{14}^2 - L_{19}^2$	.1621	.0977	.1666	.1889	.1040	.3606	.3844	.1848
.									
.	(Three iterations omitted in order to conserve space)								
.									
69	L_{58}/L_{68}	5.503	9.338	4.994	4.446	8.099	1.635	1.274	3.068
70	L_{62}/L_{68}	−1.604	−3.906	−2.111	−1.459	7.171	1.464	1.307	2.155
71	L_{67}/L_{68}	−.642	.875	−.077	−.481	−1.661	−.077	−.084	2.461
72	RL_{69}	27.279	27.270	26.172	26.492	22.155	18.610	16.674	19.115
73	$L_{72} - L_{58}$	26.404	26.395	25.332	25.642	21.448	18.016	16.142	18.503
74	$a_{j1} = L_{73}/\sqrt{L_{69} \cdot L_{73}}$	.874	.874	.838	.849	.710	.596	.534	.612
75	RL_{70}	−2.670	−3.898	−3.767	−2.932	6.931	5.869	6.015	4.720
76	$L_{75} - L_{62}$	−2.415	−3.532	−3.412	−2.653	6.305	5.337	5.469	4.290
77	$L_{76} - (L_{70} \cdot L_{74})L_{74}$	−2.553	−3.670	−3.544	−2.787	6.193	5.243	5.385	4.193
78	$a_{j2} = L_{77}/\sqrt{L_{70} \cdot L_{77}}$	−.258	−.370	−.358	−.281	.625	.529	.544	.423

Table 10.2 (*continued*)

Line	Instruction	Variable (j)							
		1	2	3	4	5	6	7	8
79	RL_{71}	$-.278$	$.215$	$-.035$	$-.250$	$-.447$	$-.125$	$-.141$	1.242
80	$L_{79} - L_{67}$	$-.176$	1.133	$-.022$	$-.158$	$-.302$	$-.097$	$-.106$	$.751$
81	$L_{80} - (L_{71} \cdot L_{74})L_{74}$	$-.147$	$.162$	$.006$	$-.130$	$-.279$	$-.077$	$-.088$	$.771$
82	$L_{81} - (L_{71} \cdot L_{78})L_{78}$	$-.167$	$.133$	$-.022$	$-.152$	$-.230$	$-.035$	$-.045$	$.804$
83	$a_{j3} = L_{82}/\sqrt{L_{71} \cdot L_{82}}$	$-.102$	$.081$	$-.013$	$-.093$	$-.141$	$-.021$	$-.028$	$.493$
84	$u_j^2 = 1 - L_{74}^2 - L_{78}^2 - L_{83}^2$	$.1592$	$.0927$	$.1694$	$.1916$	$.0854$	$.3645$	$.4181$	$.2035$

actual maximum-likelihood solution under assumption of $m = 2$ had been computed (in which the initial set of trial values came from a principal-factor solution). Hence, for the present needs, the trial values for the first two factors are taken to be the previously computed maximum-likelihood weights. For the third factor, the trial values come from the third eigenvector of a principal-factor solution that was readily available. These initial factor loadings appear in the first three rows of Table 10.2 (they are written in rows rather than columns simply for convenience of printing). The uniquenesses are computed from these values and appear in line 4. The entries in the first four lines of Table 10.2 constitute the initial set of trial values.

4. Factor weights divided by uniquenesses.—The calculations implied in the iteration equations (10.25) are organized systematically in this and the following four steps, without always translating the matrix algebra explicitly into equivalent arithmetic operations. It will be noted that in getting the second approximation for each vector of factor loadings, the original vector (a_1, a_2, or a_3) is multiplied by the inverse (U^{-2}) of the diagonal matrix of uniquenesses. This is equivalent to dividing the factor loadings of a variable by its uniqueness. These results appear in lines 5, 6, 7 of Table 10.2.

5. Determination of next trial values of first-factor weights.—The first of equations (10.25) is reduced to convenient form for arithmetic computation in lines 8, 9, 10, with the first term becoming

$$RU^{-2}a_1 = RL_5,$$

which is recorded as L_8. It should be perfectly clear when expressions that are really column vectors are recorded in rows for ease of printing, and transposes are not indicated to avoid pedantry.

The numerators for the second approximation to the first-factor weights are simply obtained in L_9. The denominators are more involved. Considering L_5 and L_9 as vectors, the expression under the radical is the dot product of these vectors as defined in **3.2** paragraph **19**. The square-root of this dot product is a constant by which each entry in line 9 is divided to get the next approximation b_{j1} according to (10.25). Actually, these factor loadings are again written as a_{j1} to simplify the notation.

6. Determination of next trial values of second-factor weights.—The next approximations to the second-factor loadings are provided by the second of equations (10.25). The rather imposing matrix manipulations are reduced to straightforward calculations in lines 11–14 of Table 10.2. The work is quite similar to that of paragraph 5 except for the additional step which corrects for the previously revised values of the first-factor weights. This correction is the term.

$$\mathbf{b_1 b_1' U^{-2} a_2}$$

from (10.25). Translated into terms of Table 10.2, this becomes

$$L_{10} L_{10}' L_6 \quad \text{or} \quad L_6' L_{10} L_{10}' \text{(transposed)},$$

wherein careful attention is paid to the designation of the elements as column vectors (without primes) or row vectors (with primes). Written more simply, the correction appears in line 13. The remaining calculations leading to b_{j2} (but written a_{j2}) are essentially the same as in the case of the first factor.

7. Determination of next trial values of third-factor weights.—The third-factor loadings are calculated in lines 15–19 of Table 10.2 on the basis of the third of the iteration equations (10.25). Again, while the matrix algebra appears very imposing, the actual calculations follow the same pattern as in the case of the first and second factors. There is now a correction for the effect of the new first-factor weights (in L_{17}) and also a correction for the new second-factor weights (in L_{18}). If there were more than three common factors there would be additional such correction terms for each of the previously computed factors.

8. Determination of next trial values of uniquenesses.—After the new approximations to the maximum-likelihood estimates of the three sets of factor loadings have been determined in lines 10, 14, and 19, the new values of the uniqueness are calculated in line 20.

9. Convergence of factor weights.—The calculations involved in paragraphs 4–8 are repeated until the factor loadings in successive iterations do not change (to a designated number of decimal places). In the illustrative example, successive values of all corresponding factor loadings agreed to within .007 after 5 iterations. This is not sufficiently accurate, and is accepted here only for illustrative purposes. Such final factor loadings appear in lines 74, 78, 83, with the associated uniquenesses in line 84 of Table 10.2.,

10. Residual matrix.—To assist in calculating the residuals, the reproduced correlations ($\hat{r}_{jk}$) are first determined according to (2.50) since the factors are orthogonal. These appear in the upper half of Table 10.3. Then, subtracting these values from the corresponding observed correlations of Table 2.3, the residual correlations ($\bar{r}_{jk}$) are obtained and recorded in the lower half of Table 10.3.

11. Statistical test of hypothesis regarding number of factors.—The hypothesis of $m = 3$ for the illustrative example can now be tested. If hand methods were employed (10.29) would be useful, but on a computer (10.27) would be programmed. In any event, for $N = 305$ cases the resulting statistic is $U_3 = 46.0$. The degrees of

Table 10.3

Reproduced Correlations and Residuals[a]

Variable	1	2	3	4	5	6	7	8
1		.851	.826	.824	.474	.387	.329	.375
2	−.005		.864	.838	.378	.323	.263	.418
3	−.021	.017		.813	.373	.310	.253	.355
4	.035	−.012	−.012		.440	.359	.303	.355
5	−.001	−.002	.007	−.004		.757	.723	.629
6	.011	.003	.009	−.030	.005		.607	.578
7	−.028	.014	−.016	.024	.007	−.024		.543
8	.007	−.003	−.010	.010	.000	−.001	−.004	

[a] Reproduced correlations appear in the upper triangle and the residuals in the lower triangle.

freedom, as given by (10.28), is $v = 7$. By referring to Table D in the Appendix it will be found that for 7 degrees of freedom a value of $\chi^2 = 18.5$ produces a probability $P = .01$. Therefore, if the hypothesis of only three common factors is correct, the probability of getting a value of $\chi^2 > 18.5$ is only 1 in 100. Since the actual value 46.0 is considerably in excess of 18.5, the hypothesis is rejected and it must be assumed that more than three common factors are required for adequate explanation of the observed data. No doubt the rejection of the hypothesis of three factors is due in large part to the poor solution (noted in paragraph **9** above). The conclusion, nonetheless, is on purely statistical grounds. It is doubtful if a factor analyst or applied statistician would look for any more (practical) relationships among the variables from the third-factor residuals in the lower half of Table 10.3.

10.6. *Numerical Illustrations*

It should be quite evident from the work in the preceding section that the maximum-likelihood method for estimating factor weights requires tremendous computations. While this method implied insuperable computing difficulties in the past—causing it to lay dormant for almost two decades—the modern electronic computers make the method feasible.

Additional problems will be considered in this section, but first a few more comments about the example of the eight physical variables. It came as a surprise to find that two factors inadequately reproduced their intercorrelations after the many crude guides pointed to precisely two clearly distinguishable clusters. What was even more surprising, then, was the large U_m for the hypothesis $m = 3$, indicating that a fourth factor really should be sought. At this point it was only natural to question the numerical calculations, and finding them to be accurate, to question the theoretical basis. One area of doubt was the approximations in going from formula (10.27) to the simpler computing formula (10.29). To this end, the determinants of the observed correlations and of the reproduced correlations (with two and with three factors) were calculated. These values were then employed in formula (10.27) to get $U_2 = 69.9$ and $U_3 = 51.0$ for the two-factor and three-factor cases, respectively. The corresponding values by use of formula (10.29) are 80.2 and 46.0. Of course the numbers differ a little, but the same conclusions would be drawn from the results of either formula—rejecting the hypothesis of two factors in the first case, and of three factors in the second case. This analysis lends credence to the use of the simpler formula.

In the course of experimenting with different maximum-likelihood procedures, the example of eight physical variables has been used extensively. Such computer programs included two provided by Donald F. Morrison (when he was associated with the National Institutes of Health); a procedure[6] of Bargmann (1963) which is based on the model developed by Howe (1955); the program (Harman 1966) outlined in (10.26); a program (Joreskog 1967a,b) that employs the method of Fletcher and Powell (1963); and a procedure by Jennrich and Robinson (1969) that uses a Newton-Raphson algorithm for solving the likelihood equations. An early solution obtained with a program from the National Institutes of Health (appearing in the second edition of this book) has since been found to be erroneous, probably for the same reason as the crude solution of Table 10.2, namely, lack of convergence. Two proper solutions are shown in Table 10.4—one produced by a program based on the algorithm (10.26)

Table 10.4

Two Maximum-Likelihood Solutions for Eight Physical Variables
(Three common factors)

Variable j	Harman Solution				Jennrich Solution			
	F_1	F_2	F_3	h_j^2	F_1	F_2	F_3	h_j^2
1	.862	.320	.164	.873	.846	.189	−.348	.873
2	.867	.432	−.243	.998	1.000	.000	.000	1.000
3	.808	.388	−.051	.807	.881	.055	−.164	.806
4	.833	.343	.180	.843	.826	.160	−.368	.843
5	.748	−.584	.090	.910	.376	.876	.031	.910
6	.625	−.499	.007	.640	.326	.725	.093	.641
7	.569	−.515	−.020	.589	.277	.704	.130	.589
8	.603	−.344	−.164	.509	.415	.543	.204	.509
V_p	4.481	1.532	.156	6.169	3.671	2.148	.352	6.171

and the other on the Newton-Raphson algorithm. The individual factor loadings are different in the two solutions because the first one is in canonical form while the second is not. They are in very close agreement, however, as can be judged from their communalities, which have a maximum difference of only .002. Diverse maximum-

---

[6]Actually a step-wise process in which each factor in turn is estimated by maximum-likelihood, but the result for a set of several factors is not the same as a maximum-likelihood solution for the specified number of factors.

likelihood solutions for the same data arise, in part, because of the different standards for convergence—only 5 iterations when calculated by hand versus hundreds of iterations in one experimental run on a computer—but also because a different relative maximum may be sought, depending on the starting point in the iteration process and other aspects of the algorithm.

It is of interest to note the statistical inference that might be drawn from these solutions. The solution in Table 10.2, based on only 5 iterations on a desk calculator, is understandably crude, and the statistical test in **10.5**, step **11**, led to the conclusion that three common factors were not sufficient to explain the observed data. The solution of Table 10.4, however, leads to a somewhat different inference. For that solution, the associated statistic $U_3 = 24.1$. While this value is greater than $\chi^2 = 18.5$ with a probability $P = .01$ for $\nu = 7$ degrees of freedom, it does not exceed $\chi^2 = 24.3$ for $P = .001$. Therefore, this solution may be accepted at the 0.1 percent level of significance.

The maximum-likelihood procedure developed by Joreskog (1967a,b) was also applied to this problem. Four different sets of initial values for the uniquenesses were attempted and identical final results were obtained in each instance. No matter what starting values, the program determined that the uniqueness for variable 2 would have to be zero to attain a maximum. The effect of that variable was partialed out, and two maximum-likelihood factors were obtained from the matrix of partial correlations among the remaining seven variables. The latter solution is then combined with the principal component through variable 2 to yield the maximum-likelihood solution for the eight variables in terms of three factors. Since the result is not in canonical form, the individual factor weights are not compared with those in Table 10.4. However, it is of interest to note that the communalities:

$$.873, \quad 1.000, \quad .806, \quad .844, \quad .910, \quad .641, \quad .589, \quad .509,$$

are almost identical with the Harman and Jennrich solutions. Also, a slightly different test of goodness of fit applied by Joreskog (1967a, p. 474) produced a test statistic of 22.67 with 8 degrees of freedom, leading to the same conclusion. It would appear that this is the true maximum-likelihood solution while the procedures that led to earlier solutions had not really converged.

This example illustrates the general principle that one tends to underestimate the number of factors that are statistically significant. For twenty years, two factors had been considered adequate, but statistically two factors do *not* adequately account for the observed correlations based on a random sample of 305 girls. However, the third factor (whose total contribution to the variance ranges from 2 percent to 5 percent for the different solutions) has little "practical significance," and certainly a fourth factor would have no practical value.

The next illustration is for the 5 socio-economic variables introduced in **2.2**. In making a choice of hypothesis regarding the number of common factors, one, two, or three, all appear somewhat reasonable, but the selection of $m = 2$ is more in keeping with the previous work. Two different computer programs were employed and with three different covergence standards (maximum change in factor loadings required to be less than .0005, .00001, and .000005) all the results were almost identical

Table 10.5

Maximum-Likelihood Solution for Five Socio-Economic Variables
(Two common factors)

Variable j	Arbitrary Form		Canonical Form		Communality
	F_1	F_2	F_1	F_2	h_j^2
1	.999	−.008	.621	.783	.998
2	.019	.899	.711	−.550	.809
3	.974	.109	.697	.689	.961
4	.446	.785	.891	−.147	.815
5	.030	.960	.766	−.580	.923
V_p	2.147	2.360	2.759	1.748	4.507

to three decimal places. In Table 10.5 the solution is shown in the arbitrary form produced by the basic maximum-likelihood program, and also after it has been put in the canonical form of **8.7**.

The similarity between this solution and the minres solution of Table 9.1 may be noted. Also, for this example, the maximum-likelihood solution is very close to the principal-factor solution of Table 8.2. The total communality produced by the maximum-likelihood solution represents 90 percent of the total variance of the five variables. This is a very exceptional situation that should not ordinarily be expected. Of course, even this high proportion must be less than the amount accounted for by the first two principal components (see Table 8.1). While the contributions of the factors and the total communality is of importance in both the minres and maximum-likelihood solutions, it must be remembered that these methods have other primary objectives than maximizing variance, which is the case only in the principal-factor methods.

One of the earliest large-scale applications of the maximum-likelihood method was made by Lord (1956) in a study of speed factors in tests and academic grades. Using Whirlwind I, an early electronic computer, he analyzed 33 variables into 10 maximum-likelihood factors. Lord originally hypothesized at least 9 common factors, but he could not arrive at such a solution directly because imaginary numbers were produced for the factor loadings. He found that the method broke down unless extremely close initial approximations to the actual solution were available whenever m was large. Hence, he carried out the computations in stages: starting with $m = 4$ and somewhat arbitrary trial values, he obtained maximum-likelihood estimates of the factor loadings; then he took the hypothesis of $m = 5$, using the previously determined weights for the first four factors and guesses based upon the residuals for the fifth; proceeding in this manner he was able to obtain ten factors without encountering further difficulty. Tests for the number of common factors produced a significant χ^2, with a probability well below the 1% level, in each instance from $m = 4$ through $m = 9$. However, the χ^2 dropped sufficiently so that ten factors were found to be significant at the 7% level. More than ten years later Joreskog

(1967a) obtained solutions for $m = 9, 10, 11$ in about 1.5 to 2 minutes each of CPU time on a CDC 3600. He showed that 10 factors were significant at the 4% level and 11 factors at the 38% level.

The final example consists of the twenty-four psychological tests whose correlations are given in Table 7.4. In the mid-1960s the determination of maximum-likelihood loadings for such a problem was still viewed as somewhat of an Herculean task. With careful choices of initial values, based upon the experience with this data set in **9.7**, a maximum-likelihood solution for four factors was reached in just under five minutes CPU time on a Philco 2000. This solution, in canonical form, is shown in Table 10.6. In 1974, using a program of Joreskog (1967b) on an IBM 360/65 with extended core (i.e., relatively slow memory) an identical solution[7] was obtained directly from the correlation matrix, along with a solution in terms of five factors,

Table 10.6

Maximum-Likelihood Solution for Twenty-four Psychological Tests (Four common factors)

Test j	F_1	F_2	F_3	F_4	h_j^2
1	.601	.019	.388	.221	.561
2	.372	−.025	.252	.132	.220
3	.413	−.117	.388	.144	.356
4	.487	−.100	.254	.192	.349
5	.691	−.304	−.279	.035	.648
6	.690	−.409	−.200	−.076	.689
7	.677	−.409	−.292	.084	.718
8	.674	−.189	−.099	.122	.515
9	.697	−.454	−.212	−.080	.743
10	.476	.534	−.486	.092	.757
11	.558	.332	−.142	−.090	.450
12	.472	.508	−.139	.256	.566
13	.602	.244	.028	.295	.510
14	.423	.058	.015	−.415	.354
15	.394	.089	.097	−.362	.304
16	.510	.095	.347	−.249	.451
17	.466	.197	−.004	−.381	.402
18	.515	.312	.152	−.147	.407
19	.443	.089	.109	−.150	.238
20	.614	−.118	.126	−.038	.408
21	.589	.227	.057	.123	.417
22	.608	−.107	.127	−.038	.399
23	.687	−.044	.138	.098	.503
24	.651	.177	−.212	−.017	.501
Variance	7.643	1.681	1.229	.911	11.464

[7]This solution is not in canonical form and hence the factor loadings cannot be compared with those in Table 10.6. However, the communalities for the twenty-four tests agreed except for an occasional round-off error and the total was identical.

in 50 seconds CPU time for both. An even more efficient program (Wingersky 1974, unpublished) produced identical results for four and five factors in the total CPU time of only 26 seconds.

Obviously, the choice of method for direct factor analysis need no longer be influenced greatly by computational costs, as was the case in the past. Whether the investigator uses the principal factor, minres, maximum-likelihood, or one of the methods of the next chapter should depend on other considerations. These include "distributional" assumptions in the maximum-likelihood method; "least-squares" assumptions in the principal-factor and minres methods, with communality estimates being of paramount importance in the former case while the diagonal values are eliminated from consideration of fit of the model in the latter case; "psycho-metric" approach (in contrast to statistical) in image and alpha factor analysis that are discussed in chapter 11.

11   Other Direct Methods

11.1. *Introduction*

In the preceding chapters of part ii, methods were presented for the direct determination of a factor solution for a given correlation matrix. After carefully arguing for the distinction between component analysis and factor analysis—the distinction between the model of (2.8) and that of (2.9)—it may come as somewhat of a surprise to learn that the more sophisticated and advanced methods of factor analysis pass back and forth between the two. Thus, the mathematically determinate components (linear combinations of observed variables) are used to approximate factors—linear combinations of unattainable common parts of the observed variables. Examples of this process are presented in the next three sections, dealing with canonical factor analysis, image analysis, and alpha factor analysis.

A concept central to these methods is that of "scaling." As noted in chapter 2, a set of variables considered for factor analysis generally is put in standard form (i.e., scaled to produce means of zero and variances of 1) in order to equalize the impact of the variables regardless of their original metrics or variances. Subsequently, such standardized variables may be rescaled in order to achieve certain desirable objectives. Any rescaling of the variables is manifested, in general, by $\mathbf{SRS}$, where at this stage $\mathbf{S}$ is an unspecified diagonal matrix that converts the correlation matrix to a dispersion matrix in which the variances are changed from 1's to s_j^2's. The resulting factor pattern based on $\mathbf{SRS}$ usually will be different from that based on $\mathbf{R}$. However, it is customary to rescale the factor results back to the standardized metric of the observed variables.

By rescaling the observed variables so that the reduced correlation matrix (denoted simply by $\mathbf{R}$ in this paragraph) is made Gramian and obtaining the characteristic roots and vectors of such rescaled matrices, some interesting factor results ensue. In particular, canonical factor analysis rescales in the metric of the unique parts ($\mathbf{U}^{-1}\mathbf{R}\mathbf{U}^{-1}$); image analysis employs the error of prediction ($\mathbf{S}$ as defined in **11.3**) in the regression of each observed variable on the remaining $n - 1$ variables

$(\mathbf{S}^{-1}\mathbf{R}\mathbf{S}^{-1})$; and alpha factor analysis rescales in the metric of the common parts $(\mathbf{H}^{-1}\mathbf{R}\mathbf{H}^{-1})$. These formal parallels, derived from the scaling operations, are noted here simply to provide an overall perspective to the methods that are described in **11.2**, **11.3**, and **11.4**.

Finally, before leaving the direct methods of factor analysis to which this part of the text is devoted, one additional procedure is presented, the multiple-group method in **11.5**.

11.2. *Canonical Factor Analysis*

The paradigm of canonical correlation (Hotelling 1936b)—the weighting of variables in each of two sets so as to attain the maximum correlation between the two composites—has been found useful in the development of an alternative method of factor analysis. The originator of canonical factor analysis poses the problem as follows: "What is that factor variable which is maximally related to [the observed variables]? The solution to this problem depends on a canonical correlation analysis of the hypothetical factor variables [the common parts] with the measurable variables" (Rao 1955, p. 102). This is in contrast to the objective of component or principal-factor analysis in which each factor is asked to explain as much as possible of the variation of the observed variables.

In the method of canonical factor analysis, a factor variable is sought that is predictable from the observed data with maximum precision; next, a second factor variable that is maximally related is determined subject to the condition that it is orthogonal to the first; and so on, until a specified number of factor variables have been extracted. These factor variables or factor scores[1] are the constructs or hypothetical factor measurements **f** in the common parts **c** in (2.36), of the observed variables **z**. To get the canonical correlations between the set **z** and the set **f** involves the unknown unique variances $\mathbf{U}^2$.

The development of the method proceeds from the determination of canonical correlations between linear composites of the observed variables (z_j) and linear composites of the factor variables (F_p). By considering n manifest variables and m hypothetical (factor) variables together, the resulting square supermatrix of correlations may be represented by

$$\begin{bmatrix} \mathbf{R} & \mathbf{A} \\ \mathbf{A}' & \mathbf{I} \end{bmatrix}$$

of order $(n + m)$, in which the factors have been assumed uncorrelated. Appealing to standard canonical analysis (Anderson 1958, pp. 288–96) of such a matrix, Harris (1962) points out that the roots ν_p of the determinantal equation

(11.1) $|\mathbf{A}\mathbf{A}' - \nu\mathbf{R}| = 0$

are the squared canonical correlations.

---

[1]The determination of factor scores for the more traditional methods of factor analysis is treated in chapter 16.

Then by considering $\mathbf{R} - \mathbf{U}^2$ as an approximation for $\mathbf{AA'}$, the method of canonical factor analysis (Rao 1955) leads to the equation

(11.2)
$$[(\mathbf{R} - \mathbf{U}^2) - \nu\mathbf{R}]\mathbf{b} = 0$$

for the maximal relationships between the z's and the F's, in which $\mathbf{b}$ is a column vector of weights for the linear composite of the z's. This may be simplified further to

(11.3)
$$[\mathbf{U}^{-1}(\mathbf{R} - \mathbf{U}^2)\mathbf{U}^{-1} - \lambda\mathbf{I}]\mathbf{q} = 0$$

or

(11.4)
$$[\mathbf{U}^{-1}\mathbf{R}\mathbf{U}^{-1} - (\lambda + 1)\mathbf{I}]\mathbf{q} = 0$$

where the relationships to the parameters in (11.2) are as follows:

(11.5)
$$\lambda = \frac{\nu}{1 - \nu}$$

and

(11.6)
$$\mathbf{q} = \mathbf{Ub}.$$

Here $\mathbf{q}$ is the eigenvector corresponding to the largest eigenvalue $(\lambda_1 + 1)$ of the matrix $\mathbf{U}^{-1}\mathbf{R}\mathbf{U}^{-1}$. As can be seen by comparing (11.3) and (11.4) with the standard statement of a characteristic equation (8.11), the eigenvalues of the matrix $\mathbf{U}^{-1}\mathbf{R}\mathbf{U}^{-1}$ in (11.4) are one greater than the corresponding eigenvalues of the matrix $\mathbf{U}^{-1}(\mathbf{R} - \mathbf{U}^2)\mathbf{U}^{-1}$ in (11.3). Also, it should be noted that the number of real, nonzero canonical correlations is equal to the number of roots of $\mathbf{U}^{-1}\mathbf{R}\mathbf{U}^{-1}$ that are greater than one, or equivalently, is equal to the number of positive roots of $\mathbf{R} - \mathbf{U}^2$ (Harris 1962, p. 250).

Next, the factor pattern $\mathbf{A}$ may be expressed by

(11.7)
$$\mathbf{A} = \mathbf{UQ}\boldsymbol{\Lambda}^{1/2}$$

where $\mathbf{Q}$ is the matrix of unit-length eigenvectors associated with the m largest eigenvalues of (11.3) and $\boldsymbol{\Lambda}$ is the diagonal matrix of these eigenvalues. It can be shown that these factor loadings are unaffected by arbitrarily rescaling the observed variables. This "scale-freeness" property of the maximum-likelihood method was observed in the earliest reports of the method (Lawley 1940). Special emphasis on the importance of the invariance of the factors under the rescaling involved in canonical factor analysis, and a simple proof of the property, is given by Kaiser and Caffrey (1965, p. 4).

Since the vector of the common parts (2.36) is the product $\mathbf{Af}$, the factors themselves are given by (see **16.3** and **16.7**)

(11.8)
$$\mathbf{f} = (\mathbf{A'A})^{-1}\mathbf{A'c}.$$

From this it might appear that the factors are determinate. They are from $\mathbf{c}$, but the common parts of the variables are not directly obtainable. Therefore, the factor measurements can only be approximated from the observable data.

The foregoing brief account of the theoretical development can be summarized in the following manner (Rao 1955, p. 103). The factor variable that is most highly correlated with a linear composite of the observed z's is the linear combination $\mathbf{q}_1'\mathbf{f}$, where

$\mathbf{q}_1$ is the characteristic vector corresponding to the largest root $(\lambda_1 + 1)$ of the characteristic equation (11.4). The second factor variable, uncorrelated with the first and having the next highest correlation with the z's is $\mathbf{q}_2'\mathbf{f}$, where $\mathbf{q}_2$ is the characteristic vector corresponding to the second largest root $(\lambda_2 + 1)$ of (11.4), and so on for as many factors as the number of non-zero values of ν or of $(\lambda + 1) > 1$.

Rao (1955) developed an iterative procedure that was programmed (Golub 1954) for the Illiac. It involves initial trial values of the uniquenesses, based on an assumed number of common factors; getting a trial value of $\mathbf{A}$ from which an estimate of the population correlation matrix is obtained and hence a new $\mathbf{U}^2$ is determined; and the process is continued until a stable value of $\mathbf{U}^2$ is reached. The procedure is slow in arriving at a solution, but since the equations of canonical factor analysis satisfy the equations (10.14)–(10.17) of the maximum-likelihood method (Rao 1955, p. 106), the more efficient computing procedures discussed in chapter 10 apply equally well to canonical factor analysis. Nonetheless, the canonical factor analysis method was one of the earliest programmed for maximum-likelihood estimates.

An example of a canonical factor analysis actually performed on the Illiac is shown in Table 11.1. It is for the problem of thirteen psychological tests for which several

Table 11.1

Canonical Factor Analysis for Thirteen Psychological Tests
(Five common factors)

Test j	Factor Coefficients					Uniqueness u_j^2	Communality h_j^2
	F_1	F_2	F_3	F_4	F_5		
1	.492	.171	.512	−.058	.056	.460	.540
2	.305	.042	.292	−.228	−.049	.766	.234
3	.347	−.024	.544	−.034	−.150	.559	.441
4	.425	.010	.392	.198	−.020	.626	.374
5	.817	−.122	−.140	−.251	−.171	.206	.794
6	.795	−.241	−.029	.068	.233	.250	.750
7	.812	−.217	−.082	.239	−.032	.229	.771
8	.716	−.008	.085	.149	−.186	.423	.577
9	.799	−.283	−.089	−.083	.053	.264	.736
10	.419	.622	−.359	.086	−.055	.298	.702
11	.488	.474	−.057	−.173	.311	.407	.593
12	.367	.663	.015	.063	−.132	.404	.596
13	.550	.476	.266	.003	.075	.395	.605
V	4.597	1.510	1.042	.291	.273	5.287	7.713

solutions in terms of three factors have been obtained previously. In this analysis, tests for the number of common factors show five factors significant at the 5% level and three factors significant at the 1% level. The latter agrees with the subjective judgments made earlier regarding the number of factors for practical consideration.

11.3. *Image Factor Analysis*

In this and the following section methods are considered that involve the concept of a "universe of content". The distinguishing notion is that the set of n variables under consideration is a subset (not necessarily a representative sample) of an infinite universe of such measures. In developing his image theory, Guttman (1953) only assumes that the universe of variables can be so arranged that the particular sample contains the first n variables. On the other hand, with respect to the individuals an indefinitely large number is assumed so that problems associated with sampling of people are avoided. Thus, a sample of n variables can be considered standardized (zero mean and unit variance) in the universe of individuals and their correlation matrix $\mathbf{R}_n$ is Gramian, with ones in the diagonal, of course. Since the correlation between any two variables does not depend on any of the other variables in the set, it follows that as more and more variables from the universe of content are added to an initial sample of variables "*there is always a limiting matrix*, which we shall denote by $\mathbf{R}_\infty$,

$$\mathbf{R}_\infty = \lim_{n \to \infty} \mathbf{R}_n.$$

$\mathbf{R}_\infty$ is an infinite Gramian matrix, and represents the correlations between all variables in the infinite universe of content" (Guttman 1953, p. 281).

Since the interest in this text is in the application of Guttman's theory to empirical data, the special notation $\mathbf{R}_n$, calling attention to the sample of n variables from a universe of content, will not be employed. Instead, the standard notation $\mathbf{R}$ will be used for the matrix of correlations among n variables.

The point of departure for image theory is the use of the multiple-correlation approach to identify "commoness." Guttman proposed this in contradistinction to the partial-correlation approach of the more traditional factor analysis, in which the new hypothetical constructs (the common factors) are partialled out to explain the correlations among the variables. Alternatively, these correlations can be explained by means of the multiple regression of each variable on the remaining $n - 1$ variables of the set. The squared multiple correlation (SMC) for a particular variable represents the proportion of its total variance that is dependent on the remaining variables or how much it has in common with the other variables. The remainder of the unit variance represents the proportion of the variance that is unique to the particular variable.

From multiple regression theory each variable can be expressed as the sum of two parts, or for the set of n variables:

(11.9) $\mathbf{z} = \mathbf{p} + \mathbf{e}$

where $\mathbf{p}$ is a vector of the predictable parts and $\mathbf{e}$ is a vector of errors of prediction. These, in a way, correspond to the factor model (2.35), in which the observable variables $\mathbf{z}$ are expressed in terms of common parts $\mathbf{c}$ and unique parts $\mathbf{e}$. Some specific conclusions that follow from multiple-regression theory are that the predictable and error parts are uncorrelated and that the error parts correlate zero with each variable. Hence, each p_j is determined entirely by the remaining $n - 1$ variables while the e_j bears no relation to the other variables. The detailed study of the common and "alien" parts of observed variables through the multiple-correlation approach is designated *image analysis* by Guttman (1953), a name suggested to him by his reading of Jackson (1924).

At the core of image analysis are the concepts of an "image" of a variable, by which is meant its multiple regression on all the other variables of a set, namely:

$$(11.10) \qquad p_j = \sum_{k=1}^{n} \beta_{jk} z_k \qquad (k \neq j)$$

where the β's are the multiple regression coefficients; and of an "anti-image," by which is meant the error of estimate of the multiple regression. These ideas may be visualized geometrically, with the image p_j of the test vector z_j being its projection into the hyperplane of the remaining $n - 1$ variables and the anti-image e_j being orthogonal to the hyperplane.

In the foregoing, the terms "image" and "anti-image" were used in a generic sense. More strictly, Guttman defines the predicted values p_j from the remaining $n - 1$ variables in a sample of n variables as the *partial image* of z_j. Then, the limit of the partial images of z_j as $n \to \infty$ is what he calls the *total image* of z_j in the universe of content (Guttman 1953). He makes a similar distinction between the partial anti-image and the total anti-image of a variable. These distinctions will not be carried out in this text since a full development of image analysis is not given here. The interested reader may wish to explore the original work of Guttman (1953, 1956, 1960) and to refer to excellent summaries by Kaiser (1963) and Muliak (1972, pp. 186–207). Of special interest is the integrating work of Harris (1962) in which he brings out the relationship of Guttman's psychometric work in image theory to the statistical factor analysis work of Rao (1955).

The rationale for image factor analysis may be stated in either of two ways: (1) as a means of analyzing the structure of a set of variables for a population of individuals; or (2) as a means of restoring the Gramian properties of a "reduced" correlation matrix in the more traditional factor analytic practice. Guttman's original endeavors are aimed at the former while its application to factor analysis rests on the latter. For studying the structure of **R**, Guttman (1953) established the fundamental identity in image analysis:

$$(11.11) \qquad \mathbf{R} = \mathbf{G} - \mathbf{\Gamma} + 2\mathbf{S}^2$$

where **G** and **Γ** are the covariance matrices of the images and anti-images (the notation being selected, no doubt, to call attention to the fact that these matrices were Gramian), and $\mathbf{S}^2$ is the diagonal matrix of variance error of estimate of each of the z_j from the remaining $n - 1$ variables (i.e., the anti-image variances). This partitioning of the correlation matrix into image and anti-image covariances corresponds roughly to the fundamental theorem of factor analysis:

$$(11.12) \qquad \mathbf{R} = \mathbf{A}\mathbf{\Phi}\mathbf{A}' + \mathbf{U}^2$$

in which the partitioning is in terms of new hypothetical constructs (the common factors—**A** being a weight matrix and **Φ** being their covariance matrix) and the diagonal matrix of uniquenesses.

It has been shown (Guttman 1956) that if the ratio of a given number of factors m to the number of variables n approaches zero as $n \to \infty$, then image analysis in the universe of content becomes identical with factor analysis. Under these circumstances, or more practically, when the number of common factors is small compared with n,

$$(11.13) \qquad \mathbf{S}^2 \to \mathbf{U}^2 \quad \text{as} \quad n \to \infty.$$

Then the traditional factor analysis of the reduced correlation matrix $\mathbf{R} - \mathbf{U}^2$ (where, of course, $\mathbf{U}^2$ is not known in advance) can be approximated from the theoretical relationship

$$(11.14) \qquad \mathbf{G} \to \mathbf{R} - \mathbf{S}^2 \quad \text{as} \quad n \to \infty,$$

by taking

$$(11.15) \qquad \mathbf{S}^2 = (\text{diag } \mathbf{R}^{-1})^{-1} = \text{diag } (1/r^{jj})$$

and factor analyzing the reduced correlation matrix $\mathbf{R} - \mathbf{S}^2$ with SMC's in the diagonal.

As noted in **5.6** the SMC for a variable j is a lower bound for the communality h_j^2, so that s_j^2 (the jth diagonal element of the matrix $\mathbf{S}^2$) is an upper bound for the uniqueness u_j^2. It can be seen, of course, that the diagonal value of $\mathbf{R} - \mathbf{S}^2$ for any variable j, namely, $(1 - s_j^2)$, is the SMC for that variable according to (5.36). Now, by taking

$$(11.16) \qquad \mathbf{S}^{-1} = \text{diag } (\sqrt{r^{jj}})$$

as a scale factor, define the rescaled correlation matrix by

$$(11.17) \qquad \mathbf{R}^* = \mathbf{S}^{-1} \mathbf{R} \mathbf{S}^{-1},$$

which is Gramian. This procedure has been likened to the traditional approach of finding communality estimates to "insert" in the diagonal: "We are inserting squared multiples in the diagonal and . . . adjusting (usually slightly lowering) the off-diagonals 'just enough' to keep the matrix honest, or Gramian" (Kaiser 1963, p. 161).

Then, the principal-factor method applied to the reduced matrix $\mathbf{R} - \mathbf{S}^2$ produces (in its real factors) results that are closely related to the components of $\mathbf{R}^*$ that have roots greater than one, and the latter can be related to the corresponding components of the image covariance matrix (Harris 1962). Thus, factoring $\mathbf{R} - \mathbf{S}^2$ may be considered as an alternative to analyzing Guttman's partial image covariance matrix.

An algorithm for image analysis can be put in the following form:
1. Starting with a correlation matrix $\mathbf{R}$, obtain $\mathbf{R}^{-1}$.
2. $\mathbf{S}^2 = (\text{diag } \mathbf{R}^{-1})^{-1} = (1/r^{jj})$; $\mathbf{S}^{-1} = \sqrt{r^{jj}}$; $(\text{SMC}) = \text{diag } (\mathbf{I} - \mathbf{S}^2)$.
3. $\mathbf{R}^* = \mathbf{S}^{-1} \mathbf{R} \mathbf{S}^{-1}$.
4. Compute eigenvalues and eigenvectors of: (a) $\mathbf{R} - \mathbf{S}^2$ and (b) $\mathbf{R}^*$.
5. Determine $\mathbf{G}$ from (11.11), as follows:

$$\mathbf{G} = \mathbf{R} + \mathbf{S}^2 \mathbf{R}^{-1} \mathbf{S}^2 - 2\mathbf{S}^2$$

where $\mathbf{S}^2 \mathbf{R}^{-1} \mathbf{S}^2 = \Gamma$ (Kaiser 1963, p. 158).
6. $\mathbf{G}^* = \mathbf{S}^{-1} \mathbf{G} \mathbf{S}^{-1}$.
7. Compute eigenvalues and eigenvectors of: (a) $\mathbf{G}$ and (b) $\mathbf{G}^*$.

8. Compute factor pattern for $R-S^2$ from step 4(a):

$$A = Q\Lambda_m^{1/2}$$

where Q = eigenvectors and Λ_m = m eigenvalues > 0.

9. Compute factor pattern for G, as in step 8 but using eigenvalues and eigenvectors from step 7(a) with m = eigenvalues > 1.

10. Compute factor pattern for R^*:

$$A = SQ\Lambda_m^{1/2}$$

where Q and Λ are from step 4(b), with m = eigenvalues > 1.

11. Compute factor pattern for G^* by postmultiplying A of step 10 by D, where

$$D = \text{diag } (I - \Lambda_m^{-1})$$

and Λ_m is the matrix of eigenvalues retained in step 10.

12. Put all factor patterns A in canonical form according to **8.7**.

Table 11.2

R Inverse and Related Matrices for Five Socio-Economic Variables*

Variable	R^{-1}				
	1	2	3	4	5
1	31.83970	7.28932	−31.20484	−1.17196	−2.28854
2	7.28932	5.62659	−7.34618	−0.25620	−3.92454
3	−31.20484	−7.34618	32.44806	−0.82277	3.72301
4	−1.17196	−0.25620	−0.82277	4.66675	−3.28140
5	−2.28854	−3.92454	3.72301	−3.28140	6.53628

Related Diagonal Matrices

	S^2	S	S^{-1}	$(SMC) = \text{diag}(I - S^2)$
1	.03141	.17722	5.64267	.96859
2	.17773	.42158	2.37204	.82227
3	.03082	.17555	5.69632	.96918
4	.21428	.46291	2.16027	.78572
5	.15299	.39114	2.55661	.84701

*The reader is reminded that the only reason for showing so many decimal places in this and the following table is to provide a means for checking computations.

The relationships noted by Harris (1962) can perhaps be appreciated best by means of a simple example. To that end let us work with the five socio-economic variables whose correlations are given in Table 2.2. Designating that matrix by **R**, its inverse is shown in Table 11.2 and the reduced matrix (ones from the principal diagonal replaced by SMC's of each variable on the remaining four variables) appears as $R - S^2$ in Table 11.3. The matrix **G** is shown in the second block and the rescaled versions of **R** and **G** are shown in the next two blocks. From inspection of the data in this table, one can see the following interesting relationships among these matrices: the diagonals (SMC's) in the first two matrices are identical—the off-diagonal values in **G** having been adjusted in order to make it Gramian; the values in the diagonal of **R*** are one greater than the corresponding values of **G***. As a consequence of the last relationship, the unit-length eigenvectors of **G*** are the same as the unit-length eigenvectors of **R***, as was first noted by Harris (1962).

In the right-hand portion of Table 11.3 are the factor patterns obtained from the several matrices. First, of course, the results of factoring the reduced matrix **R** − **S**² are essentially the same, for the first two factors, as those in Table 8.2. The third factor

Table 11.3

Image Analysis of Five Socio-Economic Variables

Variable j	**R** − **S**² (non-Gramian)					Factor Pattern			
	1	2	3	4	5	F_1	F_2	F_3	h_j^2
1	.96859	.00975	.97245	.43887	.02241	.62533	.76621	.04379	.98003
2	.00975	.82227	.15428	.69141	.86307	.71369	−.55516	−.12685	.83365
3	.97245	.15428	.96918	.51472	.12193	.71448	.67935	−.08988	.98008
4	.43887	.69141	.51472	.78572	.77765	.87899	−.15847	.10699	.80918
5	.02241	.86307	.12193	.77765	.84701	.74215	−.57806	.04490	.88696
Variance						2.73429	1.71607	.03955	4.48991
	G = **R** + **S**²**R**⁻¹**S**² − 2**S**² (Gramian)								
1	.96859	.05044	.94225	.43098	.01141	.67037	.71307		.95786
2	.05044	.82227	.11404	.68165	.75636	.66831	−.58026		.78334
3	.94225	.11404	.96918	.50929	.13948	.74549	.63373		.95737
4	.43098	.68165	.50929	.78572	.67007	.85369	−.19294		.76601
5	.01141	.75636	.13948	.67007	.84701	.66809	−.59565		.80114
Variance						2.62692	1.63881		4.26573
	R* = **S**⁻¹**RS**⁻¹ (Gramian)								
1	31.83970	.13050	31.25692	5.34968	.32329	.58101	.81020	.00892	.99408
2	.13050	5.62659	2.08462	3.54296	5.23400	.76548	−.54204	−.32026	.98233
3	31.25692	2.08462	32.44806	6.33392	1.77570	.67200	.72618	−.12784	.99526
4	5.34968	3.54296	6.33392	4.66675	4.29494	.92402	−.11007	.25953	.93328
5	.32329	5.23400	1.77570	4.29494	6.53628	.80024	−.55246	.10755	.95716
Variance						2.86932	1.79488	.19791	4.86211
	G* = **S**⁻¹**GS**⁻¹ (Gramian)								
1	30.83970	.67510	30.28609	5.25354	.16465	.66901	.71514	.00324	.95901
2	.67510	4.62659	1.54094	3.49296	4.58686	.66158	−.57610	−.07899	.77582
3	30.28609	1.54094	31.44806	6.26706	2.03135	.74907	.63040	−.03054	.95944
4	5.25354	3.49296	6.26706	3.66675	3.70080	.84984	−.19455	.06466	.76426
5	.16465	4.58686	2.03135	3.70080	5.53628	.67455	−.59918	.02669	.81475
Variance						2.62361	1.63759	.01208	4.27328

weights are shown only because they are real (i.e., $\lambda_3 > 0$), but they certainly are not significant in any practical sense. In the analysis of **G** two common factors are presented since only two eigenvalues of this matrix are greater than one. For **R*** three eigenvalues are greater than one and hence three factors are computed, while the analysis based on **G*** is derived from the solution for **R*** (indicated by step 11 of the algorithm) and always has the same number of factors. The computer output includes the unit-length eigenvectors of **R*** and **G***, which are identical but not listed in the same order. To save space only the final factor patterns (after rescaling the eigenvectors and transforming to canonical form) are presented in Table 11.3. Direct comparisons of the solutions based on the different matrices of image analysis can be made since they are in canonical form. The results based on **G** and **G*** agree to within a few units in the third decimal place for the two factors, but they account for somewhat less of the variance than the first two principal factors obtained from $\mathbf{R} - \mathbf{S}^2$. The analysis of **R*** explains most of the variance (4.862), which is just short of that explained by the first three principal components (4.885). This simple example illustrates the supposition advanced above that a principal-factor analysis of $\mathbf{R} - \mathbf{S}^2$ yields results closely related to the components of **R*** and hence can serve as an alternative to analyzing the image covariance matrix.

In order to see how image analysis results compare with the principal-factor methods for a larger data set, some statistics for the twenty-four psychological tests are presented without showing the detailed computer output, which would require entirely too much space. There are 13 roots of $\mathbf{R} - \mathbf{S}^2$ greater than zero and these real factors contribute 13.555 to the total variance of the tests. The first five of these factors (accounting for 11.912 of the variance) are identical with the principal factor solution of Table 8.14. The output for **G**, on the basis of its eigenvalues being greater than one, yields only two common factors. These are identical to the first two factors produced for **G*** (actually 13 factors were determined since that is the number of eigenvalues of **R*** greater than one). The 13 components of **R*** account for 20.102 of the total variance of the twenty-four tests, which is only slightly less than the maximum of 20.323 produced by the first 13 principal components (see Table 8.12) of the original correlation matrix **R**.

A closely related method—*image factor analysis*—is based on a model introduced by Joreskog in 1962 and subsequently fully solved by him (Joreskog 1969a). In a sense it is an extension of Guttman's image analysis but with the crucial distinction of the addition of a parameter. As noted above, when $n \to \infty$ the corresponding elements of $\mathbf{U}^2$ and $\mathbf{S}^2$ tend to the same limit and hence $\mathbf{S}^2$ may be used to replace the unknown $\mathbf{U}^2$. However, for n finite the matrix $\mathbf{S}^2$ is not a permissible $\mathbf{U}^2$ matrix since $\mathbf{R} - \mathbf{S}^2$ is not Gramian. What Joreskog (1965, 1969a) proposes is that the elements of $\mathbf{U}^2$ be chosen *proportional* to the corresponding elements of $\mathbf{S}^2$, namely:

$$(11.18) \qquad\qquad \mathbf{U}^2 = \theta \mathbf{S}^2$$

where the parameter θ is a positive scalar. This expression constitutes the fundamental postulate of image factor analysis. Also, corresponding to (11.12) is the following fundamental equation of image factor analysis:

$$(11.19) \qquad\qquad \mathbf{R} = \mathbf{AA'} + \theta \mathbf{S}^2.$$

The relationships shown by Harris (1962) to exist between the approaches of Guttman (1953) in image analysis and Rao (1955) in maximum-likelihood factor analysis is tied in to his own work in image factor analysis by Joreskog (1969a). He notes that the first iteration of Harris's method corresponds to his earlier method (Joreskog 1963), the main difference involving the parameter θ in (11.18). He then states, "If the equations of Rao and of Harris are iterated in the way suggested and if the iterations converge, the final estimates satisfy [(11.12)] but not [(11.19)], thus yielding a traditional factor analysis solution" (Joreskog 1969a, p. 53). By contrast, Joreskog considers image factor analysis "as a model in its own right" and develops an iterative procedure for getting maximum-likelihood estimates of the parameters of the model that satisfy (11.19).

An example of an image factor analysis computed by Joreskog (1965) is given in Table 11.4. Fortuitously, it is for the same 13 psychological tests for which a canonical

Table 11.4

Image Factor Analysis of Thirteen Psychological Tests

Test	Coefficients of Factors					Common Variance
	F_1	F_2	F_3	F_4	F_5	
1	.527	.251	.441	−.104	.130	.563
2	.332	.095	.325	−.298	−.253	.378
3	.379	.064	.528	.052	−.228	.482
4	.468	.057	.410	.184	.234	.479
5	.782	−.153	−.137	−.088	−.198	.701
6	.788	−.267	−.045	−.103	.114	.718
7	.795	−.246	−.093	.150	.044	.726
8	.727	−.022	.047	.295	−.121	.633
9	.782	−.312	−.091	−.096	.041	.728
10	.393	.487	−.417	.087	−.021	.574
11	.495	.448	−.208	−.244	.090	.557
12	.376	.636	−.127	.111	−.073	.580
13	.583	.523	.118	−.030	.069	.633
V	4.636	1.448	1.034	.354	.277	7.749

factor analysis (yielding maximum-likelihood estimates) is shown in Table 11.1. Furthermore, "these two sets of factor loadings are directly comparable since both have been obtained under the same normalization of the factor matrices" (Joreskog 1965, p. 21). Any differences must be ascribed to the differences between the traditional model and the image factor model. The results of his tests of significance (indicating that at least five factors are required for the data to be consistent with the image factor model) are in agreement with the conclusions reached in **11.2** regarding the canonical factor analysis.[2]

[2] Subsequently, Joreskog (1969a, p. 72) called attention to the fact that the χ^2 (yielding a probability level of .23) he reported in 1965 was incorrect. However, the inference of five significant factors is little affected by the small difference in χ^2.

Several researchers have explored additional ramifications and extensions of Guttman's image theory. Harris (1971a) introduced the notion of "ideal" images, which may or may not lead to practical results. Bentler (1969, 1970) has devised a method of "regression factor analysis," in which he uses "generalized images" as a means of estimating the parameters in the traditional factor analysis model. On the other hand, Koopman (1973) returns to Guttman's original notion of treating "image analysis as a structural decomposition . . . of interest in its own right and which, more or less accidentally, happens to be related to factor analysis."

Koopman develops a "generalized image system" in which the vector of generalized anti-images of the set of n observed variables is defined by

$$(11.20) \qquad\qquad \mathbf{q} = \mathbf{TS}^2\mathbf{R}^{-1}\mathbf{z}$$

where $\mathbf{T}$ is a diagonal matrix of unspecified but positive parameters. The generalized images are simply the differences between the observations and the anti-images, namely,

$$(11.21) \qquad\qquad \mathbf{p} = \mathbf{z} - \mathbf{q}.$$

He then seeks to determine $\mathbf{T}$, under the assumption the desired end product for interpretation is a set of reduced-rank approximate images, "so as to allow reduced spaces to be identified that account for as much image variance, but as little anti-image variance, as is possible" (Koopman 1973, p. 500). An efficient computer program is described and the procedure is applied to the problem of twenty-four psychological tests. The results point clearly to four image dimensions. Although the fifth dimension accounts for slightly more image variance than anti-image variance, its eigenvalue is not sufficiently greater than that of the sixth dimension to warrant its retention.

Some special instances of the generalized image system for certain values of the diagonal matrix $\mathbf{T}$ are pointed out by Koopman. Of course, as $\mathbf{T}$ approaches the null matrix, the anti-images in (11.20) approach a null vector and the images in (11.21) approach the observed variables. At the other extreme, if $\mathbf{T} = \mathbf{I}$ then the generalized and the Guttman system of images are identical. When the restriction

$$(11.22) \qquad\qquad\qquad \mathbf{T} = t\mathbf{I}$$

is imposed an especially interesting case arises. Koopman considers the relation between this restricted and the unrestricted general image systems as analogous to the relation between Joreskog's image factor analysis and traditional factor analysis, with his scalar t functioning in the same manner as Joreskog's θ. Since Joreskog found image factor analysis to be more psychometrically invariant than the unrestricted factor model, Koopman also expects that the restriction in his system may produce results that are more psychometrically invariant than those from the unrestricted general image system.

11.4. *Alpha Factor Analysis*

The method under consideration in this section was prompted by the scaling considerations introduced by Rao, as noted in **11.2**, and by the psychometric considerations introduced by Guttman, as noted in **11.3** (Kaiser 1965). While the notion that a set of variables might be viewed as a sample from an assumed universe of content was introduced in the course of getting images, this concept becomes even more cogent in the present method that is based on reliability considerations. Specifically, a method is developed in which the decision as to the number of "psychometrically significant" factors is made according to a measure of reliability of the factors themselves.

In statistical studies, especially in the social sciences, the sampling elements or entities usually are persons. The measurements, or attributes of these persons, are the variables analyzed for a description and understanding of the group being studied. An important aspect of such studies frequently involves a generalization of the results found in the particular sample to other groups of persons presumed to belong to the same population or universe from which the original sample was drawn. The concepts of sampling and generalization thus refer to the entities or people—the variables tacitly assumed to be determined or fixed.

When the roles of the entities and variables are interchanged,[3] the new type of generalization must be distinguished from the more traditional one, which has always been known as *statistical inference*. By contrast, when the variables are the elements being sampled, they may be presumed to belong to a universe of content and when projections are made from such a sample it may be referred to as *content-area inference*. Specifically, when working in the field of psychology, the term *psychometric inference* is generally used now.

The issue of psychometric inference was addressed in the classic paper by Hotelling (1933, p. 504) as follows:

> Instead of regarding the analysis of a particular set of tests as our ultimate goal, we may look upon these merely as a sample of a hypothetical larger aggregate of possible tests. Our aim then is to learn something of the situation portrayed by the large aggregate. . . . Instead of dealing with the degree of instability of functions of the correlations of the observed tests arising from the smallness of the number of persons tested, regarded as a sample of a larger population of persons, we are now concerned with the degree of instability resulting from the limited number of tests whose correlations enter into our analysis . . . . As in other uses of sampling theory, the reservation must be made that if the sampling is not random the results cannot be applied with accuracy.

While this consideration led to interesting theoretical results in terms of principal components (Hotelling 1933, pp. 509–14), it was some time before it was applied to the inference of common factors in the psychometric domain from a given sample of psychological variables.

---

[3]While the concern here is with the interchange of entities and variables as the sampling elements, there has been considerable interest in obtaining correlations among the entities (persons) and subjecting these to factor analysis. The first explicit references in this connection seem to have been made by Thomson (1935) and Stephenson (1935), but the most extensive use over the years has been in the work of Cattell (for summaries of alternative designs of factor analyses that may be considered, see Cattell 1952; Comrey 1973, pp. 212–22). It should be noted, however, that correlations between persons, aside from factor analytic implications, had actually been used much earlier by Burt and by Thomson and, no doubt, by others.

Except for the work of Guttman in the 1940s and 1950s (one aspect of psychometric inference relating to estimation of communality is noted in **5.6**) and that of Tryon (1957, 1959) involving domain sampling, factor analysts did not seriously explore the subject of psychometric inference until the early 1960s. However, psychologists working in classical test theory did develop much of the theory of reliability and generalizability as the basis for the psychometric approach in factor analysis (see, for example, Kuder and Richardson 1937; Cronbach 1951; Cronbach, Rajaratnam, and Gleser 1963).

To put it succinctly, then, just as inferences are made in traditional statistical inquiries from a given sample of N individuals to the universe from which they presumably came, so in psychometric considerations, inferences about a universe of psychological measures may be drawn from a sample of n variables in a particular study. While the very complex idea of attacking both types of inferences simultaneously may be way off in the future, progress has been made on the theoretical developments of the two separately. Canonical factor analysis is a result of such work on the statistical side; image factor analysis and the method of this section are instances of the psychometric developments.

The point of departure for the method of *alpha factor analysis,* as stated by its developers (Kaiser and Caffrey 1965, p. 5), "is that *common factors* [in a sample of tests] *are to be determined which have maximum correlation with corresponding universe common factors.*" A set of factors satisfies this principle if each of them has maximum *generalizability,* a term used for the squared correlation in the preceding sentence (Cronbach, Rajaratnam and Gleser 1963, p. 146). The concept of generalizability has been studied by many researchers and can be traced back to Kuder-Richardson formula 20 (Kuder and Richardson 1937, p. 158), which in its generalized form has been called "coefficient alpha" by Cronbach (1951, p. 299).

In the development of alpha factor analysis the basic factor model (2.35) is assumed, and from the expression for the common parts in (2.36) it follows that the common factors are given by an equation such as (11.8), namely:

$$(11.23) \qquad\qquad\qquad \mathbf{f} = \mathbf{W}'\mathbf{c}$$

where $\mathbf{W}$ is the $n \times m$ matrix of weights, by columns, for the linear combinations of the common parts of the observable variables $\mathbf{z}$. Written out for a particular factor p, (11.23) becomes:

$$(11.24) \qquad\qquad F_p = \sum_{j=1}^{n} w_{jp}\, c_j = \mathbf{w}'_p \mathbf{c} \qquad\qquad (p = 1, 2, \cdots, m)$$

where $\mathbf{w}_p$ is a column vector of n weights for the linear combination of the column vector of the n common parts that make up the factor. The coefficient of generalizability becomes (Kaiser and Caffrey 1965, p. 6):

$$(11.25) \qquad \alpha = [n/(n-1)]\,[1 - \mathbf{w}'\mathbf{H}^2\mathbf{w}/\mathbf{w}'(\mathbf{R} - \mathbf{U}^2)\mathbf{w}],$$

in which it is understood that a particular set of weights (say $\mathbf{w}_p$) would lead to a correspondingly particular α_p.

Kaiser and Caffrey then proceed, following Lord (1958), to maximize α by simply maximizing the following ratio of two quadratic forms:

(11.26)
$$\lambda = \frac{\mathbf{w}'(\mathbf{R} - \mathbf{U}^2)\mathbf{w}}{\mathbf{w}'\mathbf{H}^2\mathbf{w}}.$$

The mathematical process leads to the characteristic equation:

(11.27)
$$[\mathbf{H}^{-1}(\mathbf{R} - \mathbf{U}^2)\mathbf{H}^{-1} - \lambda\mathbf{I}]\mathbf{q} = \mathbf{0},$$

which is formally similar to (11.3) of canonical factor analysis. A result from (11.27) is the following (Kaiser and Caffrey 1965, p. 6):

(11.28)
$$\mathbf{q} = \mathbf{Hw} \quad \text{or} \quad \mathbf{w} = \mathbf{H}^{-1}\mathbf{q},$$

but the communalities in $\mathbf{H}^2$ are not known in advance although the eigenvectors $\mathbf{q}$ and eigenvalues λ can be determined by standard methods. What also follows immediately is the relationship between the eigenvalues λ and the coefficients of generalizability α_p, namely:

(11.29)
$$\alpha_p = \frac{n}{n-1}\left(1 - \frac{1}{\lambda_p}\right).$$

The characteristic roots and vectors of the rescaled correlation matrix in (11.27) can be obtained according to the methods described in chapter 8, for which very efficient computer programs are available. When these eigenvectors are scaled appropriately the resulting factor pattern matrix can be represented as follows:

(11.30)
$$\mathbf{A} = \mathbf{HQ\Lambda}^{1/2},$$

where $\mathbf{Q}$ is an $n \times m$ matrix of unit-length eigenvectors associated with the m largest eigenvalues of (11.27) and $\mathbf{\Lambda}$ is the diagonal matrix of these eigenvalues. The actual factors $F_1, F_2, \ldots, F_m$ are given formally by (11.8) just as in the case of canonical factor analysis but, of course, the $\mathbf{A}$'s are different in the two methods. Kaiser and Caffrey have called these "alpha factors" since each successive factor has maximum generalizability in the coefficient alpha sense.

While the foregoing brief account of alpha factor analysis emphasized the maximization of generalizability (the α-criterion), even more important is the rescaling of the variables so that "the *same* factors are found regardless of the units of measurement of the observable variables, and loadings are proportional to scaling constants (Kaiser and Caffrey 1965, p. 7)." This scale-freeness property derives from an optimal rescaling of the variables that modifies their covariances so that the factor solution is not dependent on the scale. In the present case, the first term in (11.27) represents a correlation matrix of the rescaled variables which is made to fit the correlations of the common parts ($\mathbf{AA}'$) as closely as possible. A similar approach was followed in the case of canonical factor analysis. However, the rescaling in alpha factor analysis is in the metric of the common parts while the metric of the unique parts is employed in the latter case. It should be noted that in both instances—(11.30) and (11.7)—the factor patterns obtained by the respective methods have been scaled back to the standardized metric of the observed variables.

An iterative procedure for computing an alpha factor analysis is suggested by Kaiser and Caffrey (1965, pp. 12–13), and efficient computer programs are generally available. The process is started with some initial estimates (SMC's are reasonable) of the communalities for the diagonal matrix $\mathbf{H}^2$. Using such initial values, equation (11.27) can be solved for its eigenvectors and eigenvalues. It may be clearer as to what is going on if $\mathbf{U}^2$ is replaced by $\mathbf{I} - \mathbf{H}^2$ and (11.27) is rewritten in the form:

$$(11.31) \qquad [\mathbf{H}^{-1}(\mathbf{R} - \mathbf{I})\mathbf{H}^{-1} - (\lambda - 1)\mathbf{I}]\mathbf{q} = \mathbf{0}.$$

Then the question arises as to the number of eigenvalues and the associated eigenvectors to retain for subsequent iterations.

It can be argued that the number of common factors in a universe of content must be arbitrarily large (Kaiser and Caffrey 1965, pp. 10–11). Just as a decision on the number of factors to be retained on the basis of a statistical test is a function of the size N of the sample of individuals, so on the basis of a psychometric test it must be a function of the number n of tests in the sample from the psychological universe. Then, it is further argued that any factor not having positive generalizability can certainly be rejected "as being so tenuous as not to be worthy of consideration." It can be seen from (11.29) that an alpha factor will have negative generalizability if and only if its associated eigenvalue λ_p is less than one. Hence, it is recommended that only those alpha factors be retained that have associated eigenvalues greater than one.

Now, we return to the outline of the iteration procedure for solving (11.27) or its equivalent (11.31). From the solution of (11.31) for the initial matrix $\mathbf{H}^2$ determine the m largest (all > 1) eigenvalues Λ and associated eigenvectors $\mathbf{Q}$, leading to the first trial value of $\mathbf{A}$ as given by (11.30). These factor coefficients provide an estimate of a modified $\mathbf{H}^2$, and the process is continued until a stable value of $\mathbf{H}^2$ is reached. Then the final $\mathbf{A}$, as given by (11.30) is the alpha factor matrix.

Table 11.5

Alpha Factor Analysis of Eight Physical Variables

Variable j	Factor Coefficients		Communality h_j
	F_1	F_2	
1	.813	−.420	.838
2	.803	−.496	.891
3	.758	−.494	.819
4	.787	−.432	.807
5	.805	.482	.881
6	.680	.420	.639
7	.621	.444	.582
8	.645	.290	.500
Variance	4.413	1.543	5.957
λ	5.938	2.062	
α	.950	.589	

An alpha factor analysis of the eight physical variables, whose correlations are given in Table 2.3, is shown in Table 11.5. In general appearance, of course, the alpha-factor pattern is very similar to the principal-factor pattern of Table 8.4. However, there are differences of as much as .06 in corresponding weights on the first factor and .09 on the second factor. The two solutions account for the same amount of the variance of the eight variables (74.5%). The adequacy of the alpha factor analysis is judged by the generalizability of the resulting factors. In the present case the two positive eigenvalues computed from (11.31) and the associated two α's from (11.29) are shown at the bottom of Table 11.5. Clearly these high coefficients of generalizability justify the retention of the two common factors.

Another illustration of alpha factor analysis, for the twenty-four psychological tests, is provided in Table 11.6. These results might be compared with those in Table 8.14 stemming from a principal-factor analysis of the same data. While there are sizable differences in corresponding weights, after the first factor, the overall

Table 11.6

Alpha Factor Analysis of Twenty-Four Psychological Tests

Test j	Factor Coefficients					Communality h_j^2
	F_1	F_2	F_3	F_4	F_5	
1	.620	.122	.361	−.072	−.009	.535
2	.390	.145	.263	−.044	.153	.267
3	.447	.251	.305	.035	−.249	.418
4	.490	.219	.206	−.072	−.009	.335
5	.653	.235	−.362	−.119	.082	.633
6	.652	.314	−.370	.025	−.006	.662
7	.635	.344	−.441	−.148	−.046	.740
8	.653	.203	−.173	−.120	−.118	.526
9	.660	.351	−.428	.019	−.006	.742
10	.455	−.561	−.250	−.391	.092	.745
11	.554	−.398	−.109	−.071	.005	.482
12	.469	−.420	.068	−.361	.085	.539
13	.600	−.164	.141	−.318	−.058	.512
14	.432	−.153	−.158	.364	.095	.376
15	.407	−.166	−.041	.361	.175	.356
16	.545	−.045	.216	.329	.127	.470
17	.477	−.305	−.119	.315	−.192	.472
18	.545	−.283	.172	.111	−.070	.425
19	.465	−.119	.046	.134	−.387	.401
20	.626	.180	.021	.093	.214	.479
21	.610	−.120	.143	−.159	.123	.448
22	.614	.128	.009	.058	−.018	.398
23	.696	.149	.087	−.048	.051	.519
24	.641	−.179	−.145	−.137	−.075	.488
Variance	7.613	1.617	1.279	1.013	.444	11.966
λ	15.453	2.986	2.368	2.131	1.062	
α	.976	.694	.603	.554	.061	

results are remarkably close. The corresponding contributions of the five factors agree quite well (largest discrepancy is .093 for F_4), with the total for the five alpha factors being 11.966, as compared with 11.912 for the five principal factors. Alpha factor analysis points to five factors with positive generalizability for the twenty-four tests. The fifth factor would appear to be borderline as can be seen from its α value in Table 11.6. This question—of four or five meaningful or interpretable factors for this data set—has been debated among researchers in factor analysis for many years.

11.5. *Multiple-Group Method*

In this section we return to a method that is essentially in the spirit of the early factor models of chapter 7. The distinguishing characteristic of the method involves the factoring of a correlation matrix into several multiple factors simultaneously.[4] The resulting factors usually are oblique to one another—unlike the previous methods, all of which led to orthogonal factors.

Horst (1937) anticipated the multiple-group method of factor analysis, but he did not carry the theoretical work to the stage of practical application. Similarly, Guttman (1944) presented the theory without computational procedures. It was not too surprising that shortly afterward, Holzinger (1944b) and Thurstone (1945a) presented simple computing procedures for "group factor analysis," without recognizing the similarity to the earlier theoretical developments. The several independently developed "multiple group methods" for factor analysis are compared and synthesized by Harman (1954).

Basically, the multiple-group method extracts a number of common factors in one operation. To do so, it is necessary to select a number of linearly independent groups, which number approximates the rank of the reduced correlation matrix. Except in rare circumstances, the common factors extracted in a single operation are oblique to one another. Hence, the group-factor method leads to two matrices—a factor pattern and a factor structure—the first of these gives the coefficients of the factors in the linear descriptions of the variables, while the second gives the correlations of the variables with the factors. These results can be used to obtain a matrix of reproduced correlations; and hence the residual matrix can be determined. If the residual matrix is not sufficiently close to the null matrix then the multiple-group method can be applied, again, to the residual matrix.

After it is determined that the multiple-group solution adequately reproduces the observed correlations, some investigators may consider such a solution as a preliminary step to the "rotational" problem. In seeking "simple structure" (see **6.2**) by transformation of axes, the problem is simplified if an orthogonal frame of reference is first obtained. Hence, two additional concepts are introduced—an orthogonal factor matrix and the transformation matrix from the oblique to this solution.

---

[4]The concept of group factors in factor analysis should not be confused with the group-factor method for reducing a correlation matrix to a factor matrix which satisfies the fundamental theorem (2.46). During the rapid development of factor analysis in the 1930s, several workers dealt with group factors. Notable among these were Cyril Burt, who considered the "group factor method"; R. C. Tyron, who proposed "cluster analysis"; and K. J. Holzinger, who developed the "bi-factor" method of analysis.

One of the principal differences that appears in the several developments of multiple-group methods of factor analysis really is concerned with the formulation of scientific hypotheses rather than with the *method* of analysis. Guttman and Holzinger suggest that the multiple-group methods be used to confirm some *a priori* psychological theory. Guttman emphasizes the fact that the computational procedures of multiple-group methods can be applied in any event, but most psychological meaning can be gained only through the testing by the data of preconceived hypotheses. These hypotheses are reflected in the specific manner of grouping the variables and in the resulting common factors (usually oblique).

On the other hand, Thurstone emphasizes that the multiple-group method of factoring is quite independent of the manner of grouping the variables, and in an example, deliberately sets up groups in an arbitrary fashion, with little reference to the correlations. This thought is evident when Thurstone calls attention to the "unnecessary" restrictions that Holzinger placed upon the matrix of correlations in order to use his "simple method of factor analysis." These restrictions *are* unnecessary when the object is simply to get a reduction of the correlation matrix to a factor matrix by the expedient multiple-group method; they are *not* unnecessary when the object is to test some specified hypothesis by use of a multiple-group solution.

Thus, while Holzinger considers the multiple-group method suitable only if the correlation matrix is amenable to sectioning into portions of approximate unit rank, and Guttman prefers to group the variable so as to avoid or reduce the problem of rotation of axes, Thurstone conceives of the multiple-group method primarily as another (efficient) technique for initial factoring to provide an orthogonal factor matrix "which is the starting-point for the rotational problem" (Thurstone 1947, p. 171).

If the total number of common factors is not extracted in a single operation, then the multiple-group method can be applied again to the residual matrix obtained after the first operation; and this can be repeated as many times as necessary to bring the residuals down to negligible values. In the successive application of the multiple-group method, the common factors extracted at each stage are oblique to one another, but the factors obtained in any single stage are orthogonal to all factors extracted in other stages. The implication of this is that if an *a priori* hypothesis involves an oblique structure then all the common factors must be extracted in one operation, or else subsequent rotation might be necessitated.

1. Oblique solution.—Now the procedures leading to the oblique solution are outlined. Further discussion of the geometric basis and other concepts associated with an oblique solution appears in chapter 12. However, in that chapter the oblique solution is obtained by transformation from some pre-computed orthogonal solution rather than from the correlation matrix directly as in this section.

The essence of the multiple-group method consists of representing the factors by reference axes passing through the centroids of the respective groups of variables. Since the clusters of variables would not ordinarily be at right angles to one another, the common factors obtained in a single operation of the multiple-group method are oblique also. A reduced correlation matrix is the starting point, with communalities in the principal diagonal estimated by one of the methods suggested in chapter 5. The actual analysis begins with an appropriate grouping of the n variables into m

groups G_p ($p = 1, 2, \cdots, m$) on some *a priori* basis, by the method of B-coefficients of **7.4**, or on a purely arbitrary basis.

Since sums of variables (centroids) are involved in the multiple-group method, some basic properties of such *composite variables* will be found useful. While the individual variables z_j are in standard measure, their composites are not necessarily so; and formulas for their variances and correlations have long been known (Spearman 1913). In the multiple-group method, a composite variable T_p is assumed through the cluster of n_p variables in a group G_p, namely,

$$(11.32) \qquad\qquad T_p = \sum (z_k; \quad k \in G_p) \qquad\qquad (p = 1, 2, \cdots, m)$$

Such composite variables constitute the oblique factors, which ordinarily would not have unit variances.

The calculation of variances and covariances among the factors can be expedited by the determination of certain preliminary sums of correlations. The first of these is simply the sum of the correlations of each variable z_j with all the variables in each group G_p, namely:

$$(11.33) \qquad w_{jp} = \sum (r_{jk}; \quad k \in G_p) \qquad (j = 1, 2, \cdots, n; \quad p = 1, 2, \cdots, m),$$

where the sum is on the index k which takes on all the values of the variables in group G_p. When the index k takes the value j, the "self-correlation" is assumed to be the communality, i.e., $r_{jj} = h_j^2$. Another sum which is useful is

$$(11.34) \qquad \begin{aligned} W_{pq} &= \sum (w_{jq}; \quad j \in G_p) \\ &= \sum (r_{jk}; \quad j \in G_p, k \in G_q) \quad (p, q = 1, 2, \cdots, m) \end{aligned}$$

which represents the sum of correlations between all variables in group G_p with all those in group G_q (including the case where $p = q$). The first task is to determine the correlations among the oblique factors and the correlations (structure values) of the variables with these factors. The required correlations can be expressed concisely by means of the foregoing sums of simple correlations, but first a formula will be obtained for the variances of the oblique factors. Ordinarily the variance of a composite variable T_p would be given by:

$$(11.35) \qquad s_{T_p}^2 = n_p + 2 \sum (r_{jk}; \quad j, k \in G_p, j < k),$$

since there are n_p self-correlations of unity. However, when the "self-correlations" are replaced by communalities, this formula may be written

$$(11.36) \qquad s_{T_p}^2 = \sum (r_{jk}; \quad j, k \in G_p),$$

where it is understood that $r_{jj} = h_j^2$. Employing (11.34), the last expression becomes

$$(11.37) \qquad\qquad s_{T_p}^2 = W_{pp}.$$

Now, by definition the correlation between any two composite variables, T_p and T_q, is

$$(11.38) \qquad\qquad r_{T_p T_q} = \sum T_{pi} T_{qi} / N s_{T_p} s_{T_q},$$

where summation with respect to i from 1 to N is understood. The s's in the denominator have just been expressed in (11.37) in terms of the foregoing sums of simple correlations. The remainder of (11.38) may be expanded and simplifies to:

$$(11.39) \qquad \sum_{i=1}^{N} T_{pi}T_{qi}/N = W_{pq}.$$

Substituting the values from (11.37) and (11.39) into (11.38), the latter formula for the correlation between two oblique factors becomes:

$$(11.40) \qquad r_{T_pT_q} = W_{pq}/\sqrt{(W_{pp}W_{qq})}.$$

Next, the correlations of the variables with the factors—the oblique factor structure—can be obtained in terms of the foregoing sums of simple correlations. The structure value s_{jp} is the correlation $r_{z_jT_p}$ of a variable in standard measure with a composite variable whose variance is given by (11.37). Then, it can readily be shown that the required correlation is given by the formula:

$$(11.41) \qquad s_{jp} = w_{jp}/\sqrt{W_{pp}}.$$

To complete the solution in terms of correlated factors, the linear descriptions of the variables in terms of the factors are required as well as their correlations with the factors. The coefficients in these linear equations, i.e., the pattern values, are the co-ordinates with respect to the oblique (factor) axes of the points representing the variables. The factor pattern can be obtained from the known factor structure **S** and the correlations among the factors **Φ**, according to (2.44), as follows:

$$(11.42) \qquad \mathbf{P} = \mathbf{S\Phi}^{-1}.$$

If the analysis is to be terminated with an oblique solution then appropriate computing formulas are required for the reproduced correlations and the residuals. There are several formulas for getting the reproduced correlations directly from the component parts of an oblique solution. From the relationships between a pattern and a structure in an oblique solution (see **2.9**), this formula can be put in either of the following more convenient forms for computation:

$$(11.43) \qquad \mathbf{\hat{R}} = \mathbf{PS'} \quad \text{or} \quad \mathbf{\hat{R}} = \mathbf{SP'}.$$

The residual matrix with m factors removed is defined by

$$(11.44) \qquad \mathbf{R}_m = \mathbf{R} - \mathbf{\hat{R}},$$

where it is assumed that the reproduced correlations are based on the extraction of m factors by the multiple-group method.

Before considering methods for transforming the results to an orthogonal solution, it is well to consider the cogent argument, presented by Guttman (1952, p. 215) for accepting the oblique multiple-group solution:

> A drawback is that if rotation is actually necessary, this implies that original hypotheses about the nature of the common factors are wrong. *A posteriori* hypotheses, made after

inspection of the data, may be subject to all the uncertainties and controversies which beset any *a posteriori* theory. The results of a factor analysis would seem to be more trust-worthy if the . . . [grouping of the variables] is chosen according to an *a priori* psycho-logical theory, which is then *tested* by the data. This kind of procedure carries more scientific weight than the procedure of constructing an *a posteriori* theory to fit already known facts. The latter is implied by rotation of axes (whether or not the rotation is "blind").

2. Orthogonal solution.—Whether an orthogonal solution is desired simply for completion of the multiple-group analysis (expediting some of the computational labor if done by hand) or as a stepping-stone to the rotational problem, methods for obtaining it are outlined in this paragraph. The orthogonal solution is derived by transformation from the oblique solution either from the pattern values (b_{jp}) or the structure values (s_{jp}) to the orthogonal factor weights (a_{jp}).

Of all possible transformations from oblique to rectangular coordinate axes, the special case employed in the multiple-group analysis has the following properties: the first axis of the new system coincides with the first oblique-factor axis, the second is in the plane of the first two oblique axes and orthogonal to the first, etc.[5] This type of transformation, for the case of only two factors, is illustrated in Figure 11.1. For the sake of simplicity, a general point is designated P instead of P_j, and its coordinates are shown as (b_1, b_2) instead of (b_{j1}, b_{j2}) in the oblique reference system, and as (a_1, a_2) instead of (a_{j1}, a_{j2}) in the rectangular reference system. The point P (or the vector from the origin to P) can be represented in the common-factor space as follows:

$$\tilde{z} = b_1 T_1 + b_2 T_2,$$

or

$$\tilde{z} = a_1 F_1 + a_2 F_2,$$

depending upon which reference system is employed. In the oblique reference system, the (orthogonal) projections on the coordinate axes are distinct from the coordinates, and are given by the structure values:

(11.45) $$s_1 = r_{zT_1} \quad \text{and} \quad s_2 = r_{zT_2}.$$

For the special type of transformation from oblique to rectangular axes with the properties listed above, the relationships between the two sets of coordinates are

(11.46) $$a_1 = b_1 + b_2 \cos \theta_{12}$$
$$a_2 = \qquad b_2 \sin \theta_{12}$$

where θ_{12} is the angle between the oblique axes T_1 and T_2. As noted in **4.9**, the cosine of the angle between vectors is the correlation of the variables represented by such vectors. Hence, $\cos \theta_{12} = r$, where for simplicity r is used to designate $r_{T_1 T_2}$. Then the foregoing transformation equations may be written in matrix form:

(11.47) $$(a_{j1} a_{j2}) = (b_{j1} b_{j2}) \cdot \begin{bmatrix} 1 & 0 \\ r & \sqrt{1 - r^2} \end{bmatrix}.$$

[5]In formal mathematics, this transformation is known as the Gram-Schmidt process and yields the orthogonalization of a matrix (Paige and Swift 1961, p. 78).

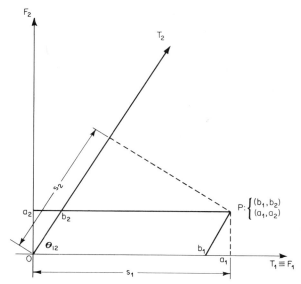

Fig. 11.1.—Transformation from oblique to rectangular axes

The transformation matrix that carries the coordinates of the oblique reference system into the coordinates of the rectangular reference system can be derived from the matrix of correlations among the oblique factors. By applying the square root operation (see **3.3**) on the matrix $\boldsymbol{\Phi}$ of factor correlations, the resulting "square root" matrix $\mathbf{T}'$ is found to be precisely the transformation matrix, as in (11.47). The general square root operation leads to

$$(11.48) \qquad\qquad \boldsymbol{\Phi} = \mathbf{T}'\mathbf{T},$$

corresponding to (3.27).

   The expression (11.47) is immediately generalizable to n variables and m factors, viz.,

$$(11.49) \qquad\qquad \mathbf{A} = \mathbf{P}\mathbf{T}',$$

where $\mathbf{A}$ and $\mathbf{P}$ are $n \times m$ matrices (a_{jp}) and (b_{jp}), respectively; and $\mathbf{T}$, a square matrix of order m, is derived by the square root operation on $\boldsymbol{\Phi}$. While (11.49) provides the transformation from oblique *coordinates* to the specified orthogonal coordinates, it is desirable to express the transformation in terms of the oblique *structure values*, because those are determined first in the course of the analysis. To accomplish this, substitute the expression for the oblique factor pattern matrix from (11.42) into (11.49), obtaining

$$\mathbf{A} = \mathbf{S}\boldsymbol{\Phi}^{-1}\mathbf{T}'.$$

Then from the square root operation (11.48) on $\boldsymbol{\Phi}$, the foregoing equation becomes

$$(11.50) \qquad\qquad \mathbf{A} = \mathbf{S}\mathbf{T}^{-1},$$

239

which is precisely the desired transformation from the oblique structure values to the orthogonal factor pattern. Stated another way, the transformation (11.50) to the orthogonal frame of reference (F's) is described in terms of projections (s_{jp}) on the oblique axes instead of coordinates (b_{jp}) in the original oblique reference system.

3. Algorithm.—The methods described in paragraphs **1** and **2** can be summarized and organized in convenient computing form. Such a schematic form is presented in the top half of Table 11.7; the numerical illustration in the bottom half of the table will be described shortly. The principal parts of this worksheet consist of: (1) the stub, listing the variables; (2) the heading, giving brief instructions; and (3) the body of the table proper, made up of three vertical sections with three blocks in each section. Also, there are instructions for checking the numerical operations.

What this computing form accomplishes is the determination of both the oblique factor pattern and the orthogonal factor solution, starting with the intercorrelations among the factors and the oblique factor structure. The work is begun by recording in the first vertical section the three known matrices: (1) the $m \times m$ matrix of correlations among the factors; (2) an identity matrix of the same order; and (3) the $n \times m$ oblique factor structure.

The next step involves the application of the square root method to the first vertical section to get the middle section. The first block, of course, yields the square root matrix of the original matrix of factor correlations. The next block, obtained by applying the square root operator to the identity matrix, contains the transformation matrix $\mathbf{T}^{-1}$. In the third block, the orthogonal factor solution is determined by the same square root operation.[6]

Finally, the third vertical section is obtained by simple matrix multiplication. Each block (matrix) in the middle section is multiplied, row-by-row, by the transformation matrix $\mathbf{T}^{-1}$ (which is set off by the bold lines) to obtain the corresponding block in the third section. The first block need not be computed, except if desired for an additional check. The next block, which gives $\boldsymbol{\Phi}^{-1}$, again is not required explicitly, but results without cost as a by-product of the square root method. The required oblique factor pattern is obtained in the last block of the algorithm by postmultiplication of the orthogonal factor matrix by the transpose of the transformation matrix,[7] i.e.,

$$(11.51) \qquad\qquad \mathbf{P} = \mathbf{A}(\mathbf{T}')^{-1}.$$

The fact that the row-by-row multiplication of $\mathbf{A}$ by $\mathbf{T}^{-1}$ actually yields $\mathbf{P}$, can be derived from (11.49) by postmultiplying both sides of that equation by $(\mathbf{T}')^{-1}$.

After the computations outlined in Table 11.7 have been made, it is a simple matter to get the matrix of reproduced correlations, and hence the residual matrix.

---

[6]It should be noted that the arrangement of work in Table 11.7 is transposed from that in Table 3.2. In Section **3.3**, the square root method is presented with the square root matrix below the original matrix, while here it is placed to the right. Because of this transposition of the blocks, the computing formulas of **3.3** must also be transposed.

[7]As indicated in **3.2**, paragraph **18**, the row-by-row multiplication of a matrix $\mathbf{A}$ by another matrix $\mathbf{B}$ is equivalent to the conventional row-by-column multiplication of $\mathbf{A}$ by $\mathbf{B}'$.

Table 11.7

Multiple-Group Factor Algorithm

Variable	Instructions		
	Original Matrices (*m* columns)	Square Root Operation ($\mathbf{T}^{-1}$) on Preceding Block (*m* columns)	Row-by-row Multiplication of Preceding Block with $\mathbf{T}^{-1}$, i.e., Postmultiplication by $(\mathbf{T}')^{-1}$ (*m* columns)
T_1 T_2 . . . T_m	Factor Correlations $\mathbf{\Phi}$ $(\mathbf{\Phi} = \mathbf{T}'\mathbf{T})$	Square Root Matrix $\mathbf{T}'$ $(\mathbf{\Phi}\mathbf{T}^{-1} = \mathbf{T}')$	(Result is $\mathbf{I}$, except for rounding errors—may be left blank, or used as check)
T_1 T_2 . . . T_m	Identity Matrix $\mathbf{I}$	Transformation Matrix $\mathbf{T}^{-1}$ $(\mathbf{I}\mathbf{T}^{-1} = \mathbf{T}^{-1})$	Inverse of Initial Matrix $\mathbf{\Phi}^{-1}$ $(\mathbf{T}^{-1}(\mathbf{T}')^{-1} = \mathbf{\Phi}^{-1})$ (not required explicitly)
1 2 3 . . . *n*	Oblique Factor Structure $\mathbf{S}$	Orthogonal Factor Matrix $\mathbf{A}$ $(\mathbf{S}\mathbf{T}^{-1} = \mathbf{A})$	Oblique Factor Pattern $\mathbf{P}$ $(\mathbf{A}(\mathbf{T}')^{-1} = \mathbf{P})$
Total	Sum of all $(2m + n)$ elements in each column		
Check	(No check in this block)	Square root operation applied to totals of preceding block	Row-by-row multiplication of totals in preceding blocks with $\mathbf{T}^{-1}$

	Example								
T_1 T_2 T_3	1.0000 .6511 .4640	a 1.0000 .5324	a a 1.0000	1.0000 .6511 .4640	.7590 .3034	.8323	1.0000 .0000 −.0000	0 1.0000 −.0000	0 0 1.0000
T_1 T_2 T_3	1.0000 0 0	0 1.0000 0	0 0 1.0000	1.0000 0 0	−.8578 1.3175 0	−.2448 −.4803 1.2015	1.7957 −1.0126 −.2941	a 1.9665 −.5771	a a 1.4436

	Oblique factor structures: **S**			Orthogonal factor matrix: **A**			Oblique factor pattern: **P**		
1	.90	.52	.37	.90	−.09	−.03	.98	−.09	−.04
2	.83	.61	.38	.83	.09	−.04	.76	.14	−.05
3	.87	.56	.46	.87	−.01	.07	.86	−.04	.08
4	.55	.96	.43	.55	.79	−.07	−.11	1.07	−.08
5	.56	.86	.49	.56	.65	.04	−.01	.84	.04
6	.63	.86	.50	.63	.60	.03	.11	.77	.04
7	.28	.39	.59	.28	.27	.45	−.06	.14	.55
8	.38	.40	.76	.38	.20	.63	.05	−.04	.76
9	.38	.39	.88	.38	.19	.77	.03	−.12	.93
Total	8.50	8.73	7.86	8.50	4.21	3.16	4.10	4.05	3.80
Check				8.50	4.21	3.17	4.12	4.03	3.80

[a]Terms above the diagonal of a symmetric matrix are deleted for simplicity. These terms, however, must be included in the totals in order for the checks to apply.

Row-by-row multiplication of **A** by itself yields the matrix $\hat{\mathbf{R}}$ of reproduced correlations according to (2.50). An alternative procedure is row-by-row multiplication of **S** by **P** according to (11.43).

The computing procedure involving the oblique solution of paragraph **1**, followed by the square root method outlined in Table 11.7, will be found very efficient for factoring if an electronic computer is not available. It might still be desirable to get a multiple-group solution with the aid of a computer in some instances (e.g., to explore a specific hypothesis involving groups of variables). A computer program for triangular decomposition (Madansky 1965a) may be very useful for such cases. In general, however, when an electronic computer is available, the principal-factor, minres, maximum-likelihood, or one of the methods of the three preceding sections would be preferred.

The calculations involved in the multiple-group method will be illustrated with a nine-variable example. The reduced correlation matrix, with the communalities estimated by single triads of equation (5.33), is contained in Table 11.8. As the first step in the analysis, the nine variables are placed in three groups, as follows:

$$G_1 : (1, 2, 3), \text{ verbal};$$
$$G_2 : (4, 5, 6), \text{ arithmetic};$$
$$G_3 : (7, 8, 9), \text{ spatial relations}.$$

This grouping is justified by the nature of the respective variables and verified by *B*-coefficients:

$$B(1, 2, 3) = 187, \quad B(4, 5, 6) = 186, \quad \text{and} \quad B(7, 8, 9) = 168.$$

The sums of correlations within groups (*w*'s) and between groups (*W*'s) are obtained as the basis for calculating the correlations among the factors, and between the factors and the variables. These correlations are the input matrices in the first vertical section of the bottom half of Table 11.7. Then applying the square root op-

Table 11.8

Intercorrelations of Nine Psychological Variables[a]

Variable	1	2	3	4	5	6	7	8	9
1. Word meaning	.81								
2. Sentence completion	.75	.69							
3. Odd words	.78	.72	.75						
4. Mixed arithmetic	.44	.52	.47	.91					
5. Remainders	.45	.53	.48	.82	.74				
6. Missing numbers	.51	.58	.54	.82	.74	.74			
7. Gloves	.21	.23	.28	.33	.37	.35	.35		
8. Boots	.30	.32	.37	.33	.36	.38	.45	.58	
9. Hatchets	.31	.30	.37	.31	.36	.38	.52	.67	.77

[a] Taken from K. J. Holzinger's unpublished class notes involving a study of 696 cases, 12 tests, and 4 factors.

eration and subsequent matrix multiplications, the end products are the orthogonal factor matrix **A** (in the lower block of the middle section) and the oblique factor pattern **P** (in the lower right hand corner). After finishing this analysis, the adequacy of the solution is judged from a comparison of the matrix of reproduced correlations with the reduced correlation matrix. A comparison of the original and reproduced correlations show only one instance of a residual as high as .02. Obviously, the multiple-group solution provides an excellent fit to the observed data of Table 11.8. The adequacy of the results, of course, is independent of whether the orthogonal or the oblique solution is preferred.

A closely related method of factor analysis is discussed by Overall (1968). The procedure involves the identification of clusters of variables from a preliminary orthogonal solution, and passing oblique primary axes through their centroids for the final solution. He illustrates such a solution with the example of twenty-four psychological tests. A computer program to accomplish the same general purpose has been developed (Bentler 1971).

Part III

Derived Factor Solutions

12 Subjective Basis for Multiple-Factor Solutions

)

12.1. *Introduction*

In the five preceding chapters, various methods were proposed for reducing a correlation matrix to a factor matrix which in some reasonable sense reproduces the original correlations. Such factor solutions could be viewed as final products, in their own right; or they could be conceived as initial products, satisfying the fundamental factor theorem of reproducing the correlation matrix, that require further manipulation to a final form for interpretation. The basic philosophy for transforming a preliminary solution into a final multiple-factor type of solution is described in **6.5**. There it is made clear that once the common-factor space has been determined, an infinitude of rotations is possible from one coordinate system to another without any effect on the adequacy of solution.

The multiple-factor solution was originally defined essentially in intuitive terms only, and so has not lent itself to precise mathematical formulation. This preferred type of solution rests upon the principles of "simple structure" set forth in **6.2**. Attempts to objectify these principles are made in chapters 13 and 14, thereby making possible the determination of multiple-factor solutions by analytical methods. Since these methods involve very extensive computations, their very conception had to await the development of the large electronic computers. Before considering such methods, there is a pedagogic value in briefly reviewing the more modest techniques that had been used for obtaining a multiple-factor solution involving subjective, graphical transformations from some arbitrary initial solution. Such techniques for getting an *orthogonal* multiple-factor solution are covered in **12.2** while those for an *oblique* solution are covered in **12.4**.

Actually, the course of the historical development of the oblique form of the multiple-factor solution was somewhat complex and indirect. To lay a foundation for it some basic geometric ideas are first presented in **12.3** before the recommended "primary-factor" method is given in **12.4**. An alternative approach is discussed in **12.5** and the relationships between these two oblique solutions are brought out in **12.6**.

The general task of obtaining a derived solution, which is the subject of the entire part iii of this text, involves the specification of the initial factor pattern and the desired properties of the final solution. On this basis, a matrix of transformation is developed that leads to the final product. When its properties are specified in exact mathematical terms it can be determined objectively, as will be seen in chapters 13 and 14; when not stated in such precise terms it can only be approached subjectively, as was the practice before computers and the newer theoretical methods were available, and which is described in this chapter.

12.2. *Orthogonal Multiple-Factor Solution*

The subjective procedures involve the build-up of a series of rotations in a plane. The angle of rotation at each stage is selected by inspection of a graph and judgment as to the attainment of the objectives of simple structure (see **6.2**). To assist in the development of orthogonal transformations, the following summary of notation will be found convenient:

$\mathbf{A} = (a_{jp})$, initial factor matrix, with factors F_p,

$\mathbf{B} = (b_{jp})$, final factor matrix, with factors M_p,

$\mathbf{T} = (\lambda_{qp})$, orthogonal transformation matrix, with θ_{qp} the angle of rotation in the plane of the original factor p and the final factor q.

The range of j is over the n variables, and the range of p and q is over the m factors.

When an initial factor pattern involves only two factors, the variables may be represented as points in a plane, with the coefficients of the factors as the coordinates. Then a transformation to some other form of solution implies the representation of these points with respect to the axes denoting the new factors. Such a transformation is merely a rotation of axes in this common-factor space. Thus, any point may be referred to either system of reference F_1, F_2, or M_1, M_2, as shown in Figure 12.1. For the sake of simplicity, a general point is designated P instead of P_j, and its coordinates in the original frame of reference are shown as (a_1, a_2) instead of (a_{j1}, a_{j2}), and in the new reference system as (b_1, b_2) in place of (b_{j1}, b_{j2}). The problem is to express the new b-coordinates in terms of the original a-coordinates when the reference axes are rotated through an angle θ *from* the original to the new.

The required transformation is accomplished by making use of the following property on projections of lines: the sum of the projections upon a straight line of the segments of any broken line connecting two points is equal to the corresponding sum for any other broken line connecting the same two points. Here the origin O and any point P are joined by two broken lines, namely, ORP and OSP. It follows that the projections of these broken lines along any direction are equal, i.e.,

$$\text{Proj. } OR = \text{Proj. } RP = \text{Proj. } OS + \text{Proj. } SP.$$

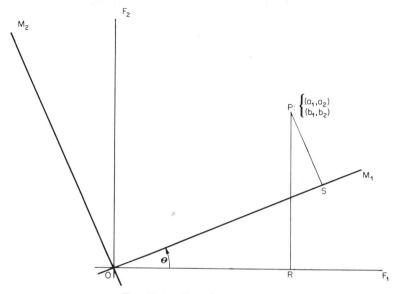

FIG. 12.1.—Rotation in a plane

If the direction is taken, first, as the positive axis of M_1 and, second, as the positive axis of M_2, the resulting expressions are

$$OR \cos \theta + RP \sin \theta = OS + 0,$$

$$-OR \sin \theta + RP \cos \theta = 0 + SP.$$

But the line segments are simply the coordinates, viz.,

$$OR = a_1, \quad RP = a_2 \quad \text{and} \quad OS = b_1, \quad SP = b_2.$$

Hence, the final coordinates are expressed in terms of the initial ones, resulting from the rotation of axes through the angle θ, by the following equations:

(12.1)
$$b_1 = a_1 \cos \theta + a_2 \sin \theta,$$
$$b_2 = -a_1 \sin \theta + a_2 \cos \theta.$$

It should be noted that the trigonometric terms are actually the direction cosines of the new axes with respect to the old ones, and the equations (12.1) may be put in the form:

(12.2)
$$b_1 = \lambda_{11} a_1 + \lambda_{21} a_2,$$
$$b_2 = \lambda_{12} a_1 + \lambda_{22} a_2.$$

For a set of n points there would be n pairs of equations (12.2) carrying each pair of coordinates (a_{j1}, a_{j2}) into the corresponding pair (b_{j1}, b_{j2}). This transformation may be put in matrix form, as follows:

$$(b_{j1} \quad b_{j2}) = (a_{j1} \quad a_{j2}) \cdot \begin{bmatrix} \lambda_{11} & \lambda_{12} \\ \lambda_{21} & \lambda_{22} \end{bmatrix},$$

or, in more compact and generalizable terms:

(12.3) $$\mathbf{B} = \mathbf{AT}.$$

In the simple example of a rotation in a plane, the matrices $\mathbf{A}$ and $\mathbf{B}$ are each of order $n \times 2$ and the matrix $\mathbf{T}$ is 2×2. The elements of $\mathbf{T}$ clearly satisfy the conditions

$$\lambda_{11}^2 + \lambda_{21}^2 = 1, \qquad \lambda_{12}^2 + \lambda_{22}^2 = 1, \qquad \lambda_{11}\lambda_{12} + \lambda_{21}\lambda_{22} = 0$$

so that the transformation is orthogonal in the sense of **4.6**.

When a factor solution involves three factors, the transformation from an initial to a final pattern takes the form:

(12.4) $$\begin{aligned} b_{j1} &= \lambda_{11}a_{j1} + \lambda_{21}a_{j2} + \lambda_{31}a_{j3}, \\ b_{j2} &= \lambda_{12}a_{j1} + \lambda_{22}a_{j2} + \lambda_{32}a_{j3}, \\ b_{j3} &= \lambda_{13}a_{j1} + \lambda_{23}a_{j2} + \lambda_{33}a_{j3}, \end{aligned}$$

where the preceding notation has been extended to an additional dimension. This transformation is covered by (12.3) if the factor matrices in that expression are presumed to be of order $n \times 3$ and the transformation matrix of order 3×3. The elements of $\mathbf{T}$, in this case, must satisfy the six independent conditions:

(12.5) $$\begin{aligned} \lambda_{11}^2 + \lambda_{21}^2 + \lambda_{31}^2 &= 1, \\ \lambda_{12}^2 + \lambda_{22}^2 + \lambda_{32}^2 &= 1, \\ \lambda_{13}^2 + \lambda_{23}^2 + \lambda_{33}^2 &= 1, \\ \lambda_{11}\lambda_{12} + \lambda_{21}\lambda_{22} + \lambda_{31}\lambda_{32} &= 0, \\ \lambda_{11}\lambda_{13} + \lambda_{21}\lambda_{23} + \lambda_{31}\lambda_{33} &= 0, \\ \lambda_{12}\lambda_{13} + \lambda_{22}\lambda_{23} + \lambda_{32}\lambda_{33} &= 0. \end{aligned}$$

Thus, the nine coefficients of (12.4), being subject to six conditions, afford only three degrees of freedom of rotation in ordinary space. Explicit equations for the b's in terms of the a's, involving only three independent parameters can be obtained,[1] but are not employed in practical analyses.

A form of transformation that was found practical in the past will now be indicated. The principle underlying the method is that the result of successive orthogonal transformations is itself an orthogonal transformation, which is said to be the *product* of the successive rotations. Since a planar rotation is the simplest type, a transformation

---

[1]These are known as Euler's formulas, a typical one being: $a_1 = b_1(\cos \varphi \cos \psi - \sin \varphi \sin \psi \cos \theta) - b_2(\cos \varphi \sin \psi + \sin \varphi \cos \psi \cos \theta) + b_3\sin \varphi \sin \theta$, where the first subscript j has been dropped from the a's and b's and θ, φ, ψ are angles of rotation (Snyder and Sisam 1914, p. 42).

in three-space may be built up from such simpler rotations. Thus a transformation in ordinary space may involve the displacement of any two axes about the third, being, in effect, a rotation in a plane. Finally, a product of such rotations may be taken as the complete transformation.

The rotations can be arranged in a systematic order so that each axis is rotated with every other axis only once. The three rotations of pairs of axes in ordinary space may be indicated conveniently in the following manner:

Old Axes	Angle of Rotation	New Axes
$F_1 F_2$	θ_{12}	$Y_1 Y_2$
$Y_1 F_3$	θ_{13}	$M_1 Y_3$
$Y_2 Y_3$	θ_{23}	$M_2 M_3$

It will be noted that the angle of rotation is denoted by θ with subscripts corresponding to the numbers of the axes involved in the rotation. The first rotation is made in the plane of F_1 and F_2, leaving F_3 unaltered. The new axes in this plane are designated by Y_1 and Y_2. Since F_3 is perpendicular to the plane of F_1 and F_2, it is perpendicular to any line in this plane. In particular, F_3 is perpendicular to the new axis Y_1. The next rotation is made in the plane of Y_1 and F_3, leaving Y_2 unchanged. The new first axis, denoted by M_1, may be regarded as final because it is the result of rotations with each of the other axes. The last rotation transforms Y_2 and Y_3 into the final coordinate axes M_2 and M_3. It will be observed that the Y's are merely auxiliary axes and, taken alone, do not comprise a transformation from the F's with the orthogonal properties (12.5). On the other hand, both sets of axes Y_1, Y_2, F_3 and M_1, Y_2, Y_3 have these orthogonal properties, and either one may be taken, in some instances, as the final reference system. The solution ordinarily desired, however, is one based upon the complete transformation of the original axes F_1, F_2, F_3 to the final M_1, M_2, M_3.

Denoting the matrix of transformation of F_1 and F_2, leaving F_3 unchanged, by

$$\mathbf{T}_{12} = \begin{bmatrix} \cos \theta_{12} & -\sin \theta_{12} & 0 \\ \sin \theta_{12} & \cos \theta_{12} & 0 \\ 0 & 0 & 1 \end{bmatrix},$$

the first of the above rotations may be denoted by

$$\mathbf{C} = \mathbf{AT}_{12},$$

where $\mathbf{C}$ is an intermediate matrix of coordinates with respect to Y_1, Y_2, F_3. The second and third rotations may be designated similarly, as follows:

$$\mathbf{D} = \mathbf{CT}_{13} \quad \text{and} \quad \mathbf{B} = \mathbf{DT}_{23},$$

where $\mathbf{D}$ is another intermediate matrix, and

$$\mathbf{T}_{13} = \begin{bmatrix} \cos \theta_{13} & 0 & -\sin \theta_{13} \\ 0 & 1 & 0 \\ \sin \theta_{13} & 0 & \cos \theta_{13} \end{bmatrix}, \quad \mathbf{T}_{23} = \begin{bmatrix} 1 & 0 & 0 \\ 0 & \cos \theta_{23} & -\sin \theta_{23} \\ 0 & \sin \theta_{23} & \cos \theta_{23} \end{bmatrix}.$$

The three preceding rotations may be combined into a single transformation. Substituting the expression for **D** and then for **C** in the expression for **B** produces

(12.6) $$\mathbf{B} = \mathbf{AT}_{12}\mathbf{T}_{13}\mathbf{T}_{23} = \mathbf{AT},$$

where **T** denotes the product of the three successive rotations. In practice this matrix **T** cannot be determined in advance, but rather, the final pattern is derived as a result of the successive rotations.

The preceding methods can be generalized to a common-factor space of m dimensions. The matrix of transformation is now

$$\mathbf{T} = \begin{bmatrix} \lambda_{11} & \lambda_{12} & \cdots & \lambda_{1m} \\ \lambda_{21} & \lambda_{22} & \cdots & \lambda_{2m} \\ \cdot & \cdot & \cdot \cdots \cdot & \cdot \\ \lambda_{m1} & \lambda_{m2} & \cdots & \lambda_{mm} \end{bmatrix},$$

and in the transformation (12.3) the initial and final factor matrices are each of order $n \times m$. The sets of λ's, by columns, are the direction cosines of the final reference axes $M_1, M_2, \cdots, M_m$ with respect to the original axes $F_1, F_2, \cdots, F_m$. These direction cosines are subject to the following set of independent conditions in order that the matrix **T** be orthogonal (see **4.6**):

(12.7) $$\sum_{r=1}^{m} \lambda_{rp}\lambda_{rq} = \delta_{pq} \qquad (p, q = 1, 2, \cdots, m; \quad p \leqq q),$$

where δ_{pq} in the Kronecker delta (zero when $p \neq q$ and unity when $p = q$). Since $p \leqq q$ and these indices range from 1 to m, the number of such conditions is $m(m + 1)/2$. There is a total of m^2 parameters in matrix **T**, and, since these are subject to $m(m + 1)/2$ restrictions, there remain

$$m(m - 1)/2$$

degrees of freedom of rotation in m-space.

The number of independent parameters may be associated with the same number of rotations in planes. The planes in which the rotations are made are determined by all possible pairs of reference axes. Of course, since the angles of rotation are determined subjectively, there is no reason to assume that the best overall transformation has been obtained after going through the $m(m - 1)/2$ unique planar rotations. Additional rotations in any plane may be made, if desired, and the new product of all the rotations becomes the final transformation.

Graphical methods are seldom used today for approximating simple structure, except by some researchers who use such methods in conjunction with the objective computer procedures. Nonetheless, a couple of illustrations are presented to clarify the general notion of transforming an initial to a final solution. An orthogonal rotation in the common-factor space of the initial pattern preserves the properties of the number of factors, their orthogonality, the communalities of the variables (or their lengths), and the total communality. The contributions of the respective factors may be quite different. The purpose of the transformation is to obtain a final pattern that exhibits low complexities for the variables, more level contributions of factors, and at least hyper-planar fit; or more specifically, approximates the simple structure principles enumerated in **6.2**.

The first illustration of a multiple-factor solution is based upon the two minres factors for the eight physical variables, given in Table 9.2. The coefficients in this pattern are the coordinates, with respect to the two minres axes, of the eight points representing the variables. The plot of these points is given in Figure 12.2, in which it is apparent that the points fall into two distinct clusters. If two lines, Y_1 and Y_2 were passed through these clusters of points, they would produce excellent geometric fit to the data. Such axes, however, are not orthogonal and therefore not appropriate for the present case.

If one axis is passed through a cluster and the other orthogonal to it, the standard of uncorrelated factors is met, but other standards are not well satisfied. In an attempt to meet the basic standards for a multiple-factor pattern, the axes M_1 and M_2 are

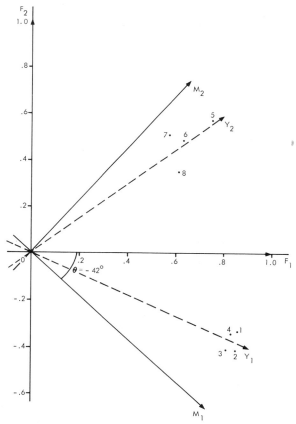

FIG. 12.2.—Rotation for eight physical variables

selected so as to be about equally removed from the two clusters of points. By inspection the resulting angle of rotation is taken to be $\theta_{12} = -42°$. Another worker, of course, might select a slightly different angle. The necessary trigonometric functions are

$$\cos(-42°) = .7431, \quad \sin(-42°) = -.6691,$$

the transformation from which may be written in the form

$$\mathbf{B} = \mathbf{A} \begin{bmatrix} .7431 & .6691 \\ -.6691 & .7431 \end{bmatrix},$$

where $\mathbf{A}$ is the pattern matrix of Table 9.2 and $\mathbf{B}$ is the final pattern which is presented in Table 12.1.

Table 12.1

Multiple-Factor Solution for Eight Physical Variables

(Initial solution: Minres, Table 9.2)

Variable j	M_1	M_2	h_j^2
1. Height	.853	.332	.838
2. Arm span	.906	.261	.889
3. Length of forearm	.874	.237	.820
4. Length of lower leg	.846	.302	.807
5. Weight	.175	.926	.888
6. Bitrochanteric diameter	.140	.788	.641
7. Chest girth	.082	.760	.584
8. Chest width	.216	.667	.492
Contribution of factor (V_p)	3.132	2.827	5.959

The pattern of Table 12.1 may be examined now to see how well it conforms to the standards for a multiple-factor solution. Since there are no sampling error formulas for this type of solution, the analyst usually must set some arbitrary level of significance. The present example is based on a large number of observations ($N = 305$), and hence even relatively small coefficients may not be insignificant. As a rough approximation, a standard error of .066 is obtained from Table B in the Appendix, for an $N = 305$ and an average correlation of .355 in the original data. If this standard error were applied to the coefficients in Table 12.1, even the smallest value might be judged significant. As crude as this test might be, it nevertheless throws doubt on the insignificance of the small values. It should be obvious that this is a poor example of an orthogonal multiple-factor solution (when the restriction of orthogonality is lifted, good approximation to simple structure can be attained, as will be seen in the next section).

The next example is based upon the centroid pattern, given in Table 8.15, for the thirteen psychological tests, involving three factors. In Figure 12.3 the thirteen points are plotted in the plane of the first two centroid axes. The first rotation is made in order to accomplish a leveling of the contributions of the first two factors. An angle $\theta_{12} = 50°$ is selected by inspection for this purpose. In such a rotation all points have negative projections on the second axis, designated as Y'_2. This rotation is immediately followed by reflection of the second axis, namely,

$$Y_2 = -Y'_2,$$

so as to yield positive coordinates. Although many points will have appreciable loadings for both Y_1 and Y_2, this can be adjusted by subsequent rotations.

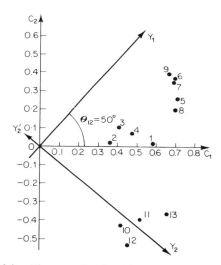

FIG. 12.3.—First rotation for thirteen psychological tests

The resulting matrix of transformation, including the reflection of the temporary second axis, takes the form:

$$\mathbf{T}_{12} = \begin{bmatrix} .6428 & .7660 \\ .7660 & -.6428 \end{bmatrix}.$$

Then, postmultiplying the first two columns of Table 8.15 by $\mathbf{T}_{12}$, yields the first two new factors Y_1, Y_2, which may be stored in a work table. These and the factor C_3 are mutually orthogonal, and their total contribution should be the same as that of the original system C_1, C_2, C_3.

The next rotation is made in the Y_1, C_3-plane. The plot of points is presented in Figure 12.4. In this transformation the first multiple-factor axis is selected. Therefore, it is important that this axis pass near a cluster of points and also be about 90° removed from a number of other points. To satisfy these requirements, the angle

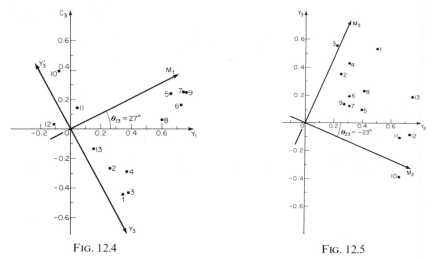

Fig. 12.4   Fig. 12.5

Figs. 12.4–12.5.—Second and final rotations for thirteen psychological tests

$\theta_{13} = 28°$ is chosen. In this case one of the axes is reflected again to obtain positive coordinates. The transformation matrix in this plane is given by

$$\mathbf{T}_{13} = \begin{bmatrix} .8829 & .4695 \\ .4695 & -.8829 \end{bmatrix}.$$

The final rotation is made in the Y_2, Y_3-plane. For this transformation the last two multiple-factor axes are selected so as to pass as near as possible to clusters of points. Thus M_2 passes near points 10, 11, 12, and 13, while M_3 lies close to the points 1, 2, 3, and 4 when the angle of rotation is taken to be $\theta_{23} = -23°$. The third transformation matrix is given by

$$\mathbf{T}_{23} = \begin{bmatrix} .9205 & .3907 \\ -.3907 & .9205 \end{bmatrix}.$$

The coefficients of the factors M_1, M_2, and M_3 are recorded in Table 12.2. The complete transformation matrix which carries the original factor weights into the final ones may be summarized, according to (12.6), as follows:

$$\mathbf{T} = \mathbf{T}_{12}\mathbf{T}_{13}\mathbf{T}_{23} = \begin{bmatrix} .5675 & .5872 & .5771 \\ .6763 & -.7322 & .0799 \\ .4695 & .3499 & -.8127 \end{bmatrix}.$$

The numerical check on the total contribution of a factor system, which can be made after each rotation, may again be employed on the final set of factors. Thus the numbers appearing in the last line of Table 12.2 sum to 6.967, which is the same as the total contribution of the original centroid factors.

256

The multiple-factor pattern of Table 12.2 satisfies the standards listed above. The contributions of the factors are relatively level in comparison with the centroid solution. The criteria of low complexity and good geometric fit also appear to be satisfied. For the present sample ($N = 145$) it is judged that a factor coefficient of two-tenths is insignificant. In general, the solution tends to satisfy the criteria for simple structure set forth in **6.2**. The above solution thus affords a good illustration of the multiple-factor type.

In naming the multiple factors, those variables having definitely significant weights, say, greater than four-tenths, are considered (indicated in bold face type in Table 12.2). The subgroups of tests identifying the multiple factors are the same as those employed in naming the first three group factors in the bi-factor solution of Table 7.6. The same names are then assigned to the multiple factors, as indicated in Table 12.2. It may be noted that each test is essentially a measure of only one of these factors, except Test 13, which appears to be reasonable, inasmuch as the test is a measure of speed of perception of simple geometric forms.

From the 1930s to the middle 50s many attempts were made to lighten the burden of the rotational task, and to set forth objective principles for the preferred multiple-factor solution. Some of these principles for simple structure were presented in **6.2**. In chapters 13 and 14 some of the more recent developments in analytical solutions are presented. For historical reasons it may be of interest to note some of the ingenious procedures that were devised during the period of dependence on graphical methods.

Because the simple-structure concept rests on subjective analysis of graphs, Thurstone has probably done more work than anyone else toward simplifying the chore

Table 12.2

Multiple-Factor Solution for Thirteen Psychological Tests

(Initial solution: centroid, Table 8.15)

Test j	Verbal M_1	Speed M_2	Spatial Relations M_3	Communality h_j^2
1. Visual perception	.096	.248	**.706**	.569
2. Cubes	.102	.089	**.425**	.199
3. Paper form board	.136	−.011	**.602**	.381
4. Flags	.193	.121	**.516**	.318
5. General information	**.702**	.324	.243	.657
6. Paragraph comprehension	**.719**	.214	.300	.653
7. Sentence completion	**.778**	.243	.237	.721
8. Word classification	**.562**	.291	.372	.539
9. Word meaning	**.791**	.198	.231	.718
10. Addition	.119	**.757**	−.100	.597
11. Code	.109	**.651**	.161	.462
12. Counting dots	−.083	**.703**	.210	.545
13. Straight-curved capitals	.070	**.619**	**.469**	.608
Contribution of factor (V_p)	2.670	2.292	2.005	6.967

of plotting graphs. As he states (Thurstone 1947, p. 377): "In the final acceptance or rejection of a simple-structure solution it is still the appearance of a set of graphs that determines the answer." Thurstone was among the first to seek an alternative graphical method to the two-dimensional operations by proposing three-dimensional sections, drawn in the plane of the paper however (Thurstone 1938a). The effect of a three-dimensional configuration in a plane is accomplished by extending the test vectors so that they all have unit projection on the first axis of the initial solution. In addition to the "method of extended vectors," Thurstone offers several other alternatives for rotation, devoting more than one-fourth of his text to the specific task of finding graphical substantiation for the simple-structure solution (Thurstone 1947).

In another attempt to reduce the computational labor of rotation to simple structure, Zimmerman (1946) proposed an ingenious scheme to eliminate the calculation of the numerical values of the intermediate coordinates. His procedure makes use of the principle of projection of a point from one graph to another, and involves only an ordinary drawing board, T-square, and drawing triangle. The two factor axes which are to be rotated are initially on two separate plots, with one coordinate for any point (representing a variable) projected horizontally from one plot and the other coordinate projected vertically from the second plot onto a new graph. Thus any axis can be rotated with any other without actual calculation of the numerical coordinates of the points. Only after all rotations have been made (to satisfy the appearance of simple structure), need one read and record the coordinates of the points with respect to the final axes. As a result of many rotations, and the inaccuracies of plotting, the basic relationship (2.50)—product of the factor matrix by its transpose—for the final rotated factors may not agree with that of the initial factors.

Another labor-saving approach was through the use of mechanical or electrical devices. One such machine, known as the "Factor Matrix Rotator"—conceived by Richard Gaylord and described by Harman and Harper (1953)—was of the analog type, that is, the readings were in the nature of displacements along a scale so that the figures had to be estimated from calibrations on the scale rather than read as precise digital values. The initial factor weights were set into the machine by means of a series of dials; then the positions of the points representing the test were viewed as points of light on a scope (cathode ray tube). At the beginning of the work, the dials representing the transformation matrix were set for the identity transformation so that the researcher could first view the plot of the points as they appear in the initial factor solution. The axes were rotated by a simple manipulation of a dial; when desirable positions of the axes were located, the researcher could cause the appropriate elements in the transformation matrix to be reset to take the new positions into account.

Of course, the plots of points viewed on the scope were for a pair of axes at a time. An immediate advantage over hand methods arose from the fact that while a decision was being made regarding the rotation of a particular pair of axes, it was possible to view each of the remaining factor axes, in turn, with each of the two under consideration. The usual procedure employed by researchers was to view the plots in relation to all possible pairs of axes and on a schematic chart to note those planes in which rotation seemed most desirable and those that might be considered in order to keep the number of rotations to a minimum. When final decisions had been made about the location of factor axes to exhibit simple structure, the elements of both the transformation matrix and the final factor matrix was obtained by turning a dial and reading a scale, the computations being done electronically.

The Factor Matrix Rotator was designed primarily to handle problems of up to 50 tests and 12 factors and involving orthogonal rotations. Nonetheless, the machine had been applied to problems involving up to 130 tests and 24 factors. Further, it had been employed in connection with oblique transformations. However, applications beyond the basic capacity of the Rotator necessarily involved extensive additional computations off the machine.

Before leaving the subject of alternatives to the complete graphical method, it should be remembered that all of these methods arose as a result of the simple structure concept, and the lack of any real objective means of arriving at such a solution. The work of Paul Horst (1941) was among the very earliest in which the transformation from an arbitrary factor matrix into a simple-structure matrix was almost completely objective. The criterion he employs is that of maximizing the ratio of the sum of squares of the "significant" factor loadings to the sum of squares of all the loadings. A variant of this method is proposed by Tucker (1944), in which he gets the solution for all factors simultaneously, using graphs for the selection of subgroups of tests.

12.3. *Geometric Basis for an Oblique Solution*

In the early history and development of factor analysis, solutions in terms of uncorrelated factors were tacitly assumed to be the only type permissible. Then, in the 1940s the notion of correlated factors not only became acceptable, but frequently preferable to uncorrelated ones. For the field of psychology, Thurstone (1947, p. vii) states the case as follows:

> If we impose the restriction that the reference frame shall be orthogonal, then we are imposing the condition that the factors or parameters shall be uncorrelated in the experimental population or in the general population . . . . It seems just as unnecessary to require that mental traits shall be uncorrelated in the general population as to require that height and weight be uncorrelated in the general population. This admission of oblique axes has also been debated and is not yet generally accepted by students of factor theory.

It is clear that a certain simplicity of interpretation is sacrificed upon relinquishing the standard of orthogonality. This disadvantage may be offset, however, if the linear descriptions of the variables in terms of correlated factors can be made simpler than in the case of uncorrelated ones. Generally this is possible.

In the remainder of this chapter the basic methods are described for transforming some initial orthogonal pattern to an oblique solution that approximates simple structure. The communalities of the variables, which are determined by the common-factor space of the preliminary solution, remain invariant under this transformation. Therefore, the entire development is made in the common-factor space.

When the factors are uncorrelated the concepts of factor pattern and structure are identical. Therefore, in the foregoing text (with the exception of **11.5**), no distinction was necessary, and the term "pattern" was used synonymously with "solution." When correlated factors are employed, however, a solution comprises both the pattern and structure. The distinction in this case can best be shown geometrically.

A pattern, in terms of common factors only, may be represented as follows:

$$(12.8) \qquad \tilde{z}_j = b_{j1}T_1 + b_{j2}T_2 + \cdots + b_{jm}T_m \qquad (j = 1, 2, \cdots, n),$$

where b's are employed to denote coefficients of correlated factors. As pointed out in **4.10**, the curl denotes a variable projected into the common-factor space. Since the analysis of this chapter is entirely in the common-factor space, it will simplify matters to drop the curl. The coefficients may be considered as the coordinates of a point P_j with respect to the factor axes. This interpretation may be made whether the factors are represented by orthogonal or oblique axes.

For the case of two factors these ideas may be illustrated by Figure 12.6. When the correlation between the factors T_1 and T_2 is known, the unit vectors representing T_1 and T_2 are separated by an angle $\theta_{12} = \text{arc cos } r_{T_1 T_2}$. The oblique reference system

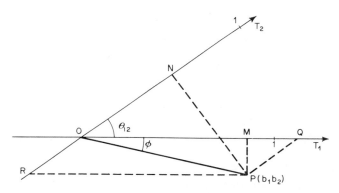

F<small>IG</small>. 12.6—Distinction between coordinate and correlation in oblique reference system

is thus determined. Any variable z_j is represented by a vector, OP, whose length and direction are determined by its coordinates. Again, for the sake of simplicity, the point representing any variable z_j is designated P instead of P_j, and its coordinates are shown as (b_1, b_2) instead of (b_{j1}, b_{j2}) with respect to the two oblique axes T_1 and T_2. From the definition of general Cartesian coordinates, given in **4.8**, it may be noted that the coordinates b_1, b_2 are given by the line segments OQ and OR, respectively. For the hypothetical variable z_j in Figure 12.6, the first coordinate is positive and greater than unity, while the second coordinate is negative and less than unity.

The length of the vector corresponding to z_j can be determined by means of formula (4.39), which in this case may be written as follows:

(12.9)
$$D^2(OP) = \sum_{p=1}^{2} \sum_{q=1}^{2} b_{jp} b_{jq} \cos \theta_{pq}$$

$$= b_{j1} b_{j1} \cos \theta_{11} + b_{j1} b_{j2} \cos \theta_{12} + b_{j2} b_{j1} \cos \theta_{21}$$
$$+ b_{j2} b_{j2} \cos \theta_{22}.$$

In this formula each of the angles θ_{11} and θ_{22} is equal to zero, and θ_{12} is the angle between the reference axes. Hence $\cos \theta_{11} = \cos \theta_{22} = 1$ and $\cos \theta_{12} = r_{T_1 T_2}$. The expression (12.9) then reduces to

(12.10)
$$D^2(OP) = b_{j1}^2 + b_{j2}^2 + 2 b_{j1} b_{j2} r_{T_1 T_2}.$$

The right-hand member is the communality h_j^2 of the variable z_j. The length of the vector is then equal to the square root of the communality, namely,

(12.11)
$$D(OP) = h_j.$$

The geometric interpretation of the correlation of a variable with a factor will be given next. Let the angle between the vector corresponding to z_j and the reference vector T_1 be denoted by ϕ. Also let the projections of the end point P upon the T_1 and T_2 axes be M and N, respectively, as indicated in Figure 12.6. From the right triangle OMP, it is apparent that

$$\cos \phi = \frac{D(OM)}{D(OP)}.$$

This formula reduces to

(12.12)
$$D(OM) = h_j \cos \phi$$

upon making use of (12.11). Employing the expression (4.56) for a reproduced correlation in the common-factor space, this formula can be simplified further. In the present example, one variable is z_j and the other is T_1 so that their scalar product, according to (4.56) is

$$\hat{r}_{jT_1} = h_j h_{T_1} \cos \phi.$$

Since the length or "communality", of any factor is unity, this expression may be written in the form

(12.13)
$$r_{jT_1} = h_j \cos \phi.$$

In this formula, and in all other representations of correlations of variables with factors, the hat is dropped for simplicity. Substituting (12.13) into (12.12), the projection of a vector upon a reference axis may finally be expressed as follows:

(12.14)
$$D(OM) = r_{jT_1}.$$

In a similar manner it can be shown that the projection, $D(ON)$, of the vector z_j on the T_2 axis is the correlation of the variable with the second factor. Of course, the correlation between two factors is also given by the projection of either reference vector upon the other.

By referring to Figure 12.6, the distinction between a coordinate and a correlation can be seen clearly. The coordinates may be positive or negative and may be greater than one. A correlation coefficient also may be positive or negative but can never exceed unity. It may also be observed that the coordinates and correlations approach coincidence as the reference vectors approach orthogonality.

A complete solution involving correlated factors must consist of a pattern and a structure. The factor pattern may be exhibited in equation form or, more compactly, in a table giving the coefficients of the factors. The structure usually is presented in tabular or matrix form. In addition to the pattern and structure, an oblique solution should include a table of intercorrelations of factors.

12.4. *Oblique Primary-Factor Solution*

The form of oblique multiple-factor solution developed in this section leads to a set of factors which have been called "primary" (Thurstone 1947, chap. XV), when considered in the context of psychological traits. Aside from the particular application, and although arrived at somewhat differently, it is convenient to designate the oblique solution of this section as "primary-factor" to distinguish it from another form of oblique solution considered in the next section.

Starting with any initial orthogonal pattern, it is possible to transform it into an oblique primary-factor solution which, more or less, satisfies the conditions of simple structure. The procedures outlined in this section are intended for hand methods, and therefore would be useful only for small problems. However, the heuristic value goes far beyond the immediate applications.

1. Initial orthogonal pattern.—Any preliminary orthogonal solution (e.g., principal-factor, minres, maximum-likelihood) may be employed. The method will be illustrated with the same data employed in **12.2**, namely, the two-factor minres solution of Table 9.2 for the eight physical variables.

2. Reduced pattern.—Since the coordinate axes representing the oblique factors will be made to pass through the centroids of clusters of variables, it is necessary to identify such groupings, say, G_p ($p = 1, 2, \cdots, m$). These groups of variables may be established from the earlier analysis which led to the orthogonal solution, or they may be found by inspection of the initial pattern or graphs of the points. By inspection of Table 9.2, it is evident from the algebraic signs of the coefficients that the plot of these eight points with respect to the two minres axes would lead to a cluster in the fourth quadrant for the first four variables, and a cluster in the first quadrant for the last four. The actual plot of these points in Figure 12.7 bears this out.

To determine the directions of the oblique reference vectors, lines may be drawn by inspection from the origin through the clusters of variables. The angles which these new axes make with the old may be measured, and the transformation may thus be determined. Such a procedure is completely subjective, and may be replaced by the following operational method.

A composite variable v_p is assumed through each cluster of n_p variables in group G_p. This type of variable was designated T_p in **11.5**, paragraph **1**, but it will be found

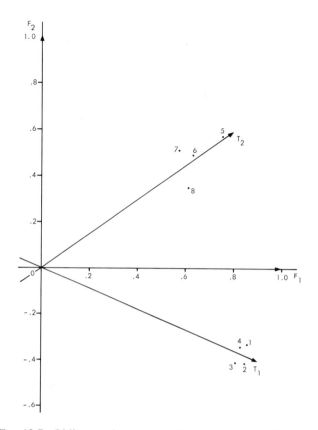

F_{IG}. 12.7—Oblique reference axes through clusters of points

more convenient in the present development to reserve T_p for the standardized form of the oblique factor. For the example, the two composite variables are defined by

$$v_1 = z_1 + z_2 + z_3 + z_4 \quad \text{and} \quad v_2 = z_5 + z_6 + z_7 + z_8.$$

The variance of a composite variable is given by

$$(12.15) \qquad\qquad s_{v_p}^2 = \sum (r_{jk}; \quad j, k \in G_p),$$

in which there are n_p self-correlations of unity. Applying this formula to the two composite variables and employing the correlations from Table 2.3, the resulting standard deviations are found to be

$$s_{v_1} = 3.7465 \quad \text{and} \quad s_{v_2} = 3.4117.$$

It is now possible to express the composite variables in terms of the factors of the initial solution. The coefficients in such linear expressions are also the correlations of the composite variables with the factors (the factors in the initial solution being uncorrelated). Since the factors are standardized variables, the correlation of any composite variable v_p with a factor F is given by

(12.16) $$r_{v_p F} = \sum (r_{jF}; \quad j \in G_p)/s_{v_p},$$

where the individual correlations of the variables with the factor are, of course, the coefficients in the initial orthogonal pattern for the variables comprising the group G_p. The correlation for the first composite variable of the example with the first minres factor is calculated as follows:

$$r_{v_1 F_1} = (.856 + .848 + .808 + .831)/3.7465 = .8923,$$

where the values in the numerator are taken from Table 9.2. In a similar manner, the correlations of each of the composite variables with each of the minres factors can be obtained, and the results presented in the form of a *reduced factor pattern,* as follows:

$$u_1 = v_1/s_{v_1} = .8923F_1 - .3969F_2,$$
$$u_2 = v_2/s_{v_2} = .7495F_1 + .5639F_2.$$

the standardized form of a composite variable v is indicated by u. The reduced pattern equations have the same properties as those for individual variables.

3. Transformation matrix.—Since the oblique primary-factors are represented by the coordinate axes passing through the points corresponding to the composite variables u_p, the reduced pattern provides the basis for determining the transformation matrix. The coefficients of the reduced pattern give the coordinates of the composite points, and division by the respective distances of these points from the origin produces the direction cosines of the lines through them. These lines are precisely the oblique factors T_p and hence these direction cosines with respect to the initial reference system constitute the elements of the transformation matrix.

For example, the distance of the first point from the origin is

$$\sqrt{(.8923)^2 + (-.3969)^2} = .9766,$$

according to (4.12). Then the direction cosines of T_1 with respect to the F_1 and F_2 axes are given by:

$$t_{11} = .8923/.9766 = .9137 \quad \text{and} \quad t_{21} = -.3969/.9766 = -.4064.$$

The direction cosines of the T_2 axis with respect to the orthogonal axes F_1 and F_2 are determined in a similar manner. The resulting transformation matrix may be written as follows:

$$\mathbf{T} = \begin{bmatrix} t_{11} & t_{12} \\ t_{21} & t_{22} \end{bmatrix} = \begin{bmatrix} .9137 & .7991 \\ -.4064 & .6012 \end{bmatrix}.$$

While this matrix is written specifically for the illustrative example, the ideas and notation are generalizable to any number of factors. The symbol $\mathbf{T}$ is used in general for the transformation matrix for any number of axes.

4. Factor correlations.—After the direction cosines of the oblique reference

264

vectors have been obtained, the correlations among such factors can be determined. The sum of paired products of the direction cosines of two vectors gives the cosine of the angle between them, according to (4.47); and, by (4.48), this cosine is equal to the correlation between the two variables represented by the vectors. Hence, the correlation between T_1 and T_2 in the present example is

$$r_{T_1 T_2} = .9137(.7991) - .4064(.6012) = .4858.$$

The self-correlations, or variances, of the factors may be calculated in the same manner. These sums of squares by columns in the transformation matrix must be unity, and thus provide a check on the calculation of the elements of the transformation matrix.

More generally, the scalar product between any pair of vectors T_p and T_q is equal to their correlation according to (4.56) and (4.54). Such scalar products can be designated in matrix form, as follows:

(12.17) $$\mathbf{\Phi} = \mathbf{T'T}.$$

From the correlation between factors the angle of separation of the reference vectors can be determined if desired. In the present case this angle is given by

$$\theta_{12} = \text{arc cos } .4858 = 61°.$$

5. Factor structure.—The projections of the vectors representing the variables upon the oblique primary-axes can now be determined. As indicated in (12.14), such projections are the correlations of variables with the factors, i.e., the elements of the factor structure. In order to derive formulas for the structure values, Figure 12.8 has been constructed. In this figure the oblique axes T_1 and T_2 have been taken in the first quadrant of the F_1, F_2 reference system only to simplify the development, the results being the same regardless of the quadrants in which the oblique axes are located. The angles from the F_1 axis to the T_1 and T_2 axes are denoted by α and β, respectively.

Any variable z_j may be represented in this figure by a point P whose coordinates (a_{j1}, a_{j2}) with respect to the original minres axes are the coefficients in the initial pattern equation. The variable may also be construed as a vector from the origin to the point P. The angle from the F_1 axis to this vector is denoted by ϕ. Then the projection of the vector upon the T_1 axis is given by

$$D(OM) = D(OP)\cos(\phi - \alpha).$$

As noted in (12.14), the projection $D(OM)$ is equal to the correlation r_{jT_1}, and from (12.11) the length of the vector $D(OP)$ is h_j. Making these substitutions and expanding the cosine of the difference of two angles, this formula becomes

$$r_{jT_1} = h_j(\cos \phi \cos \alpha + \sin \phi \sin \alpha),$$
$$= (h_j \cos \phi)\cos \alpha + (h_j \sin \phi)\sin \alpha.$$

Now $h_j \cos \phi$ and $h_j \sin \phi$ are the projections a_{j1} and a_{j2} of the vector representing z_j on the F_1 and F_2 axes, respectively. Then the formula finally becomes

$$r_{jT_1} = a_{j1} \cos \alpha + a_{j2} \sin \alpha.$$

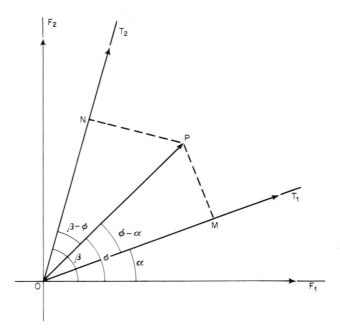

F$_\text{IG}$. 12.8—Derivation of structure values for primary-factor system

In a similar manner it can be shown that the projection $D(ON)$, of the vector representing z_j on the T_2 axis, is given by

$$r_{jT_2} = a_{j1} \cos \beta + a_{j2} \sin \beta.$$

These results may be summarized in the following matrix form:

$$(r_{jT_1} \quad r_{jT_2}) = (a_{j1} \quad a_{j2}) \cdot \begin{bmatrix} t_{11} = \cos \alpha & t_{12} = \cos \beta \\ t_{21} = \sin \alpha & t_{22} = \sin \beta \end{bmatrix}$$

where, in the last matrix, the elements of the first column are the direction cosines of T_1 with respect to F_1 and F_2, and those of the second column are the direction cosines of T_2.

The elements of a structure can be generalized to problems involving more than two factors. Thus, the transformation from an initial orthogonal factor pattern **A** to the oblique structure **S** is given by:

(12.18) $$S = AT,$$

where the transformation matrix **T** contains in its columns the direction cosines of the oblique axes with respect to the orthogonal frame of reference.

For the example the minres pattern matrix of Table 9.2 is multiplied by the transformation matrix to get the structure values of Table 12.3. The correlations of the composite variables with the oblique factors are obtained by multiplying the reduced

266

pattern matrix by the same transformation matrix. These values are presented in the reduced structure of Table 12.3.

6. Factor pattern.—To complete the solution in terms of correlated factors, the linear descriptions of the variables are required as well as their correlations with the factors. The pattern coefficients are the coordinates with respect to the oblique axes

Table 12.3

Oblique Primary-Factor Solution for Eight Physical Variables

(Initial solution: Minres, Table 9.2)

Variable j	Structure: **S**		Pattern: **P**	
			Lankiness T_1	Stockiness T_2
	r_{jT_1}	r_{jT_2}		
1	.914	.489	.885	.059
2	.942	.430	.960	−.036
3	.904	.400	.929	−.053
4	.898	.458	.884	.028
5	.453	.943	−.007	.946
6	.377	.800	−.015	.807
7	.313	.761	−.074	.797
8	.412	.696	.097	.649
	Reduced Structure		Reduced Pattern	
u_1	.977	.474	.977	−.001
u_2	.456	.938	.000	.938

of the points representing the variables and could have been obtained directly[2] from the initial factor pattern. It is more convenient, however, to calculate these values after the oblique factor structure has been obtained, making use of the relationships between pattern and structure developed in **2.9**.

If the oblique factor pattern for the illustrative example is denoted by

$$z_j = b_{j1}T_1 + b_{j2}T_2 \qquad\qquad (j = 1, 2, \cdots, 8),$$

the problem is to determine the coefficients b_{j1}, b_{j2}. For any variable z_j, multiply this expression by T_1 and T_2 in turn, sum for the N values, and divide by N. The resulting equations are

$$r_{jT_1} = b_{j1} \qquad + b_{j2}r_{T_1T_2},$$
$$r_{jT_2} = b_{j1}r_{T_2T_1} + b_{j2}.$$

[2]It is possible to obtain the coordinates of the points with respect to the oblique reference system directly by transformation of the original coordinates. Since, in factor analysis, both the coordinates and the projections (i.e., the coefficients and the correlations) are desired, the present approach is suggested as the simplest and the one best adapted to systematic calculations. First the projections are obtained, and then in the next stage of the analysis the coordinates are calculated.

There is such a pair of simultaneous equations for determining the two unknowns b_{j1}, b_{j2} for each variable z_j. In these equations the left-hand members contain the known elements of the factor structure. The correlation between the factors also is known from paragraph **4** above. Hence, the matrix of coefficients of the unknown b's is

$$\mathbf{\Phi} = \begin{bmatrix} 1 & .4858 \\ .4858 & 1 \end{bmatrix}$$

and remains the same for all variables.

   The foregoing procedures can be generalized to any number of variables and factors. The matrix relationships between the common-factor portions of an oblique pattern and structure are shown in **2.9**. In a notation more suitable to this chapter equation (2.43) becomes:

(12.19) $$\mathbf{S} = \mathbf{P\Phi},$$

which states that the factor structure $\mathbf{S}$ is equal to the pattern matrix $\mathbf{P}$ postmultiplied by the matrix $\mathbf{\Phi}$ of factor correlations. Solving this equation explicitly for the factor pattern yields:

(12.20) $$\mathbf{P} = \mathbf{S\Phi}^{-1}.$$

While this equation can be employed to get the factor pattern from the known structure values and correlations of factors, the work implied in getting the inverse of $\mathbf{\Phi}$ for many factors can be very substantial without the use of high-speed computers. For a small number of factors the work of computing the oblique factor pattern can best be done by using the square root method. This is illustrated for the simple example in Table 12.4. The resulting values of the factor coefficients are repeated in the pattern matrix in Table 12.3, including those for the composite variables.

   An alternative formula can be developed for calculating the oblique pattern, involving the initial factor pattern instead of the oblique structure. The structure is expressed in terms of the initial pattern in (12.18), and the factor correlation matrix is expressed in terms of the transformation matrix in (12.17). Making use of these relationships, formula (12.20) then becomes:

(12.21) $$\mathbf{P} = \mathbf{A}(\mathbf{T'})^{-1}.$$

This expression also involves the calculation of the inverse of a matrix of order equal to the number of factors. If one wishes to employ $\mathbf{A}$ instead of $\mathbf{S}$ for determining $\mathbf{P}$ then the worksheet of Table 11.7 will be found convenient.

   7. Contributions of oblique factors.—After an oblique factor pattern has been obtained, the direct and joint contributions of these factors can be determined. The communality of a variable z_j as given by (12.8), may be expressed as follows:

(12.22) $$h_j^2 = b_{j1}^2 + b_{j2}^2 + \cdots + b_{jm}^2 + 2b_{j1}b_{j2}r_{T_1 T_2} + \cdots + 2b_{j,m-1}b_{jm}r_{T_{m-1} T_m}.$$

The terms in the right-hand member of this equation represent the portions of the communality of z_j ascribable to the respective factors. The *direct contributions* of the

Table 12.4

Calculation of a Pattern from a Structure

	Schematic		Numerical Example			
Original Matrices	Computed Matrices		Original Matrices		Computed Matrices	
Factor Correlations† Φ (Assume $\Phi = Q'Q$)	Square Root Matrix Q' (Square root operation Q^{-1} on Φ)		1.0000 .4858	* 1.0000	1.0000 .4858	.8741
Identity Matrix **I**	Q^{-1} (Square root operation Q^{-1} on **I**)		1.0000 0	0 1.0000	1.0000 0	−.5558 1.1440
	$\Phi^{-1} = Q^{-1}(Q')^{-1}$ (Row-by-row multiplication of Q^{-1} by itself)				1.3089 −.6358	−.6358 1.3087
Factor Structure	Factor Pattern		.914 .942 .904 .898	.489 .430 .400 .458	.885 .960 .929 .884	.059 −.036 −.053 .028
S	**P**		.453 .377 .313	.943 .800 .761	−.007 −.015 −.074	.946 .807 .797
	$(P = S\Phi^{-1})$		.412 .977	.696 .474	.097 .977	.649 −.001
	(Row-to-row multiplication of **S** by Φ^{-1})		.456	.938	.000	.938

†The square root decomposition of Φ into $Q'Q$ should not be confused with (12.17) in which the correlations among the factors are obtained by premultiplying the transformation matrix **T** by its transpose.

factors are given by the first m terms, while the *joint contributions* of the factors are furnished by the remaining terms.

In **2.4** the total contribution of a factor to the variances of all the variables was defined for the case of uncorrelated factors. When the factors are correlated, their contributions to the variances of the variables can come about through their interaction with other factors as well as through their individual impact. Thus, total contributions of oblique factors can be obtained by summing the separate contributions, as exhibited in (12.22), over all the variables. It is convenient to designate these as *total direct contributions*:

$$(12.23) \qquad V_p = \sum_{j=1}^{n} b_{jp}^2 \qquad (p = 1, 2, \cdots, m),$$

and as *total joint contributions*:

$$(12.24) \qquad V_{pq} = 2r_{T_p T_q} \sum_{j=1}^{n} b_{jp} b_{jq} \qquad (p, q = 1, 2, \cdots, m; \quad p < q).$$

These two sets of expressions can be arranged conveniently in a triangular matrix in which the direct contributions are put in the diagonal and the joint contributions in the lower triangle.

In the illustrative example the total direct contributions of the two factors are given by $V_1 = 3.365$ and $V_2 = 2.611$, while the total joint contribution of these factors is $V_{12} = -.021$. The grand total of the contributions of a set of oblique factors should, of course, be equal to the total communality of the original solution. In the present example this total (5.955) agrees within a few points in the last decimal place with the original value from Table 9.2. The total direct contributions of the factors account for all but a negligible amount of the total common-factor variance in the particular example.

A striking similarity may be noted between the procedures outlined in this section and those in **11.5**, paragraph 1. The methods are quite similar, the distinction being in the data to which the methods are applied. Here the raw data are the coefficients of an initial orthogonal factor pattern, while in **11.5** the raw data are the correlations among the variables themselves.

12.5.   *Oblique Reference-Axes Solution*

An alternative form of oblique solution is presented in this section. In an endeavor to satisfy the intuitive principles of simple structure, Thurstone (1947, chap. XV) devised an ingenious procedure to guarantee a certain number of zeros in the factor solution. To this end, he introduced a reference system consisting of the normals to the coordinate hyperplanes of the primary-factor solution of the preceding section. While this procedure tends to produce the desired number of zeros, it does complicate the situation by considering a second reference system. In the remainder of this section an exposition is presented of this new "oblique reference system," and then in the following section the distinction and functional relationship between this and the "primary-factor system" is developed.

For a common-factor space of m dimensions there are, of course, m reference axes Λ_p ($p = 1, 2, \cdots, m$), each of which is normal to a coordinate hyperplane π_p (of $m - 1$ dimensions) as defined in **4.3**. In ordinary space, the hyperplanes are actual planes, and the three reference axes are normal to the three coordinate planes. For a common-factor space of only two dimensions, the hyperplane becomes a line, and its normal is another line at right-angles to it. Specifically for the example of the preceding section, the "hyperplane" π_1 in the T_1T_2-plane is the space with the T_1 axis missing—in other words, the T_2 axis; and similarly the π_2 hyperplane is the T_1 axis. Then, the reference axis Λ_1 is perpendicular to π_1 ($\equiv T_2$) and Λ_2 is perpendicular to π_2 ($\equiv T_1$), as indicated in Figure 12.9. It is evident from this figure that the four points hovering close to T_1 have projections on Λ_2 very close to zero. Similarly, the variables close to T_2 have near zero projections on Λ_1.

Without drawing a three-dimensional diagram, three oblique coordinate planes π_1, π_2, and π_3 can be imagined. The normals to these planes are the reference axes Λ_1, Λ_2, and Λ_3, respectively. For each of these axes, every point in the plane to which it is orthogonal will have zero projection upon it. This will be true whether

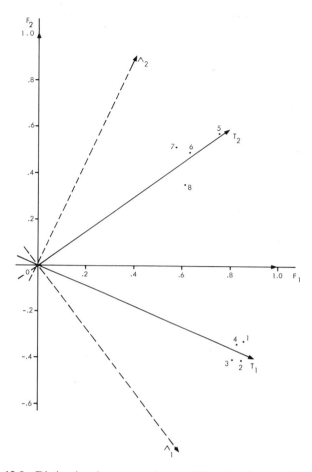

F_{IG}. 12.9—Distinction between primary (T) and reference (Λ) axes

the points in the coordinate plane cluster around the intersections of these planes (T_1, T_2, and T_3) or fan out in these planes.

The generalization of these properties to any m-space is immediate. All points lying in, or close to, a hyperplane π_p will have near zero projections on the normal Λ_p to this hyperplane. It is probably this property—which guarantees the first criterion for simple structure (see **6.2**)—that led Thurstone to the choice of the reference axes. Also, by requiring that each hyperplane by "overdetermined," i.e., contain at least m points, the second criterion for simple structure is assured. Thus it can be seen why Thurstone developed the oblique solution on the basis of reference axes which would be normal to geometric spaces, so that every point in such a space would have a zero projection at least on the axis at right angles to it. Concentrating on the zero projections, Thurstone plays down the factor pattern associated with the

271

reference axes. For heuristic reasons, the complete oblique solution in terms of such reference axes will be developed here, including the factor pattern as well as the factor structure.

Just as in the preceding section, the oblique solution in terms of the new reference axes is obtained by rotation of some initial orthogonal solution. Conventionally, the transformation in this case is designated by Λ and the resulting oblique factor structure by V, while in this text A is employed for the initial matrix of coefficients of the orthogonal factors rather than F which might be confused with the factors themselves. Then in place of (12.18) there is the following equation:

$$(12.25) \qquad\qquad\qquad V = A\Lambda.$$

Again, as in the transformation matrix T of (12.18), the matrix Λ contains in its columns the direction cosines of the oblique axes (Λ_p) with respect to the orthogonal frame of reference.

Knowing the previous transformation matrix T it is possible to determine the desired matrix Λ without resorting to graphical methods. The elements of T are the direction cosines of the T-axes (passing through the clusters of variables or determined by the intersections of the coordinate hyperplanes containing a spread of the variables). These axes may be viewed as additional vectors (like the variables) in the original orthogonal reference frame. In this manner they may be considered as extensions of the factor pattern A, just as the reduced pattern in the preceding section. Since the matrix T was written with the direction cosines in columns, it is necessary to take the transpose of T in the extension of A. Then applying the transformation (12.25) to this continuation of A, there results

$$(12.26) \qquad\qquad\qquad T'\Lambda = D,$$

which is a matrix of the scalar products or correlations among vectors T_p and Λ_p ($p = 1, 2, \cdots, m$). Since Λ_p is normal to the hyperplane

$$\pi_p = OT_1T_2 \cdots)T_p(\cdots T_m,$$

it is uncorrelated with every T-axis except T_p. Hence, the diagonal values of D are the correlations between corresponding Λ and T factors, while all values off the diagonal are zero, i.e., D is a diagonal matrix. The matrix D represents the relationships among the bi-orthogonal axes—the two oblique systems, primary and reference, whose corresponding axes are orthogonal.

From the relationship (12.26), the explicit expression for the transformation matrix Λ becomes:

$$(12.27) \qquad\qquad\qquad \Lambda = (T')^{-1}D.$$

From the previous knowledge of T, the inverse of its transpose can be computed. However, this computation may be rather laborious because T is not a symmetric matrix. From the relationship (12.17), the inverse of T can be obtained when the inverse of the symmetric matrix Φ is known. Taking the inverse of both sides of (12.17) produces

$$\Phi = T^{-1}(T')^{-1}$$

and then premultiplying both sides by $\mathbf{T}$ produces the desired result:

$$(12.28) \qquad (\mathbf{T}')^{-1} = \mathbf{T}\mathbf{\Phi}^{-1}.$$

Then $\mathbf{\Lambda}$ is obtained by normalizing the columns of this matrix, i.e., dividing each element in a column by the square-root of the sum of the squares of all the elements in that column.

After the transformation matrix $\mathbf{\Lambda}$ is determined, the initial orthogonal factor pattern is postmultiplied by it to obtain the new factor structure $\mathbf{V}$, according to (12.25). The intercorrelations of the reference factors Λ_p can be obtained by the following matrix multiplication:

$$(12.29) \qquad \mathbf{\Lambda}'\mathbf{\Lambda} = \mathbf{\Psi},$$

where the resulting matrix is designated $\mathbf{\Psi}$ to distinguish it from the matrix $\mathbf{\Phi}$ of correlations among the factors T. Then, to complete this oblique solution, the factor pattern $\mathbf{W}$ in terms of the reference axes Λ_p is computed by either of the formulas:

$$(12.30) \qquad \mathbf{W} = \mathbf{V}\mathbf{\Psi}^{-1}$$

which corresponds to (12.20), or

$$(12.31) \qquad \mathbf{W} = \mathbf{A}(\mathbf{\Lambda}')^{-1},$$

which corresponds to (12.21).

To illustrate the foregoing, the example of eight physical variables again is employed. First, the transformation matrix $\mathbf{\Lambda}$ is required, and it is obtained by use of formula (12.27). The $(\mathbf{T}')^{-1}$ for this formula is calculated by means of (12.28) using the values for $\mathbf{T}$ and $\mathbf{\Phi}^{-1}$ from the preceding section, producing

$$(\mathbf{T}')^{-1} = \begin{bmatrix} .6879 & .4649 \\ -.9142 & 1.0452 \end{bmatrix}.$$

Then, normalizing by columns produces:

$$\mathbf{\Lambda} = \begin{bmatrix} .6012 & .4064 \\ -.7991 & .9137 \end{bmatrix},$$

as the transformation matrix to the new reference axes.

The new factor structure $\mathbf{V}$ is obtained by multiplying the original minres pattern, and the reduced pattern matrix, by this transformation matrix, and the results are shown in Table 12.5. The new factor pattern $\mathbf{W}$ is calculated by (12.30), using the algorithm of Table 12.4 with $\mathbf{\Psi}$ in place of $\mathbf{\Phi}$, and $\mathbf{V}$ in place of $\mathbf{S}$. The resulting pattern $\mathbf{W}$ is given in Table 12.4. The correlation between Λ_1 and Λ_2, obtained from the general expression (12.29) is simply the sum of the two cross-products of the direction cosines in $\mathbf{\Lambda}$, namely $-.4858$.[3]

---

[3]It will be noted that this correlation is simply the negative of the correlation between the factors T_1 and T_2. From Figure 12.9 it can be seen that cos (angle between Λ_1 and Λ_2) $= \cos(180° - \theta_{12}) = -\cos\theta_{12}$, so that the correlation of one set of axes is the negative of that between the other set.

Table 12.5

Oblique Reference Solution for Eight Physical Variables

(Initial solution: Minres, Table 9.2)

Variable j	Structure: $\mathbf{V}$		Pattern: $\mathbf{W}$	
	$r_{j\Lambda_1}$	$r_{j\Lambda_2}$	Λ_1	Λ_2
1	.774	.052	1.046	.559
2	.839	−.032	1.078	.492
3	.813	−.045	1.034	.458
4	.773	.025	1.027	.524
5	−.005	.827	.518	1.079
6	−.014	.706	.431	.915
7	−.065	.697	.358	.871
8	.084	.567	.471	.796
	Reduced Structure		Reduced Pattern	
u_1	.854	−.000	1.118	.542
u_2	−.000	.820	.522	1.073

It may also be of some interest to compute the diagonal matrix $\mathbf{D}$

$$\mathbf{D} = \mathbf{T}'\mathbf{\Lambda} = \begin{bmatrix} .8741 & 0 \\ 0 & .8741 \end{bmatrix},$$

giving the correlations between corresponding T and Λ factors. For the simple case of only two factors, each of these correlations is .8741.

12.6.   *Relationship between Two Types of Oblique Solutions*

In the preceding two sections, the several parts that make up an oblique multiple-factor solution were outlined very explicitly for the set of T-axes and the set of Λ-axes. The T-factors of **12.4** are called *primary factors* by Thurstone, and the Λ-factors of **12.5** are merely called *reference axes*. He uses the structure of the latter system as an indication of the pattern of the former system, and thereby identifies the primary factors.

The reference axes lie in the common-factor space and are said to be bi-orthogonal to the primary factors. Certainly the reference factors of **12.5** would seem more like mathematical abstractions than the primary factors of **12.4**. The only reason for the strong interest of the Thurstone school in the simple reference structure $\mathbf{V}$ is its similarity to the primary-factor pattern, which is shown in (12.36) below. The bi-orthogonal system of coordinate axes may have been an ingenious idea in the 1930s, but certainly is not necessary today. This dual system—reference and primary—is presented for its historical and traditional interest; the direct approach to primary solutions (by hand methods in **11.5** and in **12.4**, and by computer means in **14.5**) is strongly recommended.

The attempt made in the preceding sections was to clearly define and distinguish the two sets of oblique axes. It was recognized that the oblique solution is dependent upon an initial orthogonal pattern from which clustering of variables might be discerned, or else some graphical means might be necessary to locate the axes. Then the primary factors T_p were passed through these clusters of variables, and the correlations among the factors were determined. Specifically, the analysis of the variables in terms of these oblique factors was shown both by the correlations with the factors (structure **S**) and by the coefficients in the linear expressions in terms of the factors (pattern **P**). Similarly, when the analysis was made in terms of the reference axes Λ_p, both the structure **V** and the pattern **W** were displayed. It would have been quite sufficient to have a single oblique solution, consisting of the structure **S** and the pattern **P**. However, since the structure **V** had been so popular it seems important to bring into clear perspective the meaning of the apparently alternative oblique solutions. To assist in the ensuing discussion, the notation employed in the oblique solutions is summarized in Table 12.6.

Table 12.6

Notation Employed in Bi-orthogonal Oblique Solutions

Type of Solution	Factor Designation	Initial Orthogonal Pattern	Transformation Matrix	Factor Correlations	Oblique Solution	
					Structure	Pattern
Sec. **12.4**	T_p (Primary)	A	$\mathbf{T} = (t_{qp})$	$\mathbf{\Phi}$	S	P
Sec. **12.5**	Λ_p (Reference)	A	$\Lambda = (\lambda_{qp})$	$\mathbf{\Psi}$	V	W

Unfortunately, the explicit designations of structure values and pattern values have not always been made in connection with oblique solutions, with a resulting state of confusion. The Thurstone school of factor analysis frequently refers to "the factor matrix **V**," implying therein the complete factor solution. This is an extremely ambiguous statement when the factors are correlated—there is no unique, single matrix! Is it the matrix of factor coefficients, or the matrix of test correlations with the factors? Both uses have been made of the term "factor matrix" in an oblique solution. The more common meaning of "the factor matrix **V**" is that defined by Thurstone (1947, p. 347) as the matrix containing the projections of the test vectors on a set of oblique reference axes Λ_p, which meaning is carried in the present text.

Along with the ambiguous use of a single matrix to describe the two distinct components of an oblique solution is the equally ambiguous use of the term factor "loading." While this may be perfectly acceptable in the case of an orthogonal solution, it lacks precision of meaning in an oblique solution. Factor "loading" is not a mathematical or statistical term meaning either "correlation" or "coefficient," and hence has been used inconsistently in both senses. Even when the term is given explicit meaning in an oblique solution it can never take the place of such well-defined concepts as correlation and coefficient. For the oblique case, Comrey (1973, p. 126) explicitly defines the term "loading" as the coordinate of a variable and distinguishes it from the correlation with a factor by simply calling the latter a "projection." Fruchter (1954, p. 193) refers to the "loading" of a variable both for the *correlation with a reference axis* and for the *coefficient of a primary factor*, probably because of the relationship between the structure of the one solution and the pattern of the other, which is indicated below in (12.36).

The confusion is not simple-minded but results from some rather subtle considerations. The fact of the matter is that a mathematical relationship exists between the structure **V** and the pattern **P** (as well as between **S** and **W**). Hence, in some sense it is unnecessary to introduce **P**, because all of its properties can be inferred from **V**. While this is true, it certainly complicates the interpretation of the primary-factor pattern to have to rely on the reference-factor structure for an indication of its values, i.e., to have to look at the structure in Table 12.5 to infer the properties of the pattern in Table 12.3. Now the exact mathematical relationships will be developed.

From (12.21), the initial orthogonal factor pattern can be expressed in terms of the primary pattern,

$$(12.32) \qquad\qquad \mathbf{A} = \mathbf{PT'},$$

and from (12.25), it can also be expressed in terms of the reference structure,

$$(12.33) \qquad\qquad \mathbf{A} = \mathbf{V\Lambda}^{-1}.$$

Equating these two expressions yields:

$$(12.34) \qquad\qquad \mathbf{PT'} = \mathbf{V\Lambda}^{-1}.$$

But, from (12.27),

$$\mathbf{\Lambda}^{-1} = \mathbf{D}^{-1}\mathbf{T'},$$

so that (12.34) becomes:

$$(12.35) \qquad\qquad \mathbf{PT'} = \mathbf{VD}^{-1}\mathbf{T'}.$$

Finally, the relationship between **P** and **V** is given by:

$$(12.36) \qquad\qquad \mathbf{P} = \mathbf{VD}^{-1} \quad \text{or} \quad \mathbf{V} = \mathbf{PD}.$$

Thus, for a given reference structure matrix and correlations between the corresponding primary and reference factors, the primary pattern matrix is determined.

In a similar fashion, the initial orthogonal factor pattern can be expressed in terms of the primary structure from (12.18), and also in terms of the reference pattern from (12.31). Then the same kind of mathematical analysis, employing the relationship (12.27) between the two transformation matrices, yields:

$$(12.37) \qquad\qquad \mathbf{S} = \mathbf{WD} \quad \text{or} \quad \mathbf{W} = \mathbf{SD}^{-1}.$$

This relationship, like (12.36), indicates that the structure of one type of oblique solution is rather simply related to the pattern of the other solution, and vice versa.

While (12.36) and (12.37) establish the exact relationships *across* the two types of oblique solutions, they do not replace the need for the clear distinction between the structure and pattern for either type of oblique solution. Of course, the structure and pattern have unique meanings, and serve rather distinct purposes, and it is in this sense that they complement each other in providing complete understanding of an oblique solution. In general, for a set of positively correlated primary factors, the factor structure will contain all positive entries, while the factor pattern will have high positive values and many values near zero (see Table 12.3). The primary-factor structure is useful in the estimation of factors (see chapter 16). On the other hand, it does not provide a very good indication of "saturation" of the variables with the factors. The primary-factor pattern gives this precisely, and thereby is most useful for identification of the factors.

By way of illustrating these points, consider variable 1 (Height) in the example of Table 12.3. From the first line of the factor structure, its correlation with the factor T_1 (Lankiness) is found to be .914 and its correlation with the factor T_2 (Stockiness), .489. However, its "saturation" with these factors can best be obtained from the linear equation:

$$z_1 = .885T_1 + .059T_2,$$

which comes from the first line of the factor pattern. The direct contributions of factors T_1 and T_2 to the variance of variable 1 are $(.885)^2 = .783$ and $(.059)^2 = .003$, respectively, while $2(.885)(.059)(.4858) = .051$ is attributable to the joint influence of the two factors. In other words, 78.3 percent of the Height variable is attributable to the Lankiness factor, while only 0.3 percent is attributable to the Stockiness factor and 5.1 percent to the joint influence of these factors (leaving 15.3 percent of the total variance of variable 1 unaccounted by the common factors).

Similar interpretations could be made of the values in Table 12.5. But actually, nobody proposes the reference axes as useful factors. The Thurstone school would exhibit the "factor matrix **V**" for purposes of identifying the factors. To this end, it is just as effective as the pattern matrix **P**, although from (12.36) it can be seen that the values in **P** are larger than those in **V** because each correlation in the diagonal matrix **D** is less than unity. However, for overall clarity and understanding, the complete primary-factor solution is recommended.

13   Objective Orthogonal Multiple-Factor Solutions

13.1. *Introduction*

In the last chapter methods were introduced for transforming some initial factor solution to another "preferred" type of solution. Such a transformation—often referred to as the "rotation problem" in factor analysis—is intended to display a solution in the most cogent and poignant manner for scientific interpretation. The multiple-factor solutions have these objectives but they are dependent in large measure on subjective judgments, and the transformations to them cannot be written explicitly from the qualitative conditions for "simple structure." Many attempts have been made to reduce the principles of simple structure to an objective form, and hence to develop an objective procedure for calculating a (simple structure) multiple-factor solution. These attempts date back to the 1930s but it took twenty years before a real breakthrough was accomplished (Carroll 1953).

One might wonder if objective procedures are really necessary when some of the solutions in chapter 12 seem so elegant even with the crude subjective procedures. These appear as choice solutions only because there were clear-cut clustering of variables into groups. Unfortunately, not all variables lend themselves to ready grouping, no matter how well an experiment is designed. Furthermore, a scientific methodology cannot be dependent on subjective operations. Now sound, objective, efficient procedures are available for determining a multiple-factor solution for any set of data. Analytical methods for transforming any initial solution to a simple-structure solution are presented in this chapter for the case of orthogonal factors and in the following chapter for the case of oblique factors.

Before developing the objective procedures a brief discussion of some semi-analytical methods is presented in **13.2**. This is done in order to provide some historical perspective to the problem of finding an objective solution. Also in this section is developed the fundamental rationale for the analytical methods. In **13.3** and **13.4** specific procedures are presented which lead to orthogonal simple-structure solutions. Essentially the same basis—the quartimax criterion—was developed independently by four researchers, and the orthogonal solution derived therefrom is presented in **13.3** both in theory and with numerical illustrations. An alternative approach to orthogonal simple structure is developed in **13.4**, employing Kaiser's varimax criterion. This procedure does a better job of approximating the classical simple-structure principles. Again, numerical examples are given to illustrate the methods. Finally, a brief discussion of a weighted combination of the quartimax and varimax criteria is presented in **13.5**

While the breakthrough in the analytic rotational methods came in 1953, the new procedures could not immediately be used because of the laborious computations involved. By 1958, however, electronic computer programs were developed which made their application feasible, and now such procedures are routine.

13.2. *Rationale for Analytic Methods*

As noted in chapter 12, many ingenious graphical and mechanical procedures were developed for transforming "arbitrary" factor matrices into "meaningful" factor matrices satisfying the simple structure principles of **6.2**. So long as the criteria for simple structure were stated in qualitative terms, rather than precise mathematical terms, it was to be expected that the quest for a simple structure solution could only lead to a subjective result. To get results that are independent of the particular investigator it would be necessary to rephrase the conditions for simple structure. That is precisely what has been taking place ever since the principles were first enunciated, although done indirectly or implicitly more often than by explicit attack on the principles themselves.

From the very beginning of the application of simple-structure principles, it was recognized that the procedure was more of an art than a science. In an endeavor to put the rotations on a more objective basis, the first improvements were directed toward eliminating graphical procedures. Nonetheless, arbitrary decisions were still required to determine "significant" factor loadings, "large" or "near zero" factor loadings, "subgroups" of variables, and the like. Of the many such semi-analytical solutions proposed, Horst's (1941) was among the first. He follows Thurstone's early principle for simple structure, namely, that each column of the factor matrix should have a minimum number of negative values and a maximum number of nearly vanishing values. He then expresses this condition in analytical terms, as follows (Horst 1941, p. 80): "For a given factor the sum of the squares of significant factor loadings divided by the sum of the squares of all the loadings shall be a maximum." This procedure lacks complete objectivity in that a subgroup of variables with "significant" factor loadings has to be selected, and since such variables cannot be determined on statistical grounds an arbitrary operational definition is introduced.

Employing Horst's criterion as a point of departure, Tucker (1944) presents a compromise procedure employing both analytical and graphical methods. In this method the positions of the trial reference axes for subgroups of variables are determined by an analytical method, while the subgroups themselves are selected subjectively employing the inter-factor graphs as guides.

Thurstone (1954) proposed another type of near-objective procedure involving the minimization of a weighted sum of projections of the test vectors on a reference vector. The selection of the weights is on a rather arbitrary basis designed to emphasize near zero projections. The method involves simple computations and yields results closely approximating the more intuitive graphical methods.

As noted above, the first truly analytical rotation criterion for determining psychologically interpretable factors was developed by Carroll (1953). He considered Thurstone's five principles of simple structure (see **6.2**) but immediately ruled out the likelihood of a single mathematical expression embodying all these characteristics. This conscious departure was aptly stated by Kaiser (1958, p. 188) as "the first attempt to break away from an inflexible devotion to Thurstone's ambiguous, arbitrary, and mathematically unmanageable qualitative rules for his intuitively compelling notion of simple structure."

In a similar attempt to objectify the definition of simple structure, Tucker (1955) proposes a list of ten requirements to be satisfied by any such criteria. While his list provides another indication of the necessity to depart from Thurstone's qualitative rules, it also is dependent on subjective judgment in several places. On the basis of the objective definition of simple structure which he proposes, Tucker develops a method for the isolation of m "linear constellations" each with dimensionality $(m - 1)$ when the common-factor space is of m dimensions. His procedure yields satisfactory results primarily for "those well-designed studies in which the vectors are concentrated along all hyperplanes" (Tucker 1955, p. 224). Since the emphasis in this chapter is on analytical procedures which completely avoid subjective decisions, and are applicable to any initial factor solution, Tucker's rotational method will not be treated further.

Several researchers,[1] working independently, almost simultaneously arrived at very similar solutions for objectifying the rotational problem in factor analysis. While three of the investigators apparently were led to their solutions by a rationale which they considered to be based on Thurstone's rules, Ferguson attempted "to develop a logical groundwork which would lead ultimately to an objective analytical solution and render explicit the meaning of such a solution" (1954, p. 288). His development centers around the concept of parsimony in factor analysis, including its philosophical kinship to the term as used in other scientific theories. This concept, with its widespread application in all aspects of the subject, provides the very foundation of factor analysis—from a simple definition of its objective to the complex considerations in the rotational problem.

Parsimony is one of the fundamental standards in selecting a preferred solution out of the infinitude of possible solutions, and is the basis of the simple-structure principles. While the notion of parsimony is implicit in much of the work in factor analysis, it does not always carry an explicit meaning. In regard to the number of factors, it is perfectly clear what is meant by parsimony. On the other hand, no such precise meaning attaches to the notion of parsimony in the rotational problem. It was

---

[1]Carroll (1953), draft August 1952; Saunders (1953); Neuhaus and Wrigley (1954), draft August 1953; and Ferguson (1954), draft July 1953.

the full realization of this fact that led Ferguson to his rationale for an analytical solution to the rotational problem:

> Since factorists in dealing with the rotational problem employ an intuitive concept of parsimony, the question can be raised as to whether the term can be assigned a precise and more explicit meaning, which will enable the rotational problem to be more clearly stated and admit the possibility of a unique and objective solution. This involves *explication* . . . [which he attributes to Carnap] . . . the process of assigning to a vague, ill-defined, and perhaps largely intuitive concept a precise, explicit and formal meaning . . . (Ferguson 1954, p. 282).

Now, Thurstone's principles of simple structure were devised as an explicit expression of parsimony in factor analysis, but they do not provide *explication* in the above sense. Ferguson points out three shortcomings: (1) The conditions for simple structure cannot be represented as terms in a mathematical expression capable of manipulation; (2) the conditions are discrete rather than continuous; and (3) because of the discrete formulations in the simple-structure concept it is insufficiently general. He therefore proposes an explication of the concept of parsimony so that a unique solution to the rotational problem would result. Of course, the extent of agreement between solutions obtained by intuitive-graphical methods and by such a precise objective method would depend on the nature of the explication.

A measure of parsimony in the rotational problem can be defined in terms of the degree to which the configuration of vectors representing the variables is structured, i.e., the position of the configuration on an hypothetical continuum of all possible configurations, from the completely chaotic to the ideal configuration in which each variable is of unit complexity. As pointed out in **6.2**, the configuration of vectors serves as the vehicle to get to a particular set of reference axes. In factor analysis the structural properties of the configuration are conveyed by the frame of reference.

While there are many approaches to the problem of assigning a precise mathematical meaning to a measure of parsimony, Ferguson suggests a simple and attractive one. Starting with a single variable, represented by a point, what is the most parsimonious description of it, upon rotation of a pair of orthogonal axes? He suggests that intuitively the most parsimonious description results when one of the axes passes through the point. Approaching this ideal, it can be seen that when the reference frame is rotated so that one of the axes approaches the point, the product of the two coordinates grows smaller. Continuing this line of reasoning, Ferguson suggests that some function of the sum of products of coordinates of a set of collinear points might be used as a measure of the amount of parsimony associated with the description of these points. Finally, for the usual situation of positive and negative coordinates, he proposes (in place of the simple sum) the sum of squares of products of coordinates as a measure of parsimony. This measure, for the case of n variables and m orthogonal factors, is

$$(13.1) \qquad \sum_{j=1}^{n} \sum_{p<q=1}^{m} (a_{jp}a_{jq})^2,$$

involving $m(m-1)/2$ sums of n pairs of coordinates.

The expression (13.1) turns out to be closely related to several of the analytical procedures that were developed independently. It will be convenient to employ the following notation for the general rotational problem in terms of orthogonal factors:

$$\mathbf{A} = (a_{jp}), \text{ initial factor matrix,}$$

(13.2) $$\mathbf{B} = (b_{jp}), \text{ final factor matrix,}$$

$$\mathbf{T} = (t_{qp}), \text{ orthogonal transformation matrix,}$$

so that

(13.3) $$\mathbf{B} = \mathbf{AT}.$$

When $\mathbf{A}$ is carried into $\mathbf{B}$ by the orthogonal transformation $\mathbf{T}$, the communality of any variable is invariant, i.e.,

(13.4) $$\sum_{p=1}^{m} b_{jp}^2 = \sum_{p=1}^{m} a_{jp}^2 = h_j^2 \qquad (j = 1, 2, \cdots, n).$$

The squared communality of any variable also remains constant, namely,

(13.5) $$\left(\sum_{p=1}^{m} b_{jp}^2 \right)^2 = \sum_{p=1}^{m} b_{jp}^4 + 2 \sum_{p<q=1}^{m} b_{jp}^2 b_{jq}^2 = \text{constant.}$$

Then, summing over the n variables produces

(13.6) $$\sum_{j=1}^{n} \sum_{p=1}^{m} b_{jp}^4 + 2 \sum_{j=1}^{n} \sum_{p<q=1}^{m} b_{jp}^2 b_{jq}^2 = \text{constant.}$$

Since the sum of the two terms in this expression must always be the same, it follows that when one of these terms increases the other must decrease, and vice versa. Hence, a transformation of $\mathbf{A}$ which maximizes one of the terms in (13.6) will, at the same time, minimize the other. Formula (13.6) provides the relationship between two independent approaches to the rotational problem, as will be indicated below.

Either term of (13.6), or some function of these terms, could serve as a precise mathematical measure of parsimony. Actually, *minimization* of the second term for maximum parsimony is implied in (13.1). On the other hand, Ferguson (1954, p. 286) suggests that

(13.7) $$Q = \sum_{j=1}^{n} \sum_{p=1}^{m} b_{jp}^4$$

be *maximized* for maximum parsimony of a factor structure. Of course the value of Q depends upon the factor loadings, which vary with the particular positions of the reference axes. The most parsimonious solution, in the least-square sense, would seem to require that rotation of the frame of reference which makes the value of Q a maximum for a given set of data. The theoretical limit is attained when the complexity of each variable is one. This might be said to constitute the maximum degree of structure or organization possible for a configuration of variables.

13.3. *Quartimax Criterion*

Without employing the "parsimony rationale" explicitly, and each starting with an independent approach, Carroll (1953), Neuhaus and Wrigley (1954), and Saunders (1953) arrived at criteria for objective analytical solutions closely related to the maximization of the function (13.7). In one way or another, each viewed the rotation of axes as an attempt to reduce the complexity of the factorial description of the variables. The ultimate objective would be a uni-factor solution, in which each variable would be of complexity one, i.e., involve only a single common factor. An orthogonal uni-factor solution is extremely unlikely with empirical data (except for the limiting case of only a general factor for the entire set of variables, or the case of several mutually uncorrelated group factors as implied by a set of correlations as in Figure 6.1).

If a uni-factor solution were possible, the variance of each variable would result from but one factor loading; and a reasonable approach to this ideal would seem to require the maximum inequality in the distribution of the variance among the several factors for each variable in the factor pattern. In other words, the transformation desired is one which will tend to increase the large factor loadings and decrease the small ones for each variable of the original factor matrix. In this attempt to increase the inequalities among the factor loadings, the size implied is independent of algebraic sign. Since absolute values are somewhat awkward for mathematical manipulation, Neuhaus and Wrigley (1954) propose that the inequalities among squares of factor loadings be maximized; or, more specifically, that the variance in the distribution of squared factor loadings should be made a maximum by the use of orthogonal transformations. Since this approach involves the maximization of fourth powers of factor loadings, they credit Burt with suggesting the term "quartimax" for this method. In this text the term "quartimax method" is used collectively for the several independent derivations of analytical procedures related to the maximization of the function (13.7).

In the notation of (13.2), the object of the quartimax method is to determine the orthogonal transformation $\mathbf{T}$ which will carry the original factor matrix $\mathbf{A}$ into a new factor matrix $\mathbf{B}$ for which the variance of squared factor loadings is a maximum. From the basic definition (2.4) the variance of the contributions (the squared factor loadings) of all m factors to the n variables is simply:

$$(13.8) \qquad s_{b^2}^2 = \frac{1}{mn} \sum_{j=1}^{n} \sum_{p=1}^{m} (b_{jp}^2 - \overline{b^2})^2$$

where the mean of all the squared factor loadings is

$$(13.9) \qquad \overline{b^2} = \frac{1}{mn} \sum_{j=1}^{n} \sum_{p=1}^{m} b_{jp}^2.$$

Upon expansion and simplification, the expression (13.8) reduces to

$$(13.10) \qquad M = \frac{1}{mn} \sum_{j=1}^{n} \sum_{p=1}^{m} b_{jp}^4 - (\overline{b^2})^2,$$

which Neuhaus and Wrigley (1954) designated the quartimax criterion that is to be maximized. Now, since $\overline{b^2}$ remains constant under orthogonal transformation according to (13.4), and constant terms have no effect on the maximizing process, this criterion is equivalent to the measure of parsimony (13.7), i.e., simply the maximization of the sum of fourth powers of factor loadings.

In Carroll's (1953) original development of an objective procedure he focused attention on criteria 3, 4, and 5 of the simple structure principles (see **6.2**). This led him to consider the minimization of some sort of inner-product function of the columns of the final factor-structure matrix. The criterion which he proposes is that

$$(13.11) \qquad N = \sum_{j=1}^{n} \sum_{p<q=1}^{m} b_{jp}^2 b_{jq}^2$$

be a minimum. It should be noted that, for the orthogonal case, the expression (13.11) is identical with the measure of parsimony (13.1) proposed by Ferguson. Also for the orthogonal case, minimizing (13.11) is equivalent to maximizing (13.10) according to (13.6). In other words, the criterion $N =$ minimum will lead to precisely the same results as $Q =$ maximum when the rotated factors are orthogonal. However, Carroll's criterion (13.11) is not restricted to the orthogonal case. As a matter of fact, its application generally will lead to oblique factors (see **14.3**).

Again, from a fresh point of view, Saunders (1953, p. 5) attempts to objectify the rotation to simple structure by maximizing "the proportion of small and large loadings at the expense of medium-sized ones." Before considering any function of the factor loadings, he notes that the direction of scoring a test is irrelevant to simple structure, so that the algebraic signs in any column of the factor matrix may be changed without affecting the criterion. In order to deal with this sign ambiguity, and at the same time preserve the sign relationships of loadings for the same variable, he suggests that each variable be considered *twice* (as originally scored and also reflected) in the frequency distribution of factor loadings. Thus, the "doubled" distribution of factor loadings is perfectly symmetric and always has a mean of zero. Then Saunders proposes as a criterion for a simple structure solution that the kurtosis of the "doubled" frequency distribution of rotated factor loadings be a maximum. The fourth moment and second moment are easily expressed about the mean of zero, so that the kurtosis to be maximized is:[2]

$$(13.12) \qquad K = \sum_{j=1}^{n} \sum_{p=1}^{m} b_{jp}^4 \Big/ \left(\sum_{j=1}^{n} \sum_{p=1}^{m} b_{jp}^2 \right)^2.$$

It will be recalled that kurtosis is a measure of the flatness or peakedness of a single-humped distribution. For the present application the special significance of this measure is that as kurtosis is increased the relative frequencies of the middle (near zero loadings) and tails (large loadings) of a distribution are increased at the expense

---

[2]Since the resulting function is to be maximized, the numerical constants that arise from the number of observations and from consideration of the "doubled" frequency may be disregarded. Thus, while the notion of the "doubled" frequency was necessary to the rationale of the method, the factor loadings actually need not be reflected.

of the intermediate regions. The denominator of (13.12) remains constant under orthogonal transformation according to (13.4), so that this criterion is equivalent to each of the preceding in the orthogonal case.

Since the four criteria (Q, M, N, and K) lead to identical results for an orthogonal solution, the theory in this section will be developed simply for the maximization of the sum of fourth powers of factor loadings (Q), following the procedure of Neuhaus and Wrigley (1954). The notation of (13.2) is employed, with b's representing all intermediate values resulting from rotation of the a's as well as the final factor loadings. For any variable z_j, the orthogonal transformation in the plane of factors p and q through an angle φ will carry the original coordinates (a's) into the new coordinates (b's), as follows:

$$(13.13) \qquad \begin{aligned} b_{jp} &= a_{jp} \cos \varphi + a_{jq} \sin \varphi \\ b_{jq} &= -a_{jp} \sin \varphi + a_{jq} \cos \varphi \end{aligned}$$

according to the basic equations of transformation in a plane (12.1). In order to measure the effect of such a transformation $\mathbf{T}_{pq}$ on the overall criterion Q, the sum of fourth powers of the new loadings of the two rotated factors is determined. This sum is defined by

$$(13.14) \qquad Q_{pq}(\varphi) = \sum_{j=1}^{n} (b_{jp}^4 + b_{jq}^4),$$

which depends on the parameter φ. The object is to determine the angle of rotation (φ_{pq} in precise notation) for any pair of factors p and q which will make the sum Q_{pq} a maximum. Then the product of the transformations of all combinations of pairs of factors produces a transformed factor matrix:

$$(13.15) \qquad \mathbf{B} = \mathbf{A}\mathbf{T}_{12}\mathbf{T}_{13} \cdots \mathbf{T}_{pq} \cdots \mathbf{T}_{(m-1),m},$$

where $p = 1, 2, \cdots, (m - 1)$, and the associated $q = p + 1, p + 2, \cdots, m$. The complete set of $m(m - 1)/2$ pairings of p and q is called a *cycle*. In each cycle of operations the value of Q for the entire matrix is as large as or larger than the preceding sum. Since the theoretical maximum of fourth powers of factor loadings cannot exceed n (even when the total unit variance of each variable is analyzed), the procedure must converge after a sufficient number of cycles.

For any rotation $\mathbf{T}_{pq}$ the angle φ which will make Q_{pq} a maximum can be determined as follows: (a) substitute the expressions for the b's from (13.13) into (13.14); (b) differentiate (13.14) with respect to φ; (c) set the derivative equal to zero; and (d) solve the equation for φ. The results (Neuhaus and Wrigley 1954, p. 83) can be put in the form:

$$(13.16) \qquad \tan 4\varphi = \frac{2 \sum_{j=1}^{n} (2a_{jp}a_{jq})(a_{jp}^2 - a_{jq}^2)}{\sum_{j=1}^{n} [(a_{jp}^2 - a_{jq}^2)^2 - (2a_{jp}a_{jq})^2]} = \frac{v}{\delta}.$$

When (13.14) is expanded and the terms involving φ are collected and simplified, they are found to involve $\sin 4\varphi$ and $\sin^2 2\varphi$. Since each of these terms has the period $\pi/2$ so does $Q_{pq}(\varphi)$. Therefore the solution (13.16) need only be considered for φ between $0°$ and $90°$. Actually, experience has shown that subsequent reflection of factors can be reduced by requiring φ to be between $-45°$ and $+45°$.

While any solution (13.16) yields a critical value of φ, necessary for a maximum value of Q_{pq}, such a critical value may produce a minimum, or stationary value of Q_{pq} as well. A sufficient condition for a maximum is a negative value of the second derivative of the function when the critical value is substituted in it. The conditions for a maximum can be summarized in the form:

(13.17)

$$\frac{dQ_{pq}}{d\varphi} = \nu \cos 4\varphi - \delta \sin 4\varphi = 0$$

$$\frac{d^2 Q_{pq}}{d\varphi^2} = -4\delta \cos 4\varphi - 4\nu \sin 4\varphi < 0$$

from which (ignoring the factor 4, since it has no effect on the algebraic sign) it follows that

(13.18)
$$-\frac{\delta^2 + \nu^2}{\nu} \sin 4\varphi < 0.$$

Actually, the formal work of computing the second derivative can be obviated since the angle which produces a maximum can be determined from the algebraic signs of the numerator and denominator of (13.16). In the expression (13.18) the numerator is always a positive number, so the algebraic sign of the entire expression is determined completely from the simpler form:

(13.19)
$$\frac{1}{\nu} \sin 4\varphi > 0.$$

It follows that the numerator of (13.16) and $\sin 4\varphi$ must have the same algebraic signs if the condition (13.19) for a maximum is to be preserved. Corresponding to each algebraic sign of the numerator, the denominator may be either positive or negative. The resulting four possibilities, with the angle of rotation associated with each, are set forth in Table 13.1.

The foregoing theory provides the basis for computation of the quartimax method. First $\tan 4\varphi$ is calculated from (13.16) and then, from the algebraic signs of ν and δ, the angle of rotation φ is determined from Table 13.1. Then the matrix of the original (or last computed) pair of columns p and q of the factor matrix is post-multiplied by the transformation matrix

$$\mathbf{T}_{pq} = \begin{pmatrix} \cos \varphi & -\sin \varphi \\ \sin \varphi & \cos \varphi \end{pmatrix},$$

where φ is understood to be the angle of rotation φ_{pq} in the plane of the factors p and q. The result leads to the maximum sum Q_{pq} of fourth powers of the rotated

Table 13.1

Angle of Rotation

Algebraic signs in (13.16)			Sign of $\cos 4\varphi$	Resulting Quadrant of 4φ	Limits for φ
Numer-ator (ν) (and $\sin 4\varphi$)	Denom-inator (δ)	$\tan 4\varphi$			
$+$	$+$	$+$	$+$	I: $\quad 0 \ < 4\varphi < \ 90°$	$0°$ to $22.5°$
$+$	$-$	$-$	$-$	II: $\quad 90° < 4\varphi < 180°$	$22.5°$ to $45°$
$-$	$-$	$+$	$-$	III: $-180° < 4\varphi < -90°$	$-45°$ to $-22.5°$
$-$	$+$	$-$	$+$	IV: $\ -90° < 4\varphi < \ \ 0°$	$-22.5°$ to $0°$

factor loadings for factors p and q. After rotation of all combinations of factors, the transformation to the final factor matrix **B** is accomplished as indicated symbolically in (13.15). The cycle of operations on all pairings of factors must be repeated as many times as necessary to assure that the Q, for the full matrix, no longer increases (to the specified number of decimal places).

In order to illustrate the quartimax method, such a solution will be calculated for the simple example of the eight physical variables. The centroid solution, taken from the first edition of this text, is repeated in Table 13.2 as the initial solution. To get the angle of rotation φ, formula (13.16) is first applied. There are essentially two types of terms in this formula—twice the products of corresponding factor loadings $(2a_{j1}a_{j2})$ and the differences of squares of factor loadings $(a_{j1}^2 - a_{j2}^2)$—and these are listed for each variable in Table 13.2. The numerator of (13.16) is twice the sum of

Table 13.2

Quartimax Solution for Eight Physical Variables

(Initial solution: Centroid)

Variable j	Initial Solution		Squares		Products $2a_{j1}a_{j2}$	Difference of squares $a_{j1}^2 - a_{j2}^2$	Final Solution	
	a_{j1}	a_{j2}	a_{j1}^2	a_{j2}^2			b_{j1}	b_{j2}
1	830	$-.396$	.6889	.1568	$-.6574$	.5321	.899	.196
2	.818	$-.469$	.6691	.2200	$-.7673$	.4491	.934	.131
3	.777	$-.470$	.6037	.2209	$-.7304$	.3828	.902	.105
4	.798	$-.401$	.6368	.1608	$-.6400$	.4760	.876	.172
5	.786	.500	.6178	.2500	.7860	.3678	.315	.877
6	.672	.458	.4516	.2098	.6156	.2418	.250	.774
7	.594	.444	.3528	.1971	.5275	.1557	.197	.715
8	.647	.333	.4186	.1109	.4309	.3077	.307	.660
Sum of Squares	4.4394	1.5263	2.5776	.3053	3.4247	1.1706	3.5563	2.4112

the products of these eight corresponding values, namely, $v = -1.2520$. From the bottom row of Table 13.2 the denominator of (13.16) is $\delta = 1.1706 - 3.4247 = -2.2541$. Substituting these values in (13.16) yields $\tan 4\varphi = .5554$.

Since the numerator and denominator are both negative, the angle 4φ falls in the third quadrant according to the third line in Table 13.1. From tables of trigonometric functions it is found that $4\varphi = -150°\ 57'$ and hence the angle of rotation is $\varphi = -37°\ 44'$. The necessary elements for the transformation matrix are $\sin \varphi = -.6120$ and $\cos \varphi = .7909$, so that it may be written as

$$T = \begin{pmatrix} .7909 & .6120 \\ -.6120 & .7909 \end{pmatrix}.$$

The expression (13.15) for the final factor matrix reduces to the simple postmultiplication of the initial factor matrix of Table 13.2 by this transformation matrix. The resulting quartimax solution appears in the last two columns of Table 13.2. The quartimax criterion for this solution is

$$Q = \sum_{j=1}^{8} \sum_{p=1}^{2} b_{jp}^4 = 4.091,$$

while the corresponding value for the initial solution is only 2.883. In the simple case of $m = 2$, only one cycle involving a single rotation leads to convergence.

Of course, the foregoing example of only two factors is extremely simple and does not bring out all the ramifications of the quartimax procedure, but it does show the fundamental properties of such a solution. It approximates a simple structure solution even though the small values are not as close to zero as one might like them to be. No doubt a much better approximation to simple structure could be obtained with an oblique solution (see chap. 14), but if an orthogonal solution is desired the result in Table 13.2 is the best possible in the sense of this section. It is interesting to note that the intuitive-graphical solution of Table 12.1 is very similar to the analytical solution, but it does not satisfy the quartimax criterion quite as well (see ex. 1, chap. 13).

While the indicated type of computation can be done with conventional punched-card equipment and desk calculators, the work is very laborious and time-consuming. However, it can be done most expeditiously on high-speed electronic computers. Such programs were first written for the IBM 701 (and later model machines), the Illiac, and several other electronic computers (Wrigley, Saunders, and Neuhaus 1958). The machine procedure involves successive pairings of factors $p < q = 1$, $2, \cdots, m$, and carrying through the full $m(m-1)/2$ transformations for each cycle. When the machine finds the angle of rotation which will give a maximal sum of fourth powers of loadings of rotated factors, it makes the transformation only if the angle is greater than some specified value (perhaps one degree; or only one minute if the computer has very large high-speed memory capacity). Cycles of operation are continued until the sum of fourth powers for the entire matrix no longer increases. The convergence is generally rapid in the first few cycles and then tends to slow down.

The application of the quartimax method to a large problem, for which an electronic computer was employed, will now be shown. Neuhaus and Wrigley (1954) performed an analytical rotation on the centroid solution (which appeared in the first edition of this text) of the twenty-four psychological tests, employing the Illiac. Their results, which took about one minute of computer time, are shown in Table 13.3.[3] The calculation of cycles was continued until convergence of Q was obtained to the eighth decimal place. This required five cycles, but from a practical standpoint the convergence was adequate at the end of two cycles.

Table 13.3

Quartimax Solution for Twenty-Four Psychological Tests

(Initial solution: Centroid)

Test j	Verbal M_1	Speed M_2	Deduction M_3	Memory M_4
1	.369	.190	**.599**	.068
2	.245	.066	.384	.039
3	.313	.010	**.475**	.013
4	.359	.070	**.463**	−.012
5	**.806**	.135	−.016	−.039
6	**.812**	.030	.000	.055
7	**.854**	.072	−.044	−.095
8	**.660**	.202	.197	−.034
9	**.857**	−.058	−.020	.098
10	.234	**.700**	−.124	.112
11	.310	**.616**	.011	.231
12	.164	**.688**	.191	−.012
13	.350	**.569**	.323	−.082
14	.324	.190	−.026	**.424**
15	.251	.114	.101	**.448**
16	.289	.134	.372	.368
17	.285	.239	.022	**.569**
18	.215	.324	.302	**.467**
19	.276	.180	.189	.323
20	**.518**	.090	.354	.142
21	.347	.385	.347	.144
22	**.526**	.041	.295	.255
23	**.546**	.187	**.441**	.087
24	**.487**	**.432**	.101	.196
V_p	5.587	2.422	1.958	1.418

There is rather good agreement between the quartimax solution of Table 13.3 and the orthogonal multiple-factor solutions obtained by intuitive-graphical methods in the first edition of this text, and summarized in Table 13.7. With few exceptions,

[3] In 1958 an independent solution was obtained on an IBM 704 at the System Development Corporation, and it was found to agree identically with that in Table 13.3.

large factor loadings in one case correspond to similarly large values in the other. In the quartimax solution, the large values tend to be somewhat larger, and the small values smaller than their counterparts in the graphical solution. Exceptions are especially noticeable in the third factor where there are fewer well-pronounced large loadings in the quartimax solution; and in the first factor (verbal) where even the small values are increased in the quartimax solution. This tendency toward a general factor is one of the main shortcomings, in the simple-structure sense, of the quartimax solution.

13.4.   *Varimax Criterion*

As outlined in the last section, the emphasis in the quartimax method is on simplification of the description of each *row*, or variable, of the factor matrix. In contradistinction, Kaiser (1958) places more emphasis on simplifying the *columns*, or factors, of the factor matrix in an attempt to meet the requirements for simple structure. Thus, while simplicity of each variable may be attained concurrent with a large loading on the same factor, such a general factor is precluded by the simplicity constraint on each factor.

The varimax method proposed by Kaiser (1956c) is a modification of the quartimax method which more nearly approximates simple structure. Following his development (1958, p. 190), the simplicity of a factor p is defined as the variance of its squared loadings, i.e.

$$(13.20) \qquad s_p^2 = \frac{1}{n} \sum_{j=1}^{n} (b_{jp}^2)^2 - \frac{1}{n^2} \left(\sum_{j=1}^{n} b_{jp}^2 \right)^2 \qquad (p = 1, 2, \cdots, m).$$

When the variance is at a maximum, the factor has the greatest interpretability or simplicity in the sense that its components (the b's) tend toward unity and zero. The criterion of maximum simplicity of a complete factor matrix is defined as the maximization of the sum of these simplicities of the individual factors, as follows:

$$(13.21) \qquad s^2 = \sum_{p=1}^{m} s_p^2 = \frac{1}{n} \sum_{p=1}^{m} \sum_{j=1}^{n} b_{jp}^4 - \frac{1}{n^2} \sum_{p=1}^{m} \left(\sum_{j=1}^{n} b_{jp}^2 \right)^2.$$

The maximization of (13.21) has been called the "raw" varimax criterion by Kaiser because of his preference for an improved version which is presented below. From empirical studies he found that the "raw" varimax and the quartimax analytical methods did not meet the standard of level contributions of factors any better than the intuitive-graphical methods. Along with this tendency for the contributions of factors to have greater dispersion in the analytic solutions, there was the tendency for the more prominent factors to have larger values in both the large and small factor loadings than their counterparts in the less prominent factors. In the intuitive-graphical solutions such systematic bias is generally avoided, yielding level contributions of factors with more equitable distribution of high and low factor loadings.

This type of bias is attributed by Kaiser (1958) to the divergent weights which implicitly are attached to the variables by the size of their communalities, namely, the square-roots of their communalities. Each variable contributes to the function (13.21) as the square of its communality. Hence, a variable with communality twice that of another will influence the rotations by four times as much. This means that a variable with communality .90 will have a weight four times that of a variable with communality .45 in determining the final solution. These relative weights are probably quite different from those intuitively assigned in graphical rotations. At Saunders' suggestion, Kaiser modified his original approach by weighting the variables equally for purposes of rotation. This is accomplished by extending the vectors representing the variables to unit length in the common-factor space, carrying out the rotations, and then bringing the vectors back to their original length.

In place of the "raw" varimax criterion (13.21), the improved standard for rotation requires that the final factor loadings be such as to maximize the function: [4]

$$(13.22) \qquad V = n \sum_{p=1}^{m} \sum_{j=1}^{n} (b_{jp}/h_j)^4 - \sum_{p=1}^{m} \left(\sum_{j=1}^{n} b_{jp}^2/h_j^2 \right)^2.$$

Kaiser refers to this as the "normal" varimax criterion, but since the earlier version will not be employed in this text, the simple term "varimax" will be understood to mean (13.22). It should be noted that the adjusted correlations of variables with factors (b_{jp}/h_j) correspond to the correlations $\bar{r}$ of (4.55), while the original correlations (b_{jp}) correspond to the $\hat{r}$ of (4.51) since the factors themselves are of unit length.

The computing procedure for a varimax solution is quite similar to that employed for a quartimax solution in the preceding section, but requires that (13.22) be maximized instead of (13.7). Factors are rotated two at a time according to the scheme indicated by (13.15), and the complete cycle of $m(m - 1)/2$ pairings of factors is repeated until the value of V to the specified number of decimal places no longer increases.

It will be convenient to introduce some additional notation in order to make the subsequent expressions more compact. First, the "normalized" factor loadings of a variable z_j for a particular pair of factors p and q, will be designated by

$$x_j = a_{jp}/h_j$$
$$y_j = a_{jq}/h_j$$

and the rotated loading by X_j, Y_j, so that the transformation corresponding to (13.13) may be put in the form:

$$(13.23) \qquad (X_j \quad Y_j) = (x_j \quad y_j) \begin{pmatrix} \cos \varphi & -\sin \varphi \\ \sin \varphi & \cos \varphi \end{pmatrix}$$

---

[4]Since a constant multiplier has no effect on the maximization process, the expression (13.21) was multiplied by n^2 for greater simplicity.

where φ is the angle of rotation in the plane of the factors p and q. Since squares and cross-products of the normalized loadings are required in the computation, the following notation will be found useful:

$$u_j = x_j^2 - y_j^2 \qquad C = \sum (u_j^2 - v_j^2)$$

(13.24)
$$v_j = 2x_j y_j \qquad D = 2 \sum u_j v_j$$

$$A = \sum u_j \qquad E = D - 2AB/n$$

$$B = \sum v_j \qquad F = C - (A^2 - B^2)/n$$

where all sums are on j from 1 to n.

The required angle of rotation is shown by Kaiser (1959, p. 415) to be given by:[5]

(13.25) $\tan 4\varphi = E/F.$

Just as before, the solution (13.25) which makes (13.22) a maximum need be considered only for values of φ between $-45°$ and $+45°$; and the sufficiency conditions for a maximum lead to the choice of the angle of rotation according to the values in Table 13.1.

Perhaps the best way to get a feel for the computing procedures is to try them on the same data of the last section. In Table 13.4 is indicated an appropriate worksheet for all the data that must be computed and recorded in the process of carrying

Table 13.4

Computation Form for Varimax Solution: Eight Physical Variables

Variable j	Initial Solution		Square root of communality h_j	Normalized loadings		Computing parameters		
	a_{j1}	a_{j2}	h_j	x_j	y_j	u_j	v_j	$u_j^2 - v_j^2$
1	.830	−.396	.9196	.9026	−.4306	.6293	−.7773	−.2082
2	.818	−.469	.9429	.8675	−.4974	.5051	−.8630	−.4896
3	.777	−.470	.9081	.8556	−.5176	.4641	−.8857	−.5691
4	.798	−.401	.8931	.8935	−.4490	.5967	−.8024	−.2878
5	.786	.500	.9316	.8437	.5367	.4238	.9056	−.6405
6	.672	.458	.8132	.8264	.5632	.3657	.9309	−.7328
7	.594	.444	.7416	.8010	.5987	.2832	.9591	−.8397
8	.647	.333	.7277	.8891	.4576	.5811	.8137	−.3244
Sum						3.8490	.2809	−4.0921

out the analytic rotation of one pair of factors, when working with a desk calculator. The values of $2u_j v_j$ for the individual variables are not recorded since only their sum D is required, namely, $D = -.6930$. On the other hand, since the difference of squares,

[5]It may be noted that expression (13.16) for the quartimax criterion is simply $\tan 4\varphi = D/C$ in terms of the notation (13.24).

$u_j^2 - v_j^2$, cannot be accumulated on the ordinary calculator, they are recorded for each variable. Only those sums (A, B, and C) required in the calculation of φ are recorded in the last row of the table.

Substituting in formula (13.25) produces $\tan 4\varphi = -.9633/-5.9341 = .1623$. In calculating the tangent, the numerator and denominator must be determined separately so that the algebraic signs may be noted. Then, referring to Table 13.1 for the case of both numerator and denominator negative, the angle 4φ must be in the third quadrant. From a table of trigonometric functions, $4\varphi = -170°\,47'$, so that $\varphi = -42°42'$. For this angle of rotation, $\sin \varphi = -.6782$ and $\cos \varphi = .7349$, and the transformation matrix is

$$\mathbf{T} = \begin{pmatrix} .7349 & .6782 \\ -.6782 & .7349 \end{pmatrix}.$$

Then the normalized rotated loadings are computed by postmultiplying the original normalized loadings by this matrix. The results (X_j, Y_j) appear in the first two columns of Table 13.5. Finally, the normalization is removed by multiplying each value by the appropriate h_j for the row. The resulting varimax solution appears in the last two columns of Table 13.5. The varimax criterion (13.22) for this solution is $V = 24.3012$, for which the necessary sums of squares and fourth-powers of rotated normalized loadings are taken from the middle two columns of Table 13.5.

A comparison of the varimax solution with the previous solutions is most enlightening. Of course, the original centroid solution is very poor from a simple structure point of view; and this is indicated by the value of only .4078 for the varimax criterion. On the other hand, the intuitive-graphical multiple-factor solution of Table 12.1 is

Table 13.5

Varimax Solution for Eight Physical Variables

(Initial solution: Centroid)

Variable *j*	Rotated Normalized Loadings		Squares		Final Solution	
	X_j	Y_j	X_j^2	Y_j^2	b_{j1}	b_{j2}
1	.9554	.2957	.9128	.0874	.879	.272
2	.9749	.2228	.9504	.0496	.919	.210
3	.9798	.1999	.9600	.0400	.890	.182
4	.9611	.2760	.9237	.0762	.858	.246
5	.2560	.9666	.0655	.9343	.238	.900
6	.2254	.9744	.0508	.9495	.183	.792
7	.1826	.9832	.0333	.9667	.135	.729
8	.3431	.9393	.1177	.8823	.250	.684
Sum			4.0142	3.9860		
Sum of Squares			3.5331	3.5049	3.316	2.648

quite as good, having a varimax criterion value of 23.75. Looked at the other way, the varimax solution of Table 13.5 comes closest to an orthogonal simple-structure solution which was arrived at intuitively in Table 12.1. The quartimax solution of Table 13.2 is also a close approximation to the desired end, but it does not meet the varimax criterion as well as the graphical method (see ex. 3, chap. 13).

While the foregoing method of hand calculation has some heuristic value, a much simpler algorithm for finding $\sin \varphi$ and $\cos \varphi$, and hence for carrying out varimax rotations, is recommended for a computer subroutine (private communication from Bary Wingersky). It is a procedure for finding $\sin \varphi$ and $\cos \varphi$ when they are not zero and one, respectively. Using the notation (13.24) and setting

$$G = \sqrt{E^2 + F^2},$$

it can be seen that if $G = 0$ the varimax criterion is maximal and no rotation is required. However, if $G \neq 0$ then

(13.26) $$\cos 4\varphi = F/G$$

and, from conventional trigonometric identities for half-angles:

$$\cos 2\varphi = \sqrt{(1 + \cos 4\varphi)/2} \quad \text{and} \quad \cos \varphi = \sqrt{(1 + \cos 2\varphi)/2}.$$

Similarly,

$$|\sin \varphi| = \sqrt{(1 - \cos 2\varphi)/2}$$

and if $E < 0$, $\sin \varphi = -|\sin \varphi|$; otherwise, $\sin \varphi = |\sin \varphi|$. Thus the elements of the orthogonal rotation matrix in (13.23) are readily obtained. When $|\sin \varphi| < .001$ the rotation is trivial and the varimax criterion can be considered reached.

As in the preceding section, the work of computing a varimax solution without the aid of high-speed electronic computers becomes prohibitive for problems involving more than a few factors. However, computer programs for the varimax rotation are available for all present-day computers, this being the most popular means of getting an orthogonal multiple-factor solution. At many computing centers, the varimax program is part of a "factor analysis package" which has the principal-factor method for the initial solution.

A varimax solution for the example of five socio-economic variables was obtained by the use of such a factor analysis program package. Starting with the correlation matrix from Table 2.2, first the principal-component solution of Table 8.1 is determined and then, specifying two factors for rotation, the varimax solution of Table 13.6 is obtained. Of course, the individual factor coefficients are altered as the result of the rotation, as is also the contribution of each of the two factors. However, the variance of each variable, and the total contribution of the two factors remain the same. Put another way, the proportion of the total variance accounted for by either set of factors is unaltered. As noted before, once the space is determined by the choice of the number of principal components, a rotation to a new basis in the same space has no effect on the lengths of the vectors representing the variables. The square of the length

Table 13.6

Varimax Solution for Five Socio-Economic Variables[a]

(Initial solution: first two principal components, Table 8.1)

Variable	M_1	M_2	Variance
1	.01602	.99377	.98783
2	.94079	−.00883	.88515
3	.13702	.98006	.97930
4	.82479	.44714	.88022
5	.96821	−.00604	.93747
Contribution of factor	2.52182	2.14815	4.66997
Percent of total variance	50.4	43.0	93.4

[a] The only reason for showing five decimal places (of the computer output) is to provide a means for checking numerical calculations.

of each vector is its variance, according to (4.52), and is given in the last column of Table 13.6.

The varimax solution is indeed a multiple-factor solution satisfying the simple structure criteria of **6.2**. Of course, for so few variables the conditions cannot be taken too literally. The factor weights of 0 or 1 in the first decimal place certainly may be viewed as essentially zero. In this sense the factor matrix exhibits one zero in each row, with the exception of variable 4; two zeros in each column; and several variables whose entries vanish in one column but not in the other. Even the exception of variable 4 is not contradictory to the set of simple-structure criteria (see number 5). Again it should be emphasized that the simple-structure criteria have compelling intuitive value but lack the precision necessary for mathematical computation. The varimax criterion, on the other hand, is a precisely defined method which indeed approximates orthogonal simple structure.

An example of a varimax solution for a large problem is presented for the twenty-four psychological tests so that the varimax solution may be compared with previous ones for these data. In Table 13.7 the varimax solution is given along with the quartimax (from Table 13.3) and a subjective graphical solution (from the first edition of this text). The coefficients are recorded to two decimal places to facilitate comparison. A quick glance will immediately lead one to the intuitive conclusion that the varimax solution somehow meets the vague notions of simple structure better than either of the other two solutions. Applying each of the five criteria for simple structure (see **6.2**), it is found that both the varimax and the subjective solutions satisfy them insofar as a non-mathematical standard can be satisfied by crude judgment. On the other hand, it is quite obvious that the quartimax solution fails to satisfy the standard of having at least four zeros in each column—the first factor tending towards a general factor as noted in the previous section.

Table 13.7

Comparison of Varimax, Quartimax, and Subjective Orthogonal
Multiple-Factor Solutions: Twenty-Four Psychological Tests

(Initial solution: Centroid)

Test j	Subjective				Quartimax				Varimax			
	M_1	M_2	M_3	M_4	M_1	M_2	M_3	M_4	M_1	M_2	M_3	M_4
1	.10	.32	.62	.20	.37	.19	.60	.07	.14	.19	.67	.17
2	.07	.15	.41	.13	.24	.07	.38	.04	.10	.07	.43	.10
3	.10	.12	.53	.13	.31	.01	.48	.01	.15	.02	.54	.08
4	.15	.18	.53	.12	.36	.07	.46	−.01	.20	.09	.54	.07
5	.75	.15	.26	.15	.81	.14	−.02	−.04	.75	.21	.22	.13
6	.72	.05	.28	.25	.81	.03	.00	.06	.75	.10	.23	.21
7	.81	.08	.27	.11	.85	.07	−.04	−.10	.82	.16	.21	.08
8	.54	.26	.38	.14	.66	.20	.20	−.04	.54	.26	.38	.12
9	.76	−.04	.29	.30	.86	−.06	−.02	.10	.80	.01	.22	.25
10	.28	.66	−.19	.14	.23	.70	−.12	.11	.15	.70	−.06	.24
11	.27	.61	−.04	.29	.31	.62	.01	.23	.17	.60	.08	.36
12	.13	.72	.09	.03	.16	.69	.19	−.01	.02	.69	.23	.11
13	.24	.63	.31	.02	.35	.57	.32	−.08	.18	.59	.41	.06
14	.23	.19	−.02	.48	.32	.19	−.03	.42	.22	.16	.04	.50
15	.11	.14	.08	.50	.25	.11	.10	.45	.12	.07	.14	.50
16	.05	.22	.34	.45	.29	.13	.37	.37	.08	.10	.41	.43
17	.15	.24	−.03	.62	.28	.24	.02	.57	.14	.18	.06	.64
18	.01	.39	.20	.52	.22	.32	.30	.47	.00	.26	.32	.54
19	.12	.22	.18	.39	.28	.18	.19	.32	.13	.15	.24	.39
20	.31	.18	.46	.29	.52	.09	.35	.14	.35	.11	.47	.25
21	.17	.46	.33	.24	.35	.38	.35	.14	.15	.38	.42	.26
22	.31	.12	.40	.40	.53	.04	.30	.26	.36	.04	.41	.36
23	.31	.29	.54	.25	.55	.19	.44	.09	.35	.21	.57	.22
24	.39	.46	.14	.31	.49	.43	.10	.20	.34	.44	.22	.34
V_p	3.43	2.92	2.68	2.36	5.59	2.42	1.96	1.42	3.50	2.44	3.08	2.36

From the nature of the tests with the large weights, the following names are suggested for the factors:

M_1: Verbal
M_2: Speed
M_3: Deduction
M_4: Memory

A word about the naming of the third factor may be in order. The first four tests used to identify this factor have previously been referred to as "spatial relations" tests, involving the deduction of relations among geometric objects. All the other tests with large weights involve logical and arithmetical relations. Hence, the factor is named from the common attribute, "deduction of relations," regardless of the specific content of the tests.

The varimax solution seems to be the "best" parsimonious analytical solution in the sense that it correlates best with the intuitive concept of that term as exemplified by the graphical solution. This can be demonstrated by a numerical index of relationship among pairs of solutions. Since each of these solutions has as its goal some ideal simple structure for a given set of variables in a fixed common-factor space, it would seem quite appropriate to make direct comparisons of corresponding factor loadings. The common statistical measure that would seem to be applicable is the root mean square. For a comparison between the varimax (V) solution and the subjective (S) solution this index may be written in the simple form:

$$(13.27) \qquad (V - S)_{rms} = \sqrt{\frac{\sum (b_V - b_S)^2}{mn}},$$

where the sum is over all *mn* corresponding factor loadings b_{jp} in the *V*-solution and b_{jp} in the *S*-solution. The root-mean-square deviations computed from Table 13.7 are as follows:

$$(V - S)_{rms} = .062,$$
$$(V - Q)_{rms} = .116,$$
$$(Q - S)_{rms} = .127.$$

Although the scale is arbitrary, perfect agreement would be indicated by a value of zero and the relative agreement between pairs of solutions may be judged by their relative magnitudes. The varimax solution agrees almost perfectly with the subjective results, while the quartimax solution is least like the subjective; and the difference between the varimax and quartimax is almost as great as between the quartimax and the subjective.

The varimax criterion will now be applied to the twenty-variable box problem to see how well it recovers the known underlying order of these data (see **8.6**, example **5**). Starting with the orthogonal solution **A** of Table 8.11, the varimax rotation leads to the results in Table 13.8. This multiple-factor solution not only satisfies the simple-structure principles but does an excellent job of bringing out the structural order that had been designed into the problem. Clearly, it can be seen that the factors designated M_1, M_2, M_3 bear a one-to-one correspondence to the x, y, z dimensions of the hypothetical boxes. Of course, the varimax rotation produces uncorrelated factors, and within this constraint the factor analytic results make very good sense. An even better fit to the inherent structure is possible when the factors are permitted to be correlated (see Tables 14.13 and 14.16).

In addition to the fact that the varimax solution tends to definitize mathematically the intuitive notion of simple structure, Kaiser (1958) points out another property of this type of solution that may be of greater significance. While the weighting system introduced in the varimax method leads to results that appear more like simple structure, it may be subject to the same criticism as the intuitive-graphical methods because different sets of weights might be selected for different problems. The rationale for the varimax criterion (13.22) must be more fundamental if it is truly to provide a mathematical definition for the rotation problem. Such a basis is developed

Table 13.8

Varimax Solution for Twenty-Variable Box Problem

(Initial solution: **A** of Table 8.11)

Variable	M_1	M_2	M_3	Communality
1	.989	.117	.045	.994
2	.144	.974	.146	.990
3	.043	.102	.981	.975
4	.572	.799	.145	.986
5	.438	.117	.877	.975
6	.097	.475	.859	.972
7	.794	.596	.115	.997
8	.876	.151	.452	.994
9	.113	.797	.589	.996
10	.698	.703	.137	1.000
11	.701	.139	.700	1.000
12	.107	.668	.737	1.000
13	.986	.144	.040	.994
14	.091	.971	.199	.990
15	.055	.047	.985	.975
16	.372	.468	.765	.943
17	.718	.565	.401	.995
18	.959	.079	.049	.928
19	.184	.943	.095	.931
20	.037	.122	.950	.919
Contribution of factor	6.518	6.235	6.800	19.553
Percent of total variance	32.6	31.2	34.0	97.8

by Kaiser (1958, p. 195) when he proves for a special case that the *"varimax solution is invariant under changes in the composition of the test battery."*[6]

The principle of factorial invariance is stated by Thurstone (1947, p. 361) as "a fundamental requirement of a successful factorial method, that *the factorial description of a test must remain invariant when the test is moved from one battery to another which involves the same common factors."* The varimax method tends to have this invariance property; so that it permits the drawing of inferences about the factors in an (indefinite) domain of psychological content from a varimax solution based on a sample of *n* tests. This does not ascribe greater "psychological meaning" to the varimax factors than to factors obtained on some other basis, but it does mean that varimax factors obtained in a sample will have a greater likelihood of portraying the universe varimax factors. While the general impression may be that simple structure is the "ultimate" objective of the rotational problem, Kaiser (1958, p. 195)

---

[6]This is done by showing that the angle of rotation which maximizes (13.22) is not dependent on the number of variables in the limiting case where all variables fall into two collinear clusters. The generalization to *m* factors suggests virtually insuperable mathematical difficulties according to Kaiser.

suggests that "the ultimate criterion is factorial invariance." Because the varimax solution was devised with a view to satisfying the simple structure criteria and subsequently found to show this kind of invariance, Kaiser also suggests that "Thurstone's intuition was basically on the trail of factorial invariance." Thus, the "invariance criterion" is proposed as an alternative or possible improvement to "simple structure."

An example of the tendency for the varimax criterion to lead to factorially invariant solutions is provided by Kaiser (1958, pp. 196–8). Starting with the initial centroid solution for the twenty-four psychological tests, he rotated the first five tests, then six, and so on, adding one test at a time until all twenty-four were rotated. It is in this sense that he considers the effect on the factor loadings of changes in the composition of the test battery. For the particular example, the first and third factors are essentially invariant from the outset while the second and fourth factors fluctuate some before becoming stable.

13.5. *Orthomax Criteria*

There are essentially but two basic procedures for accomplishing orthogonal rotations to approximate simple structure—the quartimax of **13.3** and the varimax of **13.4**. As noted in the first edition of this text (Harman 1960, p. 334), a general class of orthogonal criteria could be constructed from a weighted composite of these two distinct types of orthogonal rotations, namely:

(13.28) $$\alpha Q + \beta V = \text{maximum}.$$

Taking Q from (13.7) and using the raw form (13.21) of the varimax criterion (but multiplied by n since a constant multiplier does not effect the maximization process), the class of "orthomax" criteria may be written explicitly in the form:

(13.29) $$\sum_{p=1}^{m} \left(\sum_{j=1}^{n} b_{jp}^4 - \frac{\gamma}{n} \left(\sum_{j=1}^{n} b_{jp}^2 \right)^2 \right) = \text{maximum},$$

where $\gamma = \beta/(\alpha + \beta)$. Of course, for $\gamma = 0$ this reduces to the quartimax criterion and for $\gamma = 1$ it becomes the varimax criterion. An equally weighted ("biquartimax") criterion would be designated by $\gamma = .5$. Jennrich (1970) presents general algorithms for the class of orthomax criteria and illustrates the results for several values of γ with the example of the twenty-four psychological tests.

Instead of taking arbitrary values of the parameter γ, Saunders (1962) suggests that best results can be obtained when it is equal to approximately half the number of common factors. The expression (13.29) for $\gamma = m/2$ is called the "equamax" criterion, and Kaiser (1974c) provides a rationale for it.

14   **Objective Oblique**
                          Multiple-Factor
                          Solutions

14.1. *Introduction*

In the last chapter the rationale for analytical solutions was presented, along with some of the historical developments. Two practical methods—albeit requiring high-speed computers—were given for the determination of multiple-factor solutions approximating simple structure under the condition that the factors be uncorrelated. The restriction of orthogonality is removed in the present chapter.

While the mathematics and the computations become more involved, there is much greater flexibility in an oblique solution. Of course, an orthogonal (or near-orthogonal) solution may result out of the more general oblique conditions if, in fact, the "best" solution should tend toward orthogonality. The conditions set forth for an oblique solution do not preclude zero correlations among the factors.

The theory and procedures which lead to oblique simple-structure solutions stem from the same objective criteria underlying the orthogonal solutions of chapter 13. Upon relaxing the restriction of orthogonality several of the criteria of chapter 13 can be adapted to produce oblique solutions. In **14.2** one form of the quartimax criterion is generalized to produce the oblimax method, involving the maximization of fourth powers of oblique structure elements. The original analytical procedure due to Carroll—the quartimin method—is developed in **14.3**. Further improvements and generalizations of that method are presented in **14.4** under the oblimin methods. In all these oblique methods a rather involved procedure is followed, wherein the desired simple structure principles for the primary factor solution are introduced in an indirect manner. In **14.5**, a direct procedure is presented for getting oblimin-like solutions. Finally, a class of oblique factor transformations is arrived at by means of intermediate orthogonal rotations in **14.6**. In each of these sections the theory leading to the particular oblique solution is presented and illustrated with numerical examples.

The basic concepts that arise in the analytical methods of rotation to multiple-factor solutions, both orthogonal and oblique, are listed in Table 14.1 along with the

Table 14.1

Concepts and Notation for the Rotation Problem

Concept	Notation	
	Orthogonal Case	Oblique Case
Original factors	F_p $\quad\quad (p = 1, 2, \cdots, m)$	F_p (orthogonal)
Original factor loadings	$\mathbf{A} = (a_{jp})$ $\quad (j = 1, 2, \cdots, n)$	$\mathbf{A} = (a_{jp})$
Transformation matrix	$\mathbf{T} = (t_{qp})$ $\quad (p, q = 1, 2, \cdots, m)$	$\Lambda = (\lambda_{qp})$
Final solution	$\mathbf{B} = \mathbf{AT} = (b_{jp})$	$\mathbf{V} = \mathbf{A\Lambda} = (v_{jp})$, reference structure matrix
		$\mathbf{P} = (b_{jp})$, primary pattern matrix
Final factors	M_p	T_p if primary factors
		Λ_p if reference axes
Criteria for transformation		
Quartimax	Equivalent expressions	
	(13.7) $Q = $ max.	
	(13.10) $M = $ max.	
	(13.11) $N = $ min.	
	(13.12) $K = $ max.	
Varimax	(13.22) $V = $ max.	
Oblimax		(14.2) $K = $ max.
Oblimin methods		
Quartimin		(14.12) $N = $ min.
Covarimin		(14.21) $C = $ min.
Oblimin (general)		(14.27) $B = $ min.
Binormamin		(14.28) $D = $ min.
Direct Oblimin		(14.33) $F = $ min.
Orthoblique		
Independent Clusters		(14.44) with $\mathbf{T}_2 = \mathbf{I}, \mathbf{D}_3 = \mathbf{I}$
Proportional		(14.45) with $\mathbf{T}_2 = \mathbf{I}, \mathbf{D}_3 = \Lambda^{1/4}$

symbols employed for them in this text. This summary of concepts and notation should assist in distinguishing the methods in this chapter from those of the preceding chapter, and can serve as a ready reference for the basic notation employed in this chapter. Specific notation required for the development of the ensuing methods will be introduced as needed.

14.2. *Oblimax Criterion*

It will be recalled that four separate criteria in chapter 13 were found to be equivalent when the rotated solution is restricted to orthogonal factors. When oblique factors are permitted, the four criteria are no longer equivalent; and, as a matter of fact, each method is not immediately generalizable to the oblique case. The criterion (13.12) can be applied to the oblique case. While the criterion $K = $ maximum is equivalent to $Q = $ maximum in the orthogonal case (since the denominator of K is an invariant under orthogonal transformation), the full expression for K must be used in the oblique case.

The problem is to find a transformation matrix Λ which will carry an initial factor matrix A into a final solution V, as in (12.25):

$$(14.1) \qquad\qquad V = A\Lambda,$$

in which the elements v_{jp} of the resulting factor structure matrix V will satisfy the criterion $K = $ maximum, where

$$(14.2) \qquad\qquad K = \sum_{j=1}^{n} \sum_{p=1}^{m} v_{jp}^4 \Big/ \Big(\sum_{j=1}^{n} \sum_{p=1}^{m} v_{jp}^2 \Big)^2 .$$

This restatement of (13.3) and (13.12) in different notation should make perfectly clear the distinction between the orthogonal and the oblique case. Also, it should be noted that in the latter case the term "loading" is used for the structure value, i.e., the correlation of the variable with the reference axis:

$$(14.3) \qquad\qquad v_{jp} = r_{z_j \Lambda_p} .$$

An oblique solution obtained under the condition that (14.2) be a maximum will be called an "oblimax" solution.[1]

The development of the theory of the oblimax method will be made following the work of Pinzka and Saunders (1954). The orthogonal projections v_{jp} on an oblique reference axis Λ_p are determined in such a manner as to make

$$(14.4) \qquad\qquad K_p = \sum_{j=1}^{n} v_{jp}^4 \Big/ \Big(\sum_{j=1}^{n} v_{jp}^2 \Big)^2 \qquad (p = 1, 2, \cdots, m)$$

a relative maximum under rotation in a plane. As the structure values v_{jp} are altered in successive iterations, the function (14.2) eventually attains a maximum value. Thus, while (14.4) represents the impact of maximizing the v's on a single reference axis, the criterion (14.2) represents the ultimate effect such successive maximizations have on the final solution V. The oblimax criterion can be expressed in terms of the factor loadings of the initial solution and the direction cosines in the matrix of transformation, and thereby the latter values can be determined.

To simplify the development, the coordinates of any point in the plane of the first two factors of the original rectangular reference system are designated (a, b) instead of (a_{j1}, a_{j2}). Then the elements v_{jp} resulting from the transformation (14.1) can be expressed as follows:

$$(14.5) \qquad\qquad v_{jp} = a\lambda_{1p} + b\lambda_{2p} \qquad\qquad (p = 1, 2, \cdots, m).$$

Since the direction cosines must satisfy the conditions

$$(14.6) \qquad\qquad \sum_{k=1}^{m} \lambda_{kp}^2 = 1, \qquad\qquad (p = 1, 2, \cdots, m),$$

---

[1] This term was suggested by Saunders.

it suffices to consider the ratio of the two in (14.5) as a single unknown, $x = \lambda_{2p}/\lambda_{1p}$, and rewrite the expression in the form:[2]

$$(14.7) \qquad\qquad v_{jp} = a + bx.$$

Substituting (14.7) into (14.4), and without designating the factor p, the criterion to be maximized becomes:

$$(14.8) \qquad\qquad K = \frac{\sum (a + bx)^4}{\left[\sum (a + bx)^2\right]^2},$$

where all summations are understood to extend over the n values of a and b (viz., a_{j1} and a_{j2} for $j = 1, 2, \cdots, n$). To simplify the work further, the functions of x in the numerator and denominator are designated by:

$$N = \sum (a + bx)^4,$$

$$D = \sum (a + bx)^2.$$

A necessary condition for the maximization of $K = N/D^2$ is the vanishing of its derivative with respect to x, namely,

$$K' = \frac{D^2 N' - N(2DD')}{D^4} = 0,$$

or, more simply,

$$(14.9) \qquad\qquad f(x) = DN' - 2ND' = 0,$$

where $f(x)$ is used to designate the resulting function of x. In general this equation will be of the fifth order, but fortuitously the coefficient of x^5 is zero. Representing the quartic equation by

$$(14.10) \qquad\qquad \alpha_4 x^4 + \alpha_3 x^3 + \alpha_2 x^2 + \alpha_1 x + \alpha_0 = 0,$$

its coefficients are given by

$$
\begin{aligned}
\alpha_4 &= \sum ab \sum b^4 \quad - \sum b^2 \sum ab^3, \\
\alpha_3 &= \sum a^2 \sum b^4 \quad + 2 \sum ab \sum ab^3 - 3 \sum b^2 \sum a^2 b^2, \\
\alpha_2 &= 3 \sum a^2 \sum ab^3 \qquad\qquad - 3 \sum b^2 \sum a^3 b, \\
\alpha_1 &= 3 \sum a^2 \sum a^2 b^2 - 2 \sum ab \sum a^3 b - \sum b^2 \sum a^4, \\
\alpha_0 &= \sum a^2 \sum a^3 b \quad - \sum ab \sum a^4.
\end{aligned}
$$

(14.11)

While these coefficients appear rather imposing at first glance, a certain symmetry of form will be detected upon more careful scrutiny.

Any one of the four roots of (14.10), if real, will produce either a maximum or a minimum of K. When all four roots $x = \lambda_{2p}/\lambda_{1p}$ are real and distinct, they correspond

---

[2] It is tacitly assumed that $\lambda_{1p} \neq 0$, otherwise the ratio would not be defined. Of course, if $\lambda_{1p} = 0$ then $\lambda_{2p} = 1$ and the rotated axis is coincident with the second axis of the original reference frame.

to two relative maxima and two relative minima of K. From calculus it is known that those roots of (14.10) for which the second derivative K'' is negative make K a maximum. Differentiating $K' = f/D^3$ produces

$$K'' = \frac{D^3 f' - f(3D^2 D')}{D^6} = \frac{f'}{D^3}$$

where the last equality follows from $f = 0$. Since D is a sum of squares and is always positive, the algebraic sign of K'' is the same as that of f'.

Then the sufficient condition for a maximum involves the substitution of a root of (14.10) into the derivative of the same function to note if the result is negative. Actually the derivative of (14.10) need not be determined explicitly because its behavior in the vicinity of the root can be determined from the polynomial itself. If the polynomial is increasing in the neighborhood of the root then K must be at a minimum; if decreasing, then K must be at a maximum. The sign of α_4 determines the sign of the entire polynomial as x increases without limit. Therefore, for the largest root K will be a maximum if α_4 is negative, and a minimum if α_4 is positive. Once it is known whether the largest root produces a maximum or a minimum the same information is known for each of the other roots since the roots alternate between maxima and minima.

The two roots of (14.10) that correspond to maxima yield the direction cosines of the new reference axes, and the analytical rotation is carried out accordingly. This process is repeated for all pairs of factors $p = 1, 2, \cdots, m - 1$ and $q = p + 1, p + 2, \cdots, m$, until K stabilizes at its maximum value (to a specified number of decimal places).

The oblimax method, just as all the other analytical procedures, requires a vast amount of computing and hence becomes impractical without high-speed computing facilities. Pinzka and Saunders (1954, pp. 11–30) present a flow chart of the computations and outline a computer program for a hypothetical electronic computer. An oblimax program was written by Kern W. Dickman for the Illiac. Such a solution was obtained on this computer for the twenty-four psychological variables, and is exhibited in Table 14.2. The oblimax reference structure matrix V and its associated primary-factor pattern matrix P are recorded in this table from the direct output of the computer (except for the reflection of two factors and rounding to three decimal places for convenience of printing). The criterion (14.2) was $K = .02364$ for the initial centroid loadings and increased to a maximum $K = .04168$ for the structure values of the oblimax matrix V. The correlations among the reference factors and among the primary factors also are outputs of the computer.

The principal purpose of presenting Table 14.2 is to show the feasibility of an oblimax solution on a large electronic computer. It is also of interest to note that this objective solution is very similar to one that had been obtained by intuitive-graphical methods.

14.3. *Quartimin Criterion*

The next analytical procedure for an oblique solution is the one originally introduced by Carroll (1953). The criterion is $N = $ minimum, just as in (13.11) but without

Table 14.2

Oblimax Solution for Twenty-Four Psychological Tests

(Initial solution: Centroid)

Test	Reference Structure: V				Primary Pattern: P			
	Λ_1	Λ_2	Λ_3	Λ_4	Verbal T_1	Speed T_2	Deduction T_3	Memory T_4
1	−.095	.014	.537	−.034	−.131	.018	.832	−.050
2	−.040	−.042	.353	−.023	−.056	−.056	.547	−.034
3	−.015	−.110	.454	−.060	−.021	−.146	.704	−.087
4	.020	−.048	.440	−.087	.027	−.063	.682	−.127
5	.607	.077	−.025	−.060	.839	.103	−.038	−.087
6	.601	−.052	−.015	.036	.831	−.068	−.023	.052
7	.689	.037	−.031	−.109	.952	.049	−.048	−.159
8	.365	.110	.170	−.086	.505	.146	.263	−.125
9	.655	−.146	−.031	.085	.905	−.193	−.048	.124
10	.050	.625	−.243	.085	.069	.828	−.376	.124
11	.023	.481	−.127	.187	.032	.636	−.196	.271
12	−.132	.596	.090	−.079	−.182	.789	.139	−.115
13	−.011	.466	.250	−.165	−.016	.618	.387	−.239
14	.099	.032	−.144	.405	.137	.043	−.223	.589
15	−.013	−.065	−.016	.417	−.018	−.086	−.024	.607
16	−.109	−.077	.261	.298	−.150	−.101	.404	.434
17	−.008	.029	−.136	.541	−0.11	.039	−.211	.786
18	−.201	.090	.145	.397	−.277	.120	.224	.577
19	−.020	.015	.087	.278	−.028	.020	.135	.404
20	.151	−.065	.298	.076	.208	−.087	.462	.110
21	−.046	.223	.250	.066	−.064	.296	.387	.095
22	.168	−.134	.224	.198	.232	−.177	.347	.287
23	.119	.022	.381	.003	.165	.029	.590	.004
24	.165	.289	−.006	.146	.228	.382	−.009	.212

Factor	Correlations Among Factors							
1	1.000	−.094	−.413	−.207	1.000	.494	.661	.579
2		1.000	−.253	−.315		1.000	.590	.598
3			1.000	−.342			1.000	.663
4				1.000				1.000

the constraint that the factors be orthogonal in the rotated solution. Carroll now suggests the name "quartimin" for this method since it involves the minimization of terms of the fourth degree, viz., the sum of cross-products of squared factor "loadings."[3]

A transformation of the form (14.1) will produce a quartimin solution if the elements v_{jp} of the resulting factor structure matrix **V** minimize:

$$(14.12) \qquad N = \sum_{j=1}^{n} \sum_{p<q=1}^{m} v_{jp}^2 v_{jq}^2.$$

[3] Of course, for an oblique solution the use of the term "loading" must be made explicit (see **12.6**), and here it stands for the structure value as given by (14.3).

This criterion can be expressed in terms of the initial factor loadings and the direction cosines in the matrix of transformation. For any row j of A and any column p of Λ the resulting element of V, according to (14.1), is

$$v_{jp} = \sum_{k=1}^{m} a_{jk}\lambda_{kp},$$

so that (14.12) can be expressed in the form:

$$(14.13) \qquad N = \sum_{j=1}^{n} \sum_{p<q=1}^{m} \left(\sum_{k=1}^{m} a_{jk}\lambda_{kp}\right)^2 \left(\sum_{k=1}^{m} a_{jk}\lambda_{kq}\right)^2.$$

It would appear that by conventional calculus methods, the elements of the transformation matrix could be determined such that the expression (14.13) is a minimum. As Carroll (1953, p. 26) points out, however, the resulting equations would be so complex as not to be readily soluble. Instead, Carroll reaches a solution by iterative methods—systematically varying values of λ_{qp} until the value of N attains a minimum under the m conditions (14.6).[4]

The iterative solution is accomplished by a systematic process permitting the values in one column of Λ to vary while the remaining columns are fixed. If the column vector for which the values are going to be changed is designated

$$\Lambda_x = \{\lambda_{1x}, \lambda_{2x}, \cdots, \lambda_{mx}\},$$

then it is appropriate to designate by N_x the value of the criterion N when it changes as a function of Λ_x, namely:

$$(14.14) \qquad N_x = \sum_{j=1}^{n} \left[v_{jx}^2 \sum_{p=1}^{m} v_{jp}^2 \right], \qquad\qquad (p \neq x).$$

Now, for any variable j the sum of squares of structure values which is independent of x may be designated by:

$$w_j = \sum_{p=1}^{m} v_{jp}^2, \qquad\qquad (p \neq x),$$

so that the criterion (14.14) becomes:

$$(14.15) \qquad N_x = \sum_{j=1}^{n} w_j v_{jx}^2.$$

It will simplify the following development to employ matrix algebra. The column vector V_x of the structure matrix V which results from a change in Λ_x is, according to (14.1),

$$V_x = A\Lambda_x.$$

[4]These conditions merely state that each reference vector is of unit length, while the additional restriction that $\Lambda'\Lambda = I$ would impose orthogonality on the solution; but in that case the simpler, equivalent solution of **13.3** would be employed.

Hence, corresponding to the sum of squared structure values is

$$\mathbf{V}_x'\mathbf{V}_x = \Lambda_x'\mathbf{A}'\mathbf{A}\Lambda_x$$

and the entire expression (14.15) becomes:

(14.16) $$N_x = \Lambda_x'\mathbf{A}'\mathbf{W}\mathbf{A}\Lambda_x = \Lambda_x'\mathbf{C}\Lambda_x,$$

where $\mathbf{W}$ is a diagonal matrix of the n scalars w_j and $\mathbf{C} = \mathbf{A}'\mathbf{W}\mathbf{A}$.

The problem, then, is to minimize (14.16) under the condition

(14.17) $$\Lambda_x'\Lambda_x = 1$$

corresponding to (14.6) for the reference vector x. This can be accomplished by the method of Lagrange's multipliers, yielding the characteristic equation of $\mathbf{C}$, namely:

(14.18)
$$
\begin{vmatrix}
(c_{11} - N_x) & c_{12} & \cdots & c_{1m} \\
c_{21} & (c_{22} - N_x) & \cdots & c_{2m} \\
\cdot & \cdot \cdot \cdot & \cdot & \cdot \\
c_{m1} & c_{m2} & \cdots & (c_{mm} - N_x)
\end{vmatrix} = 0.
$$

Any latent root of this m^{th} order linear equation will make the determinant vanish; and, in order to minimize N_x, the smallest latent root is selected. Then the elements of the latent vector associated with this root are the desired solutions λ_{px}. When the smallest N_x is determined from equation (14.18), it is substituted into the following set of homogeneous linear equations (from which the condition (14.18) was derived):

(14.19)
$$
\begin{aligned}
(c_{11} - N_x)\lambda_{1x} + && c_{12}\lambda_{2x} + &&\cdots &&+ && c_{1m}\lambda_{mx} = 0, \\
c_{21}\lambda_{1x} + (c_{22} - N_x)\lambda_{2x} + &&\cdots &&+ && c_{2m}\lambda_{mx} = 0, \\
\cdot \quad \cdot \quad \cdot \quad \cdot \quad \cdot \quad \cdot \quad \cdot \quad \cdot \quad \cdot \quad \cdot \quad \cdot \quad \cdot \quad \cdot \quad \cdot \quad \cdot \quad \cdot \quad \cdot \quad \cdot, \\
c_{m1}\lambda_{1x} + && c_{m2}\lambda_{2x} + &&\cdots &&+ (c_{mm} - N_x)\lambda_{mx} = 0.
\end{aligned}
$$

The resulting solutions λ_{px} are all proportional to one arbitrary solution, and by applying the condition (14.17) the direction cosines for the new axis are obtained which will make the criterion N_x a minimum.

The theory of the quartimin method, as outlined above, clearly implies a tremendous amount of computing. The work involved in preparation for the iterations, determining $\mathbf{C}$, and the large number of iterations that are usually required, indicate that only with the capability of a high-speed electronic computer is a quartimin rotation feasible. The only practical exception is the case of only two common factors.

More will be said about computer programs for the quartimin method in **14.4**. To illustrate the preceding theory, however, a simple numerical example will be employed; and to make comparisons possible, the example of the eight physical variables again is used. The centroid solution for this example is taken as the initial solution $\mathbf{A}$ and appears in Table 14.3.

Table 14.3

Quartimin Solution for Eight Physical Variables

(Initial solution: Centroid)

Variable j	Initial Solution: A		Elements of W for First Two Iterations		Structure: V	
	a_{j1}	a_{j2}	$x = 1$ $w_j = a_{j2}^2$	$x = 2$ $w_j = a_{j1}^2$	v_{j1}	v_{j2}
1	.830	−.396	.1568	.6889	.783	.046
2	.818	−.469	.2200	.6691	.838	−.024
3	.777	−.470	.2209	.6037	.817	−.044
4	.798	−.401	.1608	.6368	.770	.027
5	.786	.500	.2500	.6178	.007	.814
6	.672	.458	.2098	.4516	−.020	.723
7	.594	.444	.1971	.3528	−.050	.673
8	.647	.333	.1109	.4186	.072	.601

The object of the iteration process is successively to alter the values of the transformation matrix

$$\Lambda = \begin{bmatrix} \lambda_{11} & \lambda_{12} \\ \lambda_{21} & \lambda_{22} \end{bmatrix}$$

in such a manner as to reduce the value of N, as given by (14.13), to a minimum. The process is begun by arbitrarily selecting the first column to be the vector Λ_x for which the values $\lambda_{11}, \lambda_{21}$ are going to be changed. Having designated $x = 1$, the w_j values are determined next. These w_j values are simply the respective a_{j2}^2 for the first iteration, and are also given in Table 14.3. The diagonal matrix **W** is made up of these elements and the matrix multiplications are carried out to produce:

$$C = \begin{bmatrix} .8561 & −.0294 \\ −.0294 & .3053 \end{bmatrix}.$$

The minimization process leads to the characteristic equation

$$\begin{vmatrix} (.8561 − N_x) & −.0294 \\ −.0294 & (.3053 − N_x) \end{vmatrix} = 0,$$

or

$$N_x^2 − 1.1614N_x + .2605 = 0,$$

from which the smallest root is found to be $N_x = .3038$. For this value of N_x, equations (14.19) become

$$.5523\lambda_{11} - .0294\lambda_{21} = 0,$$

$$-.0294\lambda_{11} + .0015\lambda_{21} = 0.$$

From the first of these equations,

$$\lambda_{21} = \frac{.5523}{.0294}\lambda_{11}$$

and, upon applying the condition (14.6), viz.,

$$\frac{.305035}{.000864}\lambda_{11}^2 + \lambda_{11}^2 = 1$$

there results $\lambda_{11}^2 = .002824$, and hence $\lambda_{21}^2 = .997176$. The direction cosines of the new position of the first reference axis are $\lambda_{11} = .0531$ and $\lambda_{21} = .9986$, while the second axis remains unchanged. The impact of this first transformation is to reduce the value of N from .8561 for the initial solution to .3038.

The second iteration is made by taking the second column of Λ to be the vector Λ_x and using the new values of the first column for the remainder of the transformation matrix. In this case, a new matrix C is set up, for which the characteristic equation is

$$\begin{vmatrix} (.8245 - N_x) & .0605 \\ .0605 & (.3037 - N_x) \end{vmatrix} = 0.$$

The least root of this equation is $N_x = .2968$, a slight drop from the previous value of .3038. Proceeding as before in applying the condition (14.6), the new direction cosines for the second reference axis are found to be $\lambda_{12} = -.1139$ and $\lambda_{22} = .9935$.

After seven iterations the value of N is found to be stable at $N = .0065$. These iterations changed the values of the elements in the transformation matrix until the following were reached:

$$\begin{pmatrix} .4756 & -.5432 \\ .8797 & .8396 \end{pmatrix}.$$

The signs of the second column are reflected and the two columns are interchanged in order to present the final results in the same order as previously. The transformation matrix may then be written:

$$\Lambda = \begin{pmatrix} .5432 & .4756 \\ -.8396 & .8797 \end{pmatrix}.$$

Postmultiplying the initial solution A by this matrix produces the factor structure of the quartimin solution in Table 14.3.

The quartimin structure V is very similar to both the intuitive-graphical solution and to the oblimax solution (given in the first edition of this text when based upon the same initial solution), the difference between corresponding elements being no greater than .003 in either case. In spite of the close agreements the differences among these solutions stem from fundamental differences in the basis underlying each one. It is of interest to note that the oblimax criterion for the quartimin solution of Table 14.3 is $K = .12890$. Of course this cannot be quite as large as the maximum value, $K = .12891$, for the oblimax solution (although the difference is only in the fifth decimal place). Theoretically the present solution is not as good as the one obtained according to the oblimax criterion. On the other hand, the quartimin criterion for Table 14.3 is $N = .0065$ while a similar computation for the oblimax solution yields $N = .0068$. In the same sense, the present solution is better than the oblimax solution according to the quartimin criterion. While the foregoing differences were rather academic, real pronounced differences can be expected in situations where the clusters are not so well-defined as in the simple example of eight physical variables.

14.4.   *Oblimin Methods*

In the preceding section an approximation to a simple-structure solution was obtained by minimizing the expression (14.12) involving terms of the fourth degree. Carroll (1960) has generalized his original criterion to a whole class of methods for oblique transformations to simple structure which involve minimization of certain expressions. This class of methods, involving oblique factors and a minimizing criterion, is designated by the term "oblimin." Carroll arrived at the general class of oblimin solutions from a consideration of his quartimin criterion and Kaiser's oblique version of the varimax criterion (1956a).

The criterion for the latter solution, which Kaiser (1958) considers the most obvious way of relaxing the restriction of orthogonality in his original varimax method, is the minimization of the function:[5]

$$(14.20) \qquad C^* = \sum_{p<q=1}^{m} \left(n \sum_{j=1}^{n} v_{jp}^2 v_{jq}^2 - \sum_{j=1}^{n} v_{jp}^2 \sum_{j=1}^{n} v_{jq}^2 \right),$$

i.e., minimization of the covariances of squared elements of the factor structure **V**. In the orthogonal case the criterion (13.21) is equivalent to (14.20). Just as (13.21) is replaced by (13.22), so Kaiser (1958, p. 198) suggests replacing (14.20) by

$$(14.21) \qquad C = \sum_{p<q=1}^{m} \left[n \sum_{j=1}^{n} (v_{jp}^2/h_j^2)(v_{jq}^2/h_j^2) - \sum_{j=1}^{n} v_{jp}^2/h_j^2 \sum_{j=1}^{n} v_{jq}^2/h_j^2 \right],$$

involving "normalized loadings." This implies the normalization by rows of the initial factor matrix, carrying through the transformation in terms of the extended vectors, and then reducing the matrix **V** thus obtained to the original-length vectors by multiplying the elements in rows of **V** by the square root of the respective communalities.

Both Kaiser and Carroll have found from empirical investigations that neither the quartimin nor the covarimin methods work very well. The trouble is that the latter procedure is almost invariably biased toward factor axes which are too orthogonal,

---

[5]Also called the "covarimin" criterion by Carroll (1957).

while the former procedure is just as biased in the opposite direction of factor axes which are too highly correlated. Since covarimin tends to be "too orthogonal" and quartimin "too oblique," Carroll (1957) proposed the following "biquartimin" criterion as a compromise:

$$(14.22) \qquad B^* = N + C^*/n = \text{minimum},$$

where N is defined in (14.12) and C^* in (14.20). In the last term, the full covarimin expression including division by n is retained, whereas it had been dropped as immaterial to the minimization of (14.20). The rationale for (14.22) is the simultaneous minimization of two quantities, each of which has a valid justification.

Subsequently, Carroll (1960) generalized this simple sum of the two separate criteria to permit varying weights of the "quartimin" and "covarimin" components. This is accomplished by introducing variable parameters α and β as follows

$$(14.23) \qquad B^* = \alpha N + \beta C^*/n = \text{minimum}.$$

Then, substituting the criteria N and C^* from (14.12) and (14.20), the new criterion becomes

$$(14.24) \qquad B^* = \sum_{p<q=1}^{m} \left\{ \alpha \sum_{j=1}^{n} v_{jp}^2 v_{jq}^2 + \beta \left[n \sum_{j=1}^{n} v_{jp}^2 v_{jq}^2 - \sum_{j=1}^{n} v_{jp}^2 \sum v_{jq}^2 \right] \middle/ n \right\}.$$

Multiplying the entire expression (14.24) by n (which has no effect on the minimum of B^*), and combining terms, produces the following:

$$B^* = \sum_{p<q=1}^{m} \left[(\alpha + \beta) \left(n \sum_{j=1}^{n} v_{jp}^2 v_{jq}^2 \right) - \beta \sum_{j=1}^{n} v_{jp}^2 \sum_{j=1}^{n} v_{jq}^2 \right].$$

Dividing this expression by the sum of the weights and setting

$$(14.25) \qquad \gamma = \beta/(\alpha + \beta),$$

the general oblimin criterion is given by:

$$(14.26) \qquad B^* = \sum_{p<q=1}^{m} \left(n \sum_{j=1}^{n} v_{jp}^2 v_{jq}^2 - \gamma \sum_{j=1}^{n} v_{jp}^2 \sum_{j=1}^{n} v_{jq}^2 \right).$$

When the analysis is carried through for "normalized loadings," the final oblimin criterion may be expressed by:

$$(14.27) \qquad B = \sum_{p<q=1}^{m} \left[n \sum_{j=1}^{n} (v_{jp}^2/h_j^2)(v_{jq}^2/h_j^2) - \gamma \sum_{j=1}^{n} v_{jp}^2/h_j^2 \sum_{j=1}^{n} v_{jq}^2/h_j^2 \right] = \text{min}.$$

It will be noted that the covarimin criterion (14.20) is a special instance of (14.26) corresponding to the value $\gamma = 1$ of the arbitrary parameter.[6] Similarly, the quartimin criterion (14.12) is another special instance of (14.26), namely, when $\gamma = 0$. Also when

[6]Or in terms of normalized elements (14.21) is a special instance of (14.27).

$\alpha = \beta = 1$, or $\gamma = .5$ from (14.25), the biquartimin criterion results. These special instances of the general oblimin criterion are summarized as follows:

Quartimin: $\gamma = 0$;   most oblique.

Biquartimin: $\gamma = .5$;   less oblique.

Covarimin: $\gamma = 1$;   least oblique.

Of course, any other value between zero and unity may be selected for γ with a corresponding variation in the criterion (14.27) and the oblimin solution resulting therefrom. Based upon empirical evidence, Carroll (1960, p. 3) suggests "that results will be most generally satisfactory when γ is set equal to $\frac{1}{2}$."

Another analytical procedure involving oblique factors and a minimizing criterion is due to Kaiser and Dickman (1959), and called "binormamin" by Dickman (1960, p. 81). Although it is not a special case of the class of oblimin solutions (14.27), it has many similarities in its formal expression, namely:[7]

$$(14.28) \qquad D = \sum_{p<q=1}^{m} \left[\sum_{j=1}^{n} (v_{jp}^2/h_j^2)(v_{jq}^2/h_j^2) \Big/ \left(\sum_{j=1}^{n} v_{jp}^2/h_j^2 \right) \left(\sum_{j=1}^{n} v_{jq}^2/h_j^2 \right) \right] = \min.$$

This criterion resulted from Kaiser's attempt to resolve the undetermined parameter γ in the oblimin class of solutions. Essentially the criterion (14.28) provides a solution which corrects for the "too oblique" bias of the quartimin criterion and the "too orthogonal" bias of the covarimin criterion without arbitrarily taking $\gamma = \frac{1}{2}$ of the biquartimin solution. In comparing their criterion with the biquartimin, Kaiser and Dickman (1959, pp. 6–7) argue that apparently the advantage of one or the other depends on the nature of the data under consideration: if the data are particularly simple, or extremely complex, criterion (14.28) is better; but if the data are moderately complex then criterion (14.27) is superior.

Actually, there has not been sufficient experience with these new analytical methods to judge whether one or another method is so effective as to justify the exclusion of all others. Kaiser and Dickman summarize their exploration by indicating examples of the two extremes: their worst result being for the twenty-variable box problem and their best for the twenty-four psychological tests. In the first case, they tend to get slightly negative loadings for the well-established zeros, and somewhat higher inter-correlations among the primary factors than the intercorrelations of the under-lying three dimensions of the boxes. On the other hand, the correspondence between their analytical solution for the twenty-four psychological tests and the subjective-graphical solution is almost uncanny. Kaiser and Dickman conclude that the degree of simplicity of structure inherent in the data accounts for these results. An example of a binormmamin solution is given later, but a detailed mathematical development involving the criterion (14.28) is not included.

Returning to the class of oblimin solutions given by the criterion (14.27), it is obvious that the task of computing such a factor solution is extremely difficult. Since

---

[7] In order to avoid confusion with the oblimax criterion, the symbol "D" is employed here instead of the symbol "K" used by Kaiser and Dickman.

there is little likelihood that the general oblimin methods will be employed with desk calculators, detailed steps for such calculations are not presented. An efficient computer program has been prepared by Carroll (1960)–written in FORTRAN for the IBM 704 originally, but since adapted to the IBM System 360 and other computers–and a general indication will be given of the form of these calculations.

Somewhat similar to the computing procedure described in **14.3**, Carroll found the most practicable procedure (even for large matrices) to be the successive modification of the transformation matrix Λ and the reference structure matrix V until it meets the condition (14.27). The process is begun by selecting one column of the matrix V, say V_x, and altering its values (with the elements in the remaining ($m = 1$) columns unchanged) until a minimum value is obtained for the following expression:

$$(14.29) \qquad B_x = \sum_{\substack{q=1 \\ (q \neq x)}}^{m} \left[n \sum_{j=1}^{n} (v_{jx}^2/h_j^2)(v_{jq}^2/h_j^2) - \gamma \sum_{j=1}^{n} v_{jx}^2/h_j^2 \sum_{j=1}^{n} v_{jq}^2/h_j^2 \right].$$

This operation on a single column is designated a "minor cycle" of the iterations. A set of m minor cycles, one for each of the m columns of V, is called a "major cycle."

For each minor cycle, the core of the electronic computations involves the solution of a characteristic equation, yielding the algebraically smallest eigenvalue and corresponding eigenvector of a non-symmetric matrix (1960, pp. 4–6). From such an eigenvector is derived a column of the transformation matrix and the desired V_x of the structure matrix, while the eigenvalue is the required minimum value of (14.29). The iterative process is continued, taking successive values of x until a major cycle is accomplished. The computer program involves successive major cycles until a satisfactory degree of convergence is attained. This is measured by the amount of change in the total value of the criterion (14.27), consisting of the sum of the m values (14.29) obtained in each major cycle; or more precisely, by the amount of change in the individual values (14.29).

To illustrate the oblimin solutions the set of eight physical variables is again used for the first example. The two-factor minres solution of Table 9.2 was taken as the initial matrix A, and three different values of the parameter γ were employed to get the factor structure matrices of Table 14.4. It will be recalled that the quartimin solution for the same example was also computed by desk calculator methods in the last section (but employing a centroid initial solution), and the structure matrix appears in Table 14.3. Of course there are some differences in structure values (the largest being .034) since the two solutions are based on different initial matrices, but also because the first employed the criterion (14.12) while the second used the normalized form (14.27) with $\gamma = 0$. Of the three solutions in Table 14.4, the covarimin less clearly satisfies the simple structure principles than either of the others. On the other hand, it may be considered the simplest because the covarimin factors are uncorrelated in this example. While the well-defined zero weights in the quartimin structure may make it appear more desirable than the biquartimin solution, the latter has the advantage of lower correlation between the primary factors. All things considered, the biquartimin solution appears to be the "best."

Table 14.4

Three Oblimin Solutions for Eight Physical Variables

(Initial solution: Minres, Table 9.2)

Variable j	Quartimin ($\gamma = 0$) Reference Structure		Biquartimin ($\gamma = .5$) Reference Structure		Covarimin ($\gamma = 1$) Reference Structure	
	v_{j1}	v_{j2}	v_{j1}	v_{j2}	v_{j1}	v_{j2}
1	.775	.051	.825	.154	.872	.278
2	.840	−.033	.884	.074	.921	.204
3	.814	−.046	.854	.056	.887	.181
4	.774	.024	.821	.126	.864	.248
5	−.003	.826	.105	.872	.233	.913
6	−.012	.706	.080	.744	.189	.778
7	−.064	.697	.024	.728	.129	.753
8	.086	.567	.165	.610	.258	.652
Criterion (15.39) Initial value Final value	11.621 .068		5.414 −2.848		−.793 −6.601	
Correlation between primary factors	.485		.275		.000	

Another, more practical, application of the oblimin procedure was made to the example of twenty-four psychological tests. For a problem of this magnitude electronic computations become imperative. Starting with the centroid solution and an initial criterion value of $B = 9.33$, seven major cycles for a total of 610 iterations later (but only a few minutes even on the computers of the early 1960s) produced the biquartimin reference structure of Table 14.5 with a final minimum criterion of $B = -4.17$. This structure matrix V is in terms of the original lengths of the test vectors, although they were first normalized and after the rotations were accomplished they were shrunken again.

The output of the computer also includes: (1) the transformation matrix Λ that carries the initial matrix V into V; (2) the matrix $\Psi = \Lambda'\Lambda$ containing the correlations among the reference factors Λ_p; (3) the matrix $\Phi = T'T$ containing the correlations among the primary factors T_p; and (4) a matrix of numbers which can easily be transformed into factor measurements (see **16.5**). From the first three of these matrices the primary factor pattern can be obtained to complete the oblique solution. The primary factor pattern P may be determined from the structure V by employing the relationship (12.36). What is needed, first, is the diagonal matrix D of correlations between corresponding Λ and T factors. This is defined in (12.26) and involves the transformation matrix T from the initial solution to the primary-factor structure. But, from formula (12.26), it follows that

$$(14.30) \qquad\qquad T' = D\Lambda^{-1},$$

Table 14.5

Biquartimin Solution for Twenty-Four Psychological Tests

(Initial solution: Centroid)

Test	Reference Structure: V				Primary Pattern: P			
	Λ_1	Λ_2	Λ_3	Λ_4	Verbal T_1	Speed T_2	Deduction T_3	Memory T_4
1	.014	.094	.598	.051	.015	.103	**.666**	.058
2	.028	.007	.392	.029	.031	.008	**.436**	.033
3	.067	−.052	.498	.000	.074	−.057	**.555**	.000
4	.106	.011	.490	−.022	.117	.012	**.545**	−.025
5	.675	.110	.075	−.008	**.748**	.120	.083	−.009
6	.670	−.016	.089	.084	**.742**	−.018	.099	.095
7	.755	.063	.068	−.061	**.836**	.069	.076	−.069
8	.449	.159	.256	−.019	**.497**	.174	.285	−.021
9	.722	−.111	.079	.130	**.800**	−.122	.087	.146
10	.080	.650	−.186	.132	.089	**.711**	−.208	.149
11	.074	.525	−.054	.245	.082	**.574**	−.060	.276
12	−.072	.641	.132	−.011	−.080	**.701**	.146	−.012
13	.074	.524	.307	−.082	.082	**.573**	.341	−.092
14	.135	.070	−.069	.437	.149	.077	−.076	**.492**
15	.029	−.019	.052	.452	.032	−.021	.058	**.508**
16	−.032	−.007	.330	.359	−.035	−.008	.368	**.404**
17	.034	.079	−.053	.579	.038	.086	−.059	**.652**
18	−.130	.161	.217	.460	−.144	.176	.242	**.518**
19	.035	.066	.151	.324	.039	.072	.168	**.365**
20	.240	−.002	.378	.143	.265	−.002	**.421**	.161
21	.038	.289	.318	.141	.042	**.316**	.353	.159
22	.250	−.071	.311	.258	.277	−.078	**.346**	.291
23	.223	.095	.464	.085	.247	.104	**.516**	.095
24	.234	.341	.082	.211	.260	**.373**	.091	.237
Factor	Correlations Among Factors							
1	1.000	−.120	−.233	−.216	1.000	.262	.341	.337
2		1.000	−.172	−.233		1.000	.295	.338
3			1.000	−.192			1.000	.329
4				1.000				1.000

which states that $\mathbf{T}'$ is obtainable from Λ^{-1} by normalizing its rows. The inverse of the non-symmetric transformation matrix Λ may involve considerable computations. To simplify the process, the symmetric matrix $\boldsymbol{\Psi}$ of correlations among the reference factors Λ_p is set up, namely:

(14.31) $$\boldsymbol{\Psi} = \Lambda'\Lambda,$$

and its inverse can be obtained by the square-root method of **3.4**. Then the desired inverse of Λ follows simply from the matrix product:

(14.32) $$\Lambda^{-1} = \boldsymbol{\Psi}^{-1}\Lambda'.$$

Finally, the algebraic factors required to normalize the rows of Λ^{-1} are the values for the principal diagonal of $\mathbf{D}$.

For the example of twenty-four psychological tests, the matrices Λ^{-1} and $\mathbf{D}$ are obtained in ex. 9, chap. 14. The proportionality factors necessary for calculating the primary pattern are contained in the matrix:

$$\mathbf{D}^{-1} = \begin{bmatrix} 1.1075 & 0 & 0 & 0 \\ 0 & 1.0939 & 0 & 0 \\ 0 & 0 & 1.1128 & 0 \\ 0 & 0 & 0 & 1.1251 \end{bmatrix}$$

Applying formula (12.36), the primary pattern of Table 14.5 is obtained.

The objective solution of Table 14.5 may be compared with the solution obtained by subjective graphical methods, and also with the oblimax solution of Table 14.2. There is a striking similarity between the biquartimin and each of the other two solutions. The biquartimin factors have smaller intercorrelations than either those arrived at by graphical methods or those determined by the oblimax method. The relative contributions of the factors to the total communality of 11.383 appear to be somewhat different. The complete analysis of the contributions of the biquartimin factors is presented in Table 14.6. These analytically determined factors have a

Table 14.6

Total Contributions of Biquartimin Primary Factors

Factor	T_1	T_2	T_3	T_4
T_1	3.070	—	—	—
T_2	.172	2.039	—	—
T_3	.581	.251	2.465	—
T_4	.267	.340	.364	1.839

Grand total = 11.388

greater variation in their direct contributions than those obtained subjectively by passing the primary factors through the points representing composite variables. In other words, there is a greater tendency toward level contributions of factors determined by intuitive-graphical methods.

Since the computation of an analytical oblique solution for a problem of twenty-four variables and four factors is now measured in seconds of CPU time, several additional solutions to the one in Table 14.5 were determined. Without presenting the detailed tables, certain interesting properties will be noted. As an empirical test of convergence, two biquartimin solutions were obtained, once starting with the centroid solution and then again starting with the varimax solution (Table 13.7).

The results were almost identical, with a maximum difference for any element of the final structure matrix **V** being less than .01.

Two other oblimin solutions were computed, for $\gamma = 0$ and $\gamma = 1$, each time starting with the same centroid solution. Of course these solutions turned out to be quite different from the biquartimin solution of Table 14.5 since they were designed to satisfy different criteria. One striking difference was that the quartimin ($\gamma = 0$) solution contained forty-one small negative entries while the covarimin ($\gamma = 1$) solution did not contain a single negative entry. While it would require too much space to show these solutions, some of the statistics associated with them are presented in Table 14.7. Either of the transformation matrices given in this table may be applied to the centroid pattern to get a corresponding oblimin reference structure by using (14.1). From the correlations among the primary factors, it will be noted that the quartimin factors are most highly correlated, the covarimin factors are least correlated, while the biquartimin factors are between these extremes. It was empirical evidence of this type, coupled with its own rationale, that led Carroll to the development of the biquartimin criterion.

The final application of the oblimin methods is to the problem of eight political variables for which the method of **14.2** broke down. The oblimin methods applied to the same difficult problem lead to satisfactory results. First, the quartimin method of **14.3** is applied, using a desk calculator, and after six iterations the criterion stablizes at the minimum $N = .1819$ (from an original value of $N = .4344$ for the initial

Table 14.7

Some Statistics for the Quartimin and Covarimin Solutions for Twenty-Four Psychological Tests

Factor	Quartimin Solution ($\gamma = 0$)				Covarimin Solution ($\gamma = 1$)			
	1	2	3	4	1	2	3	4
	Transformation Matrix Λ							
Λ_1	.234	.201	.170	.160	.671	.545	.631	.599
Λ_2	−.588	−.376	.499	.434	−.378	.625	−.576	.536
Λ_3	−.714	.737	−.530	.425	.514	−.386	−.458	.246
Λ_4	.301	−.525	−.665	.778	−.378	−.405	.246	.542
	Correlations Among Primary Factors							
T_1	1.000	.680	.564	.653	1.000	−.037	−.304	−.080
T_2		1.000	.604	.655		1.000	−.020	−.339
T_3			1.000	.724			1.000	−.044
T_4				1.000				1.000
Number of iterations	1,218				121			
Criterion								
Initial	132.22				−12.69			
Final	4.03				−21.92			

principal-factor solution). The resulting structure is the first one exhibited in Table 14.8. Alongside of this solution is a corresponding one obtained on a computer, but in which normalized loadings were employed in the course of the calculations.

Two additional oblimin solutions—the covarimin ($\gamma = 1$) and the biquartimin ($\gamma = .5$)—for the eight political variables were also obtained on a computer and are shown in Table 14.8. Again, it will be noted that the quartimin factors tend to be highly correlated, the covarimin factors tend toward orthogonality (actually so in

Table 14.8

Three Oblimin Solutions and Binormamin Solution for Eight Political Variables

(Initial solution: Principal-Factor, Table 8.8)

Variable j	Quartimin ($\gamma = 0$) Solutions*				Covarimin ($\gamma = 1$) Solution‡		Biquartimin ($\gamma = .5$) Solution				Binormamin Solution			
	On Desk Calculator† Structure **V**		On Electronic Computer Structure **V**				Structure **V**		Pattern **P**		Structure **V**		Pattern **P**	
	Λ_1	Λ_2	Λ_1	Λ_2	T_1	T_2	Λ_1	Λ_2	T_1	T_2	Λ_1	Λ_2	T_1	T_2
1	.63	.09	.71	.14	.74	−.04	.74	.09	.77	.09	.73	.12	.79	.12
2	.90	.23	.98	.30	1.00	.05	1.00	.23	1.04	.24	1.00	.27	1.07	.28
3	.64	−.07	.78	−.01	.86	−.22	.84	−.06	.87	−.06	.82	−.03	.87	−.03
4	−.44	.32	−.62	.26	−.76	.46	−.71	.32	−.74	.33	−.68	.29	−.73	.31
5	−.37	−.70	−.20	−.69	−.03	−.71	−.09	−.70	−.09	−.73	−.13	−.70	−.13	−.74
6	.51	−.25	.68	−.19	.80	−.39	.76	−.24	.79	−.25	.74	−.21	.79	−.23
7	.08	.72	−.15	.68	−.36	.79	−.29	.71	−.30	.74	−.24	.70	−.26	.74
8	−.43	.40	−.64	.34	−.80	.55	−.75	.39	−.78	.40	−.72	.36	−.77	.39
$r_{T_1 T_2}$	−.63		−.47		−.00		−.26				−.35			

* In order to save space, only the reference structures are exhibited. The primary factor pattern for the first solution is given by $\mathbf{P} = 1.291\mathbf{V}$ while the corresponding relationship for the second solution is $\mathbf{P} = 1.134\mathbf{V}$.

† This solution is the only one not based on normalized loadings.

‡ Because this oblique varimax solution actually resulted in an orthogonal frame of reference the Λ- and T-axes coincide; and the four otherwise distinct matrices—reference structure, reference pattern, primary structure, and primary pattern—all collapse into a single matrix involving orthogonal factors.

this case), while the biquartimin factors assume some intermediate positions. Any one of these solutions is a better approximation to simple structure than the one attempted by graphical methods (in first edition of this text). The results of the biquartimin solution are exhibited in Figure 14.1. Of course, after obtaining the results of the analytical solutions it is easy to see wherein the original intuitive judgments could be improved upon—and this kind of rationalization is to be expected if the objective definition of simple structure is indeed a good explication of the intuitive concept.

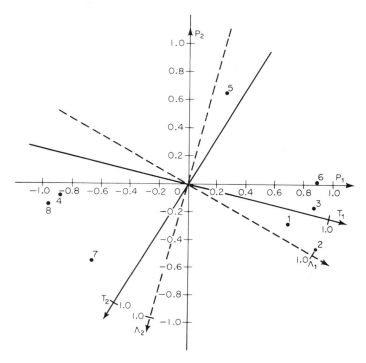

FIG. 14.1—Biquartimin factors for eight political variables

An oblique solution for the difficult example of eight political variables was also obtained by applying the binormamin criterion (14.28). This solution is shown at the extreme right of Table 14.8, and as far as meeting the simple structure principles it does about as good a job as any of the oblimin solutions, coming closest to the biquartimin form. With regard to the degree of obliqueness, its primary factors are a little more correlated than those of the biquartimin solution but less than the quartimin.

While the entire class of oblimin solutions is infinite, depending on the value of the parameter γ, three particular forms have been singled out: the quartimin for $\gamma = 0$, the covarimin for $\gamma = 1$, and the biquartimin for $\gamma = .5$. In addition, there is the binormamin solution based upon the criterion (14.28), and a fifth major form is the oblimax solution. An important consideration in making a choice of form of solution is the degree of correlation among the primary factors. All five of these methods were employed in the analysis of the eight physical variables, the eight political variables, and the twenty-four psychological variables. From these empirical studies, the covarimin criterion was found to lean very strongly toward orthogonality; the quartimin criterion was found to produce primary factors which were highly correlated; the biquartimin criterion led to an intermediate position but tending toward the lower correlations; and the binormamin criterion also led to an intermediate position but somewhat higher than the biquartimin factors. The obli-max criterion also leads to primary factors which are highly correlated like the quartimin factors. From the viewpoint of showing least bias toward orthogonality or obliqueness, either the biquartimin or the binormamin solutions are most satis-factory. As noted earlier, the superiority of any one solution over the others is apt to stem from the inherent nature of the data rather than from a theoretical consideration.

It should be noted that the problem of analytical rotation in the orthogonal case is essentially resolved. Several very competent methods are available in chapter 13 and chances are that they can be little improved upon. On the other hand analytical methods for the oblique case are fundamentally different and still in a develop-mental state. Important new developments are presented in the next two sections.

Since the trend is toward oblique simple structure, Schmid and Leiman (1957) became concerned with the difficulties that may arise in the psychological interpre-tation of oblique factors. They propose a method for transforming such a solution into an orthogonal one, still preserving simplicity but involving a larger number of orthogonal factors. Their model of an hierarchical factor solution is a natural exten-sion of the bi-factor solution, including subgroups of the group factors. Unlike the bi-factor method, or Burt's (1950) group-factor method which involves the succes-sive grouping of variables according to their sign pattern in a centroid solution, the hierarchical solution proposed by Schmid and Leiman depends upon successively obtained higher-order factor solutions. These higher-order solutions are the factori-zations of the matrices of correlations among the oblique factors. If an oblique sim-ple-structure type solution can be obtained at each level then their procedure can be used to recast the several higher-order factors into an orthogonal hierarchical factor pattern.

14.5. *Direct Oblimin*

As noted in **12.6**, the bi-orthogonal system of coordinate axes—reference and primary—played an important role in the development of oblique primary-factor solutions. Now the computational capabilities are available to make obsolete this rather awkward approach. An important breakthrough was made by Jennrich and Sampson (1966) when they derived an analytical procedure to go directly from an initial to a primary-factor pattern. Their procedure also involves a parameter, dif-ferent values of which lead to a whole class of oblimin-like solutions. Because a primary-factor pattern is obtained directly, without involving an intermediate refer-ence structure, and because the method involves oblique factors and a minimizing criterion, it is designated "direct oblimin" in keeping with the previous names. Jennrich and Sampson use the term "simple loadings."

The general procedure for getting a simple structure solution has been to maxi-mize, as in (14.2), or minimize, as in (14.12) or (14.27), some function of the refer-ence structure elements. The ultimate objective is to make the primary-factor pattern satisfy the simple structure principles. Since the reference-factor structure and the primary-factor pattern are simply related by (12.36), it follows that the latter will look simple if the former does. This property has permitted the indirect approach of simplifying the reference structure to be used as a basis for getting the desired primary-factor solution.

The point of departure in the Jennrich and Sampson approach is to seek a simple structure solution directly by minimizing a function of the primary-factor-pattern coefficients. Thus, in place of the criterion (14.26) that involves the structure values, the corresponding function for the direct oblimin method may be expressed in the form:

$$(14.33) \qquad F(\mathbf{P}) = \sum_{p<q=1}^{m} \left(\sum_{j=1}^{n} b_{jp}^2 b_{jq}^2 - \frac{\delta}{n} \sum_{j=1}^{n} b_{jp}^2 \sum_{j=1}^{n} b_{jq}^2 \right),$$

where $\mathbf{P}$ is the primary-factor-pattern matrix with elements b_{jp}. In order to avoid confusion with the (indirect) oblimin methods of the preceding section, the parameter δ is employed in the present section instead of γ, which Jennrich uses. Of course, the original factor loadings a_{jp} may be normalized by rows, i.e., divided by h_j, and the transformation to the final matrix $\mathbf{P}$ may be carried through in terms of the extended vectors. The original lengths are restored at the end of the process by multiplying the final b_{jp} by h_j. In any event, the direct oblimin solution is obtained by minimizing $F(\mathbf{P})$ in (14.33). It will be recalled from (12.21) that

$$(14.34) \qquad \mathbf{P} = \mathbf{A}(\mathbf{T}')^{-1},$$

so that the problem amounts to finding a transformation matrix $\mathbf{T}$ that will minimize $F(\mathbf{A}(\mathbf{T}')^{-1})$ under the side condition

$$(14.35) \qquad \text{diag}(\mathbf{T}'\mathbf{T}) = \mathbf{I}.$$

In the paper by Jennrich and Sampson (1966), the mathematical development is presented for the simplest case—what might be called the "direct quartimin," when $\delta = 0$ in (14.33)—and comparisons are made with the biquartimin solutions for two practical problems. The mathematical details actually are given for one elementary rotation (involving only two primary factors), from which the generalization of the process is readily evident. Rotations of this type are performed systematically using all possible pairs of factors until $F(\mathbf{P})$ converges.

A FORTRAN IV subroutine which implements the direct oblimin procedures has been written by Jennrich and Sampson, and was adapted by the author (1966a) in FORTRAN II for use on Philco 2000 and more recently in FORTRAN IV for use on IBM System 360. In this program, the criterion for convergence is

$$(14.36) \qquad (F_{i-1} - F_i)/F_0 \leqq \epsilon,$$

where i is the iteration number and ϵ is usually .00001. Actually, the function minimized in the subroutine is twice that in (14.33); the sum over the factors in the subroutine is only restricted to $p \neq q$, and since the terms are symmetric in p and q the resulting sum is twice what it would be if these indices were not permitted to be interchanged. The output of the program is an oblique factor solution satisfying the principles of simple structure, more or less. The solution consists of the factor pattern, the correlations among the factors, and the factor structure (all of these, of course, refer to the primary-factor solution).

When applying the direct oblimin criterion (14.33), it is possible for the minimum of $F(\mathbf{P})$ to approach $-\infty$ if positive values of δ are employed. Specifically, Jennrich has demonstrated (in a private communication to the author) that $F(\mathbf{P})$ approaches $-\infty$ if and only if $\delta > \frac{4}{5}$. For practical purposes, it is recommended that the value of δ in (14.33) be zero or negative (to be distinguished from the range of zero to one for γ in the indirect oblimin methods). When δ is zero, the factors are most oblique (even higher correlations among the factors can be obtained for positive fractional values of δ). For negative values of δ the factors become less oblique as δ gets smaller.

The last mentioned property is immediately evident from the three direct oblimin solutions shown in Table 14.9—the correlation between the two factors goes down

Table 14.9

Three Direct Oblimin Factor Patterns for Eight Physical Variables

(Initial solution: Minres, Table 9.2)

Variable j	$\delta = 0$		$\delta = -.5$		$\delta = -70$	
	T_1	T_2	T_1	T_2	T_1	T_2
1	.883	.065	.866	.115	.819	−.411
2	.956	−.029	.933	.027	.802	−.498
3	.926	−.045	.902	.010	.762	−.491
4	.882	.035	.863	.085	.792	−.427
5	.005	.940	.061	.918	.804	.490
6	−.006	.803	.042	.784	.678	.424
7	−.065	.793	−.017	.770	.618	.448
8	.104	.646	.140	.637	.640	.286
Criterion (14.33) Initial value Final value	1.453 .036		2.228 .968		110.071 108.597	
Correlation between primary factors	.471		.373		.002	

as the value of δ decreases. Other properties may also be determined from a study of this table, and from supplementary data obtained by running this problem for values of δ from -100 to $+1$. First, of course, it is of interest to see how the various direct solutions compare with the oblimin solutions of the preceding section. For $\delta = 0$, the solution is very similar to that of the quartimin, for which the reference structure is given in Table 14.4 and the primary factor pattern is provided in the answer to ex. 8, chap. 14. The differences between respective factor coefficients are only in the third decimal place. For $\delta = -1$ to $\delta = -4$, the resulting direct oblimin solutions are roughly like the biquartimin, with the correlation between the primary factors ranging from .337 to .285 and all factor coefficients being positive and forming the two very distinct clusters.

Experimentation was continued with different values of δ for the problem of eight physical variables. By the time δ gets down to -6.5, the resulting factor pattern has "returned" to the form of the initial minres solution (the first factor coefficients agree within .001 while the second factor coefficients differ by three units in the second decimal place). The correlation between the primary factors is .044 as contrasted with the zero correlation in the minres case. Even when the correlation is reduced to .002 (for $\delta = -70$ to $\delta = -100$), the resulting factor pattern is not materially different from that obtained for $\delta = -6.5$. Specifically, the first axis goes through the cluster of all the points and the second is essentially at right angle to it, just as in the case of the minres solution. For no value of δ was a solution found that could be said to be similar to the covarimin (reference structure given in Table 14.4) with its features of zero correlation between the primary factors and all positive factor coefficients. The direct oblimin solutions for large negative values of δ satisfy the condition of near zero correlation while the solution for $\delta = -4$ satisfies the property of positive factor coefficients, but no single value of δ produced all the features of the covarimin solution. Before leaving this problem, a couple of positive values of δ were tried also. For $\delta = .5$, the correlation between the factors reached .748 and the factor coefficients did not satisfy the simple structure principles nearly as well as for the $\delta = 0$ solution in Table 14.9. Finally, just as an empirical test it was found that for $\delta = 1$ the function in (14.33) did in fact become very large negatively before the calculations in the computer were stopped.

The behavior of the direct oblimin method was also explored for the problem of twenty-four psychological tests. This was done both with an initial minres solution and an initial centroid solution. Because of space limitations, only one complete solution is presented, in Table 14.10, but conclusions will be drawn from all of the experimental work. As a general observation, the direct oblimin solution in this table is quite similar to the biquartimin solution of Table 14.5 although the two solutions were obtained by different methods and were based on different initial matrices. The correlations among the direct oblimin factors are consistently, but only slightly, larger than the corresponding correlations of the biquartimin solution (Table 14.5), but not as large as the correlations among the quartimin factors (Table 14.7).

As δ increases negatively, it seems that the resulting factor pattern tends to return to the form of the original input and the correlations among the factors tend toward zero. The ultimate results did not appear, however, up to $\delta = -95$. No negative δ produced a solution with as high correlations among the factors as the (indirect) quartimin. When δ was permitted to be positive—experimenting with δ from .1 to .5 in .1 increments—it was found that for $\delta = .4$ the resulting solution was most nearly like the quartimin. The correlations among the factors for these two solutions are shown in the top blocks of Table 14.11.

Unlike the preceding example, for the twenty-four psychological tests the direct oblimin solution with $\delta = 0$ does not approximate the quartimin but comes closer to the biquartimin. Actually, the solution for $\delta = -.5$ is a better approximation to the biquartimin than that produced by $\delta = 0$. The correlations among the factors for each of these solutions, as well as those of the biquartimin factors are exhibited

Table 14.10

Direct Oblimin ($\delta = 0$) Solution for Twenty-Four Psychological Tests

(Initial solution: Minres, $m = 4$)

Test j	Primary Structure: S				Primary Pattern: P			
	r_{jT_1}	r_{jT_2}	r_{jT_3}	r_{jT_4}	Verbal T_1	Speed T_2	Deduction T_3	Memory T_4
1	.353	.331	.731	.344	.008	.113	**.680**	.035
2	.234	.170	.478	.198	.029	.026	**.458**	−.001
3	.283	.104	.574	.244	.053	−.095	**.564**	.039
4	.364	.202	.577	.232	.149	.014	**.523**	−.037
5	.793	.345	.365	.347	**.760**	.107	.009	−.011
6	.816	.225	.383	.412	**.785**	−.069	.024	.103
7	.849	.283	.361	.284	**.872**	.041	.009	−.096
8	.674	.361	.481	.345	**.547**	.131	.211	−.012
9	.857	.208	.376	.404	**.850**	−.094	.004	.085
10	.289	.829	.048	.308	.118	**.856**	−.273	.045
11	.336	.617	.251	.503	.074	**.493**	−.045	**.305**
12	.190	.734	.294	.259	−.084	**.734**	.124	−.029
13	.359	.621	.515	.292	.069	**.519**	.359	−.070
14	.318	.199	.177	.591	.126	−.032	−.095	**.588**
15	.244	.186	.220	.554	.022	−.029	.005	**.554**
16	.265	.205	.501	.596	−.083	−.069	.357	**.518**
17	.284	.333	.198	.631	.031	.122	−.086	**.606**
18	.220	.449	.406	.554	−.136	.267	.221	**.425**
19	.282	.279	.335	.438	.049	.096	.162	**.319**
20	.523	.252	.529	.449	**.304**	−.016	**.323**	.204
21	.361	.528	.503	.386	.061	**.376**	**.329**	.092
22	.511	.274	.516	.445	.290	.017	**.308**	.199
23	.545	.377	.627	.425	.279	.125	**.433**	.096
24	.511	.588	.346	.465	.294	**.421**	.026	.175

Factor	Correlations Among Factors				
T_1	1.000	.316	.432	.414	Criterion (14.33):
T_2		1.000	.296	.374	Initial value, 5.221
T_3			1.000	.387	Final value, 1.740
T_4				1.000	

in Table 14.11. The actual ninety-six factor coefficients for the biquartimin and each of these direct oblimin solutions were compared, yielding mean differences of .0114 and .0155 for $\delta = -.5$ and $\delta = 0$, respectively; and for the more important coefficients (i.e., $a_{jp} > .300$), these mean differences are .0109 and .0147, respectively.

Further experimentation with the twenty-four–variable problem was conducted for values of δ from -10 to -95 in increments of -5. First, it should be noted that the process failed to converge within the limit of 100 iterations (for $\delta = 0$ it only required about a dozen iterations for convergence), and the criterion function (14.33) was very large for these values of δ and changed very little in successive iterations.

Table 14.11

Comparison of Direct and Indirect Oblimin Factor Correlations:
Twenty-Four Psychological Tests, Four Factors

(Initial solution: Centroid)

	Direct Oblimin					Indirect Oblimin			
Factor	T_1	T_2	T_3	T_4	Factor	T_1	T_2	T_3	T_4
	$\delta = .4$					Quartimin ($\gamma = 0$)			
T_1	1.000	.646	.712	.717	T_1	1.000	.680	.564	.653
T_2		1.000	.633	.701	T_2		1.000	.604	.655
T_3			1.000	.673	T_3			1.000	.724
T_4				1.000	T_4				1.000
	$\delta = 0$					Biquartimin ($\gamma = .5$)			
T_1	1.000	.313	.434	.405	T_1	1.000	.262	.341	.337
T_2		1.000	.313	.412	T_2		1.000	.295	.338
T_3			1.000	.376	T_3			1.000	.329
T_4				1.000	T_4				1.000
	$\delta = -.5$					Covarimin ($\gamma = 1$)			
T_1	1.000	.270	.379	.335	T_1	1.000	$-.037$	$-.304$	$-.080$
T_2		1.000	.280	.364	T_2		1.000	$-.020$	$-.339$
T_3			1.000	.329	T_3			1.000	$-.044$
T_4				1.000	T_4				1.000

Average Correlation: $\bar{r}$

δ	$\bar{r}$	δ	$\bar{r}$	δ	$\bar{r}$	γ	$\bar{r}$	Type
.5	.841	.2	.443	$-.5$	.326	0	.647	Quartimin
.4	.680	.1	.400	-10	.283	.5	.317	Biquartimin
.3	.524	0	.375	-95	.031	1	$-.137$	Covarimin

As noted before, the factor correlations decrease as δ becomes larger negatively. The first instance where all the factor correlations are zero in the first decimal place is for $\delta = -25$. In this sense, that solution is like the covarimin; but just as in the case of the 8–variable example, it appears to be more like the original centroid pattern than the intended covarimin form with all positive factor coefficients and very low factor correlations.

Finally, the direct oblimin method is applied to the twenty–variable box problem, starting with the orthogonal solution **A** from Table 8.11. Since this is an artificial problem with a known "target" a wide range of values for the parameter δ were tried in an attempt to reach this objective. This led to various transformations, from highly correlated factors to almost orthogonal ones. The average correlation among the three factors of each solution may be used as a rough overall indicator of the degree to which the direct-oblimin solution approximates the target oblique solution (see Table 8.11), for which the "true" $\bar{r} = .202$. A somewhat better indicator of how well any one of the direct oblimin solutions fits may be surmised from the root-mean-square deviation (rms), similar to formula (13.27), between the obtained correlations and the corresponding "true" values. Both types of measures for twelve different values of δ are shown in Table 14.12. It can be seen that the best fit, on the basis of these indicators,[8] is for $\delta = -3$.

Table 14.12

Factor Correlations of Direct Oblimin Solutions for Twenty-Variable Box Problem

(Averages and comparisons with "true" values)

δ	.5	.4	.3	.2	.1	0	$-.5$	-1	-2	-3	-4	-5
$\bar{r}$	.623	.482	.398	.354	.328	.311	.274	.260	.249	.234	.017	.016
rms	.422	.281	.197	.154	.129	.113	.079	.068	.059	.042	.198	.199

The complete solution for $\delta = -3$ is given in Table 14.13. Not only are the factor correlations very close to the theoretical values, but so also are the individual correlations of the variables with the factors and the factor coefficients. The root-mean-square deviation for the sixty factor coefficients is only .097. Of course, this good a fit was obtained because the "target" was known and the particular member of the class of direct oblimin solutions was selected to accomplish this. There does not seem to be any "blind" way of arriving at the solution of Table 14.13. Not having the hypothetically "true" solution available as a target, the applied scientist must rely upon his training and experience to lead him to the formulation of the theory that this three-factor solution is a good representation (model) of the x, y, z dimensions (constructs) of the boxes as measured by the twenty manifest variables.

From the theoretical developments and the empirical investigations, certain tentative conclusions can be drawn regarding the direct oblimin methods. First, it becomes quite evident that no simple relationship exists between the direct and the indirect methods. That is not to say that striking agreements cannot be found between results obtained by the two approaches, but merely that there is not a very simple way of saying what value of δ in the direct method will lead to an equivalent result for a given γ in the indirect method. Secondly, there is no compelling reason to accept the three special instances of the indirect oblimin—quartimin ($\gamma = 0$), biquartimin ($\gamma = .5$), and covarimin ($\gamma = 1$)—as superior to direct oblimin. In some sense, the direct obli-

[8]Actually, in trying to home in on the "true" solution, as given in Table 8.11, values of δ between -3 and -4 were also investigated. For $\delta = -3.2$ the average correlation (.190) is closer to the target than for $\delta = -3.0$, but its rms $= .072$ is not as good.

Table 14.13

Direct Oblimin ($\delta = -3$) Solution for Twenty-Variable Box Problem

(Initial solution: Orthogonal solution **A**, Table 8.11)

Variable j	Primary Structure: **S**			Primary Pattern: **P**		
	r_{jx}	r_{jy}	r_{jz}	x	y	z
1. x^2	.977	.389	−.009	.962	.134	−.180
2. y^2	.178	.986	.229	−.142	1.031	−.005
3. z^2	.247	.279	.982	.105	.009	.965
4. xy	.595	.937	.183	.342	.849	−.075
5. xz	.612	.384	.854	.488	.042	.773
6. yz	.278	.626	.892	.033	.422	.783
7. $\sqrt{x^2 + y^2}$	.804	.801	.119	.624	.638	−.128
8. $\sqrt{x^2 + z^2}$	.951	.461	.406	.876	.128	.248
9. $\sqrt{y^2 + z^2}$	.240	.888	.654	−.076	.796	.469
10. $2x + 2y$	.717	.879	.157	.498	.749	−.099
11. $2x + 2z$	.832	.445	.663	.728	.087	.537
12. $2y + 2z$	.262	.789	.789	−.029	.642	.635
13. $\log x$	.973	.413	−.010	.949	.164	−.187
14. $\log y$	.138	.978	.285	−.189	1.021	.061
15. $\log z$	.259	.231	.979	.135	−.050	.972
16. xyz	.527	.677	.781	.303	∶428	.632
17. $\sqrt{x^2 + y^2 + z^2}$	.789	.801	.406	.585	.574	.181
18. e^x	.948	.345	−.006	.943	.093	−.165
19. e^y	.206	.959	.172	−.097	1.004	−.061
20. e^z	.235	.291	.953	.090	.034	.932

Factor	Correlations Among Factors		
x	1.000	.311	.144
y		1.000	.246
z			1.000

min is superior, not only because of its greater simplicity but because of the wider range of oblique solutions that are possible. However, this very flexibility may detract from the direct method. It may be advisable, in due course of time, to recommend certain "preferred" values of δ that may be expected to have special properties, depending on the number of variables, number of factors, and perhaps other parameters.

14.6. *Orthoblique Method*

Another class of oblique factor transformations, the orthoblique method (Harris and Kaiser 1964), is considered in this section. While these procedures were first reported before the second edition of this text was published, they had not yet withstood the test of time and were not included. That omission is now being rectified. The orthoblique method compares very favorably (Hakstian 1971; Hakstian and

Abell 1974) with the preceding methods treated in this chapter. Computer programs for this method are now much more generally available and used in practice.

This method takes its name from the fact that a sequence of intermediate *orthogonal* transformations are employed in arriving at an objective *oblique* solution. In general a derived factor solution, with certain desirable properties according to some criterion, is obtained from a given initial solution by generating a suitable transformation matrix. For the orthogonal case, an initial factor matrix $\mathbf{A}$ is carried into a derived form $\mathbf{B}$ by an orthogonal transformation $\mathbf{T}$, as stated in (13.3), which is dependent on the particular criterion employed (see chapter 13). When the derived factor solution is permitted to have correlated factors, the initial factor matrix $\mathbf{A}$ (with uncorrelated factors) is carried into a derived reference structure matrix $\mathbf{V}$, as in (14.1), or into a derived primary factor pattern matrix $\mathbf{P}$, as in (14.34), according to the particular method used for generating the transformation matrix by the different methods presented in this chapter. The orthoblique method is distinguished by its procedure for getting an oblique solution (a pattern $\mathbf{P}$, a structure $\mathbf{S}$, and factor correlations $\boldsymbol{\Phi}$) by means of a composite transformation that is made up of orthogonal transformation matrices and positive-definite diagonal matrices.

In any transformation from some initial to a final factor form, the question of the adequacy of the direct solution must be resolved beforehand since the "theoretical" or reproduced correlations $\hat{\mathbf{R}}$ among the variables are subsequently employed, rather than their (fallible) observed values. This becomes very explicit in the orthoblique method when Harris and Kaiser state that it is the matrix of reproduced correlations $\hat{\mathbf{R}}$ for which an oblique factor solution is desired. Such a matrix is Gramian and singular, in general, being of rank m and a direct orthogonal factor solution $\mathbf{A}$ satisfies the fundamental factor theorem (2.50), namely:

$$(14.37) \qquad\qquad \hat{\mathbf{R}} = \mathbf{A}\mathbf{A}'.$$

Now, for the initial factorization of $\hat{\mathbf{R}}$ the principal-factor method gives

$$(14.38) \qquad\qquad \mathbf{A} = \mathbf{Q}\boldsymbol{\Lambda}^{1/2}$$

so that

$$(14.39) \qquad\qquad \hat{\mathbf{R}} = \mathbf{A}\mathbf{A}' = \mathbf{Q}\boldsymbol{\Lambda}\mathbf{Q}'$$

where $\boldsymbol{\Lambda}$ is the diagonal matrix of the m nonzero eigenvalues of $\hat{\mathbf{R}}$ and $\mathbf{Q}$ is the $n \times m$ matrix of column normalized eigenvectors corresponding to these eigenvalues.

The orthoblique method emanates from the following ingenious tautology (Harris and Kaiser 1964, p. 350):[9]

$$\hat{\mathbf{R}} = (\mathbf{Q}\boldsymbol{\Lambda}^{1/2}\mathbf{T}_2\mathbf{D}_2\mathbf{T}_1\mathbf{D}_1)(\mathbf{D}_1^{-1}\mathbf{T}_1'\mathbf{D}_2^{-1}\mathbf{T}_2'\boldsymbol{\Lambda}^{-1/2}\boldsymbol{\Lambda}\boldsymbol{\Lambda}^{-1/2}\mathbf{T}_2\mathbf{D}_2^{-1}\mathbf{T}_1\mathbf{D}_1^{-1})$$
$$(14.40) \qquad (\mathbf{D}_1\mathbf{T}_1'\mathbf{D}_2\mathbf{T}_2'\boldsymbol{\Lambda}^{1/2}\mathbf{Q}'),$$

[9]The tautological expression can readily be verified by formally carrying out the indicated matrix multiplications (working outward from the product of the first and middle expressions and from the product of the middle and third expressions) to get (14.39).

in which all the **T** matrices are orthogonal ($\mathbf{TT'} = \mathbf{T'T} = \mathbf{I}$) and all the **D** matrices are positive-definite diagonal with both types being of order m. It can be seen immediately that the expression in the last set of parentheses is the transpose of that in the first set of parentheses, and hence the entire expression (14.40) may be related to the generalized form of the fundamental factor theorem (2.46), namely:

$$(14.41) \qquad \hat{\mathbf{R}} = \mathbf{P\Phi P'},$$

where **P** is used to designate the oblique factor pattern (to distinguish it from the original orthogonal pattern **A**) and **Φ** is the matrix of factor correlations. Then the entire class of orthoblique solutions may be represented by:

$$(14.42) \qquad \begin{aligned} \mathbf{P} &= \mathbf{Q\Lambda^{1/2}T_2D_2T_1D_1}, \\ \mathbf{\Phi} &= \mathbf{D_1^{-1}T_1'D_2^{-1}T_2'\Lambda^{-1/2}\Lambda\Lambda^{-1/2}T_2D_2^{-1}T_1D_1^{-1}} = \mathbf{D_1^{-1}T_1'D_2^{-2}T_1D_1^{-1}}, \\ \mathbf{S} &= \mathbf{P\Phi} = \mathbf{Q\Lambda^{1/2}T_2D_2^{-1}T_1D_1^{-1}}, \end{aligned}$$

where the third expression (for the oblique factor structure) is obtained from the first two according to (2.43).

While Harris and Kaiser develop their method in the most general form, leading to both orthogonal and oblique derived solutions, the presentation here is limited to certain of their oblique methods.[10] Particular solutions are obtained depending on the choices of the matrices $\mathbf{T_1}$, $\mathbf{T_2}$, and $\mathbf{D_2}$ (it being understood that **A**, or **Q** and **Λ**, are known in advance). The matrix $\mathbf{D_1}$ merely provides the appropriate scaling, being chosen so that $\mathbf{D_1^{-1}}$ normalizes the expression for **Φ** to insure that it has unities in the diagonal and is a proper correlation matrix. The orthoblique transformations considered here fall in the Case II category of Harris and Kaiser (1964, p. 352) in which $\mathbf{T_2} = \mathbf{I}$ and $\mathbf{D_2} \neq \mathbf{I}$ (or else $\mathbf{\Phi} = \mathbf{I}$ and an orthogonal transformation arises). By restricting the class of oblique solutions so that $\mathbf{T_2} = \mathbf{I}$ implies certain constraints on the possible location of the primary-factor axes. Thus, for the two-factor case the primary factors must lie in adjacent quadrants—not in the same or nonadjacent quadrants—and for a solution involving three or more factors there are corresponding constraints. While this is a non-negligible restriction, there may be many sets of data for which oblique solutions of this class would be perfectly satisfactory. To obtain a particular oblique solution from (14.42) as restricted to the general class specified as Case II, a choice must be made for $\mathbf{T_1}$ and $\mathbf{D_2}$ (other than the identity matrix) and determining $\mathbf{D_1^{-1}}$ so that it normalizes $\mathbf{T_1'D_2^{-2}T_1}$ and thereby produces **Φ**. The formal representation of such a solution (with $\mathbf{T_2} = \mathbf{I}$) simplifies to:

$$(14.43) \qquad \begin{aligned} \mathbf{P} &= \mathbf{Q\Lambda^{1/2}D_2T_1D_1} = \mathbf{QD_3T_1D_1}, \\ \mathbf{\Phi} &= \mathbf{D_1^{-1}T_1'D_2^{-2}T_1D_1^{-1}} = \mathbf{D_1^{-1}T_1'D_3^{-1}\Lambda D_3^{-1}T_1D_1^{-1}}, \\ \mathbf{S} &= \mathbf{Q\Lambda^{1/2}D_2^{-1}T_1D_1^{-1}} = \mathbf{Q\Lambda D_3^{-1}T_1D_1^{-1}}, \end{aligned}$$

---

[10]Not covered in this text is Harris-Kaiser Case I, orthogonal solution, and Harris-Kaiser Case III, oblique solution for which $\mathbf{T_2} \neq \mathbf{I}$—the former because of its triviality, the latter because of its complexity and lack of resolution. A good start on the Case III orthoblique method is made by Hakstian and Abell (1974).

where $\mathbf{\Lambda}^{1/2}\mathbf{D}_2$ is set equal to $\mathbf{D}_3$ since the eigenvalues, as derived from the given data, also constitute a positive-definite diagonal matrix. In getting the last two expressions in terms of the newly defined matrix $\mathbf{D}_3$ it should be remembered that diagonal matrices may be replaced by their transposes. Now, the choice of $\mathbf{T}_1$ and $\mathbf{D}_2$ should be made so that the resulting oblique pattern $\mathbf{P}$ meets some designated criteria. If, for a given matrix of reproduced correlations $\hat{\mathbf{R}}$, a satisfactory Case II solution exists, then (14.43) "shows that the desired pattern matrix is proportional by columns to an orthogonal transformation of the rescaled principal-axes factors of [$\hat{\mathbf{R}}$, author's notation]" (Harris and Kaiser 1964, p. 353). The crux of the problem, then, is the rescaling of the principal factors $\mathbf{Q}\mathbf{\Lambda}^{1/2}$. Once this rescaling matrix $\mathbf{D}_2$ is determined, the generation of the orthogonal transformation matrix $\mathbf{T}_1$ can proceed according to any of the methods of chapter 13.

The first definite type of solution sets $\mathbf{D}_3 = \mathbf{I}$ and specifies that $\mathbf{T}_1$ be generated according to the quartimax criterion (13.10), and is designated the independent clusters solution (Harris and Kaiser 1964, p. 356). Of course, the observed correlations (and the model representation $\hat{\mathbf{R}}$ of these data) must exhibit the inherent property of distinct clusters for this oblique solution to hold. In such event the common parts ($\mathbf{c}$) of the observed variables ($\mathbf{z}$) fall into m independent (not necessarily orthogonal) clusters. In the pattern matrix $\mathbf{P}$ each row would contain one and only one nonzero entry and the (common part) variable would be of complexity one. It would then follow that $\mathbf{P'P}$ was necessarily diagonal.

Setting $\mathbf{D}_3 = \mathbf{I}$ in (14.43) leads to the following expressions for the *independent clusters* solution:

$$\mathbf{P} = \mathbf{Q}\mathbf{T}_1\mathbf{D}_1,$$

(14.44)
$$\mathbf{\Phi} = \mathbf{D}_1^{-1}\mathbf{T}_1'\mathbf{\Lambda}\mathbf{T}_1\mathbf{D}_1^{-1},$$

$$\mathbf{S} = \mathbf{Q}\mathbf{\Lambda}\mathbf{T}_1\mathbf{D}_1^{-1}.$$

It can be verified immediately that $\mathbf{P'P} = \mathbf{D}_1^2$, a diagonal matrix. While this condition is necessary, Harris and Kaiser argue that any arbitrary orthogonal transformation matrix $\mathbf{T}_1$ may not be sufficient to guarantee this *ideal* $\mathbf{P}$. "Instead, some restriction must be put on $\mathbf{T}_1$. One way which may be shown to do this is to develop $\mathbf{T}_1$, using the quartimax criterion, as an orthogonal transformation of $\mathbf{Q}$. Note that it is the matrix $\mathbf{Q}$ that is being 'rotated,' not the principal-axes factor matrix [$\mathbf{Q}\mathbf{\Lambda}^{\frac{1}{2}}$, author's notation]" (Harris and Kaiser 1964, p. 356). In the early work with the orthoblique method emphasis was placed on generating the matrix $\mathbf{T}_1$ by the quartimax criterion (13.10), but subsequently the varimax criterion (13.22) or other orthomax criteria (13.29) were found to serve equally well (Kaiser 1970; Hakstian and Abell 1974).

A simple example of independent clusters is that of the eight physical variables. Instead of using the principal-factor solution of Table 8.4 (based on prior estimates of communality), however, the minres solution of Table 9.2 is taken as the initial factor matrix $\mathbf{A}$, and which is repeated in Table 14.14 as the starting point for the calculations. The first step in the orthoblique method is to normalize the columns of $\mathbf{A}$ and thus obtain the matrix $\mathbf{Q}$ of unit-length eigenvectors. An immediate indication

Table 14.14

Orthoblique (Independent Clusters) Solution for Eight Physical Variables

(Initial solution: Minres, Table 9.2)

Variable j	Given Matrices				Derived Solution			
	Principal-Factor*		Column Normalized		Primary Structure: S		Primary Pattern: P	
	$A = Q\Lambda^{\frac{1}{2}}$		$Q = (Q\Lambda^{\frac{1}{2}})(\Lambda^{-\frac{1}{2}})$		r_{jT_1}	r_{jT_2}	T_1	T_2
1	.856	−.324	.406	−.264	.914	.488	.883	.063
2	.848	−.412	.402	−.335	.942	.429	.958	−.032
3	.808	−.409	.383	−.333	.905	.398	.927	−.047
4	.831	−.342	.394	−.278	.898	.457	.882	.033
5	.750	.571	.356	.465	.450	.943	−.004	.945
6	.631	.492	.299	.400	.374	.800	−.014	.807
7	.569	.510	.270	.415	.310	.761	−.073	.797
8	.607	.351	.288	.286	.410	.696	.098	.649
Sum of squares	4.449	1.510	1.000	1.000	Factor Correlations		3.352	2.609
Factor	Scaling Matrix D_1^{-1}						Matrix T_1	
T_1	.5463	0			1.0000	.4808	.7915	.6111
T_2	0	.6193			.4808	1.0000	−.6111	.7915

*It should be noted that minres yields a principal-factor type solution.

of how well the model fits the observed data is provided by the computer output of the eigenvalues of $\hat{R}$, which are practically identical with the eigenvalues of the observed, reduced (with communalities), correlation matrix R. Then applying the quartimax rotation on Q produces the transformation matrix T_1. Next, $T_1'\Lambda T_1$ is computed and D_1^{-1} is determined so as to normalize this expression and thus get the matrix Φ of factor correlations as shown in the second of equations (14.44). Having derived T_1 and D_1, with Q and Λ given, the complete oblique solution can be determined according to (14.44). These results are shown in Table 14.14. A remarkable agreement (less than one unit in the second decimal place) may be noted between this primary-factor pattern and that obtained by the direct oblimin method ($\delta = 0$) in Table 14.9. From the various analyses of this problem throughout the text, it is well known that there are two clear-cut clusters inherent in the data, and that is why the independent clusters type of orthoblique works so well for it.

Another problem with considerable structure built into it is the example of twenty-four psychological tests, in which five groups of tests were identified (see **7.6**) and hence it would be quite reasonable to hypothesize five "independent clusters" factors. As a guide to the practical capability or limitation of the independent clusters ortho-blique method, it is attempted for this near-structured problem. Starting with the 5-factor minres solution of Table 9.5, the results of the analysis is shown in Table 14.15.

Table 14.15

Orthoblique (Independent Clusters) Solution for
Twenty-Four Psychological Tests

(Initial Solution: Minres, Table 9.5)

Test	Primary Structure: S					Primary Pattern: P				
j	r_{jT_1}	r_{jT_2}	r_{jT_3}	r_{jT_4}	r_{jT_5}	T_1	T_2	T_3	T_4	T_5
1	.719	.393	.325	.454	.443	**.692**	−.061	−.119	.046	.225
2	.478	.253	.197	.265	.180	**.541**	−.067	.003	−.025	−.018
3	.554	.312	.103	.321	.264	**.569**	.023	−**.308**	.065	.176
4	.587	.383	.240	.317	.219	**.611**	.056	−.025	−.074	−.003
5	.489	.794	.431	.435	.224	−.018	**.785**	.094	−.044	.004
6	.494	.829	.311	.488	.194	−.067	**.868**	−.165	.117	.062
7	.487	.845	.378	.376	.177	−.005	**.913**	.041	−.146	−.011
8	.567	.687	.419	.442	.300	.199	**.542**	.054	−.038	.071
9	.508	.852	.332	.473	.094	−.004	**.868**	−.041	.059	−.114
10	.170	.300	.846	.363	.456	−.293	.041	**.962**	−.029	.028
11	.312	.378	.592	.573	.603	−.286	.139	.188	**.406**	**.428**
12	.349	.218	.691	.343	.538	.122	−.166	**.645**	−.071	.186
13	.555	.409	.565	.406	.826	.216	.131	.052	−.094	**.712**
14	.240	.342	.245	.584	.171	−.250	.156	−.139	**.711**	.049
15	.276	.264	.248	.540	.105	−.048	−.024	−.015	**.627**	−.095
16	.515	.301	.243	.623	.249	**.302**	−.145	−.195	**.611**	.043
17	.275	.308	.384	.622	.209	−.181	−.001	.100	**.689**	−.032
18	.453	.252	.481	.588	.319	.224	−.256	.257	**.460**	−.029
19	.376	.306	.310	.469	.241	.120	.009	.026	**.361**	.039
20	.613	.535	.364	.512	.087	**.464**	.154	.150	.165	−.288
21	.587	.384	.585	.428	.381	**.483**	−.087	**.457**	−.065	−.032
22	.588	.525	.367	.509	.155	**.393**	.177	.103	.176	−.174
23	.702	.564	.463	.515	.242	**.563**	.133	.208	.036	−.153
24	.461	.526	.658	.533	.320	.057	.197	**.521**	.133	−.098

Factor	Correlations Among Factors				
T_1	1.000	.622	.461	.614	.410
T_2		1.000	.468	.555	.242
T_3			1.000	.560	.570
T_4				1.000	.374
T_5					1.000

Factor coefficients greater than .300 are shown in boldface type, and the five groups
of tests are separated to call attention to the original assumptions about structure of
the test battery. By way of a general conclusion, this solution provides a fair approximation to the hypothesized structure, but with some marked departures. These are
pointed out in the following more specific observations:

T_1: Tests intended to identify a "spatial relations" factor did not separate from
tests intended to identify a "logical reasoning" factor; instead these two groups
of tests seem to define a "deduction" factor.

T_2: Verbal factor is very clearly identified; no test outside this group has a large coefficient on this factor.

T_3: Perceptual speed factor intended, but only Tests 10 (Addition) and 12 (Counting Dots) have pronounced coefficients, while Tests 11 (Code) and 13 (Straight-Curved Capitals) also in this group have negligible coefficients (the former showing up in T_4 and T_5, and the latter in T_5). Also, three other tests (3, 21, 24) have substantial coefficients on this factor.

T_4: Memory factor is clearly defined; no test outside this group has a sizable coefficient on it except for the complex Test 11.

T_5: This may be a "pseudo" common factor (only picking up Tests 11 and 13), that would disappear under an assumption of four common factors.

Somewhat similar conclusions might have been drawn from the 4-factor direct oblimin solution (Table 14.10), but the independent clusters solution of Table 14.15 shows the extent of inherent structure in this data set most clearly.

When a data set is not so simply structured that each variable is of complexity one, then a more elaborate type of orthoblique solution is needed. The previous condition that $\mathbf{P'P}$ be diagonal is relaxed to require that it only be proportional to $\mathbf{\Phi}$. This modified condition is arrived at by Harris and Kaiser (pp. 360–61) by considering a generalization for the choice of $\mathbf{D}_3$ in (14.43)—in place of the simple choice $\mathbf{D}_3 = \mathbf{I}$ that led to the independent clusters solution of (14.44). Noting that the latter condition can be put in the form $\mathbf{D}_3 = \mathbf{I} = \mathbf{\Lambda}^0$ and that the condition for the orthogonal case (Harris and Kaiser 1964, p. 352) is $\mathbf{D}_3 = \mathbf{\Lambda}^{\frac{1}{2}}$, they propose trying $\mathbf{D}_3$ equal to some power of $\mathbf{\Lambda}$ intermediate between these two. Thus, setting $\mathbf{D}_3 = \mathbf{\Lambda}^{\frac{1}{4}}$ in (14.43) leads to the following expressions for the *proportional* solution:

$$\mathbf{P} = \mathbf{Q}\mathbf{\Lambda}^{\frac{1}{4}}\,\mathbf{T}_1\mathbf{D}_1,$$

(14.45)
$$\mathbf{\Phi} = \mathbf{D}_1^{-1}\mathbf{T}_1'\mathbf{\Lambda}^{\frac{1}{2}}\,\mathbf{T}_1\mathbf{D}_1^{-1},$$

$$\mathbf{S} = \mathbf{Q}\mathbf{\Lambda}^{\frac{3}{4}}\,\mathbf{T}_1\mathbf{D}_1^{-1}.$$

By carrying out the matrix multiplications of the expressions for $\mathbf{P}$ and $\mathbf{P'}$ it is readily found that

$$\mathbf{P'P} = \mathbf{D}_1\mathbf{T}_1'\mathbf{\Lambda}^{\frac{1}{2}}\,\mathbf{T}_1\mathbf{D}_1,$$

which shows that $\mathbf{P'P}$ is proportional to $\mathbf{\Phi}$, within the scaling by the matrix $\mathbf{D}_1$. To compute a proportional orthoblique solution from (14.45) there remains only the task of generating a suitable transformation matrix $\mathbf{T}_1$. Note that in this case it is not the matrix $\mathbf{Q}$ but the matrix $\mathbf{Q}\mathbf{\Lambda}^{\frac{1}{4}}$ that is being "rotated." Harris and Kaiser (p. 362) again recommend the quartimax criterion. However, the selection of (1) a power of $\mathbf{\Lambda}$ for the determination of $\mathbf{D}_3$ and (2) the criterion function—from the class of orthomax criteria, by choosing γ in (13.29)—to generate the matrix $\mathbf{T}_1$ may be crucial to the particular data set, and much more theoretical and experimental work is needed before definitive guidelines can be established.

The example selected to illustrate the proportional orthoblique method is the twenty-variable box problem. These artificial data were designed by Thurstone to be factorially complex in order to put the technique of factor analysis to the test to see if it can recover an existing underlying order in the data. The underlying order, of course, consists of the three basic dimensions of the boxes, but the twenty variables (see Table 8.10) involve these dimensions in a very complex way. Certainly the independent clusters form (with the requirement that groups of variables measure only a single dimension) is not expected to provide a good fit. On the other hand, it is worthwhile investigating how well the proportional form of the orthoblique method might approach the "target" oblique solution of Table 8.11. Starting with the initial matrix A from Table 8.11, and applying the method outlined in (14.45), the proportional orthoblique solution is determined as shown in Table 14.16. This solution does, in fact, fit the hypothetical data very well, but it is not quite the "target" sought. The correlations between factors x and y, and between y and z, are almost identical with the theoretical values shown in Table 8.11, but the correlation between factors x and z differs by nine units in the second decimal place. Comparison of the sixty separate

Table 14.16

Orthoblique (Proportional) Solution for Twenty-Variable Box Problem

(Initial solution: Orthogonal solution **A**, Table 8.11)

Variable j	Primary Structure: S			Primary Pattern: P		
	r_{jx}	r_{jy}	r_{jz}	x	y	z
1. x^2	.996	.245	.147	1.005	−.003	−.044
2. y^2	.276	.994	.284	.017	.981	.037
3. z^2	.141	.214	.986	−.044	−.024	1.001
4. xy	.677	.876	.298	.481	.747	.020
5. xz	.525	.268	.920	.372	−.041	.859
6. yz	.231	.575	.919	−.024	.375	.830
7. $\sqrt{x^2 + y^2}$	.869	.700	.261	.738	.512	−.007
8. $\sqrt{x^2 + z^2}$	.924	.309	.543	.852	−.005	.382
9. $\sqrt{y^2 + z^2}$	.263	.866	.696	−.027	.744	.516
10. $2x + 2y$	.790	.796	.288	.625	.632	.012
11. $2x + 2z$	.772	.303	.771	.654	−.028	.654
12. $2y + 2z$	.253	.753	.824	−.029	.591	.682
13. $\log x$	.995	.271	.146	.998	.027	−.051
14. $\log y$	.229	.990	.331	−.041	.977	.096
15. $\log z$	.147	.162	.984	−.025	−.082	1.009
16. xyz	.493	.592	.850	.268	.346	.712
17. $\sqrt{x^2 + y^2 + z^2}$	.814	.692	.534	.641	.452	.299
18. e^x	.961	.204	.143	.977	−.039	−.033
19. e^y	.307	.963	.233	.066	.950	−.016
20. e^z	.135	.230	.957	−.050	.002	.966

Factor	Correlations Among Factors		
x	1.000	.257	.191
y		1.000	.249
z			1.000

factor coefficients shows a maximum difference of six units in the second decimal place, with most of the larger discrepancies appearing for the smaller coefficients while the agreement between the very large coefficients is remarkably close. The root-mean-square deviation is only .031. This fit to the "target" is actually better than the direct oblimin for $\delta = -3$, which was arrived at only after trying many values of δ.

A variety of methods for oblique transformations to arrive at better interpretable final solutions have been presented in this and the preceding sections of this chapter. Not covered in this text are the *promax* (Hendrickson and White 1964) and *maxplane* (Cattell and Muerle 1960; Eber 1966) methods, which some investigators have found useful. What should be evident is that there are many options open to an investigator, and also that different methods may be appropriate for different data sets. Hakstian and Abell (1974) wind up an excellent comparison of such methods with the following: "One conclusion that appears inescapable is that no *single* computing procedure— general paradigm or specialization . . . can be expected to yield uniformly optimal oblique solutions *for all kinds of data*" (p. 444). It is certainly sound scientific practice for an investigator to use whatever tools are available to try to get the "best" inter- pretation of the data—so long as the procedures are clearly identified and can be repli- cated by another investigator. In particular, one could try several values of the parameter in a particular class of oblique solutions. Thus, for the oblimin methods try $\gamma = 0, .5, 1$; for direct oblimin, in addition to $\delta = 0$, try $\delta = -5$ and $\delta = .1, .2,$ $\cdots, .5$; and for orthoblique try both the independent clusters and proportional forms, and perhaps other power of Λ in the choice of $\mathbf{D}_3$. In the last analysis, the user of these methods should view them only as aids toward his scientific objectives: if any procedure fails to produce a meaningful result, discard it and try something else; if a particular method yields a meaningful solution, retain it.

15

Congruent and Prescribed Factor Solutions

15.1. *Introduction*

In the preceding three chapters various procedures were developed for transforming a direct factor analysis of a given body of data to a derived form that in some sense is more meaningful or interpretable. These procedures were designed to yield a final factor pattern that exhibited "simple structure" (see **6.2**, par. **10**) to a greater or lesser degree, dependent on the inherent nature of the data. In this chapter two further aspects of the final factor solution are addressed: (1) to what extent can two factor solutions be related to one another, and (2) to what extent can a given body of data be described in terms of a prescribed factor pattern.

A very considerable literature has been building up on the subjects addressed in this chapter, which are frequently referred to as *procrustes* transformations—a term borrowed (Hurley and Cattell 1962) from Greek mythology in which a highwayman named Procrustes is supposed to have made all his victims fit his bed, cruelly stretching those who were too short and cutting down to size those who were too tall. The specific situation to which Hurley and Cattell refer is the possible misuse of their computer program to perform "the brutal feat of making almost any data fit almost any hypothesis! Because of this possible proclivity we gave the code name Procrustes to this program, for this reference describes what it does, for better or worse" (p. 260). While procrustes has come to mean almost any forced transformation in factor analysis, it seems advisable to distinguish among several aspects of the problem, such as factor invariance, measures of relationships among factors, matching of factors, and obtaining best-fitting transformations to prescribed or target solutions.

The earliest paper on the subject of procrustes rotation is now credited to Mosier (1939). However, Holzinger's bi-factor method (see **7.5**) is also in the spirit of procrustes since it tries to fit a target pattern, albeit a very specialized one in which a general factor and non-overlapping group factors are hypothesized. The next major contribution (Green 1952) to procrustes transformations was still ten years before the term was coined. Since 1962, many papers have been published on various aspects of the subject and these will be noted as the methods are presented in this chapter.

In the next section, the basic transformation matrix is developed as a general method for arriving at the relationship between two factor solutions in the same common-factor space. This is followed, in **15.3**, by some measures of congruence between factors from two studies where either the samples of individuals or the variables differ. In addition to measures of the extent of agreement between factors, it is of interest to get the best possible matching of pairs of factors from separate studies. This problem is addressed in **15.4**. Finally, in **15.5** is presented the usual procrustes transformation of a given factor matrix to a specified target matrix.

In Table 15.1 is presented a summary of the key concepts and the notation involved in the various kinds of factor comparisons that are made in this chapter. This table is

Table 15.1

Concepts and Notation for Factor Comparisons

Concept	Notation
Relationships between solutions	
Known factor patterns	$\mathbf{A} = (a_{jp})$ and $\mathbf{B} = (b_{jp})$
(or initial and target patterns)	$(j = 1, 2, \cdots, n; p = 1, 2, \cdots)$
	(same notation used for factor patterns whether orthogonal or oblique)
Known factors (or initial and final)	F_p and K_p $(p = 1, 2, \cdots)$
Transformation matrix	(15.4) $\mathbf{T}$
Factor congruence across studies	
Any concept in study 1	Prefix "1" on the symbol for that concept
	e.g., $_1\mathbf{A} = (_1a_{jp})$ for the factor pattern matrix, and factor coefficients, in study 1 (similarly, of course, for study 2, etc.)
Root-mean-square deviation	(15.7) rms_{pq} (p in study 1; q in study 2)
between two factors	
Coefficient of congruence	(15.8) φ_{pq} (p in study 1; q in study 2)
(same variables, different samples)	
Coefficient of congruence	(15.9) ψ_{pq} (p in study 1; q in study 2)
(different variables, same sample)	
Matching factor solutions	
Factor patterns before rotation	$_1\mathbf{A}$ and $_2\mathbf{A}$
After orthogonal rotation	
Factor patterns and factors	$_1\mathbf{B}$ and $_2\mathbf{B}$; $_1K_p$ and $_2K_q$ ($p, q = 1, 2, \cdots$)
After oblique transformation	
Pattern, Structure, Factor correlations	$_k\mathbf{P}$, $_k\mathbf{S}$, $_k\boldsymbol{\Phi}$, for study k
Procrustes transformations	
Groups of variables with specified	$j \epsilon \, G_p$ $(p = 1, 2, \cdots)$
weights for factors	
Orthogonal case	
Initial pattern and factors	$\mathbf{A}$ and F_p
Final pattern and factors	$\mathbf{B}$ and K_p
Angle of rotation	φ
Objective function	(15.18) $f(\varphi) = \text{min.}$
Oblique case	
Initial pattern and factors	$\mathbf{A}$ and F_p
Final pattern and factors	$\mathbf{P}$ and T_p
Angles between oblique axes	θ_{pq} $(p, q = 1, 2, \cdots)$
Angle of rotation of a single axis in plane	φ
of each of the other axes	
Objective function	(15.28) $f(\varphi) = \text{min.}$

intended to serve as a general guide to the topics treated and as a reference source. The more explicit or detailed notation is introduced, as needed, in the discussion of the different methods and illustrations.

15.2.   *Relationship between Two Known Solutions*

Several types of comparisons among factor solutions are of interest, both from a methodological viewpoint and from the viewpoint of an applied science, such as psychology, in which it is desired to establish basic factors on the strength of many independent studies. The most obvious type of comparison, of course, is between any two solutions derived from the same correlation matrix (Holzinger and Harman 1937). That is the subject of the present section. Other comparisons are discussed in the next section.

In mathematics the reference system plays a very minor role; the particular configuration of points is of prime importance, and the coordinate system is of much lesser significance. Thus, if it is desired to describe an ellipse, i.e., get an algebraic equation for the ellipse, it is quite irrelevant whether rectangular Cartesian coordinates, nonrectangular Cartesian coordinates, or polar coordinates are employed. Furthermore, the particular orientation of axes is immaterial. With each change of the coordinate system, of course, the equation of the ellipse will generally change, but the fact remains that the equation in each case describes the ellipse with respect to the given reference system.

The object of factor analysis, on the other hand, is the selection of an appropriate frame of reference, the configuration of points representing the variables being of lesser significance. Then the indeterminateness of the factor problem is obvious. In selecting a particular reference system, the unit vectors along the coordinate axes represent the factors, and, since the reference system can be rotated about its origin in an infinitude of ways in the common-factor space, there arises an infinite number of factor systems for a given body of data.

As a general procedure, it might be advisable to put any factor solution in some standard form, e.g., the canonical form of **8.7**. Then, if two independent solutions are each brought to canonical form it will be obvious whether they are indeed alike or not. When it is desired to study the relationships between two distinct factor solutions, that may be accomplished by finding a matrix of transformation which carries the coordinates of one into the other. Thus, if the first factor pattern is denoted by **A** and the second factor pattern by **B**, then the problem is to find a matrix **T** such that

$$(15.1) \qquad\qquad \mathbf{AT} = \mathbf{B}.$$

The matrix **A** represents the coordinates a_{jp} of the n points with respect to one set of m common-factor axes, say $F_1, F_2, \cdots, F_m$; the matrix **B** represents the coordinates b_{jp} of the points with respect to a new set of axes, say $K_1, K_2, \cdots, K_m$; while the matrix **T** represents the transformation of the coordinates in **A** to those in **B**.

If the number of factors were equal to the number of variables then the matrix $\mathbf{A}$ would have an inverse and the solution for $\mathbf{T}$ would simply be

$$(15.2) \qquad \mathbf{T} = \mathbf{A}^{-1}\mathbf{B}.$$

Since the number of common factors is usually much smaller than the number of variables, however, the matrix $\mathbf{A}$ does not have an inverse and $\mathbf{T}$ cannot be calculated directly. It may be noted that, for any matrix $\mathbf{A}$,

$$(15.3) \qquad (\mathbf{A'A})^{-1}(\mathbf{A'A}) = \mathbf{I},$$

and hence, if both members of (15.1) are premultiplied by $(\mathbf{A'A})^{-1}\mathbf{A'}$, there results

$$(15.4) \qquad \mathbf{T} = (\mathbf{A'A})^{-1}\mathbf{A'B}$$

This formula gives the desired matrix of transformation.

The relationships among the *factors themselves* (or the factor measurements) may also be obtained by means of the matrix $\mathbf{T}$. In the given common-factor space the column vectors of the first and second sets of factors may be taken to be $\mathbf{f} = \{F_1 F_2 \cdot \cdot \cdot\}$ and $\mathbf{k} = \{K_1 K_2 \cdot \cdot \cdot\}$, respectively. From the definitions of the two factor patterns, and their assumed equality, it follows that

$$(15.5) \qquad \mathbf{Af} = \mathbf{Bk}.$$

Premultiplying both sides of this equation by $(\mathbf{A'A})^{-1}\mathbf{A'}$, and again employing (15.3) and (15.4) there results

$$(15.6) \qquad \mathbf{f} = (\mathbf{A'A})^{-1}\mathbf{A'Bk} = \mathbf{Tk}.$$

This is the matrix formulation of the relationships between the F factors and the K factors.

A system of equations represented by (15.1) gives the actual transformation of coordinates between the two factor solutions. Thus the factor weights for any variable in one solution are expressed linearly in terms of the weights of the other solution. An alternative way of expressing the relationship between two factor solutions is afforded by a system of equations implied by (15.6). Thus, the contributions of the K factors to the variance of each F factor can be obtained. Also, these equations may be used to estimate the measurements of F factors from known equations of measurements of the K factors.

A detailed numerical illustration of these procedures will now be given, employing the example of thirteen psychological tests. The relationships will be developed between the multiple-factor solution of Table 12.2 and an oblique primary-factor solution for the same data (see ex. 11, chap. 12). A schematic worksheet is presented in Table 15.2 along with the specific example. The matrix of coefficients of the multiple-factor pattern is denoted by $\mathbf{B}$ and appears in the extreme right-hand block of the table, and just to the left of it is the oblique factor pattern denoted by $\mathbf{A}$. These two solutions may be considered equivalent (or in the same common-factor space) since both solutions were obtained by transformation of the same centroid solution.

Table 15.2

Transformation Between Solutions in a Fixed Common-Factor Space

A. Computing Algorithm

Calculation of Transformation Matrix		j	Known Factor Patterns					
			a_{j1}	a_{j2}	$\cdots$	b_{j1}	b_{j2}	$\cdots$
A'A Col.-by-col. multiplication of **A** by itself	**I**	1 2 . .						
Square root method of Table 3.2 is applied to compute $(\mathbf{A'A})^{-1}$		. .		**A**			**B**	
	$(\mathbf{A'A})^{-1}$	. .						
$\mathbf{T'} = (\mathbf{B'A})(\mathbf{A'A})^{-1}$ Row-by-row multiplication of $(\mathbf{B'A})$ $(\mathbf{A'A})^{-1}$	**B'A** Col.-by-col. multiplication of **B** by **A**	n						

B. Example of Thirteen Psychological Tests

Calculation of Transformation Matrix						j	Primary Factor Pattern[b]			Multiple-Factor Pattern[c]		
							a_{j1}	a_{j2}	a_{j3}	b_{j1}	b_{j2}	b_{j3}
1.823	−.232	−.058	1	0	0	1	.731	−.089	.142	.096	.248	.706
[a]	3.394	−.017		1	0	2	.441	.004	.004	.102	.089	.425
[a]	[a]	2.103			1	3	.721	−.090	−.142	.136	−.011	.602
						4	.508	.090	−.003	.193	.121	.516
1.350	−.172	−.043	.741	0	0							
	1.834	−.013	.069	.545	0	5	−.058	.801	.087	.702	.324	.243
		1.449	.023	.005	.690	6	.037	.809	−.051	.719	.214	.300
						7	−.068	.901	−.030	.778	.243	.237
			.554	.038	.016	8	.155	.591	.078	.562	.291	.372
			[a]	.297	.003	9	−.068	.919	−.081	.791	.198	.231
			[a]	[a]	.476							
						10	−.385	.164	.809	.119	.757	−.100
.250	.883	.070	.246	2.939	.121	11	−.039	.077	.659	.109	.651	.161
.198	.314	.962	.230	1.008	2.006	12	.073	−.177	.773	−.083	.703	.210
.950	.344	.262	1.635	.944	.490	13	.351	−.061	.594	.070	.619	.469

[a]Terms below the diagonal of a symmetric matrix are deleted for simplicity, while blanks actually denote zeros.
[b]Obtained by the graphical methods of chapter 12 in exercises 5–11 for that chapter.
[c]From Table 12.2.

After the known factor patterns are recorded in the right half of Table 15.2, the computations leading to the transformation matrix **T** are performed in the left half of the table. First, the product **A'A** is determined and placed in the upper left block of the table; and the inverse of this product is calculated by the square root method (see **3.4**). This provides the first part of the expression (15.4) for **T**. In place of the second part of (15.4), its transpose is determined (primarily for computational convenience). This product $(\mathbf{B}'\mathbf{A})$ is recorded in the block below $(\mathbf{A}'\mathbf{A})^{-1}$. Finally, the transpose of the desired transformation matrix (15.4) is computed in the extreme lower left corner of the table.

The actual transformation from the primary factor coordinates to the multiple-factor coordinates is given by

$$b_{j1} = .250a_{j1} + .883a_{j2} + .070a_{j3},$$
$$b_{j2} = .198a_{j1} + .314a_{j2} + .962a_{j3},$$
$$b_{j3} = .950a_{j1} + .344a_{j2} + .262a_{j3},$$

where the a's and b's are the coordinates in the matrices $\mathbf{A}$ and $\mathbf{B}$, respectively. It is evident from these equations that the coefficients of the first multiple factor can be described mostly in terms of the coefficients of the second primary factor; the second multiple factor in terms of the third primary factor; and the third multiple factor in terms of the first primary factor.

Similarly, by means of the matrix $\mathbf{T}$, the relationships among the factors may be exhibited as follows:

$$T_1 = .250M_1 + .198M_2 + .950M_3,$$
$$T_2 = .883M_1 + .314M_2 + .344M_3,$$
$$T_3 = .070M_1 + .962M_2 + .262M_3,$$

where the T's represent the (oblique) primary factors and the M's the (orthogonal) multiple factors. From these equations it is apparent that each of the oblique factors consists primarily of one of the multiple factors, with some slight contribution of each of the other two. For example, the factor M_3 contributes 90 percent to the unit variance of T_1, while M_1 and M_2 contribute only 6 percent and 4 percent, respectively.

While the foregoing development may seem to be somewhat trivial, there was a period of time in the development of factor analysis when such relationships were not completely understood. As noted in chapter 1, it may have been the failure to recognize the fact that a given matrix of correlations could be factored in an infinite number of different ways that led to the many controversies about the "true," the "best," or the "invariant" solution for a set of data. It is now obvious that any two factorizations of a given set of data are related by (15.1), where the transformation from one to the other solution is given by (15.4).

15.3. *Measuring Factor Congruence*

In the preceding section both factor patterns $\mathbf{A}$ and $\mathbf{B}$ were assumed to have come from the same data set and known, the problem being to find the transformation matrix $\mathbf{T}$ that would show the relationship between them. Now, situations are considered in which two solutions are given in advance, but *not* from a common data set—either the sampling elements or the variables are permitted to differ—and the problem is to determine what relationships might exist between such factor solutions.

It should be perfectly clear that many different factor solutions are possible for a given set of variables for a single sample of individuals. Not only is this evident from the several techniques for factoring a correlation matrix, developed earlier in the text, but more particularly from the considerations of derived solutions covered in the last three chapters.

A procedure developed by Tucker (1966) for factor analysis of a three-mode matrix (individuals measured on a number of variables on several occasions) may be considered as an alternative to the comparison of ordinary factor solutions (for a group of individuals measured on a number of variables) obtained on several different occasions. For further guidance on the applicability of three-mode factor analysis the reader is referred to Tucker (1963, 1966). A related approach (called "longitudinal factor analysis") for describing changes in structure from one time period to another for a fixed sample and fixed variables has been developed (Corballis and Traub 1970; Corballis 1973; Nesselroade 1972).

There are two additional problems that seem to be of more importance to the development of content-area (e.g., psychological) theories based upon factor analysis. Suppose the same variables (or, at least, several variables common to the two betteries) are measured for two distinct groups of individuals. What can be said about the resulting factors used in the description of the identical variables? The other problem is concerned with two distinct sets of variables (designed to measure the same traits) for which factor analyses are obtained for a single sample of individuals.

In each situation two sets of factors are obtained and the problem is to determine the extent of similarity or dissimilarity between them. Of course, factorial similarity is a matter of degree rather than coincidence. While the ultimate objective in psychology may be the formulation of some theories on the invariance of factors, the treatment in the present section is limited to an exposition of several measures of factor similarity.

Before considering these measures, it might be well to point out some of the principal work on the "invariance" problem. Perhaps the point of departure for the present-day theoretical work in this area was the demonstration by Ahmavaara (1954) of the invariance of a factor solution upon the selection of samples (satisfying certain conditions) from a population. Essentially, the method extends the procedure of the last section from two known factor analyses of the same data set to the case where the variables are the same but the samples are different. By assuming the two sets of factors are in the same common-factor space, the transformation matrix (15.4) gives the relationship between them (for an application of Ahmavaara's method, see Hamilton 1967). Several other works—(Barlow and Burt 1954), (Cattell 1949), (Cattell and Cattell 1955), (Horst 1961b)—have made some contributions to this area, but two papers by Meredith (1964a, b) are of special significance. In the first of these, he shows that there exists a factor pattern for a given set of variables that is invariant with respect to sampling from a parent population, provided the "selection does not occur directly on the observable variables and does not reduce the rank of the system." In the second paper, Meredith develops procedures for transforming factor solutions based on different populations to conform to a single "best fitting" factor pattern, and illustrates these procedures with examples involving four groups of individuals. In addition to the foregoing work of Meredith, the serious student on the subject of "factor invariance" may want to refer to the research papers of Bloxom (1972), Joreskog (1971) and Please (1973). Also, an excellent exposition of the topic is presented by Muliak (1972, pp. 337–60).

1. Fixed variables, different samples.—Since factor analysis has been employed as a tool in the development of psychological theories, dealing with cognitive, educational, and temperamental traits, considerable interest has been directed toward the "identification" of factors from one study to another. Ideally, the problem could be solved in a manner similar to the establishment of standards for weight or mass in the physical sciences, as suggested by Mosier (1939) and Young and Householder (1940). Thus, in the field of psychological aptitudes, a "set of r independent tests is to be assigned any non-singular $r \times r$ array of factor loadings once and for all, and then future testing is to be linked to the standard by always carrying a set of r independent tests (or individuals) from each experiment to the next" (Young and Householder 1940, p. 51). It is not very likely that psychologists will take this approach very seriously. Instead, they are more likely to appeal to statistical criteria for a measure of coincidence or agreement of factors obtained in one study with those of another.

Attempts to link factors of separate investigations go back to the earliest days of the development of factor analysis. Generally, rough methods of inspection and personal impressions are offered as the basis of the "identification." In notes by Barlow and Burt (1954) and Leyden (1953), attention is called to a variety of measures that have been proposed over the years, and to the divergent values that can be obtained with the different indices.

A common statistical measure—the *root-mean-square deviation*, which has been used for comparing two derived factor solutions in chapters 13 and 14—might be used to determine the extent of agreement between corresponding factor weights in the two studies, since the variables are the same. Such an index for comparing factor p of study 1 and factor q of study 2 may be put in the form:

$$(15.7) \qquad rms_{pq} = \sqrt{\sum_{j=1}^{n} (_1a_{jp} - {}_2a_{jp})^2/n},$$

where the notation of Table 15.1 is employed. Of course, this is a very simple kind of index from which it might be difficult to ascertain what is really "good agreement," knowing that perfect agreement would yield a root-mean-square deviation of zero.

The simple expedient of employing an index roughly resembling a coefficient of correlation has been used by several investigators to compare the weights of a fixed set of variables on two factors (presumed to be identical, or at least, suspected to have a high degree of relationship). Burt (1948, p. 185) proposes as a proportionality criterion the "unadjusted correlation" between the two sets of factor coefficients.[1] Tucker (1951, p. 43) develops a *coefficient of congruence*, to study the agreement

---

[1]Actually, Burt compares a set of factor coefficients of twelve temperamental traits for a "general emotionality" factor with a teacher's set of independent gradings for "general emotionality."

between factors in two studies, which is precisely the same as Burt's unadjusted correlation. Again, Wrigley and Neuhaus (1955b) present the same formula for measuring the *degree of factorial similarity*. In the notation of Table 15.1, the coefficient of congruence is simply

$$
(15.8) \qquad \varphi_{pq} = \frac{\sum\limits_{j=1}^{n} {}_1 a_{jp} \cdot {}_2 a_{jq}}{\sqrt{\left(\sum\limits_{j=1}^{n} {}_1 a_{jp}^2\right) \left(\sum\limits_{j=1}^{n} {}_2 a_{jq}^2\right)}}.
$$

While this formula is similar in form to the product-moment coefficient defined in (2.7), it certainly is not a correlation—the a's are not deviates from their respective means and the summations are over the n variables instead of the number of individuals. If the n variables of study 1 are identical with those of study 2 the application of formula (15.8) is straightforward to the corresponding numbers in the two columns representing the factors p and q. If only a subset of the variables are common to the two studies, the summations must be understood to apply only to such variables. Since a small number of variables usually will be common to two studies, it is evident that the coefficient of congruence will be high so long as there are factor weights with like algebraic signs in the two instances. The coefficient of congruence can range in value from $+1$ for perfect agreement (or -1 for perfect inverse agreement) to zero for no agreement whatsoever.

To illustrate the calculation of (15.8), the data of Table 15.2 will be employed. While it is convenient to use the data at hand, it should be clear that a coefficient of congruence would not ordinarily be of interest for two different factor solutions of a set of variables for the same individuals. Considering the two solutions **A** and **B** as the studies "1" and "2," respectively, the only new calculations required are the denominators of (15.8), and the quotients, to get all nine coefficients of congruence; the numerators are the elements of **B′A** in Table 15.2. The results are shown in Table 15.3. Of course, the coefficients of congruence confirm the relationships among these factors discussed in **15.2**.

In situations where factors from two studies can be matched visually, and the number of variables common to the studies is small, it can be expected that the co-

Table 15.3

Coefficients of Congruence between Oblique Primary
and Orthogonal Multiple Factors

p	q		
	M_1	M_2	M_3
T_1	.112	.113	.855
T_2	.976	.361	.362
T_3	.051	.913	.239

efficient (15.8) will be very high. Tucker (1951) analyzes two studies—one involving eighteen variables for a sample of Naval Recruits and the other involving forty-four variables for a sample of Airmen and Soldiers—in which ten variables are common and the six factors of the smaller study are matched with six out of the twelve factors of the larger. He accepts coefficients ranging from .999984 down to .939811 as defining congruent factors, but rejects a value of .459717 as "definitely low so that this factor will not be considered as a congruent factor" (p. 19).

It is recommended that each factor of one study be compared with all the factors of the other study, and be paired with the one with which it has the highest coefficient of congruence. This implies a considerable amount of work, for which high-speed electronic computers have been applied. While the statistical relationships between factors of different studies have certain intrinsic values, a number of workers (e.g., Cattell, Guilford, Royce, Tucker, Wrigley) are even more concerned with the development of psychological theories through these means. They would employ the indices of proportionality as stepping stones to an objective basis for the matching of factors and the subsequent rotation to identical positions of the factor axes in the two studies. Tucker, for example, defines a congruent space between two studies as that spanned by their congruent factors, where the two matrices of these factor loadings are "considered as congruent if they are generally similar, with only relatively small random differences" (Tucker 1951, p. 18). He then discusses the degree of confidence a psychologist might have in the representation of the same mental function by congruent factors in two studies.

Several other indices are proposed by Pinneau and Newhouse (1964) for the comparison of factors based on a fixed set of variables on the same or different samples. Their "coefficient of invariance" and "coefficient of factor similarity" involve the correlation between the measurements of the factors (see chap. 16) for the individuals. This procedure follows the work of Horst (1961a, b).

A more general approach to the problem of relating factors from two studies based on different individuals is developed by Kaiser, Hunka, and Bianchini (1971). It does not require that the set of variables be identical in the two studies but that *some* of the variables be the same. Conceptualization of the method can be aided by the geometric considerations of **4.10**. The vectors representing the common factors of study 1 (with the larger number of factors) determines a space containing $_1\tilde{z}_j$ (the projections of the observed variables of study 1 into the common-factor space). The factor vectors of study 2 and its variables $_2\tilde{z}_j$ can also be placed in the common-factor space of study 1—but not uniquely, since the angular separations (or correlations) between the vectors of the two studies are not known. These angular separations (or their cosines or reproduced correlations) are known among the variables and factors of each study separately, but not between studies. The problem is to find an optimal way of placing the two studies in the same space and thereby provide a means of measuring the relationships among the factors of the two studies.

The method developed by Kaiser, Hunka, and Bianchini (1971) places the subset of variables common to the two studies in the common-factor space of study 1 in such a way that the pairs of variables are as close together as possible. This is accomplished computationally by rotating the common variables and factors of study

2 until the sum of the inner products of the pairs of common variables from the two studies is maximized. After the rotation has been made, the cosines of the angles among all factor vectors are computed. These are the factor correlations (I or Φ depending on whether the given solutions were orthogonal or oblique) in each of the two studies separately. However, these cosines between a factor of one study with that of the other are not correlations in the usual sense "but they may surely be taken as a measure of relationship between the factors represented, and a measure which certainly can be interpreted in the same way as a correlation coefficient" (Kaiser, Hunka, and Bianchini 1971, p. 411). To help judge the confidence that might be attached to such a solution of the relationship between the factors of the two studies, they propose an index derived from the subset of common variables. It is simply the mean of the cosines between the pairs of vectors representing the common variables, and ranges in value from zero to one.

To illustrate the procedure, they employ two distinct studies of anthropometric variables: one study on 100 North Ireland adult males for whom twelve measurements were made, leading to four correlated factors; the other study was on fifty London University male students for whom fourteen measurements were obtained and resulting in two uncorrelated factors. The comparative analysis was made on the basis of six variables that were apparently common[2] to the two studies. The results show the correlation-like relationships between each of the four correlated factors of the first study and the two uncorrelated factors of the second study, with an index of .85, "suggesting that the pairing of the six variables was reasonable" (p. 419).

Returning to the measure (15.8) as an indicator of the consistency of factors from sample to sample for a fixed set of variables, it is suggested only as a practical guide in lieu of more refined techniques. While this sounds like a classical problem in the theory of statistical sampling, the fact of the matter is that little progress has been made toward its resolution. Some notable exceptions of theoretical work (Joreskog 1971; Please 1973) indicate the direction that might be pursued to get statistical tests for the variations in factor structures among several samples of individuals for whom a common set of measures have been obtained. Nonetheless, the empirical approach, employing indices of proportionality of factors, which is suggested in this section seems not inappropriate at this time for the "identification" of factors across different studies.

2. Different variables, fixed sample.—Another situation where it is of interest to compare factors from different studies is when the sample of individuals is fixed but the sets of variables in two studies are different. While a statistical theory of the stability of factors under sampling variation of variables may be developed some day, the present approach to the problem is along empirical lines.

Wrigley and Neuhaus (1955) propose what appears like the most natural method for matching factors determined from two different sets of variables for the same sample of individuals. In each study the measurements of the respective factors for

---

[2]Caution is advised against assuming that two variables from different studies are identical simply because they are given the same name (Kaiser, Hunka, and Bianchini 1971, pp. 419–21).

the individuals can be obtained by the methods of chapter 16. Then, for a given sample of individuals, the measurements of a factor p from one set of variables may be compared with the measurements of a factor q from the other set of variables in a manner similar to that above. As before, *a coefficient of congruence* can be defined for measuring the *degree of factorial similarity,* namely:

$$(15.9) \qquad \psi_{pq} = \frac{\sum\limits_{i=1}^{N} {}_1F_{pi} \cdot {}_2F_{qi}}{\sqrt{\left(\sum\limits_{i=1}^{N} {}_1F_{pi}^2\right) \left(\sum\limits_{i=1}^{N} {}_2F_{qi}^2\right)}},$$

where ${}_1F_{pi}$ is the factor measurement for individual i on a factor p for study 1, with similar interpretation for measurements of factor q of study 2. The coefficient of congruence (15.9) may range in value from -1 to $+1$ just as the index (15.8).

Assuming m_1 and m_2 factors in the two studies, there is possible a total of $m_1 \times m_2$ comparisons of each factor of one study with every factor of the other. A given factor of one study may be said to be "matched with" or "congruent to" that factor of the other study with which it has the highest coefficient of congruence. If there should be any conflicts, Wrigley and Neuhaus (1955) propose that the factors be paired in such a way as to make the sum of the indices (15.9) a maximum.

While the foregoing index provides a means for comparing factors obtained from different sets of variables, there is considerable interest in bringing the factors from such studies into confluence. That is the subject of the remainder of this chapter.

15.4. *Matching Factor Solutions*

The problem of *matching* factors should be distinguished from the related problem of *measuring* the degree of relationship between factors, which is the subject of the preceding section. By matching factors between two studies is meant the process of transforming (rotating) the two sets of factors so as to bring corresponding (or matching) pairs from the two studies as close together as possible. The matching problem should also be distinguished from another related problem: the transformation of a given factor matrix to best fit a specified target matrix, which is treated in the following section.

Here we are interested not simply in measuring the degree of relationship between pairs of factors as exhibited in the two studies, but in making pairs of corresponding factors in these studies as congruent as possible. While Meredith (1964a) has shown that in general good matching cannot be obtained if the factors are required to be uncorrelated, there are situations where an investigator may wish to compare the factors from one sample (or study) with another when they are restricted to orthogonality. Cliff (1966) addresses the problem of orthogonally rotating two such sets of factors to a best-fitting position (as well as the more typical procrustes problem of selecting one of the two matrices as a target and rotating the other as closely to it as possible). The task of matching factors orthogonally may be perceived as involving a rotation of each system of factor axes so that: the first axis in each system has the respective factor coefficients of the variables as similar as possible; the second pair of factor axes, orthogonal to the first, be such that makes the coefficients of the variables on them as similar as possible; and so on for as many factor axes that can be paired up.

The procedure developed here, for the orthogonal case, follows closely the factor matching method of Cliff (1966). Using the notation of Table 15.1, the two sets of original factors may be designated by

$$_1F_p \quad (p = 1, 2, \cdots, {_1}m) \qquad \text{and} \qquad _2F_q \quad (q = 1, 2, \cdots, {_2}m)$$

and, after rotation by

$$_1K_p \quad (p = 1, 2, \cdots, {_1}m) \qquad \text{and} \qquad _2K_p \quad (p = 1, 2, \cdots, {_1}m)$$

where $_1m$ and $_2m$ are the respective numbers of common factors in the two studies, with $_1m \leq {_2}m$. The designations of the two factor patterns before rotation are

$$_1\mathbf{A} = ({_1}a_{jp}) \qquad \text{and} \qquad _2\mathbf{A} = ({_2}a_{jq}),$$

and after rotation are

$$_1\mathbf{B} = ({_1}b_{jp}) \qquad \text{and} \qquad _2\mathbf{B} = ({_2}b_{jp}).$$

Similarly, the prefixes "1" and "2" are used to distinguish all other elements in the two studies.

Now, the desired orthogonal rotations may be represented by

(15.10) $$_1\mathbf{A} \cdot {_1}\mathbf{T} = {_1}\mathbf{B} \qquad \text{and} \qquad _2\mathbf{A} \cdot {_2}\mathbf{T} = {_2}\mathbf{B}$$

where the transformation matrices $_1\mathbf{T}$ and $_2\mathbf{T}$ are to be determined in such a way as to make the corresponding columns of $_1\mathbf{B}$ and $_2\mathbf{B}$ as similar as possible. Thus, the sets of direction cosines (in the columns of the transformation matrices) may be determined for one corresponding pair at a time by maximizing some measure of similarity. To this end, the numerator of (15.8) is employed, which for any factor p in the two studies may be expressed in the form

(15.11) $$\varphi_p = \sum_{j=1}^{n} {_1}b_{jp} \cdot {_2}b_{jp} \qquad (p = 1, 2, \cdots, {_1}m).$$

The least-squares maximization of this function for a particular p is equivalent to finding corresponding columns of the two transformation matrices for which

(15.12) $$\text{tr}\,({_1}\mathbf{B} \cdot {_2}\mathbf{B}') = \text{tr}\,({_1}\mathbf{A} \cdot {_1}\mathbf{T} \cdot {_2}\mathbf{T}' \cdot {_2}\mathbf{A}') = \text{max}.$$

The maximization of (15.12) can be accomplished most expeditiously by making use of the Eckart-Young decomposition of a matrix (Eckart and Young 1936; Johnson 1963). Thus, the product of the two original factor pattern matrices may be decomposed as follows:

(15.13) $$_1\mathbf{A}' \cdot {_2}\mathbf{A} = \mathbf{U}\mathbf{\Lambda}\mathbf{V}'$$

where **U** and **V** are orthonormal matrices and Λ is diagonal, consisting of the eigenvalues of the symmetric matrices

$$(15.14) \quad L = (_1A' \cdot _2A)(_2A' \cdot _1A) \quad \text{and} \quad M = (_2A' \cdot _1A)(_1A' \cdot _2A).$$

Then the eigenvectors corresponding to the largest eigenvalue of **L** (and **M**) will constitute the first columns of $_1T$ and $_2T$ (Cliff 1966, p. 35). These represent the direction of greatest congruence, while the eigenvectors corresponding to succeeding eigenvalues, in order, represent directions orthogonal to the previous ones with successively maximum remaining congruence. These conclusions may be put succinctly,

$$(15.15) \quad U = {}_1T \quad \text{and} \quad V' = {}_2T$$

in (15.13). Also, it can be shown that the eigenvalues in Λ correspond to the values φ_p in (15.11). Hence the problem of factor matching can be solved by finding **U** and **V**, using standard eigenvalue-eigenvector computer routines, and applying the transformations (15.15) to $_1A$ and $_2A$ to get the maximally congruent $_1B$ and $_2B$. The coefficients of congruence (15.8) can be computed to judge the degree of agreement of corresponding columns of the best fitting solution.

To illustrate the best orthogonal matching of two sets of factors consider the familiar problem of eight physical variables. Even though we don't have two separate studies, consider the 2-factor subjective solution of Table 12.1 and the 3-factor minres solution of Table 9.2 *as if* they had come from two *different* groups of individuals for whom the eight physical variables had been measured. These are repeated in the left portion of Table 15.4 as the original solutions $_1A$ and $_2A$ for which simultaneous orthogonal rotations are sought that will produce solutions having the greatest agreement. Using

Table 15.4

Matching Factors of Eight Physical Variables: Two Assumed Studies

Variable	Original Factor Solutions					Best Matching Solutions			
	$_1A$ (Table 12.1)		$_2A$ (Table 9.2)			$_1B = {}_1A \cdot {}_1T$		$_2B = {}_2A \cdot {}_2T$	
	$_1F_1$	$_1F_2$	$_2F_1$	$_2F_2$	$_2F_3$	$_1K_1$	$_1K_2$	$_2K_1$	$_2K_2$
1	.853	.332	.860	−.322	−.160	.857	−.323	.859	−.324
2	.906	.261	.867	−.432	.242	.849	−.411	.866	−.433
3	.874	.237	.803	−.396	.031	.809	−.407	.802	−.398
4	.846	.302	.835	−.340	−.163	.831	−.340	.834	−.342
5	.175	.926	.751	.583	−.113	.749	.572	.752	.581
6	.140	.788	.626	.492	.019	.631	.493	.627	.491
7	.082	.760	.565	.508	.001	.569	.511	.566	.507
8	.216	.667	.611	.362	.182	.606	.352	.612	.361
Factor						$_1T$		$_2T$	
F_1						.744	−.668	1.000	−.002
F_2						.668	.744	.002	1.000
F_3								−.001	.003

a computer program (Pennell and Young 1967) the transformation matrices $_1\mathbf{T}$ and $_2\mathbf{T}$ are determined and these lead to the best matching factor weights, shown in the right half of Table 15.4. Comparing the corresponding coefficients of the K_1 (and K_2) factors in the two studies, it can be seen that the maximum difference is only two units in the second decimal place (for either factor), and the root-mean-square deviation (15.7) is $rms_{11} = .0073$ (and $rms_{22} = .0097$). A formal indication of the degree of matching can be obtained by computing the coefficients of congruence (15.8). Thus,

$$\varphi_{11} = .99996 \quad \text{and} \quad \varphi_{22} = .99978$$

showing, what we already knew, that the two sets of final factors are practically identical. Of course, the remarkable agreement between $_1\mathbf{B}$ and $_2\mathbf{B}$ stems from the fact that the "two studies" are really only two different models of the same data.

The best matching solutions $_1\mathbf{B}$ and $_2\mathbf{B}$ may not be in the form for ready interpretation. If desired they may be transformed to approximate simple structure by the methods of chapter 13 for the orthogonal case, or by the methods of chapter 14 for the oblique case, or to some prescribed form as will be presented in the next section. Whichever method is used for getting a derived solution, the same transformation should be applied to $_1\mathbf{B}$ and $_2\mathbf{B}$ since they have already been established as best matching and any subsequent transformation is only to facilitate interpretation.

As noted at the beginning of this section, it is difficult to get good matching of factors when they are required to be uncorrelated. Removing this restriction, Meredith (1964b) developed more general procedures. These methods are not presented in detail here, but some understanding can be gleaned through an illustration of his results and a comparison with matching orthogonal factors. The example selected by Meredith (pp. 197–204) consists of nine tests—three for each of the intended factors: spatial relations, verbal, memory—from the total set of twenty-four psychological tests featured throughout this text. He obtained the raw data (Holzinger and Swineford 1939) not only for the 145 children in a Chicago suburban school (see Table 7.3), but also for 156 children, many of whose parents were factory workers and foreign born, from another school. On the basis of these data, especially Test 10 (Addition), Meredith divided the students in each school into two approximately equal groups, making a total of four groups for his investigation into factorial invariance. His first two groups came from the other school, while Groups 3 and 4 were from the school used in this text. Thus, the total sample ($N = 145$) was split into two subsamples, consisting of $_3N = 74$ low scoring and $_4N = 71$ high scoring students on Test 10. The correlation matrices for Groups 3 and 4 are presented in Table 15.5.

The method of this section is applied to get the best matching orthogonal solutions for Groups 3 and 4. Applying the minres method to $_3\mathbf{R}$ and $_4\mathbf{R}$ produces the original factor solutions shown in Table 15.6. Then the factor matching program produces the transformation matrices and the best matching orthogonal factor weights, shown in the right half of Table 15.6. The coefficients of congruence (15.8) between the two groups are:

$$\varphi_{11} = .9966, \quad \varphi_{22} = .9419, \quad \text{and} \quad \varphi_{33} = .9281.$$

These values indicate quite good agreement for real empirical data.

Table 15.5

Correlations Among Nine Psychological Tests: Two Samples*

Test†	1	2	3	5	7	8	16	17	18
1. Visual Perception		.34	.41	.38	.40	.42	.35	.16	.35
2. Cubes	.32		.21	.32	.16	.13	.27	.01	.27
3. Paper Form Board	.34	.18		.31	.24	.35	.30	.09	.09
5. General Information	.31	.24	.31		.69	.55	.17	.31	.34
7. Sentence Completion	.22	.16	.29	.62		.65	.20	.30	.27
8. Word Classification	.27	.20	.32	.57	.61		.31	.34	.27
16. Figure Recognition	.48	.31	.32	.18	.20	.29		.31	.38
17. Object-Number	.20	.01	.15	.06	.19	.15	.36		.38
18. Number-Figure	.42	.28	.40	.11	.07	.18	.35	.44	

*The Group 3 matrix of correlations ($_3\mathbf{R}$) is in the upper triangle, and $_4\mathbf{R}$ is in the lower triangle.
†The numbers of the tests correspond to those of the total set of twenty-four tests as given in Table 7.3.

Table 15.6

Matching Factors of Nine Psychological Tests: Two Samples

Test	Original Factor Solutions						Best Matching Solutions					
	$_3\mathbf{A}$ (Minres)			$_4\mathbf{A}$ (Minres)			$_3\mathbf{B} = {}_3\mathbf{A} \cdot {}_3\mathbf{T}$			$_4\mathbf{B} = {}_4\mathbf{A} \cdot {}_4\mathbf{T}$		
	$_3F_1$	$_3F_2$	$_3F_3$	$_4F_1$	$_4F_2$	$_4F_3$	$_3K_1$	$_3K_2$	$_3K_3$	$_4K_1$	$_4K_2$	$_4K_3$
1	.628	.219	−.265	.597	.160	.331	.636	.073	−.321	.584	.257	−.291
2	.365	.262	−.244	.383	.014	.303	.374	.127	−.324	.377	.099	−.295
3	.439	.122	−.266	.522	.031	.155	.443	−.011	−.285	.517	.089	−.148
5	.733	−.247	−.062	.627	−.447	−.060	.724	−.272	.057	.647	−.419	−.045
7	.772	−.453	−.015	.648	−.454	−.294	.756	−.442	.185	.672	−.477	.181
8	.718	−.194	.010	.653	−.339	−.113	.711	−.194	.100	.669	−.325	.030
16	.486	.430	.079	.561	.253	.171	.500	.410	−.097	.546	.311	−.114
17	.472	.069	.582	.484	.657	−.578	.473	.288	.510	.464	.533	.707
18	.508	.279	.215	.514	.427	.178	.516	.327	.090	.491	.479	−.081
Factor							$_1\mathbf{T}$			$_2\mathbf{T}$		
F_1							.999	−.030	.017	.999	.047	−.007
F_2							.034	.911	−.410	−.044	.974	.224
F_3							−.003	.411	.912	−.017	.223	−.975

Next, a comparison is made with the Meredith results, even though the latter are derived from all four groups and from entirely different procedures. His original factor solutions $_k\mathbf{A}$ ($k = 1, 2, 3, 4$) were obtained by the canonical factor analysis method (see **11.2**), but rescaled by the normalized (across the four groups) standard deviations in each group. These four factor pattern matrices are then employed to generate a key matrix in the analysis (Meredith 1964b, pp. 190–91), namely:

$$(15.16) \qquad \mathbf{G} = \frac{1}{4} \sum_{k=1}^{4} {}_k\mathbf{A} \left({}_k\mathbf{A}' \, {}_k\mathbf{A} \right)^{-1} {}_k\mathbf{A}'.$$

Such a symmetric matrix can be decomposed into its eigenvalues and eigenvectors, as in (8.53). Thus, the matrix $\mathbf{Q}$, shown in Table 15.7, contains in its columns the normalized eigenvectors corresponding to the three largest eigenvalues of $\mathbf{G}$. The matrix $\mathbf{Q}$, which is orthogonal, is described as the "best fit factor pattern matrix" (p. 201) because it satisfies the objective function that must be minimized for a solution. Then the four transformation matrices, corresponding to (15.4), are given by (p. 191):

$$(15.17) \qquad {}_k\mathbf{T} = \left({}_k\mathbf{A}' \, {}_k\mathbf{A} \right)^{-1} {}_k\mathbf{A}'\mathbf{Q} \qquad (k = 1, 2, 3, 4)$$

and the (oblique) rotated factor pattern matrices are given by expressions that are formally similar to (15.10). The oblique factor patterns for Groups 3 and 4, as well as the correlations among the factors in each of these groups, are shown in Table 15.7. The coefficients of congruence between each factor (in the two sets of results) and its counterpart in $\mathbf{Q}$ are shown in the last line of this table. Considering the different numbers of subgroups being matched, the different methods of factoring, and the different matching algorithms used in the two methods, it is rather surprising to find such excellent agreement between the best matching orthogonal and oblique factors for Groups 3 and 4.

Table 15.7

Comparison of Two Methods of Matching Factors for Nine Psychological Tests

Test	Results from Table 15.6*						Results from Meredith (1964b)†								
	$_3\mathbf{B}$ (normalized)			$_4\mathbf{B}$ (normalized)			Matrix $\mathbf{Q}$			Group 3 Pattern			Group 4 Pattern		
	$_3K_1$	$_3K_2$	$_3K_3$	$_4K_1$	$_4K_2$	$_4K_3$	I	II	III	I	II	III	I	II	III
1	.36	.09	.41	.35	.23	.34	.34	.27	.43	.34	.13	.42	.28	.26	.40
2	.21	.15	.41	.22	.09	.34	.18	.13	.53	.20	.14	.49	.17	.07	.36
3	.25	−.01	.36	.31	.08	.17	.21	.02	.41	.24	.01	.41	.29	.14	.17
5	.41	−.33	−.07	.39	−.38	.05	.48	−.32	−.12	.49	−.24	−.12	.49	−.30	.03
7	.43	−.53	−.24	.40	−.43	−.21	.51	−.29	−.23	.51	−.33	−.24	.46	−.25	−.28
8	.41	−.23	−.13	.40	−.30	−.03	.48	−.10	−.17	.44	−.08	−.15	.50	−.19	−.13
16	.28	.49	.12	.32	.28	.13	.22	.45	.12	.15	.54	.10	.22	.34	.12
17	.27	.35	−.65	.28	.49	−.82	.13	.52	−.46	.16	.47	−.53	.13	.53	−.59
18	.29	.39	−.11	.29	.44	.09	.16	.51	−.21	.19	.51	−.12	.16	.54	.09

Factor							Factor Correlations								
I							1.00	0	0	1.00	.25	.03	1.00	.27	.06
II								1.00	0		1.00	.17		1.00	.10
III									1.00			1.00			1.00

| φ_{pp} | .97 | .93 | .96 | .96 | .96 | .82 | | | | .99 | .98 | .98 | .99 | .97 | .88 |

*These factor patterns have been normalized by columns to make them comparable to Meredith's results. Also, the factors $_3K_3$ and $_4K_3$ were reflected to coincide with the directions of the factors obtained by Meredith.
†Method 1, rotational procedures (Meredith 1964b, pp. 190–93, 200–201).

15.5. *Fitting a Prescribed Factor Model*

The problem of describing a given body of data in terms of a prescribed factor pattern is addressed in this section. The earliest attempt to find a transformation of an arbitrary factor solution that would lead to a least-squares fit to a specified (or hypothesized) factor structure was made by Mosier (1939). The equations derived by Mosier could not be solved algebraically so he proposed an approximate least squares fit. An exact solution had to wait about thirty years, when an effective iterative procedure for "oblique procrustes rotation" was developed (Browne 1967; 1972b). In the meantime, methods for orthogonal rotations to least-squares fit to fully prescribed target solutions had been developed (Green 1952; Fischer and Roppert 1964; Kristof 1964; Cliff 1966; Schonemann 1966a). Elaboration of the orthogonal procedures to cover the case when the target is only partially specified has been carried out by Lawley and Maxwell (1964) and by Browne (1972a).

Before discussing general procedures for fitting a target matrix, in which zeros or specific values are assigned to some or all elements, we first consider the related question of how such a target might be inferred. One way of prescribing a factor solution is to specify or hypothesize which variables should identify each factor. This can be done in a variety of ways: from the observed data by grouping the n variables into m mutually exclusive groups (as in the multiple-group method of **11.5**); according to an experimental design that postulates certain variables as potential measures of putative factors; from the pattern of algebraic signs of the factor coefficients obtained by the principal-factor, minres, or maximum-likelihood methods; from the largest factor coefficient for each variable in a derived orthogonal multiple-factor solution (such as varimax in **13.4**). However the variables are grouped, an axis can be passed through each of their centroids in the m-dimensional common-factor space to yield an oblique solution as developed in **11.5**. Such a procedure based on an initial orthogonal solution is discussed by Overall (1968) and illustrated with the example of twenty-four psychological tests. Bentler (1971) presents a general computer program for an oblique factor solution that is prescribed by grouping of variables.

1. Orthogonal procrustes rotation.—In the course of developing a procrustes transformation, first a choice of either orthogonal or oblique factors must be made. For this simpler, orthogonal case, the problem is to determine a matrix **T** that will transform a given factor pattern **A** to a target factor pattern **B**, corresponding to the formal expression (15.1). It is understood that such a best fit is in the least-squares sense—the sum of squares of differences between corresponding elements of **AT** and **B** is a minimum—subject to the constraint that **T** is orthogonal, i.e., $\mathbf{TT'} = \mathbf{I}$.

The approximate fit can be accomplished by carrying out a series of planar rotations, arranged in a systematic order so that each factor axis is rotated with every other axis only once to constitute a single cycle (see **12.2**), and the process repeated as necessary until convergence has been reached. As the rotations are carried out the intermediate values of **A** may be designated by **A*** for each cycle until the target **B** values are reached. Thus, for an angle of rotation φ for any two axes in a plane, the familiar relations (12.1) or (13.13) apply, and the new factor weights a_{jp}^* are functions of the angle φ with the original weights a_{jp} as known coefficients. Then the objective function that is to be minimized in order to attain a best fit to the target may be represented by

(15.18)
$$f(\varphi) = \sum_{p=1}^{m} \sum_{j \in G_p} (a_{jp}^* - b_{jp})^2,$$

where the sum on j is only over the group of variables (G_p) that have specified weights for factor p in the target matrix $\mathbf{B}$.

To facilitate the minimization process, for the case of a rotation in the plane of the first two factors, we follow Browne (1972a) and put the criterion to be minimized in the form (p. 116):

(15.19) $f(\varphi) = c_1 \sin^2 \varphi + c_2 \cos\varphi\sin\varphi + c_3 \cos\varphi + c_4 \sin\varphi + c_o$

where

(15.20)
$$c_1 = \sum_{j \in G_1} a_{j2}^2 + \sum_{k \in G_2} a_{k1}^2 - \sum_{j \in G_1} a_{j1}^2 - \sum_{k \in G_2} a_{k2}^2$$
$$c_2 = 2 \left(\sum_{j \in G_1} a_{j1} a_{j2} - \sum_{k \in G_2} a_{k1} a_{k2} \right)$$
$$c_3 = -2 \left(\sum_{j \in G_1} a_{j1} b_{j1} + \sum_{k \in G_2} a_{k2} b_{k2} \right) \leq 0$$
$$c_4 = 2 \left(\sum_{k \in G_2} a_{k1} b_{k2} - \sum_{j \in G_1} a_{j2} b_{j1} \right)$$

and c_o is a constant that is irrelevant to the minimization. The terms $\sum_{j \in G_p} a_{jp} b_{jp}$ are made non-negative (by interchanging or reflecting factors in $\mathbf{A}$, as necessary, before rotation) in order to simplify the minimization process. A necessary condition for a minimum is the vanishing of the first derivative of (15.19), namely:

(15.21) $f'(\varphi) = c_1 \sin 2\varphi + c_2 \cos 2\varphi - c_3 \sin\varphi + c_4 \cos\varphi = 0.$

For two special cases (where all specified elements in the two columns of $\mathbf{B}$ are zero, or if both columns are fully specified) this equation can be solved readily. However, for the more usual case the specified elements of the two columns of $\mathbf{B}$ would not be expected to satisfy the special conditions. Then the most expedient way of determining $\sin\varphi$ involves the solution of the non-linear equation (Browne 1972a, p. 117):

(15.22) $f'(\varphi) = 2 c_1 \sin \varphi + c_4 + [c_2(1 - 2 \sin^2\varphi) - c_3 \sin \varphi] / \sqrt{1 - \sin^2\varphi} = 0.$

He solves this equation iteratively using the Newton-Raphson method (Henrici 1964, p. 105) and has provided the computer program.

An application of the foregoing procedure is given in Table 15.8. Here, again, the two-factor minres solution of Table 9.2 was taken as the given factor pattern $\mathbf{A}$. The theoretical target pattern was set up according to the experimental design in which the first four variables are measures of "lankiness" and the last four are measures of "stockiness." On this basis, zeros are specified for the first four coefficients on the second factor and for the last four coefficients on the first factor. No specific values (denoted by 9's in the computer program) are assigned to the coefficients that are expected to be sizeable in this example. The best least-squares fit to this theoretical target, obtained by Browne's program, is shown in the right-hand block of the table. As a measure of success in fitting the prescribed model the root-mean-square devi-

Table 15.8

Orthogonal Procrustes Solution for Eight Physical Variables

Variable	Original Factor Pattern: **A**		Target Pattern		Final Factor Pattern: **B**	
	F_1	F_2	K_1	K_2	K_1	K_2
1	.856	−.324	9	0	.881	.247
2	.848	−.412	9	0	.927	.172
3	.808	−.409	9	0	.893	.150
4	.831	−.342	9	0	.872	.218
5	.750	.571	0	9	.265	.905
6	.631	.492	0	9	.216	.771
7	.569	.510	0	9	.155	.748
8	.607	.351	0	9	.280	.643

ation between the specified elements in the target matrix and their computed values in the rotated matrix is also produced by the program. This value is .218. While this indicates that the target is approximated fairly well, under the constraint of orthogonality, it will be seen below that a much better fit can be achieved when the factors are permitted to be oblique. It should be noted that the orthogonal method of Cliff (1966, pp. 35–36) yields a solution which, although differing slightly in the individual coefficients, fits the target equally well.

2. Oblique procrustes transformation.—Now, the more general oblique procrustes transformations are considered. The mathematical development can be made somewhat similar to that in the orthogonal case but with the important difference of allowing for correlations among the factors, that is, of oblique angles between pairs of primary axes. Thus, the objective function to be minimized may be expressed formally by (15.18). However, in the present case this function is not of the angles of rotation of successive pairs of orthogonal axes in planes, but it is a function of the angles of successive rotations of a single axis around a fixed axis in the plane of these oblique axes.

The method proceeds by means of a sequence of rotations of each factor F_p (from a set of m oblique factors) in the planes of the $(m - 1)$ remaining factors. Specifically, for the first two factors, such a rotation of F_1 in the plane of F_1 and F_2 may be expressed by

$$(15.23) \qquad F_1^* = t_1 F_1 + t_2 F_2$$

where t_1 and t_2 are chosen so that the rotated factor F_1^* has unit length. This requires that

$$(15.24) \qquad t_1^2 + 2t_1 t_2 c_{12} + t_2^2 = 1$$

where $c_{12} = \cos\theta_{12}$ is the known cosine of the angle between the two factor axes before rotation. Denoting any intermediately derived factor pattern matrix by $\mathbf{A}^* = (a_{jp}^*)$, as before, the transformation yields (Jennrich and Sampson 1966, p. 316):

(15.25) $a_{j1}^* = \dfrac{1}{t_1} a_{j1}, \quad a_{j2}^* = -\dfrac{t_2}{t_1} a_{j1} + a_{j2}, \quad$ and $\quad a_{jp}^* = a_{jp} \quad$ for $p \neq 1, 2.$

To facilitate the minimization process, Jennrich and Sampson propose the change of variables

(15.26) $$t_1 = \frac{1}{\gamma} \text{ and } t_2 = \frac{\delta}{\gamma}$$

so that the condition (15.24) becomes

(15.27) $$\gamma^2 = 1 + 2c_{12}\delta + \delta^2.$$

Browne (1972b) starts with this relationship and adapts the rotation process of Jennrich and Sampson to the case of fitting a partially specified target matrix. First, he notes that the criterion to be minimized may be expressed in the form (p. 208):

(15.28) $$f = c_2\delta^2 + c_1\delta + c_3\gamma + c_0,$$

where

(15.29)
$$c_2 = \sum_{j \varepsilon G_1} a_{j1}^2 + \sum_{k \varepsilon G_2} a_{k1}^2$$
$$c_1 = 2c_{12} \sum_{j \varepsilon G_1} a_{j1}^2 - 2 \sum_{k \varepsilon G_2} a_{k1}^2 (a_{k2} - b_{k2})$$
$$c_3 = -\sum_{j \varepsilon G_1} a_{j1}b_{j1} \leq 0,$$

and c_0 is a constant that does not effect the minimization. As before, the terms $\sum_{j \varepsilon G_p} a_{jp}b_{jp}$ are made non-negative (by interchanging or reflecting factors in **A**, as necessary, before rotation) in order to simplify the development. Then, by treating γ as a function of δ and taking the positive root in (15.27), the criterion function (15.28) is regarded as a function of δ alone. Its first derivative must vanish, i.e.,

(15.30) $f'(\delta) = c_1 + 2c_2\delta + c_3(c_{12} + \delta)/\sqrt{1 + 2c_{12}\delta + \delta^2} = 0,$

as a necessary condition for a minimum.

For the special case when all the coefficients of the variables in G_p are specified to be zero for the factor p that is being rotated, it will be noted from (15.29) that $c_3 = 0$. Then the solution to (15.30) follows immediately:

(15.31) $$\delta = -c_1/2c_2,$$

which is the unique minimum of the parabola $f(\delta)$ in (15.28). When some of the coefficients of a factor being rotated are specified to be other than zero then a solution for (15.30) cannot be obtained by direct means. Browne (1972b, pp. 209–10) proceeds to solve this equation iteratively by using the Newton-Raphson method and has made a computer program available for the calculation of a general oblique procrustes solution.

After the value of δ has been found, either by (15.31) or iteratively, the next stage of the factor pattern matrix $\mathbf{A}^*$ is determined. This can be accomplished by (15.25).

However, in terms of the changed variables (15.26), the transformation matrix is

(15.32)
$$\begin{bmatrix} \gamma & -\delta \\ 0 & 1 \end{bmatrix},$$

which, when applied to the two affected columns of **A** yields the corresponding new values of **A***. The correlations between the rotated factor (1) and the others are given by

(15.33)
$$c_{1p}^* = t_1 c_{1p} + t_2 c_{2p} = (c_{1p} + \delta c_{2p})/\gamma \qquad\qquad (p \neq 1),$$

while the correlations among all the other factors remain unchanged. The cosine of the angle of rotation is given by (Browne, 1972b, p. 210):

(15.34)
$$\cos\varphi = (1 + \delta c_{12})/\gamma.$$

Rotations are performed by systematically taking each factor in the plane with each of the other $(m - 1)$ factors, stopping when, in a cycle of $m(m - 1)$ possible rotations, none requires an angle of rotation φ in excess of a sufficiently small one (say, one minute of one degree).

The first illustration of an oblique procrustes rotation is shown in Table 15.9 for the familiar example of eight physical variables. Only the specified elements in the target matrix (8 zeros) are indicated. There are no theoretical reasons for specifying any other values. The computer program produces the final factor pattern **P** that best fits the target and the correlation matrix **Φ** for the oblique factors, while the factor structure **S** can be obtained simply by postmultiplying **P** by **Φ**. The root-mean-square deviation for the eight fitted elements is only .054, naturally showing a much better

Table 15.9

Oblique Procrustes Solution for Eight Physical Variables

(Initial solution: 2-factor minres, Table 9.2)

Variable	Target Pattern		Final Pattern: **P**	
	T_1	T_2	T_1	T_2
1		0	.883	.062
2		0	.958	−.033
3		0	.928	−.048
4		0	.883	.032
5	0		.001	.942
6	0		−.010	.805
7	0		−.069	.795
8	0		.101	.647
Factor			Factor Correlations: **Φ**	
T_1			1.000	.477
T_2			.477	1.000

fit than in the orthogonal case. The oblique procrustes solution is almost identical with the orthoblique (independent clusters) solution of Table 14.14, with differences at most being only a few units in the third decimal place for corresponding elements. This, of course, is due to the fact that the experimental design of these data provides clear-cut clusters for the orthoblique method and obvious zeros for the target matrix in the procrustes method. Such simple results cannot be expected for more complex data.

Next, we perform an oblique procrustes rotation on the twenty-four psychological tests, using as the original input matrix the 5-factor minres solution of Table 9.5. For the target pattern zeros are specified for all coefficients except on the putative factor

Table 15.10

Oblique Procrustes Solution for Twenty-Four Psychological Tests

(Initial solution: Minres, Table 9.5)

Variable	Target Pattern					Final Pattern: **P**				
	T_1	T_2	T_3	T_4	T_5	T_1	T_2	T_3	T_4	T_5
1	9	0	0	0	0	**.565**	.024	.162	.113	.152
2	9	0	0	0	0	**.338**	.004	−.006	.038	.246
3	9	0	0	0	0	**.508**	.084	−.021	.110	.046
4	9	0	0	0	0	**.394**	.127	−.008	.000	.263
5	0	9	0	0	0	−.033	**.743**	.105	−.040	.088
6	0	9	0	0	0	.019	**.813**	−.007	.090	−.053
7	0	9	0	0	0	−.022	**.862**	.050	−.133	.079
8	0	9	0	0	0	.143	**.538**	.138	−.011	.119
9	0	9	0	0	0	−.043	**.825**	−.099	.050	.107
10	0	0	9	0	0	−.391	.028	**.710**	−.021	.277
11	0	0	9	0	0	−.039	.108	**.598**	.342	−.200
12	0	0	9	0	0	.013	−.129	**.641**	−.025	.231
13	0	0	9	0	0	**.427**	.140	**.760**	−.061	−.212
14	0	0	0	9	0	−.100	.133	.008	**.609**	−.121
15	0	0	0	9	0	−.060	−.009	−.059	**.561**	.070
16	0	0	0	9	0	.263	−.087	−.046	**.579**	.073
17	0	0	0	9	0	−.143	.001	.090	**.607**	.038
18	0	0	0	9	0	.080	−.193	.186	**.451**	.248
19	0	0	0	9	0	.092	.035	.091	**.341**	.080
20	0	0	0	0	9	.143	.218	−.150	.207	**.436**
21	0	0	0	0	9	.193	−.010	.299	.013	**.419**
22	0	0	0	0	9	.156	.228	−.068	.207	**.333**
23	0	0	0	0	9	.249	.206	.019	.103	**.430**
24	0	0	0	0	9	−.120	.214	.296	.147	**.327**
Factor						Factor Correlations: **Φ**				
T_1						1.000	.303	.142	.276	.256
T_2							1.000	.300	.469	.445
T_3								1.000	.394	.456
T_4									1.000	.408
T_5										1.000

expected by each of the five groups of tests identified in **7.6**. The latter, unspecified but expected large weights, are designated by 9s according to the program requirements. This target matrix and the derived procrustes pattern for these data, along with the correlations among the factors, are shown in Table 15.10. This solution provides an excellent fit to the hypothesized factors, as can be seen by visual inspection or from the root-mean-square deviation of .148. A comparison with the orthoblique (independent clusters) solution of Table 14.15 also indicates the superiority of the present solution, which does not have the marked departures from the hypothesized pattern that had been noted in the former case.

The twenty-variable box problem, which has eluded a simple orthoblique solution, is now considered for procrustes rotation. Of course, the input matrix is the orthogonal solution **A** of Table 8.11. The target pattern matrix was constructed by specifying zeros according to the formula for each variable, as shown in Table 15.11 (the unspecified

Table 15.11

Oblique Procrustes Solution for Twenty-Variable Box Problem

(Initial solution: Orthogonal solution **A**, Table 8.11)

Variable	Target Pattern			Procrustes Pattern: **P**		
	x	y	z	x	y	z
1. x^2		0	0	.997	.000	$-.002$
2. y^2	0		0	.008	.994	$-.006$
3. z^2	0	0		$-.001$	.013	.985
4. xy			0	.471	.759	.007
5. xz		0		.406	$-.008$	.863
6. yz	0			.008	.411	.800
7. $\sqrt{x^2 + y^2}$			0	.728	.522	.001
8. $\sqrt{x^2 + z^2}$		0		.863	.014	.411
9. $\sqrt{y^2 + z^2}$	0			$-.013$	.773	.474
10. $2x + 2y$			0	.615	.643	.009
11. $2x + 2z$		0		.678	$-.001$	.672
12. $2y + 2z$	0			$-.007$	.624	.645
13. $\log x$		0	0	.990	.030	$-.011$
14. $\log y$	0		0	$-.047$	.993	.050
15. $\log z$	0	0		.019	$-.046$	.996
16. xyz				.293	.378	.697
17. $\sqrt{x^2 + y^2 + z^2}$				.645	.472	.301
18. e^x		0	0	.970	$-.036$	.009
19. e^y	0		0	.055	.962	$-.055$
20. e^z	0	0		$-.009$	.038	.950

Factor	Factor Correlations: **Φ**		
x	1.000	.257	.099
y		1.000	.246
z			1.000

values are left blank in the table so that the missing latent variables may be seen more clearly). While such a theoretical design might not be known in an empirical study, this hypothetical problem provides a good test of the effectiveness of the procrustes method. The resulting pattern and factor correlations are given in Table 15.11. The root-mean-square deviation for the specified elements is only .026, indicating an exceptionally excellent fit. What is even more striking is that the procrustes pattern compared with the "target" oblique pattern of Table 8.11 leads to rms = .011. The maximum difference between corresponding coefficients in the two factor patterns is only two units in the second decimal place and the factor correlations differ only in the third decimal place (.005, .003, and .006). Truly, the procrustes method demonstrates how factor analysis recovers the postulated order built into the box problem.

In this section we covered briefly some general and efficient methods for attaining the objective of procrustes rotations. Basically, that is to minimize, in a least-squares sense, the differences between the final rotated matrix and the target matrix. While the foregoing presentation may be adequate for the general user of these methods, there are some complex problems, especially in the oblique case, not treated here—for example: the type of target matrix (primary pattern or structure, or reference structure); the number of elements specified in the target matrix, and their values; starting values for the iteration process; a possible singularity in the objective function; the general problem of convergence. For more details and some of the finer technical points and proofs, the reader is referred to Browne (1967); Browne (1972b); Browne and Kristof (1969); Cramer (1974); Gruvaeus (1970).

Part IV   Factor Measurements

16   Measurement of Factors

16.1. *Introduction*

There are two basic problems with which factor analysis is concerned. The first of these deals with the methods for obtaining the linear resolution of a set of variables in terms of hypothetical factors. Most of the preceding work has been devoted to the solution of this problem, leading to the several orthogonal and oblique factoring methods. The second problem is concerned with the description of the factors in terms of the observed variables, and is the subject matter of the present chapter.

While there has been much research, and new theory and computing techniques for determining the factor weights of the variables in terms of the factors, there has not been a corresponding effort directed toward the expression of the factors in terms of the variables. The limited work on factor measurements done in the 1940s and 1950s included a brief note on oblique factors (Thomson 1949), a rather fundamental theoretical paper (Kestelman 1952), a sound statistical treatment of the problem (Anderson and Rubin 1956), and the development of several computer programs. In the 1960s and 1970s researchers paid much more attention to this area of factor analysis, refining and consolidating the established procedures for getting factor measurements. Among the many contributions during this period were empirical comparisons of methods (Horn 1965; Horn and Miller 1966; Velicer 1975) and studies of the analytical relationships among them (Harris 1967; McDonald and Burr 1967).

Methods for expressing the hypothetical constructs—the factors—in terms of the observed variables are developed in this chapter. First, the need for "estimation" rather than determining factor measurements directly is discussed in **16.2**. This is followed, in **16.3**, by the special situation for the measurement of principal components. Then various means are considered for estimating factor measurements when the classical factor analysis model is employed. The best prediction, in the least-square sense, is that obtained by ordinary regression methods. In **16.4** the linear regression of any factor on the n observed variables is obtained by the usual method. Next, an alternative regression method is developed in which the observed correlation matrix is replaced by the matrix of reproduced correlations that ensues from the theoretical factor model.

Three other methods for estimating factor scores are presented in the next two sections. In **16.6** a regression method is developed in which the sum of squares of unique factors is minimized. Also presented in that section is a modification of the procedure so that the estimated factors are guaranteed to be uncorrelated. These two methods have certain advantages over the preceding regression methods, while not quite attaining the validity level of the latter. The final method, developed in **16.7**, involves the mathematical solution of a set of equations rather than the statistical estimation by regression. Hence the factors themselves, instead of estimates of them, are obtained. However, this solution is in terms of "ideal" variables and therefore when the observed variables are used, in place of the ideal variables, these equations yield approximations to the factor scores that may be considered as another estimation method. A brief summary and comparison of the alternative methods is given in **16.8**.

To facilitate the development of the theory and methods of this chapter, as well as to bring together many of the concepts of the previous chapters, a summary of the relevant matrix notation is presented in Table 16.1. Because it is practically impossible to use a separate and distinct symbol for each new concept, and to retain the particular symbol every place that it occurs, the intent of the table is to call attention to the

Table 16.1

Notation for Matrices Frequently Used

Matrix	Order	Definition and Use
$\mathbf{R}$	$n \times n$	Matrix of observed correlations among the n variables.
$\hat{\mathbf{R}}$	$n \times n$	Matrix of reproduced correlations.
$\hat{\mathbf{R}} + \mathbf{U}^2$	$n \times n$	Matrix of reproduced correlations with unities in diagonal.
$\mathbf{Z} \equiv (z_{ji})$	$n \times N$	Matrix of N measurements on each of the n variables.
$\mathbf{z} \equiv \{z_j\}$	$n \times 1$	Column vector of the n variables.
$\mathbf{F} \equiv (F_{pi})$	$m \times N$	Matrix of N measurements on each of the m common factors.
$\mathbf{f} \equiv \{F_p\}$	$m \times 1$	Column vector of the m common factors.
$\mathbf{y} \equiv \{Y_j\}$	$n \times 1$	Column vector of the n unique factors.
$\mathbf{M} \equiv (\mathbf{A}\|\mathbf{U})$	$n \times m + n$	Complete pattern matrix.
$\mathbf{A}$	$n \times m$	General matrix of common-factor coefficients. Also, initial orthogonal solution when transformation to oblique solution is involved.
$\mathbf{U}$	$n \times n$	Matrix of unique-factor coefficients. Also matrix for unique-factor portion of factor structure.
$\mathbf{S}$	$n \times m$	Factor structure matrix. Only the common-factor portion is usually of interest; both the common and unique portions may be represented by $(\mathbf{S}\|\mathbf{U})$.
$\boldsymbol{\Phi}$	$m \times m$	General matrix of correlations among a set of oblique common factors.
$\boldsymbol{\Psi}$	$m \times m$	Matrix of correlations among common factors when these are reference axes and have to be distinguished from the primary factors.
$\mathbf{P}$	$n \times m$	Primary-factor pattern matrix (in oblique factor analysis an initial principal-factor solution is designated $\mathbf{A}$ rather than $\mathbf{P}$).
$\mathbf{S}$	$n \times m$	Primary-factor structure matrix (in oblique factor analysis this is not mistaken for a general factor structure matrix).
$\mathbf{V}$	$n \times m$	Reference-factor structure matrix.
$\mathbf{W}$	$n \times m$	Reference-factor pattern matrix.

specific uses of the notation and to provide a ready reference source. In addition to the basic concepts in this table, other definitions will be made, as needed, in the course of the development of the various procedures.

16.2. *Direct Solution versus Estimation*

A set of n variables can be analyzed either (a) in terms of common factors only, by inserting unities in the diagonal of $\mathbf{R}$; or (b) in terms of common and unique factors, by inserting communalities in the diagonal of $\mathbf{R}$. These two approaches, of course, correspond to the component analysis and the classical factor analysis models, respectively, as first presented in **2.3**. In the first instance $\mathbf{R}$ is a Gramian matrix, generally of rank n, and the factor solution

$$(16.1) \qquad\qquad \mathbf{z} = \mathbf{Af}$$

is in terms of n common factors. Since $\mathbf{A}$ is a square non-singular matrix, in this instance, it will have an inverse. Then the required factor measurements are given simply by:

$$(16.2) \qquad\qquad \mathbf{f} = \mathbf{A}^{-1}\mathbf{z}.$$

This solution is determined exactly, is unique, and involves no "estimation."

However, when the factor model involves common and unique factors the solution is not so simple. Then the total number of factors exceeds the number of variables, and an inverse does not exist for the factor matrix $\mathbf{M}$. The generally accepted procedure, in this case, is to resort to the "best fit" in the least squares sense. Such methods are developed in the ensuing sections.

Kestelman (1952) proves that even when the total number of factors exceeds the number of variables, exact numerical specifications can be found for the factors (but not unique values) such that

$$\mathbf{FF'} = \mathbf{I},$$

i.e., the factor measurements are in standard form and uncorrelated. He also indicates that such theoretical measurements are not necessarily superior, from a statistical standpoint, to the correlated estimates obtained by regression methods.

The concern with the fact that the regression methods lead to correlated estimates of factor measurements is taken up by Heermann (1963). He develops two procedures for transforming the least-squares estimates of orthogonal factors so as to produce uncorrelated measurements. These he calls "orthogonal approximations." He also derives "univocal estimates" (see Guilford and Michael 1948) of orthogonal factors that have the property of not correlating with any of the factors except those they were designed to estimate. Of course, in making any of these transformations there is bound to be a loss in the validity of the estimators—the regression methods determine estimates that give the "best" fit according to the least-squares principle. However, in considering alternative advantages of uncorrelated factor measurements and lack of correlations with other factors, Heerman argues that "it would appear that the orthogonal estimators represent something of a compromise between the maximum validity of least-squares estimators and the purity of the univocal estimators" (1963, p. 172). We will return to some of these issues in **16.8** after first presenting the case of principal components and then developing five alternative methods for estimating factor measurements.

16.3.   *Measurement of Principal Components*

When the analysis is in terms of principal components, then the factor measurements can be obtained directly. Not only does the inverse of the factor matrix exist when all n components have been obtained, so that the factor measurements are given by (16.2), but actually it is not necessary to calculate the inverse of the factor matrix. Furthermore, in the more practical situation when only a few of the larger components are used, the simplified procedure still applies. Also, for the methods described in **11.2**, **11.3**, and **11.4**, where in the course of getting a traditional factor analysis the variables are rescaled in order to make the matrices under consideration Gramian, the following procedures are applicable in obtaining the factors that are derived from the eigenvectors of those matrices.

In the factor model (16.1) it need not be assumed that $\mathbf{A}$ is square, but can be of order $n \times m$. Premultiplying both sides of (16.1) by $\mathbf{A}'$ produces

$$\mathbf{A}'\mathbf{z} = \mathbf{A}'\mathbf{Af},$$

and solving for $\mathbf{f}$ explicitly, the final result is

$$(16.3) \qquad \mathbf{f} = (\mathbf{A}'\mathbf{A})^{-1}\mathbf{A}'\mathbf{z} = \Lambda_m^{-1}\mathbf{A}'\mathbf{z},$$

where Λ_m is the diagonal matrix of the m eigenvalues retained, corresponding to (8.17). From this expression, or the equivalent algebraic form:

$$(16.4) \qquad F_p = \sum_{j=1}^{n} \frac{a_{jp}}{\lambda_p} z_j \qquad (p = 1, 2, \cdots, m),$$

it is clear that the principal components are described mathematically as linear combinations of the variables, with no question of statistical estimation. The coefficients in the equation for any principal component in terms of the variables are obtained simply by dividing its "factor loadings" by its eigenvalue. This property was first derived by Hotelling (1939) and generalized by Kaiser (1962).

To illustrate the foregoing, consider the principal component solution of Table 8.1 for the five socio-economic variables. The necessary eigenvalues are equal to the variances in the second to last row of that table. Then dividing the numbers in the columns by the respective eigenvalue produces the required coefficients. For example, the resulting equation in the case of the second component (P_2) is:

$$F_2 = .4488z_1 - .3032z_2 + .4041z_3 - .0581z_4 - .3107z_5.$$

Another important property of component analysis is that the measurements of any rotated components can also be obtained more simply than in the case of classical factor analysis. Consider a rotation of the principal component solution (say, to the varimax form) by means of the transformation

(16.5) $$\mathbf{B} = \mathbf{AT},$$

where $\mathbf{A}$ is the initial matrix of coefficients of the principal components, $\mathbf{B}$ is the corresponding matrix for the rotated component solution, and $\mathbf{T}$ is the matrix of transformation. The new solution may be represented by

(16.6) $$\mathbf{z} = \mathbf{Bg}$$

where $\mathbf{g}$ is used to distinguish the new column vector from the original $\mathbf{f}$. Then, pre-multiplying both sides of (16.6) by $\mathbf{B}'$ and solving for $\mathbf{g}$ produces

(16.7) $$\mathbf{g} = (\mathbf{B}'\mathbf{B})^{-1}\mathbf{B}'\mathbf{z}.$$

Again using the five socio-economic variables for illustration, the rotated varimax components are given in Table 13.6. The matrix $\mathbf{B}$ can be read from this table, as follows (actually, its transpose for printing convenience):

$$\mathbf{B}' = \begin{pmatrix} .0160 & .9408 & .1370 & .8248 & .9682 \\ .9938 & -.0088 & .9801 & .4471 & -.0060 \end{pmatrix}.$$

Simple computations produce:

$$\mathbf{B}'\mathbf{B} = \begin{pmatrix} 2.5218 & .5048 \\ .5048 & 2.1481 \end{pmatrix} \quad \text{and} \quad (\mathbf{B}'\mathbf{B})^{-1} = \begin{pmatrix} .4161 & -.0978 \\ -.0978 & .4885 \end{pmatrix}.$$

Then, equation (16.7) can be applied to get the equation for each of the rotated components, namely:

$$G_1 = -.0905z_1 + .3923z_2 - .0388z_3 + .2995z_4 + .4035z_5,$$
$$G_2 = .4839z_1 - .0963z_2 + .4654z_3 + .1378z_4 - .0976z_5.$$

The measurements of these (varimax) components for the sample of $N = 12$ entities (census tracts) are presented in Table 16.2. The rotated components are designated by M's instead of G's because that was the notation used in chapter 13. To check any of these values by hand methods, the standard scores for the variables would first have to be calculated from Table 2.1 and then substituted in the above equations. Alternatively, these equations could be transformed to raw score form and the values from Table 2.1 used directly.

While the above procedure, which led to (16.7), is relatively simple, there is still another approach for getting the measurements of rotated components. From (16.1) and (16.6) it follows that

(16.8) $$\mathbf{f} = \mathbf{Tg},$$

which relationship between the two sets of components corresponds to (15.6). Pre-multiplying by $\mathbf{T}'$, and remembering that $\mathbf{T}'\mathbf{T} = \mathbf{I}$ for an orthogonal transformation, this relationship becomes

(16.9) $$\mathbf{g}' = \mathbf{T}'\mathbf{f},$$

Table 16.2

Measurements of Varimax Components: Five Socio-Economic Variables

(Solution of Table 13.6)

Case	M_1	M_2
1	1.20	−.03
2	−.66	−1.38
3	−1.26	−.77
4	1.11	−.80
5	.94	−.76
6	−1.23	.55
7	−.17	−1.55
8	−.44	.73
9	.32	.91
10	1.58	1.03
11	−.95	.96
12	−.45	1.11

and, upon substituting (16.3) for **f**,

$$(16.10) \qquad \mathbf{g} = \mathbf{T'}\mathbf{\Lambda}_m^{-1}\mathbf{A'z}.$$

Now, the transformation matrix itself can be expressed in the form

$$(16.11) \qquad \mathbf{T} = \mathbf{\Lambda}_m^{-1}\mathbf{A'B},$$

which corresponds to (15.4) and which can be obtained directly from (16.5). Finally, substituting (16.11) into (16.10), the formula for the rotated components becomes:

$$(16.12) \qquad \mathbf{g} = \mathbf{B'A}\mathbf{\Lambda}_m^{-2}\mathbf{A'z}.$$

Either (16.7) or this formula yields the equations for the rotated components. The difference between these two expressions is that the former employs the eigenvalues of **B'B**, involving the rotated matrix, while the latter uses the initial factor matrix. Thus, (16.7) may actually require more computations if m is of fair size because the matrix to be inverted is not diagonal as it is in (16.12). The results of applying formula (16.12) to the example of five socio-economic variables are identical to those obtained above; the computations are left as an exercise.

16.4. *Estimation by Regression*

The remainder of this chapter deals primarily with the classical factor analysis model (2.9). In this section conventional regression methods are employed to obtain estimates of factor measurements. The linear regression of any factor F_p on the n variables may be expressed in the form:

$$(16.13) \qquad \hat{F}_p = \beta_{p1}z_1 + \beta_{p2}z_2 + \cdots + \beta_{pn}z_n \qquad (p = 1, 2, \cdots, m).$$

From the general theory of multivariate regression, it follows that the normal equations for determining the β's are

$$(16.14) \quad \begin{cases} \beta_{p1} + r_{12}\beta_{p2} + \cdots + r_{1n}\beta_{pn} = s_{1p}, \\ r_{21}\beta_{p1} + \beta_{p2} + \cdots + r_{2n}\beta_{pn} = s_{2p}, \\ \cdots \cdots \cdots \cdots \cdots \cdots \\ r_{n1}\beta_{p1} + r_{n2}\beta_{p2} + \cdots + \beta_{pn} = s_{np}, \end{cases}$$

where $s_{jp} = r_{z_j F_p}$. The coefficients of the unknown β's are the elements of the symmetric matrix of observed correlations. Thus, any factor can be estimated when the correlations of the variables with the factor and the correlations among the variables themselves are known.

The regression method can best be developed by constituting a matrix made up of the two sets of variables: the n observed **Z** and the m common hypothetical constructs **F**. By postmultiplying this $(n + m) \times N$ partitioned matrix by its transpose, it follows that:

$$(16.15) \quad \begin{pmatrix} \mathbf{Z} \\ \mathbf{F} \end{pmatrix} (\mathbf{Z'} \quad \mathbf{F'}) = \begin{pmatrix} \mathbf{ZZ'} & \mathbf{ZF'} \\ \mathbf{FZ'} & \mathbf{FF'} \end{pmatrix} = \begin{pmatrix} \mathbf{R} & \mathbf{S} \\ \mathbf{S'} & \mathbf{\Phi} \end{pmatrix},$$

where **Z** is assumed to be appropriately scaled (as noted in **2.9**) so that division by N is obviated. Next, express the regression equations (16.13) in matrix form:

$$(16.16) \quad \mathbf{F} = \mathbf{BZ} + \mathbf{E}$$

where **B** is the $m \times n$ matrix of β-weights and **E** is the matrix of errors, or residuals, assumed to be uncorrelated with **Z**. Then, by performing the following matrix operations on (16.16)

$$(16.17) \quad \mathbf{FZ'} = \mathbf{BZZ'}$$

$$\mathbf{FZ'} (\mathbf{ZZ'})^{-1} = \mathbf{B}$$

and making use of the definitions indicated in the last equality of (16.15), the desired solution becomes

$$(16.18) \quad \mathbf{B} = \mathbf{S'} \, \mathbf{R}^{-1}.$$

Hence, the measurements of all the factors can be expressed compactly, as follows:

$$(16.19) \quad \mathbf{\hat{F}} = \mathbf{S'R}^{-1}\mathbf{Z}.$$

While the foregoing development employed the factor structure, it is possible to estimate the factors by use of the factor pattern instead. Substituting the expression (2.43) for the structure in terms of the pattern, equation (16.19) becomes

$$(16.20) \quad \mathbf{\hat{F}} = \mathbf{\Phi A'R}^{-1}\mathbf{Z}.$$

When the factors are uncorrelated, **Φ** is the identity matrix, and the matrix equation for the prediction of such factors becomes

$$(16.21) \quad \mathbf{\hat{F}} = \mathbf{A'R}^{-1}\mathbf{Z} \qquad \text{(uncorrelated factors)}$$

which is also immediately evident from (16.19) since the pattern and structure coincide. If the factors are correlated, of course the distinction between a pattern and a structure is of paramount importance.

A measure of the accuracy of estimating a factor F_p by means of equation (16.13) is given by the coefficient of multiple correlation R_p. Several important and useful formulas involving R_p will be developed next. The normal equations (16.14) may be written in the condensed form

$$(16.22) \qquad \sum (F_{pi} - \hat{F}_{pi})z_{ji} = 0 \qquad (j = 1, 2, \cdots, n),$$

where the summation extends over the N observations of each variable. In the following development, summation on i from 1 to N will be understood although the i is omitted. Since the set of residuals $(F_p - \hat{F}_p)$ is orthogonal to each of the n sets of numbers z_j, it is orthogonal to any linear combination of these z_j. In particular, the set $\hat{F}_p$ is such a linear combination, and hence

$$\sum (F_p - \hat{F}_p)\hat{F}_p = 0,$$

which, upon dividing through by N, reduces to

$$(16.23) \qquad s_{F_p} r_{F_p \hat{F}_p} = s_{\hat{F}_p}^2,$$

since F_p is in standard form. The coefficient of multiple correlation of F_p in terms of $z_1, z_2, \cdots, z_n$ is defined to be the simple correlation coefficient of F_p and $\hat{F}_p$. The expression (16.23) may finally be written in the form

$$(16.24) \qquad R_p = r_{F_p \hat{F}_p} = s_{\hat{F}_p}.$$

This formula shows that the standard deviation of the factor estimates is equal to the coefficient of multiple correlation.

A simple formula for calculating R_p may be obtained by multiplying both sides of (16.13) by F_p, summing for the N individuals, and dividing by N. the result is

$$s_{F_p} r_{F_p \hat{F}_p} = \beta_{p1} s_{1p} + \beta_{p2} s_{2p} + \cdots + \beta_{pn} s_{np},$$

where the symbol for the sample standard deviation $(s_{\hat{F}})$ should not be confused with the symbol for a factor structure element (s_{jp}). Then, according to (16.24),

$$(16.25) \qquad R_p^2 = \beta_{p1} s_{1p} + \beta_{p2} s_{2p} + \cdots + \beta_{pn} s_{np}.$$

While (16.25) is the simplest formula for computing the multiple correlation, another form can be derived with other useful features. To this end, multiply the first of equations (16.14) by β_{p1}, the second by β_{p2}, etc., obtaining

$$\beta_{p1} s_{1p} = \beta_{p1}^2 \qquad + \beta_{p1} \beta_{p2} r_{12} + \cdots + \beta_{p1} \beta_{pn} r_{1n},$$

$$(16.26) \qquad \cdot \quad \cdot \quad \cdot \quad \cdot \quad \cdot \quad \cdot \quad \cdot \quad \cdot \quad \cdot \quad \cdot$$

$$\beta_{pn} s_{np} = \beta_{pn} \beta_{p1} r_{n1} + \beta_{pn} \beta_{p2} r_{n2} + \cdots + \beta_{pn}^2.$$

Adding these equations, and employing (16.25), there results

$$(16.27) \qquad R_p^2 = \sum_{j=1}^{n} \beta_{pj}^2 + 2 \sum_{j<k=1}^{n} \beta_{pj} \beta_{pk} r_{jk}.$$

This formula, although not so simple as (16.25) for computing R_p, illustrates an important property. Any product term $\beta_{pj}s_{jp}$ in (16.25) measures the *total* (*direct* and *indirect*) contribution of the corresponding variable X_j to R_p^2, or the importance of that variable as a "determiner" of F_p. The resolution of the total contribution of any variable into its direct and indirect effect upon F_p is indicated in (16.26). Thus, while $\beta_{p1}s_{1p}$ represents the total portion of R_p^2 which is due to X_1, the right-hand member of the first of equations (16.26) shows that this is composed of the direct contribution (β_{p1}^2) of X_1 and of the indirect contribution $(\beta_{p1}\beta_{pk}r_{1k})$ of X_1 through its correlations with each of the other variables X_k $(k = 2, 3, \cdots, n)$. It may be noted that the indirect or joint contribution of any two variables is distributed equally between them.

The formulas for the multiple correlation coefficients were developed in detailed algebraic form for heuristic reasons. They can also be expressed compactly in matrix form, as follows:

$$(16.28) \qquad\qquad (R_p^2) = \text{diag } \mathbf{BS}$$

where the m squared multiple correlations appear in the diagonal of the matrix product of the β-matrix and structure matrix.

In the preceding section involving component analysis it was demonstrated that the principal components (or orthogonal rotations of them) are linear combinations of the original variables involving no estimation. One immediate implication of this is that the multiple correlation for any principal component must be precisely unity. It must also be unity for any rotation of the principal components. On the other hand, when the analysis is in terms of classical factor analysis then the multiple correlation will be less than one for each factor. The extent of this reduction can be seen from the following analysis.

Suppose the factor coefficients have been estimated by the principal-factor method of **8.2**; that is, the columns of factor loadings are appropriately normalized eigenvectors of $\mathbf{R} - \mathbf{U}^2$, where $\mathbf{R}$ is the full correlation matrix and $\mathbf{U}^2$ is the diagonal uniqueness matrix. Designating the eigenvalues by λ_p and the corresponding unit-length eigenvectors by $\boldsymbol{\alpha}_p$, it follows from (8.11) that

$$(16.29) \qquad\qquad (\mathbf{R} - \mathbf{U}^2)\boldsymbol{\alpha}_p = \lambda_p\boldsymbol{\alpha}_p \qquad\qquad (p = 1, 2, \cdots, m)$$

and

$$(16.30) \qquad\qquad \boldsymbol{\alpha}_p'\boldsymbol{\alpha}_p = 1.$$

The column vector $\mathbf{a}_p$ of factor coefficients is scaled according to (8.10) as follows:

$$(16.31) \qquad\qquad \mathbf{a}_p = \sqrt{\lambda_p}\,\boldsymbol{\alpha}_p.$$

Now, let $\boldsymbol{\beta}_p$ be the column vector of regression coefficients for the estimation of F_p from $z_1, \cdots, z_n$. Also let $\mathbf{s}_p$ designate the column vector of correlations of the variables with factor F_p. Then, an expression corresponding to (16.18) for the regression coefficients can be put in the following matrix form:

$$(16.32) \qquad\qquad \boldsymbol{\beta}_p = \mathbf{R}^{-1}\mathbf{s}_p = \mathbf{R}^{-1}\mathbf{a}_p,$$

where the last equality follows from the fact that the structure elements are identical with the pattern coefficients in the case of an orthogonal factor solution. Similarly, an expression for the multiple correlation corresponding to (16.28) may be put in the form:

$$(16.33) \qquad R_p^2 = s'_p \beta_p = a'_p \beta_p.$$

Substituting the value for β_p from (16.32), the last expression becomes

$$(16.34) \qquad R_p^2 = a'_p R^{-1} a_p,$$

or, making use of (16.31),

$$(16.35) \qquad R_p^2 = \sqrt{\lambda_p} \alpha'_p R^{-1} \alpha_p \sqrt{\lambda_p} = \alpha'_p R^{-1} (\lambda_p \alpha_p),$$

where the last equality follows from the fact that λ_p is a scalar. Then, according to the basic relationship (16.29), the last equation can be put in the form

$$R_p^2 = \alpha'_p R^{-1} (R - U^2) \alpha_p$$
$$= \alpha'_p (I - R^{-1} U^2) \alpha_p$$
$$= \alpha'_p \alpha_p - \alpha'_p R^{-1} U^2 \alpha_p,$$

and, finally

$$(16.36) \qquad R_p^2 = 1 - \alpha'_p R^{-1} U^2 \alpha_p,$$

by use of (16.30). This indicates the extent to which the multiple correlation is reduced from unity when the factor solution includes uniqueness variance. On the other hand, when the correlation matrix with ones in the diagonal is factored, then $U^2 = 0$ and the multiple correlation is exactly one for each principal component.

Returning to the formulas (16.19) or (16.20) for the estimation of factor measurements, it can be seen that they require the calculation of the inverse of the correlation matrix, and hence the regression method is practical only with large computers. While hand procedures like the square root method could be used for a small number of variables (as illustrated in earlier editions of this text), in a realistic sense, computers are a must for estimation of factor measurements.

A simple example to show the computer produced β's will now be presented for the prediction of the two oblique factors from the five socio-economic variables. The direct oblimin ($\delta = 0$) factor pattern, structure, and correlation between the two factors come from ex. 15, chap. 14, while the correlations among the five variables are given in Table 2.2 and the raw measurements for the twelve census tracts are in Table 2.1. It is immaterial whether (16.19) or (16.20) is programmed. Either one produces, for this example, the following regression equations:

$$\hat{T}_1 = -.58737z_1 - .06657z_2 + .67417z_3 + .07303z_4 + .91362z_5,$$
$$\hat{T}_2 = 1.12140z_1 + .14066z_2 - .13686z_3 + .02006z_4 - .06387z_5,$$

where five decimal places are shown not because of such presumed accuracy but only to better serve as a test case for computer check-out. The multiple correlations for these estimates, according to (16.25), are $R_1 = .9960$ and $R_2 = 1.0007$ (no doubt the value in excess of one is simply a round-off error). The regression estimates of these two factors for the twelve cases are shown in Table 16.3. Of course, these estimated values of the two oblique factors are different from the exact measurements of the two orthogonally rotated principal components in Table 16.2.

Table 16.3

Measurements of Factors Estimated by Regression Method:
Five Socio-Economic Variables

(Solution of ex. 15, chap. 14)

Case	$\hat{T}_1$	$\hat{T}_2$
1	1.38	−.14
2	−1.10	−1.51
3	−1.36	−.92
4	1.15	−.63
5	1.09	−.62
6	−.83	.41
7	−.40	−1.44
8	−.44	.85
9	.10	1.16
10	1.35	1.10
11	−.72	.89
12	−.22	.88

In the foregoing illustration standardized values were used. The calculation of such values for many variables for a large sample of individuals is laborious. The work can be reduced by formally expressing the equations of estimation in terms of observed values by the use of formula (2.5). Thus, in general, an equation of the form (16.13) may be written as follows:

(16.37)
$$\hat{F}_p = \frac{\beta_{p1}}{s_1}X_1 + \frac{\beta_{p2}}{s_2}X_2 + \cdots + \frac{\beta_{pn}}{s_n}X_n - C,$$

where

(16.38)
$$C = \frac{\beta_{p1}}{s_1}\overline{X}_1 + \frac{\beta_{p2}}{s_2}\overline{X}_2 + \cdots + \frac{\beta_{pn}}{s_n}\overline{X}_n.$$

It should be noted that an estimated factor is not in standard form. Such a variable, however, has a mean of zero and a standard deviation which is equal to the coefficient of multiple correlation as shown by (16.24).

The regression equations in terms of the raw score form of the five socio-economic variables are as follows:

$$\hat{T}_1 = -.00017X_1 - .03698X_2 + .00054X_3 + .00064X_4 + .00014X_5 - 2.29580,$$
$$\hat{T}_2 = .00033X_1 + .07815X_2 - .00011X_3 + .00017X_4 - .00001X_5 - 2.51900.$$

373

If these are used to get the factor scores for the twelve census tracts, of course the same results will be obtained as those in Table 16.3.

The factor estimates by equation (16.13), or (16.37) may be positive or negative numbers. If it is desirable to eliminate the negative values, a transformation can be made to an arbitrary positive scale. This can be accomplished by standardizing the values $\hat{F}_{pi}$ given by (16.37) and equating the variable to an arbitrary variable in standard form. Thus, if the arbitrary variable Y is assigned a mean of 50 and standard deviation of 10, the required transformation can be written in the form

$$(16.39) \qquad Y_p = 10\hat{F}_p/R_p + 50,$$

where the multiple correlation coefficient has been substituted for the standard deviation of the estimated factor according to (16.24). Such transformations have been found especially useful in psychological studies employing factor estimates (Holzinger and Swineford 1939; Wenger, Holzinger, and Harman 1948).

Another familiar example is that of the eight physical variables whose correlations are given in Table 2.3, and whose means and standard deviations as well as raw and standardized values for two girls are given in Table 16.4. The two oblique primary

Table 16.4

Means and Standard Deviations of Eight Physical Variables,* and Values for Two Girls

Variable j	Mean $\overline{X}_j$	Standard Deviation s_j	Case 1		Case 2	
			X_{j1}	z_{j1}	X_{j2}	z_{j2}
1. Height	63.96 in.	2.09 in.	63.98 in.	0.01	66.34 in.	1.14
2. Arm span	64.25 in.	2.50 in.	63.19 in.	−0.42	66.89 in.	1.06
3. Length of forearm	17.10 in.	.67 in.	16.89 in.	−0.31	17.99 in.	1.33
4. Length of lower leg	19.62 in.	.86 in.	19.09 in.	−0.62	20.71 in.	1.27
5. Weight	119.22 lb.	15.19 lb.	149.25 lb.	1.98	125.5 lb.	0.41
6. Bitrochanteric diameter	12.27 in.	.66 in.	13.15 in.	1.33	12.44 in.	0.26
7. Chest girth	31.21 in.	1.91 in.	34.37 in.	1.65	32.52 in.	0.69
8. Chest width	9.92 in.	.67 in.	10.87 in.	1.42	10.55 in.	0.94

* For 305 fifteen-year old girls.

factors, found in Table 12.3, will now be estimated by the regression method and their measurements determined for the two girls. The β-weights, as given by (16.18) in terms of the factor structure or in (16.20) using the factor pattern, can easily be programmed for any computer. The values obtained for predicting the oblique factors T_1 (Lankiness) and T_2 (Stockiness) are shown in Table 16.5, both in terms of standardized and raw scores of the variables. The measurements of these factors for a particular individual are obtained by substituting the appropriate values in these equations.

Table 16.5

Regression Equations for Predicting Oblique
Primary Factors: Eight Physical Variables

(Solution of Table 12.3)

Factor p	Coefficients of Variables								
	1	2	3	4	5	6	7	8	
	Standardized Form								R_p^2
$\hat{T}_1$	.239	.399	.189	.199	.031	.007	−.003	−.004	.9568
$\hat{T}_2$	−.016	.117	−.065	.013	.650	.157	.121	.107	.9273
	Raw Score Form								Constant
$\hat{T}_1$	.114	.159	.282	.231	.002	.011	−.002	−.005	27.169
$\hat{T}_2$	−.008	.047	−.096	.015	.043	.238	.063	.159	12.728

Thus, for the two girls whose values for the eight variables are given in Table 16.4, the factor measurements are:

$$\text{Case 1:} \quad \hat{T}_{11} = -0.29, \ \hat{T}_{21} = 1.81;$$

$$\text{Case 2:} \quad \hat{T}_{12} = 1.20, \ \hat{T}_{22} = 0.53.$$

Clearly, the first girl is of the stocky type, while the second is tall or lanky. The original measurements reveal these facts, of course, but not so simply as the factor measurements. Although the estimated factors are not in standard form, their standard deviations (.9782 and .9630) are nearly the same, and so the estimated values are reasonably comparable. The measurements for the first girl indicate that she is almost two standard deviations above the mean in the factor "stockiness" and slightly below the average in "lankiness." The second girl is a less extreme type—being less lanky than the other girl is stocky and also being above average in "stockiness."

An illustration of the proportions of the variance of one of the above estimated factors due to the eight physical variables will now be given. The direct and indirect contributions of these variables to the prediction of the factor $T_1 =$ Lankiness are indicated in Table 16.6. Each entry in the table proper represents the total indirect contribution $(2\beta_{1j}\beta_{1k}r_{jk})$ of variables X_j and X_k. The total indirect contribution of any variable is equal to one-half of the sum in the row and column representing that variable and is given in the last row of the table. The direct contributions (β_{1j}^2) are given in the row preceding the last. The total contribution $(\beta_{1j}s_{j1})$ of each variable is presented in the last column of the table. Of course, the sum of the direct and indirect contributions of each variable must be equal to its total contribution. Finally, the sum of the entries in the last column (or last two rows) is equal to the square of the multiple correlation.

Table 16.6

Proportions of Variance of $\hat{T}_1$ Due to the Independent Variables

Variable	1	2	3	4	5	6	7	8	Total $\beta_{1j}s_{j1}$
1									.218
2	.164								.376
3	.073	.133							.171
4	.082	.131	.060						.179
5	.007	.009	.004	.005					.014
6	.001	.002	.001	.001	.000				.003
7	−.000	−.001	−.000	−.000	−.000	−.000			−.001
8	−.001	−.001	−.001	−.001	−.000	−.000	.000		−.002
Direct	.057	.159	.036	.040	.001	.000	.000	.000	$R_1^2 = .958$
Indirect	.162	.217	.135	.139	.012	.002	−.000	−.002	

Since it is a well known fact that adding variables to a regression equation can only increase a multiple correlation, one might wonder about the small negative numbers in the last column of Table 16.6. No doubt these are spurious, insignificant values that have arisen from the rather involved mathematical computations, and no significance should be attached to the values appearing in the third decimal place as a result of a matrix inversion.

One practical use of the contributions of variables to the variance of a factor is to measure their relative importance for predictive purposes. In building a psychological test, for example, many items might be analyzed by factorial methods, and then the question might arise about the "importance" of the different items. A simple measure of validity is the correlation of an item with the factor. However, a much better indicator is the total contribution of an item to the variance of the computed factor. The correlation of an item with the factor does not reflect sufficiently the indirect contributions of the item through its correlations with each of the other items. Returning to the example of eight physical variables, this point might be made by comparing the importance of variable 1 (Height) with variable 5 (Weight) as to their effect on the prediction of factor T_1 (Lankiness). Their correlations with the factor are .914 and .453, respectively; while their total contributions to the prediction of the factor are .218 and .014, respectively. While one would not take direct ratios of these pairs of numbers, nonetheless it seems that the large difference in the proportions of the variance of the estimated factor make the latter numbers much more meaningful in judging the relative importance of the two variables.

16.5. *Estimation by Theoretical Model*

In an attempt to preserve the principle of least-squares regression but at the same time to reduce the computational labor, Ledermann (1939) developed a "shortened method" for estimating factors and Harman (1941) generalized it to the case of oblique factors. While the justification for these approaches was understandable in the pre-computer days, that would no longer be the case today. However, the method —not its original purpose—makes perfectly good sense as an alternative approach to factor estimation. The essence of the method involves the replacement of the observed correlation matrix by the reproduced correlation matrix, leading to a matrix to be inverted that is of order m instead of n. What we focus on now is not the reduction of computing work but the acceptance of the theoretical model as the basis for estimating the factors.

Stated explicitly, the assumption made in this section is that

$$(16.40) \qquad \hat{R} + U^2 = R,$$

i.e., the reproduced correlations, with ones in the diagonal, are set equal to the observed correlations. Then, according to (2.46), this condition leads to:

$$(16.41) \qquad R = A\Phi A' + U^2.$$

This relation will now be used in modifying formula (16.20) for the estimation of the m common factors. Premultiplying both sides of (16.41) by $A'U^{-2}$ there arises[1]

$$(16.42) \qquad A'U^{-2}R = (A'U^{-2}A\Phi + I)A' = (J\Phi + I)A',$$

where the $m \times m$ matrix J is defined by:

$$(16.43) \qquad J = A'U^{-2}A.$$

Now, premultiplying (16.42) by $(J\Phi + I)^{-1}$ and postmultiplying by R^{-1}, it becomes

$$(16.44) \qquad A'R^{-1} = (J\Phi + I)^{-1}A'U^{-2}.$$

Then, substituting this expression for $A'R^{-1}$ in (16.20), there results

$$(16.45) \qquad \hat{F} = \Phi(J\Phi + I)^{-1}A'U^{-2}Z.$$

This expression can be simplified by premultiplying both sides by $[\Phi(J\Phi + I)^{-1}]^{-1}$, obtaining

$$(16.46) \qquad (J + \Phi^{-1})\hat{F} = A'U^{-2}Z,$$

and by making use of the definition of J from (16.43) the final form becomes:

$$(16.47) \qquad \hat{F} = (A'U^{-2}A + \Phi^{-1})^{-1}A'U^{-2}Z.$$

Although this formula may appear to be more complex than (16.20), it is actually much simpler to apply. Aside from inverting the squares of the unique-factor coefficients, the only matrix whose inverse must be calculated is of order m. Again, it should be noted that this gain in computing efficiency is of lesser importance today than when the method was first developed; of utmost conceptual importance is the use of the factor model in estimating the factors—in effect, accepting the theoretical relationships among the variables in preference to the observed (but fallible) data.

[1]Throughout this and the following section it is tacitly assumed that none of the uniquenesses vanishes. For an excellent treatment of the contrary case see Guttman (1940).

In previous editions of this text, detailed procedures using the square root method with a desk calculator were outlined for estimating factors by means of the reproduced correlations. Also, as a byproduct, a procedure was developed to approximate $\mathbf{R}^{-1}$ by calculating $(\hat{\mathbf{R}} + \mathbf{U}^2)^{-1}$. These short-cut methods for hand calculation have little to recommend them when computers are so generally available, and so they have been omitted from the present edition.

By way of illustrating the method of this section, the same data sets are considered as in the last section. Before attempting to apply (16.47) it should be noted that the factor pattern for the five socio-economic variables contains a Heywood case, so that the uniqueness of the first variable is zero, and the method breaks down. Hence, the illustration will be only for the example of eight physical variables for the same oblique primary factors. The expression (16.47) was programmed and the computer output has been put in Table 16.7. While these weights are in general agreement with

Table 16.7

Estimation by Theoretical Model: Oblique Primary Factors for Eight Physical Variables

(Solution of Table 12.3)

Factor p	Coefficients of Variables								
	1	2	3	4	5	6	7	8	
	Standardized Form								R_p^2
$\hat{T}_1$	.235	.370	.222	.198	.021	.004	$-.002$	.012	.9997
$\hat{T}_2$	.042	.000	$-.007$	.024	.629	.165	.141	.095	.9998
	Raw Score Form								Constant
$\hat{T}_1$	.113	.148	.331	.230	.001	.007	$-.001$	.018	27.273
$\hat{T}_2$	.020	.000	$-.011$	.027	.041	.250	.074	.141	13.348

their corresponding values in Table 16.5, there is a striking exception for the coefficient of z_2 for $\hat{T}_2$. Nonetheless, the factor measurements by the present method for the two girls, namely,

$$\text{Case 1:} \quad \hat{T}_{11} = -0.29, \quad \hat{T}_{21} = 1.82,$$

$$\text{Case 2:} \quad \hat{T}_{12} = 1.22, \quad \hat{T}_{22} = 0.56,$$

are almost identical to those obtained by the previous method.

It should be remembered that the method developed in this section is dependent upon the vanishing of the residuals resulting from the factor analysis. If the condition (16.40) is satisfied only approximately then the β-weights and multiple correlations produced by this method will approach the actual least-squares values as the residuals approach zero. Dwyer (1940, p. 216) suggests that the multiple correlation resulting from the use of the factor solution will generally differ in absolute value from the actual multiple R determined from the observed correlations by an amount approximately equal to the average of the absolute residual error.

While the method of this section cannot be applied when any uniqueness vanishes, it does apply in a situation when the regression method of the previous section breaks down—if R is singular, or near-singular, as will be the case when multicollinearity exists. The present method can be used because in the common-factor space the dimensions (factors) are linearly independent and the $m \times m$ matrix to be inverted in (16.47) is nonsingular.

16.6. *Estimation by Minimizing Unique Factors*

An alternative to the ordinary regression method for estimating factors has been proposed by Bartlett (1937). Whereas in the previous methods the sum of the squares of discrepancies between the true and estimated factors over the range of individuals is minimized, now the sum of squares of the unique factors over the range of variables will be minimized. This method is in harmony with Bartlett's principle that unique factors should be introduced only in order to explain discrepancies between observed values and postulated common factors.

To indicate how the theory is developed, consider the case of only two common factors with the following factor pattern:

$$(16.48) \qquad z_j = a_{j1} F_1 + a_{j2} F_2 + u_j Y_j \qquad (j = 1, 2, \cdots, n).$$

The explicit expression for the unique factor of any variable z_j is

$$(16.49) \qquad Y_j = (z_j - a_{j1} F_1 - a_{j2} F_2)/u_j,$$

and the sum of the squares of all such factors may be denoted by the function

$$(16.50) \qquad Y(F_1, F_2) = \sum_{j=1}^{n} Y_j^2 = \sum_{j=1}^{n} (z_j - a_{j1} F_1 - a_{j2} F_2)^2/u_j^2.$$

Then to minimize the sum of squares of the unique factors over the range of variables, it is necessary that the partial derivatives of the function Y with respect to F_1 and F_2 vanish, leading to:

$$(16.51) \qquad \begin{cases} \left(\sum \dfrac{a_{j1}^2}{u_j^2}\right) \hat{F}_1 + \left(\sum \dfrac{a_{j1} a_{j2}}{u_j^2}\right) \hat{F}_2 = \sum \dfrac{a_{j1}}{u_j^2} z_j, \\ \left(\sum \dfrac{a_{j2} a_{j1}}{u_j^2}\right) \hat{F}_1 + \left(\sum \dfrac{a_{j2}^2}{u_j^2}\right) \hat{F}_2 = \sum \dfrac{a_{j2}}{u_j^2} z_j, \end{cases}$$

where the summations extend from $j = 1$ to $j = n$, and hats have been placed on the F's to distinguish the estimates of the factors from the true factors. This pair of simultaneous equations can be solved for the two unknowns, $\hat{F}_1$ and $\hat{F}_2$, using the methods of chapter 3 for small problems or a computer generally.

The foregoing development can be generalized to the case of m factors. The set of equations (16.51), written in matrix form, and solved for the factor estimates becomes:

$$\text{(16.52)} \qquad \hat{\mathbf{F}} = \mathbf{J}^{-1}\mathbf{A}'\mathbf{U}^{-2}\mathbf{Z}$$

in which the matrix $\mathbf{J}$ is defined in (16.43). Although formula (16.52) is not a special case of formula (16.47), it may be noted that if the term $\mathbf{\Phi}^{-1}$ is dropped in that formula it becomes identical with (16.52).

Again, the eight physical variables example is used to illustrate the estimation method contained in (16.52). This was programmed and run on an IBM system 360 to obtain the "regression" weights of Table 16.8. Applying these equations to the two girls previously considered, the estimates of their factor measurements are found to be:

$$\text{Case 1:} \quad \hat{T}_{11} = -0.35, \ \hat{T}_{21} = 2.03;$$

$$\text{Case 2:} \quad \hat{T}_{12} = 1.28, \ \hat{T}_{22} = 0.55.$$

While these are similar to the estimates obtained by regression in the ordinary manner and by use of the theoretical model, the degree of agreement may be due to the simplicity of the example.

Table 16.8

Estimation by Minimizing Unique Factors: Oblique Primary Factors for Eight Physical Variables

(Solution of Table 12.3)

Factor p	Coefficients of Variables								Constant
	1	2	3	4	5	6	7	8	
	Standardized Form								
$\hat{T}_1$	.248	.392	.235	.209	.005	.000	−.006	.010	
$\hat{T}_2$	.035	−.019	−.019	.016	.694	.183	.156	.104	
	Raw Score Form								
$\hat{T}_1$	.119	.157	.351	.243	.000	.000	−.003	.015	28.507
$\hat{T}_2$	.017	−.007	−.029	.019	.046	.277	.081	.156	13.383

The reliability of prediction can be judged by the appropriate standard error or multiple correlation coefficient. It should be noted, however, that formula (16.25) does not yield the required multiple correlation for the present method. If formula (16.25) is applied, the resulting "multiple correlation" will be found to approach unity. This follows from the fact that the common factors are estimated under the condition that the unique factors are minimized, and the uniqueness is the standard error of estimate in a pattern equation.

Bartlett (1937, p. 100) proposes as a measure of the "information (reciprocal of the error variance)" for any factor p, the expression

(16.53) $$|\mathbf{J}|/|\mathbf{J}_{pp}|,$$

where $|\mathbf{J}_{pp}|$ is the minor of the element in row and column p of $|\mathbf{J}|$. From this expression, a measure of "multiple correlation" for the prediction of a factor p by the method discussed in this section may be put in the form:

(16.54) $$R_p^2 = 1 - |\mathbf{J}_{pp}|/|\mathbf{J}|.$$

This form corresponds to the multiple correlation for the conventional regression estimate of a factor p, shown for the orthogonal case by Dwyer (1940, p. 229), namely:

(16.55) $$R_p^2 = 1 - |\mathbf{L}_{pp}|/|\mathbf{L}|,$$

where $\mathbf{L} = \mathbf{I} + \mathbf{J}$ and $|\mathbf{L}_{pp}|$ is the minor of the element in row and column p of $|\mathbf{L}|$.

The multiple correlations for the factors estimated in Table 16.8, as given by formula (16.54) are $R_1^2 = .9571$ and $R_2^2 = .9262$. These values are very close to those obtained by the regression and theoretical methods. For the particular example it may be concluded that, statistically, the different methods for estimating factors are equally good. For other data the method of this section may lead to radically different results than the conventional regression methods. The choice of the method of this section instead of one of the other methods must be made on the basis of the principle of prediction which is involved.

The estimates of the common factors by means of formula (16.52) provide an alternative solution to the regression estimates of the preceding sections. Bartlett pointed out that the principle of estimation adopted in this section does not completely agree with the solution that has usually been employed, although the difference does not affect the relative weights assigned to the variables in estimating a single general factor. When several common factors are involved, however, the discrepancy between equations (16.47) and (16.52) is even more serious. Bartlett (1937) states: "One point of view appears to have been to consider all the persons with different possible factorial make-ups that would give rise to the observed test scores of a particular person, whereas I have regarded the test scores as a sample of all possible scores that might have arisen for that person according to the different values of specific [unique] factors he may happen to have."

A modification to Bartlett's approach was introduced by Anderson and Rubin (1956) to insure orthogonality of the estimated factors. The resulting solution (Anderson & Rubin 1956, pp. 139–40) can be put in the form:

(16.56) $$\hat{\mathbf{F}} = (\mathbf{A}'\mathbf{U}^{-2}\mathbf{R}\mathbf{U}^{-2}\mathbf{A})^{-\frac{1}{2}}\mathbf{A}'\mathbf{U}^{-2}\mathbf{Z}$$

where the symmetric square root of the matrix in parentheses is to be taken. This formula requires more programming than (16.52). While the matrix to be inverted is still of order $m \times m$, it is the symmetric-square-root process that entails an eigenvalue-eigenvector routine. Also, it should be noted that the development assumes that the initial factor weights have been determined by the maximum-likelihood method

(Anderson & Rubin 1956, p. 140). Nonetheless, Harris (1967) presents this as a general method for getting uncorrelated estimated factors.

The modified procedure (16.56) was programmed and run on a computer to produce the equations in Table 16.9 for the example of eight physical variables. We follow Harris in accepting this method as a means of getting uncorrelated estimated factors even though the initial factor weights were not maximum-likelihood. To verify

Table 16.9

Modified Estimation by Minimizing Unique Factors:
Oblique Primary Factors for Eight Physical Variables

(Solution of Table 12.3)

Factor p	Coefficients of Variables								Constant
	1	2	3	4	5	6	7	8	
	Standardized Form								
$\hat{T}_1$	.254	.414	.250	.216	−.122	−.033	−.035	−.009	
$\hat{T}_2$	−.045	−.149	−.098	−.052	.737	.194	.168	.108	
	Raw Score Form								
$\hat{T}_1$	.121	.166	.373	.251	−.008	−.050	−.018	−.013	27.443
$\hat{T}_2$	−.021	−.059	−.146	−.060	.049	.294	.088	.161	4.870

the orthogonality property empirically would require the factor measurements for all 305 girls in the sample. Although these are not available, it can be shown analytically that the correlation between $\hat{T}_1$ and $\hat{T}_2$ is zero (see ex. 6). For the two girls with known data the factor measurements by (16.56) are:

$$\text{Case 1:} \quad \hat{T}_{11} = -0.74, \qquad \hat{T}_{21} = 2.27;$$

$$\text{Case 2:} \quad \hat{T}_{12} = 1.24, \qquad \hat{T}_{22} = 0.17.$$

These values are considerably different from all the previous estimates and especially accentuate the "stockiness" of the first girl.

16.7. *Estimation by Ideal Variables*

The final method of estimating factor measurements involves an approximation of the unavailable variables $\bar{z}_j$ in the common-factor space by the observable variables z_j. It is possible to get a mathematical solution for the factors in terms of $\bar{z}$ by starting with the factor model (2.36), namely:

(16.57) $$\mathbf{c} = \mathbf{Af}$$

where **c** stresses the "common" parts of the variables and corresponds to the column vector $\{\tilde{z}_1 \tilde{z}_2 \ldots \tilde{z}_n\}$ of the variables projected into the common-factor space. The factors may be determined as linear combinations of the hypothetical variables $(\tilde{z}_j)$ much as was done in **16.3** for the case of principal components. Premultiplying (16.57) by **A'** and designating the diagonal matrix of m eigenvalues by

(16.58) $$\mathbf{\Lambda}_m = \mathbf{A'A}$$

as in (8.17), the explicit solution for **f** becomes:

(16.59) $$\mathbf{f} = \mathbf{\Lambda}_m^{-1}\mathbf{A'c}.$$

This result is very similar to (16.3) for principal components except for the fact that the observed variables are replaced by "ideal" variables in the present case.

To illustrate the present method, formula (16.59) will be applied to the example of five socio-economic variables. The methods of the previous two sections broke down for this example because the factor analysis contained a Heywood case (i.e., a zero uniqueness). The method of the present section can be applied to these data. The programming of (16.59) is readily accomplished, and the computer produces:

$$T_1 = -.04328\tilde{z}_1 + .37375\tilde{z}_2 + .01196\tilde{z}_3 + .31589\tilde{z}_4 + .42335\tilde{z}_5,$$

$$T_2 = .48408\tilde{z}_1 - .04925\tilde{z}_2 + .46143\tilde{z}_3 + .15494\tilde{z}_4 - .06504\tilde{z}_5.$$

These equations give the descriptions of the two oblique factors (not their estimates) in terms of the "common-factor portions" of the original variables. The values of the variables $\tilde{z}_j$ are not known, and hence such equations cannot be applied directly to obtain the measurements of the factors for the individuals.

A reasonable approximation can be obtained by replacing each $\tilde{z}_j$ by z_j. Indicating such approximations by "curls" on the factor designations, and writing (16.59) for the N measurements, the final form becomes:

(16.60) $$\tilde{\mathbf{F}} = (\mathbf{A'A})^{-1}\mathbf{A'Z}.$$

The factor measurements for the twelve census tracts are shown in Table 16.10. These values differ rather significantly in some instances from the corresponding measurements by the regression method given in Table 16.3. Of course, this doesn't mean that one method is "right" and the other "wrong." It only points up the fact that different estimation methods can be expected to lead to different results; the choice rests with the investigator whose decision should rest upon knowledge of the content area and purpose of the study as well as the technical basis of the estimation method.

Another application of (16.60), to the eight-physical-variable problem, is summarized in Table 16.11, with the estimated factor measurements for the two girls given by:

Case 1: $\tilde{T}_{11} = -0.36, \quad \tilde{T}_{21} = 1.99;$

Case 2: $\tilde{T}_{12} = 1.32, \quad \tilde{T}_{22} = 0.68.$

Similar values were obtained for these girls by each of the four preceding estimation methods. It is not our intent to make detailed comparisons here, but only to call

Table 16.10

Measurements of Factors Estimated by Ideal Variables:
Five Socio-Economic Variables

(Solution of ex. 15, chap. 14)

Case	$\tilde{T}_1$	$\tilde{T}_2$
1	1.24	.07
2	−.82	−1.45
3	−1.35	−.89
4	1.07	−.70
5	.90	−.68
6	−1.17	.43
7	−.33	−1.57
8	−.37	.71
9	.42	.95
10	1.72	1.16
11	−.85	.88
12	−.35	1.08

attention to the fact that the similarities may be caused by the ideal variables not being too different from the observed variables in this example. In a sense, it is almost unfortunate that the eight physical variables constitute such a simple, well-structured data set that many different approaches lead to nearly equivalent results.

Table 16.11

Estimation by Ideal Variables: Oblique Primary Factors
for Eight Physical Variables

(Solution of Table 12.3)

Factor p	Coefficients of Variables								Constant
	1	2	3	4	5	6	7	8	
	Standardized Form								
$\tilde{T}_1$	.263	.285	.276	.263	.000	−.002	−.020	.030	
$\tilde{T}_2$	.025	−.011	−.018	.013	.362	.309	.305	.249	
	Raw Score Form								
$\tilde{T}_1$	.126	.114	.412	.306	.000	−.004	−.010	.045	28.505
$\tilde{T}_2$	.012	−.005	−.027	.015	.024	.468	.160	.371	17.557

16.8.   *Comparison of Factor Estimation Methods*

Five different methods for estimating factor scores have been presented in the last four sections. Also presented were numerical results based on two data sets to illustrate the several procedures. While some similarities and differences in the results were pointed out, certainly these simple examples cannot be used as a basis for assessing the merits and possible preference of one method over another.

Comparison of the several methods might be approached empirically (Horn 1965; Horn and Miller 1966; Glass and Maguire 1966). On the other hand, this can be done analytically to highlight certain properties of each method and relationships among the methods. One property, noted in **16.2**, that has caused considerable concern is the fact that regression methods yield factor estimates that are correlated. Attempts to circumvent this have led to the loss of other desirable properties, and trade-offs are clearly indicated. The most clear-cut properties that are desired may be identified as follows:

1. Valid: $r_{\hat{F}_p F_p}$ should be high.

2. Orthogonal: $r_{\hat{F}_p \hat{F}_q} = \begin{cases} 1 \text{ for } p = q, \\ 0 \text{ for } p \neq q. \end{cases}$

3. Univocal: $r_{\hat{F}_p F_q} = 0$ for $p \neq q$.

The extent to which these properties are satisfied by the several estimation methods is indicated in Table 16.12. The analytical developments in support of these conclusions are provided by Harris (1967) and McDonald and Burr (1967).

Table 16.12

General Properties of Alternative Estimation Methods

Estimation Method	Reference Equation	Properties		
		Valid	Orthogonal	Univocal
Regression	(16.20)	×		
Theoretical model	(16.47)	×		
Minimizing unique f.	(16.52)	×		×
Modified min. unique f.	(16.56)	×	×	
Ideal variables	(16.60)	×		×

In general, all the methods satisfy the property of having high validity, with the regression method showing up best. On the other hand, the regression method (and the method using the theoretical model) fails to satisfy either the "orthogonal" or "univocal" properties. Only the (Anderson-Rubin) modified method of minimizing unique factors satisfies the property of orthogonal estimated factors. The univocal property is met by both the (Bartlett) method of minimizing unique factors and the method of ideal variables. Since the orthogonal and univocal conditions are basically in conflict, it seems that the latter—the estimated factor being correlated only with its corresponding true factor—is more important than the former, which requires that the set of estimated factors be mutually orthogonal.

It has been tacitly assumed throughout this chapter that the derived factors (i.e., after rotation) were the ones of interest, not those obtained directly by the factor analysis. To emphasize this point, the numerical examples were purposely set in terms of oblique factors. Harris (1967) and McDonald and Burr (1967) show that for the special case when the initial solution is obtained by canonical factor analysis (see **11.2**), these factors can be estimated so that they satisfy both the orthogonal and univocal properties.

The approach employed by Harris (1967) considers the "true" factors as uncorrelated and of unit length (as assumed throughout part ii of this text) and obtains the formal expressions for the variances and covariances of these with five types of estimated factor scores. These include four of the five methods covered in the preceding sections. He does not cover estimation by use of the theoretical model (**16.5**). On the other hand, he includes a "quick and dirty" procedure that simply uses the factor coefficients of a factor pattern as the weights for the variables in estimating the factors, a method not recommended in this chapter. From the analytical comparisons, Harris concludes that "for an initial solution it is possible to secure factor score estimates that are both orthogonal and univocal. However for derived orthogonal solutions one still must choose. One can retain the univocal character of factor score estimates at the expense of orthogonality or one can retain orthogonality at the expense of the univocal character" (p. 378). In either event he strongly urges the estimation principle employed in **16.6**.

In a paper devoted to factor indeterminacy, Schönemann and Wang (1972) call attention to the obscure nature of the concept of true "factor scores" and of the equally vague notion of "factor score estimates." A further inquiry into the relation between these and component scores concludes that "there is little practical difference between principal component scores, rescaled image scores, and factor score estimates" (Velicer 1975). Another aspect of the competing methods of factor score estimates is considered by Tucker (1971). Unlike the preceding investigations—all of which are concerned with the relationships among the several methods—Tucker directs his attention to the properties of estimates when the objective is to determine the relationships of external measures (i.e., not part of the set that was factor analyzed) with the theoretical factors of the analysis. He then concludes that the nature of the use—e.g., for predicting group differences in factor level, for estimating correlations of other attributes with the factors, for counseling individuals on the basis of factor profiles—is vital to the choice of a particular method of estimating factor scores.

Certain consequences of the factor analysis model should be noted. The fundamental assumption that the observed variables are linear functions of the factor variables implies that certain kinds of data (e.g., color of eyes, nationality) cannot be studied in the framework of factor analysis. A corollary condition is that all observed variables must be linearly related to one another. In general if factor-analysis methods were to be applied to qualitative or non-linear data, new equations would have to be derived to fit the data. Hence, the first step to take in a factor analysis is to make certain that the n observed variables are linearly related. At least a visual inspection if not a formal statistical check should be made for each pair of observed variables. If non-linearity appears, then at least one of the non-linear pair is not a linear function of the factors.

Sometimes factor analysis is applied to non-linearly related variables, provided their relationships are monotonic. This is done with the belief that a straight line is always a good approximation to a monotonic function. Under this premise, most of the variance will be explained by the common-factor coefficients, even though a portion may be lost due to the inadequate fit of a straight line to a curve. Hence, while the factor analysis model may not be appropriate in a strict sense, it may be very useful in explaining the correlations and extracting as much variance as possible by means of the factors.

A purely statistical restriction is the requirement that each observed variable be normally distributed. While considerable latitude might be allowed, nevertheless a variable which is distinctly non-normal should not be included in the analysis. It must be remembered that the n variables are presumed to have a multivariate normal distribution in the mathematical developments leading to the large sample χ^2 tests of **9.5** and **10.4**. In other words, the powerful statistical methods of chapters 9 and 10 will lead to sound conclusions provided the basic assumptions are met.

Factor analysis has made tremendous progress in recent years. Much of this modern development is included in the text. However, what has been presented certainly is not all there is to say about factor analysis. Some of the areas touched very lightly, or omitted entirely, include: (a) practical uses and interpretations of factor analytical results; (b) specific use of factor analysis in the construction of theories and systems in the behavioral and biological sciences; (c) inverted factor techniques as expounded principally by Cattell and Stephenson; (d) three-mode factor analysis as developed and applied by Tucker and his students; and (e) confirmatory factor analysis as developed by Jöreskog.

The basic intent of this book is to provide the logical foundation for factor analysis upon which the major methods of analysis and computing procedures can be built. Hopefully, it will provide the practitioners with the means to proceed with applications in a meaningful way, and the serious student with a basis for subsequent independent exploration of new developments in the research literature.

Part V

Problems and Exercises

Problems

CHAPTER 2

1. Why are each of the following types of factors postulated:
   (a) common, (b) unique, (c) specific, (d) error?

2. Why are all variables and factors taken to be in standard form?

3. Write equations (2.9) for $n = 5$ and $m = 2$.

4. (a) What elements of these equations must be calculated in obtaining a factor solution?
   (b) How many of these elements are there to be determined in the case of exercise 3?

5. (a) Write the contributions of the common factors to the variance of z_1 in the following pattern equation:

$$z_1 = .5F_1 + .8F_2 + .33Y_1$$

   (b) Write the contributions of the common factors to the variance of z_2 in exercise 3.

6. Obtain the total contributions of the common factors in exercise 3.

7. What is the communality of z_1 in exercise 5?

8. Why cannot the communality of a variable exceed its reliability?

9. In the following table there are eight exercises in which two quantities are given and the remaining three can be determined therefrom. Complete the table.

Problems and Exercises

Variance Component	a	b	c	d	e	f	g	h
Specificity	.10	.15	.20	.25				
Error variance	.20				.05	.10		
Communality		.75			.60		.50	
Uniqueness			.35			.45		.30
Reliability				.85			.75	.90

Exercises 10–25 are based upon the data of Table I.

Table I
Coefficients of Two Uncorrelated Common Factors

Variable	F_1	F_2
1	.7	.3
2	.8	0
3	.7	0
4	.8	.6
5	.6	.5
6	.5	0
7	.6	.4
8	.7	.6

10. Calculate the communality of variable 8.

11. Which variable has the highest communality?

12. Which variable has the lowest communality?

13. Calculate the uniqueness of variable 1.

14. Which variable has the lowest uniqueness?

15. Which variable has the highest uniqueness?

16. Is a general factor present in this solution?

17. Is a group factor present in this solution?

18. Find the total contributions of F_1 and F_2.

19. What percent of the total variance is attributable to each of the common factors?

20. What percent of the total communality is attributable to each of the common factors?

21. If the reliability of variable 5 is .84, write the complete linear description of this variable, including the specific and error factors.

392

22. Calculate the index of completeness of factorization for variable 5.

23. What is the complexity of variable 1? Of variable 2?

24. Calculate the correlations $\hat{r}_{12}$, $\hat{r}_{14}$, $\hat{r}_{25}$, $\hat{r}_{26}$.

25. Are any of the reproduced correlations equal to zero?

CHAPTER 3

Evaluate the determinants in exercises 1–6:

1. $\begin{vmatrix} 5 & 3 \\ 2 & 4 \end{vmatrix}$ 2. $\begin{vmatrix} 3 & 4 \\ -2 & 6 \end{vmatrix}$ 3. $\begin{vmatrix} 4 & -2 \\ -7 & 3 \end{vmatrix}$

4. $\begin{vmatrix} 4 & 3 & 4 \\ 2 & 1 & 5 \\ 1 & 5 & 3 \end{vmatrix}$ 5. $\begin{vmatrix} 3 & -2 & 4 \\ 8 & 5 & -3 \\ 1 & 2 & 1 \end{vmatrix}$ 6. $\begin{vmatrix} 1 & 2 & 1 \\ 0 & 1 & 2 \\ 1 & 3 & 3 \end{vmatrix}$

Find the ranks of the matrices in exercises 7–9:

7.
$$\mathbf{A} = \begin{bmatrix} -4 & 2 & -6 \\ 6 & -3 & 9 \end{bmatrix}$$

8.
$$\mathbf{B} = \begin{bmatrix} 1 & 2 & 1 \\ 0 & 1 & 2 \\ 1 & 3 & 3 \end{bmatrix}$$

9.
$$\mathbf{C} = \begin{bmatrix} .81 & .54 & .72 \\ .54 & .40 & .54 \\ .72 & .54 & .73 \end{bmatrix}$$

10. Are the matrices **B** and **C** singular or nonsingular?

11. Which of the matrices **A**, **B**, **C** is symmetric?

12. Postmultiply the matrix **A** by the matrix **B**. What is the rank of the product matrix?

13. Write the transpose of: (a) the pattern matrix of ex. 3, chap 2; (b) the pattern matrix of Table I.

14. Assume the following pattern (with uncorrelated factors):

$$z_1 = .5F_1 + .8F_2 + .33Y_1$$
$$z_2 = .8F_1 + .3F_2 \qquad\qquad + .52Y_2$$
$$z_3 = .6F_1 + .6F_2 \qquad\qquad\qquad + .53Y_3$$
$$z_4 = .7F_1 + .4F_2 \qquad\qquad\qquad\qquad + .59Y_4$$
$$z_5 = .7F_1 + .7F_2 \qquad\qquad\qquad\qquad\qquad + .14Y_5$$

(a) Calculate the matrix $\hat{\mathbf{R}}$ of reproduced correlations (to 2 decimal places) by means of equation (2.50).
(b) Interpret the diagonal elements.

15. Assume the following factor solution:

$$z_1 = .80F_1 + .60F_2$$
$$z_2 = .73F_1 + .68F_2$$
$$z_3 = .87F_1 + .49F_2$$
$$z_4 = .51F_1 + .86F_2$$
$$z_5 = .64F_1 + .77F_2$$

(a) Calculate $\hat{\mathbf{R}}$.

(b) Interpret the diagonal elements.

16. For the numerical examples:

$$\mathbf{A} = \begin{bmatrix} 1 & 2 \\ 3 & 4 \end{bmatrix} \quad \text{and} \quad \mathbf{B} = \begin{bmatrix} 0 & 1 \\ 2 & 3 \end{bmatrix},$$

show that:

(a) $\mathbf{AB} \neq \mathbf{BA}$, i.e., multiplication of matrices is not commutative;

(b) $|\mathbf{AB}| = |\mathbf{A}| \cdot |\mathbf{B}|$, i.e., the determinant of the product of two square matrices is equal to the product of their determinants;

(c) $|\mathbf{AB}| = |\mathbf{BA}|$, i.e., the determinant of the product of two square matrices is independent of the order of multiplication of the matrices.

17. Compute the product matrices $\mathbf{AB}$, $\mathbf{BA}$, $\mathbf{A'B}$, $\mathbf{BA'}$, $\mathbf{B'A}$, $\mathbf{AB'}$, $\mathbf{A'B'}$, $\mathbf{B'A'}$ when the individual matrices are given by:

$$\mathbf{A} = \begin{bmatrix} 1 & 2 & 3 \\ 0 & 1 & 4 \\ 0 & 0 & 1 \end{bmatrix} \quad \text{and} \quad \mathbf{B} = \begin{bmatrix} 6 & 0 & 0 \\ 7 & 8 & 0 \\ 7 & 4 & 2 \end{bmatrix}.$$

Verify, with these particular examples, that multiplication of matrices is not commutative. Also verify the theorem on the transpose of products of matrices, viz., $(\mathbf{AB})' = \mathbf{B'A'}$, $(\mathbf{A'B})' = \mathbf{B'A}$, etc.

18. For the matrices of the preceding exercise, obtain the values of the determinants $|\mathbf{A}|$, $|\mathbf{B}|$, $|\mathbf{AB}|$, and $|\mathbf{BA}|$.

19. Given the following two matrices:

$$\mathbf{C} = \begin{bmatrix} 2 & 4 & 6 \\ 3 & 1 & 2 \end{bmatrix} \quad \text{and} \quad \mathbf{D} = \begin{bmatrix} 9 & 1 \\ 3 & 2 \\ 2 & 7 \end{bmatrix}.$$

(a) Compute the product matrices $\mathbf{CD}$ and $\mathbf{DC}$.

(b) Are the determinants of the resulting matrices equal?

20. Show that the product (in either order) of a matrix by its transpose is a symmetric matrix.

21. The determinant of the inverse of a matrix is equal to the reciprocal of the determinant of the matrix, i.e.,

$$|\mathbf{A}^{-1}| = \frac{1}{|\mathbf{A}|}.$$

Demonstrate this theorem in the following two instances:

(a) $\mathbf{A} = \begin{bmatrix} a & b \\ c & d \end{bmatrix}$ (b) $\mathbf{A} = \begin{bmatrix} 2 & 1 & 1 & 2 \\ 1 & 2 & 1 & 0 \\ 3 & 1 & 1 & 1 \\ 0 & 0 & 3 & 0 \end{bmatrix}.$

22. Calculate the inverse of the matrix

$$\begin{bmatrix} 1.000 & .693 & .216 \\ .693 & 1.000 & .295 \\ .216 & .295 & 1.000 \end{bmatrix}$$

by the square root method indicated in Table 3.2, and check the results by (3.14).

23. Compute the inverse of the matrix in ex. 21 (b), employing the square root method of Table 3.2 and check the result by comparing the value of its determinant with that obtained in ex. 21. (Hint: Use idea of ex. 20.)

CHAPTER 4

1. (a) Construct a 2-dimensional rectangular Cartesian coordinate system and plot the following points: $(1, 2)$, $(0, 4)$, $(3, 0)$, $(-2, 5)$, $(-3, 0)$, $(2, -2)$, $(-3, -1)$, $(0, -4)$.
   (b) Plot the points whose coordinates are given in (a) with respect to a reference system in which the axes form an angle of $45°$.

2. In a non-homogeneous Cartesian coordinate system in a 5-dimensional Euclidean space, how many of each of the following occur:
   (a) coordinate axes, (b) coordinate hyperplanes, (c) planes through pairs of axes, (d) three-flats through sets of three axes?

3. In a rectangular coordinate system, plot the points $P:(3, 4)$ and cP for $c = 2, 3$. What is the relationship among these three points?

4. Determine the linear combination of the two points $P_1:(1, 3)$ and $P_2:(2, 4)$ for $t_1 = 3$, $t_2 = -2$. Plot these three points.

5. Determine the linear combination of the three points $P_1:(1, 3, 4)$, $P_2:(2, 1, 5)$, and $P_3:(3, -2, -1)$ for $t_1 = 2$, $t_2 = -3$, and $t_3 = 1$.

6. Show that the three points $P_1:(1, 2)$, $P_2:(3, 4)$, $P_3:(5, 1)$ are linearly dependent by employing the conditions (4.3). Express the coordinates of P_3 explicitly as linear combinations of the coordinates of P_1 and P_2.

7. (a) By use of Theorem 4.1 determine the number of linearly independent points in the set of four points of exercise 5.
   (b) What is the smallest space containing these four points?
   (c) For the set of three points of exercise 6, how many are linearly independent and what is the smallest space containing them?

8. Given two points $P_1:(3, 4)$ and $P_2:(4, 1)$ in a rectangular Cartesian coordinate system, find (a) $D(OP_1)$, (b) $D(OP_2)$, (c) $D(P_1P_2)$.

9. Write equations (4.22) for the rotation about the origin:
   (a) in the plane; (b) in ordinary space.

10. (a) In a rectangular coordinate system, find the direction cosines of the straight line through the origin and the point P:(4, 3).
    (b) Find the sum of the squares of the direction cosines.

11. (a) In a four dimensional rectangular coordinate system, find the direction cosines of a line through the origin and the point P:(.4, .2, .1, $-.2$).
    (b) Find the sum of the squares of the direction cosines.

12. Find the angle between the line of exercise 11 and the line going through the origin and the point Q:(.5, .6, .4, .2).

13. Find the scalar product of the two vectors of exercise 12.

14. (a) Given two points P_1:(0, 4) and P_2:(3, 0) in a reference system in which the axes form an angle of 60°, find $D(P_1 P_2)$.
    (b) Find the distance between two points with the preceding coordinates in a rectangular reference system.
    (c) Plot these points employing the same horizontal line for the first axis in each case and the same origin. Verify the distances.

Exercises 15–19 are based upon the data of Table II.

Table II

Values of Two Variables for Three Individuals

Individual i	X_{1i}	X_{2i}
1	1	2
2	5	2
3	6	8

15. Exhibit the point representation and also the vector representation of the data.

16. Obtain the lengths of the vectors representing the variables.

17. Calculate the direction cosines of these vectors.

18. (a) Find the angle of separation of these vectors.
    (b) Determine the coefficient of correlation by use of formula (4.48).

19. Check the value of the correlation coefficient by employing the standardized values in formula (2.7).

Exercises 20–22 are based upon the data of Table I.

20. Are the two columns of the pattern matrix linearly independent?

21. What is the rank of the reproduced correlation matrix $\hat{R}$ (determined in ex. 25, chap. 2)?

22. What subset of variables would give a correlation matrix of rank one?

Exercises 23–25 are based upon the data of Table III.

Table III

Coefficients of Two Uncorrelated Common Factors

Variable	F_1	F_2
1	.86	.43
2	.48	.24
3	.70	.35
4	.50	.25
5	.64	.32
6	.56	.28

23. Plot the points representing the six variables in the common factor space.

24. (a) Are the two columns of the pattern matrix linearly independent?
    (b) Do all the second order minors vanish?
    (c) Why can these six variables be described in terms of only one common factor?

25. Obtain a factor solution in terms of only one common factor, calculating the factor weights: (a) from the plot of exercise 23; (b) by employing formula (4.52).

26. Given the following portion of an orthogonal factor pattern:

$$\tilde{z}_1 = .4F_1 + .2F_2 + .1F_3 - .2F_4,$$
$$\tilde{z}_2 = .5F_1 + .6F_2 + .4F_3 + .2F_4.$$

Calculate:
(a) the correlation corrected for uniqueness;
(b) the reproduced correlation, as the scalar product of the two vectors in the common-factor space;
(c) the reproduced correlation, as the cosine of the angle between the two vectors in the total factor space.

CHAPTER 5

1. In a properly designed experiment with expected relationships among the correlations (i.e., not arbitrary or independent), how would you use Table 5.2 to find the smallest number of variables required to determine:
   (a) four factors,
   (b) six factors?

2. Why is it not desirable to employ only eleven variables to determine six factors?

Problems and Exercises

Exercises 3–6 are based upon the data of Table IV, Set A:

Table IV

Intercorrelations of Two Sets of Five Variables

Variable	Set A					Set B				
	1	2	3	4	5	1	2	3	4	5
1		.48	.56	.32	.40		.64	.78	.67	.91
2	.48		.42	.24	.30	.64		.66	.68	.77
3	.56	.42		.28	.35	.78	.66		.66	.84
4	.32	.24	.28		.20	.67	.68	.66		.77
5	.40	.30	.35	.20		.91	.77	.84	.77	

3. Show that the five variables can be described in terms of only one common factor by employing the conditions (5.9).

4. (a) Calculate the communality of the first variable by means of equations (5.8).
   (b) Why are the numerical values of the six distinct expressions of (5.8) exactly equal?

5. For a given variable, how many different (a) tetrads and (b) triads are there?

6. Obtain the coefficients of the common factor.

7. Assume a matrix of correlations among five variables, with unknown communalities h_j^2 ($j = 1, \cdots, 5$). Equations (5.9) constitute five linearly independent conditions that the correlations must satisfy if the five variables are to be described in terms of only one common factor. Equations (5.9) were obtained as a result of formally solving for h_1^2. Obtain an equivalent set of equations by solving for h_2^2, and show that they are linear combinations of equations (5.9).

Exercises 8–13 are based upon the data of Table IV, Set B:

8. Test the set of correlations to see if the five variables can be described in terms of only one common factor:
   (a) Calculate the communalities under the assumption that the rank of the correlation matrix is one.
   (b) Write the factor pattern.
   (c) Calculate the matrix of reproduced correlations.
   (d) Calculate the residuals.

9. Show that the intercorrelations of the five variables satisfy the condition (5.15) exactly.

10. Calculate the communalities under the assumption that the rank of the correlation matrix is two.

398

11. Obtain a solution in terms of two common factors. Hint: Select one of the factor coefficients, say, a_{11}, arbitrarily.

12. Check that the correlations are reproduced exactly by the solution of exercise 11.

13. Discuss the relative merits of the solutions in exercises 8 and 11 considering the data (a) as exact, (b) as observations subject to fluctuations of sampling.

14. Check that the rank of the correlation matrix in Table V can appropriately be assumed to be equal to two.

Table V

Intercorrelations of Six Physical Variables for 305 Girls

Variable	1	2	3	4	5	6
1. Height						
2. Length lower leg	.859					
3. Sitting height	.740	.451				
4. Weight	.473	.436	.507			
5. Chest girth	.301	.327	.327	.730		
6. Chest depth	.201	.227	.211	.611	.484	

15. Calculate the communalities of the variables in Table V by means of formula (5.18).

16. Calculate the communalities for the eight political variables of Table 8.7.

17. Why are communalities put in the principal diagonal of a correlation matrix?

18. Make an outline of various methods that may be employed in estimating communalities, and comment on their relative merits.

19. The communalities of the five fictitious variables of Table IV, Set B were computed under the assumption of unit rank in exercise 8, and under the assumption of rank 2 in exercise 10. Compare these values with the "arbitrary estimates" given by:
    (a) the highest correlation for each variable;
    (b) the average correlation;
    (c) the single triad, formula (5.31).
    Also compare these values with the "complete estimates" given by:
    (d) the first centroid factor, formula (5.34).

20. Determine the estimates of communality (a), (b), (c), and (d), as in exercise 19, for the six physical variables of Table V and compare with the communalities computed in exercise 15, under the assumption of rank 2.

CHAPTER 6

1. The following questions are intended to be provocative and for general class discussion.
    (a) Why can a set of variables be interpreted in terms of a factorial solution involving correlated or uncorrelated factors?
    (b) What are some advantages in employing uncorrelated factors?
    (c) How may several workers arrive at the same factorial solution for a given matrix of correlations?
    (d) How can one judge the relative significance of the factors of a given solution.
    (e) Why would the uni-factor solution be the most desirable form? Why is this form not likely to be obtained with observed data?
    (f) Why is a more complex solution than the uni-factor type likely to furnish a more satisfactory description of observed data?
    (g) Why is the multiple-factor solution formulated so as not to include a general factor?
    (h) How may the selectivity of the sample affect the intercorrelations of a set of variables, and the subsequent factorial analysis?
    (i) Can a new variable be added to a given set without changing the factorial solution of the original portion?
    (j) When new variables are added to a set for which a factorial solution has been obtained, is any one of the preferred forms likely to be more "invariant" than the others?
    (k) How would you justify the co-existence of several preferred solutions for a given body of data? How would you make a choice among them?

2. Give illustrations, other than those in the text, in which bipolar factors furnish more convenient interpretations than those with all positive coefficients.

3. (a) What happens to the factorial composition of a variable when its scale is reversed?
    (b) What is the effect on the reproduced correlations when all the coefficients of any factor are multiplied by -1?

CHAPTER 7

Exercises 1–2 are based upon the correlations among the variables 5, 6, 7, 8, 9 in Table 7.4:

1. Assume rank one for the matrix of correlations, and calculate a "two-factor" pattern by means of formula (7.7).

2. (a) Compute the residuals.
    (b) Check the significance of these residuals, by use of Table A in Appendix (justifying the assumption of exercise 1).

3. Obtain another permissible solution (with more than one common factor) for the correlation matrix of Table 7.2 which led to the Heywood case.

4. Consider a set of ten variables $(z_1, z_2, \cdots, z_{10})$ grouped as follows:

$$G_1 = (1, 2, 3,), \quad G_2 = (4, 5, 6, 7,), \quad G_3 = (8, 9, 10,).$$

Use the set theory notations of (7.8) to express the following:
(a) variable 6 is included in group 2;
(b) the system of elements consisting of variables 1, 2, 3 and 8, 9, 10;
(c) the sum of the first 100 values of variable 5.

Exercises 5–13 are based upon the data of Table VI.

Table VI

Intercorrelations of Twelve Psychological Tests for 355 Pupils

Variable	1	2	3	4	5	6	7	8	9	10	11	12
1. Perception of brightness												
2. Counting dots	.690											
3. Straight and curved letters	.596	.655										
4. Speed in simple code	.515	.557	.600									
5. Verbal completion	.421	.397	.386	.255								
6. Understanding paragraphs	.350	.300	.252	.200	.611							
7. Reading vocabulary	.376	.349	.329	.258	.642	.576						
8. General information	.405	.448	.351	.310	.660	.545	.738					
9. Arithmetic proportions	.342	.381	.284	.241	.407	.428	.435	.478				
10. Permutations-combinations	.325	.377	.324	.286	.359	.407	.392	.385	.460			
11. Mechanical ability I	.260	.285	.255	.252	.321	.370	.408	.379	.406	.384		
12. Mechanical ability II	.165	.200	.146	.145	.162	.236	.303	.285	.278	.213	.398	

Source: Holzinger (1936, No. 9, Table 2).

5. From the definition in **7.4**, calculate the following *B*-coefficients and interpret the results: (a) *B* (1, 2, 3); (b) *B* (1, 6, 12).

6. Starting with the *B*-coefficient of exercise 5(a), determine *B* (1, 2, 3, 4) by means of the following steps:
(a) Denote the sums in the calculation of *B* (1, 2, 3) by S_3 and T_3.
(b) Add test 4 to the group and determine L_4 by formula (7.15).
(c) Calculate S_4 and T_4 by means of (7.16) and (7.17).
(d) Employing the results of (c), calculate *B* (1, 2, 3, 4) by means of formula (7.13).

7. Allocate the twelve tests to appropriate groups, employing the *B*-coefficient technique as outlined in Table 7.5.

8. Make a bi-factor pattern plan, using the groups determined in the last exercise.

9. Write formula (7.21) for the determination of the general-factor coefficient for the first variable: (a) in the set theory notation, (b) in the conventional summation

401

notation, indicating the limits, (c) in expanded form, indicating the individual correlations.

10. Calculate the general-factor coefficients.

11. Obtain the general-factor residuals and check the satisfactoriness of the pattern plan.

12. (a) Calculate the group-factor coefficients, and write the complete factor pattern.
    (b) Determine the communalities.

13. Obtain the final residuals and test the adequacy of the solution.

Exercises 14–18 are based upon the data of Table VII.

Table VII

Correlations and Portion of Bi-Factor Solution for Five Physical Variables for 305 Girls

Variable	Correlations (r_{jk})					General Factor F_0	Residuals ($\dot{r}_{jk}$)				
	1	2	3	4	5		1	2	3	4	5
1. Height						.691					
2. Arm span	.846					.591	.438				
3. Length of forearm	.805	.881				.581	.404	.538			
4. Length of lower leg	.859	.826	.801			.598	.446	.473	.454		
5. Sitting height	.740	.497	.494	.451		.674	.274	.099	.102	.048	

Source: Mullen (1939, p. 20).

14. In a study (Mullen 1939) involving 17 physical variables the five variables of Table VII were found to belong together according to their B-coefficient, and a bi-factor pattern was postulated with a general physical (or growth) factor F_0 and a group factor F_1 through these variables. Given the general-factor coefficients and the residuals, determine whether the original hypothesis of a single group factor for the five variables is warranted. Proceed as follows:
    (a) Compute the B-coefficients of variable 5 with each of the other four variables, one at a time, employing the residuals.
    (b) Compute the B-coefficients of variable 5 with all combinations of the other four variables, two at a time.
    (c) Compute the B-coefficients of variable 5 with all combinations of the other four variables, three at a time.
    (d) Compute B (1, 2, 3, 4).
    (e) What conclusion may be drawn from the contrast of (d) and the preceding B-coefficients?

15. Test the statistical significance of the general-factor residuals for variable 5, employing an average correlation $r = .355$ (based on all 17 variables and $N = 305$ of the original study).

16. Formulate a revised pattern plan for the five variables, based upon the findings in exercises 14 and 15.

17. Determine the new group-factor coefficients.

18. Assuming a doublet factor for variables 1 and 5, and allowing one standard error for chance error, why cannot the remaining variance be divided equally between the two variables?

CHAPTER 8

1. In earlier editions of this text, when more emphasis was placed on hand computing, eight separate exercises were given for obtaining a principal-factor solution for the data of Table V using the communalities determined in ex. 15, chap. 5. Now, with the aid of a computer: (a) get the first two principal factors for these data; (b) calculate the residuals with two factors removed; (c) check the properties (8.18).

2. Compute the principal-factor solution for the six hypothetical variables of Table 5.4, employing the "actual" communalities of Table 5.5. What is exceptional about the six eigenvalues?

3. Obtain the first two principal factors for the eight physical variables example of Table 2.3, employing the SMC's (determined in ex. 21, chap. 5) for the diagonal values of the correlation matrix. Compare the results with the solution in Table 8.4 for which communalities were employed.

CHAPTER 9

1. Starting with the objective function (9.9) for the sum of squares of residual correlations with a fixed variable j, derive a formula for the minres solution for the case of $m = 1$ (i.e., a single common factor).

2. For the five hypothetical variables of Table 7.2:
   (a) Obtain a minres solution in terms of one factor, using the formulas derived in the preceding exercise.
   (b) Compare the minres solution (after 3 iterations) with the original Heywood solution, in terms of the residuals and of the size of the objective function.

3. For the problem of five socio-economic variables, apply the asymptotic χ^2 test to determine the significance of one, two, and three factors at the .1%, 1%, and 5% levels. While the illustrative example actually contains only 12 cases, and the approximations made in arriving at the statistic (9.31) assumed a large sample, nonetheless as an exercise apply the tests for $N = 12, 50, 100, 200$. (The necessary determinants were produced by a computer as follows: $|\mathbf{R}| = .0016908$ for the

original correlations; and $|\hat{\mathbf{R}}_1| = .1273853, |\hat{\mathbf{R}}_2| = .0023976, |\hat{\mathbf{R}}_3| = .0016908$ for the reproduced correlations for minres solutions with $m = 1, 2, 3$, respectively.)

4. Obtain a minres solution, with $m = 2$, for the six hypothetical variables of Table 5.4.

CHAPTER 10

1. For the binomial distribution

$$f(X; p) = p^X(1 - p)^{1-X} \qquad\qquad (X = 0, 1)$$

involving samples of size N, a particular set of observations $X_1, X_2, \cdots X_N$ consists of a sequence of zeros and ones. Suppose that in a sample of $N = 100$ a total of 18 successes were noted. Determine the following for this case:
(a) The likelihood function L (i.e., the joint distribution of the sample values).
(b) The logarithm (to base e) of L.
(c) The derivative of log L with respect to p.
(d) The maximum-likelihood estimator $\hat{p}$.

Exercises 2 and 3 are based on the data of Table 7.1, and employ the computing procedures of **10.5**.

2. Since Spearman used these data to demonstrate the two-factor theory, it is reasonable to hypothesize a single common factor and to take the general-factor coefficients from Table 7.1 as first approximations for the calculation of maximum-likelihood estimates. Set up a worksheet in the form of Table 10.2, but for $m = 1$, and determine: (a) the first iteration; (b) additional iterations, as necessary, to obtain convergence of the factor weights.

3. Test the hypothesis of $m = 1$, proceeding as follows:
   (a) calculate the reproduced correlations and residuals, and determine the sum for formula (10.29);
   (b) complete the calculation of U_1;
   (c) determine the number of degrees of freedom;
   (d) for this number of degrees of freedom, what value of χ^2 produces a probability of $P = .01$?
   (e) how does the actual U_1 compare with this value?
   (f) what conclusion may be drawn regarding the hypothesis?

4. For the five socio-economic variables the observed correlations are given in Table 2.2 and the maximum-likelihood solution, under the hypothesis of $m = 2$, is in Table 10.5. Test this hypothesis.

Exercises 5–8 are based on the data of Table V. Although it is reasonable to assume two common factors for these data (see ex. 14, chap. 5), other assumptions are made for the sake of exercise.

5. Obtain a maximum-likelihood solution under the assumption $m = 1$, employing the coefficients of the first principal factor (ex. 1, chap. 8) as first approximations.

6. Since the natural choice of ex. 5 for first approximations to the maximum-likelihood loadings led to lengthy computations, start with the following trial values to see how soon convergence is obtained:

Exercise	1	2	3	4	5	6
a	1.000	.800	.700	.600	.500	.400
b	.900	.700	.600	.500	.400	.300
c	.950	.850	.750	.500	.350	.250

(In order to get the full value of the convergence problem indicated in exs. 5 and 6, without requiring the laborious calculations on the part of each student, it is suggested that teams be formed and the work shared.)

7. Test the hypothesis of $m = 1$.

8. Assume $m = 2$ and take as starting values the principal-factor coefficients from ex. 1, chap. 8, to set up a worksheet like Table 10.2 and carry through one complete iteration.

9. If a computer and a suitable program are available, obtain a maximum-likelihood solution for the twenty-four psychological tests for $m = 5$ factors. How does it compare with the minres results of Table 9.5?

CHAPTER 11

Since the methods developed in **11.2, 11.3**, and **11.4** require a computer for the calculations, the student can use the illustrative examples in the text for checking out any programs. No additional problems are provided for this purpose. The following exercises are designed for practice in applying the multiple-group method, and are based on the data for the eight physical variables:

1. Set up the reduced correlation matrix by employing the correlations from Table 2.3 and the communalities from Table 5.3. Assume the previously determined grouping of variables:

G_1:(1, 2, 3, 4), lankiness; G_2:(5, 6, 7, 8), stockiness.

Determine the sums (11.33).

2. Obtain the sums (11.34) of correlations between groups and calculate the standard deviations of the composite variables according to (11.37).

3. Calculate the correlation between the two oblique factors, T_1 and T_2, by means of (11.40).

4. Determine the oblique factor structure, the elements of which are given by (11.41).

5. Obtain the oblique factor pattern and the orthogonal factor matrix by setting up a worksheet like Table 11.7 and following the instructions given therein.

6. Compute the reproduced correlations by employing the orthogonal factor matrix and check the results by using the oblique structure and pattern.

7. Show the residuals. Are these residuals of the order of magnitude of final residuals of previous solutions? What percent of the original communality assumed in exercise 1 is accounted for by two multiple-group factors?

CHAPTER 12

1. The multiple-factor solution (Table 12.2) for the thirteen psychological tests was obtained by graphical methods, considering two factors at a time, as described in **12.2**. Check the coefficients for z_1 and z_{13} in the multiple-factor pattern of Table 12.2 by applying the complete transformation matrix to the original centroid pattern of Table 8.15.

2. When a multiple-factor solution is obtained by intuitive-graphical methods it is not expected that a particular solution obtained by one worker could be replicated by another, or by the same individual at another time. As exercises in applying the methods of **12.2**, the eight, thirteen, and twenty-four variable examples can be employed, with independent graphing and calculations, and checked against the results obtained in the text.

3. Rotate the minres solution of ex. 4, chap. 9 to "simple structure" by the hand methods of **12.2**. Compare the results with the direct solution of Table 5.7.

4. Compare the primary-factor solution (Table 12.3) for the eight physical variables with the multiple-group solution given in the table of ex. 5, chap. 11.

Exercises 5–12 are designed for practice in obtaining a primary-factor solution according to the outline in **12.4**, and employ the thirteen psychological tests with the initial centroid solution of Table 8.15.

5. Available information about these data (chap. 7) suggest the three composite variables:

$$v_1 = z_1 + z_2 + z_3 + z_4$$
$$v_2 = z_5 + z_6 + z_7 + z_8 + z_9$$
$$v_3 = z_{10} + z_{11} + z_{12} + z_{13}$$

Calculate the standard deviations of these composite variables.

6. Express the composite variables (standardized) in terms of the factors of the initial solution.

7. Determine the distances of the three composite points from the origin.

8. Obtain the transformation matrix from the centroid factors (C_p) to the primary factors (T_p).

9. Calculate the correlations among the primary factors by use of formula (12.17).

10. Obtain the primary-factor structure by applying (12.18).

11. Obtain the primary-factor pattern by using the computing algorithm of Table 12.4.

12. Determine the contributions of the primary factors according to formulas (12.23) and (12.24).

13. Develop formula (12.31) starting with (12.30).

14. Set up a worksheet like Table 12.4 and show the detailed calculations for the pattern **W** of the oblique reference solution of Table 12.5.

CHAPTER 13

1. Compute the sum of fourth powers of the factor loadings for the eight physical variables in the graphical solution of Table 12.1, and compare with the value for the analytical solution of Table 13.2.

2. (a) Using the principal-factor solution (Table 8.8) for the eight political variables as the initial matrix **A**, compute the quartimax solution.
   (b) Compare the quartimax criterion of the final solution with that of the initial solution.

3. Compute the varimax criterion V for the quartimax solution for the eight physical variables (Table 13.2), and compare the result with the values for the graphical solution (Table 12.1) and the varimax solution (Table 13.5).

4. (a) Starting with the principal-factor solution for the eight political variables (Table 8.8), compute the corresponding varimax solution.
   (b) Compare the varimax criterion for the initial and the final solutions.

5. Compute the root-mean-square values for the differences between the following pairs of solutions for the eight physical variables:

   (a) Varimax and Subjective
   (b) Varimax and Quartimax
   (c) Quartimax and Subjective.

CHAPTER 14

1. Compute the oblimax criterion K for the centroid solution of the eight physical variables (initial solution **A** in Table 14.3).

2. Show that the value of the quartimin criterion N for the factor structure of Table 12.5 does not differ significantly from the value for the quartimin solution of Table 14.3, although the minres solution served as the starting point for the former while the centroid solution was used in the latter.

3. The quartimin solution (obtained on a desk calculator) for the eight political variables is shown in Table 14.8. The initial matrix **A** is the principal-factor solution of Table 8.8. Determine the final quartimin solution through the following procedures of **14.3**:

   (a) Select the first column (i.e., $x = 1$) of the transformation matrix Λ to initiate the iteration process and determine the values w_j for $p \neq 1$.

   (b) Employing the values from (a) for the diagonal matrix **W**, determine the matrix **C**.

   (c) Write the characteristic equation and solve for the least root $N_x(x = 1)$.

   (d) Obtain the values of λ_{11} and λ_{21}.

   (e) Determine the new elements v_{j1} resulting from the first iteration.

   (f) Select $x = 2$ for the second iteration and repeat the process (a)–(e), arriving at new elements v_{j2}.

   (g) Perform as many iterations as necessary, alternating between $x = 1$ and $x = 2$, until the value of N converges (to the minimum of $N = .1819$ as indicated in the text). Write the final transformation matrix.

   (h) Verify a few entries in the final structure matrix **V** by applying (14.1) with the transformation matrix determined in (g).

4. Calculate the following matrices for determining the primary-factor pattern corresponding to the structure **V** in Table 14.3.

   (a) The inverse of the transformation matrix Λ.

   (b) The transformation matrix **T**.

   (c) The diagonal matrix **D**.

   (d) The primary-factor pattern **P**.

   Also calculate:

   (e) The correlation between the two primary factors.

Problems 5–7 are based on the first two principal components (see Table 8.1) for the five socio-economic variables as the initial factor matrix **A**, and certain results produced by a computer.

5. Get the quartimin primary-factor pattern corresponding to the reference structure matrix

$$
\mathbf{V} = \begin{bmatrix}
-.0954 & .9857 \\
.9359 & -.1142 \\
.0264 & .9585 \\
.7695 & .3519 \\
.9628 & -.1145
\end{bmatrix},
$$

and the transformation matrix

$$
\Lambda = \begin{pmatrix}
.7515 & .4758 \\
-.6597 & .8795
\end{pmatrix}.
$$

6. Get the biquartimin primary-factor pattern corresponding to the reference structure matrix

$$V = \begin{bmatrix} -.0366 & .9909 \\ .9399 & -.0669 \\ .0850 & .9697 \\ .8000 & .3954 \\ .9672 & -.0658 \end{bmatrix},$$

and the transformation matrix

$$\Lambda = \begin{pmatrix} .7893 & .5196 \\ -.6140 & .8544 \end{pmatrix}.$$

7. Determine the common-factor variance of variable 1 from the primary-factor pattern found in ex. 5 and compare it with the value from the initial factor matrix **A**.

8. The quartimin reference structure for the eight physical variables is given in Table 14.4. This solution, based on the minres initial matrix of Table 9.2, was produced by a computer which also gave the transformation matrix

$$\Lambda = \begin{pmatrix} .6032 & .4052 \\ -.7976 & .9142 \end{pmatrix}.$$

Obtain the quartimin primary-factor pattern corresponding to this reference structure.

9. The reference structure **V** in Table 14.5 was computed on an electronic computer. One of the outputs of the computer program is the transformation matrix:

$$\Lambda = \begin{bmatrix} .3520 & .2699 & .3684 & .2944 \\ -.6047 & .5822 & -.3846 & .5051 \\ -.6432 & -.4960 & .6839 & .3712 \\ .3109 & -.5849 & -.4985 & .7214 \end{bmatrix}.$$

(a) Obtain the inverse of **Λ**. First apply the square root method of **3.4** to the symmetric matrix

$$\Psi = \Lambda'\Lambda$$

to get Ψ^{-1}, and then the desired result follows from (14.32).

(b) Determine the diagonal matrix **D**, i.e., the normalizing factors of the rows of Λ^{-1}.

(c) Determine the transformation matrix **T** for the primary-factor solution.

Problems 10–13 are based on the 3-variable example employed by Jennrich and Sampson (1966) for which they assume the following initial pattern matrix (in terms of orthogonal factors):

$$A = \begin{bmatrix} .960 & .140 \\ .480 & .070 \\ -.560 & .300 \end{bmatrix}.$$

10. Get the value of the criterion (14.33) for the initial factor pattern for each of the following values of the parameter δ:

$$0, \ -.5, \ -1, \ -5, \ .1, \ .5, \ .8, \ 1.$$

11. Normalize matrix **A** by rows, and determine the value of the criterion function for $\delta = 0$ in this case.

12. Plot the three variables with reference to the orthogonal common-factor axes. What is special about these points?

13. For $\delta = 0$, a computer produced the following factor pattern:

j	b_{j1}	b_{j2}
1	.97015	.00000
2	.48508	.00000
3	.00000	.63530

The correlation between the primary factors is $-.80411$.
(a) What is the value of the criterion function for this solution?
(b) Determine the primary-factor structure for this solution.

Problems 14–15 are based on the minres solution (Table 9.1) for the five socio-economic variables as the initial factor matrix **A**.

14. Compute the criterion (14.33) for **A**, with $\delta = 0$.

15. Normalize matrix **A** by rows and, for $\delta = 0$, determine the initial value of the criterion function and the final value after the function has been minimized. Show the complete direct oblimin ($\delta = 0$) solution. (This exercise requires the use of a computer, and may be useful as a test case.)

16. In spite of the fact that an independent clusters orthoblique solution for the 20-variable box problem must be expected to fit poorly (the variables were explicitly designed by Thurstone to be complex and not fall into clusters), obtain such a solution and contrast it with the proportional orthoblique of Table 14.16.

CHAPTER 15

1. Determine the transformation matrix **T** in (15.1) for the twenty-four psychological tests when **A** is the biquartimin pattern (Table 14.5) and **B** is the quartimax pattern (Table 13.3).

2. Employing the transformation equation (15.1), calculate $b_{11}, b_{12}, b_{13}, b_{14}, b_{53}, b_{24,4}$ and compare the results with the original values in Table 13.3.

The remaining exercises of this chapter are based upon the data of Table VIII (Harman et al. 1975, Technical Report No. 6). The portion of the study selected for these exercises consists of the correlations among 12 self-report temperament scales

Table VIII

Correlations among Twelve Temperament Scales*

Scale	1	2	3	4	5	6	7	8	9	10	11	12
1. Ca 1		.614	.688	−.072	.157	.068	.469	.392	.430	.059	.116	.207
2. Ca 2	.705		.471	−.046	.166	.158	.502	.450	.372	.132	.110	.210
3. Ca 3	.684	.626		−.102	.056	.114	.385	.305	.276	.085	.148	.107
4. Om 1	.123	.186	.037		.428	.333	−.013	.028	.069	.251	.203	.116
5. Om 2	.190	.309	.268	.580		.273	.150	.156	.190	.307	.220	.319
6. Om 3	.300	.448	.267	.500	.447		.130	.130	.093	.288	.208	.086
7. Sc 1	.433	.654	.426	.300	.349	.495		.658	.558	.151	.220	.158
8. Sc 2	.423	.600	.462	.370	.394	.477	.662		.532	.128	.160	.133
9. Sc 3	.435	.567	.392	.281	.342	.391	.598	.587		.232	.270	.247
10. To 1	.202	.157	.075	.148	.142	.273	.109	.140	.204		.449	.408
11. To 2	.197	.267	.260	.274	.356	.307	.249	.098	.275	.274		.418
12. To 3	.188	.200	.253	.394	.499	.398	.277	.220	.291	.311	.305	

*College sample correlations are in the upper triangle; Navy sample correlations are in the lower triangle.

for two samples (Navy recruits and College students). Three scales were constructed to measure each of four postulated factors, namely:

Ca = Calmness
Om = Open-mindedness
Sc = Self-confidence
To = Tolerance

and are designated in Table VIII in a manner to bring out this design. Minres factorizations for $m = 4$ factors were obtained for each sample and were rotated according to the varimax criterion to yield the results in Table IX.

3. Following the procedure of **15.4**, and with the use of a computer, obtain the best orthogonal matching factor weights and the transformation matrices that carry the varimax solutions into them.

4. With the aid of a computer, perform an oblique procrustes rotation on the twelve temperament scales for the Navy sample and the College sample, using the varimax solutions of Table IX as the original input matrices.

CHAPTER 16

1. In **16.3** the measurements of the rotated varimax components for the five socio-economic variables were obtained by use of (16.7). The same results can be obtained by use of (16.12); show the computations leading to the two equations by means of the latter formula.

2. Designate by **L** the $m \times m$ matrix in (16.47) that requires inversion, namely:

$$\mathbf{L} = (\mathbf{\Phi}^{-1} + \mathbf{A}'\mathbf{U}^{-2}\mathbf{A}),$$

and prove that it is symmetric.

Table IX

Varimax Solutions for Twelve Temperament Scales:
Navy and College Samples

(Initial solutions: Minres)

	Navy: $_N\mathbf{A}$				College: $_C\mathbf{A}$			
	$_NF_1$	$_NF_2$	$_NF_3$	$_NF_4$	$_CF_1$	$_CF_2$	$_CF_3$	$_CF_4$
1. Ca 1	.355	.048	.700	.165	.261	.917	.069	.029
2. Ca 2	.616	.111	.598	.106	.403	.557	.102	.067
3. Ca 3	.242	.139	.834	−.003	.211	.677	.078	−.017
4. Om 1	.290	.678	−.112	.050	−.020	−.125	.096	.766
5. Om 2	.204	.788	.136	−.013	.090	.094	.273	.526
6. Om 3	.455	.481	.108	.220	.085	.068	.151	.438
7. Sc 1	.733	.226	.268	.045	.769	.298	.117	.042
8. Sc 2	.758	.234	.232	−.013	.774	.207	.053	.090
9. Sc 3	.595	.228	.278	.158	.585	.238	.253	.082
10. To 1	.075	.160	.051	.719	.092	.006	.614	.283
11. To 2	.066	.388	.214	.274	.144	.040	.614	.169
12. To 3	.094	.571	.145	.267	.073	.137	.624	.108

3. The quartimin solution for the eight physical variables consists of the reference structure (in Table 14.3) and the primary-factor pattern which was determined in ex. 4, chap. 14. Starting with this factor pattern and correlation of .483 between the primary factors, compute the regression weights for these factors by using the method of **16.5**.

4. Let the $m \times n$ matrix of coefficients in (16.52) be defined by:

$$\mathbf{\Gamma} = \mathbf{J}^{-1}\mathbf{A}'\mathbf{U}^{-2}$$

where the special type of "regression" coefficients are designated γ's to distinguish them from the conventional β's. Prove that this matrix when postmultiplied by the factor-structure matrix produces the matrix of correlations among the factors, namely:

$$\mathbf{\Gamma S} = \mathbf{\Phi}.$$

5. Verify the relationship proven in ex. 4 for the eight physical variables example for which the matrix of coefficients $\mathbf{\Gamma}$ is in Table 16.8 and the structure matrix $\mathbf{S}$ is in Table 12.3.

6. Prove that the factors estimated by the modified method of (16.56) are orthogonal by formally carrying out the matrix product $\mathbf{\hat{F}\hat{F}'}$.

Answers

1. Discussion in **2.4**.　　　　　　2. For computational convenience.

3. $\hat{z}_1 = a_{11}F_1 + a_{12}F_2 + u_1Y_1,$
$\hat{z}_2 = a_{21}F_1 + a_{22}F_2 \qquad\quad + u_2Y_2,$
$\hat{z}_3 = a_{31}F_1 + a_{32}F_2 \qquad\qquad\quad + u_3Y_3,$
$\hat{z}_4 = a_{41}F_1 + a_{42}F_2 \qquad\qquad\qquad\quad + u_4Y_4,$
$\hat{z}_5 = a_{51}F_1 + a_{52}F_2 \qquad\qquad\qquad\qquad\qquad u_5Y_5.$

4. (a) The a's and u's; (b) 15.　　　　5. (a) .25, .64; (b) a_{21}^2, a_{22}^2.

6. $a_{11}^2 + a_{21}^2 + a_{31}^2 + a_{41}^2 + a_{51}^2$ and $a_{12}^2 + a_{22}^2 + a_{32}^2 + a_{42}^2 + a_{52}^2$.

7. $h_1^2 = .89$.

8. Reliability $= 1 - e^2 = h^2 + b^2 \geqq h^2$.

9. The given quantities are x'd out.

Variance Component	Formula	a	b	c	d	e	f	g	h
Specificity	$b^2 = u^2 - e^2$	×	×	×	×	.35	.35	.25	.20
Error variance	$e^2 = 1 - r = u^2 - b^2$	×	.10	.15	.15	×	×	.25	.10
Communality	$h^2 = 1 - u^2$	.70	×	.65	.60	×	.55	×	.70
Uniqueness	$u^2 = 1 - h^2 = b^2 + e^2$	.30	.25	×	.40	.40	×	.50	×
Reliability	$r = 1 - e^2$	.80	.90	.85	×	.95	.90	×	×

10. $h_8^2 = .85$.　　　　　　　　　　11. z_4 (since $h_4^2 = 1.00$).

12. z_6 (since $h_6^2 = .25$).　　　　　13. $u_1^2 = .42$.

14. z_4 (since $u_4^2 = 0$).　　　　　　15. z_6 (since $u_6^2 = .75$).

16. Yes, F_1.   17. Yes, F_2.

18. $\sum_{j=1}^{8} a_{j1}^2 = 3.72$, $\sum_{j=1}^{8} a_{j2}^2 = 1.22$.   19. 46.50% and 15.25%.

20. 75.3% and 24.7%.   21. $z_5 = .6F_1 + .5F_2 + .48S_5 + .4E_5$.

22. $C_5 = 72.6\%$.   23. 2, 1.

24. $\hat{r}_{12} = .56$, $\hat{r}_{14} = .74$, $\hat{r}_{25} = .48$, $\hat{r}_{26} = .40$.

25. No.

CHAPTER 3

1. 14.   2. 26.   3. -2.   4. -15.   5. 139.   6. 0.

7. 1.   8. 2.   9. 2.   10. Singular. 11. **C**.   12. 1.

13. (a) $\mathbf{A}' = \begin{bmatrix} a_{11} & a_{21} & a_{31} & a_{41} & a_{51} \\ a_{12} & a_{22} & a_{32} & a_{42} & a_{52} \end{bmatrix}$

(b) $\mathbf{A}' = \begin{bmatrix} .7 & .8 & .7 & .8 & .6 & .5 & .6 & .7 \\ .3 & 0 & 0 & .6 & .5 & 0 & .4 & .6 \end{bmatrix}$

14. (a) $\hat{\mathbf{R}} = \begin{bmatrix} .89 & .64 & .78 & .67 & .91 \\ .64 & .73 & .66 & .68 & .77 \\ .78 & .66 & .72 & .66 & .84 \\ .67 & .68 & .66 & .65 & .77 \\ .91 & .77 & .84 & .77 & .98 \end{bmatrix}$

15. (a) $\hat{\mathbf{R}} = \begin{bmatrix} 1.00 & .99 & .99 & .92 & .97 \\ .99 & 1.00 & .97 & .96 & .99 \\ .99 & .97 & 1.00 & .87 & .93 \\ .92 & .96 & .87 & 1.00 & .99 \\ .97 & .99 & .93 & .99 & 1.00 \end{bmatrix}$

16. (a) $\mathbf{AB} = \begin{bmatrix} 4 & 7 \\ 8 & 15 \end{bmatrix}$, $\mathbf{BA} = \begin{bmatrix} 3 & 4 \\ 11 & 16 \end{bmatrix}$;

(b) $|\mathbf{AB}| = 4$, $|\mathbf{A}| \cdot |\mathbf{B}| = (-2)(-2)$;   (c) $|\mathbf{AB}| = 4$, $|\mathbf{BA}| = 4$.

17.

$\mathbf{AB} = \begin{bmatrix} 41 & 28 & 6 \\ 35 & 24 & 8 \\ 7 & 4 & 2 \end{bmatrix}$ $\mathbf{BA} = \begin{bmatrix} 6 & 12 & 18 \\ 7 & 22 & 53 \\ 7 & 18 & 39 \end{bmatrix}$

$\mathbf{A}'\mathbf{B} = \begin{bmatrix} 6 & 0 & 0 \\ 19 & 8 & 0 \\ 53 & 36 & 2 \end{bmatrix}$ $\mathbf{BA}' = \begin{bmatrix} 6 & 0 & 0 \\ 23 & 8 & 0 \\ 21 & 12 & 2 \end{bmatrix}$

$\mathbf{B}'\mathbf{A} = \begin{bmatrix} 6 & 19 & 53 \\ 0 & 8 & 36 \\ 0 & 0 & 2 \end{bmatrix}$ $\mathbf{AB}' = \begin{bmatrix} 6 & 23 & 21 \\ 0 & 8 & 12 \\ 0 & 0 & 2 \end{bmatrix}$

$$\mathbf{B'A'} = \begin{bmatrix} 41 & 35 & 7 \\ 28 & 24 & 4 \\ 6 & 8 & 2 \end{bmatrix} \qquad \mathbf{A'B'} = \begin{bmatrix} 6 & 7 & 7 \\ 12 & 22 & 18 \\ 18 & 53 & 39 \end{bmatrix}$$

18. $|\mathbf{A}| = 1$, $\quad |\mathbf{B}| = 96$, $\quad |\mathbf{AB}| = |\mathbf{BA}| = 96$.

19. (a) $\mathbf{CD} = \begin{bmatrix} 42 & 52 \\ 34 & 19 \end{bmatrix}$, $\qquad \mathbf{DC} = \begin{bmatrix} 21 & 37 & 56 \\ 12 & 14 & 22 \\ 25 & 15 & 26 \end{bmatrix}$.

(b) No, since $|\mathbf{CD}| = -970$ and $|\mathbf{DC}| = 0$.

20. Suppose the given matrix is $\mathbf{A}$ and let $\mathbf{B} = \mathbf{AA'}$, then

$$\mathbf{B'} = (\mathbf{AA'})' = (\mathbf{A'})'(\mathbf{A'}) = \mathbf{AA'} = \mathbf{B}.$$

Similarly, if $\mathbf{C} = \mathbf{A'A}$, then $\mathbf{C'} = (\mathbf{A'A})' = \mathbf{A'A} = \mathbf{C}$. Since the matrix $\mathbf{B}$ (or $\mathbf{C}$) is equal to its transpose, the product (in either order) of any matrix by its transpose is symmetric according to the definition in **3.2**, paragraph **14**.

21. (a) $|\mathbf{A}| = ad - bc$, $\quad \mathbf{A}^{-1} = \begin{bmatrix} d/|\mathbf{A}| & -b/|\mathbf{A}| \\ -c/|\mathbf{A}| & a/|\mathbf{A}| \end{bmatrix}$,

$$|\mathbf{A}^{-1}| = \frac{ad - bc}{(ad - bc)^2} = \frac{1}{ad - bc} = \frac{1}{|\mathbf{A}|}.$$

(b)
$$|\mathbf{A}| = 21, \qquad \mathbf{A}^{-1} = \begin{bmatrix} -6/21 & -3/21 & 12/21 & -1/21 \\ 3/21 & 12/21 & -6/21 & -3/21 \\ 0 & 0 & 0 & 7/21 \\ 15/21 & -3/21 & -9/21 & -1/21 \end{bmatrix},$$

$$|\mathbf{A}^{-1}| = \frac{3 \cdot 3 \cdot 3 \cdot 1}{21 \cdot 21 \cdot 21 \cdot 21} \begin{vmatrix} -2 & -1 & 4 & -1 \\ 1 & 4 & -2 & -3 \\ 0 & 0 & 0 & 7 \\ 5 & -1 & -3 & -1 \end{vmatrix}$$

$$= \frac{-7}{7 \cdot 7 \cdot 7 \cdot 21}[-2(-14) - 1(7) + 5(-14)] = \frac{(-1)(-49)}{49 \cdot 21} = \frac{1}{21}.$$

22.

R	I						
		1	.693	.216	1	0	0
		*	1	.295		1	0
		*	*	1			1
S	$(\mathbf{S'})^{-1}$	1	.693	.216	1	0	0
			.721	.202	−.961	1.387	0
				.955	−.023	−.293	1.047
	$\mathbf{R}^{-1}$				1.924	−1.326	−.024
					*	2.010	−.307
					*	*	1.096

Check:

$$\mathbf{R}\mathbf{R}^{-1} = \begin{bmatrix} 1.000 & .001 & -.000 \\ * & 1.001 & -.000 \\ * & * & 1.000 \end{bmatrix}.$$

23. First obtain a symmetric matrix by multiplying the given matrix by its transpose, namely:

$$\mathbf{B} = \mathbf{A}\mathbf{A}' = \begin{bmatrix} 10 & 5 & 10 & 3 \\ 5 & 6 & 6 & 3 \\ 10 & 6 & 12 & 3 \\ 3 & 3 & 3 & 9 \end{bmatrix}.$$

Apply the method of Table 3.2 to the matrix $\mathbf{B}$ to obtain

$$\mathbf{B}^{-1} = \begin{bmatrix} .612 & .021 & -.511 & -.041 \\ .021 & .367 & -.184 & -.068 \\ -.511 & -.184 & .594 & .034 \\ -.041 & -.068 & .034 & .136 \end{bmatrix}.$$

But $\mathbf{B}^{-1} = (\mathbf{A}\mathbf{A}')^{-1} = (\mathbf{A}')^{-1}\mathbf{A}^{-1}$. Therefore premultiplying $\mathbf{B}^{-1}$ by $\mathbf{A}'$ yields $\mathbf{A}^{-1}$, as follows:

$$\mathbf{A}^{-1} = \begin{bmatrix} -.288 & -.143 & .576 & -.048 \\ .143 & .571 & -.285 & -.143 \\ -.001 & .000 & .001 & .333 \\ .713 & -.142 & -.428 & -.048 \end{bmatrix}.$$

Check: $|\mathbf{A}^{-1}| = .048.$

CHAPTER 4

2. (a) 5; (b) 5; (c) $\binom{5}{2} = 10$; (d) $\binom{5}{3} = 10$.

3. The three points $P:(3, 4)$, $2P:(6, 8)$, and $3P:(9, 12)$ lie on a line.

4. $P(3, -2):(-1, 1)$.

5. $P(2, -3, 1):(-1, 1, -8)$.

6. $x_{31} = -8.5x_{11} + 4.5x_{21}$,
   $x_{32} = -8.5x_{12} + 4.5x_{22}$,

7. (a) 3; (b) Ordinary space; (c) 2, a plane.

8. (a) 5; (b) $\sqrt{17}$; (c) $\sqrt{10}$.

9. (a) $y_{j1} = \alpha_{11}x_{j1} + \alpha_{12}x_{j2}$,
   $y_{j2} = \alpha_{21}x_{j1} + \alpha_{22}x_{j2}$,
   where $\alpha_{1k}\alpha_{1l} + \alpha_{2k}\alpha_{2l} = \delta_{kl}$. When

$$\alpha_{11} = \cos\theta \qquad \alpha_{12} = \sin\theta$$
$$\alpha_{21} = -\sin\theta \qquad \alpha_{22} = \cos\theta$$

it can be verified by (4.24) that the conditions for an *orthogonal transformation* are satisfied.

(b) $y_{j1} = \alpha_{11}x_{j1} + \alpha_{12}x_{j2} + \alpha_{13}x_{j3}$,
$y_{j2} = \alpha_{21}x_{j1} + \alpha_{22}x_{j2} + \alpha_{23}x_{j3}$,
$y_{j3} = \alpha_{31}x_{j1} + \alpha_{32}x_{j2} + \alpha_{33}x_{j3}$,

10. (a) $\lambda_1 = .8$, $\lambda_2 = .6$; (b) 1.

11. (a) $\lambda_1 = .8$, $\lambda_2 = .4$, $\lambda_3 = .2$, $\lambda_4 = -.4$; (b) 1.

12. $\varphi = 44°41'$. 13. $P \cdot Q = .32$.

14. (a) $D(P_1 P_2) = \sqrt{13} = 3.6$; (b) $D(P_1 P_2) = \sqrt{25} = 5$.

16. $\rho_1 = 3.74$, $\rho_2 = 4.90$.

17. $\lambda_{11} = -.802$, $\lambda_{12} = .267$, $\lambda_{13} = .535$;
$\lambda_{21} = -.408$, $\lambda_{22} = -.408$, $\lambda_{23} = .816$.

18. (a) $\varphi_{12} = -49°$; (b) $r_{12} = \cos\varphi_{12} = .655$.

20. Yes, matrix is of rank 2. 21. 2. 22. Variables 2, 3, and 6.

24. (a) No; (b) Yes; (c) By Theorem 4.6.

25. (b) $a_{10} = .96$, $a_{20} = .54$, $a_{30} = .78$, $a_{40} = .56$, $a_{50} = .72$, $a_{60} = .63$.

26. (a) $\tilde{r}_{12} = .71$ by formula (4.54); (b) $\hat{r}_{12} = .32$ by formula (4.56);
(c) $\hat{r}_{12} = .32$.

CHAPTER 5

1. (a) Read across in row $m = 4$ to the first positive entry, and the number $n = 8$ at the head of that column is the minimum number of variables required for the determination of 4 factors;
(b) $n = 11$.

4. (a) $h_1^2 = .64$;
(b) Rank of the matrix is one mathematically, not just statistically.

5. (a) 15; (b) 6. 6. .8, .6, .7, .4, .5.

7. There are six linear equations for the solution of h_2^2, namely,

$$h_2^2 = \frac{r_{21}r_{23}}{r_{13}} = \frac{r_{21}r_{24}}{r_{14}} = \frac{r_{21}r_{25}}{r_{15}} = \frac{r_{23}r_{24}}{r_{34}} = \frac{r_{23}r_{25}}{r_{35}} = \frac{r_{24}r_{25}}{r_{45}}.$$

On eliminating h_2^2, the consistency conditions may be put in the form:

(i)	$r_{23}r_{14} - r_{24}r_{13} = 0,$
(ii)	$r_{23}r_{15} - r_{25}r_{13} = 0,$
(iii)	$r_{12}r_{34} - r_{24}r_{13} = 0,$
(iv)	$r_{12}r_{35} - r_{25}r_{13} = 0,$
(v)	$r_{23}r_{45} - r_{24}r_{35} = 0.$

To show that these equations are linear combinations of those in (5.9), note that equations (i) and (ii) are equivalent to (5.9_1) and (5.9_2), respectively; equation (iii) is the difference of (5.9_1) and (5.9_3); and equation (iv) is the difference of (5.9_2) and (5.9_4). To show that (v) is linearly dependent on (5.9), substitute $r_{13} = r_{14}r_{23}/r_{24}$, obtained from (5.9_1), into (5.9_5). The result is

$$r_{14}r_{23}r_{45} - r_{14}r_{35}r_{24} = 0,$$

which reduces to (v) by factoring out r_{14}.

8. (a) $h_1^2 = .7620$ (b) $a_{11} = .87$
$\quad\quad h_2^2 = .6163$ $a_{21} = .79$
$\quad\quad h_3^2 = .7289$ $a_{31} = .85$
$\quad\quad h_4^2 = .6351$ $a_{41} = .80$
$\quad\quad h_5^2 = .9530$ $a_{51} = .98$

(c)

	1	2	3	4
1				
2	.69			
3	.75	.67		
4	.70	.63	.68	
5	.85	.77	.83	.78

(d)

	1	2	3	4
1				
2	−.05			
3	.03	−.01		
4	−.03	.05	−.02	
5	.06	.00	.01	−.01

10. .89, .73, .72, .65, .98

11. One solution is the factor pattern given in ex. 14, chap. 3.

15. .718, .494, .414, .945, .546, .363.

16. .52, 1.00, .78, .82, .36, .80, .63, .97.

17. According to the "common-factor" model set forth in (2.9).

19.

Variable	Assumed Rank		Arbitrary Estimate			Complete Estimate
	1	2	(a)	(b)	(c)	(d)
1	.76	.89	.91	.75	.84	.81
3	.62	.73	.77	.69	.68	.65
3	.73	.72	.84	.74	.72	.75
4	.64	.65	.77	.70	.68	.67
5	.95	.98	.91	.82	.98	.93

20.

Variable	Ex. 15	(a)	(b)	(c)	(d)
1	.718	.859	.515	1.409	.644
2	.494	.859	.460	.524	.545
3	.414	.740	.447	.793	.484
4	.942	.730	.551	.922	.664
5	.546	.730	.434	.578	.459
6	.363	.611	.347	.405	.301

CHAPTER 6

2. A few examples follow: friendliness–hostility; active–inactive; impulsiveness–restraint; demonstrative–inhibitive; dominance–submissiveness; heat–cold; difficulty–ease; radicalism–conservatism.

3. (a) Its factor weights are changed in sign; (b) No effect.

CHAPTER 7

1.

2. (a)

Variable	F_0
5	.809
6	.811
7	.854
8	.680
9	.840

Variable	5	6	7	8	9
5					
6	−.034				
7	−.035	.029			
8	.031	−.021	.042		
9	.043	.033	−.032	−.036	

4. (a) $6 \in G_2$; (b) $(z_j; j \in G_p, p = 1, 3)$; (c) $\sum (z_{5i}; i = 1, 2, \cdots, 100)$.

5. (a) $B(1, 2, 3) = 186$; (b) $B(1, 6, 12) = 69$.

6. (a) $S_3 = 1.941$, $T_3 = 9.380$; (b) $L_4 = 1.672$;
   (c) $S_4 = 3.613$, $T_4 = 9.655$; (d) $B(1, 2, 3, 4) = 200$.

7. $G_1 = (1, 2, 3, 4)$, $G_2 = (5, 6, 7, 8)$, $G_3 = (9, 10, 11, 12)$.

9. (a) $a_{10}^2 = \sum (r_{1j}r_{1k}; \ j \in G_2, k \in G_3) \big/ \sum (r_{jk}; \ j \in G_2, k \in G_3)$.

   (b) $a_{10}^2 = \sum_{k=9}^{12} \sum_{j=5}^{8} r_{1j}r_{1k} \big/ \sum_{k=9}^{12} \sum_{j=5}^{8} r_{jk}$.

10 and 12.

Variable	Common Factors				Communality
j	F_0	F_1	F_2	F_3	h_j^2
1	.543	.555			.603
2	.568	.624			.712
3	.481	.650			.654
4	.405	.564			.482
5	.653		.519		.696
6	.610		.342		.489
7	.688		.506		.729
8	.736		.382		.688
9	.636			.223	.454
10	.613			.245	.436
11	.537			.380	.433
12	.347			.435	.310

11 and 13. The general-factor residuals are below the diagonal and the final residuals are above.

Variable	1	2	3	4	5	6	7	8	9	10	11	12
1		.036	−.026	−.018								
2	.382		−.024	−.025								
3	.335	.382		.038								
4	.295	.327	.405									
5	.066	.026	.072	−.009		.036	−.070	−.019				
6	.019	−.046	−.041	−.047	.213		−.017	−.035				
7	.002	−.042	−.002	−.021	.193	.156		.039				
8	.005	.030	−.003	.012	.179	.096	.232					
9	−.003	.020	−.022	−.017	−.008	.040	−.003	.010		.015	−.021	−.040
10	−.008	.029	.029	.038	−.041	.033	−.030	−.066	.070		−.038	−.107
11	−.032	−.020	−.003	.035	−.030	.042	.039	−.016	.064	.055		.047
12	−.023	.003	−.021	.004	−.065	.024	.064	.030	.057	.000	.212	

14. (a) $B(5, 1) = 107$, $B(5, 2) = 32$, $B(5, 3) = 34$, $B(5, 4) = 16$.
   (b) $B(5, 1, 2) = 81$, $B(5, 1, 3) = 77$, $B(5, 1, 4) = 78$, $B(5, 2, 3) = 71$,
   $B(5, 2, 4) = 55$, $B(5, 3, 4) = 54$.
   (c) $B(5, 1, 2, 3) = 87$, $B(5, 1, 2, 4) = 79$, $B(5, 1, 3, 4) = 74$, $B(5, 2, 3, 4) = 73$.
   (d) $B(1, 2, 3, 4) = 164$.
   (e) In the set of five variables, there is no doubt that 1, 2, 3, 4 belong together, while variable 5 does not group with any of the others; except that variables 5 and 1 belong together to about the same extent to which they belong with the other three variables.

15. $\sigma_r = .074$ from Table A in Appendix.
   For $\hat{r}_{51}$: $.274/.074 = 3.70$, $P = 1 - \alpha = .0002$ from Table C in Appendix.
   For $\hat{r}_{52}$: $.099/.074 = 1.34$, $P = .1802$.

For $\dot{r}_{53}$: $.102/.074 = 1.38$, $P = .1676$.
For $\dot{r}_{54}$: $.048/.074 = 0.65$, $P = .5092$.
The probability P for the residual $\dot{r}_{51} = .274$ indicates that the observed value would be exceeded in less than a fraction of one per cent in sampling from a true value of zero; and hence it may be concluded that the true value of this residual is different from zero. The probabilities for the other three residuals are each greater than .05, the standard level of significance usually recommended, so that the deviations of these values from zero may be attributed to chance errors.

16.

Variable	F_0	F_1	D_1
1	a_{10}	a_{11}	d_{11}
2	a_{20}	a_{21}	—
3	a_{30}	a_{31}	—
4	a_{40}	a_{41}	—
5	a_{50}	—	d_{51}

17. $a_{11} = .616$, $a_{21} = .732$, $a_{31} = .689$, $a_{41} = .679$.

18. Since $\sigma_{\dot{r}} = .074$, to divide the remaining variance between the two variables means that

$$d_{11} = d_{51} = \sqrt{.274 - .074} = .447.$$

If this value were taken for d_{11}, then the communality for the first variable would be:

$$h_1^2 = .691^2 + .616^2 + .447^2 = 1.057,$$

an impossible value if there is to be a real unique factor.

CHAPTER 8

1. (a)

j	a_{j1}	a_{j2}
1	.793	.508
2	.682	.362
3	.651	.243
4	.882	−.423
5	.646	−.381
6	.501	−.376

(b)

$$\mathbf{R}_2 = \begin{bmatrix} -.169 & .134 & .101 & -.011 & -.017 & -.005 \\ .134 & -.102 & -.081 & -.013 & .024 & .021 \\ .101 & -.081 & -.069 & .036 & -.001 & -.024 \\ -.011 & -.013 & .036 & -.012 & -.001 & .010 \\ -.017 & .024 & -.001 & -.001 & -.016 & .017 \\ -.005 & .021 & -.024 & .010 & .017 & -.029 \end{bmatrix}$$

(c) $\sum a_{j1}^2 = 2.964 = \lambda_1,$ $\sum a_{j2}^2 = .914 = \lambda_2,$ $\sum a_{j1}a_{j2} = .000.$

2.

Variable	P_1	P_2
1	.8600	−.0169
2	.8341	−.1559
3	.8646	−.3773
4	.5776	.3956
5	.4950	.3391
6	.3300	.2261

The two largest eigenvalues are $\lambda_1 = 2.8704$ and $\lambda_2 = .4896$, while the remaining four are zero. This property follows from the fact that the reduced correlation matrix (with communality) is of rank 2, mathematically.

3.

Variable	P_1	P_2
1	.857	−.317
2	.846	−.398
3	.810	−.402
4	.832	−.335
5	.728	.537
6	.627	.494
7	.567	.516
8	.607	.360
Contribution of factor	4.410	1.461

This solution agrees very closely with the solution in Table 8.4, with corresponding factor coefficients differing by less than .02 in the case of the first factor, and by less than .03 for the second factor. The total common-factor variance accounted for in Table 8.4 is 5.966 while the present solution (with minimal values of communalities) accounts for 5.871.

CHAPTER 9

1. For the simple case of $m = 1$ formula (9.9) becomes

$$f_j = \sum_{\substack{k=1 \\ k \neq j}}^{n} (r_{jk} - a_k b_j)^2 \qquad (j \text{ fixed})$$

Then, expanding the quadratic, this becomes

$$f_j = l_j b_j^2 - 2Q_j b_j + C_j$$

or, by completing the square,

$$f_j = l_j\left(b_j - \frac{Q_j}{l_j}\right)^2 + K_j$$

where

$$l_j = \sum a_k^2, \quad Q_j = \sum r_{jk}a_k, \quad C_j = \sum r_{jk}^2, \quad \text{and} \quad K_j = C_j - \frac{Q_j^2}{l_j}$$

and it is understood that all summations extend over the range $k = 1$ to n but not equal to j. From the last formula for f_j it is seen that its minimum value occurs when $b_j = Q_j/l_j$. Thus, the minres solution is given by:

$$b_j = \frac{Q_j}{l_j} \quad \text{if} \quad \left|\frac{Q_j}{l_j}\right| \leq 1,$$

$$b_j = 1 \quad \text{if} \quad \left|\frac{Q_j}{l_j}\right| > 1.$$

2. (a) Denoting the original loadings by a_j and the minres loadings by b_j with a superscript for the iteration number, the solutions are given in the following table:

j	a_j	$b_j^{(1)}$	$b_j^{(2)}$	$b_j^{(3)}$
1	1.05	1.000	1.000	1.000
2	.90	.918	.913	.912
3	.80	.810	.809	.809
4	.70	.706	.707	.707
5	.60	.604	.605	.605

(b) For the Heywood solution (with the communality of the first variable being greater than one) all the residuals vanish and the objective function is precisely zero. The minres solution yields an $f = .004441$ from the residuals in the following table:

j	1	2	3	4	5
1					
2	.033				
3	.031	−.018			
4	.028	−.015	−.012		
5	.025	−.012	−.009	−.008	

3.

m	U_m for N equal to:				ν	χ^2			Action regarding null hypothesis
	12	50	100	200		0.1%	1%	5%	
1	47.5	211.8	427.9	860.1	10	29.6	23.2	18.3	Reject at all levels, all N.
2	3.8	17.1	34.6	69.6	6	22.5	16.8	12.6	For $N = 12$, accept at all levels; for $N = 50$, accept at 0.1% level, reject at 5% level; for $N > 50$, reject at all levels.
3	0	0	0	0	3	16.3	11.3	7.8	Accept at all levels, all N.

4.

j	F_1	F_2	h_j^2
1	.860	−.017	.740
2	.834	−.156	.720
3	.865	−.377	.890
4	.577	.396	.490
5	.495	.339	.360
6	.330	.226	.160
Variance	2.870	.490	3.360

CHAPTER 10

1. (a) $L = \prod_{i=1}^{N} f(X_i;\ p) = \prod_{i=1}^{N} p^{X_i}(1-p)^{1-X_i} = p^{\Sigma X_i}(1-p)^{N-\Sigma X_i}$

In the example, $N = 100$ and $\sum X_i = 18$, so that the likelihood function becomes: $L = p^{18}(1-p)^{82}$.

(b) $\log L = 18 \log p + 82 \log(1-p)$

(c) $\dfrac{d(\log L)}{dp} = \dfrac{18}{p} - \dfrac{82}{1-p}$

(d) $18(1-\hat{p}) - 82\hat{p} = 0,\quad \hat{p} = 0.18$.

2. (a)

First Iteration for Maximum-Likelihood Estimates of General-Factor Weights for Five Psychological Tests of Table 7.1

Line	Instruction	1	2	3	4	5
1	a_{j1}	.707	.673	.604	.554	.398
2	$u_j^2 = 1 - a_{j1}^2$	.5002	.5471	.6352	.6931	.8416
3	L_1/L_2	1.413	1.230	.951	.799	.473
4	RL_3	2.847	2.727	2.402	2.259	1.611
5	$L_4 - L_1$	2.140	2.054	1.798	1.705	1.213
6	$a_{j1} = L_5/\sqrt{L_3 \cdot L_5}$	.706	.677	.593	.562	.400
7	$u_j^2 = 1 - L_6^2$	.5016	.5417	.6484	.6842	.8400

The uniquenesses are in line 2 of the above table, and the first iteration is contained in lines 3–7. The square-root of the inner product of the vectors in line 3 and line 5 is $\sqrt{L_3 \cdot L_5} = 3.033$.

(b) The convergence is considered satisfactory after four iterations when four of the five weights have stabilized to three decimal places, and the coefficient for test 2 differs by one unit in the third decimal place from its preceding value. The maximum-likelihood estimates of the five coefficients are: .705, .682, .587, .566, .399.

3. (a) The work can be organized conveniently as in Table 10.3, and the required sum is

$$\sum_{j<k=1}^{5} \bar{r}_{jk}^2 / u_j^2 u_k^2 = .007626.$$

(b) $U_1 = 757(.007626) = 5.77.$ (c) $\nu = 5.$ (d) $\chi^2 = 15.1.$

(e) The calculated U_1 is well below the χ^2 required for the 1% significance level.

(f) The hypothesis stands unrejected, i.e., on the basis of random sampling a fit as bad or worse than that observed can be expected in about 1 out of 2 cases ($P = .46$) if the real description of the data were actually in terms of a single common factor.

4. In order to provide a means for checking numerical calculations, the data are presented to five decimal places (certainly, with no implications of such degree of accuracy). The reproduced correlations are given in the upper triangle and the residuals in the lower triangle of the following table:

Variable	1	2	3	4	5
1		.01118	.97243	.43866	.02195
2	−.00143		.11660	.71458	.86422
3	.00002	.03768		.52000	.13429
4	.00021	−.02317	−.00528		.76768
5	.00046	−.00115	−.01236	.00997	

For $N = 12$, the resulting statistic (10.29) is $U_2 = 2.21306$. From (10.28), the number of degrees of freedom is one and the associated χ^2 is 3.841 at the .05 level of significance. The hypothesis of 2 common factors would be accepted since U_2 is less than χ^2. (It should be remembered that this was merely an exercise; the large-sample test certainly should not be applied to cases of $N < 100$.)

5. Starting with the coefficients of the first principal factor (ex. 1, chap 8) it took 36 iterations for convergence. To assist the reader, some of the intermediate results are shown in addition to the final factor weights.

Trial	1	2	3	4	5	6
Initial	.793	.682	.651	.882	.646	.501
1st iteration	.735	.678	.674	.843	.669	.535
5th iteration	.764	.698	.687	.795	.643	.508
10th iteration	.862	.784	.727	.691	.533	.407
20th iteration	.966	.867	.727	.527	.363	.254
30th iteration	.980	.865	.734	.506	.339	.233
Final	.984	.864	.736	.499	.330	.226

7. It should be immediately obvious upon computing the residuals that at least a second common factor is necessary to explain the correlations. Simply as an exercise in applying formula (10.29), it is found that

$$\sum_{j<k=1}^{6} (\bar{r}_{jk}^2 / u_j^2 u_k^2) = 1.477737$$

and that $U_1 = 450.7$ since $N = 305$. This tremendously large value of χ^2 falls off Table D for $\nu = 9$ degrees of freedom. Without question the hypothesis is rejected, and at least a second factor should be sought for an adequate fit to the correlations.

8.

First Iteration for Maximum-Likelihood Estimates of Two Factors for Six Physical Variables of Table V

Line	Instruction	1	2	3	4	5	6
1	a_{j1}	.793	.682	.651	.882	.646	.501
2	a_{j2}	.508	.362	.243	−.423	−.381	−.376
3	$u_j^2 = 1 - a_{j1}^2 - a_{j2}^2$	.1131	.4038	.5172	.0431	.4375	.6076
4	L_1/L_3	7.011	1.689	1.259	20.464	1.477	.825
5	L_2/L_3	4.492	.896	.470	−9.814	−.871	−.619
6	RL_4	19.683	17.872	18.241	26.737	19.889	16.102
7	$L_6 - L_1$	18.890	17.190	17.590	25.855	19.243	15.601
8	$a_{j1} = L_7/\sqrt{L_4 \cdot L_7}$	.688	.626	.641	.942	.701	.568
9	RL_5	.581	.262	−1.193	−8.074	−6.536	−5.831
10	$L_9 - L_2$	.073	−.100	−1.436	−7.651	−6.155	−5.455
11	$L_{10} - (L_5 \cdot L_8)L_8$	4.376	3.815	2.573	−1.760	−1.771	−1.903
12	$a_{j2} = L_{11}/\sqrt{L_5 \cdot L_{11}}$	.658	.573	.387	−.265	−.266	−.286
13	$u_j^2 = 1 - L_8^2 - L_{12}^2$	.0937	.2798	.4394	.0424	.4378	.5956

The method broke down after eleven iterations when the uniqueness of the first variable became negative. With an electronic computer the process would be started over again, with a different set of initial values—perhaps the first maximum-likelihood factor obtained in ex. 5, and some arbitrary values for the second factor based upon the residuals determined in ex. 7.

9. The maximum-likelihood solution obtained by use of a program of Joreskog (1967b) on an IBM 360/65 is given in the following table.

Test j	F_1	F_2	F_3	F_4	F_5	h_j^2
1	.560	.019	.462	−.147	−.021	.550
2	.344	−.034	.288	−.044	−.120	.219
3	.376	−.132	.433	−.120	−.028	.361
4	.461	−.100	.298	−.118	−.160	.351
5	.726	−.253	−.219	−.059	.015	.643
6	.723	−.378	−.162	.001	.141	.712
7	.722	−.354	−.240	−.137	−.017	.723
8	.689	−.153	−.030	−.105	−.066	.515
9	.726	−.424	−.172	.025	.029	.738
10	.513	.595	−.388	.038	−.128	.786
11	.574	.380	−.035	.073	.366	.614
12	.476	.546	−.015	−.119	−.131	.556
13	.626	.345	.192	−.386	.217	.744
14	.403	.012	.051	.369	.245	.361
15	.359	.026	.123	.373	.104	.294
16	.453	.031	.386	.288	.105	.450
17	.437	.139	.040	.402	.114	.386
18	.471	.265	.218	.253	−.031	.404
19	.417	.062	.155	.177	.057	.236
20	.592	−.152	.171	.153	−.228	.479
21	.574	.234	.145	.020	−.177	.436
22	.587	−.126	.175	.122	−.119	.420
23	.668	−.054	.213	.025	−.251	.557
24	.658	.186	−.134	.132	−.137	.522
Variance	7.557	1.707	1.308	.928	.560	12.057

CHAPTER 11

1.

G_p	j	w_{j1}	w_{j2}
G_1	1	3.352	1.554
	2	3.434	1.394
	3	3.304	1.281
	4	3.301	1.457
G_2	5	1.665	2.993
	6	1.372	2.569
	7	1.142	2.436
	8	1.507	2.247

2.

q p	1	2
1	13.391	5.686
2	5.686	10.245
s_q	3.659	3.201

3. $r_{T_1 T_2} = 5.686/(3.659)(3.201) = .4855$.

4. The factor structure appears as the 8×2 matrix in the lower left corner of the answer to ex. 5.

5. The oblique factor pattern is the 8×2 matrix, calculated in the right-hand block of the table, while the orthogonal factor matrix is obtained in the middle block.

Variable	Original Matrices		Square Root Operation		Row-by-Row Multiplication with $\mathbf{T}^{-1}$	
T_1	1.0000	*	1.0000		1.0000	0
T_2	.4855	1.0000	.4855	.8742	−.0000	1.0000
T_1	1.0000	0	1.0000	−.5554	1.3085	*
T_2	0	1.0000	0	1.1439	−.6353	1.3085
1	.916	.485	.916	.046	.890	.053
2	.939	.435	.939	−.024	.952	−.027
3	.903	.400	.903	−.044	.927	−.050
4	.902	.455	.902	.020	.891	.023
5	.455	.935	.455	.817	.001	.935
6	.375	.803	.375	.710	−.019	.812
7	.312	.761	.312	.697	−.075	.797
8	.412	.702	.412	.574	.093	.657
Total	7.699	7.461	7.699	4.259	5.333	4.873
Check			7.699	4.259	5.334	4.872

6. The reproduced correlations in the table were obtained by row-by-row multiplication of the orthogonal factor matrix $\mathbf{A}$ by itself. These numbers may be checked by row-by-row multiplication of the oblique structure $\mathbf{S}$ by the oblique pattern $\mathbf{P}$, or in reverse order.

Variable	1	2	3	4	5	6	7	8
1	.841							
2	.859	.882						
3	.825	.849	.817					
4	.827	.846	.814	.814				
5	.454	.408	.375	.427	.875			
6	.376	.335	.307	.352	.751	.645		
7	.318	.276	.251	.295	.711	.612	.583	
8	.404	.373	.347	.383	.656	.562	.529	.499

7. The residuals are recorded in the table. It seems reasonable to conclude that these residuals are random deviations around zero. Two multiple-group factors account for 99.93% of the original communality of 5.960.

Variable	1	2	3	4	5	6	7	8
1	.001							
2	−.013	−.001						
3	−.020	.032	.000					
4	.032	−.020	−.013	.001				
5	.019	−.032	.005	.009	−.003			
6	.022	−.009	.012	−.023	.011	.002		
7	−.017	.001	−.014	.032	.019	−.029	.001	
8	−.022	.042	−.002	−.018	−.027	.015	.010	.003

8. $s_{T_1}^2 = \sum T_{1i}^2/N = \sum (z_{1i} + z_{2i} + z_{3i})^2/N$

$\qquad = \sum z_{1i}^2/N + \sum z_{2i}^2/N + \sum z_{3i}^2/N$

$\qquad\quad + 2\left(\sum z_{1i}z_{2i}/N + \sum z_{1i}z_{3i}/N + \sum z_{2i}z_{3i}/N \right)$

$\qquad = s_1^2 + s_2^2 + s_3^2 + 2(r_{12} + r_{13} + r_{23})$

$s_{T_1}^2 = \sum_{j,k=1}^{3} r_{jk}$, where $r_{jj} = 1$ or $r_{jj} = h_j^2$ depending on the model.

CHAPTER 12

1. $b_{11} = .096$, $b_{12} = .248$, $b_{13} = .706$;
   $b_{13,1} = .070$, $b_{13,2} = .619$, $b_{13,3} = .469$.

   These values agree perfectly with those obtained in Table 12.2 (by successive rotations in a plane).

3. It should be noted that variables 4, 5, 6 fall on a straight line. Hence, one axis can be passed through these three points and the other at right angles to it. The direction of the second axis may have to be reversed in order to make the algebraic signs of the factor loadings agree with those in Table 5.7.

4. There is generally close agreement between corresponding values in the two solutions, with a number being identical. The largest discrepancy in structure values is .008 and the largest in pattern coefficients is .011.

5. $s_{v_1} = 2.843$, $s_{v_2} = 4.214$, $s_{v_3} = 3.147$.

6. $u_1 = .6535C_1 + .0735C_2 - .5012C_3$
   $u_2 = .8448C_1 + .3759C_2 + .2330C_3$
   $u_3 = .6841C_1 - .5697C_2 + .1405C_3$

7. $D(Ou_1) = .8268$, $D(Ou_2) = .9536$, $D(Ou_3) = .9013$.

8. $$T = \begin{bmatrix} .7904 & .8859 & .7590 \\ .0889 & .3942 & -.6321 \\ -.6062 & .2443 & .1559 \end{bmatrix}.$$

9.
$$\Phi = T'T = \begin{bmatrix} 1.000 & .587 & .449 \\ .587 & 1.000 & .461 \\ .449 & .461 & 1.000 \end{bmatrix}$$

10.
$$S = CT = \begin{bmatrix} .743 & .406 & .430 \\ .445 & .264 & .204 \\ .604 & .324 & .157 \\ .559 & .386 & .266 \\ .451 & .807 & .429 \\ .489 & .807 & .339 \\ .447 & .846 & .355 \\ .537 & .717 & .420 \\ .435 & .841 & .311 \\ .075 & .311 & .712 \\ .302 & .357 & .677 \\ .316 & .222 & .724 \\ .582 & .419 & .723 \end{bmatrix}$$

11. The primary-factor pattern P for these data is exhibited as the matrix A in Table 15.2.

12. The total direct contributions are given in the diagonal and the total joint contributions below the diagonal of the table:

Factor	T_1	T_2	T_3
T_1	1.823		
T_2	−.272	3.394	
T_3	−.052	−.015	2.103

The grand total of the contributions is 6.981 as compared with the centroid total communality of 6.966.

13.
$$W = V\Psi^{-1} = V(\Lambda'\Lambda)^{-1} = V\Lambda^{-1}(\Lambda')^{-1} = A(\Lambda')^{-1}$$

CHAPTER 13

1. $Q = 3.983$ for the graphical solution of Table 12.1 (for a graphical solution based on a centroid pattern, which was given in the first edition of this text, $Q = 4.061$), while the maximum $Q = 4.091$ is for the quartimax solution of Table 13.2.

2. (a) Quartimax solution for eight political variables:

j	b_{j1}	b_{j2}
1	.74	.10
2	.97	.25
3	.89	−.05
4	−.83	.30
5	.11	−.70
6	.86	−.23
7	−.50	.70
8	−.89	.38

(b) $Q = 4.040$ for the quartimax solution; $Q = 4.009$ for the principal-factor solution.

3. $V = 23.61$ for quartimax solution; $V = 23.75$ for graphical solution; $V = 24.30$ for varimax solution.

4. (a) Varimax solution for eight political variables:

j	b_{j1}	b_{j2}
1	.74	.08
2	1.00	.00
3	.85	.26
4	−.73	−.50
5	−.06	.70
6	.78	.43
7	−.31	−.81
8	−.77	−.59

(b) $V = 9.58$ for principal-factor solution; $V = 15.95$ for varimax solution.

5. (a) $(V - S)_{rms} = .040$; (b) $(V - Q)_{rms} = .052$; (c) $(Q - S)_{rms} = .091$.

CHAPTER 14

1. $K = .0810$.

3. (a)

j	$w_j = a_{j2}^2$
1	.0784
2	.2304
3	.0289
4	.0081
5	.4225
6	.0001
7	.3136
8	.0225

(b) $C = \begin{bmatrix} .4344 & .0799 \\ .0799 & .3375 \end{bmatrix}$

(c) $N_1^2 - .7719N_1 + .1402 = 0$; $N_1 = .2924$.

(d) $\lambda_{11} = .4904$, $\lambda_{21} = -.8715$

(e)

j	v_{j1}
1	.5824
2	.8499
3	.5748
4	−.3531
5	−.4292
6	.4277
7	.1644
8	−.3401

(f)

j	$w_j = v_{j1}^2$	v_{j2}
1	.3392	−.0695
2	.7223	−.2064
3	.3304	.0876
4	.1247	−.3394
5	.1842	.7030
6	.1829	.2657
7	.0270	−.7262
8	.1157	−.4199

$$C = \begin{bmatrix} 1.3451 & -.3478 \\ -.3479 & .2925 \end{bmatrix}$$

$$N_2^2 - 1.6376N_2 + .2724 = 0$$
$$N_2 = .1879$$
$$\lambda_{12} = .2878, \quad \lambda_{22} = .9576.$$

(g) $$\Lambda = \begin{bmatrix} .5784 & -.2659 \\ -.8158 & -.9640 \end{bmatrix}$$

4. (a) $$\Lambda^{-1} = \begin{bmatrix} 1.0030 & -.5422 \\ .9574 & .6194 \end{bmatrix}$$

(b) $$T = \begin{bmatrix} .8797 & .8396 \\ -.4755 & .5432 \end{bmatrix}$$

(c) $$D = T'\Lambda = \begin{bmatrix} .877 & .000 \\ .000 & .877 \end{bmatrix}$$

(d) $$P' = D^{-1}V' = \begin{bmatrix} .893 & .955 & .931 & .878 & .008 & -.023 & -.057 & .082 \\ .052 & -.027 & -.050 & .031 & .928 & .824 & .767 & .685 \end{bmatrix}$$

(e) $r_{T_1 T_2} = .4803$.

5. $$\Lambda^{-1} = \begin{pmatrix} .9022 & -.4881 \\ .6767 & .7709 \end{pmatrix}.$$

The matrix for normalizing the rows of Λ^{-1} is:

$$D = \begin{pmatrix} .97488 & 0 \\ 0 & .97488 \end{pmatrix}, \quad \text{and} \quad D^{-1} = \begin{pmatrix} 1.02577 & 0 \\ 0 & 1.02577 \end{pmatrix}.$$

The primary-factor pattern is given by:

$$P = VD^{-1} = \begin{bmatrix} -.0979 & 1.0111 \\ .9600 & -.1171 \\ .0271 & .9832 \\ .7893 & .3610 \\ .9876 & -.1175 \end{bmatrix}.$$

6. $$\Lambda^{-1} = \begin{pmatrix} .8601 & -.5231 \\ .6181 & .7945 \end{pmatrix}; \quad D = \begin{pmatrix} .9934 & 0 \\ 0 & .9934 \end{pmatrix}; \quad D^{-1} = \begin{pmatrix} 1.0066 & 0 \\ 0 & 1.0066 \end{pmatrix};$$

$$P = VD^{-1} = \begin{bmatrix} -.0368 & .9974 \\ .9461 & -.0673 \\ .0856 & .9761 \\ .8053 & .3980 \\ .9736 & .0662 \end{bmatrix}.$$

7. From the solution of ex. 5, the first variable may be expressed as follows:

$$\hat{z}_1 = -.0979T_1 + 1.0111T_2 + .1104Y_1,$$

and its common-factor variance is given by

$$h_1^2 = (-.0979)^2 + (1.0111)^2 + 2(-.0979)(1.0111)r_{T_1 T_2}$$

where the correlation between the two oblique factors is required. This may be obtained by use of (14.30),

$$T' = D\Lambda^{-1} = \begin{pmatrix} .8795 & -.4758 \\ .6597 & .7515 \end{pmatrix},$$

and then from (12.17) it follows that $r_{T_1 T_2} = .2226$. Hence,

$$h_1^2 = .0096 + 1.0223 - .0441 = .9878.$$

This value is precisely the same as the sum of the squares of the coefficients of the first two principal components for variable 1.

8. $\Lambda^{-1} = \begin{pmatrix} 1.0452 & -.4633 \\ .9119 & .6897 \end{pmatrix}$; $D = \begin{pmatrix} .8746 & 0 \\ 0 & .8747 \end{pmatrix}$; $D^{-1} = \begin{pmatrix} 1.1446 & 0 \\ 0 & 1.1434 \end{pmatrix}$;

$$P = 1.144V = \begin{bmatrix} .886 & .058 \\ .961 & -.038 \\ .931 & -.053 \\ .885 & .027 \\ -.004 & .945 \\ -.013 & .807 \\ -.073 & .797 \\ .099 & .648 \end{bmatrix}.$$

9. (a)

$$\Lambda^{-1} = \begin{bmatrix} .7956 & -.5068 & -.5031 & .2891 \\ .6893 & .5767 & -.3975 & -.4806 \\ .8223 & -.3133 & .5514 & -.3999 \\ .7842 & .4695 & .2755 & .5955 \end{bmatrix}.$$

(b)

$$\begin{bmatrix} .9029 & 0 & 0 & 0 \\ 0 & .9142 & 0 & 0 \\ 0 & 0 & .8986 & 0 \\ 0 & 0 & 0 & .8888 \end{bmatrix}.$$

(c) **T** is determined by use of (14.30):

$$T = \begin{bmatrix} .7183 & .6302 & .7389 & .6970 \\ -.4576 & .5272 & -.2815 & .4173 \\ -.4542 & -.3634 & .4955 & .2449 \\ .2610 & -.4394 & -.3594 & .5293 \end{bmatrix}.$$

10. $F_0 = .0474$, $F_{-.5} = .0754$, $F_{-1} = .1033$, $F_{-5} = .3271$
    $F_{.1} = .0418$, $F_{.5} = .0194$, $F_{.8} = .0026$, $F_1 = -.0085$.

433

Problems and Exercises

11.

j	a_{j1}/h_j	a_{j2}/h_j
1	.9895	.1443
2	.9895	.1443
3	−.8815	.4722

$F_0 = .2140$ for normalized $\mathbf{A}$.

12. The first two variables are represented by two collinear points with the origin. An "obvious" oblique solution would consist of an axis through the first two variables and another through the third variable, which would make an obtuse angle with the first axis.

13. (a) $F_0 = 0$.

(b) The structure matrix is obtained by postmultiplying the pattern matrix by the factor correlation matrix, according to (2.43). The result is

$$\begin{bmatrix} .97015 & -.78011 \\ .48508 & -.39005 \\ -.51085 & .63530 \end{bmatrix}.$$

14. $F_0 = .83956$. The computer program calculates the sum over the factors only under the constraint that the indices for the factors be different. Formula (14.33) requires that one index always be less than the other. Hence, the computer output, $F_0 = 1.679149$, is just twice that calculated by (14.33).

15. In terms of the expression (14.33), but with each b_{jp} replaced by b_{jp}/h_j, the initial value is .976 and the final value is .138. The complete direct oblimin ($\delta = 0$) solution consists of the following:

j	Factor Pattern		Factor Structure	
	b_{j1}	b_{j2}	r_{jT_1}	r_{jT_2}
1	−.07316	1.01078	.12028	.99678
2	.88580	−.08021	.87045	.08931
3	.05653	.96704	.24160	.97786
4	.76056	.34397	.82638	.48953
5	1.00303	−.10971	.98203	.08224
			Factor Correlations	
T_1			1.	.19137
T_2			.19137	1.

16. The orthoblique (independent clusters) solution, derived from the initial orthogonal solution $\mathbf{A}$ of Table 8.11, consists of the following:

434

Variable	Pattern			Structure		
j	x	y	z	r_{jx}	r_{jy}	r_{jz}
1	1.095	−.118	−.140	.979	.368	.244
2	−.121	1.087	−.082	.397	.985	.401
3	−.116	−.143	1.086	.249	.329	.969
4	.417	.773	−.114	.763	.928	.432
5	.347	−.195	.897	.610	.420	.942
6	−.138	.320	.851	.367	.666	.952
7	.731	.484	−.139	.920	.786	.392
8	.899	−.154	.333	.955	.465	.620
9	−.170	.770	.468	.409	.913	.776
10	.590	.628	−.122	.859	.867	.423
11	.667	−.189	.648	.832	.466	.824
12	−.163	.579	.666	.399	.822	.884
13	1.084	−.083	−.151	.981	.393	.245
14	−.188	1.082	−.012	.356	.981	.442
15	−.088	−.212	1.100	.248	.282	.961
16	.192	.267	.701	.609	.707	.909
17	.611	.392	.207	.893	.803	.645
18	1.069	−.156	−.121	.941	.326	.233
19	−.060	1.054	−.140	.418	.955	.352
20	−.124	−.109	1.046	.242	.340	.943

Factor				Factor Correlations		
x				1.000	.507	.403
y					1.000	.489
z						1.000

CHAPTER 15

1.
$$T = \begin{bmatrix} .990 & .016 & -.130 & -.044 \\ .257 & .961 & .076 & -.012 \\ .456 & .112 & .878 & .026 \\ .386 & .250 & .109 & .881 \end{bmatrix}$$

2. $b_{11} = .367$, $b_{12} = .188$, $b_{13} = .597$, $b_{14} = .067$, $b_{53} = -.016$, $b_{24,4} = .195$.

3. The best matching solutions for the Navy and College samples based on their varimax analyses of the temperament scales are given in the following table.

Scale	$_N B = {_N}A \cdot {_N}T$				$_c B = {_c}A \cdot {_c}T$			
	$_N K_1$	$_N K_2$	$_N K_3$	$_N K_4$	$_c K_1$	$_c K_2$	$_c K_3$	$_c K_4$
1. Ca 1	.680	−.342	.257	.007	.727	−.471	.315	−.254
2. Ca 2	.813	−.313	−.001	.034	.637	−.276	.054	−.060
3. Ca 3	.679	−.380	.333	−.238	.546	−.363	.244	−.142
4. Om 1	.446	.529	−.220	−.175	.220	.615	−.191	−.386
5. Om 2	.560	.478	−.046	−.372	.401	.415	.002	−.187
6. Om 3	.629	.293	−.123	.038	.305	.309	−.051	−.189

table continued

Scale	$_NB = {_N}A \cdot {_N}T$				$_cB = {_c}A \cdot {_c}T$			
	$_NK_1$	$_NK_2$	$_NK_3$	$_NK_4$	$_cK_1$	$_cK_2$	$_cK_3$	$_cK_4$
7. Sc 1	.749	−.098	−.299	.059	.715	−.231	−.295	.210
8. Sc 2	.735	−.098	−.364	.027	.658	−.188	−.389	.184
9. Sc 3	.688	−.035	−.149	.104	.633	−.063	−.144	.212
10. To 1	.317	.331	.322	.488	.401	.480	.199	.187
11. To 2	.398	.263	.219	−.018	.413	.378	.211	.265
12. To 3	.460	.429	.160	−.084	.407	.309	.325	.242

Factor	$_NT$				$_cT$			
F_1	.669	−.196	−.658	.286	.629	−.217	−.641	.382
F_2	.446	.752	.019	−.484	.573	−.512	.494	−.407
F_3	.547	−.523	.588	−.285	.392	.521	.531	.541
F_4	.233	.349	.470	.776	.349	.648	−.252	−.629

4. Zeros are specified for all coefficients of the target patterns except on the putative factor expected by each of the four groups of three scales. The resulting oblique procrustes factor patterns and correlations are given in the table.

Scale	Navy Pattern: $_NP$				College Pattern: $_cP$			
	T_1	T_2	T_3	T_4	T_1	T_2	T_3	T_4
1. Ca 1	.741	−.138	.082	.125	1.006	.025	−.072	−.035
2. Ca 2	.577	−.051	.410	.041	.519	.036	.245	.001
3. Ca 3	.946	.026	−.118	−.050	.729	−.033	−.031	.013
4. Om 1	−.214	.664	.205	.096	−.081	.818	−.030	−.089
5. Om 2	.106	.783	−.023	.034	.101	.500	.005	.151
6. Om 3	−.004	.344	.339	.244	.077	.438	.030	.036
7. Sc 1	.166	.128	.661	−.015	.064	−.030	.800	−.007
8. Sc 2	.126	.167	.706	−.082	−.036	.038	.849	−.088
9. Sc 3	.187	.084	.493	.127	.050	−.014	.579	.171
10. To 1	−.067	.188	−.017	.822	−.065	.130	.014	.619
11. To 2	.192	.237	−.130	.332	−.054	.001	.070	.641
12. To 3	.102	.434	−.114	.342	.083	−.061	−.054	.672

Factor	Correlations: $_N\Phi$				Correlations: $_c\Phi$			
T_1	1.000	.282	.551	.327	1.000	.029	.606	.258
T_2		1.000	.347	.420		1.000	.167	.475
T_3			1.000	.344			1.000	.341
T_4				1.000				1.000

CHAPTER 16

1. In formula (16.12) the matrix **A** consists of the first two principal components from Table 8.1, the matrix **B** comes from Table 13.6, and the matrix Λ_m is the diagonal

matrix of the first two eigenvalues retained. The key parts of the computations include:

$$\mathbf{B'A} = \begin{pmatrix} 2.35810 & -1.02656 \\ 1.64172 & 1.47451 \end{pmatrix},$$

$$\mathbf{\Lambda_2^2} = \begin{pmatrix} 8.25591 & 0 \\ 0 & 3.22799 \end{pmatrix},$$

$$\mathbf{B'A\Lambda_2^{-2}} = \begin{pmatrix} .28562 & -.31801 \\ .19885 & .45678 \end{pmatrix}.$$

Finally, postmultiplying the last matrix by $\mathbf{A'}$ produces the identical values for the coefficients of the z's as those arrived at in the text by use of (16.7).

2. To prove that $\mathbf{L}$ is a symmetric matrix it is sufficient to show that its transpose is equal to the matrix itself, namely,

$$\mathbf{L'} = (\mathbf{\Phi^{-1}} + \mathbf{A'U^{-2}A})' = (\mathbf{\Phi^{-1}})' + (\mathbf{A})'(\mathbf{U^{-2}})'(\mathbf{A'})' = \mathbf{\Phi^{-1}} + \mathbf{A'U^{-2}A} = \mathbf{L},$$

since $\mathbf{\Phi}$ (and hence $\mathbf{\Phi^{-1}}$) is symmetric, as is also the diagonal matrix $\mathbf{U^{-2}}$.

3.
$$\mathbf{B'} = \begin{bmatrix} .248 & .367 & .226 & .185 & .020 & .003 & -.001 & .011 \\ .042 & .000 & .011 & .023 & .578 & .200 & .140 & .120 \end{bmatrix}.$$

This answer is based upon a computer output which produced the quartimin reference structure of Table 14.3, and therefore may vary slightly from the results that will be obtained by applying (16.47) directly.

4. $\mathbf{\Gamma S} = \mathbf{J^{-1}A'U^{-2}S}$, postmultiplying the matrix in (16.52) by $\mathbf{S}$,
$= \mathbf{J^{-1}A'U^{-2}A\Phi}$, substituting for $\mathbf{S}$ from (2.43),
$= \mathbf{J^{-1}J\Phi}$, substituting for the definition (16.43) of $\mathbf{J}$,
$= \mathbf{\Phi}$.

5.
$$\mathbf{\Gamma S} = \begin{pmatrix} 1.001 & .487 \\ .486 & 1.001 \end{pmatrix}$$

6.
$$\hat{\mathbf{F}}\hat{\mathbf{F}}' = \overbrace{[(\mathbf{A'U^{-2}RU^{-2}A})^{-\frac{1}{2}}]'}^{\hat{\mathbf{F}}}[\mathbf{A'U^{-2}}\underbrace{\mathbf{ZZ'}}_{\mathbf{R}}\mathbf{U^{-2}A}]\overbrace{(\mathbf{A'U^{-2}RU^{-2}A})^{-\frac{1}{2}}}^{\hat{\mathbf{F}}'}$$

Let $\mathbf{M} = (\mathbf{A'U^{-2}RU^{-2}A})$ so that the expression may be written:

$$\hat{\mathbf{F}}\hat{\mathbf{F}}' = (\mathbf{M^{-\frac{1}{2}}})'\mathbf{MM^{-\frac{1}{2}}},$$

$$= \mathbf{M^{-\frac{1}{2}}MM^{-\frac{1}{2}}}, \text{ since } \mathbf{M} \text{ is symmetric,}$$

$$= \mathbf{I}.$$

Appendix

Statistical
Tables

The sampling distribution of statistics arising in factor analysis has been largely neglected during the rapid development of descriptive procedures. An early exception was the work of Spearman and Holzinger (1924) on the sampling error of tetrad differences. When Hotelling (1933) presented the general theory and computing procedures for the principal-factor method, he also included discussions of the sampling errors of the roots of the characteristic equation and of the sampling of variables from a hypothetical infinite population of such variables. In 1940 came the next major contribution to the statistical theory of factor analysis, when Lawley (1940) introduced the maximum likelihood methods into factor analysis.

Because of the lack of precise sampling error formulas for factor coefficients and residuals, approximation procedures were developed by Holzinger and Harman (1941, pp. 122–36). Without repeating this development here, nor giving the details of the various assumptions, the principal results are presented in the first two tables. The basic assumption is that the individual correlations may be replaced by the mean (r) of the set. Additional assumptions which led to the approximations tabled were out of consideration of computational labor. For each successive approximation the sampling error formulas generally became smaller. Knowing that the sampling errors are probably underestimated, a more stringent level of significance should be required. In Table A the standard error of a residual (with one factor removed) is given for samples from $N = 20$ to $N = 500$ for an average correlation from $r = .10$ to $r = .75$. For the same range of values of N and r, the standard error of a factor coefficient a is given in Table B.

Tables C and D contain more conventional statistical information. Areas under the normal curve are given in Table C where the frequency or probability of occurrence ($\frac{1}{2}\alpha$) in the interval from the mean to a deviate x/s is shown for values of x/s from 0 to 4 by steps of .02. Then the probability of exceeding a deviation of $\pm x/s$ is given by $P = 1 - \alpha$.

In Table D the χ^2 distribution is presented for a few selected values of P, where

$$P(\chi^2) = \int_0^{\chi^2} \frac{(\chi^2)^{(\nu-2)/2}e^{-\chi^2/2}\,d(\chi^2)}{2^{\nu/2}[(\nu-2)/2]!}$$

and for the number of degrees of freedom ν from 1 to 30. The value of P is the probability that on random sampling a value of χ^2 would be obtained as great as, or greater than, the value actually obtained.

Table A

Standard Errors of Residuals with One Factor Removed

$$\sigma_{\tilde{r}} = (1 - r)\sqrt{(5 + 8r + 2r^2)/2N}$$

N \ r	.10	.15	.20	.25	.30	.35	.40	.45	.50	.55	.60	.65	.70	.75
20	.343	.336	.327	.317	.305	.292	.277	.261	.244	.225	.205	.184	.161	.138
30	.280	.274	.267	.258	.249	.238	.226	.213	.199	.184	.167	.150	.132	.112
40	.243	.237	.231	.224	.215	.206	.196	.185	.172	.159	.145	.130	.114	.097
50	.217	.212	.207	.200	.193	.184	.175	.165	.154	.142	.130	.116	.102	.087
60	.198	.194	.189	.183	.176	.168	.160	.151	.141	.130	.118	.106	.093	.079
70	.183	.180	.175	.169	.163	.156	.148	.139	.130	.120	.110	.098	.086	.074
80	.172	.168	.163	.158	.152	.146	.138	.130	.122	.113	.103	.092	.081	.069
90	.162	.158	.154	.149	.144	.137	.131	.123	.115	.106	.097	.087	.076	.065
100	.154	.150	.146	.142	.136	.130	.124	.117	.109	.101	.092	.082	.072	.062
110	.146	.143	.139	.135	.130	.124	.118	.111	.104	.096	.087	.078	.069	.059
120	.140	.137	.133	.129	.124	.119	.113	.107	.099	.092	.084	.075	.066	.056
130	.135	.132	.128	.124	.120	.114	.109	.102	.096	.088	.080	.072	.063	.054
140	.130	.127	.124	.120	.115	.110	.105	.099	.092	.085	.078	.070	.061	.052
150	.125	.123	.119	.116	.111	.106	.101	.095	.089	.082	.075	.067	.059	.050
160	.121	.119	.116	.112	.108	.103	.098	.092	.086	.080	.073	.065	.057	.049
170	.118	.115	.112	.109	.105	.100	.095	.090	.084	.077	.070	.063	.055	.047
180	.114	.112	.109	.106	.102	.097	.092	.087	.081	.075	.068	.061	.054	.046
190	.111	.109	.106	.103	.099	.095	.090	.085	.079	.073	.067	.060	.052	.045
200	.109	.106	.103	.100	.096	.092	.088	.083	.077	.071	.065	.058	.051	.044
250	.097	.095	.092	.090	.086	.082	.078	.074	.069	.064	.058	.052	.046	.039
300	.089	.087	.084	.082	.079	.075	.071	.067	.063	.058	.053	.047	.042	.036
350	.082	.080	.078	.076	.073	.070	.066	.062	.058	.054	.049	.044	.039	.033
400	.077	.075	.073	.071	.068	.065	.062	.058	.054	.050	.046	.041	.036	.031
450	.072	.071	.069	.067	.064	.061	.058	.055	.051	.047	.043	.039	.034	.029
500	.069	.067	.065	.063	.061	.058	.055	.052	.049	.045	.041	.037	.032	.028

Note: r is the average value in the correlation matrix.

Table B

Standard Errors of Factor Coefficients

$$\sigma_a = \tfrac{1}{2}\sqrt{(3/r - 2 - 5r + 4r^2)/N}$$

N	.10	.12	.14	.16	.18	.20	.22	.24	.26	.28	.30	.35	.40	.45	.50	.55	.60	.65	.70	.75
20	.587	.530	.485	.448	.417	.390	.366	.345	.326	.309	.293	.258	.227	.201	.177	.155	.134	.115	.097	.079
30	.479	.433	.396	.366	.340	.318	.299	.282	.266	.252	.239	.210	.186	.164	.144	.126	.110	.094	.079	.065
40	.415	.375	.343	.317	.295	.276	.259	.244	.231	.218	.207	.182	.161	.142	.125	.109	.095	.081	.068	.056
50	.371	.335	.307	.283	.264	.247	.232	.218	.206	.195	.185	.163	.144	.127	.112	.098	.085	.073	.061	.050
60	.339	.306	.280	.259	.241	.225	.211	.199	.188	.178	.169	.149	.131	.116	.102	.089	.077	.066	.056	.046
70	.314	.283	.259	.239	.223	.208	.196	.184	.174	.165	.157	.138	.122	.107	.094	.083	.072	.061	.052	.042
80	.293	.265	.242	.224	.208	.195	.183	.173	.163	.154	.146	.129	.114	.100	.088	.077	.067	.057	.048	.040
90	.277	.250	.229	.211	.196	.184	.173	.163	.154	.146	.138	.121	.107	.095	.083	.073	.063	.054	.046	.037
100	.262	.237	.217	.200	.186	.174	.164	.154	.146	.138	.131	.115	.102	.090	.079	.069	.060	.051	.043	.035
110	.250	.226	.207	.191	.178	.166	.156	.147	.139	.132	.125	.110	.097	.086	.075	.066	.057	.049	.041	.034
120	.240	.216	.198	.183	.170	.159	.150	.141	.133	.126	.120	.105	.093	.082	.072	.063	.055	.047	.039	.032
130	.230	.208	.190	.176	.163	.153	.144	.135	.128	.121	.115	.101	.089	.079	.069	.061	.053	.045	.038	.031
140	.222	.200	.183	.169	.158	.147	.138	.130	.123	.117	.111	.097	.086	.076	.067	.058	.051	.043	.036	.030
150	.214	.193	.177	.164	.152	.142	.134	.126	.119	.113	.107	.094	.083	.073	.065	.056	.049	.042	.035	.029
160	.207	.187	.171	.158	.147	.138	.129	.122	.115	.109	.104	.091	.080	.071	.062	.055	.047	.041	.034	.028
170	.201	.182	.166	.154	.143	.134	.126	.118	.112	.106	.100	.088	.078	.069	.061	.053	.046	.039	.033	.027
180	.196	.177	.162	.149	.139	.130	.122	.115	.109	.103	.098	.086	.076	.067	.059	.052	.045	.038	.032	.026
190	.190	.172	.157	.145	.135	.126	.119	.112	.106	.100	.095	.084	.074	.065	.057	.050	.044	.037	.031	.026
200	.186	.168	.153	.142	.132	.123	.116	.109	.103	.098	.093	.081	.072	.064	.056	.049	.042	.036	.031	.025
250	.166	.150	.137	.127	.118	.110	.104	.098	.092	.087	.083	.073	.064	.057	.050	.044	.038	.032	.027	.022
300	.151	.137	.125	.116	.108	.101	.095	.089	.084	.080	.076	.067	.059	.052	.046	.040	.035	.030	.025	.020
350	.140	.127	.116	.107	.100	.093	.088	.083	.078	.074	.070	.062	.054	.048	.042	.037	.032	.027	.023	.019
400	.131	.118	.108	.100	.093	.087	.082	.077	.073	.069	.065	.058	.051	.045	.040	.035	.030	.026	.022	.018
450	.124	.112	.102	.094	.088	.082	.077	.073	.069	.065	.062	.054	.048	.042	.037	.033	.028	.024	.020	.017
500	.117	.106	.097	.090	.083	.078	.073	.069	.065	.062	.059	.052	.045	.040	.035	.031	.027	.023	.019	.016

Note: r is the average value in the correlation matrix.

Appendix

Table C

Area under the Normal Curve

$$\tfrac{1}{2}\alpha = \frac{1}{\sqrt{2\pi s}} \int\limits_{0}^{x/s} e^{-\frac{1}{2}(x/s)^2}\, dx$$

x/s	$\tfrac{1}{2}\alpha$	x/s	$\tfrac{1}{2}\alpha$	x/s	$\tfrac{1}{2}\alpha$	x/s	$\tfrac{1}{2}\alpha$	x/s	$\tfrac{1}{2}\alpha$
.00	.0000	.80	.2881	1.60	.4452	2.40	.4918	3.20	.4993
.02	.0080	.82	.2939	1.62	.4474	2.42	.4922	3.22	.4994
.04	.0160	.84	.2995	1.64	.4495	2.44	.4927	3.24	.4994
.06	.0239	.86	.3051	1.66	.4515	2.46	.4931	3.26	.4994
.08	.0319	.88	.3106	1.68	.4535	2.48	.4934	3.28	.4995
.10	.0398	.90	.3159	1.70	.4554	2.50	.4938	3.30	.4995
.12	.0478	.92	.3212	1.72	.4573	2.52	.4941	3.32	.4995
.14	.0557	.94	.3264	1.74	.4591	2.54	.4945	3.34	.4996
.16	.0636	.96	.3315	1.76	.4608	2.56	.4948	3.36	.4996
.18	.0714	.98	.3365	1.78	.4625	2.58	.4951	3.38	.4996
.20	.0793	1.00	.3413	1.80	.4641	2.60	.4953	3.40	.4997
.22	.0871	1.02	.3461	1.82	.4656	2.62	.4956	3.42	.4997
.24	.0948	1.04	.3508	1.84	.4671	2.64	.4959	3.44	.4997
.26	.1026	1.06	.3554	1.86	.4686	2.66	.4961	3.46	.4997
.28	.1103	1.08	.3599	1.88	.4699	2.68	.4963	3.48	.4997
.30	.1179	1.10	.3643	1.90	.4713	2.70	.4965	3.50	.4998
.32	.1255	1.12	.3686	1.92	.4726	2.72	.4967	3.52	.4998
.34	.1331	1.14	.3729	1.94	.4738	2.74	.4969	3.54	.4998
.36	.1406	1.16	.3770	1.96	.4750	2.76	.4971	3.56	.4998
.38	.1480	1.18	.3810	1.98	.4761	2.78	.4973	3.58	.4998
.40	.1554	1.20	.3849	2.00	.4772	2.80	.4974	3.60	.4998
.42	.1628	1.22	.3888	2.02	.4783	2.82	.4976	3.62	.4999
.44	.1700	1.24	.3925	2.04	.4793	2.84	.4977	3.64	.4999
.46	.1772	1.26	.3962	2.06	.4803	2.86	.4979	3.66	.4999
.48	.1844	1.28	.3997	2.08	.4812	2.88	.4980	3.68	.4999
.50	.1915	1.30	.4032	2.10	.4821	2.90	.4981	3.70	.4999
.52	.1985	1.32	.4066	2.12	.4830	2.92	.4982	3.72	.4999
.54	.2054	1.34	.4099	2.14	.4838	2.94	.4984	3.74	.4999
.56	.2123	1.36	.4131	2.16	.4846	2.96	.4985	3.76	.4999
.58	.2190	1.38	.4162	2.18	.4854	2.98	.4986	3.78	.4999
.60	.2257	1.40	.4192	2.20	.4861	3.00	.4987	3.80	.4999
.62	.2324	1.42	.4222	2.22	.4868	3.02	.4987	3.82	.4999
.64	.2389	1.44	.4251	2.24	.4875	3.04	.4988	3.84	.4999
.66	.2454	1.46	.4279	2.26	.4881	3.06	.4989	3.86	.4999
.68	.2517	1.48	.4306	2.28	.4887	3.08	.4990	3.88	.4999
.70	.2580	1.50	.4332	2.30	.4893	3.10	.4990	3.90	.5000
.72	.2642	1.52	.4357	2.32	.4898	3.12	.4991	3.92	.5000
.74	.2703	1.54	.4382	2.34	.4904	3.14	.4992	3.94	.5000
.76	.2764	1.56	.4406	2.36	.4909	3.16	.4992	3.96	.5000
.78	.2823	1.58	.4429	2.28	.4913	3.18	.4993	3.98	.5000

Table D

Distribution of χ^2 for Selected Probabilities P and Degrees of Freedom v

v \\ P	.001	.01	.02	.05	.10	.20	.30	.50	.70	.80	.90	.95	.98	.99
1	10.827	6.635	5.412	3.841	2.706	1.642	1.074	.455	.148	.064	.016	.004	.001	.000
2	13.815	9.210	7.824	5.991	4.605	3.219	2.408	1.386	.713	.446	.211	.103	.040	.020
3	16.268	11.345	9.837	7.815	6.251	4.642	3.665	2.366	1.424	1.005	.584	.352	.185	.115
4	18.465	13.277	11.668	9.488	7.779	5.989	4.878	3.357	2.195	1.649	1.064	.711	.429	.297
5	20.517	15.086	13.388	11.070	9.236	7.289	6.064	4.351	3.000	2.343	1.610	1.145	.752	.554
6	22.457	16.812	15.033	12.592	10.645	8.558	7.231	5.348	3.828	3.070	2.204	1.635	1.134	.872
7	24.322	18.475	16.622	14.067	12.017	9.803	8.383	6.346	4.671	3.822	2.833	2.167	1.564	1.239
8	26.125	20.090	18.168	15.507	13.362	11.030	9.524	7.344	5.527	4.594	3.490	2.733	2.032	1.646
9	27.877	21.666	19.679	16.919	14.684	12.242	10.656	8.343	6.393	5.380	4.168	3.325	2.532	2.088
10	29.588	23.209	21.161	18.307	15.987	13.442	11.781	9.342	7.267	6.179	4.865	3.940	3.059	2.558
11	31.264	24.725	22.618	19.675	17.275	14.631	12.899	10.341	8.148	6.989	5.578	4.575	3.609	3.053
12	32.909	26.217	24.054	21.026	18.549	15.812	14.011	11.340	9.034	7.807	6.304	5.226	4.178	3.571
13	34.528	27.688	25.472	22.362	19.812	16.985	15.119	12.340	9.926	8.634	7.042	5.892	4.765	4.107
14	36.123	29.141	26.873	23.685	21.064	18.151	16.222	13.339	10.821	9.467	7.790	6.571	5.368	4.660
15	37.697	30.578	28.259	24.996	22.307	19.311	17.322	14.339	11.721	10.307	8.547	7.261	5.985	5.229
16	39.252	32.000	29.633	26.296	23.542	20.465	18.418	15.338	12.624	11.152	9.312	7.962	6.614	5.812
17	40.790	33.409	30.995	27.587	24.769	21.615	19.511	16.338	13.531	12.002	10.085	8.672	7.255	6.408
18	42.312	34.805	32.346	28.869	25.989	22.760	20.601	17.338	14.440	12.857	10.865	9.390	7.906	7.015
19	43.820	36.191	33.687	30.144	27.204	23.900	21.689	18.338	15.352	13.716	11.651	10.117	8.567	7.633
20	45.315	37.566	35.020	31.410	28.412	25.038	22.775	19.337	16.266	14.578	12.443	10.851	9.237	8.260
21	46.797	38.932	36.343	32.671	29.615	26.171	23.858	20.337	17.182	15.445	13.240	11.591	9.915	8.897
22	48.268	40.289	37.659	33.924	30.813	27.301	24.939	21.337	18.101	16.314	14.041	12.338	10.600	9.542
23	49.728	41.638	38.968	35.172	32.007	28.429	26.018	22.337	19.021	17.187	14.848	13.091	11.293	10.196
24	51.179	42.980	40.270	36.415	33.196	29.553	27.096	23.337	19.943	18.062	15.659	13.848	11.992	10.856
25	52.620	44.314	41.566	37.652	34.382	30.675	28.172	24.337	20.867	18.940	16.473	14.611	12.697	11.524
26	54.052	45.642	42.856	38.885	35.563	31.795	29.246	25.336	21.792	19.820	17.292	15.379	13.409	12.198
27	55.476	46.963	44.140	40.113	36.741	32.912	30.319	26.336	22.719	20.703	18.114	16.151	14.125	12.879
28	56.893	48.278	45.419	41.337	37.916	34.027	31.391	27.336	23.647	21.588	18.939	16.928	14.847	13.565
29	58.302	49.588	46.693	42.557	39.087	35.139	32.461	28.336	24.577	22.475	19.768	17.708	15.574	14.256
30	59.703	50.892	47.962	43.773	40.256	36.250	33.530	29.336	25.508	23.364	20.599	18.493	16.306	14.953

This table is taken from R. A. Fisher and Frank Yates, *Statistical Tables for Biological, Agricultural and Medical Research*, and is published with the kind permission of the authors and publishers.

Bibliography

Included in the bibliography are not only all the books and papers cited in the text, but also certain other works that may be useful to the researcher and student. The items have been culled from the vast literature on the basis of their relevance to the theory or technique of factor analysis. Practical applications are not included unless they are referenced in the text. The following abbreviations are employed for journals with long titles that are cited more than once.

AMM = *American Mathematical Monthly*
A. Psych. = *American Psychologist*
Ann. Math. Stat. = *The Annals of Mathematical Statistics*
B Sci. = *Behavioral Science*
Biom. = *Biometrika*
BrJ Math. Stat. Psych. = *British Journal of Mathematical and Statistical Psychology*
BrJP Stat. Sec. = *former designation for British Journal of Mathematical and Statistical Psychology*
BrJ Stat. Psych. = *former designation for British Journal of Mathematical and Statistical Psychology*
BrJP = *British Journal of Psychology*
CompJ = *Computer Journal*
Ed. Psych. Meas. = *Educational and Psychological Measurement*
JACM = *Journal of the Association for Computing Machinery*
JASA = *Journal of the American Statistical Association*
JEP = *Journal of Educational Psychology*
J. Exp. Ed. = *Journal of Experimental Education*
J. Roy. Stat. Soc. = *Journal of the Royal Statistical Society*
MBR = *Multivariate Behavioral Research*
Phil. Trans. Roy. Soc. = *Philosophical Transactions of the Royal Society of London, Series A*
Proc. Nat. Acad. Sci. = *Proceedings of the National Academy of Sciences*
Proc. Roy. Soc. Edin. = *Proceedings of the Royal Society of Edinburgh*

Proc. Roy. Soc. Lon. = *Proceedings of the Royal Society of London,* Series A
Psych. Bull. = *Psychological Bulletin*
Psych. Rep. = *Psychological Reports*
Psych. Rev. = *Psychological Review*
Psych. = *Psychometrika*

Adcock, C. J. 1964. Higher-order factors. *BrJ Stat. Psych.* 17:153–60.
Adelman, I., and Morris, C. T. 1966. A factor analysis of the interrelationship between social and political variables and per capita GNP. *Econometrica,* ser. B, 34:37–39.
Ahmavaara, Y.
    1954. The mathematical theory of factorial invariance under selection. *Psych.* 19:27–38.
    1957. On the unified factor theory of mind. *Annales Akademiae Scientiarum Fennicae,* ser. B, 106.
Aitchison, J., and Silvey, S. D. 1960. Maximum-likelihood estimation procedures and associated tests of significance. *J. Roy. Stat. Soc.,* B, 22:154–71.
Aitken, A. C. 1942. *Determinants and matrices.* 2d ed. Edinburgh: Oliver and Boyd.
Albert, A. A.
    1941. *Introduction to algebraic theories.* Chicago: University of Chicago Press.
    1944a. The matrices of factor analysis. *Proc. Nat. Acad. Sci.* Pp. 90–95.
    1944b. The minimum rank of a correlation matrix. *Proc. Nat. Acad. Sci.* Pp. 144–46.
Alker, H. 1964. Dimensions of conflict in the General Assembly. *Am. Pol. Sci. Rev.* 58:642–57.
Andersen, E. B. 1968. Review of H. H. Harman, *Modern factor analysis. Review of the Intl. Statistical Institute* 36:355–57.
Anderson, T. W.
    1958. *An introduction to multivariate statistical analysis.* New York: Wiley.
    1963a. Asymptotic theory for principal-component analysis. *Ann. Math. Stat.* 34:122–48.
    1963b. The use of factor analysis in the statistical analysis of multiple time series. *Psych.* 28:1–25.
Anderson, T. W., and Rubin, H. 1956. Statistical inference in factor analysis. *Proc. of the Third Berkeley Symposium on Mathematical Statistics and Probability* 5: 111–50.
Andrews, T. G. 1948. Statistical studies in allergy. II: A factorial analysis. *J. of Allergy* 19:43–46.
Apostol, T. M. 1957. *Mathematical analysis: A modern approach to advanced calculus.* Reading, Mass.: Addison-Wesley Publishing Co.
Aubert, E. J., Lund, I. A., and Thomasell, A. J. 1959. Some objective six-hour predictions prepared by statistical methods. *J. of Meteorology* 16:436–46.

Baggaley, A., and Cattell, R. B. 1956. A comparison of exact and approximate linear function estimates of oblique factor scores. *BrJ Stat. Psych.* 9:83–86.

Balloun, J. L., and Kearns, J. 1974. A relative interaction criterion and its use in orthogonal rotation. Research Bulletin 74–21. Princeton, N.J.: Educational Testing Service.

Banachiewicz, T. 1938. Methode de resolution numerique des equations lineaires, du calcul de determinants et des inverses et de reduction des formes quadratiques. *Bull. Int. Acad. Polonaise des Sciences et Lettres.* Pp. 393–404.

Banks, C., and Burt, C. 1954. The reduced correlation matrix. *BrJ Stat. Psych.* 7: 107–17.

Bargmann, R. 1963. *Factor analysis program for 7090, preliminary version.* IBM Research Center, Inter. Doc. 28-126.

Barlow, J. A., and Burt, C. 1954. The identification of factors from different experiments. *BrJ Stat. Psych.* 7:52–56.

Bartlett, M. S.
> 1937. The statistical conception of mental factors. *BrJP* 28:97–104.
> 1948. Internal and external factor analysis. *BrJP Stat. Sec.* 1:73–81.
> 1950. Tests of significance in factor analysis. *BrJP Stat. Sec.* 3:77–85.
> 1951a. A further note on tests of significance in factor analysis. *BrJP Stat. Sec.* 4:1–2.
> 1951b. The effect of standardization on a χ^2 approximation in factor analysis. *Biom.* 38:337–44.
> 1953. Factor analysis in psychology as a statistician sees it. *Uppsala symposium on psychological factor analysis.* Uppsala: Almqvist & Wiksell. Pp. 23–34.
> 1954. A note on the multiplying factors for various χ^2 approximations. *J. Roy. Stat. Soc.,* B. 16:296–98.

Bechtoldt, H. P.
> 1961. An empirical study of the factor analysis stability hypothesis. *Psych.* 26:405–32.
> 1974. A confirmatory analysis of the factor statibility hypothesis. *Psych.* 39: 319–26.

Benoit, C. 1924. Note sur une methode de resolution des equations normales. *Bull. Geodesique.* Pp. 67–77.

Bentler, P. M.
> 1968a. Alpha-maximized factor analysis (Alphamax): Its relation to alpha and canonical factor analysis. *Psych.* 33:335–45.
> 1968b. A new matrix for the assessment of factor contributions. *MBR* 3:489–94.
> 1969. Some extensions of image analysis. *Psych.* 34:77–83.
> 1970. A comparison of monotonicity analysis with factor analysis. *Ed. Psych. Meas.* 30:241–50.
> 1971. CLUSTRAN, a program for oblique transformation. *B. Sci.* 16:183–85.
> 1976. Multistructure statistical model applied to factor analysis. *MBR* 11:3–25.

Bernyer, G. 1957. Psychological factors: Their number, nature, and identification. *BrJ Stat. Psych.* 10:17–27.

Berry, B. J. L.
  1961. Basic patterns of economic development. In *Atlas of Economic Development*, ed. N. Ginsburg, pp. 110–19. Chicago: University of Chicago Press.
  1962. Some relations of urbanization and basic patterns of economic development. In *Urban Systems and Economic Development*, ed. F. R. Pitts, pp. 1–15. Eugene: University of Oregon, School of Business, Bureau of Business Research.
Berry, B. J. L., and Rees, P. H. 1969. The factorial ecology of Calcutta. *Am. J. of Sociology* 74:445–89.
Binder, A. 1959. Considerations of the place of assumptions in correlational analysis. *A. Psych.* 14:504–10.
Black, M. A. 1965. Institute for Juvenile Research statistical package (IJRPAC). IBM 7094 program. Mimeographed. University of Chicago Computation Center.
Bliss, G. A. 1933. Mathematical interpretations of geometrical and physical phenomena. *AMM* 40:472–80.
Bloxom, B.
  1968a. Factorial rotation to simple structure and maximum similarity. *Psych.* 33:237–47.
  1968b. A note on invariance in three-mode factor analysis. *Psych.* 33:347–50.
  1972. Alternative approaches to factorial invariance. *Psych.* 37:425–40.
BMD: Biomedical Computer Programs. 1973. Los Angeles: University of California School of Medicine, Health Sciences Computing Facility.
Bock, R. D., and Bargmann, R. E. 1966. Analysis of covariance structures. *Psych.* 31:507–34.
Boldt, R. F. 1964. Least-squares factoring to fit off-diagonals. *A. Psych.* 19:582.
Borko, H. 1965. A factor analytically derived classification system for psychological reports. *Perceptual and Motor Skills* 20:393–406.
Bowdler, H., Martin, R. S., Reinsch, C., and Wilkinson, J. H. 1968. The QR and QL algorithms for symmetric matrices. *Numerische Mathematik* 11:293–306.
Braverman, E. M. 1972. Introductory article in Russian translation of H. H. Harman, *Modern factor analysis*, 2d ed. Moscow: Statistics.
Brogden, H. E. 1969. Pattern, structure, and the interpretation of factors. *Psych. Bull.* 72:375–78.
Brown, R. H. 1962. A comparison of the maximum determinant solution in factor analysis with various approximations. In *Representative ordering and selection of variables. Part B*, ed. R. E. Bargmann. Blacksburg, Va.: Virginia Polytechnic Institute.
Browne, M. W.
  1967. On oblique procrustes rotation. *Psych.* 32:125–32.
  1968a. A comparison of factor analytic techniques. *Psych.* 33:267–334.
  1968b. Gauss-Seidel computing procedures for a family of factor analytic solutions. Research Bulletin 68–61. Princeton, N.J.: Educational Testing Service.
  1969. Fitting the factor analysis model. *Psych.* 34:375–94.

1972a. Orthogonal rotation to a partially specified target. *BrJ Math. Stat. Psych.* 25:115–20.

1972b. Oblique rotation to a partially specified target. *BrJ Math. Stat. Psych.* 25:207–12.

Browne, M. W., and Kristof, W. 1969. On the oblique rotation of a factor matrix to a specified pattern. *Psych.* 34:237–48.

Buhler, R. 1964. P-STAT: A system of statistical programs for the 7090/7094. Mimeographed Report. Princeton, N.J.: Princeton University Computer Center, Programming Notes no. 12.

Burch, E. E. 1972. Evaluating systems within systems. *Journal of Systems Management* December, pp. 18–33.

Burns, L. S., and Harman, A. J. 1966. *The complex metropolis.* Part V of *Profile of the Los Angeles Metropolis: Its people and its homes.* Los Angeles: University of California Press.

Burroughs, G. E. R., and Miller, H. W. L. 1961. The rotation of principal components. (With Appendix "A note on factor patterns" by C. Burt.) *BrJ Stat. Psych.* 14:35–49.

Burt, C.

1917. *The distribution and relations of educational abilities.* London: P. S. King & Son.

1937. Correlations between persons. *BrJP* 28:59–96.

1938. The unit hierarchy and its properties. *Psych.* 3:151–68.

1939. The factorial analysis of emotional traits. *Character and Personality* 7: 238–54, 285–99.

1941. *The factors of the mind: An introduction to factor analysis in psychology.* New York: Macmillan.

1947. A comparison of factor analysis and analysis of variance. *BrJP Stat. Sec.* 1:3–26.

1948a. Factor analysis and canonical correlations. *BrJP Stat. Sec.* 1:95–106.

1948b. The factorial study of temperamental traits. *BrJP Stat. Sec.* 1:178–203.

1949. The structure of mind: A review of the results of factor analysis. *Br. J. Ed. Psych.* 19:100–11, 176–99.

1950. Group factor analyses. *BrJP Stat. Sec.* 3:40–75.

1952. Tests of significance in factor analysis. *BrJP Stat. Sec.* 5:109–33.

1966. The early history of multivariate techniques in psychological research. *MBR* 1:24–42.

Burt, C., and Howard, M. 1956. The multifactorial theory of inheritance and its application to intelligence. *BrJ Stat. Psych.* 9:95–131.

Burt, C., and Stephenson, W. 1939. Alternative views on correlations between persons. *Psych.* 4:269–81.

Butler, J. M.

1968. Descriptive factor analysis. *MBR* 3:355–70.

1969. Simple structure reconsidered: Distinguishability and factorial invariance in factor analysis. *MBR* 4:5–28.

Cady, L. D., Gertler, M. M., Gottsch, L. G., and Woodbury, M. A. 1961. The factor structure of variables concerned with coronary artery disease. *B Sci.* 6:37–41.

Cady, L. D., Gertler, M. M., and Nowitz, L. A. 1964. Coronary disease factors. *B Sci.* 9:30–32.

Caldwell, M. 1971. WECOS: A direct, noniterative, oblique rotation procedure. *B Sci.* 16:567–70.

Canter, D., and Wools, R. 1970. A verbal measure for buildings. *Building* 25/73.

Carroll, J. B.
  1953. Approximating simple structure in factor analysis. *Psych.* 18:23–38.
  1957. Biquartimin criterion for rotation to oblique simple structure in factor analysis. *Science* 126:1114–15.
  1960. IBM 704 program for generalized analytic rotation solution in factor analysis. Harvard University, unpublished.
  1961. The nature of the data, or how to choose a correlation coefficient. *Psych.* 26:347–72.

Cattell, R. B.
  1949. A note on factor invariance and the identification of factors. *BrJP Stat. Sec.* 2:134–39.
  1952. *Factor analysis.* New York: Harper & Bros.
  1965. Factor analysis: An introduction to essentials. *Biometrics* 21:190–215, 405–35.
  1966. The scree test for the number of factors. *MBR* 1:245–76.
  1970. The isopodic and equipotent principles for comparing factor scores across different populations. *BrJ Math. Stat. Psych.* 23:23–41.

Cattell, R. B., and Baggaley, A. R. 1960. The salient variable similarity index for factor matching. *BrJ Stat. Psych.* 13:33–46.

Cattell, R. B., Breuel, H., and Hartman, H. P. 1952. An attempt at more refined definition of the cultural dimensions of syntality in modern nations. *Am. Sociological Rev.* 17:408–21.

Cattell, R. B., and Cattell, A. K. S. 1955. Factor rotation for proportional profiles: Analytical solution and an example. *BrJ Stat. Psych.* 8:83–91.

Cattell, R. B., Eber, H. W., and Tatsuoka, M. M. 1970. Handbook for the sixteen personality factor questionnaire (16PF). Champaign, Ill.: Institute for Personality and Ability Testing.

Cattell, R. B., and Dickman, K. 1962. A dynamic model of physical influences demonstrating the necessity of oblique simple structure. *Psych. Bull.* 59:389–400.

Cattell, R. B., and Muerle, J. L. 1960. The "maxplane" program for factor rotation to oblique simple structure. *Ed. Psych. Meas.* 20:569–90.

Chayes, F. 1971. *Ratio correlation.* Chicago: University of Chicago Press.

Christian, P., Kropf, R., and Kurth, H. 1964. Eine Faktorenanalyse der subjektiven Symptomatik vegetativer Herz- und Kreislaufstorungen. *Archiv fuer Kreislaufforschung* 45:171–94.

Christoffersson, A. 1975. Factor analysis of dichotomized variables. *Psych.* 40:5–32.

Clarke, M. R. B. 1970. A rapidly convergent method for maximum-likelihood factor analysis. *BrJ Math. Stat. Psych.* 23:43–52.

Cliff, N.
  1962. Analytic rotation to a functional relationship. *Psych.* 27:283–95.
  1966. Orthogonal rotation to congruence. *Psych.* 31:33–42.
  1970. The relation between sample and population characteristic vectors. *Psych.* 35:163–78.
Cliff, N., and Pennell, R. 1967. The influence of communality, factor strength, and loading size on the sampling characteristic of factor loadings. *Psych.* 32:309–26.
Comrey, A. L.
  1962. The minimum residual method of factor analysis. *Psych. Rep.* 11:15–18.
  1967. Tandem criteria for analytic rotation in factor analysis. *Psych.* 32:143–54.
  1973. *A first course in factor analysis.* New York: Academic Press.
Coombs, C. H. 1941. A criterion for significant common factor variance. *Psych.* 6:267–72.
Coombs, C. H., and Kao, R. C. 1960. On a connection between factor analysis and multidimensional unfolding. *Psych.* 25:219–31.
Corballis, M. C. 1973. A factor model for analysing change. *BrJ Math. Stat. Psych.* 26:90–97.
Corballis, M. C., and Traub, R. E. 1970. Longitudinal factor analysis. *Psych.* 35:79–98.
Cramer, E. M. 1974. On Browne's solution for oblique procrustes rotation. *Psych.* 39:159–63.
Crawford, C. B., and Ferguson, G. A. 1970. A general rotation criterion and its use in orthogonal rotation. *Psych.* 35:321–32.
Creager, J. A. 1958. General resolution of correlation matrices into components and its utilization in multiple and partial regression. *Psych.* 23:1–8.
Cronbach, L. J. 1951. Coefficient alpha and the internal structure of tests. *Psych.* 16:297–334.
Cronbach, L. J., and Gleser, G. C. 1953. Assessing similarity between profiles. *Psych. Bull.* 50:456–73.
Cronbach, L. J., Rajaratnam, N., and Gleser, G. C. 1963. Theory of generalizability: A liberalization of reliability theory. *BrJ Stat. Psych.* 16:137–63.
Cureton, E. E. 1939. The principal compulsions of factor-analysts. *Harvard Ed. Rev.* 9:287–95.
Cureton, E. E., and Muliak, S. A.
  1971. On simple structure and the solution to Thurstone's "invariant" box problem. *MBR* 6:375–87.
  1975. The weighted varimax rotation and the promax rotation. *Psych.* 40:183–95.
Cureton, T. K., and Sterling, L. F. 1964. Factor analyses of cardiovascular test variables. *J. of Sports Medicine and Physical Fitness* 4:1–24.
Danford, M. B. 1953. Factor analysis and related statistical techniques. Unpublished Ph.D. dissertation, North Carolina State College.
Darroch, J. N. 1969. Some further inequalities and an identity in factor analysis. *Psych.* 34:45–49.
Dempster, A. P. 1969. *Elements of continuous multivariate analysis.* Reading, Mass.: Addison-Wesley.

Bibliography

Dickman, K. W.
  1960. Factorial validity of a rating instrument. Ph.D. dissertation, University of Illinois.
  1964. SSUPAC (Statistical Service Unit Package): Manual of computer programs for statistical analysis. Urbana: University of Illinois.
Dickson, L. E. 1930. *Modern algebraic theories*. New York: Benj. H. Sanborn & Co.
Digman, J. M. 1967. The procrustes class of factor-analytic transformations. *MBR* 2:89–94.
Dodd, S. C. 1929. On the sampling theory of intelligence. *BrJP* 19:306–27.
Dwyer, P. S.
  1937. The determination of the factor loadings of a given test from the known factor loadings of other tests. *Psych.* 2:173–78.
  1939. The contribution of an orthogonal multiple factor solution to multiple correlation. *Psych.* 4:163–71.
  1940. The evaluation of multiple and partial correlation coefficients from the factorial matrix. *Psych.* 5:211–32.
  1944. A matrix presentation of least squares and correlation theory with matrix justification of improved methods of solution. *Ann. Math. Stat.* 15:82–89.
  1945. The square root method and its use in correlation and regression. *JASA* 40:493–503.
  1951. *Linear computations*. New York: John Wiley & Sons.
Eber, H. W. 1966. Toward oblique simple structure: Maxplane. *MBR* 1:112–25.
Eckart, C., and Young, G. 1936. The approximation of one matrix by another of lower rank. *Psych.* 1:211–18.
Elmgren, J., and Löwenhard, P. 1969. A factor analysis of the human EEG. Goteborg, Sweden: University of Goteborg, Reports from the Psychological Laboratory.
Elfving, G., Sitgreaves, R., and Solomon, H. 1959. Item selection procedures for item variables with a known factor structure. *Psych.* 24:189–205.
Emmett, W. G.
  1936. Sampling error and the two-factor theory. *BrJP* 26:362–87.
  1949. Factor analysis by Lawley's method of maximum likelihood. *BrJP Stat. Sec.* 2:90–97.
Evans, G. T. 1971. Transformation of factor matrices to achieve congruence. *BrJ Math. Stat. Psych.* 24:22–48.
Eysenck, H. J.
  1950. Criterion analysis—An application of the hypothetico-deductive method to factor analysis. *Psych. Rev.* 57:38–53.
  1952. Uses and abuses of factor analysis. *Applied Statistics* 1:45–49.
  1953. The logical basis of factor analysis. *A. Psych.* 8:105–14.
Faddeev, D. K., and Faddeeva, V. N. 1963. *Computational methods of linear algebra*. San Francisco and London: W. H. Freeman & Co.
Farrar, D. E. 1962. *The investment decision under uncertainty*. Englewood Cliffs, N.J.: Prentice-Hall.

Fee, F. 1973. Orthogonal transformation to hypothesized factors of different orders. *BrJ Math. Stat. Psych.* 26:188–94.

Ferguson, G. A. 1954. The concept of parsimony in factor analysis. *Psych.* 19: 281–90.

Fischer, G., and Roppert, J. 1964. Bemerkungen zu einem Verfahren der Transformations-analyse. *Arch. ges. Psychol.* 116:98–100.

Fisher, R. A.
   1922. On the mathematical foundations of theoretical statistics. *Phil. Trans. Roy. Soc.* 222:309–68.
   1925. Theory of statistical estimation. *Proc. Camb. Phil. Soc.* 22:700–725.

Fletcher, R., and Powell, M. J. D. 1963. A rapidly convergent descent method for minimization. *CompJ.* 6:163–68.

Forsyth, A. R. 1930. *Geometry of four dimensions*, Vol. 1. Cambridge: Cambridge University Press.

Francis, J. G. F. 1961. The QR transformation: Parts 1 and 2. *CompJ.* 4:265–71, 332–45.

French, J. W. 1951. The description of aptitude and achievement factors in terms of rotated factors. *Psychometric Monographs*, no. 5. Chicago: University of Chicago Press.

Fruchter, B. 1954. *Introduction to factor analysis*. New York: D. Van Nostrand Co.

Fuller, E. L., Jr., and Hemmerle, W. J. 1966. Robustness of the maximum-likelihood estimation procedure in factor analysis. *Psych.* 31:255–66.

Garnett, J. C. M. 1919. On certain independent factors in mental measurement. *Proc. Roy. Soc. Lon.* 96:91–111.

Gebhardt, F.
   1968. A counterexample to two-dimensional varimax-rotation. *Psych.* 33:35–36.
   1971. Maximum likelihood solution to factor analysis when some factors are completely specified. *Psych.* 36:155–63.

Gengerelli, J. A. 1948. A simplified method for approximating multiple regression coefficients. *Psych.* 13:135–46.

Gibson, W. A.
   1952. Orthogonal and oblique simple structure. *Psych.* 17:317–23.
   1959. Three multivariate models: Factor analysis, latent structure analysis, and latent profile analysis. *Psych.* 24:229–52.
   1960a. Nonlinear factors in two dimensions. *Psych.* 25:381–92.
   1960b. Orthogonal from oblique transformations. *Ed. Psych. Meas.* 20:713–21.
   1961. An asymmetric approach to multiple-factor analysis. *BrJ Stat. Psych.* 14:97–107.
   1967. Properties and applications of Gramian factoring. *Psych.* 32:425–34.

Girshick, M. A.
   1936. Principal components. *JASA* 31:519–28.
   1939. On the sampling theory of roots of determinantal equations. *Ann. Math. Stat.* 10:203–24.

Gittus, E. 1964. The structure of urban areas: A new approach. *The Town Planning Review* 35:5–21.

Givens, W. 1954. *Numerical computation of the characteristic values of a real symmetric matrix*. Oak Ridge, Tenn.: Oak Ridge National Laboratory.

Glass, G. V. 1966. Alpha factor analysis of infallible variables. *Psych.* 31:545–60.

Glass, G. V., and Maguire, T. O. 1966. Abuses of factor scores. *Am. Ed. Res. J.* 3:297–304.

Goldberger, A. S. 1971. Econometrics and psychometrics: A survey of communalities. *Psych.* 36:83–107.

Goldstine, H. H., Murray, F. J., and von Neumann, J. 1959. The Jacobi method for real symmetric matrices. *JACM* 6:59–96.

Gollob, H. F. 1968. A statistical model which combines features of factor analytic and analysis of variance techniques. *Psych.* 33:73–115.

Golub, G. H.
 1954. On the number of significant factors as determined by the method of maximum likelihood. Unpublished paper, University of Illinois.
 1955. Eigenvalues and Eigenvectors of a real symmetric matrix. Computing programs J124 and J125 for the JOHNNIAC. Santa Monica: The RAND Corp.

Gosnell, H. F., and Schmidt, M. 1936. Factorial and correlational analysis of the 1934 vote in Chicago. *JASA* 31:507–18.

Gower, J. C. 1975. Generalized procrustes analysis. *Psych.* 40:33–51.

Graybill, F. A. 1969. *Introduction to matrices with applications in statistics*. Belmont, Calif.: Wadsworth Publishing Co.

Green, B. F. 1952. The orthogonal approximation of an oblique structure in factor analysis. *Psych.* 17:429–40.

Gregg, L. W., and Pearson, R. G. 1961. Factorial structure of impact and damage variables in lightplane accidents. *Human Factors* 3:237–44.

Gruvaeus, G. T. 1970. A general approach to procrustes pattern rotation. *Psych.* 35:493–505.

Guilford, J. P.
 1952. When not to factor analyze. *Psych. Bull.* 49:26–37.
 1956. The structure of intellect. *Psych. Bull.* 53:267–93.

Guilford, J. P., and Hoepfner, R. 1969. Comparisons of varimax rotations with rotations to theoretical targets. *Ed. Psych. Meas.* 29:3–23.

Guilford, J. P., and Michael, W. B. 1948. Approaches to univocal factor scores. *Psych.* 13:1–22.

Gullahorn, J. E. 1967. Multivariate approaches in survey data processing: Comparisons of factor, cluster, and Guttman analyses and of multiple regression and canonical correlation methods. *Multivariate Behavioral Research Monograph*, no. 67–1.

Gulliksen, H. 1936. The relationship between the multiple correlation and the communality (abstract only). *Psych. Bull.* 33:781.

Gulliksen, H., and Tucker, L. R 1951. A mechanical model illustrating the scatter diagram with oblique test vectors. *Psych.* 16:233–38.

Guttman, L.
  1940. Multiple rectilinear prediction and the resolution into components. *Psych.* 5:75–99.
  1944. General theory and methods for matric factoring. *Psych.* 9:1–16.
  1952. Multiple group methods for common-factor analysis: Their basis, computation, and interpretation. *Psych.* 17:209–22.
  1953. Image theory for the structure of quantitative variates. *Psych.* 18:277–96.
  1954. Some necessary conditions for common-factor analysis. *Psych.* 19:149–61.
  1955a. The determinacy of factor score matrices with implications for five other basic problems of common-factor theory. *BrJ Stat. Psych.* 8:65–81.
  1955b. A generalized simplex for factor analysis. *Psych.* 20:173–92.
  1956. "Best possible" systematic estimates of communalities. *Psych.* 21:273–85.
  1957a. Simple proofs of relations between the communality problem and multiple correlation. *Psych.* 22:147–57.
  1957b. Successive approximations for communalities. Research Report, no. 12. Berkeley: University of California. P. 13.
  1958a. To what extent can communalities reduce rank? *Psych.* 23:297–308.
  1958b. What lies ahead for factor analysis? *Ed. Psych. Meas.* 18:497–515.
  1960. The matrices of linear least-squares image analysis. *BrJ Stat. Psych.* 13:109–18.
Guttman, L., and Cohen, J. 1943. Multiple rectilinear prediction and the resolution into components: II. *Psych.* 8:169–83.
Hadley, G. 1961. *Linear algebra.* Reading, Mass.: Addison-Wesley Publishing Co.
Haitovsky, Y. 1966. A note on regression on principal components. *Am. Statistician* 20:28–29.
Hakstian, A. R.
  1971. A comparative evaluation of several prominent methods of oblique factor transformation. *Psych.* 36:175–93.
  1972. Optimizing the resolution between salient and non-salient factor pattern coefficients. *BrJ Math. Stat. Psych.* 25:229–45.
  1973a. Procedures for the factor analytic treatment of measures obtained on different occasions. *BrJ Math. Stat. Psych.* 26:219–39.
  1973b. Procedures for weighting factors and variables in orthogonal confirmation factor analysis. *MBR* 8:379–90.
  1975a. Brief report: Asymmetric simplicity criteria for orthogonal factor transformation. *MBR* 10:119–25.
  1975b. Procedures for Φ-constrained confirmatory factor transformation. *MBR* 10:245–53.
Hakstian, A. R., and Abell, R. A. 1974. A further comparison of oblique factor transformation methods. *Psych.* 39:429–44.
Hakstian, A. R., and Boyd, W. M. 1972. An empirical investigation of some special cases of the general "orthomax" criterion for orthogonal factor transformation. *Ed. Psych. Meas.* 32:3–22.
Hakstian, A. R., and Muller, V. J. 1973. Some notes on the number of factors problem. *MBR* 8:461–75.

457

Hamburger, C. D. 1965. Factorial stability as a function of analytic rotation method, type of factor pattern and size of sample. Ph.D. dissertation, University of Southern California.

Hamilton, M. 1967. Comparison of factors by Ahmavaara's method. *BrJ Math. Stat. Psych.* 20:107–10.

Harman, H. H.
- 1938. Extensions of factorial solutions. *Psych.* 3:75–84.
- 1941. On the rectilinear prediction of oblique factors. *Psych.* 6:29–35.
- 1954. The square root method and multiple group methods of factor analysis. *Psych.* 19:39–55.
- 1960. Factor analysis. In *Mathematical methods for digital computers*, eds. H. S. Wilf and A. Ralston, pp. 204–12. New York: John Wiley & Sons.
- 1966a. *Direct oblimin program for the Philco 2000*. Santa Monica: System Development Corp., TM-2956.
- 1966b. *Program for the maximum-likelihood method of factor analysis*. Santa Monica: System Development Corp., TM-2960.
- 1972. How factor analysis can be used in classification. *Proceedings of the First Specialized International Symposium on Yeasts*. Bratislava: Slovak Academy of Sciences. Pp. 273–95.
- 1976. Minres method of factor analysis. In *Statistical methods for digital computers*, eds. K. Enslein, A. Ralston, and H. S. Wilf. New York: John Wiley & Sons. In press.

Harman, H. H., Principal investigator, and staff including Dermen, D., Ekstrom, R. B., and French, J. W. 1975. Reports of a study of factor-referenced cognitive tests and temperament scales. Princeton, N.J.: Educational Testing Service.

Harman, H. H., and Fukuda, Y. 1966. Resolution of the Heywood case in the minres solution. *Psych.* 31:563–71.

Harman, H. H., and Harper, B. P. 1954. AGO machines for test analysis. *Proceedings of the 1953 Invitational Conference on Testing Problems*. Princeton, N.J.: Educational Testing Service. Pp. 154–57.

Harman, H. H., and Jones, W. H. 1966. Factor analysis by minimizing residuals (minres). *Psych.* 31:351–68.

Harris, C. W.
- 1948. Direct rotation to primary structure. *JEP* 39:449–68.
- 1951. The symmetrical idempotent matrix in factor analysis. *J. Exp. Ed.* 19: 238–46.
- 1956. Relationships between two systems of factor analysis. *Psych.* 21:185–90.
- 1962. Some Rao-Guttman relationships. *Psych.* 27:247–63.
- 1963. Canonical factor models for the description of change. In *Problems in measuring change*, ed. C. W. Harris, pp. 138–55. Madison: University of Wisconsin Press.
- 1964. Some recent developments in factor analysis. *Ed. Psych. Meas.* 24: 193–206.
- 1967. On factors and factor scores. *Psych.* 32:363–79.

1971a. Image analysis illustrated with a Spearman case. *MBR* 6:423–32.

1971b. On Brogden's interpretation of factors. *Psych. Bull.* 5:360–61.

Harris, C. W., and Kaiser, H. F. 1964. Oblique factor analytic solutions by orthogonal transformations. *Psych.* 29:347–62.

Harris, C. W., and Knoell, D. M. 1948. The oblique solution in factor analysis. *JEP* 39:385–403.

Harris, M. L., and Harris, C. W.

1971. A factor analytic interpretation strategy. *Ed. Psych. Meas.* 31:589–606.

1973. A structure of concept attainment abilities. Wisconsin Monograph Series. Madison: Wisconsin Research and Development Center for Cognitive Learning.

Hattori, K., Kagaya, and Inanaga, S. 1960. The regional structure of surrounding areas of Tokyo. *Geographical Review of Japan* 495–514.

Heermann, E. F.

1963. Univocal or orthogonal estimators of orthogonal factors. *Psych.* 28:161–72.

1964. The geometry of factorial indeterminancy. *Psych.* 29:371–81.

1966. The algebra of factorial indeterminancy. *Psych.* 31:539–43.

Hemmerle, W. J. 1965. Obtaining maximum-likelihood estimates of factor loadings and communalities using an easily implemented iterative computer procedure. *Psych.* 30:291–302.

Hendrickson, A. E., and White, P. O. 1964. PROMAX: A quick method for rotation to oblique simple structure. *BrJ Stat. Psych.* 17:65–70.

Henrici, P. 1964. *Elements of numerical analysis*. New York: John Wiley & Sons.

Henrysson, S.

1957. *Applicability of factor analysis in the behavioral sciences: A methodological study*. Stockholm: Almqvist & Wiksell.

1962. The relation between factor loadings and biserial correlations in item analysis. *Psych.* 27:419–24.

Heywood, H. B. 1931. On finite sequences of real numbers. *Proc. Roy. Soc. Lon.* 134:486–501.

Hoel, P. G. 1939. A significance test for minimum rank in factor analysis. *Psych.* 4:245–53.

Hofmann, R. J. 1975. Brief report: On the proportionate contributions of transformed factors to common variance. *MBR* 10:507–8.

Holzinger, K. J.

1930. *Statistical resume of the Spearman two-factor theory*. Chicago: University of Chicago Press.

1936. *Preliminary reports on Spearman-Holzinger unitary trait study*, nos. 1–9. Chicago: University of Chicago, Statistical Laboratory, Dept. of Education.

1942. Why do people factor? *Psych.* 7:147–56.

1944a. Factoring test scores and implications for the method of averages. *Psych.* 9:155–67.

1944b. A simple method of factor analysis. *Psych.* 9:257–62.

1945. Interpretation of second-order factors. *Psych.* 10:21–25.

Holzinger, K. J., and Harman, H. H.
  1937. Relationships between factors obtained from certain analyses. *JEP* 28: 321–45.
  1938. Comparison of two factorial analyses. *Psych.* 3:45–60.
  1941. *Factor analysis*. Chicago: University of Chicago Press.
Holzinger, K. J., and Swineford, F.
  1937. The bi-factor method. *Psych.* 2:41–54.
  1939. A study in factor analysis: The stability of a bi-factor solution. *Supplementary Educational Monographs*, no. 48. Chicago: University of Chicago, Dept. of Education.
Holzinger, K. J., assisted by Swineford, F., and Harman, H. H. 1937. *Student manual of factor analysis*. Chicago: University of Chicago, Dept. of Education.
Horan, L. G., Flowers, N. C., and Brody, D. A. 1964. Principal factor wave forms of thoracic QRS complex. *Circulation Research* 15:131–45.
Horn, J. L.
  1965a. An empirical comparison of various methods for estimating common factor scores. *Ed. Psych. Meas.* 25:313–22.
  1965b. A rationale and test for the number of factors in factor analysis. *Psych.* 30:179–85.
  1969a. On the internal consistency reliability of factors. *MBR* 4:115–25.
  1969b. Factor analyses with variables of different metric. *Ed. Psych. Meas.* 29:753–62.
  1973. On extension analysis and its relation to correlations between variables and factor scores. *MBR* 8:477–89.
Horn, J. L., and Miller, W. C. 1966. Evidence on problems in estimating common factor scores. *Ed. Psych. Meas.* 26:617–22.
Horst, P.
  1937. A method of factor analysis by means of which all coordinates of the factor matrix are given simultaneously. *Psych.* 2:225–36.
  1941. A non-graphical method for transforming an arbitrary factor matrix into a simple structure factor matrix. *Psych.* 6:79–99.
  1956. Simplified computations for the multiple group method of factor analysis. *Ed. Psych. Meas.* 16:101–9.
  1961a. Relations among *m* sets of measures. *Psych.* 26:129–49.
  1961b. Generalized canonical correlations and their applications to experimental data. *J. Clinical Psych.* 14:331–47.
  1962. Matrix reduction and approximation to principal axes. *Psych.* 27:169–78.
  1965. *Factor analysis of data matrices*. New York: Holt, Rinehart, & Winston.
  1972. Factor matching transformations. Tech. Report 12, no. 3. Eugene: Oregon Research Institute.
Horst, P., and Schaie, K. W. 1956. The multiple group method of factor analysis and rotation to a simple structure hypothesis. *J. Exp. Ed.* 24:231–37.
Hotelling, H.
  1933. Analysis of a complex of statistical variables into principal components. *JEP* 24:417–41, 498–520.

1935.   The most predictable criterion. *JEP* 26:139–42.

1936a.   Simplified calculation of principal components. *Psych.* 1:27–35.

1936b.   Relations between two sets of variates. *Biom.* 28:321–77.

1943.   Some new methods in matrix calculation. *Ann. Math. Stat.* 14:1–34.

1949.   Practical problems of matrix calculation. *Proc. of the Berkeley Symposium on Mathematical Statistics and Probability.* Berkeley: University of California Press. Pp. 275–93.

1953.   New light on the correlation coefficient and its transforms. *J. Roy. Stat. Soc.* 15:193–232.

1957.   The relations of the newer multivariate statistical methods to factor analysis. *BrJ Stat. Psych.* 10:69–79.

Householder, A. S. 1958. The approximate solution of matrix problems. *JACM* 5:205–43.

Householder, A. S., and Young, G. 1938. Matrix approximation and latent roots. *AMM* 45:165–71.

Howe, W. G. 1955. Some contributions to factor analysis. Report No. ORNL-1919. Oak Ridge, Tenn.: Oak Ridge National Laboratory. Ph.D. dissertation, University of North Carolina.

Humphreys, L. G. 1964. Number of cases and number of factors: An example where N is very large. *Ed. Psych. Meas.* 24:457–66.

Humphreys, L. G., and Ilgen, D. R. 1969. Note on a criterion for the number of common factors. *Ed. Psych. Meas.* 29:571–78.

Humphreys, L. G., Ilgen, D. R., McGrath, D., and Montanelli, R. 1969. Capitalization on chance in rotation of factors. *Ed. Psych. Meas.* 29:259–71.

Hurley, J. R., and Cattell, R. B. 1962. The Procrustes Program: Producing direct rotation to test a hypothesized factor structure. *B Sci.* 7:258–62.

Imbrie, J., and van Andel, T. F. 1964. Vector analysis of heavy-mineral data. *Geological Society of America Bulletin* 75:1131–56.

Indow, T. 1960. The logic of factor analysis. *Annals of the Japan Assoc. for Philosophy of Science* 1:313–28.

Irwin, J. O. 1933. A critical discussion of the single-factor theory. *BrJP* 23:371–81.

Jackson, D. N., and Messick, S., eds. 1967. *Problems in human assessment.* New York: McGraw-Hill.

Jackson, D. 1924. The trigonometry of correlation. *AMM* 31:275–80.

Jacobi, C. G. J. 1846. Ueber ein leichtes Verfahren die in der Theorie der Saecularstoerungen vorkommenden Gleichungen numerisch aufzuloesen. *J. Reine Angewandte Mathematik* 30:51–94.

Jennrich, R. I.

1970.   Orthogonal rotation algorithms. *Psych.* 35:229–35.

1973.   On the stability of rotated factor loadings: The Wexler phenomenon. *BrJ Math. Stat. Psych.* 26:167–76.

1974.   Simplified formulae for standard errors in maximum-likelihood factor analysis. *BrJ Math. Stat. Psych.* 27:122–31.

Jennrich, R. I., and Robinson, S. M. 1969. A Newton-Raphson algorithm for maximum-likelihood factor analysis. *Psych.* 34:111–23.

Jennrich, R. I., and Sampson, P. F.
    1966. Rotation for simple loadings. *Psych.* 31:313–23.
    1968. Application of stepwise regression to non-linear estimation. *Technometrics* 10:63–72.
Jensema, C. 1972. Computers in behavioral science. *B Sci.* 17:235–40.
Johnson, R. M. 1963. On a theorem stated by Eckart and Young. *Psych.* 28:259–63.
Jones, K. J. 1964. The multivariate statistical analyzer. Mimeographed report. Cambridge, Mass.: Harvard University Press.
Jones, W. B., and Foster, G. L. 1964. Determinants of duration of left ventricular ejection in normal young men. *J. of App. Physiology* 19:279–83.
Jordan, C. 1875. Essai sur la géométrie à *n* dimensions. *Bull. S. M. France* 3:103–74.
Jöreskog, K. G.
    1962. On the statistical treatment of residuals in factor analysis. *Psych.* 27:335–54.
    1963. *Statistical estimation in factor analysis.* A new technique and its foundation. Stockholm: Almqvist & Wiksell.
    1965. Image factor analysis. Research Bulletin 65–5. Princeton, N.J.: Educational Testing Service.
    1966. Testing a simple structure hypothesis in factor analysis. *Psych.* 31:165–78.
    1967a. Some contributions to maximum likelihood factor analysis. *Psych.* 32:443–82.
    1967b. UMLFA: A computer program for unrestricted maximum likelihood factor analysis. Research Memorandum 66–20, rev. ed. Princeton, N.J.: Educational Testing Service.
    1969a. Efficient estimation in image factor analysis. *Psych.* 34:51–75.
    1969b. A general approach to confirmatory maximum likelihood factor analysis. *Psych.* 34:183–202.
    1970a. Estimation and testing of simplex models. *BrJ Math. Stat. Psych.* 23:121–45.
    1970b. A general method for analysis of covariance structure. *Biom.* 57:239–51.
    1971. Simultaneous factor analysis in several populations. *Psych.* 36:409–26.
Jöreskog, K. G., and Goldberger, A. S. 1972. Factor analysis by generalized least squares. *Psych.* 37:243–60.
Jöreskog, K. G., and Gruvaeus, G. 1967. RMLFA: A computer program for restricted maximum likelihood factor analysis. Research Bulletin 67–21. Princeton, N.J.: Educational Testing Service.
Jöreskog, K. G., and Lawley, D. N. 1968. New methods in maximum likelihood factor analysis. *BrJ Math. Stat. Psych.* 21:85–96.
Jöreskog, K. G., and van Thillo, M. 1970. SIFASP: A general computer program for simultaneous factor analysis in several populations. Research Bulletin 70–62. Princeton, N.J.: Educational Testing Service.
Kaiser, H. F.
    1956a. The varimax method of factor analysis. Unpublished Ph.D. dissertation, University of California, Berkeley.

1956b. Solution for the communalities: A preliminary report. Research Report 5. Berkeley: University of California.

1957. Further numerical investigation of the Tryon-Kaiser solution for the communalities. Research Report 14. Berkeley: University of California.

1958. The varimax criterion for analytic rotation in factor analysis. *Psych.* 23: 187–200.

1959. Computer program for varimax rotation in factor analysis. *Ed. Psych. Meas.* 19:413–20.

1960. The application of electronic computers to factor analysis. *Ed. Psych. Meas.* 20:141–51.

1962. Formulas for component scores. *Psych.* 27:83–87.

1963. Image analysis. In *Problems in measuring change*, ed. C. W. Harris, pp. 156–66. Madison: University of Wisconsin Press.

1965. Psychometric approaches to factor analysis. *Proceedings of the 1964 Invitational Conference on Testing Problems.* Princeton, N.J.: Educational Testing Service. Pp. 37–45.

1970. A second-generation Little Jiffy. *Psych.* 35:401–15.

1974a. A computational starting point for Rao's canonical factor analysis: Implications for computerized procedures. *Ed. Psych. Meas.* 34:691–92.

1974b. An index of factorial simplicity. *Psych.* 39:31–36.

1974c. A note on the equamax criterion. *MBR* 9:501–3.

Kaiser, H. F., and Caffrey, J. 1965. Alpha factor analysis. *Psych.* 30:1–14.

Kaiser, H. F., and Dickman, K. W. 1959. Analytic determination of common factors. Unpublished manuscript, University of Illinois, pp. 7–12.

Kaiser, H. F., and Horst, P. 1975. A score matrix for Thurstone's box problem. *MBR* 10:17–25.

Kaiser, H. F., Hunka, S., and Bianchini, J. C. 1971. Relating factors between studies based upon different individuals. *MBR* 6:409–22.

Kaiser, H. F., and Michael, W. B. 1975. Domain validity and generalizability. *Ed. Psych. Meas.* 35:31–35.

Kalimo, E. 1971. Notes on approximate procrustes rotation to primary pattern. *Ed. Psych. Meas.* 31:363–69.

Katz, J. O., and Rohlf, F. J.

1974. Functionplane: A new approach to simple structure rotation. *Psych.* 39: 37–51.

1975. Primary product functionplane: An oblique rotation to simple structure. *MBR* 10:219–31.

Keller, J. B. 1962. Factorization of matrices by least squares. *Biom.* 49:239–42.

Kelley, T. L.

1935. Essential traits of mental life. *Harvard studies in education*, no. 26. Cambridge, Mass.: Harvard University Press.

1940a. Comment on Wilson and Worcester's "Note on factor analysis." *Psych.* 5:117–20.

1940b. Talents and tasks: Their conjunction in a democracy for wholesome living and national defense. *Harvard education papers*, no. 1. Cambridge, Mass.: Harvard University, Graduate School of Education.

Kendall, M. G. 1953. The analysis of economic time series. *J. Roy. Stat. Soc.*, A. 116:11–34.

Kendall, M. G., and Babington-Smith, B. 1950. Factor analysis. *J. Roy. Stat. Soc.*, B, 12:60–94.

Kendall, M. G., and Lawley, D. N. 1956. The principles of factor analysis. *J. Roy. Stat. Soc.*, A. 119:83–84.

Kestelman, H. 1952. The fundamental equation of factor analysis. *BrJP Stat. Sec.* 5:1–6.

Kilchenmann, A. 1970. *Statistisch/Analytische Arbeitsmethoden in der Regionalgeographischen Forschung.* Monograph. Ann Arbor: University of Michigan.

King, B. F. 1964. The latent statistical structure of security price changes. Ph.D. dissertation, University of Chicago, Graduate School of Business.

Kloek, T., and Mennes, L. B. M. 1960. Simultaneous equations estimation based on principal components of predetermined variables. *Econometrica* 28:45–61.

Koopman, R. F. 1973. Determining parameter values in the generalized image system. *Psych.* 38:495–511.

Kristof, W.

    1964. Die beste orthogonale Transformation zur gegenseitigen Uberfuhrung zweier Faktorenmatrizen. *Diagnostica* 10:87–90.

    1967. Orthogonal inter-battery factor analysis. *Psych.* 32:199–227.

    1970. Some general results on fit in factor rotation. Research Bulletin 70–60. Princeton, N.J.: Educational Testing Service.

Krumbein, W. C., and Imbrie, J. 1963. Stratigraphic factor maps. *The Bull. of Amer. Assoc. of Petroleum Geologists* 47:698–701.

Kuder, G. F., and Richardson, M. W. 1937. The theory of the estimation of test reliability. *Psych.* 2:151–60.

Lawley, D. N.

    1940. The estimation of factor loadings by the method of maximum likelihood. *Proc. Roy. Soc. Edin.* 60:64–82.

    1942. Further investigations in factor estimation. *Proc. Roy. Soc. Edin.* 61:176–85.

    1953. A modified method of estimation in factor analysis and some large sample results. *Uppsala symposium on psychological factor analysis.* Uppsala: Almqvist & Wiksell. Pp. 35–42.

    1956. Tests of significance for the latent roots of covariance and correlation matrices. *Biom.* 43:128–36.

    1960. Approximate methods in factor analysis. *BrJ Stat. Psych.* 13:11–17.

    1967. Some new results in maximum likelihood factor analysis. *Proc. Roy. Soc. Edin.*, A. 67:256–64.

Lawley, D. N., and Maxwell, A. E.

    1963. *Factor analysis as a statistical method.* London: Butterworth.

    1964. Factor transformation methods. *BrJ Stat. Psych.* 17:97–103.

Lazarsfeld, P. F. 1950. The logical and mathematical foundation of latent structure analysis. In *Measurement and prediction*, eds. S. A. Stouffer, et al., pp. 362–412. Princeton, N.J.: Princeton University Press.

Ledermann, W.

1937. On the rank of the reduced correlation matrix in multiple-factor analysis. *Psych.* 2:85–93.

1938. The orthogonal transformations of a factorial matrix into itself. *Psych.* 3:181–87.

1939. On a shortened method of estimation of mental factors by regression. *Psych.* 4:109–16.

1940. On a problem concerning matrices with variable diagonal elements. *Proc. Roy. Soc. Edin.* 60:1–17.

Lev, J. 1936. A note on factor analysis by the method of principal axes. *Psych.* 1: 283–86.

Levin, J. 1966. Simultaneous factor analysis of several Gramian matrices. *Psych.* 31: 413–19.

Levine, R. L., and Hunter, J. E. 1971. Statistical and psychometric inference in principal components analysis. *MBR* 6:105–17.

Lingoes, J. C., and Guttman, L. 1967. Nonmetric factor analysis: A rank reducing alternative to linear factor analysis. *MBR* 2:485–505.

Lingoes, J. C., and Schonemann, P. H. 1974. Alternative measures of fit for the Schonemann-Carroll matrix fitting algorithm. *Psych.* 39:423–37.

Linn, R. L. 1968. A Monte Carlo approach to the number of factors problem. *Psych.* 33:37–71.

Linn, R. L., Snyder, F. W., Appelbaum, M. I., and Tucker, L. R 1967. A FORTRAN II program for three-mode factor analysis. Report. Urbana: University of Illinois, Department of Psychology.

Lockhard, R. S. 1967. Asymptotic sampling variances for factor analytic models identified by specified zero parameters. *Psych.* 32:265–77.

Lord, F. M.

1956. A study of speed factors in tests and academic grades. *Psych.* 21:31–50.

1958. Some relations between Guttman's principal components of scale analysis and other psychometric theory. *Psych.* 23:291–96.

Lord, F. M., and Wingersky, M. A. 1971. Efficiency of estimation when there is only one common factor. *BrJ Math. Stat. Psych.* 25:169–73.

Lorr, M., Jenkins, R. L., and Medland, F. F. 1955. Direct versus obverse factor analysis: A comparison of results. *Ed. Psych. Meas.* 15:441–49.

Lubin, A., and Summerfield, A. 1951. A square root method of selecting a minimum set of variables in multiple regression. *Psych.* 16:271–84, 425–37.

Macrae, D., Jr. 1960. Direct factor analysis of sociometric data. *Sociometry* 23: 360–70.

Madansky, A.

1964. Instrumental variables in factor analysis. *Psych.* 29:105–13.

1965a. Triangular decomposition program. Unpublished. The RAND Corp.

1965b. On admissible communalities in factor analysis. *Psych.* 30:455–58.

Martin, J. K., and McDonald, R. P. 1975. Bayesian estimation in unrestricted factor analysis: A treatment for Heywood cases. *Psych.* 40:505–17.

Maxwell, A. E.
  1956. Factor models. *JEP* 47:129–32.
  1959. Statistical methods in factor analysis. *Psych. Bull.* 56:228–35.
  1961. Canonical variate analysis when the variables are dichotomous. *Ed. Psych. Meas.* 21:259–71.
  1964. Calculating maximum-likelihood factor loadings. *J. Roy. Stat. Soc.*, A. 127:238–41.
  1972. Factor analysis: Thomson's sampling theory recalled. *BrJ Math. Stat. Psych.* 25:1–21.

McDonald, R. P.
  1967. Nonlinear factor analysis. *Psychometric Monographs*, no. 15. Chicago: University of Chicago Press.
  1968. A unified treatment of the weighting problem. *Psych.* 33:351–81.
  1969. A generalized common factor analysis based on residual covariance matrices of prescribed structure. *BrJ Math. Stat. Psych.* 22:149–63.
  1970a. The theoretical foundations of principal factor analysis, canonical factor analysis, and alpha factor analysis. *BrJ Math. Stat. Psych.* 23:1–21.
  1970b. Three common factor models for groups of variables. *Psych.* 35:111–28.
  1974. Testing pattern hypotheses for covariance matrices. *Psych.* 39:189–201.
  1975. Descriptive axioms for common factor theory, image theory and component theory. *Psych.* 40:137–52.

McDonald, R. P., and Burr, E. J. 1967. A comparison of four methods of constructing factor scores. *Psych.* 32:381–401.

McKeon, J. J. 1965. Canonical analysis: Some relations between canonical correlation, factor analysis, discriminant function analysis, and scaling theory. *Psychometric Monographs*, no. 13. Chicago: University of Chicago Press.

McMahon, J. 1923. Hyperspherical goniometry; and its application to correlation theory for *N* variables. *Biom.* 15:173–208.

McNemar, Q.
  1942. On the number of factors. *Psych.* 7:9–18.
  1951. The factors in factoring behavior. *Psych.* 16:353–59.

Meredith, W.
  1964a. Notes on factorial invariance. *Psych.* 29:177–85.
  1964b. Rotation to achieve factorial invariance. *Psych.* 29:187–206.
  1965. A method for studying differences between groups. *Psych.* 30:15–29.

Meyer, E. P.
  1973. On the relationship between ratio of number of factors and factorial determinacy. *Psych.* 38:375–78.
  1975. A measure of the average intercorrelation. *Ed. Psych. Meas.* 35:67–72.

Montanelli, R. G., Jr. 1974. The goodness of fit of the maximum-likelihood estimation procedure in factor analysis. *Ed. Psych. Meas.* 34:547–62.

Mood, A. M., and Graybill, F. A. 1963. *Introduction to the theory of statistics.* 2d. ed. New York: McGraw-Hill.

Morrison, D. 1967. *Multivariate statistical methods*. New York: McGraw-Hill.

Mosier, C. I.

1939a. Influence of chance error on simple structure. *Psych.* 4:33–44.

1939b. Determining a simple structure when loadings for certain tests are known. *Psych.* 4:149–62.

Moulton, F. R. 1939. The velocity of light. *Scientific Monthly* 48:481–84.

Mukherjee, B. N. 1973. Analysis of covariance structures and exploratory factor analysis. *BrJ Math. Stat. Psych.* 26:125–54.

Mulaik, S. A.

1971. A note on some equations of confirmatory factor analysis. *Psych.* 36:63–70.

1972. *The foundations of factor analysis*. New York: McGraw-Hill.

Mullen, F. 1939. Factors in the growth of girls seven to seventeen years of age. Ph.D dissertation. University of Chicago, Department of Education.

National Bureau of Standards 1953–60. On the solution of linear equations and the determination of eigenvalues. *Applied Mathematics Series*, nos. 29, 39, 49, 57. Washington, D.C.: Government Printing Office.

Nesselroade, J. R. 1972. Note on the "longitudinal factor analysis" model. *Psych.* 37:187–91.

Neuhaus, J. O.

1956a. The quartimax method. Computing program for the CRC 102-A. Berkeley: University of California.

1956b. Tucker's rotational procedure. Computing program for the CRC 102-A. Berkeley: University of California.

Neuhaus, J. O., and Wrigley, C. 1954. The quartimax method: An analytical approach to orthogonal simple structure. *BrJ Stat. Psych.* 7:81–91.

Ortega, J. M., and Kaiser, H. F. 1963. The LL^T and QR methods for symmetric tridiagonal matrices. *CompJ* 6:99–101.

Overall, J. E.

1962. Orthogonal factors and uncorrelated factor scores. *Psych. Rep.* 10:651–62.

1968. Cluster oriented factor solutions: Oblique powered vector factor analysis. *MBR* 3:479–88.

1974. Marker variable factor analysis: A regional principal axes solution. *MBR* 9:149–64.

Overall, J. E., and Hollister, L. E. 1964. Computer procedures for psychiatric classification. *J. Am. Med. Assoc.* 187.

Overall, J. E., and Porterfield, J. L. 1963. Powered vector method of factor analysis. *Psych.* 28:415–22.

Overall, J. E., and Williams, C. M. 1961. Models for medical diagnosis: Factor analysis. Part I, theoretical. *Medical Documentation* 5:51–56.

Paige, L. W., and Swift, J. D. 1961. *Elements of linear algebra*. Boston: Ginn & Company.

Pawlik, K. 1968. *Dimensionen des Verhaltens*. Bern, Stuttgart: Hans Huber.

Pearson, K. 1901. On lines and planes of closest fit to systems of points in space. *Phil. Mag.*, ser. 2, 6:559–72.

Pearson, K., and Filon, L. N. G. 1898. On the probable errors of frequency constants and on the influence of random selection on variation and correlation. *Phil. Trans. Roy. Soc.* 191:229–311.

Pearson, K., and Moul, M. 1927. The mathematics of intelligence. I. The sampling errors in the theory of a generalized factor. *Biom.* 19:246–92.

Pennell, R. J.
  1968a. The influence of communality and n on the sampling distributions of factor loadings. *Psych.* 33:423–39.
  1968b. Matching factor solutions. In *Manual of scientific programs*. Princeton, N.J.: Educational Testing Service.
  1972.   Routinely computable confidence intervals for factor loadings using the "jack-knife." *BrJ Math. Stat. Psych.* 25:207–14.
  1973.   Coherent factor analysis. *Contemp. Psych.* 18:180–81.

Pennell, R. J., and Young, F. W. 1967. An IBM system/360 program for orthogonal rotation to congruence. *B Sci.* 12:165.

Petersen, R. J., Komorita, S. S., and Quay, H. C. 1964. Determinants of sociometric choices. *J. of Soc. Psych.* 62:65–75.

Petrinow, L., and Hardyck, C. 1964. Behavioral changes in Parkinson patients following surgery: Factor analytic study. *J. of Chronic Diseases* 17:225–33.

Pinneau, S. R., and Newhouse, A. 1964. Measures of invariance and comparability in factor analysis for fixed variables. *Psych.* 29:271–81.

Pinzka, C., and Saunders, D. R. 1954. Analytic rotation to simple structure: II. Extension to an oblique solution. Research Bulletin 54–31. Princeton, N.J.: Educational Testing Service.

Please, N. W. 1973. Comparison of factor loadings in different populations. *BrJ Math. Stat. Psych.* 26:61–89.

Ralston, A. 1965. *A first course in numerical analysis*. New York: McGraw-Hill.

Rao, C. R. 1955. Estimation and tests of significance in factor analysis. *Psych.* 20:93–111.

Redman, C. 1973. Multistage fieldwork and analytical techniques. *American Antiquity* 38:61–79.

Reuchlin, M. 1964, *Methodes d'analyse factorielle a l'usage des psychologues*. Paris: Presse Universitaires de France.

Reyburn, H. A., and Raath, M. J. 1949. Simple structure: A critical examination. *BrJP Stat. Sec.* 2:125–33.

Rippe, D. D. 1953. Application of a large sampling criterion to some sampling problems in factor analysis. *Psych.* 18:191–205.

Rodgers, D. A. 1957. A fast approximate algebraic factor rotation method to maximize agreement between loadings and predetermined weights. *Psych.* 22:199–205.

Roff, M.
  1936. Some properties of the communality in multiple factor theory. *Psych.* 1:1–6.
  1937. The relation between results obtainable with raw and corrected correlation coefficients in multiple factor analysis. *Psych.* 2:35–39.
  1940. Linear dependence in multiple correlation work. *Psych.* 5:295–98.

Rohlf, F. J. 1965. Multivariate methods in taxonomy. In *Proceedings of IBM scientific computing symposium on statistics*, pp. 3–14. White Plains, N.Y.: IBM, Data Processing Division.

Rohlf, F. J., and Sokal, R. R. 1962. The description of taxonomic relationships by factor analysis. *Systematic Zoology* 11:1–16.

Rosner, B. 1948. An algebraic solution for the communalities. *Psych.* 13:181–84.

Ross, J. 1962. Informational coverage and correlational analysis. *Psych.* 27:297–306.

Royce, J. R. 1973. The conceptual framework for a multi-factor theory of individuality. In *Multivariate analysis and psychological theory*, ed. J. R. Royce, pp. 305–407. New York: Academic Press.

Rummel, R. J., Sawyer, J., Guetzkow, H., and Tanter, R. 1968. *Dimensions of nations*. Evanston, Ill.: Northwestern University Press.

Sackman, H., and Munson, J. B. 1964. Investigation of computer operating time and system capacity for man-machine digital systems. *JACM* 11:450–64.

Saunders, D. R.
>   1949. Factor analysis II: A note concerning rotation of axes to simple structure. *Ed. Psych. Meas.* 9:753–56.
>   1950. Practical methods in the direct factor analysis of psychological score matrices. Unpublished Ph.D. dissertation, University of Illinois.
>   1953. An analytic method for rotation to orthogonal simple structure. Research Bulletin 53-10. Princeton, N.J.: Educational Testing Service.
>   1960. A computer program to find the best-fitting orthogonal factors for a given hypothesis. *Psych.* 25:199–205.
>   1961. The rationale for an "oblimax" method of transformation in factor analysis. *Psych.* 26:317–24.
>   1962. Trans-varimax. *A. Psych.* 17:395.

Sawanobori, Y. 1957. Characteristic roots and vectors. Computing program N.Y. CRV3 for the IBM 704 at SBC N.Y. Data Processing Center, IBM Corp.

Scher, A. M., Young, A. C., and Meredith, W. M. 1960. Factor analysis of the electrocardiogram. *Circulation Research* 8:519–26.

Schmid, J., and Leiman, J. M. 1957. The development of hierarchical factor solutions. *Psych.* 22:53–61.

Schnorre, L. F. 1961. The statistical measurement of urbanization and economic development. *Land Economics* 37:229–45.

Schönemann, P. H.
>   1966a. A generalized solution of the orthogonal procrustes problem. *Psych.* 31:1–10.
>   1966b. Varisim: A new machine method for orthogonal rotation. *Psych.* 31:235–54.
>   1968. On two-sided orthogonal procrustes rotation. *Psych.* 33:19–33.
>   1971. The minimum average correlation between equivalent sets of uncorrelated factors. *Psych.* 36:21–30.

Schönemann, P. H., and Wang, M-M. 1972. Some new results on factor indeterminancy. *Psych.* 37:61–91.

469

Schubert, G. 1962. The 1960 term of the Supreme Court: A psychological analysis. *Am. Pol. Sci. Rev.* 56:90–113.

Scott, J. T., Jr.
   1966. Factor analysis and regression. *Econometrica* 34:552–62.
   1969. Factor analysis and regression revisited. *Econometrica* 37:719.

Shiba, S. 1969. New estimates of factor scores. *Japanese Psych. Res.* 11:129–33.

Snyder, V., and Sisam, C. H. 1914. *Analytic geometry of space.* New York: Henry Holt & Co.

Sokal, R. R. 1956. Quantification of systematic relationships and of phylogenetic trends. *Proceedings of the Tenth International Congress on Entomology* 2:409–15.

Sokal, R. R., and Sneath, P. H. A. 1963. *Principles of numerical taxonomy.* San Francisco: Freeman.

Solomon, H., and Rosner, B. 1954. Factor Analysis. *Rev. Ed. Res.* 24:421–38.

Solow, B. 1966. The pattern of craniofacial associations. *Acta Odontologica Scandinavica* 24. Copenhagen: Royal Dental College.

Sommerville, D. M. Y. 1958. *An introduction to the geometry of N dimensions.* New York: Dover Publications.

Spearman, C.
   1904. General intelligence, objectively determined and measured. *Am. J. of Psychology* 15:201–93.
   1913. Correlations of sums and differences. *BrJP* 5:417–26.
   1927. *The abilities of man.* New York: Macmillan.
   1937. Abilities as sums of factors, or as their products. *JEP* 28:629–31.

Spearman, C., and Holzinger, K. J.
   1924. The sampling error in the theory of two factors. *BrJP* 15:17–19.
   1925. Note on the sampling error of tetrad differences. *BrJP* 16:86–88.
   1929. Average value for the probable error of tetrad-difference. *BrJP* 20:368–70.

Stephenson, W.
   1935. Correlating persons instead of tests. *Character and Personality* 4:17–24.
   1936. The foundations of psychometry: Four factor systems. *Psych.* 1:195–209.
   1953. *The study of behavior.* Chicago: University of Chicago Press.

Swain, A. J. 1975. A class of factor analysis estimation procedures with common asymptotic sampling properties. *Psych.* 40:315–35.

Swineford, F. 1941. Some comparisons of the multiple-factor and the bi-factor methods of analysis. *Psych.* 6:375–82.

Tanter, R. 1964. Dimensions of conflict behavior within and between nations, 1958–1960. Ph.D. dissertation, Northwestern University.

Taylor, P. A. 1967. The use of factor models in curriculum evaluation: A mathematical model relating two factor structures. *Ed. Psych. Meas.* 27:305–21.

Thompson, J. R. 1929. The general expression for boundary conditions and the limits of correlation. *Proc. Roy. Soc. Edin.* 49:65–71.

Thomson, G. H.
   1916. A hierarchy without a general factor. *BrJP* 8:271–81.
   1934. Hotelling's method modified to give Spearman's g. *JEP* 25:366–74.

1935. On complete families of correlation coefficients and their tendency to zero tetrad-differences: Including a statement of the sampling theory of abilities. *BrJP* 26:63–92.

1936. Boundary conditions in the common-factor-space, in the factorial analysis of ability. *Psych.* 1:155–63.

1938a. Methods of estimating mental factors. *Nature* 141:246.

1938b. The estimation of specific and bi-factors. *JEP* 29:355–62.

1949. On estimating oblique factors. *BrJP Stat. Sec.* 2:1–2.

1951. *The factorial analysis of human ability.* 5th ed. New York: Houghton Mifflin.

Thorndike, R. M. 1970. Method of extraction, type of data, and adequacy of solutions in factor analysis. Ph.D. dissertation, University of Minnesota.

Thurstone, L. L.

1931. Multiple factor analysis. *Psych. Rev.* 38:406–27.

1935. *The vectors of mind.* Chicago: University of Chicago Press.

1938a. A new rotational method in factor analysis. *Psych.* 3:199–218.

1938b. Primary mental abilities. *Psychometric Monographs.* No. 1. Chicago: University of Chicago Press.

1940. Current issues in factor analysis. *Psych. Bull.* 37:189–236.

1944. Second-order factoring. *Psych.* 9:71–100.

1945a. A multiple group method of factoring the correlation matrix. *Psych.* 10:73–78.

1945b. The effects of selection in factor analysis. *Psych.* 10:165–98.

1947. *Multiple factor analysis.* Chicago: University of Chicago Press.

1954. An analytical method for simple structure. *Psych.* 19:173–82.

1955. A method of factoring without communalities. *Proceedings of the 1954 Invitational Conference on Testing Problems.* Princeton, N.J.: Educational Testing Service. Pp. 59–62, 64–66.

Topmiller, D. A. 1964. A factor analytic approach to human engineering analysis and prediction of system maintainability. AMRL-TR-64-115. Wright-Patterson Air Force Base, Ohio: Air Force Systems Command, Behavioral Sciences Laboratory.

Tryon, R. C.

1939. *Cluster analysis: Correlation profile and orthometric (factor) analysis for the isolation of unities in mind and personality.* Ann Arbor, Mich.: Edwards Bros.

1957. Communality of a variable: Formulation by cluster analysis. *Psych.* 22:241–60.

1958a. Cumulative communality cluster analysis. *Ed. Psych. Meas.* 18:3–35.

1958b. General dimensions of individual differences: Cluster analysis vs. multiple factor analysis. *Ed. Psych. Meas.* 18:477–95.

1966. Unrestricted cluster and factor analysis, with applications to the MMPI and Holzinger-Harman problems. *MBR* 1:229–44.

Tryon, R. C., and Bailey, E. E. 1970. *Cluster analysis.* New York: McGraw-Hill.

Tucker, L. R
    1940. The role of correlated factors in factor analysis. *Psych.* 5:141–52.
    1944. A semi-analytical method of factorial rotation to simple structure. *Psych.* 9:43–68.
    1951. A method for synthesis of factor analysis studies. Personnel Research Section Report No. 984. Washington, D.C.: Department of the Army.
    1955. The objective definition of simple structure in linear factor analysis. *Psych.* 20:209–25.
    1958. An inter-battery method of factor analysis. *Psych.* 23:111–36.
    1963. Implications of factor analysis of three-way matrices for measurement of change. In *Problems in measuring change*, ed. C. W. Harris, pp. 122–37. Madison: University of Wisconsin Press.
    1964. The extension of factor analysis to three-dimensional matrices. In *Contributions to mathematical psychology*, eds. N. Frederiksen and H. Gulliksen, pp. 109–27. New York: Holt, Rinehart, & Winston.
    1966. Some mathematical notes on three-mode factor analysis. *Psych.* 31:279–311.
    1971. Relations of factor score estimates to their use. *Psych.* 36:427–36.
Tucker, L. R, Cooper, L. G., and Meredith, W. 1972. Obtaining squared multiple correlations from a correlation matrix which may be singular. *Psych.* 37:143–48.
Tucker, L. R, Koopman, R. F., and Linn, R. L. 1969. Evaluation of factor analytic research procedures by means of standard correlation matrices. *Psych.* 34:421–59.
Tucker, L. R, and Lewis, C. 1973. A reliability coefficient for maximum likelihood factor analysis. *Psych.* 38:1–10.
Uppsala symposium on psychological factor analysis 1953. *Nordisk Psykologi's* Monograph Series, no. 3. Uppsala: Almqvist & Wiksell.
Veblen, O., and Whitehead, J. H. C. 1932. The foundations of differential geometry. Cambridge Tracts in Mathematics and Mathematical Physics, No. 29. Cambridge: University Press.
Velicer, W. F.
    1974. A comparison of the stability of factor analysis, principal component analysis and rescaled image analysis. *Ed. Psych. Meas.* 34:563–72.
    1975. The relation between factor scores, image scores, and principal component scores. *Ed. Psych. Meas.* In press.
Versace, J. 1960. Factor analysis of roadway and accident data. *Highway Research Board Bulletin*, no. 240. Washington, D.C.: National Research Council. Pp. 24–32.
Voiers, W. D. 1964. Perceptual bases of speaker identity. *J. of Acoustical Society of America* 36:1065–73.
Wackwitz, J. H., and Horn, J. L. 1971. On obtaining the best estimates of factor scores within an ideal simple structure. *MBR* 6:389–408.
Wainer, H., Gruvaeus, G., and Zill, N., II. 1973. Senatorial decision making: I. The determination of structure. *B Sci.* 18:7–19.
Walsh, J. A. 1964. An IBM 709 program for factor analyzing three-mode matrices. *Ed. Psych. Meas.* 24:669–73.

Warburton, F. W. 1963. Analytic methods of factor rotation. *BrJ Stat. Psych.* 16: 165–74.

Wenger, M. A., Holzinger, K. J., and Harman, H. H. 1948. The estimation of pupil ability by three factorial solutions. *U. of Calif. Publ. in Psych.* 5:161–252.

Westley, B. H., and Jacobson, H. K. 1962. Dimensions of teachers' attitudes toward instructional television. *AV Communication Rev.* 10:179–85.

Wherry, R. J. 1959. Hierarchical factor solutions without rotation. *Psych.* 24:45–51.

Wherry, R. J., and Winer, B. J. 1953. A method for factoring large numbers of items. *Psych.* 18:161–79.

White, P. A. 1958. The computation of eigenvalues and eigenvectors of a matrix. *J. SIAM* 6:393–437.

Whitla, D. K., ed. 1968. *Handbook of measurement and assessment in behavioral sciences.* Reading, Mass.: Addison-Wesley Publishing Co.

Whittaker, E. T., and Robinson, G. 1944. *The calculus of observations.* London: Blackie & Son.

Whittle, P.

    1952. On principal components and least square methods of factor analysis. *Skand. Aktuar.* 35:223–39.

    1963. On the fitting of multivariate autoregressions and the approximate canonical factorization of a spectral density matrix. *Biom.* 50:129–34.

Wiley, D. E., Schmidt, W. H., and Bramble, W. J. 1973. Studies of a class of covariance structure models. *JASA* 68:317–23.

Wilkinson, J. H.

    1958. The calculation of the eigenvectors of codiagonal matrices. *CompJ* 1:90–96.

    1960. Householder's method for the solution of the algebraic eigenproblem. *CompJ* 3:23–27.

    1965. *The algebraic eigenvalue problem.* New York: Oxford University Press.

Wilks, S. S.

    1938a. Weighting systems for linear functions of correlated variables when there is no dependent variable. *Psych.* 3:23–40.

    1938b. The large-sample distribution of the likelihood ratio for testing composite hypotheses. *Ann. Math. Stat.* 9:60–62.

Wilson, E. B. 1928. On hierarchical correlation systems. *Proc. Nat. Acad. Sci.* 14:283–91.

Wilson, E. B., and Worcester, J. 1939. A note on factor analysis. *Psych.* 4:133–48.

Wishart, J.

    1928a. The generalized product-moment distribution in samples from a normal multivariate population. *Biom.* 20:32–52.

    1928b. Sampling errors in the theory of two factors. *BrJP* 19:180–87.

    1955. Multivariate analysis. *Applied Statistics* 4:103–16.

Wold, H. 1953. Some artificial experiments in factor analysis. *Uppsala symposium on psychological factor analysis.* Uppsala: Almqvist & Wiksell. Pp. 43–64.

Wolfle, D. 1940. Factor analysis to 1940. *Psychometric Monographs*, no 3. Chicago: University of Chicago Press.

Wood, K. R., McCornack, R. L., and Villone, L. T. 1964. Non-linear factor analysis program A-78A. TM-1764. Santa Monica: System Development Corp.

Wood, R. C. 1961. *1400 governments*. Cambridge, Mass.: Harvard University Press.

Wright, T. W., and Hayford, J. F. 1906. The adjustment of observations. New York: D. Van Nostrand Co.

Wrigley, C.

    1956. An empirical comparison of various methods for the estimation of communalities. Contract Report no. 1. Berkeley: University of California.

    1957. The distinction between common and specific variance in factor theory. *BrJ Stat. Psych.* 10:81–98.

    1958. Objectivity in factor analysis. *Ed. Psych. Meas.* 18:463–76.

    1959. The effect upon the communalities of changing the estimate of the number of factors. *BrJ Stat. Psych.* 12:35–54.

Wrigley, C., and Neuhaus, J. O.

    1952. A re-factorization of the Burt-Pearson matrix with the ORDVAC electronic computer. *BrJP Stat. Sec.* 5:105–8.

    1955a. The use of an electronic computer in principal axes factor analysis. *JEP* 46:31–41.

    1955b. The matching of two sets of factors. Contract Memorandum Report A-32, Task A. Urbana: University of Illinois.

Wrigley, C., Saunders, D. R., and Neuhaus, J. O. 1958. Application of the quartimax method of rotation to Thurstone's Primary Mental Abilities study. *Psych.* 23: 151–70.

Young, G.

    1937. Matrix approximation and subspace fitting. *Psych.* 2:21–26.

    1939. Factor analysis and the index of clustering. *Psych.* 4:201–8.

    1941. Maximum likelihood estimation and factor analysis. *Psych.* 6:49–53.

Young, G., and Householder, A. S. 1940. Factorial invariance and significance. *Psych.* 5:47–56.

Yule, G. U., and Kendall, M. G. 1969. *An introduction to the theory of statistics*. 14th ed. New York: Hafner.

Zimmerman, W. S. 1946. A simple graphical method for orthogonal rotation of axes. *Psych.* 11:51–55.

Author
Index

Subject Index

Subject Index

Variance, 12
  in terms of factors, 18–20
Varimax method, 290–99
  angle of rotation, 292
  computer program, 294
  contrasted with quartimax
    method, 290
  criterion, 290–91, 293, 310, 330

  invariance property, 298–99
  theoretical development, 290–92
Vector, 36
Vector representation of variables, 63, 66–69, 97

When to stop factoring, 26, 151, 160, 163, 185,
    191, 195–96
Wishart distribution, 184, 201

Problem
Index

Notes to Problem Index

[1]Includes raw data, correlations, communality estimates; also, factor measurements (FM).

[2]Code for direct methods:

AFA	= Alpha	M-G	= Multiple-group
BiF	= Bi-factor	Min	= Minres
C	= Centroid	M-L	= Maximum-likelihood
CFA	= Canonical	PC	= Principal Component
D	= Directly from model	PF	= Principal Factor
IFA	= Image	T-F	= Two-factor

[3]Code for derived solutions:

Binorm	= Binormamin	Ort-IC	= Independent clusters ⎫ Orthoblique
D-Obl	= Direct Oblimin	Ort-Pr	= Proportional ⎭
Match	= Matching factors	Procr	= Procrustes
Obl-B	= Biquartimin ⎫	Qmax	= Quartimax
Obl-C	= Covarimin ⎬ Oblimin	Subj	= Subjective (graphical)
Obl-Q	= Quartimin ⎭	Var	= Varimax
Omax	= Oblimax		